DATE DUE

BRODART, CO.   Cat. No. 23-221

The Great Inflation

A National Bureau of
Economic Research
Conference Report

The Great Inflation
The Rebirth of Modern Central Banking

Edited by **Michael D. Bordo
and Athanasios Orphanides**

The University of Chicago Press

Chicago and London

MICHAEL D. BORDO is professor of economics at Rutgers University and a research associate of the National Bureau of Economic Research. ATHANASIOS ORPHANIDES is former governor of the Central Bank of Cyprus.

The University of Chicago Press, Chicago 60637
The University of Chicago Press, Ltd., London
© 2013 by the National Bureau of Economic Research
All rights reserved. Published 2013.
Printed in the United States of America

22 21 20 19 18 17 16 15 14 13   1 2 3 4 5

ISBN-13: 978-0-226-06695-0 (cloth)
ISBN-13: 978-0-226-04355-5 (e-book)

Library of Congress Cataloging-in-Publication Data

The great inflation : the rebirth of modern central banking / edited by
    Michael D. Bordo and Athanasios Orphanides.
        pages. cm. — (A National Bureau of Economic Research
    conference report)
        ISBN 978-0-226-06695-0 (cloth : alk. paper) — ISBN 978-0-226-
    04355-5 (e-book) 1. Inflation (Finance)—History—20th century.
    2. Economic history—1945–1971. 3. Economic history—
    1971–1990. I. Bordo, Michael D. II. Orphanides, Athanasios.
    III. Series: National Bureau of Economic Research conference
    report.
        HG229.G6756 2013
        332.4'109045—dc23
                                                    2012039104

♾ This paper meets the requirements of ANSI/NISO Z39.48-1992
(Permanence of Paper).

**Relation of the Directors to the
Work and Publications of the
National Bureau of Economic Research**

1. The object of the NBER is to ascertain and present to the economics profession, and to the public more generally, important economic facts and their interpretation in a scientific manner without policy recommendations. The Board of Directors is charged with the responsibility of ensuring that the work of the NBER is carried on in strict conformity with this object.

2. The President shall establish an internal review process to ensure that book manuscripts proposed for publication DO NOT contain policy recommendations. This shall apply both to the proceedings of conferences and to manuscripts by a single author or by one or more co-authors but shall not apply to authors of comments at NBER conferences who are not NBER affiliates.

3. No book manuscript reporting research shall be published by the NBER until the President has sent to each member of the Board a notice that a manuscript is recommended for publication and that in the President's opinion it is suitable for publication in accordance with the above principles of the NBER. Such notification will include a table of contents and an abstract or summary of the manuscript's content, a list of contributors if applicable, and a response form for use by Directors who desire a copy of the manuscript for review. Each manuscript shall contain a summary drawing attention to the nature and treatment of the problem studied and the main conclusions reached.

4. No volume shall be published until forty-five days have elapsed from the above notification of intention to publish it. During this period a copy shall be sent to any Director requesting it, and if any Director objects to publication on the grounds that the manuscript contains policy recommendations, the objection will be presented to the author(s) or editor(s). In case of dispute, all members of the Board shall be notified, and the President shall appoint an ad hoc committee of the Board to decide the matter; thirty days additional shall be granted for this purpose.

5. The President shall present annually to the Board a report describing the internal manuscript review process, any objections made by Directors before publication or by anyone after publication, any disputes about such matters, and how they were handled.

6. Publications of the NBER issued for informational purposes concerning the work of the Bureau, or issued to inform the public of the activities at the Bureau, including but not limited to the NBER Digest and Reporter, shall be consistent with the object stated in paragraph 1. They shall contain a specific disclaimer noting that they have not passed through the review procedures required in this resolution. The Executive Committee of the Board is charged with the review of all such publications from time to time.

7. NBER working papers and manuscripts distributed on the Bureau's web site are not deemed to be publications for the purpose of this resolution, but they shall be consistent with the object stated in paragraph 1. Working papers shall contain a specific disclaimer noting that they have not passed through the review procedures required in this resolution. The NBER's web site shall contain a similar disclaimer. The President shall establish an internal review process to ensure that the working papers and the web site do not contain policy recommendations, and shall report annually to the Board on this process and any concerns raised in connection with it.

8. Unless otherwise determined by the Board or exempted by the terms of paragraphs 6 and 7, a copy of this resolution shall be printed in each NBER publication as described in paragraph 2 above.

Contents

Preface

The idea for this conference came from several conversations Michael Bordo had with Athanasios Orphanides in the early 2000s at the Board of Governors of the Federal Reserve System. We were encouraged to go forward with the project by Ben Bernanke, who at that time was a governor of the Federal Reserve. Marty Feldstein, then president of the NBER, was most supportive of the project from the outset. We would like to thank Marty and the NBER Conference Department for all their efforts in creating a memorable conference. The conference was generously funded by the Smith Richardson Foundation, and we would like to thank Mark Steinmeyer for his guidance in preparing the grant proposal.

The conference was held on September 26–27, 2008, at the Woodstock Inn in Woodstock, Vermont, shortly after the collapse of Lehman Brothers and the bailout of AIG—the most critical episode of the subprime mortgage crisis. As a consequence of the fast-emerging global banking crisis that followed these events, some of the participants from central banks could not make the conference. Meryvn King, governor of the Bank of England notified us a few days before the conference that he would not be able to attend. Lucas Papademos, then vice president of the European Central Bank, canceled his flight from Frankfurt at the last moment but subsequently sent us the remarks that he had already prepared. Remarkably, Don Kohn, then vice chairman of the Federal Reserve, managed to arrive from Washington, DC, on time to participate in the closing panel on Saturday. The late Anna Jacobson Schwartz, despite declining health, also attended the conference, her last NBER event after close to seventy years of service.

The financial crisis, the Great Recession, and the European debt crisis delayed the publication of this conference volume. Despite the delay, we believe the subject of the Great Inflation will continue to be of great interest to both scholars and policymakers. While inflation in most countries is at present subdued, the risk of a run-up of global inflation in the not too distant future is not negligible in the light of the extraordinary monetary accommodation that was engineered by central banks around the world to contain the crisis. And some of the challenges facing central banks today have parallels to those faced in the period leading to and during the Great Inflation. We hope that the lessons learned from the historical experience of the Great Inflation in this conference volume will be a reminder of the costs of allowing high and persistent inflation to reoccur.

Introduction

Michael D. Bordo and Athanasios Orphanides

> For eight years economic policy and the news about the economy have been dominated by inflation. . . . Many programs have been launched to stop it—without success. Inflation seemed a Hydra-headed monster, growing two new heads each time one was cut off.
> —Council of Economic Advisers (1974, 21)

Overview

Maintaining an environment of low and stable inflation is widely regarded as one of the most important objectives of economic policy, in general, and the single most important objective for monetary policy, in particular. The reasons are clear. An environment of price stability reduces uncertainty, improves the transparency of the price mechanism, and facilitates better planning and the efficient allocation of resources, thereby raising productivity.

The Great Inflation from 1965 to 1982 caused significant damage to the US economy and to the economies of many other countries and was a serious policy concern. Inflation in the United States rose from below 2 percent in 1962 to above 15 percent by 1979. Attempts to control it in the early 1970s included the Nixon administration imposition of wage and price controls, which were largely ineffective but that added to distortions in the US economy and likely contributed to the deep slump of 1974. The inflation rate in the 1970s also contributed to a marked decline in the US stock market and volatility in the US dollar, including a serious exchange rate crisis in 1978 and 1979. The period was also coincident with a marked decline in productivity growth, which by the end of the 1970s was only a fraction of its performance during the 1960s.

Since the early 1980s, the United States, as well as other industrialized and

Michael D. Bordo is professor of economics at Rutgers University and a research associate of the National Bureau of Economic Research. Athanasios Orphanides is former governor of the Central Bank of Cyprus.

For acknowledgments, sources of research support, and disclosure of the authors' material financial relationships, if any, please see http://www.nber.org/chapters/c9155.ack.

some emerging countries, has been highly successful in controlling inflation. This is evident in the ability of the monetary authorities to stick to their basic low inflation objectives in the face of significant recent oil price shocks and other supply shocks.

By the end of the twentieth century, a consensus view had developed that the Great Inflation represented the most costly deviation from a period of stable prices and output growth in the period between the Great Depression and the recent financial crisis in the United States, as well as many other developed countries. It would appear self-evident that understanding the fundamental causes of this event, and avoiding its repetition, should be viewed as an important issue for macroeconomists. Many attempts to understand what happened can be identified, but over the past three decades there have been substantial disagreements, misconceptions, and misunderstandings of the period, which makes it quite hard to compare even seemingly reasonable and plausible alternatives and to draw useful lessons. In addition, recent research has produced new useful perspectives on what might have led to the unprecedented peacetime run-up in inflation.

The objective of the conference was to bring together this research, helping put the pieces together and to draw the important policy lessons necessary to help avoid the repetition of the Great Inflation. Because of the likelihood that once the present recession is past, inflationary pressure may return, this would seem an opportune time to revisit the Great Inflation. The findings of the research in this volume could have lasting influence on policy.

This introduction briefly describes the dimensions of the Great Inflation. The next section surveys the themes that have dominated the research on the Great Inflation from the 1970s to the present. We summarize the conference proceedings in the final section.

The Dimensions of the Great Inflation

The Great Inflation was a worldwide phenomenon, experienced throughout the developed world. As can be seen from a plot of inflation in the G7 countries (figure I.1), inflation started to trend upwards in the second half of the 1960s, although the defining decade when its virulence was better understood was the 1970s. Two sharp increases resulting in two peaks, one in the middle of the 1970s and the second around 1980, are evident in all countries. The second peak was followed by disinflation, sharp in some cases, during the first half of the 1980s. Though the contours of inflation were similar, there were significant differences in the extent of the problem. Inflation exceeded 20 percent in the United Kingdom and Italy, reached double digits rather briefly in the United States, but did not exceed single digits in Germany.

In addition to the adverse developments in inflation, the 1970s saw increases in unemployment and a notable slowdown in growth, relative to

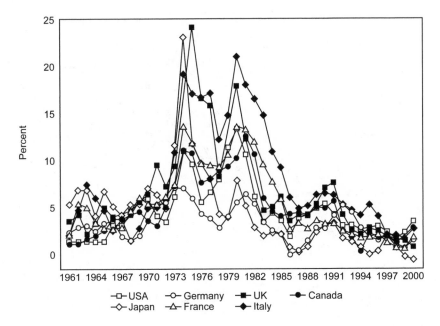

Fig. I.1   Inflation

what had been experienced earlier in the post–World War II period (figures I.2 and I.3). Unemployment levels were historically low in the 1950s and 1960s and productivity increased rapidly. In this light, the relative stagnation of the 1970s, together with the increases in inflation, raised alarms that the worst of both outcomes was being observed, popularizing a description of the period with one word—stagflation.[1] Following a long period of relative stability, the Great Inflation developments surprised policymakers and academics alike. Inflation ran higher than anticipated for long stretches. In the United States, survey data indicate that business economists were notably biased in their forecasts, expecting lower inflation than materialized for several years. Similarly, policy forecasts proved over optimistic. For example, at the Federal Reserve, the staff forecasts prepared for (Federal Open Market Committee) FOMC meetings and shown in the Green Book were on average predicting lower inflation.

The surprises did not end with developments in inflation. Another area where a deterioration was slowly recognized was in productivity. In the 1950s and 1960s rapid productivity growth in much of the developed world raised expectations of the prospects for sustained increases in prosperity. In this environment, estimates of potential output growth—the natural rate of growth that could be expected to be achieved with price stability—were

---

1. See Nelson and Nikolov (2004) for the origin of the word in the United Kingdom.

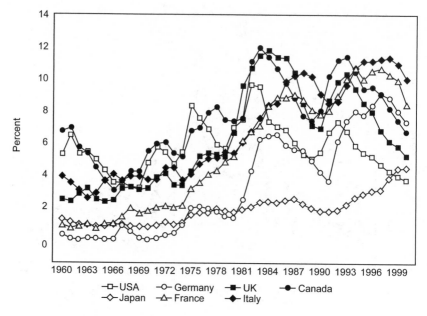

Fig. I.2   Unemployment rate

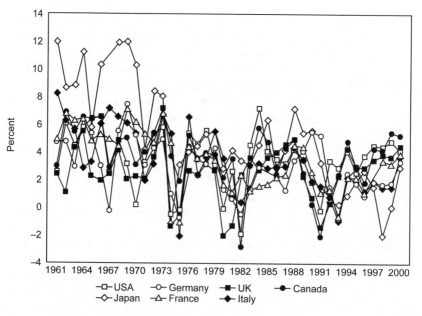

Fig. I.3   Real output growth

increased. But, as was noted in an Organization for Economic Cooperation and Development (OECD) report by a group of independent experts
headed by Paul McCracken (OECD 1977), throughout the developed world
subsequent developments disappointed and potential output prospects were
marked down as the 1970s progressed. In the United States, suspicions that
productivity was slowing down were already expressed by some before the
end of the 1960s but the degree of deterioration and successively more pessimistic assessments of productivity and potential output became common
as the 1970s progressed.

The malaise was also evident in deteriorating outcomes on employment
during the period. During the 1970s, a secular upward trend in the rate of
unemployment became evident. In the United States, whereas during the
1950s and 1960s it was increasingly accepted that an unemployment rate
of 4 percent or so corresponded to the economy's full employment potential, by the end of the Great Inflation 6 percent of even higher unemployment rates were considered more appropriate reflections of the natural
rate. Similar developments were observed elsewhere, and in Europe, in
particular, the deterioration in what constituted full employment was even
more dramatic.

The deterioration in both inflation stability and economic growth and
employment prospects experienced during the Great Inflation were disap-
pointing but also perplexing as they challenged the view prevailing during
the 1960s regarding advances in the understanding of the workings of the
economy and associated improvements in policy conduct. The timing of
the deterioration was especially disheartening to policy economists as it
came following a period of what was thought to be a great advance in doctrine. In the United States, the "New Economics" that guided economic
policy starting with the Kennedy administration was seen as a period of
great promise. (See the accounts of some of the protagonists: Heller 1966;
Tobin 1966, 1972; and Okun 1970.) Whereas before the 1960s, policymakers
appeared content to ensure that the economy was growing satisfactorily
and recessions were avoided, starting with the 1960s, active management
of aggregate demand counteracting any shortfall or excess relative to the
economy's potential was pursued. As Arthur Okun, whose work on the measurement of potential was critical for the implementation of this strategy
explained: "The revised strategy emphasized, as the standard for judging
economic performance, whether the economy was living up to its potential
rather than merely whether it was advancing" (Okun, 1970, 40). Following
many years of growth and declining unemployment with relative price stability, the Great Inflation proved a tremendous letdown. Characteristic of the
sentiment were the titles of some postmortems written after the destructive
forces of the Great Inflation were fully recognized. Arthur Burns titled his
1979 Per Jacobson lecture delivered shortly after he stepped down as Federal
Reserve chairman, *The Anguish of Central Banking.* The title of an essay

written in 1980 by Robert Solow (1982) in honor of Walter Heller was an apt question: "Where Have All the Flowers Gone?"

The Debate over the Causes of the Great Inflation

The Great Inflation posed a major intellectual challenge because considerable disagreement prevailed as to its immediate causes in both policy and academic circles, both while it was happening and in the decades since.

A number of hypotheses have been advanced as possible explanations, or at least as contributing answers to some of the questions that must be addressed on the way to providing a thorough understanding of the possible causes. Questions such as: What went wrong? What started the Great Inflation? What stopped it? Why did the inflation start in the mid-1960s and accelerate in the 1970s? What accounts for the disinflation of the 1980s? Was the increase in inflation intentional or was it an unavoidable consequence of exogenous factors against which policy was helpless? Were exogenous factors ("bad luck") or endogenous decisions ("bad policy") or a deficient institutional structure ("bad institutions") to blame? To what extent was the initial realization of higher inflation a surprise to policymakers? When was the threat of persistently higher inflation recognized by policymakers? How did households' and businesses' perceptions and attitudes regarding inflation evolve? Did policymakers try to contain inflation and fail or did they decide to let it continue once they understood its persistence? Alternatively, did policymakers perceive constraints that discouraged or rendered infeasible the adoption of policies that could have stopped it? To what extent was the inflation a conscious policy choice responding to the sociopolitical environment of the times? Was it preordained by the institutional environment that evolved following the world wars? Or was it the outcome of the prevalent economic reasoning during the period?

Price changes arise from imbalances in demand and supply and either supply or demand shocks can have influence. In the aggregate, inflation could arise from either source. Identifying the relative importance of "demand" and "supply" shocks as drivers of inflationary developments is a perennial issue, and, unsurprisingly, a matter of controversy with regard to the Great Inflation. In the post–World War II era, including during the Great Inflation, the identification of "cost push" versus "demand pull" inflation occupied many discussions but perceptions varied with schools of thought. Among the economists identified as "monetarists," overexpansionary monetary conditions and excessive nominal aggregate demand, virtually axiomatically, were given prominence in explaining inflation outcomes. Among those identified as "Keynesians," the adverse inflationary outcomes were more often than not identified as due to adverse supply.

During the 1970s in the United States, a common explanation of the inflationary developments was that it resulted from a series of adverse supply shocks. Based on the analysis by Gordon (1975, 1977), Eckstein (1978), and Blinder (1979, 1982), one could argue that the bulk of the two sharp increases in inflation during the 1970s, in 1973 to 1975 and in 1978 to 1980, could be explained due to the unusual developments in food, energy, and other commodities were taken into account to supply shocks in food and energy. In addition to the oil-cartel–induced increases in energy prices, reference was made to agricultural shortages due to unusual weather phenomena, and price increases in other commodities. In his 1977 analysis, Gordon found that structural wage and price equations that were developed to fit the 1954 to 1971 sample, prior to the realization of the unusual supply shocks observed during the first half of the 1970s, tracked the inflation developments well. According to this view, the 1970s experience represented a break from earlier history as a result of the unique supply shocks that hit the economy. The state of aggregate demand and macroeconomic policy did not need to be invoked as an important part of the explanation, and policy directed toward managing aggregate demand—either fiscal or monetary— did not play a major role in determining the adverse inflationary outcomes of the period.

Perhaps the Great Inflation would not have been characterized as such if it were not for the spikes in inflation experienced during the 1970s. While the supply shock hypothesis makes contact with the sharp increases in inflation associated in time with the two sharp increases in oil prices during the 1970s, it does not address the upward drift in inflation evident already from the mid-1960s and through the end of the 1970s. Thus, other factors must have contributed to an underlying aggregate demand pressure that may have persisted for over a decade and could have played a role over and above the supply shock explanation. Further, Barsky and Kilian (2001) suggest skepticism regarding the exogeneity of the commodity shocks of the 1970s and argue that the oil shocks, in particular, were largely the endogenous outcome of accumulated worldwide aggregate demand pressures. If this interpretation is correct, then at least some—if not all—of what is attributed to temporary supply factors should also be attributed to inflationary demand developments and the understanding of the Great Inflation must center on explaining the causes of what may have been a persistently inflationary aggregate demand imbalance.

An underlying element in a number of explanations of the Great Inflation is that policymakers accepted the increase in inflation as an unavoidable choice, necessary to advance overall economic welfare. One such mechanism is based on the time-inconsistency problem of discretionary monetary policy advanced by Kydland and Prescott (1977) and Barro and Gordon (1983). In that model, the time-consistent inflation rate that arises from the monetary policymaker's decisions increases with the economy's natural rate of unemployment. Parkin (1993) and Ireland (1999) use this link to argue that the upward drift in inflation was due to a corresponding drift in the natural rate of unemployment. Indeed, exogenous factors including demographic changes and a productivity slowdown seem to have caused an upward drift in the natural rate of unemployment during the late 1960s and 1970s so the time-inconsistency problem could serve as an explanation if policymakers recognized the upward drift in the natural rate at that time and set policy accordingly. The disinflation of the 1980s is harder to reconcile with this explanation alone, however, as it does not similarly coincide with a downward drift in the natural rate.

Another mechanism relating to the time-inconsistency issue that potentially explains episodes of high inflation is the presence of expectations traps, as argued by Chari, Christiano, and Eichenbaum (1998) and Christiano and Gust (2000). An expectations trap arises when an increase in private agents' inflation expectations in the economy pressures the monetary authority to accommodate those expectations to meet other objectives, for example, to avoid a costly recession. A key element in the story is the presence of multiple expectational equilibria. While under commitment a unique equilibrium with low inflation obtains, episodes of high and low inflation can arise in the absence of commitment in monetary policy. The expectations traps provide a mechanism for translating temporary shocks that influence adversely inflation expectations to permanent changes in the inflation tolerated by discretionary policymakers. Thus, it can explain the Great Inflation as due to the combination of adverse shocks and the policymakers' decision to accommodate their inflation consequences permanently. Although policymakers did not seek higher inflation in this story, they decided to accept it as they considered the costs associated with pursuing disinflation too high. Under these circumstances, the disinflation started once policymakers became unwilling to continue to tolerate high inflation.

The willingness of policymakers to accept high inflation is also a feature of the monetary neglect hypothesis advanced in Hetzel (1998, 2008), Nelson and Nikolov (2004), and Nelson (2005a). In this story, monetary policymakers appear unwilling to push for a disinflation once inflation starts because they doubt the effectiveness of monetary policy to tackle inflation relative to alternative policies. The story emphasizes the role of nonmonetary explanations of inflation, such as the belief that inflation can be a purely cost-push phenomenon. The prevalence of such beliefs is thus identified as culprit for the neglect toward achieving price stability. Disinflation started once the dominance of such beliefs receded.

Tolerance for inflation and an aversion to the monetary policy actions needed to end it is also at the heart of political explanations of the Great Inflation. Politics are always an unavoidable part of economic policy design and this was not different during the Great Inflation period (see Mayer 1999 and Stein 1984). Even if fiscal policy is politically motivated, however, price stability should prevail if the monetary authority can independently decide and implement its policies. The question is whether independent central banks tolerated inflation or whether central banks lacked the necessary independence to do so. Documenting several episodes of political pressure at the Federal Reserve, Meltzer (2005, 2010) argues that politics was an important part for the start, the continuation, and the end of the Great Inflation. The unprecedented public bashing by both the administration and the Congress of Chairman Martin following a policy-tightening with which the administration disagreed in December 1965 marked the start of the episode. According to Meltzer, monetary policy in the second half of the 1960s became more accommodative of the administration's policy objectives. As inflation rose, lack of political consensus for incurring the costs that disinflation would induce tied Chairman Burns's hands. Inflation was ended only when the high costs of inflation were recognized and sufficient political support for disinflation mustered.

An alternative set of explanations, dubbed the "Berkeley story" by Sargent (2002), gives prominence to the rise of views during the 1960s regarding the policy trade-offs implied by a downward sloping Phillips curve. Samuelson and Solow (1960) presented a menu of choices between unemployment and inflation that could be available to policymakers, according to the statistical relationship between inflation and unemployment following World War II. Although they were careful to qualify the stability of this relationship, the policy menu was interpreted as suggesting that if unemployment was deemed intolerably high (as it was in the early 1960s), it could be reduced by pursuing expansionary policies that corresponded to a higher level of inflation. According to DeLong (1997) and Romer and Romer (2002), following Kennedy's election as president in the 1960s, economic policy in the United States was guided by this reasoning and higher inflation was sought and tolerated during the 1960s in an attempt to achieve full employment. DeLong argues that in light of the erroneous beliefs regarding the Phillips curve, the Great Inflation of the 1970s was an accident waiting to happen as policymakers aimed to reduce unemployment toward 4 percent or lower throughout the 1960s. At some point in time, such a policy would trigger accelerating inflation, as implied by the natural rate hypothesis. By the time policymakers accepted the natural rate hypothesis, and adopted an accelerationist view of the Phillips curve (during the Nixon administration), inflation was already embedded in the economy and was difficult to reverse as that would require raising unemployment above the natural rate. Thus, inflation persisted.

Sargent (1999) embeds the discretionary policy of Kydland and Prescott and doubts regarding the natural rate hypothesis in an adaptive model where the policymaker relies on adaptive estimation of the Phillips curve to learn about the policy trade-off. He demonstrates that policy formulated based on the evolving views that arise from the changing statistical relationships between inflation and unemployment in the data gives rise to endogenously determined episodes of high inflation. Using quarterly US data, Cogley and

Sargent (2002) confirm that the pattern of evolving statistical relationships is consistent with the story where policymakers could be misled by the data into exploiting a Phillips curve, resulting in higher inflation. In a related model of learning dynamics, Primiceri (2006) shows that the combination of changing beliefs about the persistence of inflation and the inflation–unemployment trade-offs can account for the evolution of policy during the rise of inflation and also the disinflation that followed.

A different theoretical error is involved in yet another explanation of what might have caused monetary policy to be overly expansionary during the period. The starting point for this explanation is the characterization of monetary policy in terms of a simple policy rule that captures the response of the nominal short-term interest rate to developments in the economy and real economy. As Taylor (1993) suggested, if correctly specified, such policy rules can capture desirable elements of systematic monetary policy and deliver good outcomes with respect to both price stability and economic stability. Taylor (1999) and Clarida, Galí, and Gertler (2000) suggested that a policy rule responding to inflation and the output gap provided a good characterization of the period of monetary stability that followed the Great Inflation and argued that had a similar policy rule been followed during the Great Inflation, that episode would have been avoided. Instead, their analysis suggests that in the late 1960s and 1970s the Federal Reserve failed to increase the nominal rate enough to offset the negative effect of inflation on real interest rates. In this explanation, the Federal Reserve inadvertently eased monetary conditions with inflation, causing a rise in inflation during the period. The episode ended when this error was recognized and policy became more responsive to inflation. Supporting this explanation is the fact that ex post real short-term rates remained quite low or were even negative for much of the 1970s. This view, however, rests on the hypothesis of widespread policy confusion of real and nominal interest rates. The validity of this hypothesis was doubted in work by Orphanides (2003a, 2004), who argued that the empirical results presented by Taylor (1999) and Clarida, Galí, and Gertler (2000) were statistical artifacts of the use by these authors of retrospectively revised data for characterizing policy decisions. If, instead, real-time data and forecasts available to the FOMC when decisions were taken were used to characterize policy decisions, the evidence of insufficient responsiveness of policy to inflation was overturned.

Examining the information available to the FOMC during the Great Inflation reveals misinformation as another potential explanation of the Great Inflation. Orphanides (2003b) points to substantial misperceptions regarding the measurement of full employment as the cause of overly expansionary monetary policy. Using a model with an accelerationist Phillips curve, Orphanides compares the results of counterfactual simulations with policy following the Taylor (1993) policy rule. He shows that while the

Great Inflation would have been avoided had the output gap been properly measured, when the mismeasurement of the output gap observed during the late 1960s and 1970s is introduced then policy following the Taylor rule delivers inflation outcomes similar to the Great Inflation. Alternative policy rules that deemphasize the output gap are more robust to misperceptions. According to this story, the reliance on the output gap (and related unemployment gap) as a guide for stabilization policy was responsible for the inflationary outcomes. A significant lag of recognition of the productivity slowdown and increase in the natural rate of unemployment implied that estimates of potential output in the late 1960s and throughout the 1970s proved overly optimistic. Although monetary policy was properly responding to inflation it was deliberately easy to counter what were perceived as substantial output gaps and unemployment gaps. The perceived gaps were consistent with projected declining paths of inflation, as suggested by the historical record of policy discussions and the Green Books. Thus, policy was not deliberately inflationary. A persistent overestimation of potential output, an activist policy toward closing output or unemployment gaps, and a significant lag of recognition of its implications on inflation during the 1970s are necessary elements for this hypothesis. Narrative evidence confirms the prominence of the output gap following the rise of activist monetary policy during the 1960s and the delayed recognition of the over optimism reflected in real-time estimates. (See, e.g., Solow 1982, who attributes most of the error to the unexpected unfavorable shift in trend productivity that started in the 1960s.)

Whether an activist policy responding to the output gap like the Taylor (1993) rule can explain the large increase in inflation observed in the 1970s in the presence of misperceptions about the natural rate of unemployment or the output gap alone depends on the persistence of inflation dynamics. Since inflation was not very persistent before the Great Inflation, part of the explanation for the episode must account for the increase in the persistence of inflation during the 1970s. Orphanides and Williams (2005) introduce learning dynamics to examine the evolution of inflation expectations and show that the combination of activist policies and natural rate misperceptions could explain the slow rise of inflation persistence and disanchoring of inflation expectations during the 1970s. Had policy been less activist, inflation expectations would have remained well-anchored throughout the 1970s and the Great Inflation would have been avoided. Once Paul Volcker became chairman of the Federal Reserve, the destabilizing role of activist policies on inflation expectations was recognized and less activist policies adopted, ending the inflation episode.

The Great Inflation was an international phenomenon. Inflation was elevated in all advanced countries in the late 1960s and 1970s. Until 1973 most advanced countries were part of the Bretton Woods international monetary system, which operated as a gold dollar standard. The Bretton Woods articles required that member countries' exchange rates be pegged to the dollar and the dollar be pegged to gold at the official parity of $35 per ounce. Member countries also used the dollar as their international reserve. Like the gold standard that preceded it, monetary shocks would be transmitted between countries in the pegged exchange rate regime through the balance of payments.

There was considerable research in the 1970s and 1980s on the global transmission of inflation under Bretton Woods (see Bordo 1993). Expansionary US monetary policy beginning in 1965 was transmitted through a rising balance of payments deficit that led to dollar flows to the surplus countries of continental Europe and Japan. The central banks in these countries attempted to sterilize the dollar inflows but most led to increases in their money supplies and rising prices. Transmission occurred mainly through the traditional price specie flow plus capital flows channel, less so through commodity market arbitrage (Darby et al. 1983). An alternative, global monetarist view, posited that US monetary growth raised the global money supply and global prices and individual country prices converged to global prices via commodity market arbitrage (Genberg and Swoboda 1977).

In the face of this inflationary pressure, the Europeans, beginning in 1968, staged a series of runs on US gold reserves, converting their outstanding dollar liabilities into gold. The runs ended when President Nixon closed the US gold window on August 15, 1971. An attempt to restart Bretton Woods at different parities at the Smithsonian Agreement in Washington, DC, in December 1971 was unsuccessful. Following a series of currency crises and devaluations in the next two years, all of the advanced countries dropped their pegs by 1973 and began floating their currencies.

The run-up of inflation after the collapse of Bretton Woods was attributed by some to the termination of the Bretton Woods nominal anchor to gold and the departure of the last vestiges of the gold standard. In the 1970s the central banks of other advanced countries followed similar expansionary policies to the Fed. Like the Fed, they were influenced by Keynesian doctrine and many attributed the rise in inflation to nonmonetary cost push forces that could only be contained by incomes policies (see DiCiccio and Nelson for the United Kingdom, this volume, and Nelson 2005b for the cases of Australia, Canada, and New Zealand). Moreover, these countries (like the United States) accommodated the oil price shocks of 1974 and 1979. Germany and Switzerland were notable exceptions to this pattern. Policymakers there did not hold Keynesian views nor did they believe in cost push inflation. They viewed inflation to be a monetary phenomenon (see Beyer and colleagues, this volume). The central banks also appeared to enjoy greater independence. Unlike the other countries, they did not accommodate the oil price shocks. Japan also, after accommodating the first oil price shock in 1974, resisted doing so for the second one (see Ito, this volume).

The Conference Volume

The conference volume covers several salient themes on the causes of the Great Inflation. The first theme covers two of the earliest and most basic explanations for the rapid inflation in the late 1960s and 1970s—the monetarist explanation attributing the inflation to expansionary monetary policy (in chapter 1 by Poole, Rasche, and Wheelock) and the supply shock explanation, especially the oil price shocks in 1973 and 1979 in chapter 2 by Blinder and Rudd.

The second theme contains three chapters (3, 4, and 5) that expand on the failure of monetary policy hypothesis. The first, by Goodfriend and King, states that the Fed followed a "business as usual policy" in the 1960s and 1970s that explains how focus on the output gap and interest-rate smoothing at the expense of low inflation raised trend inflation. Levin and Taylor state that rising long-term inflationary expectations became embedded in the Taylor rule. In chapter 5, Orphanides and Williams state that misperception of the natural rate of unemployment and excessive weight on high employment was responsible for making an optimal control (fine-tuning) strategy an engine for high and variable inflation.

The third theme is evidence on the experience of three other major countries during the Great Inflation: Germany, which followed a monetarist framework and largely avoided the Great Inflation; Japan, which had a severe inflation after the Organization of the Petroleum Exporting Countries (OPEC) I reflecting government pressure to keep interest rates low; and the United Kingdom, which had very high inflation and whose monetary authorities had a cost push explanation for inflation that influenced Arthur Burns policies in the 1970s.

The final theme explains the international dimension—the connection between the collapse of the Bretton Woods system and expansionary Federal Reserve monetary policy—the Fed abandoned concern over the balance of payments after 1965 in favor of domestic employment on the assumption that the Treasury would handle external balance considerations.

The conference began and ended with panel sessions. In the first panel session two central bankers (Don Brash of New Zealand and John Crow of Canada) review how they successfully broke the back of inflationary expectations and instituted inflation targeting. In the concluding panel Don Kohn, former vice chairman of the Federal Reserve, reflected on several lessons for policymakers from the experience of the Great Inflation, and Harold James considered the lessons from the Great Inflation from an historical perspective.

Early Explanations

Two early conflicting explanations for the run-up of inflation from the mid-1960s to 1980 were the monetarist views of Milton Friedman and others who blamed the inflation on overly expansionary monetary policy, and the supply shock view of Alan Blinder, Robert Gordon, and others who attributed the high inflation of the 1970s to a series of oil and other supply shocks.

In chapter 1, Poole, Rasche, and Wheelock explain how the run-up of inflation beginning in the mid-1960s led to criticism by the monetarists Milton Friedman, Anna Schwartz, Karl Brunner, and Alan Meltzer, who attributed it to expansionary monetary policy. Brunner, Meltzer, and Schwartz established the Shadow Open Market Committee (SOMC) in 1973 to monitor and critique the actions by the FOMC. Using a simple quantity theoretic model based on stable demand for money function, the SOMC proposed that a gradualist monetary rule reducing the monetary base by 1 percent per year would achieve price stability with minimal variability in output and employment. The authors simulate such an SOMC rule using a modern New Keynesian model with rational expectations and forward-looking agents. Their analysis shows that price stability could have been successfully achieved in the 1970s and with a much lower cost in real output than the "cold turkey" strategy followed in 1979 to 1981 by Paul Volcker.

Christina Romer, in her comments, suggests that a better counterfactual comparison would have been between the SOMC rule and the interest rate control procedure actually used. Her comparison of the prescriptions for monetary aggregate growth given at each of the SOMC biannual meetings with the actual aggregate growth rates reveals that the only period between 1973 and 1990 that the SOMC prescription would have significantly outperformed the Fed was in the mid-1970s under Burns and Miller.

Blinder and Rudd revisit the supply shock explanation for the Great Inflation in the 1970s using revised data and new theoretical and econometric techniques. They show that the OPEC I oil price shocks combined with rises in food prices and the end of the Nixon wage price controls account for the rapid run-up of headline inflation between 1973 and 1975 followed by a quick reversal. A second price hill from 1979 to 1980 is explained by OPEC II, food price shocks, and other exogenous supply side factors.

Using Phillips curve analysis they also show that some of the supply-side shocks passed through via wages and prices to the core Consumer Price Index (CPI), which followed a more muted drift upwards. The shocks also largely explained the recessions of 1973 to 1975 and 1979 to 1980. According to these authors, monetary policy only played a minor role in accommodating the exogenous shocks.

The Failure of Monetary Policy

Goodfriend and King, in chapter 3, explain the rise and variability in the trend rate of inflation in the United States in the 1970s by two aspects of Federal Reserve policy behavior during the period: smoothing short-term interest rates and stabilizing the output gap. These objectives were held to be more important than a third objective—keeping inflation low. This strategy they call "business as usual." Under this approach, shocks to the real interest rate (such as the negative productivity shocks that occurred in the 1970s) will raise the trend inflation rate. The Fed may later tighten policy to roll back inflation but if their credibility is low they will quickly return to business as usual and inflation will pick up again. This process will generate a pattern of stop-go inflation.

These views are developed in a three-equation New Keynesian Phillips curve model. Their approach predicts the stochastic (IMA, integrated moving average) inflation trend pattern shown by Stock and Watson (2002) and also the stop-go policies following four Romer and Romer (1989) policy-tightening dates: December 1968, April 1974, August 1979, and October 1979.

Lars Svensson, in his comments, recommends an alternative modeling strategy based on a central bank loss function and optimizing policy for this loss function.

Chapter 4, by Levin and Taylor, develops several measures of long-term inflationary expectations (based on the Livingston and other surveys and the term structure of interest rates) to show that the Great Inflation began in the 1960s and not the 1970s, as argued by Blinder and Rudd and others. Moreover, long-run inflationary expectations ratcheted up from 1965 to 1980 through a series of plateaus (1968–1970, 1974–1976, and 1979–1980). They explain the pattern by a series of temporary anti-inflation policies that were reversed, reflecting political pressure (as unemployment rose and real output fell) against tightening sufficiently to break the back of inflationary expectations. The pattern changed with the Volcker shock of 1980. Their interpretation is backed up by the estimation of a Taylor rule using real-time data and the shifting measures of long-term inflationary expectations, which showed the Fed acting as if its inflation targets had kept rising.

Bennett McCallum, in his comment, compares the Taylor rule used in the chapter to his preferred base growth rule. The latter, he claims, better explains the patterns observed.

In chapter 5, Orphanides and Williams use a three-equation model based on a New Keynesian Phillips curve, real-time data on the unemployment gap, and forecasted survey data on expected inflation, to test the efficiency of the Fed's pursuit of an optimal control approach to monetary policy that approximates the fine-tuning views of the New Economics prevalent in the 1960s and 1970s. They also assume a high weight to low unemployment relative to low inflation, as prevailed after 1965. They find that if policymakers knew the true parameters of the structural model and had correctly estimated the natural rate of unemployment and if all agents had rational expectations, that such a strategy would have anchored inflationary expectations in the 1960s and 1970s and prevented the Great Inflation.

If however, policymakers had underestimated the true natural rate of unemployment, then the optimal control approach would have led inflation expectations to become unhinged so that in the face of the supply shocks of the 1970s, the Great Inflation (high and variable inflation) would have prevailed. Had policymakers attached a very low weight to unemployment stability, relative to price stability, then even in the presence of the misperceived natural rate of unemployment the Great Inflation could have been avoided, although the variability of inflation would still have been high.

The authors also show that simulation of a simple first difference instrument policy rule (in which changes in the policy rate respond slowly to deviation of inflation from trend and changes in unemployment) based on learning dynamics rather than on rational expectations, closer to the policy that appears to have been followed in the 1980s and 1990s, would have led to even better performance in the 1960s and 1970s than if the optimal control policy were followed.

Seppo Honkapohja, in his comment, makes the case for models based on dynamic learning rather than rational expectations. He interprets the authors results as driven by misperceptions about the true natural rate of unemployment. He argues that a model based on learning by private agents rather than being based on rational expectations best explain why the Great Inflation arose.

Other Countries' Experiences during the Great Inflation

Germany (and Switzerland) were two advanced countries that largely avoided the Great Inflation. Chapter 6, by Beyer, Gaspar, Gerberding, and Issing, explains the monetary targeting framework followed by the Bundesbank from 1974 to 1998. The Bundesbank was founded in 1953 as an independent central bank whose sole mandate was to maintain monetary stability. During the Bretton Woods era its domestic price stability objective was constrained by the external peg. After the breakup of the Bretton Woods system in 1973, the Bundesbank shifted to a quantity theoretic monetary targeting strategy in 1974. The policy followed used a short-term policy rate to hit the preannounced monetary targets based on forecasts of money demand. With the exception of the OPEC I oil price shock in 1973, which was partially accommodated, the Bundesbank was the most successful major central bank in keeping inflation low in the 1970s and 1980s.

The chapter describes how the monetary targeting framework was used, both to control inflation and anchor inflationary expectations. Thus, when the Bundesbank missed its targets it would always clearly state its reasons. The authors embedded the Bundesbank monetary targeting rule in a dynamic stochastic general equilibrium (DSGE) model. Based on the model, they derive an interest instrument rule like the Taylor rule. Estimation of the rule over the period 1965 to 1998 demonstrates that the Bundesbank always followed the Taylor principle that real interest rates would rise sufficiently to offset inflation. This is compared to the United States, where the Taylor principle was violated in the Burns/Miller era and the United Kingdom, where it was violated throughout the Great Inflation.

Bejmamin Friedman, in his comments, is critical of the authors' derivation of their Taylor rule, which, he argues, does not clearly isolate the contribution of monetary targeting to the outcomes of monetary policy described by the Taylor rule.

Takatoshi Ito analyzes Japan's experience during the Great Inflation in the 1970s in chapter 7. The Bank of Japan followed a loose monetary policy in 1972 under government pressure to restrain appreciation of the yen after the breakdown of Bretton Woods. Then when OPEC I hit in 1973 the bank was too slow to tighten, leading to an inflation rate of 20 percent in 1974. Ito attributes this outcome to the bank's lack of independence. Later, in the fall of 1975, the bank tightened monetary policy, aggressively attenuating the inflation spike. In the face of OPEC II in 1979 the bank, according to Ito, having learned from its mistake in the early 1970s, kept monetary policy tight and avoided the inflation that affected the United States, United Kingdom, and other countries. The author argues that the bank had achieved de facto monetary policy independence since the Japanese government did not oppose the tight policy in 1979.

To back up his story, Ito estimates a Taylor rule for the period of low inflation from 1982 to 1995 and then uses the coefficients of the Taylor rule and real-time data to calculate counterfactual best practice interest rate policy for the 1970s. He finds that such interest rates between 1972 and 1975 would have been much higher than they were, but between 1979 to 1980 actual policy rates were very close to those based on the Taylor rule.

Frederic Mishkin, in his comments, doubts that the Bank of Japan achieved de facto independence in 1975. Rather, he sees the bank as continuously subordinated to government pressure throughout the period. What differed at the end of the 1970s was that the government favored tightening. He also posits that the Japanese experience demonstrates that if the central bank has credibility for low inflation that oil price shocks need not be inflationary.

In chapter 8, Riccardo DiCecio and Edward Nelson argue that the UK experience with inflation in the 1970s was very similar to that of the United States. This they attribute to common adherence to the same mistaken nonmonetary views of the source of inflation. A narrative analysis of the UK Treasury's views in the 1960s and 1970s shows their emphasis on cost push factors (wage push) rather than monetary expansion as the key source of the run-up of inflation in the 1970s. The dominant role of wage driven inflation was used to make the case for incomes policy rather than tight money to reduce inflation. The authors argue that the UK Treasury did not believe in a long-run Phillips curve trade-off nor did they emphasize the output gap in their analysis. Instead their analysis posits that the economy has a "speedbump"—the first difference of the output gap—that if exceeded would in a nonlinear way trigger inflation. Hence monetary policy would be ineffective in stemming inflation without wage price controls.

The authors further posit, based on narrative analysis, that Arthur Burns adopted this framework after he became Federal Reserve chairman in 1970. This framework, they argue, explains Burns's advocacy of the wage-price controls adopted by the Nixon administration in 1971.

To back up their story they estimate a DSGE model with sticky wages and prices for the United Kingdom. They show that the United Kingdom did not follow a Phillips curve in the 1970s but did follow the speed-bump theory—policy rates did not respond to the output gap.

Matthew Shapiro, in his comments, doubts that US policymakers acquired their nonmonetary sources of inflation view from the United Kingdom. Nonmonetary control of inflation was a very prominent feature of US economic policy in the early 1960s (e.g., the wage-price guidelines of the Kennedy administration). He also criticizes the authors for not explicitly including nonmonetary considerations in their model.

International Considerations

Bordo and Eichengreen, in chapter 9, posit that international considerations had an important influence on Federal Reserve policymaking in the early 1960s and that adherence to the Bretton Woods peg of the price of gold at $35 per ounce served as an anchor for a low inflation policy. After 1965, international considerations became less important to FOMC deliberations. This reflects (in part) aggressive policy actions by the US Treasury and the administration to protect the balance of payments and stem gold losses in the early 1960s—policies such as the Interest Equalization Tax Act of 1963, Roosa bonds, and the Gold Pool. On the understanding that the Treasury would deal with international considerations, the Fed placed more emphasis after 1965 on domestic considerations, especially maintaining high employment. Proponents of tight money to stem inflation and protect the balance of payments such as Alfred Hayes, president of the New York Fed, were increasingly overruled by those who placed greater weight on high employment than low inflation.

A narrative analysis of FOMC meetings from 1959 to 1971 showed considerable attention being placed to protecting the dollar in the Eisenhower and Kennedy years. On several occasions, policy was tightened for external balance reasons. After 1965 external considerations received less and less attention and then only during episodes of financial crisis—1967 after sterling was devalued, 1968 after the collapse of the Gold Pool, and 1971 during the final crisis of the dollar. The narrative evidence is backed up by estimation of a Taylor rule from 1959 to 1971 that shows that policy rates erred on the side of tightness before 1965 and on the side of ease thereafter. Several measures of inflation persistence and of inflationary expectations also display a significant break after 1965.

Allan Meltzer, in his comments, emphasizes the changing environment in the US Treasury and the Council of Economic Advisers over the period. In the Kennedy years, Douglas Dillon and Robert Roosa formulated the defense of the dollar strategy. They were succeeded by the New Economics advocates who downplayed external balance considerations in favor of rapid domestic economic growth and full employment.

The Panel Sessions

The conference began with a panel session, "Pioneering Central Bankers Remember," in which two former central bank governors, on whose watch the Great Inflation was vanquished, reflected on their experiences. Donald Brash, governor of the Reserve Bank of New Zealand (RBNZ) from 1988 to 2002, the first country to adopt inflation targeting, described the experience of New Zealand in the Great Inflation era and the events that led to formal inflation targeting. New Zealand had the worst inflation experience from 1970 to 1984 in the OECD. A series of policy moves were attempted with limited success in reducing inflation, including draconic wage price controls in 1982. A major sea change in the economic policy framework occurred in 1984 with the election of the Labour party, which deregulated much of the economy including the financial sector, reduced tariffs and tax rates, floated the exchange rate, and gave the central bank independence with a mandate to reduce inflation. Inflation declined from double digits to well below 10 percent by the late 1980s.

In 1989 the government introduced radical legislation that gave the central bank de jure independence and a clear mandate to produce price stability (defined as an inflation rate of 2 percent or less) as its sole target. The governor of the RBNZ was made accountable to the government in achieving its inflation objective. By 1991 inflation was below 2 percent.

John Crow, governor of the Bank of Canada from 1987 to 1994, describes the background of inflation in Canada and the events that led to the adoption of formal inflation targeting in 1991. Canada was the second country to follow such a path. Canada's inflation experience in the 1970s and 1980s clearly followed that of the United States'. As in the United States, monetary (M1) aggregate targeting was followed in the 1970s in an attempt to gradually reduce the inflation rate. As in the United States, financial innovation weakened the connection between M1 growth and inflation and the bank abandoned the strategy in 1982. The bank then followed an implicit exchange rate target that implied a close shadowing of US monetary developments. By 1987, inflation was down to 4 percent.

Upon becoming governor, John Crow was convinced of the need for the bank to attach the highest priority to maintaining price stability (which he originally defined as 0 percent inflation) and he forcefully presented his views in a series of speeches. In 1991 the government of Canada took the initiative in having the Bank of Canada adopt an inflation target. The bank was made the agent responsible for hitting the inflation target and for the design of the targets, with the Department of Finance's approval. The target was set at 2 percent in 1993. As in New Zealand, inflation quickly dropped below 2 percent.

The conference ended with Panel Session II, "Lessons from History," involving Federal Reserve Vice Chairman Donald Kohn, Deputy Governor of the European Central Bank Lucas Papademos, and Harold James of Princeton University. Kohn emphasized the lessons that central banks need to learn after experiences like the Great Inflation. The first lesson is that central banks need to focus on price stability as their most important long-run objective. The second lesson is the importance of inflationary expectations for the control of inflation. The third lesson is the importance of vigorous debate inside central banks as well as the input by outside experts to safeguard against serious policy errors. The fourth lesson is that once inflation becomes embedded in inflationary expectations that, to avoid high economic and social costs, central bankers should go to great lengths to diffuse them. His final lesson is for central banks to be humble about what they know.

Papademos, in his remarks, emphasized the role that sound monetary policy made in Germany in not accommodating the commodity price shocks in the 1970s compared to the US case, which accommodated the shocks and exacerbated inflation. He viewed the key lessons learned from the Great Inflation as the importance of the central bank's pursuit of low inflation, the importance of not exploiting a trade-off between inflation and unemployment, the avoidance of fine tuning, not accommodating supply shocks, and the importance of anchoring inflation expectations.

Harold James discussed the nonmonetary aspects of great inflations in the past—of inflation as a way to buy social peace in a politically precarious environment. Viewing inflation as a monetary phenomenon was key to its resolution both in Germany in the 1920s and in the Great Inflation of the 1970s. The development of inflation targeting is the culmination of this process. James warned of the difficulties of measuring inflation, especially of the role of asset price booms.

References

Barro, Robert, and David Gordon. 1983. "A Positive Theory of Monetary Policy in a Natural Rate Model." *Journal of Political Economy* 91:589–610.
Blinder, Alan. 1979. *Economic Policy and the Great Stagflation.* New York: Academic Press.
———. 1982. "The Anatomy of Double-Digit Inflation in the 1970s." In *Inflation: Causes and Effects,* edited by Robert Hall, 261–82. Chicago: University of Chicago Press.
Barsky, Robert, and Lutz Kilian. 2001. "Do We Really Know Oil Caused the Great

Stagflation? A Monetary Alternative." In *NBER Macroeconomics Annual 2001,* edited by Ben Bernanke and Kenneth Rogoff, 137–183. Cambridge, MA: MIT Press.

Bordo, Michael D. 1993. "The Bretton Woods International Monetary System: An Historical Overview." In *A Retrospective on the Bretton Woods System: Lessons for Monetary Reform,* edited by Michael D. Bordo and Barry Eichengreen, Chapter 1. Chicago: University of Chicago Press.

Chari, V. V., Lawrence Christiano, and Martin Eichenbaum. 1998. "Expectations Traps and Discretion." *Journal of Economic Theory* 81:462–92.

Christiano, Lawrence J., and Christopher Gust. 2000. "The Expectations Trap Hypothesis." *Federal Reserve Bank of Chicago—Economic Perspectives* 24 (2): 21–39.

Clarida, Richard, Jordi Galí, and Mark Gertler. 2000. "Monetary Policy Rules and Macroeconomic Stability: Evidence and Some Theory." *Quarterly Journal of Economics* 115:147–80.

Cogley, Timothy, and Thomas Sargent. 2002. "Evolving Post-World War II US. Inflation Dynamics." *NBER Macroeconomics Annual 2001,* edited by Ben S. Bernanke and Kenneth Rogoff, 331–73. Cambridge, MA: MIT Press.

Council of Economic Advisers. 1974. *Economic Report of the President.* Washington, DC: United States Printing Office.

Darby, Michael R., James R. Lothian, Artur Gandolfi, Anna J. Schwartz, and Alan Stockman. 1983. *The International Transmission of Inflation.* Chicago: University of Chicago Press.

DeLong, J. Bradford. 1997. "America's Peacetime Inflation: The 1970s." In *Reducing Inflation: Motivation and Strategy,* edited by Christina Romer and David Romer, 247–80. Chicago: University of Chicago Press.

Eckstein, Otto. 1978. *The Great Recession with a Postcript on Stagflation.* Amsterdam: North-Holland.

Genberg, Hans, and Alexander Swoboda. 1977. "Causes and Origins of the Current Worldwide Inflation." In *Inflation Theory and Anti-Inflation Policy,* edited by Erik Lundberg, 72–93. London: MacMillan.

Gordon, Robert. 1975. "Alternative Response of Policy to External Supply Shocks." *Brookings Papers on Economic Activity* 1:183–205.

———. 1977. "Can the Inflation of the 1970s Be Explained?" *Brookings Papers on Economic Activity:* 253–79. Washington, DC: Brookings Institution.

Heller, W. W. 1966. *New Dimensions in Political Economy.* Cambridge, MA: Harvard University Press.

Hetzel, Robert. 1998. "Arthur Burns and Inflation." *Federal Reserve Bank of Richmond Economic Quarterly* 84:21–44.

———. 2008. *The Monetary Policy of the Federal Reserve: A History.* New York: Cambridge University Press.

Ireland, Peter. 1999. "Does the Time-Consistency Problem Explain the Behaviour of Inflation in the United States?" *Journal of Monetary Economics* 44:279–91.

Kydland, Finn, and Edward Prescott. 1977. "Rules Rather Than Discretion: The Inconsistency of Optimal Plans." *Journal of Political Economy* 85 (3): 473–91.

Mayer, T. 1999. *Monetary Policy and the Great Inflation in the United States: The Federal Reserve and the Failure of Macroeconomic Policy, 1965–1979.* Cheltenham, UK: Edward Elgar.

Meltzer, Allan. 2005. "Origins of the Great Inflation." *Federal Reserve Bank of St. Louis Review* 87 (2, part 2): 145–75.

———. 2010. *A History of the Federal Reserve,* vol. 2. Chicago: University of Chicago Press.

Nelson, Edward. 2005a. "The Great Inflation of the 1970s: What Really Happened?" *Advances in Macroeconomics* 3: Article 3.

———. 2005b. "Monetary Policy Neglect and the Great Inflation in Canada, Australia and New Zealand." *International Journal of Central Banking* 1 (1): 133–79.

Nelson, Edward, and Kalin Nikolov. 2004. "Monetary Policy and Stagflation in the UK." *Journal of Money Credit and Banking* 36 (3, part 1): 293–318.

OECD. 1977. *Toward Full Employment and Price Stability.* Paris: Organization for Economic Cooperation and Development.

Okun, Arthur. 1970. *The Political Economy of Prosperity.* Washington, DC: Brookings Institution.

Orphanides, Athanasios. 2003a. "Historical Monetary Policy and the Taylor Rule." *Journal of Monetary Economics* 50:983–1022.

———. 2003b. "The Quest for Prosperity without Inflation." *Journal of Monetary Economics* 50 (3): 633–63.

———. 2004. "Monetary Policy Rules, Macroeconomic Stability and Inflation: A View from the Trenches." *Journal of Money Credit and Banking* 36 (2): 151–75.

Orphanides, Athanasios, and John C. Williams. 2005. "The Decline of Activist Stabilization Policy: Natural Rate Misperceptions, Learning and Expectations." *Journal of Economic Dynamics and Control* 29:1927–50.

Parkin, Michael. 1993. "Inflation in North America." In *Price Stabilization in the 1990s: Domestic and International Policy Requirements,* edited by K. Shigehara, 47–83. Bank of Japan.

Primiceri, Giorgio. 2006. "Why Inflation Rose and Fell: Policymaker's Beliefs and US Postwar Stabilization Policy." *Quarterly Journal of Economics* 121 (3): 867.

Romer, Christina D., and David H. Romer. 1989. "Does Monetary Policy Matter? A New Test in the Spirit of Friedman and Schwartz." In *NBER Macroeconomics Annual 1989,* edited by O. J. Blanchard and S. Fisher, 121–69. Cambridge, MA: MIT Press.

Romer, Christina, and David Romer. 2002. "The Evolution of Economic Understanding and Postwar Stabilization Policy." In *Rethinking Stabilization Policy,* Federal Reserve Bank of Kansas City, 11–78.

Samuelson, Paul, and Robert M. Solow. 1960. "Analytical Aspects of Anti-Inflation Policy." *American Economic Review* 50 (2): 177–94.

Sargent, Thomas. 1999. *The Conquest of American Inflation.* Princeton, NJ: Princeton University Press.

———. 2002. "Commentary: The Evolution of Economic Understanding and Postwar Stabilization Policy." Federal Reserve Bank of Kansas City, *Proceedings* 2002:79–94.

Solow, Robert M. 1982. "Where Have All the Flowers Gone? Economic Growth in the 1960s." In *Economics in the Public Service: Essays in Honor of Walter W. Heller,* edited by Joseph A Pechman and N. J. Simler, 46–74. New York: Norton.

Stein, Herbert. 1984. *Presidential Economics.* New York: Simon and Schuster.

Stock, James W., and Mark W. Watson. 2007. "Why Has Inflation Become Harder to Forecast?" *Journal of Money, Credit, and Banking* 29 (1 suppl.): 3–33.

Taylor, John. 1993. "Discretion versus Policy Rules in Practice." *Carnegie-Rochester Series on Public Policy* 39, pp. 195–214.

———. 1999. "A Historical Analysis of Monetary Policy Rules." In *Monetary Policy Rules,* edited by John Taylor, Chapter 7. Chicago: University of Chicago Press.

Tobin, James. 1966. *National Economic Policy.* New Haven, CT: Yale University.

———. 1972. *New Economics One Decade Older.* Princeton, NJ: Princeton University Press.

Panel Session I
Pioneering Central
Bankers Remember

Practical Experiences in Reducing Inflation
The Case of New Zealand

Don Brash

Introduction

It was a privilege and a pleasure to address the illustrious audience during the conference: a privilege because I am all too conscious that I left the rarefied world of central banking for the anything-but-rarefied world of politics more than six years ago now, and a pleasure because so many conference attendees became old friends during the time I was governor at the Reserve Bank of New Zealand from 1988 to 2002—old friends who added enormously to my understanding of the monetary policy challenges that face all central banks.

Here I want to sketch very briefly the course of inflation in New Zealand through the 1970s and early 1980s but focus most of my attention on the factors that led New Zealand to becoming the first country to formally adopt inflation targeting as we now understand it, on the reasons why that approach to monetary policy seems to have worked very well in New Zealand, and finally on some of the unresolved issues facing us all.[1]

Don Brash is former governor of the Reserve Bank of New Zealand.

For acknowledgments, sources of research support, and disclosure of the author's material financial relationships, if any, please see http://www.nber.org/chapters/c11630.ack.

1. For a slightly fuller discussion of these issues, see "Inflation Targeting 14 Years on," by D. T. Brash, a speech delivered to the American Economics Association conference in January 2002, on the Reserve Bank of New Zealand's website (www.rbnz.govt.nz). For a much fuller discussion, see John Singleton, Arthur Grimes, Gary Hawke, and Frank Holmes, *Innovation in Central Banking: A History of the Reserve Bank of New Zealand* (Auckland University Press, 2006).

Before 1984

Prior to 1984, New Zealand had inflation that was not only high in an absolute sense but had inflation that was markedly higher than the average in other OECD countries, as the graph makes clear. Indeed, with one or two very minor exceptions, our inflation record during the period from 1970 to 1984 was the worst in the Organization for Economic Cooperation and Development (OECD) (see figure PI1.1).

That inflation was driven at least in part by the rapid escalation in international oil prices, as of course it was in all other countries also. But we added to that exogenous factor weak macroeconomic policy—large fiscal deficits and weak monetary policy. The central bank had no independence from government at all, and monetary policy was repeatedly used for cynical political purposes.

The best known example was 1981: we now know that the central bank repeatedly warned the minister of finance throughout that year, confidentially, that inflationary pressures were building, and urged him to authorize a tightening of monetary policy. But the minister of finance, who was also the prime minister, was facing an election late in the year, and did not want to do anything that might jeopardize his chances of winning that election.

He and his party did win the election by a very narrow margin and, faced with the reality of rapidly increasing inflation, in 1982 imposed sweeping

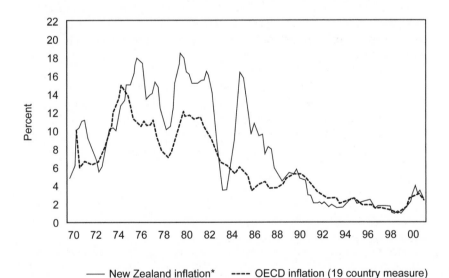

—— New Zealand inflation*   ---- OECD inflation (19 country measure)

*CPI inflation excluding interest rates and GST.

Fig. PI1.1   New Zealand and OECD inflation compared

controls on prices, wages, dividends, and rent that would have made even Richard Nixon blush. Price increases were suppressed for a time but, as so many others who have tried such controls have found, inflationary pressures continued to build.

The Arrival of the Lange/Douglas Labour Government

The election of the Lange/Douglas Labour Government in July 1984 radically changed New Zealand's economic policy framework. This is not the place to describe the extent of the changes wrought. They covered a huge range of policies: import controls were phased out and tariffs drastically reduced; export subsidies were abolished; all price, wage, dividend, and rent controls were removed; the company tax rate was reduced from 48 percent to 33 percent, the top personal tax rate was cut from 66 percent to 33 percent, and a value added tax (VAT) was introduced; many government trading enterprises were privatized; and the banking sector was substantially liberalized.

Most relevant for the present discussion, the incoming government floated the New Zealand dollar, and made it clear that the Reserve Bank was to focus on getting inflation under control. It was also made clear that the minister of finance would not be involved in the day-to-day-decisions about how best to achieve that. The Reserve Bank was granted de facto independence to operate monetary policy with the specific objective of getting inflation down.

Initially, this was a tough challenge. The extensive deregulation of the economy and reform of the tax system induced an extended period of euphoria in much of the business community. The end of the freeze on prices and wages led to a sharp increase in both, and this was compounded in late 1986 when the value added tax was introduced at a rate of 10 percent on all goods and services (except financial services). Indeed, for the twelve months to June 30, 1987—a period that included the introduction of the value added tax—inflation as measured by the Consumer Price Index (CPI) rose to 18.9 percent. Despite monetary policy being tightened substantially following the clear instruction to the Reserve Bank to get inflation under control, with ninety-day bank bills briefly peaking above 25 percent, many in the media and in the general public saw the anti-inflationary fight as a failure, and high inflationary expectations were well entrenched.

Typical of the general skepticism about the prospect for getting inflation under control was the cartoon (figure PI1.2) that appeared in early April 1988. It followed a prediction from the Reserve Bank that inflation would be reduced to below 4 percent within two years.

This was the apparently inauspicious environment in which I was appointed governor and told to get the inflation rate as measured by the CPI

Fig. PI1.2   There was widespread public skepticism that inflation would be brought under control.

Source: Used by permission of the cartoonist, Malcolm Walker.

to between zero and 2 percent. But although inflationary expectations were certainly high, and the challenge of reducing inflation therefore looked substantial, there were a number of extremely helpful factors working toward a constructive outcome.

First, there was the political situation. The Labour Government was strongly committed to getting inflation down to a very low level, and New Zealand's unicameral Westminster-style Parliament meant that cabinet decisions could be rammed through Parliament with little risk of being slowed or diluted. The leader of the Opposition National Party—the man who had been both prime minister and minister of finance between 1975 and 1984—had been toppled, and a slim majority of the National Party caucus was willing to support focusing the Reserve Bank on getting inflation under control.

Second, there was a substantial degree of unanimity between the Reserve Bank and the Treasury about the importance of getting inflation under control, and no opposition on the part of the Treasury to the Reserve Bank's making the essential decisions about monetary policy implementation.

Third, we were lucky in coming to the fight against inflation after major countries—particularly the United States—had proved that firm monetary policy could achieve a huge reduction in inflation. It was not an impossibility: it could be done; Paul Volcker had proved it.

And finally an intangible factor: perhaps because Bill Phillips was a New Zealander, the idea that tolerating a bit more inflation would deliver a bit more economic growth and a bit less unemployment was deeply ingrained in the New Zealand psyche. Yet we had seen with our own eyes that tolerating more inflation than almost every other developed country had not brought us faster economic growth in the 1970s and early 1980s. Our growth had in fact been *slower* than that in other developed countries. Perhaps those who argued that there is no trade-off between growth and inflation in the long run were right after all.

The Advent of Inflation Targeting and the 1989 Reserve Bank Act

It is not entirely clear when inflation targeting in New Zealand was "born." But it is known that then-Minister of Finance Roger Douglas was very concerned in March 1988 that, with inflation moving into single figures for almost the first time in fifteen years (with the exception of the brief period of the freeze in the early 1980s), the public would expect the Reserve Bank to ease monetary policy, and settle for inflation in the 5 percent to 7 percent range. It was in that context that the minister announced, during the course of a television interview on April 1, 1988, that he was thinking of genuine price stability, "around 0, or 0 to 1 percent."

Certainly by the time I actually became governor on September 1 of that year it was clearly understood that my task was to get inflation above zero and below 2 percent. We believed that would reflect genuine price stability— a 1 percent annual increase in the Consumer Price Index, corresponding to genuine price stability after an assumed measurement bias of 1 percent was allowed for, plus or minus 1 percent to allow for the inevitable imprecision of monetary policy.

In preparing the Reserve Bank's annual report for the year to March 1989 in the middle of 1989, I wrote that I was confident that inflation could be reduced below 2 percent by the year to March 1993. I discussed this with the minister of finance, and he asked whether it might be feasible to achieve that by the end of calendar year 1992—he liked the sound of "0 to 2 by '92"! And so it was that "0 to 2 by '92" became the mantra, repeated endlessly by my colleagues and me.

When I became governor in September 1988, the Reserve Bank still had only de facto independence. The legislation governing the bank still left all power over monetary policy in the hands of the minister of finance, and required the bank to use monetary policy to achieve a wide range of economic and social objectives. Like the legislation under which many central banks still labor to this day, New Zealand's central bank legislation had been passed into law when the conventional wisdom was that monetary policy *could* in fact deliver full employment, faster growth, and the secret of eternal life as well. The great advantage of having completely new legislation drafted in the late 1980s was that thinking had moved on considerably since those days. My predecessor as governor had formed a working party to design a new institutional structure, and this process included two senior staff members (Peter Nicholl and Arthur Grimes) talking to central bankers and academic economists around the world. The results formed the basis of the new central bank legislation, which was passed into law in late 1989.

That law was then—and still is, in my opinion—as good as any central bank legislation in the world. Its essential features were the following six items:

- First, the law made it clear that the function of monetary policy was to "achieve and maintain stability in the general level of prices." No reference to growth, or employment, or the balance of payments, or anything else.
- Second, the law required that, on the appointment or reappointment of a governor, there must be a written, public, agreement between the governor and the minister of finance defining what "stability in the general level of prices" means for the five-year term of the governor's appointment.
- Third, the law gave the minister of finance the power to "override" the agreement between governor and minister in case of need, provided that—and it was a crucially important proviso—the "override" was made public.
- Fourth, the governor was to have completely unfettered independence to operate monetary policy as he (or she) thought appropriate to deliver the agreed-upon definition of "stability in the general level of prices."
- Fifth, the governor was required to publish at least once every six months (and in practice, once every three months) a full explanation of how he saw the inflation outlook, and what he was proposing to do about it.
- Sixth, having been given independence to deliver the agreed-upon target, the governor was to be held accountable for any failure to reach that target.

Why do I believe that the legislation was as good as any in the world? Because it was honest and realistic about what monetary policy can actually deliver, namely an inflation rate. Because it was explicit about allowing for a political input into the goal-setting process—thus dealing with what Charles Goodhart has termed the "democratic deficit" problem. Because it constrained that political input both by making it clear that the overriding objective of monetary policy is to maintain stability in the general level of prices and by obliging the political input to be open and transparent for the public and financial markets to see. Because it obliged the governor to explain his actions to the public and financial markets. And because it held the governor to account for any failure to reach the agreed-upon objective, with the law making it explicit that failure could result in dismissal.[2]

Did It Work?

But did the framework established by the 1989 act work? I have no doubt at all that it did.

Most obviously, the inflation rate came down, and came down even faster than originally planned. The original goal had been to get the inflation rate below 2 percent by the end of 1992. Following the election of late 1990, and a widespread belief that the exchange rate needed to come down to ease a substantial balance of payments deficit, the goal was changed so that my task was to get inflation below 2 percent by the end of 1993. It was below 2 percent by the end of 1991, to the considerable surprise of many people both inside and outside the Reserve Bank! To be sure, the inflation rate briefly exceeded the top of the 0 to 2 percent range in the mid-1990s, and is well outside the now 1 to 3 percent range at the present time, driven in large part by the rapid increase in the price of oil and other commodities. But taking the last seventeen or eighteen years as a whole, the framework has kept New Zealand inflation at a very moderate level, certainly no higher on average than that in major developed countries.

Yes, there was a cost in reducing inflation from the high level of the 1970s and early 1980s—I know of no case where inflation has been reduced *without* cost. But the cost is always to some extent a function of how entrenched inflationary expectations have become. And although I cannot prove it, I believe that the framework established by the 1989 act, with its mandatory transparency and clear accountability for the governor, did help to reduce inflationary expectations in New Zealand in the very late 1980s and early 1990s.

I well recall that, in late 1990, not many months after the minister of finance and I had formally agreed on the 0 to 2 percent target after the 1989 act became law, the head of the New Zealand Council of Trade Unions, Ken Douglas, wrote an article that appeared in one of New Zealand's major newspapers.[3] The article argued strongly that the Reserve Bank was focused on an undesirably narrow objective (namely, low inflation), but that, as long as that was the case, unions would need to moderate their wage demands to avoid increases in unemployment. In the weeks that followed, he actively,

2. I well recall discussing the wording of the legislation with the minister in early 1989. I expressed surprise that the legislation envisaged an agreement between the minister and the governor, not between the minister and the Reserve Bank. "Ah yes," I was told, "but we can't fire the whole bank. We can't even realistically fire the whole board. But we sure as hell can fire the governor!"

3. *The Dominion,* October 31, 1990.

and with very considerable personal courage, campaigned for moderate wage settlements as a way of reducing unemployment.

I have little doubt that the inflation target played a part in encouraging employers and unions to adjust their wage settlements to levels that were quite quickly consistent with the inflation target, thus reducing the social cost of achieving that target. My colleagues and I certainly devoted a huge amount of effort to making it clear to everybody who would listen—and some who were reluctant to listen—that we were deadly serious about our commitment to getting inflation below 2 percent within the agreed time-frame. This involved not simply formal monetary policy statements every three months but many hundreds of informal speeches to Rotary Clubs, Chambers of Commerce, farmers' groups, church groups, women's groups, and schools.

The framework also had an effect on fiscal policy. We saw this most dramatically in mid-1990 when the minister of finance announced an expansionary budget just months before the general election scheduled for late that year. Markets were concerned about the loosening in fiscal policy, and became uneasy about the future direction of policy. This was reflected in a rise in long-term interest rates and a fall in the exchange rate, to which we responded by tightening monetary policy. Immediately, an editorial in New Zealand's largest daily paper noted that the budget had "rekindled inflationary expectations. The [Reserve Bank] was bound to lift interest rates. . . . Electors are frequently bribed to their ultimate cost. This time the independence of responsible monetary control quickly exposes a fiscal fraud."[4] The main Opposition party campaigned in the election on a commitment to get interest rates reduced, not by leaning on the central bank but by "giving monetary policy some mates" through tighter fiscal policy and deregulation of the labor market.

Five years later, with the party that had been in Opposition now in government, and with several years of fiscal surplus behind it, the government undertook to reduce income taxes subject to several conditions being met, one of which was that the Reserve Bank was satisfied that such tax cuts would not require a significant tightening of monetary policy.

The framework established by the 1989 act has also been a very effective way of protecting the central bank from political criticism, at least by the governing party. In my fourteen years as governor, I cannot recall a single instance where a minister, or a member of Parliament in the governing party, criticized the bank for having monetary policy too tight. Because the inflation target was agreed in writing between the minister of finance and me, it would have been difficult for the minister, or any member of his political party, to attack me for having policy too tight

---

4. *New Zealand Herald,* August 3, 1990.

unless inflation fell below the bottom of the 0 to 2 percent target range (later the 0 to 3 percent target range), or appeared likely to do so. And the same situation has continued for my successor: yes, I got plenty of brickbats for having policy too tight from members of the public, and the same has been true of my successor, but to have a supportive government is hugely helpful.

The framework not only encourages *government* to be fiscally responsible, and to refrain from attacking the central bank, it also encourages the *governor* to behave responsibly. I recall reflecting on that in 1996. At that time, monetary policy was very tight, as it needed to be, with inflation slightly over the top of the agreed 0 to 2 percent target. The National Party Government was facing an election at the end of the year. I had myself been a candidate for that party in 1981, and although I had not been a member of that party, or of any other party, since the mid-1980s, some people might have suspected that I would be tempted to ease monetary policy to help the National Party's chances of reelection. I was certainly never tempted to do that, but had I been so tempted, the framework established by the 1989 act would have effectively constrained me. I could only have eased policy if I could have shown, in the bank's quarterly monetary policy statement, that a policy easing was justified by the inflation outlook. And any attempt to show that a policy easing was justified would have required me to convince not only the bank's own economics staff but also the scores of economists and other analysts in the financial market. If they even suspected that I was playing fast and loose with the facts for political ends, interest rates would have been more likely to rise sharply than to fall, as capital fled the country.

There is no doubt in my mind that the framework established by the 1989 act has worked extremely well.

Why Did Inflation Fall?

But what were the factors that led inflation to fall so steadily in the late 1980s and early 1990s—certainly more steadily than most of us expected? Many of my central bank colleagues thought that it would be relatively easy to reduce inflation to about 5 percent, but that we would have huge difficulty in getting it any lower than that, and getting it below 2 percent would be well nigh impossible.

We were helped by the fact that international inflation had also fallen markedly since the early 1980s. We did not have any huge increases in the price of oil to deal with, though of course there was a brief spike in oil prices associated with the Gulf War. The clean float of the New Zealand dollar after March 1985 meant that the Reserve Bank had effective control over primary liquidity in the banking system. The government was running fiscal deficits, but these were gradually reducing and in any event were being fully funded by the sale of bonds on the domestic market.

And of course monetary policy was tight, with the result that both interest rates and the exchange rate were putting downwards pressure on the economy.

One of the fascinating things about the disinflation experience in New Zealand is that monetary conditions tended to adjust almost automatically to the market's understanding of what was needed. The Reserve Bank did not determine a single interest rate and did not intervene in the foreign exchange market to influence the currency. We sought to influence monetary conditions by varying the amount of primary liquidity in the banking system.

Initially, we were very much focused on the direct price effects of exchange rate movements on the inflation rate, and if the exchange rate fell "too far," or conversely rose "too far"—in other words, if the direct price effects of movements in the exchange rate seemed likely to push the inflation rate outside the target range—we would in principle adjust primary liquidity so that the exchange rate moved back to a place where it seemed consistent with the inflation target. But years went by without our actually having to change primary liquidity. Occasionally we would need to "clear our throat," or engage in "open mouth operations," to indicate that the exchange rate was moving in a way that seemed inconsistent with the inflation target, but we rarely had to actually change primary liquidity to achieve the desired change in monetary conditions. It seemed to be sufficient that financial markets knew that we *could* inflict pain on financial markets if we had to. And while it is always best when a deterrent does not have to be used, we were frankly astonished at how much impact our relatively small deterrent seemed to have!

By the mid-1990s, we had moved away from a focus on the direct price effects of movements in the exchange rate and instead were more focused on the effect that interest rates and the real exchange rate had on the output gap, and so on inflation. We still made no attempt to control any interest rate or any exchange rate but in mid-1997 adopted the Monetary Conditions Index (MCI) from the Bank of Canada as a way of signaling to the market whether we wanted overall monetary conditions to be tighter or easier, and by how much. This seemed to be a helpful way of making it clear to the financial market that we had no target exchange rate. But for reasons which I will not debate here, this MCI experiment was not a success, and the bank moved to a conventional approach to the implementation of monetary policy in March 1999, setting an overnight interest rate at which it is willing to lend money to, and receive money from, the banking system. Prior to that time, however, we may well have been the only central bank that set neither an interest rate nor an exchange rate.

Is It the End of History?

Is inflation targeting "the end of history" from a monetary policy point of view?[5] Certainly, I believe it has a huge amount to commend it, and the arguments advanced against it recently, by people like Joseph Stiglitz, seem completely unfounded.[6]

But there remain a number of important unresolved issues, in inflation targeting as in other approaches to monetary policy. How best should central banks communicate the conditionality of their inflation forecasts, while still conveying useful information? To what extent can central banks make sufficiently reliable estimates of the output gap, and to what extent do changes in the output gap now affect the inflation rate?

And is there more to achieving monetary stability than keeping the prices of goods and services purchased by the household sector stable? During the last decade or so, consumer price inflation has been exceptionally well behaved in most major economies. But at the same time, we have experienced severe episodes of monetary instability in other guises, including asset price instability and financial system instability. These experiences leave us with plenty of unanswered questions.

For a small open economy like New Zealand, one of the big policy issues is whether anything can be done to moderate the big swings in the real exchange rate that appear to be inherent in the current policy framework. New Zealand is seen by financial markets as a stable, English-speaking democracy, so when we raise the policy interest rate to restrain inflation we often see a pronounced increase in the exchange rate, with most of the monetary policy pressure being exerted on tradable sectors and too little being exerted on nontradable sectors. The consequence is that the current account deficit increases—recently to some 9 percent of GDP.

We know, because Milton Friedman told us so, that ultimately current account deficits do not matter where the public sector is in surplus and the exchange rate is floating, as is true in New Zealand. But we also know that running a very large current account deficit for decades on end inevitably builds up a very substantial amount of net foreign liabilities, and makes a

5. The suggestion that monetary policy might have reached the "end of history" in the sense that Francis Fukuyama had in mind was first raised, and rejected, by Stephen Grenville, then deputy governor of the Reserve Bank of Australia, in an address to the 30th Anniversary Conference hosted by Monetary Authority of Singapore on July 20, 2001.

6. In one recent article by Stiglitz that appeared in *The Independent Financial Review,* New Zealand, on May 21, 2008, he asserted that "today, inflation targeting is being put to the test and it will almost certainly fail." He extended his sympathies "to the unfortunate citizens" of the twenty-three countries he listed as having adopted inflation targeting. But his description of inflation targeting was a caricature, totally misrepresenting inflation targeting as practiced by all the central banks that I know.

country vulnerable to any interruption in its ability to access world capital markets. I have more than a passing suspicion that we will eventually come to recognize that the central bank needs an additional policy instrument, one that affects the level of spending in the economy without having any direct effect on the exchange rate.

Practical Experiences in Reducing Inflation
The Case of Canada

John Crow

This discussion is in two parts because there are two stories. The first looks at the experience with inflation from the early 1970s up to 1987. The second examines what happened in the years after, focusing mainly on what happened during my seven-year term as central bank governor, from early 1987 to early 1994. I should add that I was at the Bank of Canada from 1973, and for a few years before that was working on Canada for the International Monetary Fund (IMF). So this account reflects considerable direct knowledge of, and substantial involvement in, what happened throughout this period and the reasons why. It is also, of course, unofficial.

The Period to 1987

For many years up until 1987 the Bank of Canada, and from time to time the Federal government, were preoccupied with struggling over, and pushing back, an escalation of inflation. This escalation stemmed from bad luck, compounded by policy misadventures. The bad luck was twofold: first, in the late 1960s being tied under Bretton Woods to the US economy as inflationary demand pressures accumulated there; and second, being the recipient, like everyone else, of two oil (mostly) shocks in the 1970s. The misadventures were: first, while taking the bold step of moving to a floating exchange rate in early 1970 and seeing it appreciate, not taking in the end advantage of its inflation protection properties; and second, compounding this lapse by pursuing demand policies (particularly fiscal policies) that helped propagate

John Crow is former governor of the Bank of Canada.

For acknowledgments, sources of research support, and disclosure of the author's material financial relationships, if any, please see http://www.nber.org/chapters/c11173.ack.

the relative price shocks generally and cumulatively. Monetary policy, while always concerned over inflation, was imbued with a spirit of gradualism when it did address inflation directly. Put another way, the Bank of Canada was largely in a reactive mode to what turned up, whether in terms of what the Federal government thought could or should be done by Canada about inflation, or in terms of what happened in the United States regarding inflation control.

It should be added for completeness that in the early 1970s there was genuine uncertainty as to the amount of slack in the economy. This arose mainly because of changes to the economic meaning of the unemployment statistics—a change brought about by increases in the incentives to remain unemployed stemming from substantially improved terms for unemployment insurance that were introduced in 1971 and 1972. The general assessment of the likely growth of Canadian productivity (about 2 percent) also turned out to be over-optimistic. However, these difficulties for analysis and forecasting were a secondary factor in the general, somewhat tentative and episodic, approach to inflation control taken in that period. The basic rule was that whatever was to be done regarding inflation, there was to be no recession on this account. So policy in general, and monetary policy in particular, was fighting inflation with at least one hand behind its back.[1]

Floating for What?

When Canada in 1970 broke the Bretton Woods rules by floating, it contended that this was done to gain better control over its money supply. But interestingly enough, while the Bank of Canada (of course) supported the government's decision to change the exchange rate regime, it did so with a touch of reluctance. My interpretation of this is that the bank was going to lose the fixed exchange-rate anchor for monetary policy, and did not really know what to put in its place. The bank also appeared to believe that there was more scope for Canadian monetary policy to affect domestic demand under the fixed-rate regime than in fact there was. In any case, then and in the years following, the bank was continually looking to coordination with governmental actions to control inflation. In short, monetary policy was a follower.

However, governmental attention to inflation was episodic. With a close to 10 percent rise in the currency as an early result of the float, pressure from government switched from any focus on monetary control to one of avoiding further appreciation.

This bias continued even as the grain-oil shock hit from 1972, and was

1. The focus in this discussion is on inflation reduction, not prevention. However, it is worth emphasizing, on a cautionary note and in a more contemporaneous context, that the amount of slack (or recession) that monetary policy might need to produce to *prevent* inflation is surely less than what it takes subsequently to reduce it.

compounded explicitly by fiscal policy. By way of illustration, in early 1973, just as my predecessor entered office, the federal minister of finance, in his budget speech, declared himself ready to run the risk of still higher inflation as a trade-off for lower unemployment. He also congratulated the Bank of Canada for running a monetary policy sufficiently expansionary to ward off Canadian dollar appreciation.[2]

From then until 1987, inflation developments in Canada basically mirrored inflation flows and ebbs in the United States—but with somewhat more inflation overall in Canada. This situation should not be taken to imply that Canada gave up trying to do something about inflation through domestic policies. But what it did mean was that in reflection of this difference in inflation outcomes, the Canadian dollar had a pronounced tendency to depreciate bilaterally after the mid-1970s. This tendency was also something that the bank had continually to struggle with, lest the decline of the currency gather its own momentum and also feed into domestic interest rates, which already seemed far too high to most people.

Giving Monetary Aggregate Targets a Chance

In 1975 Governor Bouey delivered a speech that came to be known as the "Saskatoon Manifesto." In it, he stated that "whatever else may need to be done to bring inflation under control, it is absolutely essential to keep the rate of monetary expansion within reasonable limits."

The context for these remarks, seen as dramatically Friedmanesque by many in Canada but as simply practical at the Bank of Canada, was twofold: first, work had been done at the bank for several years on monetary aggregate targeting in response to the burgeoning academic literature, and there was pressure on the governor from senior staff to apply it; second, there was in 1975 a need for the bank to put something quantitative and of a decelerating nature in the policy shop window to go along with soon-to-be-announced governmental prices and incomes controls. The general plan was to use interest rates to generate a progressive slowing in monetary expansion that was in line with the implicit control targets for inflation of 8 percent for the first year, 6 percent for the second, and 4 percent for the third (Sargent 2005). This was taken to mean annual growth rates for narrow money (M1) within a 10 to 15 percent range for the first year (but biased toward the lower end of that range) and declining year-by-year thereafter to approach a rate consistent with "price stability." The prices and incomes controls came into

---

2. The way it was actually put was that "monetary policy . . . encouraged Canadians to borrow in domestic rather than in foreign markets." Two and a half years later, in June 1975 and with inflation much higher still, the minister noted in his budget speech that "the faster rise in costs in this country than in the United States is casting a shadow over our economic future." However, in the same speech, he rejected "again, and in the most categorical manner . . . the policy of deliberately creating, by severe measures of fiscal and monetary restraint, whatever level of unemployment is required to bring inflation to an abrupt halt. . . . The cost would be much too high. In human terms for me it would be unthinkable."

force in 1975 and were taken off in 1978.[3] However, the bank stayed with money targets until the early 1980s.

Others will delve into the advantages or otherwise of monetary aggregate targets, or indeed how exactly to look at "money" (or "credit") besides other things, for useful policy information. Here it should be sufficient to note that because of the strong interest elasticity of demand for checking balances and the increasing substitution of interest-bearing checking deposits for noninterest ones, the M1 aggregates slowed drastically even as inflation was accelerating in the latter part of the 1970s. The targets were increasingly ignored both within the bank and outside, and finally dropped in 1982. Or, as Governor Bouey put it soon after: "We didn't abandon M1, M1 abandoned us!" The bank pondered for quite some years after the possibility of using a broader, less interest-elastic and by definition more inclusive, monetary aggregate as a target. But neither Mr. Bouey nor I ever felt sufficient confidence in possible successors to M1 to take that plunge a second time.

Forced Back to the Exchange Rate

The Bank of Canada's attempt to use a money target to slow inflation, whether as a worthy attempt to generate a decelerating path for nominal demand in line with the wage–price objectives of controls or on a stand-alone basis, was in any event preempted by the great US disinflation, beginning in 1979. As already noted, inflation in Canada was tending then to run at least as high as in the United States.

What was the bank to do in the face of the dramatic rise in US short-term interest rates? At first, it aimed basically to match those increases, with the immediate goal of avoiding a dive in the currency. But this did not stop the Canadian dollar from weakening sharply and threatening to cause yet more inflation. Accordingly, the tactic shifted to one of squeezing domestic liquidity harder and forcing Canadian interest rates somewhat higher than US rates at the short end, so as to provide a more persuasive story to savers and investors.[4] This reaction mitigated the impact on the currency, though it did not stop it out completely. Canada was by no means targeting the exchange rate, either bilaterally or in terms of its effective (G10) exchange rate. However, it might be fairly said to have had (for want of something better, i.e., a clear domestic anchor) a de facto "crawling peg" for the Canada–US exchange rate, and thereby a dragging monetary anchor on inflation.

As interest rates escalated, there were many calls for a "made in Canada" monetary policy. This was accompanied by strong questioning as to what the bank thought it was up to through the regular consultations "on monetary

3. The author was seconded from the bank to the body administering the controls for a few months, beginning in late 1975.
4. To assist the process, the bank moved from a fixed to a floating bank rate.

policy and on its relation to general economic policy" that the governor is required to undertake with the minister of finance under the Bank of Canada Act. It was in this tense domestic context that the Bank of Canada made its concerns, indeed fears, known forcefully at one of the regular G10 governors' meetings held at the Bank for International Settlements (BIS). By Governor Bouey's informal oral account, he emphasized there that without an easing in the US policy stance on monetary expansion, "we will all be shoveling out money soon by the bucketful to save failed businesses," or words close to that. In any event, US policy backed off somewhat beginning in 1982, to the significant relief of the Bank of Canada.

A Temporary Peace

In the mid-1980s and up to 1987, Canadian monetary policy was essentially running in neutral—paying some attention still to the exchange rate but not being particularly preoccupied by much else. This was in part perhaps because the bank was coping with the fallout from the twin failures in 1985 of two small banks, an event that had the shock value of being the first such event in Canada since 1923. In any case, as monetary conditions eased in the United States, so did they in Canada. And inflation eased off as well. By early 1987 inflation in Canada was down to about 4 percent—and somewhat less than it had been when Mr. Bouey entered office fourteen years earlier.

By way of a conclusion for this part of the account and as a lead-in to the next, I want to note Gerald Bouey's key remarks in his 1982 Per Jacobssen Lecture, "Finding a Place to Stand." There, he made a point of observing that "monetary policy must therefore give high priority to the preservation of the value of money," and concluded by saying that "economic performance over time will be better if monetary policy never loses sight of the goal of maintaining the value of money." My own thinking was that since this was true, the important question still to be faced was how the Bank of Canada should go about having these sensible observations be not only true but also more real. This meant that we needed to test further the meaning of the phrase "high priority."

What Happened After?

Monetary policy for several years after 1987 affords some contrast with the earlier period. The bank set out its stall early, and pursued the objective of inflation reduction with consistent focus—a single-mindedness that at the time seemed praiseworthy to some and noxious to many. Inflation did come down significantly (though not easily), and from about 1992 inflation in Canada, as measured by the Consumer Price Index (CPI), has stayed around 2 percent. That is to say, there have been no further reductions in inflation, and therefore the subsequent years lie outside the mandate for this review.

Bank of Canada's Authority to Act

This is territory that is both tricky and sensitive. Judging by its statutory mandate as set out in the preamble to the Bank of Canada Act, the bank has considerable scope to set the course of monetary policy. This scope is subject to "regular consultation" with the minister of finance and, ultimately, a ministerial directive. However, it should be emphasized that regular consultation is not the same as taking instructions, although it surely does mean listening very carefully. And if it did mean taking instructions, there would be no need for the explicit provisions in the Bank of Canada Act under which the minister may issue a directive to the bank on the specific policy to be followed, provided the directive is published forthwith. No directive has ever been issued. (For specifics regarding the bank's mandate as set out in the preamble to the Bank of Canada Act, and also the consultation/directive provisions in the act, see the appendix.)

That being said, it can be taken for granted that however these provisions are read, the governor will always wish to get along with the minister of finance and his officials, and in particular to find common ground regarding the monetary policy to be pursued. In my time, Michael Wilson (the minister of finance for most of the period) was fundamentally supportive of the clear anti-inflationary stance taken, because he thought that this was the way the world was going, and also the way it needed to go. However, some of his senior officials clearly were not so supportive, government in general was manifestly ambivalent, and the Opposition openly hostile.[5] However, and contrary to the earlier period, it is worth noting that in this one the Federal government said relatively little about inflation. Thereby, it emphasized at least implicitly the bank's responsibility for both monetary policy goals and instrumentation. At the same time, the bank itself said a great deal, in speech after speech of the governor's.[6]

That is to say, and since I was concerned not to leave a policy vacuum that others might seek to fill, I was quick to set forth publicly my views that the central purpose of Canadian monetary policy was to promote confidence in the future value of Canadian money by establishing and maintaining domestic price stability. Salient features of that publicity program were a lecture in early 1988 at the University of Alberta (Crow 1988b) that folk afterwards termed the "Edmonton Manifesto," and a follow-up speech in

5. As is well illustrated in the recently published memoirs of Prime Ministers Chrétien (2007) and Mulroney (2007). Paul Martin, minister of finance for quite a few years from October 1993 on, is about to publish his.

6. It is also worth noting, and somewhat contrary to tendencies often prevailing elsewhere, that the bank did not cast aspersions on fiscal policy. One important consideration here, besides the fact that the minister of finance knew very well that he had issues, was that it would not be useful to leave any impression that monetary policy might be pushed off its anti-inflationary path by problems with other policies.

the spring at the annual meetings of the Canadian Economics Association (Crow 1988a). There, my remarks were met with particular interest—though with more attentive curiosity than general enthusiasm. The thoughts being expressed were not, it seemed to me, very different in substance from those enunciated by my predecessor in his Per Jacobssen lecture, but there seemed to be a sense around that more monetary policy action to implement them was in store.

So What Is "Price Stability"?

Everyone at this conference probably knows, and central bankers certainly do, that it is much easier to talk about price stability than to define it. And at no point did the bank volunteer a numerical price stability target—although early on I did, in response to a media question, indicate that as regards a desirable rate of inflation, "three is better than four, two better than three, one better than two, and zero better than any of them." In any case, for the earlier part of my term inflation was, notwithstanding anything the bank said or did, moving up as a result of general demand pressures—not a single inflationary supply shock in sight. So the bank could hardly be faulted that severely for raising interest rates, and then keeping them up. However, what was made clear even then was that as far as the bank was concerned, "price stability" would be distinctly less than 4 percent inflation (where we had started) and that zero inflation was not being ruled out.[7] It also became clear that the bank insisted on being judged on how it did regarding inflation and regarding progress toward price stability.

While no timetable for progress was set, it soon was evident that the bank was setting about fighting inflation in a more vigorous way than before. In regard to its monetary operations, one difference that showed up prominently for several years from 1987 was a wider spread of Canadian short-term interest rates over US ones. Traditionally, Canadian short rates had stayed close to US equivalents—almost always above, but not by a great deal—a percentage point or two. But in my time they moved up progressively to some 5 percentage points above US rates by the end of 1990—and without any apology from the central bank as it tried to turn the tide in inflation to a better direction. This was done basically by having Canadian rates go up, but more, as US ones rose in 1987 and 1988, and, by keeping a tight rein on central bank liquidity, not letting ours go down nearly as much when US rates declined. This change in the "rules of the game"—this "made in Canada" policy, or decoupling—got widespread attention, especially because the Canadian dollar was moving up also.

7. Just to note here that when the "Edmonton Manifesto" was being drafted, a point of considerable discussion between myself and Charles Freedman, a deputy governor, was whether the goal should be termed "price stability" or, rather, "very low inflation." My preference on terminology prevailed. I leave it to others to decide whether what exists now in Canada as an inflation target—namely, 2 percent—is "low" or "very low" inflation.

Overlap with Other Policies

Fiscal Policy

The relationship between fiscal policy (both federal and provincial) and a focused anti-inflationary monetary policy was a contentious and awkward issue throughout the period. Governments had not taken advantage of earlier, stronger, economic conditions to improve their fiscal situations. So difficult fiscal debts and deficits only worsened as monetary policy fought inflation with interest rates that went higher than anyone was counting on, and that shifted down only in a cautious manner as economic activity weakened beginning in 1990.

The fact that inflation initially was tending to move up not down, strengthened the Bank of Canada's arguments for its policy position in one sense but made it awkward in another. The minister of finance, in pressing in Cabinet for action to deal with the federal debt and deficit (this had been publicized as a source of serious concern by the government as early as 1985), apparently would point out that fiscal tightening would lead to an easing in interest rates. This was correct as far as it went. The difficulty was that it meant only that interest rates would be lower than otherwise, and not necessarily lower than they were at the time—because Canada was in a situation where, despite monetary policy's initial efforts, inflation pressures were persisting. In short, for this reason at least, there could be no compelling grand bargain between monetary and fiscal policy in regard to interest rate relief—at least, not one that those unfamiliar with ceteris paribus conditions would readily understand.

In point of fact, strong action on the fiscal front was a long time coming. Federal fiscal policy did not make a sharp turn in that direction, with major expenditure cuts, until early 1995, and then as a direct consequence of the "Hudson Bay peso" confidence crisis that was provoked by the Mexican financial crisis that started in late 1994, and a consequent heightened awareness in markets that Canada had a serious fiscal problem. This was after my watch (which ended in early 1994), but it is worth noting that the turn did occur in an environment where inflation was already way down and interest rates (apart from the immediate crisis-induced effects) were much lower.

Finally, it can be noted here that a change in tax policy did come to play a triggering role in the birth of the inflation-targeting regime in early 1991. That development will be addressed a little later.

Trade Policy and the Exchange Rate

As already noted, the widened short-term interest rate differentials sponsored by the bank exerted upward pressure on the Canada–US dollar exchange rate—the bilateral rate that matters far above all others for Canada. This appreciation was bound to be unpopular among exporters. But it also came under more widespread criticism, including in government circles, because at that time Canada was heavily engaged in promoting and negotiating its bilateral Canada–US Free Trade Agreement, and subsequently working to conclude the North American Free Trade Agreement (NAFTA) upon the inclusion of Mexico in the negotiations.

However, there was one sense in which the bank's stance eased the negotiation of the free trade agreements—something that Canada sorely wanted. It was evident that one of the sticking points on the US side was concern among its domestic constituencies (particularly, it seems, US labor) that Canada, with its floating currency, would engage in competitive depreciation, thereby undermining the short-term US economics behind the deal. But while Canada's currency had in fact depreciated significantly after the earlier burst of appreciation upon its 1970 float, the bank was able to demonstrate that because of Canada's greater inflation from 1973 on, this was not reflected particularly in the real bilateral rate. Furthermore, the US Treasury could hardly hold that Canada's monetary policy stance in the late 1980s was contrary to the US immediate trade bargaining interest.

More broadly, the bank took an attitude of what might be termed "benign neglect" toward the currency. For one thing, this meant that we stayed out of currency entanglements such as the short-lived and unlamented Louvre exchange-rate accord of February 1987, notwithstanding Canada's burning desire to be seen as a full-fledged participating member of G7. My express concern at the time was that this would stop Canada from doing the right thing with its monetary policy, for fear of upsetting a prepackaged US–Canada dollar exchange rate—that is, going back to the late 1960s. For another thing, in terms of ongoing policy, we did not adjust interest rates either to try to bring the currency down or to hold it up (except at times of confidence crisis). And in fact the currency did behave in a broadly appropriate way from the viewpoint of desired monetary policy results. It moved up during the time that inflation was being battled, and subsequently (the latter part of my term) moved down as inflation came under better control, but without provoking renewed inflation. Canadian short-term interest rates, of course, also adjusted upwards and then in a downward direction over the period in question.[8]

Getting on Top of Inflation

In terms of drama, political economy implications and interest among other policymakers and monetary economists generally, the big event in the period from 1987 to 1994 was introduction of inflation reduction targets (yes, inflation *reduction*) in early 1991.

---

8. On a mildly technical plane, it can be noted that for a number of years the bank attempted to "measure" monetary policy through the use of a monetary conditions index—a weighted average of interest rate and exchange rate changes. However, this approach was finally discarded, essentially because exchange rate changes were not provoked solely by interest rate developments, thus making the index a challenge to interpret from a monetary point of view.

This is not the occasion to examine the pros and cons of such targets. In any event, when Canada adopted them there was no literature available except through the example shown by New Zealand about a year earlier. Rather, what is done here is to note some features in the early Canadian experience that may be of broader interest.

First, the adoption of targets was the result of an approach by the minister of finance to the governor, in the fall of 1990. While I can only speculate on the reasons for this approach, I am inclined to believe that it was the product of two things. On the one hand, the government's decision to introduce a value added tax would by itself push prices up by about 1 1/2 percent. On the other, the bank had already made clear that, while conceding this first-round effect, it would move determinedly against any knock-on effects; that is, through wages. This latter likelihood seemed real enough, inasmuch as the tax was not at all popular and powerful union leaders were claiming 7 percent wage increases to offset, as they chose to see it, the 7 percent Good and Services Tax, or GST.[9] (Coincidentally with introduction of the targets and the tax, the government also froze the salaries of all federal public servants. This would increase their interest in a good inflation outcome, although it is unlikely that the government did it for this particular reason.)

Second, the fact that the Federal government took the initiative because of its pressing GST problem put the bank in a good position to bargain for more ambitious targets for inflation reduction than the Department of Finance originally envisaged. These included getting specific targets for inflation lower than 3 percent, and including commitments to inflation reduction for a longer rather than shorter span of years. The bank did this in recognition of the very fact that in signing on to such an agreement, it would itself be committed with government in decisions over monetary policy in a way that it had not been before. Such commitment was fine, as long as it was on the basis of strong anti-inflationary numbers that government was also committed to, and that had a decently lengthy policy horizon. The result of some strenuous negotiations was a series of announced targets that foresaw a reduction in inflation over four years from the early 1991 year-to-year peak (with the GST effect) of close to 7 percent, to 2 percent by 1995.

Third, while this was as far as matters could be pressed at that time in terms of specific targets, the bank also obtained agreement that 2 percent was not necessarily the endpoint, though admittedly further work needed to be done to establish what would constitute price stability. Also, it was declared, the experience gained over the time that it was expected to take to get to 2 percent, should itself be expected to produce evidence on what more might, or might not, be done. In other words, the bank was trying

9. For some reason, the term "VAT" was unpopular in Canada and shunned by government.

very hard to embed a long-term and progressive commitment from both parties.

Fourth, while inflation targets these days are principally seen as a means of *anchoring* inflation expectations, as initially employed in Canada they were supposed to steer expectations, along with inflation itself, in a *downward* direction.

Fifth, while refinements such as the concept of flexible inflation targeting came much later, it is worth noting that the Canadian set-up made explicit provision for coping with adverse inflation shocks (such as another hike in the GST, for example). Specifically, provision was made for an agreement between the bank and the Department of Finance as to what would be an appropriate path back to the inflation target in the event of a shock of sufficient magnitude. What would be "sufficient magnitude"? At my news conference upon the announcement on the targets, when questioned as to what size shock would qualify for special treatment, I told the media (to their evident disappointment) that we would know a shock of sufficient magnitude when we saw one. None has, to date, been identified as large enough to merit such treatment.

Sixth, the fact is inflation dropped rapidly, and more rapidly than provided for.

Seventh, the fact is there was already a store of disinflationary pressure from monetary policy.

Eighth, and not least important for the longer run, it was recognized by the Federal government then, and since then apparently also, that not only was the Bank of Canada the agent responsible for inflation performance, but it was also to play a central role in the design and further development of the targets. This means that the Department of Finance has limited itself to approval or otherwise of Bank of Canada initiatives in regard to targets. However, this has also included approval as to the extent to which there should be any officially-sponsored, publicly disseminated, discussion of those targets. The latter might well be seen as a monetary policy transparency issue, and one that is deeper than the kinds that central banks and the financial markets customarily focus on.

The one occasion when government's role became active, except for the start, was in late 1993 when, coincident with the appointment of a new Bank of Canada governor, the government in a joint communiqué with the Bank of Canada announced that the target would now be 2 percent (midpoint of a 1 to 3 percent range), at least until 1998. Also, the government and the Bank of Canada, earlier, in 1991, agreed commitment to "price stability" (and to "price stability" being a rate of inflation "clearly below 2 percent" as the probable eventual goal) was expunged. While the incoming minister of finance (Paul Martin) was not, at least initially, a fan of inflation targeting, he may have considered that the arrangement was too risky to drop wholesale. The obvious question he faced, especially for an economy such as Canada's, was what to say instead of inflation targeting that would pass muster with holders of claims on Canada, whether domestic or foreign.[10] Since that time, inflation has stayed broadly consistent with the official Bank of Canada goal, currently, of low and stable inflation. The term "price stability" virtually disappeared from the bank's lexicon in later years.

Finally, in a more positive vein, note might be taken that the bank (with a sign-off from the current minister of finance) announced in November 2006, after many years of promising to undertake a review of the inflation targeting framework, began a wide-ranging program of research designed to reexamine many aspects of it. This reexamination is going to go so far as looking at the value of lowering the current 2 percent inflation target, as well as at *price level* targeting—something that was quite recently advocated, but not actually tried, for Japan.

Lessons

This discussion has contrasted two experiences with inflation reduction—the drawn out Canadian battle over the period from the early 1970s to 1987, and the shorter one from 1987 to 1992. Shorter is clearly better. But was that shorter, sharper, campaign even necessary, when the end result was a mere 2 percentage points off inflation? That is to say, critics of the second campaign (a war of continuation?) might argue that it was not needed—that the "great inflation" was over by 1987 and that 4 percent inflation was good enough.

However, the question that would then still remain was what monetary policy was going to do in regard to inflation. And that was, and is, a crucial question for a central bank. In this regard, I did not think that 4 percent was a credible goal because I did not believe that economic agents would believe that the authorities would stick to a number that promised, essentially, "inflation." That is to say, if 4 was okay, why not 5, why not 6, and so on? And why would policy then fight to bring it down when it moved up? The test here may be whether it can be demonstrated that strong expectations regarding an unchanged future course of inflation are likely to form at a rate as "high" as 4 percent. My own view is that we would discover that there is no such demonstration, and that only generating a number appreciably closer to "price stability" would provide an adequate basis for expectations that buttress the objective. The Canadian experience, while not as ambitious as it might well have been from 1994 on, does not, at least, disprove that view.

10. Canadian monetary policy had become a political issue, at least for the Opposition. What, then, was the alternative? The new government, when in opposition, had announced in the fall 1993 election campaign that its "two-track policy of economic growth and fiscal responsibility will make possible a monetary policy that produces lower real interest rates and keeps inflation low, so that we can be competitive with our partners." However, no one explained what that meant in terms of monetary policy actions, and I have been unable to either.

My second observation is that the Canadian experience supports the maxim that "inflation is always and everywhere a monetary phenomenon"— in the following particular sense. What that experience suggests is that there will not be a fully convincing stance against inflation, whether prevention or reduction, unless the central bank takes a prominent role, or better still the lead, through its monetary policy actions and through a clear articulation of its monetary policy priorities. Relying on general government to give sufficient focus to inflation control, whether through income controls or fiscal policy, is inherently and demonstrably implausible. This is because of both the multiplicity of governmental objectives and the speed with which governmental objectives and priorities are inevitably shuffled. It is, of course, helpful if government recognizes this, and thereby recognizes that the central bank has to take the lead as regards to what is done and also, quite likely, what has to be done. That is essentially the difference between the second period and the first. Those who, as is commonplace in Canada, place the big change in inflation performance in Canada on the introduction of inflation targeting in 1991, overlook the way monetary policy laid the groundwork in the years before. That is to say, without downplaying the contribution of government, monetary policy was decisive for a remarkably successful entry into those targets.

Another lesson that may be worth broader attention is that while Canada is now (as I have emphasized many times here) a relatively small and very open economy, it has, in the end, been able to turn in a very decent domestic inflation performance on the basis of its homegrown monetary efforts. This is not to say that external conditions do not matter, but on the Canadian evidence to date they cannot be taken to be decisive.[11]

Finally, and as a variant on the abovementioned, an encouraging development has been the broad appropriateness of the behavior of the Canadian dollar exchange rate as an adjustment mechanism. This allows, among other things, Canadian monetary policy to focus properly on the value of the Canadian dollar within Canada. Whether a floating rate regime is truly the best system for Canada is a topic that surfaces periodically, but one that is not central to this conference's agenda. However, what can be said with some assurance is that Canadian monetary policy can work appropriately under such a regime, inasmuch as it can in the end deliver a decent domestic inflation outcome as a contribution to domestic economic well-being. Put another way, if Canada were to move to some other exchange-rate regime, it would not be because its monetary policy cannot, in practice as well as in theory, deliver the goods on inflation.

---

11. It would be fascinating, of course, to stress test this proposition further by repeating the experience of the late 1970s and early 1980s, with the same US conditions and monetary policy as in that period, but with the more robust Canadian domestic monetary policy stance that has developed since then. However, it is also to be hoped that nothing like this is in the works.

Appendix

Selections from the Bank of Canada Act

1. Preamble[12]

WHEREAS it is desirable to establish a central bank in Canada to regulate credit and currency in the best interests of the economic life of the nation, to control and protect the external value of the national monetary unit and to mitigate by its influence fluctuations in the general level of production, trade, prices, and employment, so far as may be possible within the scope of monetary action, and generally to promote the economic and financial welfare of Canada.

2. Government direction

Consultations

(1) The minister and the governor shall consult regularly on monetary policy and on its relation to general economic policy.

Minister's directive

(2) If, notwithstanding the consultations provided for in subsection (1), there should emerge a difference of opinion between the minister and the bank concerning the monetary policy to be followed, the minister may, after consultation with the governor and with the approval of the governor in council, give to the governor a written directive concerning monetary policy, in specific terms and applicable for a specified period, and the bank shall comply with that directive.

Publication and report

(3) A directive given under this section shall be published forthwith in the Canada Gazette and shall be laid before Parliament within fifteen days after the giving thereof, or, if Parliament is not then sitting, on any of the first fifteen days next thereafter that either House of Parliament is sitting.

---

12. This appendix is a reproduction of portions of the Bank of Canada Act (R.S.C., 1985, c. B-2). Taken from the Department of Justice, Canada, website: http://laws-lois.justice.gc.ca /eng/acts/B-2/page-1.html#docCont.

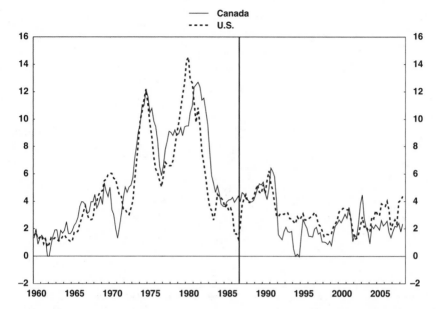

Fig. PI2.1   Consumer Price Index (quarterly year-over-year percentage change)

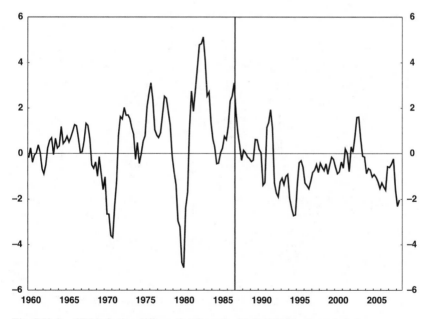

Fig. PI2.2   CPI inflation differential Canada–United States (quarterly)

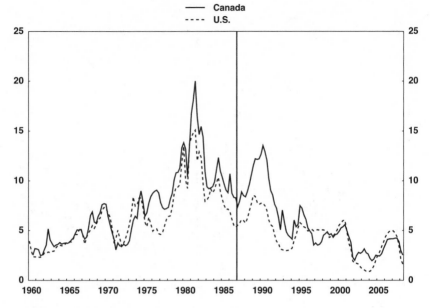

Fig. PI2.3   Three-month Treasury bill rates (quarterly)

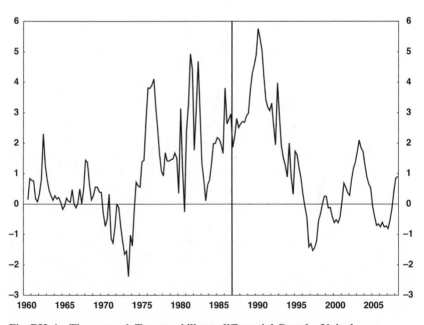

Fig. PI2.4   Three-month Treasury bill rate differential Canada–United States (quarterly)

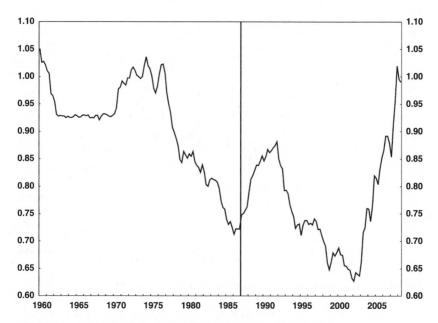

Fig. PI2.5   Canadian dollar/US dollar exchange rate (quarterly)

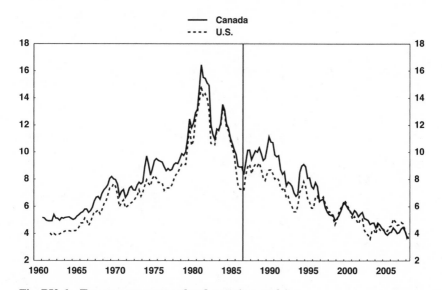

Fig. PI2.6   Ten-year government bond rates (quarterly)

Note: Prior to June 1982, gov. of Canada Bond Yield Averages (excl. extendible)—ten years and over.

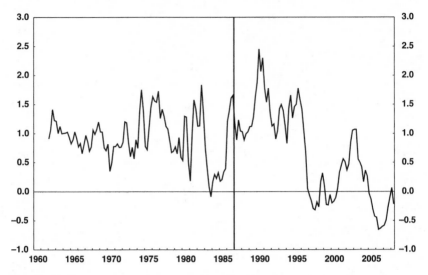

Fig. PI2.7   Ten-year government bond rate differential Canada–United States (quarterly)

Note: Prior to June 1982, gov. of Canada Bond Yield Averages (excl. extendible)—ten years and over.

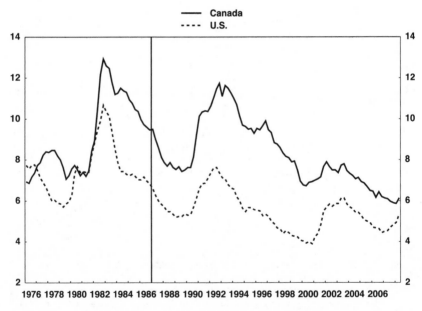

Fig. PI2.8   Unemployment rate (seasonally adjusted, quarterly)

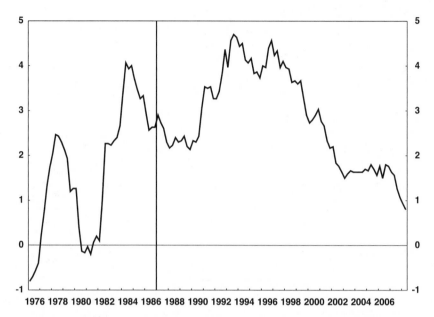

Fig. PI2.9   Unemployment rate differential Canada–United States (seasonally adjusted, quarterly)

References

Bouey, Gerald K. 1975. "Saskatoon Manifesto." Remarks from the 46th Annual Meeting of the Canadian Chamber of Commerce, Saskatoon, Saskatchewan, September 22. Mimeo, Bank of Canada Library.

———. 1982. "Monetary Policy—Finding a Place to Stand." 1982 Per Jacobssen Lecture, Toronto, Ontario. Washington, DC: Per Jacobssen Foundation.

Chrétien, Jean. 2007. *My Years As Prime Minister.* Toronto: Alfred A. Knopf Inc.

Crow, John W. 1988b. "The Work of Canadian Monetary Policy." Eric John Hanson Memorial Lecture Series, University of Alberta, January.

———. 1988a. "Some Responsibilities and Concerns of the Bank of Canada." Address at the Annual Meeting of the Canadian Economic Association, University of Windsor, June 4. *Bank of Canada Review,* June 1988.

———. 2002. *Making Money.* Toronto: John Wiley & Sons.

Department of Finance. 1975. Budget speeches delivered by the Honourable John N. Turner, Ottawa, February 19, 1973, and June 23, 1975. Mimeo, Bank of Canada Library.

Mulroney, Brian. 2007. *Memoirs: 1939–1993.* Toronto: Douglas Gibson Books.

Sargent, John. 2005. "The 1975–78 Anti-Inflation Program in Retrospect." Working Paper 2005–43, Bank of Canada, December.

Panel Session I Discussion

Michael Bordo questioned Crow on the backlash that ensued due to the policy tightening during his tenure, given the political noise that followed. Crow pointed out that his predecessor was wildly unpopular through 1972 and 1987, and he took a different approach to policymaking by making speeches about the role of monetary policy, most notably his speech in Alberta that came to be known as the Edmonton Manifesto. The minister of finance was sympathetic to Crow, and the opposition was opposed to his policies without having any clear picture of what it wanted to do. While he could have stayed longer at the Bank of Canada, Crow decided to leave given the insistence that the government was placing on him to change the inflation target, as well as the bank's mandate. In the end, Crow fundamentally believed that price stability should be a central role, not the central role.

Lars Svensson inquired about Crow's opinion on the exact number for the inflation target, as well as his views on price-level targeting. Crow felt that an inflation target of zero was better than one, yet had no real grasp on the exact number it should be. When the inflation targets were put into effect, the Bank of Canada was targeting a level of two, and then would reexamine the situation once they reached that level. Admittedly, an inflation target of two now seems to have a lot of acceptance and an iconic status in Canada as a decent number, and it is pleasing to know that the bank is reexamining the target now. In terms of price-level targeting, Crow had very little opinion other than selling it the way it was sold in Japan, in the sense that you should give inflation when you need it. But in the end, Crow felt that Canada, as a medium-sized open economy with a floating exchange rate, has to be tough on inflation.

Edward Nelson began the questions to Donald Brash, wanting more detail on the influence of the New Zealand experience on Australia. Brash described how the governor of the Reserve Bank of Australia in the 1990s was negative about inflation targeting, yet his successor was quite keen on it. There was a bit of trading going on between the two countries; Australia adopted the inflation target, while New Zealand adopted the interest rate instrument of the cash rate. Australia's framework was similar, except that interest rate decisions were made by a board rather than by the government. Brash also commented that he benefitted a lot from interactions with Crow and the Bank of Canada. Crow interjected that the Reserve Bank of Australia jokingly got inflation down without even knowing it in the 1990s, mostly due to the influence of inflation-targeting practices.

Allan Meltzer asked about the bank's reaction to onetime price shocks, pointing out that Milton Friedman always stressed how inflation is always and everywhere a monetary phenomenon. But Friedman also understood that if you have excise tax increases, onetime devaluations, oil price shocks, and so forth, then it is not inflation, but relative price changes that matter.

Brash was quick to clarify that the policy agreements of the Reserve Bank of New Zealand stressed that price level shocks that are totally exogenous are not included in the definition of the central bank's target. He cited the example of the introduction of 10 percent value added tax, which tacked on approximately 8.9 percent to the Consumer Price Index. This is something that the bank did not try to offset. In terms of exchange rate movements, the bank was less clear. Thus, if the shock is totally exogenous, do not react. If there is some sort of pass-through into the economy, then the bank should look into it more. Meltzer worried that explaining this to the public was difficult. Brash agreed, and added that by and large the public understood. But he remembered that in the early 1990s, the minister of finance was proposing amending the mandate of the bank, but there was fear that it would be thrown out. The bank had instituted a forward track policy, with which they predicted a path for inflation and set a target band for inflation in the future. Alan Blinder wondered whether there were arguments against these forward tracks, and Brash stressed that if the bank was projecting an inflation rate far outside the target under the current policy, then this was not sensible policy and it would not be allowed to happen voluntarily. When inflation was being predicted, they needed to simultaneously predict what path of interest rates would deliver that path of inflation. Blinder clarified by specifying that the rationale for it was then to explain the inflation path and how to get it back on track.

Benjamin Friedman expressed wonderment about how the empirical literature that studies industrialized countries has not found a difference across countries in terms of macroeconomic performance when comparing inflation-targeting versus non-inflation-targeting monetary policy regimes. Brash did not seem surprised, and claimed that inflation targeting is not magic. It is an effort to be more explicit to the public about what the central bank is doing. Regardless of being an inflation-targeting central bank, if your objective is to keep inflation under control, then your reaction function might look similar to that of a central bank that explicitly has an inflation target. Friedman continued by asking whether it would matter if one said that the objective was to simultaneously keep inflation low and to achieve maximal sustainable employment. Brash concluded by referring to a former governor of the Reserve Bank of Australia, who emphasized that he interpreted his inflation target as achieving the maximal possible growth rate of Australia along with stable prices.

I

Early Explanations

1

The Great Inflation
Did the Shadow Know Better?

William Poole, Robert H. Rasche, and
David C. Wheelock

> The failure to control inflation was not inevitable. The policies
> did not fail because they were poorly executed. They failed
> because they were poorly conceived.
> —Shadow Open Market Committee, August 23, 1973[1]

The Shadow Open Market Committee (SOMC) held its first meeting on
September 14, 1973. The SOMC was formed in response to rising inflation
in the United States and the apparent failure of either the Nixon administration or the Federal Reserve to formulate effective policies to control
inflation. Under the leadership of Karl Brunner and Allan Meltzer, the
SOMC met twice a year to review US economic policy and discuss policy-
related research. At the conclusion of every meeting, the committee issued
a statement evaluating current policy and proposing an alternative course
of action.[2] In this chapter, we describe the monetary policy framework of
the SOMC and the statements the committee issued during the Great Inflation period. Further, we simulate a New Keynesian macroeconomic model
embedding a representation of the SOMC policy rule to evaluate whether
the committee's proposals could have resulted in a lower average and more
stable rate of inflation than actually occurred.

William Poole is former president of the Federal Reserve Bank of St. Louis, senior fellow of
the Cato Institute, and Distinguished Scholar in Residence at the University of Delaware, and
was a member of the Shadow Open Market Committee from 1985 to 1998. Robert H. Rasche
is former executive vice president and senior policy advisor at the Federal Reserve Bank of
St. Louis, and was a member of the Shadow Open Market Committee from 1973 to 1999.
David C. Wheelock is vice president and deputy director of research at the Federal Reserve
Bank of St. Louis.

The authors thank the conference participants, especially Allan Meltzer and Christina
Romer, and two referees, for their comments on previous versions of this chapter. The views
expressed in this chapter are not necessarily official positions of the Federal Reserve Bank of
St. Louis or the Federal Reserve System. For acknowledgments, sources of research support,
and disclosure of the authors' material financial relationships, if any, please see http://www
.nber.org/chapters/c9156.ack.

1. Invitation issued to the press and other guests to attend the first meeting of the Shadow
Open Market Committee, held on September 14, 1973. Quoted in Meltzer (2000).
2. See Meltzer (2000) for a short history of the SOMC.

First, we describe the economic environment in which the SOMC was created and the policy views that the SOMC sought to counter. We then describe the SOMC policy framework by highlighting how the views of SOMC members differed from most Federal Reserve officials and many academic macroeconomists. That discussion is followed by a description of the SOMC policy rule. Importantly, the SOMC rule called for a transparent and gradual adjustment of money stock growth to a steady-state rate. We simulate a New Keynesian macroeconomic model embedding the SOMC policy rule to gauge how different the path of inflation might have been if the Federal Reserve had followed the SOMC's policy recommendations. Our simulations illustrate that a gradual adjustment of money stock growth similar to that advocated by the SOMC is likely to result in less impact on output growth and less variability in inflation or output growth than a large onetime adjustment.

1.1   The Great Inflation and the SOMC

When the SOMC first met in September 1973, the United States had already experienced eight years of rising and increasingly variable inflation. Whereas inflation averaged a mere 1.4 percent between January 1952 and December 1964, it averaged 3.9 percent between January 1965 and August 1973, and reached 7.4 percent for the twelve months ending in August 1973.[3]

The Nixon administration's response to inflation, with the strong support of Federal Reserve Chairman Arthur Burns and many academic and professional economists, was to impose controls on wages and prices.[4] A first round of controls was announced on August 15, 1971, and some controls remained in effect into 1974. Burns continued to champion wage and price controls even when most observers had concluded that they were not working. For example, in a speech on June 6, 1973, Burns argued that "the persistence of rapid advances in wages and prices in the United States and other countries, even during periods of recession, has led me to conclude that governmental power to restrain directly the advance of prices and money incomes constitutes a necessary addition to our arsenal of economic stabilization weapons."[5]

Burns attributed the inflation of the late 1960s and early 1970s mainly to rising factor costs, especially labor and energy costs, as well as to government

---

3. We measure the inflation rate here as the year-over-year percentage change in the seasonally-adjusted all-items Consumer Price Index (1982–84 = 100).

4. Nearly 93 percent of respondents to a 1971 survey of members of the National Association of Business Economists favored the use of wage and price controls or guidelines ("Top Economists Are Extremely Ebullient Over 1972 Prospects, Back Nixon Program," *Wall Street Journal,* September 28, 1971, 3), and 61 percent of surveyed members of the American Economics Association supported the administration's freeze on wages and prices ("President to Give Post-Freeze Plan in Speech Tonight," *New York Times,* October 7, 1971, 1).

5. "Some Problems of Central Banking." Quoted in Burns (1978, 156).

budget deficits, social programs, and regulations.[6] He argued that wage and price controls were necessary to stem "cost-push" inflation. For example, in a 1970 speech, he contended that "[g]overnmental efforts to achieve price stability continue to be thwarted by the continuance of wage increases substantially in excess of productivity gains. . . . The inflation that we are still experiencing is no longer due to excess demand. It rests rather on the upward push of costs—mainly, sharply rising wage rates." He argued, moreover, that "monetary and fiscal tools are inadequate for dealing with sources of price inflation such as are plaguing us now—that is pressures on costs arising from excessive wage increases."[7]

Burns's views about inflation were widely shared by leading economists and policymakers throughout the 1960s and 1970s. For example, Samuelson and Solow (1960, 181) argued that "the essence of the [inflation] problem" stemmed from the absence of perfect competition in factor and product markets, whereas Bronfenbrenner and Holzman (1963) cited the power of "economic pressure groups," such as labor unions and monopolistic firms. Throughout the 1960s, the *Economic Report of the President* blamed inflation on "excessive" wage and price increases. For example, the *Economic Report* for 1965 explained that "in a world where large firms and large unions play an essential role, the cost-price record will depend heavily upon the responsibility with which they exercise the market power that society entrusts to them" (1966, 179).

Like Burns, some economists and policymakers claimed that government budget deficits contributed to rising inflation. Federal Reserve Governor Sherman Maisel (1973, 12), for example, wrote that the increasing rate of inflation of the late 1960s and early 1970s was caused by "government deficits; . . . speculative investment in plant, equipment, and labor by business corporations; . . . use of economic power to raise wages and profits; . . . But most significant were the government deficits."

The SOMC was formed to promote an alternative to these widely entrenched views about the causes of inflation and to recommend policies for restoring price stability. The policy analysis and recommendations of the SOMC reflected the monetarist orientation of its members. Accepting Milton Friedman's dictum that "inflation is always and everywhere a monetary phenomenon," the SOMC argued that price stability could be restored only by slowing the growth of monetary aggregates. The SOMC advocated a policy rule characterized by an announced, gradual reduction in money growth to a rate consistent with long-run price stability. The SOMC made specific recommendations for money stock growth at its twice-yearly

---

6. Retrospectively, Burns (1979) cast blame for the Great Inflation widely but emphasized the effects of government budget deficits, social programs, and regulations, as well as a political and economic climate that favored the pursuit of full employment over price stability.

7. "The Basis for Lasting Prosperity" (speech, December 7, 1970). Quoted in Burns (1978, 112–13).

meetings throughout the Great Inflation period and for several years thereafter (provided in appendix A).

1.2   The Shadow's Framework

The SOMC represented a monetarist challenge to the Keynesian views
that dominated the economics profession and the Federal Reserve during the
1960s and 1970s.[8] The fundamental differences between the monetarist and
Keynesian views have been elaborated at length elsewhere.[9] Here we highlight key differences between the SOMC and Federal Reserve policymakers
about the causes of inflation and conduct of monetary policy to bolster our
contention that monetary policy would have been radically different during
the 1970s under a Shadow-led Fed.[10]

1. *Inflation is a monetary phenomenon:* Fed officials often blamed inflation on labor unions, monopolistic pricing, energy price shocks, and government budget deficits and dismissed the notion that money growth and
inflation are closely connected. Burns, for example, testified in 1974 that
"[t]he role of more rapid monetary turnover rates . . . warns against assuming any simple causal relation between monetary expansion and the rate
of inflation either during long or short periods." Burns acknowledged that
"excessive increase in money and credit can be an initiating source of excess
demand and a soaring price level. But the initiating force may primarily lie
elsewhere, as has been the case in the inflation from which this country is
now suffering."[11]

By contrast, SOMC members and other monetarists dismissed "special
factors" explanations for inflation and remained adamant that inflation is
caused solely by excessively rapid growth of the money stock. For example,
Karl Brunner argued that "Persistent increases in the price level are
hardly likely to occur . . . without a similarly persistent monetary growth.
Alternatively, in the absence of persistent and excessive monetary growth
we will not experience any persistent inflation. Moreover, any persistent
acceleration of the money stock eventually unleashes a rising inflation. On

---

8. We do not wish to leave the impression that all Federal Reserve officials shared the same
views. In particular, Darryl Francis, president of the Federal Reserve Bank of St. Louis from
1966 to 1975, advocated policies that were much closer to those recommended by the SOMC
than to those accepted by a majority of his Fed colleagues. See Hafer and Wheelock (2003).

9. For example, see Laidler (1981) or Nelson and Schwartz (2007).

10. Romer and Romer (2004) argue that throughout the Fed's history, the success of monetary policy, or lack thereof, has been mainly due to policymakers's views about how the economy works and what monetary policy can accomplish. They attribute the Fed's inflationary
policy during the 1960s and 1970s initially to a belief in a permanent trade-off between inflation
and unemployment, and later to a natural rate view with a highly optimistic estimate of the
natural rate of unemployment and a highly pessimistic estimate of the sensitivity of inflation
to economic slack.

11. "Key Issues of Monetary Policy" (statement before the House Banking Committee,
July 30, 1974). Quoted in Burns (1978, 177).

the other side, no inflation was ever terminated without lowering monetary growth to the relevant benchmark level."[12]

2. *The market system is inherently stable and economic growth reverts to a natural rate:* Keynesians often argued that expansionary fiscal or monetary policy might be required to ensure that aggregate demand is sufficient to generate full employment, especially in the face of downwardly rigid wages and prices. Samuelson (1960, 265), for example, wrote that "with important cost-push forces assumed to be operating, there are many models in which it can be shown that some sacrifice in the requirement for price stability is needed if short- and long-term growth are to be maximized, if average long-run unemployment is to be minimized, if optimal allocation of resources as between different occupations is to be facilitated." Further, Samuelson and Solow (1960) argued that policies directed at limiting inflation in the short run might increase structural unemployment and reduce economic growth over the long term. The long-run trade-off between inflation and unemployment would worsen, they argued, because an increase in structural unemployment would increase the amount of inflation required to achieve a given reduction in the unemployment rate.

Monetarists held a very different view. Brunner, for example, argued that "the market system acts as a shock absorber and tends to establish a normal level of output. This means that we consider the market system to be inherently stable." Further, he argued that the trend in output "is dominated by real conditions and shocks summarized by technology, preferences, and institutions."[13] And, "monetary impulses do not produce permanent real effects on output, employment, and real interest rates, apart from longer-run real effects exerted via the expected inflation rate or distortionary institutional constraints (e.g., tax rates specified in nominal terms)."[14] In other words, as Friedman (1968) and Phelps (1967) argued, in the long run, output growth converges to a natural rate that is independent of the rate of inflation.[15]

3. *Monetary policy should focus on price stability:* In addition to believing that monetary policy has little or no impact on output in the long run, monetarists were skeptical of using policy to "fine-tune" economic activity in the short run. Monetarists argued that the Fed's attempts to steer a path between inflation and unemployment in the face of inevitable uncertainty about the short-run impact of policy actions and other shocks had exacerbated instability in both inflation and unemployment. For example, William Poole (1975) argued that "By trying to do too much, policymakers

12. "Another View at Fashionable Fallacies." SOMC position paper, February 4, 1980. Reprinted in Lys (1997, 92–96).

13. "Conversation with a Monetarist." Quoted in Lys (1997, 6).

14. "Has Monetarism Failed?," *Cato Journal* 3 (1), Spring 1983. Quoted in Lys (1997, 24).

15. If anything, monetarists believed that inflation would depress economic growth (e.g., Friedman 1977).

have put themselves into a vicious 'stop-go' cycle with ever-widening oscillations. Each period of monetary expansion has been higher than the previous one—considering the 1965, 1967–68, and the 1972–73 expansions. Each of the inflations since 1965 has been worse than the previous one. And each setback in real activity since 1965 has been deeper than its predecessor—in the sequence 1967, 1968–70, 1974–75. This pattern must be broken, and the only method in which I have any confidence is that of stabilizing money growth."[16]

Brunner argued similarly: "The best contribution monetary policy can make to lower the variability of output relative to normal output is the committed adherence to a predictable and stable monetary control path credibly understood by the mass of price and wage setters."[17]

4. *Adverse supply shocks reduce potential output:* The SOMC members argued against basing policy actions on estimates of the gap between actual and potential output, noting that there was little evidence that doing so reduces fluctuations in output. For example, Brunner argued that "short-run adjustments of monetary growth to the magnitude of the gap in the context of an economy with long inflation experience contributes little to the closure of gaps over time." Furthermore, the occurrence of supply shocks "reminds us that we cannot infer from output movements alone whether or not a recession has occurred."[18]

The decline in output and increase in unemployment that followed the first oil shock in 1973 prompted calls for expansionary monetary policy to return the economy to full employment. Brunner, however, argued that the shock had increased the natural rate of unemployment and lowered potential output. Further, he argued that "[t]he distinction between a 'real shock decline' in output and a 'cyclic decline' in output . . . [is] important for policy making. The latter creates an 'output gap' absent from the former. A disregard of the two distinct processes thus magnifies estimates of the 'potential gap' to be removed by expansionary policies. An inadequate analysis of the decline in output observed since November 1973 thus reinforces the danger of inflationary financial responses on the part of policymakers."[19] He also argued that if a decline in output reflects a decline in potential, then "no increase in money stock whatever its magnitude will raise output again."[20] Allan Meltzer argued similarly: "Money cannot replace oil, and monetary policy cannot offset the loss of real income resulting from the oil shock.

16. Quoted by Karl Brunner in "Monetary Policy, Recovery, and Inflation" (SOMC position paper, September 12, 1975, 23).

17. "Our Perennial Issue: Monetary Policy and Inflation" (SOMC position paper, September 1979, 7). Reprinted in Lys (1997, 80–92).

18. "Our Perennial Issue: Monetary Policy and Inflation" (SOMC position paper, September 1979, 7–8). Reprinted in Lys (1997, 80–92).

19. Brunner, "Monetary Policy, Recovery and Inflation" (SOMC position paper, September 12, 1975, 15).

20. "Our Perennial Issue: Monetary Policy and Inflation" (SOMC position paper, September 1979, 8). Reprinted in Lys (1997, 80–92).

The attempt to do so converts the one-time increase in the price level into a permanently higher maintained rate of inflation."[21] Although the impact of oil shocks on potential output was noted in the academic literature (e.g., Phelps 1978), Fed policymakers seem to have relied on overly optimistic estimates of full-employment output growth produced by the Council of Economic Advisers.[22]

5. *The cost of disinflation reflects the monetary authority's credibility:* Whereas the SOMC argued that money growth should be gradually reduced to lower the inflation rate, Burns and many other economists often claimed that reducing money growth to the extent required to halt inflation would result in excessively high unemployment and lost output. For example, in testifying about the rise of inflation in the late 1960s and early 1970s, Burns argued that "an effort to use harsh policies of monetary restraint to offset the exceptionally powerful inflationary forces of recent years would have caused serious financial disorder and economic dislocation. That would not have been a sensible course for monetary policy."[23]

Brunner countered that the cost of disinflation reflects the clarity and credibility of the announced policy, and, echoing Lucas (1976), argued that estimates of the resulting loss in output associated with tighter policy generated by standard models are highly suspect: "The structural properties and response patterns of an economic system are not invariant relative to different policies and policy patterns. The mechanical simulation of a policy program substantially different from the policy patterns prevailing over the sample period used to estimate the model yield . . . little information about the consequences of the program proposed. In particular, the simulations of a model estimated over a period of accelerating inflation probably exaggerate the longer-run unemployment effects of an anti-inflationary program."[24]

Brunner (1983) argued that "[t]he social cost of a disinflationary policy is not predetermined by the magnitude or duration of monetary retardation. . . . The social cost depends crucially on the public's belief in the persistence of the disinflationary action." And, "Credibility depends . . . on the history

21. Draft of proposed statement (SOMC, September 17, 1979, 3).

22. Orphanides (2003) and Romer and Romer (2004) conclude that reliance on an overestimate of potential output can explain much of the Fed's failure to rein in inflation during the 1970s. Orphanides (2003) estimates a Taylor rule using original (i.e., real-time) data and concludes that policy was broadly consistent with a 2 percent inflation target throughout the 1960s and 1970s. Orphanides shows, for example, that estimates of potential output available to policymakers at the time suggested that during 1978 and 1979 output was far below potential when in fact revised data suggest a much smaller gap in 1975 and 1976 and little or no gap in 1977 to 1979. The SOMC estimated that the 1973 oil shock had reduced normal output by about 5 percent (SOMC policy statement, September 17, 1979). For an extended discussion, see Brunner's SOMC position paper, "Monetary Policy, Inflation and Economic Expansion" (September 13, 1976, 16–18).

23. "Key Issues of Monetary Policy" (statement before the House Banking Committee, July 30, 1974). Quoted in Burns (1978, 177–78).

24. "Assessment of Monetary Policy" (SOMC position paper, September 6, 1974, p. 10).

of policymaking and the behavior of the policy institution. Low credibility offers little incentive to modify price-wage setting behavior, and the social cost of disinflation rises correspondingly." Further, "A dominant conviction by market participants that the Federal Reserve Authorities truly, unwaveringly and persistently lower monetary growth produces a decline in the rate of inflation with a comparatively small and rapidly eroding gap [between actual and potential output]. Emergence and magnitude of a gap in the context of an anti-inflationary policy depends foremost on the credibility of the policy."[25]

6. *Policy should be rules based and transparent:* Most Fed officials rejected the call for rules-based policy, especially those involving control of monetary aggregates. Fed Governor Andrew Brimmer, for example, argued that "it would be a disastrous error for the Federal Reserve to try to conduct monetary policy on the basis of a few simple rules governing the rate of expansion of the money supply" (1972, 351). And Burns claimed that "[t]he appropriate monetary growth rates will vary with economic conditions. They are apt to be higher during periods of economic weakness . . . than when the economy is booming. . . . Special circumstances may, however, call for monetary growth rates that deviate from this general rule."[26]

By contrast, the SOMC favored rules-based policy, arguing that discretionary policy can succeed only if monetary authorities have full knowledge of the deterministic and stochastic structure of the economy. Hence, Brunner (1983) argued, "A constant monetary growth regime [is] . . . an optimal risk-minimizing strategy in a state of uncertain and shifting information" (32). Brunner's preferred policy did, however, allow changes in the monetary growth rate in response to changes in the trend of normal real growth and velocity.

7. *Money market (nominal interest rate) targeting is flawed:* The Fed used a "money market" strategy to implement its policy. This strategy evolved from the Fed's borrowed reserves strategy of the 1920s and the interest rate-pegging regime of World War II.[27] After the Fed-Treasury Accord in 1951, the Fed remained committed to maintaining an "orderly" market for government securities and policy often reflected a desire to keep the government securities market on an "even keel," especially when the Treasury was issuing new debt. Fed officials gauged the "tone and feel" of the money markets and judged the stance of policy by movements in nominal interest rates—rising rates were interpreted as reflecting tighter policy and falling rates as looser policy.[28]

Fed officials justified their focus on the money market by claiming that

25. "Another View at Fashionable Fallacies" (SOMC position paper, February 4, 1980). Reprinted in Lys (1997, 982–96).
26. "Key Issues of Monetary Policy" (statement before the House Banking Committee, July 30, 1974). Quoted in Burns (1978, 174).
27. See Brunner and Meltzer (1968), Calomiris and Wheelock (1998), and Meltzer (2003).
28. For additional discussion of Fed policy during the 1950s, see Brunner and Meltzer (1964a), Calomiris and Wheelock (1998), and Romer and Romer (2002).

"financial market behavior is too complex for simple monetary rules to work" (Gramley and Chase 1965, 1403–04). Burns explained that "we pay close attention to interest rates because of their profound effects on the working of the economy."[29]

Monetarists, however, argued that the Fed's focus on interest rates had misled policymakers into thinking that they were tightening policy in response to rising inflation when, in fact, policy was increasingly loose. Brunner, for example, noted that "[a]n interest rate target policy misleads monetary authorities and many spectators into believing that expansive (or restrictive) actions have been initiated when nothing has been done or even worse, when actually restrictive (expansive) measures have been introduced. A decline in interest rates resulting from falling credit demand possesses no expansionary meaning and simply reflects one aspect of the ongoing deflationary process. Its interpretation as an expansive action by the Fed is a dangerous illusion."[30] Allan Meltzer argued similarly in testimony before the Senate Banking Committee in 1975: "Changes in interest rates convey inaccurate information about the direction or thrust of current monetary policy." He described the use of nominal interest rates as a guide to policy as "one of the principal errors that the Federal Reserve has made throughout its history."[31]

8. *Money demand is stable:* Many economists and monetary policymakers dismissed monetary growth rules, arguing that money demand is too unstable to permit the use of such rules. Policymakers often claimed that financial innovations and changes in regulation unpredictably altered the relationship between monetary growth and nominal spending. Burns, for example, claimed that "[f]rom one month to the next, the public's demand for money is subject to variations that are usually of a short-run nature. . . . If the Federal Reserve tried to maintain a rigid monetary growth rate . . . [then] interest rates could fluctuate widely, and to no good end. The costs of financial intermediation would be increased, and the course of monetary policy would be misinterpreted."[32]

The SOMC members questioned the Fed's analysis, however, especially estimates of money demand equations that included only short-term interest rates. Brunner, for example, conjectured that "money demand functions using long term in lieu of short term interest rates supplemented with a measure of returns on equities produces different results."[33]

29. "Monetary Targets and Credit Allocation" (testimony before the Subcommittee on Domestic Monetary Policy, US House Banking, Currency, and Housing Committee, February 6, 1975). Quoted in Burns (1978, 369).

30. "Monetary Policy and the Economic Decline" (SOMC position paper, March 7, 1975, 12).

31. "The Senate Concurrent Resolution on Monetary Policy" (testimony before the Senate Committee on Banking and Currency, February 25, 1975, 3).

32. "Key Issues of Monetary Policy" (statement before the US House Banking, Currency, and Housing Committee, July 30, 1974). Quoted in Burns (1978, 175).

33. "Monetary Policy, Inflation and Economic Expansion" (SOMC position paper, September 13, 1976, 8).

9. *The money stock is controllable:* Fed officials often claimed that they had little control over the money stock and, hence, that monetary aggregate targeting would not be feasible even if it were desirable. Board staff economists Lyle Gramley and Samuel Chase (1965) argued, for example, that "[t]raditional [i.e., monetarist] analysis . . . fails to recognize that substitution between time deposits and securities may be an important source of procyclical variations in the stock of money even in the face of countercyclical central bank policy."[34] Burns argued similarly that the growth of monetary aggregates can give a misleading indication of the stance of policy. In testimony before the House Banking Committee in July 1975, he stated that "the narrowly defined money supply, M1, can actually be a misleading guide to the degree of monetary ease or restriction. For example, in periods of declining economic activity both the transaction demand for cash and the private demand for credit will tend to weaken and thus slow the growth of M1."[35]

By contrast, Brunner and other SOMC members argued that the apparent endogeneity of money to movements in income reflected the Fed's practice of targeting nominal interest rates. According to Brunner (1983), "Interest rate targeting is the most important condition contributing to 'reverse causation.' Interest rate policy converts the monetary base, and consequently the money stock, into an endogenous magnitude sensitively exposed to all ongoing shocks affecting market rates of interest. These shocks are transmitted via interest rate targeting into accelerations or decelerations of monetary growth." Further, he argued, "The effect on the base is a consequence of the Federal Reserve's interest target policy and would disappear with proper monetary control."[36]

In 1975, Congress adopted House Concurrent Resolution 133, which required the Fed to establish target ranges for monetary growth. The Fed set ranges as required, but growth frequently fell outside those ranges. Fed officials blamed the deviation of monetary growth from the target ranges on financial innovations and changes in regulation that affected money demand. The SOMC rejected that explanation, however, contending that their studies showed that by controlling the growth of the monetary base, the Fed could control the growth of the money stock at a horizon of some two to four quarters.[37] Brunner noted, however, that "effective monetary control also requires some adaptations of inherited institutions . . . [including] radical simplification of reserve requirements [and] in the manner of computing required reserves."[38]

34. Quoted in Brunner (1968, 10).

35. Quoted by Brunner in "Monetary Policy, Economic Expansion and Inflation" (SOMC position paper, March 8, 1976, 18).

36. "Monetary Policy, Economic Expansion and Inflation" (SOMC position paper, March 8, 1976, 18–19).

37. See Brunner, "Monetary Policy, Economic Expansion and Inflation" (SOMC position paper, March 8, 1976), and "Our Perennial Issue: Monetary Policy and Inflation" (Working Paper, University of Rochester, September 1979).

38. "Monetary Policy and the Economic Decline" (SOMC position paper, March 7, 1975, 14).

The preceding discussion should clarify how the SOMC's views diverged from those of the Fed. The SOMC reflected the emerging New Classical views of Friedman, Lucas, and others, many of which are features of mainstream macroeconomic models today. Although today there are few proponents of money supply policy rules, many aspects of the SOMC policy framework are now widely accepted. These include the natural rate hypothesis; the value of transparent, rules-based policies; the importance of credibility; and the notion that in the long run, inflation is determined solely by monetary policy.[39] Like many monetary economists today, the SOMC held that price stability should be the paramount objective of monetary policy, and that efforts to limit fluctuations in economic activity or to promote financial stability are unlikely to succeed in the absence of price stability.

The following section describes the SOMC policy rule and presents results from simulation of a modern macroeconomic model that embeds the SOMC rule in an effort to determine how different the path of inflation might have been if the Fed had followed such a rule.

1.3   The Shadow's Policy Rule

The SOMC articulated a consistent and transparent policy rule throughout the Great Inflation era. Karl Brunner explained the rule in a position paper written in September 1979:

> This procedure is based on an estimate of the desired target of monetary growth. This selection depends on the desired longer-rate movements of the price-level and the economy's normal real growth. A second step formulates estimates of the time profile for the monetary multiplier. These two steps imply the required growth rate of the monetary base. Projections of the source components of the base other than Federal Reserve Credit determine ultimately the anticipated path of the Fed's net open market operations over various horizons ahead. . . . [T]he "ultimate target" for the growth of the monetary base should be announced together with the stepwise reduction proceeding over the next three to five years.[40]

Although the SOMC policy rule specified a steady-state growth rate for the monetary base, it was more than a simple, fixed-rate monetary rule. As noted previously, Brunner indicated that it might be necessary to adjust the steady-state monetary growth rate in response to permanent changes

---

39. See McCallum (1999) for a favorable recent discussion of money supply rules. Long-run monetary neutrality is a feature many New Keynesian and hybrid macroeconomic models (e.g., Goodfriend and King 1997; Kimball 1995; King and Wolman 1996; McCallum and Nelson 1999), as well as standard real business cycle models (e.g., Prescott 1986). Clarida, Galí, and Gertler (1999); Woodford (2003); and many others emphasize the importance of credibility and of transparent, rules-based policies.

40. "Our Perennial Issue: Monetary Policy and Inflation" (SOMC Position Paper, September 1979, 5). Reprinted in Lys (1997, 80–92).

in economic growth or velocity. Moreover, the SOMC rule emphasized the transition from the current monetary growth rate to the steady-state growth rate. As the previous statement makes clear, the SOMC rule implied that the adjustment of monetary base growth to the ultimate target should be gradual and publicly announced.

The SOMC statements often called for transparent, consistent policies, and the SOMC was critical of the Federal Open Market Committee's (FOMC's) practice of announcing monetary growth targets starting from the most recently observed level of the money stock—a practice that came to be known as "base drift." In contrast, the SOMC's rule avoided base drift by establishing a growth rate from the previous target value:

$$(1) \qquad \ln(M^T_{t,t+1}) - \ln(M^T_{t-1,t}) = \alpha_t,$$

where $M^T_{t,t+1}$ is the target value for the money stock at time $t + 1$ established at time t. Base drift was avoided by recognizing the most recent policy error:

$$(2) \qquad \ln(M_t) = \ln(M^T_{t-1,t}) + \varepsilon_t.$$

An example of this approach can be found in the SOMC policy recommendation of March 1975:

> We renew the recommendation made at our September meeting that the growth rate of money be held at 5-1/2 percent. However growth should not start at that rate from the current low level. We recommend that the money stock be brought to a level it would have reached in March 1975, if our policy had been followed. A one-time increase in money—currency and demand deposits—to $290 billion should be announced and provided by April 15. This increase would put money growth back on the path leading the economy toward full employment at lower rates of inflation than in recent years.[41]

The SOMC's policy rule was forward-looking, extending reductions in the money growth rate into the future until a noninflationary monetary growth rate had been achieved. The SOMC never advocated an abrupt, "cold turkey" adjustment of the monetary growth rate to a long-run target. Instead, the policy rule was inherently gradualist, calling for adjustments in the monetary growth rate depending on initial conditions and the historical trend.

Typically, SOMC recommendations advocated a 1 percentage point reduction in the target growth rate of the money stock per year until a noninflationary rate of growth was achieved. At that point, the policy rule called for a constant noninflationary monetary growth rate.[42]

---

41. Policy Recommendations of the Shadow Open Market Committee, March 7, 1975.
42. The SOMC rule also permitted adjustments to monetary base growth for structural shifts in velocity. Note that the SOMC rule differed from that of McCallum (1988), who proposes a monetary base growth rule that responds to deviations between actual and desired growth in nominal output, as well as to long-run shifts in velocity.

(3) $$\ln(M_{t,t+2}^T) - \ln(M_{t,t+1}^T) = \alpha_t - .01$$

(4) $$\ln(M_{t,t+3}^T) - \ln(M_{t,t+2}^T) = \alpha_t - .02$$

The sequence continues over time until the constant growth rate has been achieved:

(5) $$\ln(M_{t,t+n}^T) - \ln(M_{t,t+n-1}^T) = \alpha$$

(6) $$\ln(M_{t,t+n+k}^T) - \ln(M_{t,t+n+k-1}^T) = \alpha, k = 1, \ldots$$

For example, this approach is reflected in the policy statement of March 1978:

> One, the rate of monetary expansion in the past year was between 7% and 7.5%. We urge that the rate be maintained at 6% in 1978.
> Two, we recommend reductions of 1% a year in the average rate of monetary expansion until a noninflationary rate of monetary expansion is achieved.[43]

The SOMC policy statements generally specify 4 percent as the noninflationary rate of money growth.[44] We use this value in our simulation of a model of money demand discussed later.

Two equations are necessary for a complete specification of the SOMC policy rule: (a) a definition of velocity:

(7) $$\ln(V_t) \equiv \ln(Y_t) + \ln(P_t) - \ln(M_t);$$

and (b) a model of the demand for money (or the monetary base).

The SOMC documents rarely articulated an explicit demand for money.[45] However, Brunner and Meltzer (1963), Meltzer (1963), and Brunner and Meltzer (1964b) present a demand for money (or velocity) that depends on a long-term interest rate. Subsequent research found evidence of a stable money demand relationship, at least through the 1970s.[46]

The relationship between base-money velocity and a long-term nominal interest rate is shown in figure 1.1, which is adapted from Anderson and Rasche (2001). This figure shows a scatter plot of annual data on the natural log of base velocity and the inverse of the Aaa bond rate over the years 1919 through 2006. The years of the Great Depression, starting in 1931 and extending until 1940, are outliers, but otherwise the relationship is highly

43. Policy statement, Shadow Open Market Committee, March 13, 1978.
44. See, for example, the SOMC policy statements of September 6, 1974 (4 percent M1 growth); March 8, 1976 (4.5 percent M1 growth is too high for price stability); September 13, 1976 (4 percent M1 growth); September 21, 1986 (3 to 4 percent base growth); March 11, 1996 (4 percent base growth); and September 14, 1998 (4 percent base growth).
45. However, see Brunner, "Monetary Policy, Inflation and Economic Growth" (SOMC position paper, September 13, 1976).
46. See, for example, Hetzel (1984), Hoffman and Rasche (1991), or Rasche (1987).

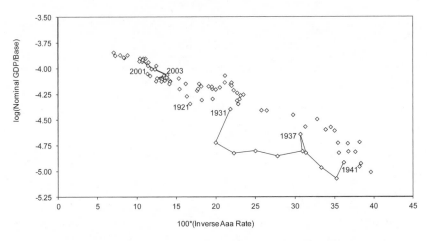

Fig. 1.1   Log base velocity and inverse Aaa bond rate, annual 1919–2006

linear. The values for the years 2000 to 2006 are also highlighted in figure 1.1. These years are after the sample that Anderson and Rasche (2001) examined. Note that the data for 2000 to 2006 fall on top of the scatter from the earlier sample. Table 1.1, reproduced from Anderson and Rasche (2001), shows the estimated values of the slope of the scatter in figure 1.1 over a sample period from 1919 through 1999. The estimated equation is also augmented with an additional variable that measures the rate of default on corporate bonds to capture the increase in risk during the Great Depression period and the flight to currency that occurred after the first wave of bank failures in 1931. The estimated slope of the relationship between the log of base velocity and the inverse of the long rate is robust across estimators and invariant to the addition of the risk variable. The lower part of the table relaxes the restriction that the income elasticity of the demand for real base money is unity. The restriction is not rejected.

Following the SOMC, and in light of the evidence from Anderson and Rasche (2001), we specify the following nonlinear demand function for base money:

$$(8) \qquad \ln(V_t) = \zeta_1 + \zeta_2(i_t^L),^{-1}$$

where i_t^L is the long-term nominal interest rate.

The noninflationary rate of money growth, α, can be defined in terms of this model. If inflation is constant and expected to be constant, then, assuming that the equilibrium real rate of interest is constant, the long-term nominal interest rate is also expected to be constant. Thus, velocity is expected to be constant in this equilibrium. The noninflationary money growth rate is then the growth rate of trend output θ plus the trend inflation

Table 1.1   Estimated linear regressions using the adjusted monetary base and the Aaa bond rate (1919–1999)

Dependent variable: GDP velocity of the adjusted monetary base = log(GDP/adjusted monetary base)

Estimation method ↓	Constant	Inverse of Aaa bond rate, times 100	Rate of new bond defaults, percent of outstanding stock	Standard error of estimate
OLS	−3.631	−0.032	—	0.144
DOLS (2 leads, 2 lags)	−3.606	−0.034	—	0.115
OLS	−3.622	−0.030	−0.0004	0.090
DOLS (1 lead, 1 lag)	−3.606	−0.031	−0.0003	0.082
FIML	—	−0.031	−0.0000[a]	

Dependent variable: Deflated adjusted monetary base = log(adjusted monetary base/GDP chain-type price index)

Estimation method ↓	Constant	Real GDP (chained 1996$)	Inverse of Aaa bond rate, times 100	Rate of new bond defaults, percent of outstanding stock	Standard error of estimate
OLS	4.490	0.903	0.027	—	0.131
DOLS (2 leads, 2 lags)	3.892	0.970	0.032	—	0.091
OLS	3.452	1.019	0.031	0.0004	0.090
DOLS (1 lead, 1 lag)	3.227	1.044	0.034	0.0003	0.073
FIML	—	1.069	0.033	−0.0000[a]	

Note: OLS = ordinary least squares; DOLS = dynamic ordinary least squares; FIML = full information maximum likelihood.

[a]Coefficient estimates rounds to this value.

rate that is defined as price stability π^*. For simplicity, we assume $\pi^* = 0$. A low positive and steady trend in measured inflation could be consistent with the SOMC's position on price stability, although various SOMC policy statements explicitly advocated a target of zero inflation or a stable price level.[47] Under these conditions, the number of years expected until a return to price stability under the SOMC's rule is $n = 100*(\alpha_t - \theta)$, and the noninflationary growth rate of money is $\alpha = \theta$.

The model of money supply and demand can be respecified in terms of deviations of money growth from the assumed trend growth of real output and in terms of an output gap. Define:

$$\ln Y_t^T \equiv \ln Y_{t-1}^T + \theta; \theta > 0.0$$

$$x_t \equiv \ln(Y_t) - \ln(Y_t^T)$$

$$\pi_t = \ln(P_t) - \ln(P_{t-1}).$$

Then the policy rule equations and the definition of velocity can be written in terms of deviations from trend output growth as follows:

(1') $\quad [\ln(M_{t,t+1}^T) - \ln Y_{t+1}^T] - [\ln(M_{t-1,t}^T) - \ln Y_t^T] = m_{t,t+1}^T - m_{t-1,t}^T = \alpha_t - \theta$

(2') $\quad m_t = [\ln(M_t) - \ln Y_t^T] = [\ln(M_{t-1,t}^T) - \ln(Y_{t-1}^T)] - \theta + \varepsilon_t$

$$= m_{t-1,t}^T - \theta + \varepsilon_t$$

(3') $\quad [\ln(M_{t,t+2}^T) - \ln(Y_{t+2}^T)] - [\ln(M_{t,t+1}^T) - \ln(Y_{t+1}^T)]$

$$= m_{t,t+2}^T - m_{t,t+1}^T = \alpha_t - \theta - .01$$

(4') $\quad [\ln(M_{t,t+3}^T) - \ln(Y_{t+3}^T)] - [\ln(M_{t,t+2}^T) - \ln(Y_{t+2}^T)]$

$$= m_{t,t+3}^T - m_{t,t+2}^T = \alpha_t - \theta - .02$$

The sequence continues over time until the constant growth rate has been achieved:

(5') $\quad [\ln(M_{t,t+n}^T) - \ln(Y_{t+n}^T)] - [\ln(M_{t,t+n-1}^T) - \ln(Y_{t+n-1}^t)]$

$$= m_{t,t+n}^T - m_{t,t+n-1}^T = \alpha - \theta = 0.0$$

(6') $\quad [\ln(M_{t,t+n+k}^T) - \ln(Y_{t+n+k}^T)] - [\ln(M_{t,t+n+k-1}^T) - \ln(Y_{t,t+n+k-1}^T)]$

$$= m_{t,t+n+k}^T - m_{t+n+k-1}^T = \alpha - \theta = 0.0, k = 1, \ldots$$

---

47. See SOMC policy statements of September 9, 1996; March 3, 1997; and September 14, 1998.

(7') $\ln(V_t) \equiv [\ln(Y_t) - \ln(Y_t^T)] + \ln(P_t) - [\ln(M_t) - \ln(Y_t^T)]$

$$= x_t + \ln P_t - m_t = x_t + \ln P_t - m_{t-1,t}^T + \theta - \varepsilon_t.$$

To complete the analysis, we embed the SOMC's policy rule and the money demand function in a model of the real economy—specifically, the New Keynesian model of Clarida, Galí, and Gertler (CGG 1999).

Investment/Savings (IS) curve (CGG, equation 2.1):

(9) $$x_t = -\varphi[i_t^S - E_t\pi_{t+1}] + E_t x_{t+1} + g_t.$$

Phillips curve (CGG, equation 2.2):

(10) $$\pi_t = \lambda x_t + \beta E_t \pi_{t+1} + u_t.$$

We augment the model with a term structure approximation from Shiller (1979):

(11) $$i_t^{L,(n)} = \frac{1-\gamma}{1-\gamma^n} \sum_{k=0}^{n-1} \gamma^k E_t(i_{t+k}^S) + \Phi_{n,t}, \quad 0 < \gamma < 1,$$

which for large n can be approximated as:

$$i_t^{L,(n)} \cong (1-\gamma)(1-\gamma F)^{-1} i_t^S + \Phi_n \text{ where } F^k i_t^S = E_t(i_{t+k}^S).$$

Then,

$$i_t^S \cong [1 - \gamma F]\left[\left(\frac{1}{1-\gamma}\right)(i_t^L - \Phi_{n,t})\right]$$

or

(12) $$i_t^S \cong \left(\frac{1}{1-\gamma}\right)(i_t^L - \gamma E_t i_{t+1}^L) - \left(\frac{1}{1-\gamma}\right)(1-\gamma F)\Phi_{n,t}.$$

1.4   Simulation of the SOMC Policy Rule for the Great Inflation

1.4.1   Linearized Model

The only nonlinearity in the previous model is the interest elasticity of the demand for money. In the following analysis, we present a linearized version of the model, recognizing that the semielasticity of money demand (ζ_3, following) varies inversely with the nominal interest rate. We examine the sensitivity of the model to various assumptions about the value of this parameter.

We define the linear operator F such that $F^j z_t = E_t z_{t+j}$. Hence, $F^{-j} = E_t z_{t-j}$ $= z_{t-j} = L^j z_t$. With this notation the five equations (1), (7'), (9), (10), and (11) can be written as

$$
\begin{bmatrix}
\ln V_t - \zeta_3 i_t^L \\
\ln V_t - x_t - \ln P_t \\
x_t + \phi i_t^s - \phi F\pi_t - Fx_t \\
\pi_t - \lambda x_t - \beta F\pi_t \\
i_t^s - (1-\gamma)^{-1} i_t^L + \gamma(1-\gamma)^{-1} F i_t^L \\
\ln P_t - \ln P_{t-1} - \pi_t
\end{bmatrix}
=
\begin{bmatrix}
\zeta_1 + \eta_t \\
-m_t \\
g_t \\
u_t \\
(1-\gamma)^{-1}\left(1-\gamma F\right)\Phi_t \\
0
\end{bmatrix}.
$$

Equations (1) and (7′) can be used to eliminate $\ln V_t$ from the model; equations (11) and (9) can be used to eliminate i_t^s, and the definition of inflation to eliminate π_t, leaving a three-equation model:

$$
\begin{bmatrix}
1.0 & 1.0 & -\zeta_3 \\
1 - F & \phi(1 - F) & \phi(1-\gamma)^{-1}(1-\gamma F) \\
-\lambda & [-F^{-1} + (1+\beta) - \beta F] & 0
\end{bmatrix}
$$

$$
\begin{bmatrix}
x_t \\
\ln P_t \\
i_t^L
\end{bmatrix}
=
\begin{bmatrix}
m_t + \zeta_1 + \eta_t \\
g_t + (1-\gamma)^{-1}(1-\gamma F)\Phi_t \\
u_t
\end{bmatrix}
$$

or

$$
A(F) * Y_t = X_t.
$$

Define the determinantal polynomial of $A(F)$ as $\det A(F)$ and the adjoint polynomial matrix of $A(F)$ as $\mathrm{adj} A(F)$. Then $\det A(F) Y_t = \mathrm{adj} A(F) X_t$. The determinant of $A(F)$ is

$$
det[A(F)] = -\lambda\phi(1-\gamma)^{-1}(1-\gamma F) + \phi(1-\gamma)^{-1}(1-\gamma F)[F^{-1} - (1+\beta) + \beta F]
$$
$$
+ \zeta_3(1-F)[F^{-1} - (1+\beta) + \beta F] - \lambda\zeta_3\phi(1-F)
$$

and the adjoint matrix of $A(F)$ is:

$$
\begin{bmatrix}
\phi(1-\gamma)^{-1}(1-\gamma F)[F^{-1} - (1+\beta) + F] & \zeta_3[F^{-1} - (1+\beta) + F] & \phi[(1-\gamma)^{-1}(1-\gamma F) + \zeta_3(1-F)] \\
-\lambda\phi(1-\gamma)^{-1}(1-\gamma F) & -\lambda\zeta_3 & -\phi(1-\gamma)^{-1}(1-\gamma F) - \zeta_3(1-F) \\
-(1-F)[F^{-1} - (1+\beta) + \beta F] + \phi\lambda(1-F) & [F^{-1} - (1+\beta) + F] - \lambda & -(1-\phi)(1-F)
\end{bmatrix}.
$$

However, $[F^{-1} - (1+\beta) + \beta F] = -(1-L)(1-\beta F)$, which when substituted into the adjoint matrix gives:

$$
\begin{bmatrix}
-\phi(1-\gamma)^{-1}(1-\gamma F)(1-\beta F)(1-L) & -\zeta_3(1-\beta F)(1-L) & \phi[(1-\gamma)^{-1}(1-\gamma F) + \zeta_3(1-F)] \\
-\lambda\phi(1-\gamma)^{-1}(1-\gamma F) & -\lambda\zeta_3 & -\phi(1-\gamma)^{-1}(1-\gamma F) - \zeta_3(1-F) \\
(1-F)(1-\beta F)(1-L) + \phi\lambda(1-F) & -(1-\beta F)(1-L) - \lambda & -(1-\phi)(1-F)
\end{bmatrix}.
$$

1.4.2   Deterministic Steady State (F = L = 1)

The value of the determinant in the steady state is $-\lambda\phi$, and the value of the steady-state adjoint matrix is

$$\begin{bmatrix} 0 & 0 & -\lambda \\ 1 & \zeta_3\phi^{-1} & 0 \\ 0 & \phi^{-1} & 0 \end{bmatrix}.$$

Hence, the steady-state solution of the model is independent of γ, and the only steady-state impact that is affected by ζ_3 is that of the price level in response to a real interest rate shock, g_t. From one steady state to another, the price level varies one-to-one with the money stock. Across steady-state equilibria with a nonzero growth of money, both the nominal interest rate and the inflation rate vary one-to-one with the growth rate of the money stock. Hence, the Fisher effect holds across steady states.

Across steady states with nonzero money growth, the only effect that depends on the value of β is the response of real output to the change in money growth. Beginning in 1968, monetarists consistently assumed that the long-run Phillips curve is vertical (see, e.g., Friedman 1968; Andersen and Carlson 1970; Poole 1978; Brunner and Meltzer 1976, 1993; and Mayer 1978), which, as noted previously, has become a standard feature of mainstream macroeconomic models. Hence we assume $\beta = 1.0$, with the result that the steady-state impact of money growth on real output is zero.

1.4.3   Dynamics

We need to calibrate the four remaining parameters to investigate the dynamics of the model. We chose a range of values for ζ_3 corresponding to a nominal interest rate from 14 percent to 8 percent and assume $\zeta_2 = -0.032$, consistent with the estimates reported in table 1.1.[48] We set $\gamma = 0.94$ following Shiller (1979, table 1, 1206), and we use estimates of $\phi = 0.125$ and $\lambda = 0.025$, consistent with typical values found in the literature adjusted to a model calibrated to annual data.[49] With these assumptions, we compute the roots of the determinantal polynomial of $A(F)$, which are the primary drivers of the dynamics of the model. These roots are shown in table 1.2.

For the parameter values that we have chosen, the polynomial always has one real root that lies within the unit circle and two roots that lie outside the unit circle. At high nominal interest rates (> 10 percent) the latter two roots are real. At lower nominal rates these roots are complex. However, when

---

48. The Aaa corporate rate in 1981 was 14.17 percent. By 1986 this rate had fallen to 7.78 percent.

49. We thank, without implicating, Ed Nelson for helpful suggestions on values for these parameters.

Table 1.2   **Polynomial roots and parameter values for linearized model**

Determinantal polynomial:

$$\det[A(F)] = \lambda\phi(1-\gamma)^{-1}(1-\gamma F) + \phi(1-\gamma)^{-1}(1-\gamma F)[(1-L)(1-\beta F)]$$
$$- \zeta_3(1-F)[(1-L)(1-\beta F)] - \lambda\zeta_3\phi(1-F)$$

or:

$$\det[A(F)] = -\beta(\phi\gamma/(1-\lambda) + \zeta_3)r_2r_3F^{-1}[(F-r_1)(1-r_2^{-1}F)(1-r_3^{-1}F)]$$

	Polynomial roots			Parameter values				
Nominal rate	$r(1)$	$r(2)*r(3)$	Omega	Beta	Lambda	Phi	Gamma	Zeta
0.14	0.876688	1.180727	0.000000	1.00	0.025	0.125	0.94	1.60
0.13	0.879409	1.174064	0.000000	1.00	0.025	0.125	0.94	1.89
0.12	0.882195	1.167449	0.000000	1.00	0.025	0.125	0.94	2.22
0.11	0.885345	1.160207	0.000000	1.00	0.025	0.125	0.94	2.64
0.10	0.888993	1.152117	0.008305	1.00	0.025	0.125	0.94	3.20
0.09	0.893114	1.143369	0.011773	1.00	0.025	0.125	0.94	3.95
0.08	0.897810	1.133831	0.013491	1.00	0.025	0.125	0.94	5.00

expressed in polar coordinates, the polar angle of the complex roots (θ in table 1.2) is always close to zero.[50]

The determinantal polynomial can be written in terms of its roots as

$$(14) \quad \det A(F) = -\beta\left(\frac{\phi\gamma}{(1-\lambda)} + \zeta_3\right)r_2r_3F^{-1}(F-r_1)(1-r_2^{-1}F)(1-r_3^{-1}F).$$

Assume that r_2 and r_3 are outside the unit circle and define the invertible polynomial

$$(15) \quad R(F) = -\beta\left(\frac{\phi\gamma}{(1-\gamma)} + \zeta_3\right)r_2r_3(1-r_2^{-1}F)(1-r_3^{-1}F),$$

so

$$(16) \quad \det A(F) = F^{-1}(F-r_1)R(F).$$

Since $F^{-1}(F-r_1) = (1-r_1F^{-1}) = (1-r_1L)$, the model can be rewritten as

$$(17) \quad (1-r_1L)Y_t = R^{-1}(F) * \text{Adj}[A(F)]X_t.[51]$$

The elements of the first column of $B(F)$ (coefficients of the current and expected future money stock) for the parameter values in table 1.2 are shown in figures 1.2 through 1.4. The low-order polynomial coefficients

50. We computed the roots of this polynomial assuming values of β in the range of [0.96, 1.0], λ in the range of [0.005, 0.045], ϕ in the range of [0.075, 0.145], γ in the range of [0.92, 0.98], and ζ_3 corresponding to nominal interest rates in the range of [0.08, 0.14]. In all cases, we found one real root less than unity. The other two roots were sometimes complex, but in all cases were outside the unit circle.

51. Expressions for $R(F)^{-1}$ are shown in appendix B.

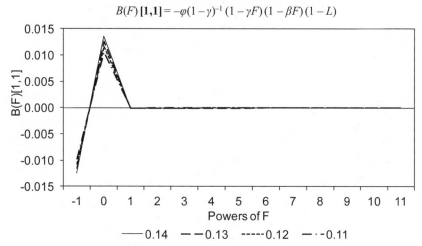

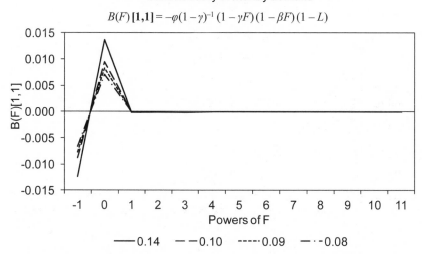

Fig. 1.2   Moving average coefficients for the response of output in a model that includes the SOMC policy rule

for the response of output and the long-term nominal interest rate are moderately sensitive to the level of the nominal interest rate around which the model is linearized, but the sensitivity of the higher-order coefficients in these polynomials disappears as the coefficients rapidly approach zero. The polynomial coefficients in the response of the price level die off much more slowly than those for output and the long-term nominal rate and

A. Coefficients of B(F)[2,1] for various values of interest
semielasticity of money demand

$$B(F)\,[\mathbf{2,1}] = -\lambda\varphi(1-\gamma)^{-1}\,(1-\gamma F)$$

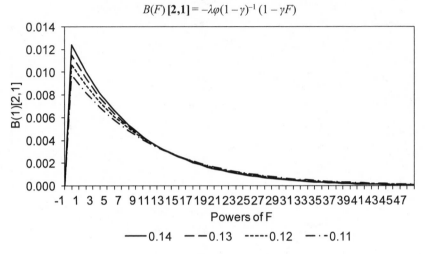

B. Coefficients of B(F)[2,1] for various values of interest
semielasticity of money demand

$$B(F)\,[\mathbf{2,1}] = -\lambda\varphi(1-\gamma)^{-1}\,(1-\gamma F)$$

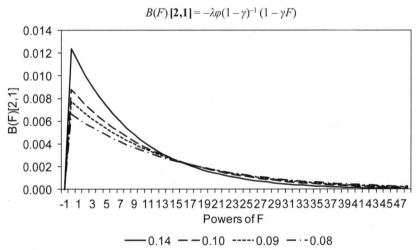

Fig. 1.3   Moving average coefficients for the response of the price level in a model that includes the SOMC policy rule

the low-order coefficients show considerable sensitivity to the level of the nominal interest rate around which the model is linearized. Consequently, we simulate the model with different assumptions about the value of ζ_3 corresponding to different assumed levels for the long-term nominal interest rate.

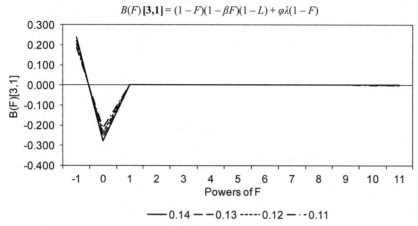

A. Coefficients of B(F)[3,1] for various values of interest
semielasticity of money demand

$$B(F)[3,1] = (1 - F)(1 - \beta F)(1 - L) + \varphi\lambda(1 - F)$$

—— 0.14 — — 0.13 ----- 0.12 — ·· 0.11

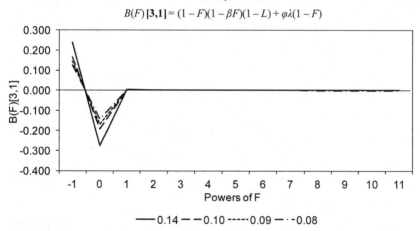

B. Coefficients of B(F)[3,1] for various values of interest semielasticity of
money demand

$$B(F)[3,1] = (1 - F)(1 - \beta F)(1 - L) + \varphi\lambda(1 - F)$$

—— 0.14 — — 0.10 ----- 0.09 — ·· 0.08

**Fig. 1.4   Moving average coefficients for the response of the long-term interest rate
in a model that includes the SOMC policy rule**

1.4.4   Policy Experiments

Clearly, if money demand is stable, prices and wages are flexible, and
supply shocks are limited, then a monetary growth rule like that advocated
by the SOMC would yield superior inflation control with less output variability than the "stop-go" policies actually pursued by the Fed during the
1970s. Monetary policy can affect real output in the short-run in the modern
New Keynesian model, such as CGG (1999) and some other models with
nominal rigidities. We compare two policy rules for money stock growth in

the previously specified model. The first experiment is the gradualist monetarist proposal of the SOMC. We assume the economy is initially in a steady state with an expected constant nominal money growth rate of 10 percent. This translates into a nominal interest rate of 14 percent, since we assume a 4 percent equilibrium real interest rate. At some point in time after expectations of future money growth, output, and inflation have been set, the monetary authority surprises private agents by implementing an immediate 1 percentage point reduction in the money growth rate and announcing that money growth will be reduced by an additional 1 percentage point in each subsequent year until the growth rate reaches 4 percent. We assume that the policy announcement is fully credible so that agents adjust their expectations in future periods accordingly. The only policy shock occurs in the first period.[52]

The second policy experiment is a onetime "cold turkey" adjustment of money stock growth. We again assume that the economy is initially in a steady-state equilibrium with a constant nominal money growth rate of 10 percent. In this case, the monetary authority surprises agents by implementing a onetime 6 percentage point reduction in money growth and announcing that the money growth rate will be maintained at the new value. Again, the announcement is assumed to be fully credible so that agents adjust their expectations in future periods accordingly.

Figure 1.5 shows the response of the model economy to the gradualist experiment. With expectations set for future periods, the economy moves along a very flat short-run Phillips curve. The inflation rate is almost unchanged in the first period, while real output falls sharply. As a result, real money balances fall (inflation is higher than money growth) and the long- and short-term nominal rates increase slightly. In subsequent periods, the continued reduction in the growth rate of the nominal money stock is fully anticipated, so the inflation rate falls in advance of the decline in money growth, as does future expected inflation, and real balances rise. With the sharp decline in near-term expected inflation, the short-run Phillips curve shifts down and output rises above the steady-state level. The long-term and short-term nominal interest rates fall, but the short-term nominal rate falls more precipitously. Adjustment to full equilibrium takes time because of the autoregressive structure built into the model.

The assumed credibility of the monetary policymaker's commitment to the announced policy is obviously a key determinant of the adjustment paths traced by our simulations, as is our assumption of rational expectations. The time path of the economy after the initial policy surprise depends on the announcement being accepted at face value and expectations being

---

52. If the policy announcement occurred before agents set their expectations, there would not be any policy surprise, output would be unaffected, and inflation would fall in advance of the expected future reductions in money growth.

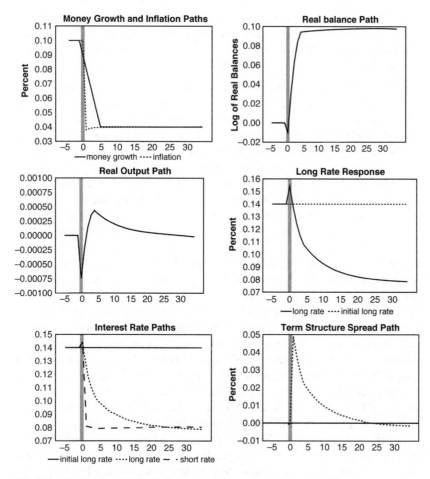

Fig. 1.5   Gradualist (SOMC) 6 percent reduction in money growth

adjusted accordingly.[53] The SOMC frequently stressed that the impact of a disinflationary policy depends crucially on the transparency and credibility of the change in policy. For example, Brunner and Meltzer (1993, 75) note

> In our analysis, if the policy of monetary control is credible, control errors are perceived as transitory deviations, so they are absorbed by changes in

---

53. Ball (1994) analyzes a model with staggered price setting and a credible disinflation. He finds that a gradual disinflation can produce a "boom," defined as "an output path that rises above the natural rate temporarily and never falls below the natural rate" (286). Ball's model differs from the one used here in that his demand for real balances is not interest sensitive (his equation [2]), and the path of the money stock is perfectly perceived at all points in time (he assumes that the announcement of the disinflation is made at $t = 0$), and that "the expectations operator can be dropped for all $t \geq 0$, because firms have perfect foresight after the Fed's announcement" (286).

interest rates at the shortest end of the yield curve. . . . The consequences differ, of course, if monetary control policies lack sufficient credibility. Control errors, particularly those exhibiting serial correlation, are interpreted partly as permanent changes.

Clearly the Fed did not have much credibility when it announced a disinflationary policy in late 1979, and the trajectory of the economy in the early 1980s was significantly different from that simulated here. As Brunner and Meltzer (1993, 75) argue, "Experience in the United States from 1979 to 1982 is an example of the increase in uncertainty that can result from inappropriate control procedures and operations that lack credibility."[54]

Figure 1.6 shows the reaction of the model economy to the alternative policy of an immediate reduction in money growth from 10 percent to 4 percent with a credible announcement that it will be maintained at that rate henceforth. Again, inflation falls little at first in response to the surprise reduction in money growth as the economy moves along a flat short-run Phillips curve. The reduction in real balances is much larger, however, because the instantaneous reduction in nominal money growth is much larger than in the gradualist case (6 percent vs. 1 percent). The increase in the long-term nominal interest rate is also much larger. In the subsequent period, assuming that the pledge to maintain nominal money growth at the lower rate is fully credible, inflation adjusts and overshoots the new steady-state rate, real balances increase, long-term and short-term nominal interest rates fall, and output begins a gradual increase back to the new steady-state equilibrium. During this adjustment period the inflation rate approaches the steady-state rate from below, real balances continue to rise, and the long-term nominal interest rate gradually declines to the equilibrium level.

In sum, the transition to the steady state implied by a large, onetime reduction in money stock growth involves a larger decline in output growth, and more variability in inflation and output growth, than that implied by a gradual reduction in money stock growth. Although our model is highly stylized, our simulations favor the gradualist approach advocated by the SOMC over more abrupt changes in policy.[55]

1.4.5   Analysis of Sensitivity to Linearization

The abovementioned results were derived by linearization of the money demand function at a long-term nominal interest rate of 14 percent. It is

---

54. Taylor (1993, 207) argues similarly: "In the period after a new policy rule has been put in place, people are unlikely either to know about or understand the new policy or to believe that policymakers are serious about maintaining it. . . . Because expectations only gradually converge during this transition period, the impact of the policy rule on the economy may be quite different than projected by an analysis that assumes rational expectations."

55. Taylor (1993) notes that the presence of natural rigidities, such as long-term wage commitments, can prevent the public from changing behavior instantly in response to a change in monetary policy, which suggests further that transitions to a new policy rule should be gradual and announced publicly.

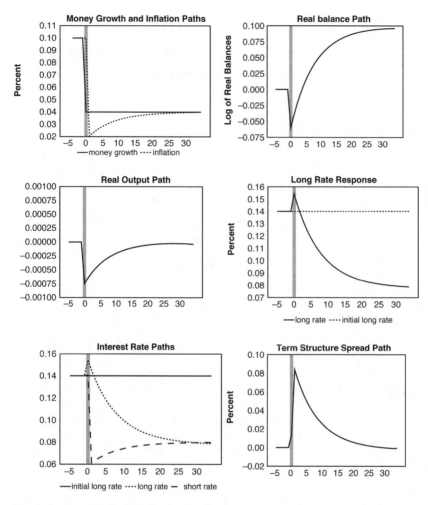

Fig. 1.6   6 percent "cold turkey" reduction in money growth

clear from figure 1.2, panel A, and figure 1.3 that the coefficients on future expected money growth vary somewhat with the assumed value of the interest rate (particularly the coefficients in the price equation). The values of the autoregression coefficient in table 1.2 ($r(1)$) also are somewhat larger, the lower the value of the nominal rate assumed for linearization. The responses of real output growth, the long-term nominal interest rate, and inflation are shown in figure 1.7 for two experiments: the "cold turkey" immediate reduction of money growth by 6 percent and the monetarist gradual reduction of 1 percent per year for linearization of the model at 14 and 11 percent nominal rates. Qualitatively the results are the same regardless which interest rate value we use (no surprise given the coefficient values in figure 1.2, panel A, and figure 1.3) and quantitatively the results

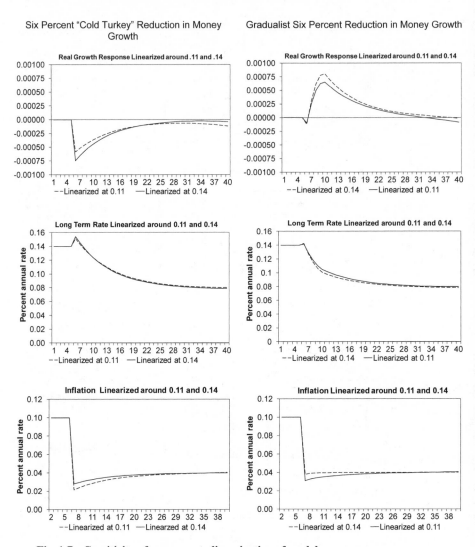

Fig. 1.7   Sensitivity of responses to linearization of model

in each experiment are quite robust to the change in the slope coefficient in the money demand function. With a lower assumed value of the nominal interest rate, the peak output response in each experiment is somewhat smaller in both experiments, but the timing of the peak and the speed of return to equilibrium are virtually the same. The price level responses are somewhat larger when the lower interest rate is used, but again the timing of the peak response is the same. The return to equilibrium is somewhat faster when we use the lower interest rate value for linearization, particularly in the gradualist experiment.

1.4.6   Shocks to a Money Growth Path: Base Drift or No Base Drift

Our final experiment considers the impact of an unexpected deviation from the target money growth path that (a) is perfectly foreseen to return to the target path in future periods (the no-base-drift case), or (b) is perfectly foreseen to remain for all future periods (the base-drift case). As noted previously, the SOMC criticized the Fed's practice of engaging in base drift, which it considered one tactic the Fed used to evade Congress's desire for better control of the monetary aggregates.

The response to the no-base-drift rule is shown in figure 1.8. The money growth rate decreases to 4 percent in the period of the unexpected shock and then jumps to 16 percent in the following period to return the money stock to the target path. Real output falls by a small amount in response to the unexpected shortfall from the target money path and quickly reverts to equilibrium with a small overshoot. That pattern is reflected in the deviation of the long-term rate from its equilibrium value. The inflation rate is virtually unaffected by this shock (again, the short-run Phillips curve in the model is flat), and so the transitory deviation of money from the target path is almost perfectly reflected in the deviation of real balances from an unchanged equilibrium value.

In the base-drift experiment (figure 1.9), money growth is reduced by 6 percent for one period but then returns to its assumed equilibrium value of 10 percent, although the money stock remains at 1 percent below the original target growth path. The initial response of inflation to the unexpected shortfall in money is very small, but once the future shortfall in money is foreseen, the inflation rate falls and only gradually returns to the equilibrium value of 10 percent. The persistence of inflation below the equilibrium value and below the maintained growth rate of the nominal money stock is required to restore the value of real balances to the unchanged equilibrium value. Again, the initial impact of the unexpected shortfall in the money stock is to reduce real output below its equilibrium value and increase the long-term nominal rate above its equilibrium value. Both of these variables return to their equilibrium values only gradually, given the slow autoregressive process inherent in the structure of the model.

A final experiment (figure 1.10), allows a persistent but not permanent deviation of the level of the money stock from the 10 percent growth path (the shock to the money stock is assumed to decay at a rate of 50 percent per period). The growth rate of the money stock decreases in the period of the shock, then increases to 13 percent in the following period (deviates from 10 percent by one-half of the deviation in the no-base-drift case), and then declines gradually to 10 percent. The deviations of real output and the long-term nominal interest rate from their equilibrium values are quite similar to the deviations in the no-base-drift case and do not show the persistence noted in the base-drift experiment. Initially inflation is barely affected,

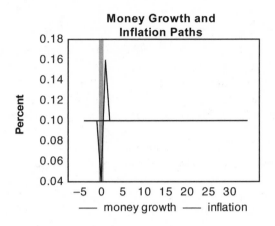

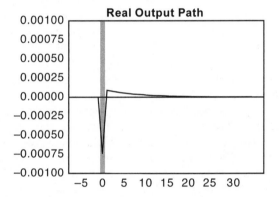

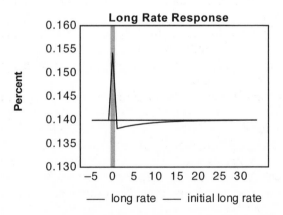

Fig. 1.8 **Response to a transitory deviation from target money growth path (no base drift)**

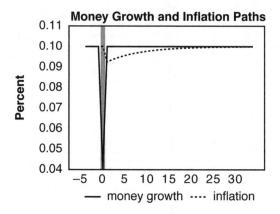

Money Growth and Inflation Paths

— money growth ···· inflation

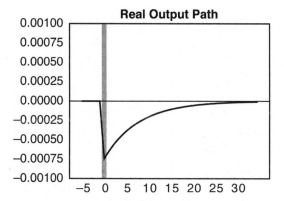

Real Output Path

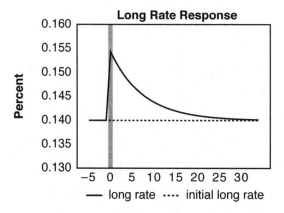

Long Rate Response

— long rate ···· initial long rate

Fig. 1.9   Response to a permanent change in the level of the money stock (base drift)

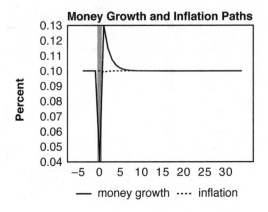

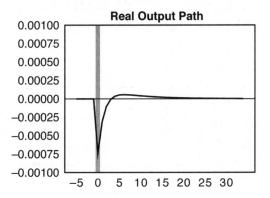

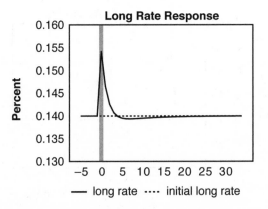

Fig. 1.10   **Response to a persistent change in the level of the money stock (base drift decays at 50 percent per period)**

although it falls below the equilibrium 10 percent rate once the persistence of the shortfall of the money stock is anticipated. Thus, our simulations indicate that base drift is relatively costly in terms of increased variability of output, at least in the context of the present model.

1.5   Conclusion

From its creation in 1973, the Shadow Open Market Committee was highly critical of Federal Reserve policy. Throughout the Great Inflation period, the SOMC consistently pushed for a gradual reduction in money stock growth to control inflation, and then a policy of fixing monetary growth at a level consistent with price stability. The views expressed by SOMC members reflected their acceptance of the natural rate hypothesis; the value of transparent, credible, rules-based policies; and the notion that, in the long run, inflation is determined solely by monetary policy. Such views were not widely held within the Federal Reserve System at the time and were just beginning to gain wide acceptance among academic economists.

Our evaluation of the SOMC policy rule in the context of the New Keynesian model of Clarida, Galí, and Gertler (1999) suggests that the gradual reduction in money growth advocated by the SOMC would have lowered inflation with less impact on output growth and less inflation and output variability than a large onetime reduction in money growth. However, our simulations are based on the extreme assumption that the adoption of a disinflation path for monetary growth is fully credible, as well as the assumption that expectations are forward-looking. As the SOMC stressed, the impact of a disinflationary monetary policy on the real economy depends crucially on the transparency and credibility of the change in policy. After some fifteen years of "stop-go" policy, the Fed had little credibility remaining. With that history, the public may have interpreted a large, one-shot cut in monetary growth (similar to what the Fed actually did in October 1979) as just another "stop" before the next "go." By contrast, the implementation of a gradual reduction in monetary growth (with no base drift) may have been perceived increasingly over time as reflecting a change to a stable price regime, and thus less costly in terms of foregone output than a "cold turkey" disinflation. Of course, without additional research, this is simply conjecture.

Regardless whether a gradual reduction in monetary growth would have resulted in a smaller reduction in output than a large onetime reduction, we are convinced that the policy rule advocated by the SOMC would have generated lower inflation, with less foregone output, than the policies actually implemented by the Federal Reserve during the Great Inflation. The SOMC articulated a policy based on a modern, well-thought-out economic model. We conclude that the Shadow did, in fact, know better than the Fed.

Appendix A
SOMC Policy Recommendations

September 14, 1973

"A policy of gradually reducing inflation can be initiated by lowering the average growth rate of money to 5 1/2% for the next six months. In March, a further reduction in the growth rate may be appropriate. The amount of additional reduction will depend on the economic conditions prevailing in March and expected to prevail thereafter."[56]

March 8, 1974

"During the first half of 1973, the rate of monetary growth was moderated somewhat to a 7.4% annual rate, and in the second half, the rate was reduced further to approximately 5%. We recommend that a growth rate of 5% to 5.5% be maintained for the coming six months."

September 6, 1974

"For the next six months the Committee recommends the objective of a 5 to 5 1/2% annual increase in money. It should be the goal of the Federal Reserve to attain that growth rate and reduce variability. This is the same short-term monetary policy that we recommended last March. A rate of growth of 5 to 5 1/2% would be appropriate as a step toward further reduction to an ultimate non-inflationary rate of about 4% a year."

March 7, 1975

"We renew the recommendation made at our September meeting that the growth rate of money be held at 5 1/2 percent. However growth should not start at that rate from the current low level. We recommend that the money stock be brought to a level it would have reached in March 1975, if our policy had been followed. A one-time increase in money—currency and demand deposits—to $290 billion should be announced and provided by April 15. This increase would put the money growth back on the path leading the economy toward full employment at lower rates of inflation than in recent years."

September 12, 1975

"Starting from the level of the money stock in August 1975, the Federal Reserve should maintain the growth rate of money at a steady 5.5 percent annual rate, so that the level in the first quarter of 1976 totals $304 billion. Such a growth rate will be adequate to support recovery but with a lower rate of inflation than more expansionary policy will produce."

56. All quotes in this appendix are from meetings of the SOMC.

March 8, 1976

"The Committee recommends that the Federal Reserve maintain a 4.5% growth rate from March 1976 onward. This growth rate should start from a base of $300 billion in March 1976 or a first-quarter average of 297.5 billion. Such a rate would mean that the money stock would rise to $304 billion by the third quarter of 1976 and $311 billion by the first quarter of 1977. A 4.5 percent rate is below the rate we recommended in March and September 1975 but above the recent rate of monetary expansion. It essentially extends the annual average rate the Federal Reserve produced for 1975. The rate of monetary expansion for the near future that we recommend is above the long-term rate consistent with zero inflation. Further reductions will be required as the economy recovers and uses resources more fully."

September 13, 1976

"The Committee concluded that the policy of gradually reducing the growth rate of the stock of money should be continued. A 4 percent annual rate of growth of money—currency and demand deposits—was recommended as appropriate policy for the next six months. A 4 percent rate of monetary growth would bring the stock of money to an average of $310 billion in the first quarter of 1977 and an average of $316 billion in the third quarter of 1977. Most importantly, 4 percent monetary growth would move the rate of monetary expansion closer to the range that permits sustained economic expansion without inflation."

March 7, 1977

"The Committee recommends that the growth rate of money—currency and demand deposits—be held in the range of 4 to 4 1/2% for the next year. A 4 to 4 1/2% rate of monetary growth would bring the stock of money to approximately $320 billion in the third quarter 1997 and to $326 billion in the first quarter 1978. These projections are made from the average $313 billion that would have prevailed in the first quarter 1977 if our previous recommendations had been followed. Currently, we anticipate an average money stock of $315 billion for the first quarter, so the policy requires the Federal Reserve to offset the recent surge in money and then maintain a less inflationary policy."

September 19, 1977

"[T]he Shadow Open Market Committee recommends that the summer bulge in money be removed by reducing the current level of the money stock by $4 billion, the reduction accompanied by an announcement that the step has been undertaken to return the money stock to the level it would have reached if the most recent error in monetary policy had not occurred.

Subsequent to the correction, money growth should resume at a constant annual rate of 4 1/2%."

March 13, 1978

"One, the rate of monetary expansion in the past year was between 7% and 7.5%. We urge that the rate be maintained at 6% in 1978.

Two, we recommend reductions of 1% a year in the average rate of monetary expansion until a noninflationary rate of monetary expansion is achieved."

September 11, 1978

"One, the rate of monetary expansion in the past year has been 7.75%. We urge that the rate be reduced to an annual rate of 6% over the next year. The stock of M-1—currency and demand deposits—will average $376 billion in the third quarter of 1979 if the 6% growth rate is attained.

Two, we recommend reduction in the average rate of monetary expansion by 1% a year until a noninflationary rate of monetary expansion is achieved."

March 12, 1979

"Two, the growth of the monetary base should be 8% for the year ending in August 1979. This is consistent with the recommendation of this Committee at our meeting in September 1978, when we selected the monetary base, as published by the Federal Reserve Bank of St. Louis, as the most reliable measure of monetary growth currently available in this period of uncertainty about the interpretation of growth rates of monetary aggregates. . . .

Three, we have urged repeatedly that the Federal Reserve adopt a five-year program to end inflation by reducing the growth rate of the monetary base by 1% a year for the next five years."

September 17, 1979

"To restore stability to the economy and permanently reduce inflation, the growth rate of the monetary base should now be reduced to an annual rate of 7% for the year ending August 1980."

February 4, 1980

"The SOMC favors an immediate return to the 6% growth rate for base money that was achieved in the first and second quarters of 1979. A 6% average rate of growth of the base in each quarter of 1980 will continue the policy we advocated at our September 1979 meeting. Base money by the end of the fourth quarter of 1980 will reach $162 billion if our recommendation is followed. The proposed policy is likely to be accompanied by a mild recession in 1980 and a slight reduction in the rate of inflation.

Large, permanent reductions in the rate of inflation can be achieved in

1981 and beyond only if there are further reductions in the growth rate of the base. We recommend reductions of one percentage point in 1981 and 1982, so the level of the base will reach $170 billion at the end of 1981 and $177 billion at the end of 1982."

September 22, 1980

"We favor an immediate end to the highly inflationary monetary policy of the past three to four months. We state our objectives in terms of the growth rate of the monetary base pending the prospective institutional change affecting the growth rates of other monetary aggregates. We urge the Federal Reserve to return the monetary base to the 6% growth rate reached in the second quarter of 1980 and to reduce the growth of the base to 5% in 1981 and to 4% in 1982."

March 16, 1981

"For 1981, we favor a 6% rate of increase in the monetary base, as computed by the Federal Reserve Bank of St. Louis. Current institutional changes have less effect on the growth of the base than on most other aggregates, so we continue to specify targets for the base. A 6% rate of growth of the base would bring the level of the monetary base to $172 billion in the fourth quarter of 1981."

September 14, 1981

"For 1982, we urge the Federal Reserve to increase the monetary base, as reported by the Federal Reserve Bank of St. Louis, by no more than 5%. Our targets being the level of the monetary base of $171 billion in the fourth quarter of 1981 and $180 billion in the fourth quarter of 1982."

March 15, 1982

"We repeat our recommendation for monetary policy in 1982. The Federal Reserve should control the monetary base, return to a sustained 5% growth path, and aim for a target of $180 billion in the fourth quarter 1982, as we urged six months ago."

September 13, 1982

"We recommend that the Federal Reserve manage the monetary base so as to increase the money supply (M1) by 4% to 4.5% from the average of the fourth quarter of 1982 to the fourth quarter of 1983. For the balance of 1982, the money supply should remain in a 5% to 5.5% growth path."

March 7, 1983

"The current inflationary policy should end. The growth of money should return to a disinflationary path. We recommend an annual growth rate of money (M1) not to exceed 5 1/2% in the year ending fourth quarter 1983."

"Again, we urge the Federal Reserve to improve control procedures and we challenge them to produce some evidence to support their statements about the effects of deregulation on the monetary aggregates. Proposals to set targets for interest rates—real or nominal—would be destabilizing."

September 19, 1983

"We urge the Federal Reserve to hold the growth rate of the monetary base to 6% from fourth quarter 1983 to fourth quarter 1984. This will be consistent with a growth rate of M1 of 6–7%, and if followed by further deceleration, would prevent a renewed burst of inflation and would help the economy to return to stable real growth with falling inflation in subsequent years."

March 11–12, 1984

"The alternative is to return monetary base growth to 6% this year. This is the path consistent with the Federal Reserve's target and our September recommendation. We urge but do not expect the Federal Reserve to implement this policy to avoid the resurgence of inflation and another prolonged recession."

October 1, 1984

"Money growth in 1985 should not exceed the mid-point of the Fed's 1984 target range (6%). Fears that further gradual reduction of money growth next year will lead to recession are unwarranted. The adjustment costs associated with sustaining a long-run disinflation would be minimized if the Fed announced and adhered to a multi-year policy of continually decreasing money growth."

March 25, 1985

"In order to eliminate 'base drift' and establish a coherent framework for steady progress towards lower money growth, the SOMC urges the federal Reserve to increase M1 in 1985 by 5% from the mid-point of the original target range for 1984. This policy would result in an increase for 1984 and 1985 taken together. In the event that money growth in 1985 exceeds this target, as we think highly likely, the target for 1986 would still be based on the target level for year-end 1985, rather than the actual level of fourth quarter 1985."

September 23, 1985

"We urge the Federal Reserve to achieve its targets, to stop rebasing and to return the money stock to a growth path of 5.5% from the second quarter of 1985 through the fourth quarter of 1986 as had been announced. The target for policy should be M1, and other monetary and credit aggregates should be discarded."

March 17, 1986

"We urge the Federal Reserve to announce—and achieve—a growth rate of the monetary base of 5% for the four quarters ending in the fourth quarter of 1986 and modest further reductions in subsequent years. This growth rate would be two and a half percentage points below the average rate of growth of the monetary base over the past five years."

September 21, 1986

"To avoid the coming inflation, the growth rate of the monetary base should be reduced to a rate consistent with price stability. Research prepared for this committee suggests that that rate is in the neighborhood of 3% to 4%. This goal should be achieved by the end of the decade."

March 9, 1987

"To avoid another costly inflation and disinflation, we again urge the Federal Reserve to abandon its inflationary policy and set the growth rate of the monetary base on the path toward sustained lower inflation. We recommend that the rate of growth of the monetary base be reduced to 7 percent for the four quarters ending in December 1987 and further reduced each year until non-inflationary growth is achieved."

September 14, 1987

"You have inherited an inflation rate that has been reduced substantially since 1981. However, inflation remains at rates that are high by past standards. We urge you to adopt a policy of reducing the strategy of consistently lowering the annual growth rate of the monetary base and maintaining the fluctuating exchange rate system."

"A 6% growth rate of the monetary base in the next 12 months is a step in a program to achieve price stability. Others urge you in different directions. They talk about testing your opposition to inflation or your commitment to current exchange rates. It is a mistake to be driven by the changing views of day traders and speculators in the markets. You cannot prevent changes in the value of the dollar, you can only delay them. It is a mistake to try."

March 14, 1988

"In 1988, monetary policy should initiate a policy of gradual disinflation. The policy should continue until price stability is achieved. At our September 1987 meeting, we praised the Federal Reserve for reducing the growth rate of the monetary base from the very high rates of 1986. We recommended a growth rate of 6 percent for 1988. This rate of money growth is consistent with administration and Federal Reserve forecasts of real growth and inflation. We repeat the recommendation today."

September 19, 1988

"We urge the Federal Reserve to resist political pressures to do the impossible—namely, to attempt to alter levels of interest rates from what freely competitive financial markets would produce. The Federal Reserve should declare its intent to focus exclusively on quantitative measure of reserves and monetary growth, and allow the price of credit to be determined by private competition."

March 20, 1989

"The present acceleration of inflation stems from overly expansive monetary policy in 1985 and 1986. The Federal Reserve has announced target ranges for monetary growth in 1989. We believe that the midpoints of the announced target ranges—if achieved as part of a continuing, long-run program to reduce money growth—would result in a gradual reduction in inflation. We urge the Federal Reserve (1) to reject fine tuning; (2) to publicly disavow the Phillips curve and concerns about policy mix; (3) to achieve its announced targets for money growth. Growth of the monetary base should be maintained in the range of 5% to 6% this year."

September 18, 1989

"Restrictive monetary policy remains in effect. During the past year, the Federal Reserve has held the growth rate of the monetary base—bank reserves and currency—at the lowest level since the early 1960s. Relatively slow growth of the base and other monetary aggregates is part of a pattern of slower money growth that is now entering its third year."

"Continuation of this pattern will bring more than 20 years of inflation to an end. We urge the Federal Reserve to continue on the path toward stable prices. To remain on this path, growth of the monetary base should remain in the neighborhood of 4 percent in the year ahead."

March 19, 1990

"The recent large increase in the base appears to be mainly a onetime increase in demand by foreigners for US currency. For 1990, we recommend that the Federal Reserve keep the growth rate of the monetary base close to an annual rate of 4 percent measure from first quarter 1990. Due regard should be taken to accommodate continued foreign demand for currency."

October 1, 1990

"We urge the Federal Reserve to maintain the long-run policy that it has emphasized in the past three years. Money growth should be brought to a level consistent with sustained long-term growth of real output and stable prices. Currently, the Federal Reserve's announced target for growth of M2 has a midpoint of 5 percent for the four quarters ending fourth quarter 1990 and 4 1/2 percent for the four quarters of 1991. A 5 percent growth rate is consistent with the Federal Reserve's goal of reducing inflation. With the economy on the edge of recession, we urge that this target be maintained and achieved."

March 4, 1991

"We welcome the Federal Reserve's renewed attention to money growth. We urge officials to meet their announced targets for 1991. We caution however, that weekly or monthly rates of change in money supply are not reliable as weekly indicators of the thrust of monetary policy. What matters is whether moderate money growth is maintained for intervals of three to six months."

"Concern for recovery should not be allowed to cause a new round of rising inflation. A 4.5 percent rate would bring money growth back to the average rate since 1987. A 4.5 percent growth rate of M2 is consistent with recovery in the economy and a declining rate of inflation."

September 30, 1991

"To achieve sustained economic growth and stable prices, we urge the Federal Reserve to limit the growth rate of the monetary base to the range of 5 percent to 6 percent. The Federal Reserve should desist from making loans to failing banks. This practice only adds to the price that taxpayers must pay to protect depositors. The Treasury Department should overhaul bidding practices in the government securities market. However, an increase in regulation would be counterproductive. Proposals to bail out the Soviet economy would waste scarce resources. We reject them."

March 9, 1992

"The shift to slower money growth causes slower growth of output or a new recession. We urge the Federal Reserve now to slow the growth of the monetary base from the current 8 percent annual rate to a 5 to 6 percent range, even at the cost of a temporary rise in short-term interest rates."

"We believe that a 5 to 6 [percent] base growth rate will provide sufficient monetary stimulus for a durable expansion. Stable monetary growth can contribute to stable growth and stable prices. Money growth that is consistent with low inflation will increase economic efficiency."

September 14, 1992

"A reduced spread between long- and short-term rates can occur either because short-term rates rise or long-term rates fall. Since short-term rates, adjusted for inflation, are now zero, these rates are likely to rise. The Federal Reserve should lower long-term rates by reducing expectations of future inflation. The policy we urge the Federal Reserve to adopt [is a] 5 to 6 percent growth in the monetary base [which] would accomplish that result. It is consistent with economic recovery and lower inflation."

March 8, 1993

"We believe growth of the domestic base should be reduced in 1993. To achieve this reduction, growth of the reported base (as published including foreign holdings of currency) should be reduced to about 8% annual rate. The Federal Reserve should measure the domestic monetary base and release this information to the public."

September 13, 1993

"A prudent monetary policy requires slower growth of the monetary base. We urge the Federal Reserve to slow the growth of the monetary base by 3 percentage points to an annual rate of no more than 8%. That is the maximum rate of base growth currently consistent with the Federal Reserve's repeated statements that it seeks to hold annual inflation to 2% or less."

March 7, 1994

"We believe that excessive money growth, not real growth, brings inflation. More decisive action is required to restrict the growth of spending by slowing money growth enough to prevent a rise in inflation. Based on recent growth of output and average cash balances, growth of the monetary base should be reduced immediately by two percentage points. The monetary base should grow at no more than an 8% annualized rate."

September 12, 1994

"Since March, year-to-year growth of the monetary base—bank reserves and currency—has fallen from above 10 1/2 percent to about 9 1/4 percent. For the past six months the base has increased at an 8 percent annual rate. This is the maximum rate we recommended at our meetings in September 1993 and March 1994. We are now on a path that, if sustained, is consistent with inflation of 2 to 3 percent. Modest further reductions are necessary if price stability is to be achieved. Therefore, the Federal Reserve should reduce base growth to 7 percent in 1995."

"We continue to urge the Federal Reserve to control growth of monetary aggregates and to use the information about future inflation provided by sustained growth of the monetary aggregates."

March 6, 1995

"At our September meeting, we recommended that Federal Reserve officials reduce growth of the monetary base to 7 percent. We now recommend that they maintain a 7 percent growth rate of the base. The Federal funds rate should move up or down as needed to maintain this policy."

September 11, 1995

"The Federal Reserve should promptly reduce short-term interest rates until the monetary base grows at a 6 percent annual rate. A 6 percent growth of the base is the rate consistent with steady real growth without inflation. If the present growth of the base—4.5 percent for the past year—continues, the economy risks recession or deflation in 1996."

March 11, 1996

"Growth of the monetary base and money remain below the rate that our rule suggests is consistent with steady growth in output and price stability. We again urge the Federal Reserve to lower its interest rate target until the monetary base grows at an annual rate of 4 percent. The Federal Reserve can, at last, achieve price stability with sustained economic growth. Current Federal Reserve policy will not do that."

September 9, 1996

"For five years, Federal Reserve policy has sustained expansion without increasing inflation. This is an historical achievement. There are few comparable periods in the eighty-two years of the Fed's existence."

"Price stability has not been achieved, however. Inflation has remained in the 2 percent to 3 percent range, a range that once was, and we believe should again be, regarded as too high. We believe that current policy, if maintained, will not substantially reduce inflation below current levels. We recommend that the Federal Reserve reduce the growth rates of the monetary base and other monetary aggregates to achieve zero inflation. Monetary acceleration of the past year should not be permitted to continue."

March 3, 1997

"At our last meeting, we urged the Federal Reserve to reduce the growth rates of the monetary base and other monetary aggregates to achieve zero inflation. We repeat that recommendation and add another: Reduce money growth both to prevent inflation from rising and to end inflation. Growth of the monetary base should not exceed 2 percent this year. This policy will require a near-term increase in the Federal fund rate target."

September 1997—No SOMC meeting.

March 15, 1998

"We urge the Federal Reserve to reduce the growth rate of monetary aggregates by reducing the growth of the monetary base by two percentage points to an annual rate of 4 percent."

September 14, 1998

"We again urge the Federal Reserve to slow the growth of the monetary base to 4 percent per year, a rate consistent with steady long-term growth and a stable price level. We urge this policy though we are aware of the risks in the world economy. We believe that, in the event of a flight to liquidity, the Federal Reserve's overriding responsibility is to satisfy the demand for money by expanding the monetary base as much as required. At present, there is no evidence of a flight to money in the US. Stability of the US economy should continue to be the Federal Reserve's primary goal."

March 8, 1999

"The FOMC should act now to reduce growth of the monetary base. By the end of the year, base growth should be brought to 4 to 5 percent from the current 7 to 8 percent."

September 27, 1999

"To slow future inflation, the Federal Reserve should act promptly to bring the growth rate of the monetary base back to 4 percent. Base growth has fallen to 6 percent in the last few months, but we believe the decline is too small, and its duration is too short, to prevent the inflationary pressure of risking aggregate demand from increasing inflation."

Appendix B

Expressions for $R(F)^{-1}$

From Sargent (1979, 179) for real roots, $r_2 < r_3$, the inverse of $R(F)$ can be written as

$$R(F)^{-1} = \left[\frac{-1}{\beta\left(\frac{\phi\gamma}{(1-\gamma)} + \zeta_3\right)r_2 r_3}\right](1 - r_2^{-1}F)^{-1}(1 - r_3^{-1}F)^{-1}$$

$$= \left[\frac{-1}{\beta\left(\frac{\phi\gamma}{(1-\gamma)} + \zeta_3\right)r_2 r_3}\right]\left[\frac{1}{r_2^{-1} - r_3^{-1}}\right][r_2^{-1}(1 - r_2^{-1}F)^{-1} - r_3^{-1}(1 - r_3^{-1}F)^{-1}].$$

When the roots are complex, the inverse of $R(F)$ can be written as

$$R(F)^{-1} = \left[\frac{-1}{\beta\left(\frac{\phi\gamma}{(1-\gamma)} + \zeta_3\right)r_2 r_3}\right]\sum_{j=0}^{\infty} r^j \left[\frac{\sin\omega(j+1)}{\sin\omega}\right]F^j,$$

where $r = \sqrt{-[r_2 r_3]^{-1}}$ and $\omega = \cos^{-1}[(r_2 + r_3)/2r]$ (Sargent 1979, 181–82).

References

Anderson, L. C., and K. M. Carlson. 1970. "A Monetarist Model for Economic Stabilization." *Federal Reserve Bank of St. Louis Review* April:7–25.

Anderson, R. A., and R. H. Rasche. 2001. "The Remarkable Stability of Monetary Base Velocity in the United States: 1919–1999." Federal Reserve Bank of St. Louis Working Paper 2001-008A, August.

Ball, L. 1994. "Credible Disinflation with Staggered Price-Setting." *American Economic Review* March:282–89.

Brimmer, A. F. 1972. "The Political Economy of Money: Evolution and Impact of Monetarism in the Federal Reserve System." *American Economic Review* May:344–52.

Bronfenbrenner, M., and F. D. Holzman. 1963. "Survey of Inflation Theory." *American Economic Review* 52:593–661.

Brunner, K. 1983. "Has Monetarism Failed?" *Cato Journal* 3 (1): 23–62.

Brunner, K., and A. H. Meltzer. 1963. "Predicting Velocity: Implications for Theory and Policy." *Journal of Finance* 18 (2): 319–54.

———. 1964a. *The Federal Reserve's Attachment to the Free Reserves Concept.* Washington, DC: Committee on Banking and Currency, United States House of Representatives.

———. 1964b. "Some Further Investigations of Demand and Supply Functions for Money." *Journal of Finance* 19 (2): 240–83.

———. 1968. "What Did We Learn from the Monetary Experiences of the United States in the Great Depression?" *Canadian Journal of Economics* 2:334–48.

———. 1976. "An Aggregative Theory for a Closed Economy." In *Monetarism*, edited by J. Stein, 69–103. Amsterdam: North-Holland Publishing Company.

———. 1993. *Money and the Economy: Issues in Monetary Analysis*, Raffaele Mattiolli Lectures. Cambridge: Cambridge University Press.

Burns, A. F. 1978. "Reflections of an Economic Policy Maker." *Speeches and Congressional Statements: 1969–1978.* Washington, DC: American Enterprise Institute for Public Policy Research.

———. 1979. "The Anguish of Central Banking." *The Per Jacobsson Lecture.* Per Jacobsson Foundation, International Monetary Fund, Belgrade, September 30.

Calomiris, C. W., and D. C. Wheelock. 1998. "Was the Great Depression a Watershed for American Monetary Policy?" In *The Defining Moment: The Great Depression and the American Economy in the Twentieth Century*, edited by M. D. Bordo, C. Goldin, and E. N. White, 23–66. Chicago: University of Chicago Press.

Clarida, R. H., J. Galí, and M. Gertler. 1999. "The Science of Monetary Policy—A New Keynesian Perspective." *Journal of Economic Literature* 37 (4): 1661–707.

Economic Report of the President. 1966. Lyndon B. Johnson, Council of Economic Advisers. Washington, DC: Government Printing Office.

Friedman, M. 1968. "The Role of Monetary Policy." *American Economic Review* March:1–17.

———. 1977. "Nobel Lecture: Inflation and Unemployment." *Journal of Political Economy* 85 (3): 451–72.

Goodfriend, M., and R. G. King. 1997. "The New Neoclassical Synthesis and the Role of Monetary Policy." In *NBER Macroeconomic Annual 1997*, edited by Ben S. Bernanke and Julio J. Rotemberg, 231–83. Cambridge, MA: MIT Press.

Gramley, L. E., and S. B. Chase Jr. 1965. "Time Deposits in Monetary Analysis." *Federal Reserve Bulletin* October:1380–404.

Hafer, R. W., and D. C. Wheelock. 2003. "Darryl Francis and the Making of Monetary Policy, 1966–1975." *Federal Reserve Bank of St. Louis Review* 85 (2): 1–12.

Hetzel, R. L. 1984. "Estimating Money Demand Functions." *Journal of Money, Credit, and Banking* 16 (2): 185–93.

Hoffman, D. L., and R. H. Rasche. 1991. "Long-Run Income and Interest Elasticities of Money Demand in the United States." *Review of Economics and Statistics:* 665–74.

Kimball, M. S. 1995. "The Quantitative Analytics of the Basic Neomonetarist Model." *Journal of Money, Credit and Banking* 27 (no. 4, pt. 2): 1241–77.

King, R. G., and A. L. Wolman. 1996. "Inflation Targeting in a St. Louis Model of the 21st Century." *Federal Reserve Bank of St. Louis Review* May/June:83–107.

Laidler, D. 1981. "Monetarism: An Interpretation and an Assessment." *Economic Journal* 91 (361): 1–28.

Lucas, R. 1976. "Econometric Policy Evaluation: A Critique." *Carnegie-Rochester Conference Series on Public Policy* 1:19–46.

Lys, T. 1997. *Monetary Theory and Policy: Selected Essays of Karl Brunner,* vol. 2. Cheltenham: Edward Elgar Publishing, Inc.

Maisel, S. J. 1973. *Managing the Dollar.* New York: W. W. Norton & Company.

Mayer, T. 1978. *The Structure of Monetarism.* New York: W. W. Norton & Company.

McCallum, B. T. 1988. "Robustness Properties of a Rule for Monetary Policy." *Carnegie-Rochester Conference Series on Public Policy* 29:173–203.

———. 1999. "Issues in the Design of Monetary Policy Rules." In *Handbook of Macroeconomics,* edited by J. B. Taylor and M. Woodford. Amsterdam: North-Holland Publishing Co.

McCallum, B. T., and E. Nelson. 1999. "An Optimizing IS-LM Specification for Monetary Policy and Business Cycle Analysis." *Journal of Money, Credit, and Banking* 31 (no. 3, pt. 1): 296–16.

Meltzer, A. H. 1963. "The Demand for Money: Evidence from the Time Series." *Journal of Political Economy* 71 (3): 219–46.

———. 2000. "The Shadow Open Market Committee: Origins and Operations." *Journal of Financial Services Research* 18 (2-3): 119–28.

———. 2003. *A History of the Federal Reserve. Volume 1:1913–1951.* Chicago: University of Chicago Press.

Nelson, E., and A. J. Schwartz. "The Impact of Milton Friedman on Modern Monetary Economics: Setting the Record Straight on Paul Krugman's 'Who Was Milton Friedman?'" Federal Reserve Bank of St. Louis Working Paper 2007-048A.

Orphanides, A. 2003. "Historical Monetary Policy Analysis and the Taylor Rule." *Journal of Monetary Economics* 50:983–1022.

Phelps, E. S. 1967. "Phillips Curves, Expectations of Inflation and Optimal Unemployment over Time." *Economica* August:254–81.

———. 1978. "Commodity-Supply Shock and Full-Employment Monetary Policy." *Journal of Money, Credit, and Banking* 10 (2): 206–21.

Poole, W. 1975. "Monetary Policy during the Recession." *Brookings Papers on Economic Activity* 1975 (1): 123–39.

———. 1978. *Money and the Economy: A Monetarist View.* Reading, MA: Addison-Wesley Publishing Company.

Prescott, E. C. 1986. "Theory Ahead of Business Cycle Measurement." *Federal Reserve Bank of Minneapolis Quarterly Review* 10 (4): 9–22.

Rasche, R. H. 1987. "M1-Velocity and Money-Demand Functions: Do Stable Relationships Exist?" *Carnegie-Rochester Conference Series on Public Policy* 27:9–88.

Romer, C. D., and D. H. Romer. 2002. "A Rehabilitation of Monetary Policy in the 1950s." *American Economic Review* 92 (2): 121–27.

———. 2004. "Choosing the Federal Reserve Chair: Lessons from History." *Journal of Economic Perspectives* 18 (1): 129–62.

Samuelson, P. A. 1960. "Reflections on Monetary Policy." *Review of Economics and Statistics* August:263–69.

Samuelson, P. A., and R. M. Solow. 1960. "Problem of Achieving and Maintaining a Stable Price Level: Analytical Aspects of Anti-Inflation Policy." *American Economic Review, Papers and Proceedings* May:177–94.

Sargent, T. J. 1979. *Macroeconomic Theory.* New York: Academic Press.

Shiller, R. J. 1979. "The Volatility of Long-Term Interest Rates and Expectations Models of the Term Structure." *Journal of Political Economy* 87 (6): 1190–219.

Taylor, J. B. 1993. "Discretion versus Policy Rules in Practice." *Carnegie-Rochester Conference Series on Public Policy* 39:195–214.

Woodford, M. 2003. *Interest and Prices: Foundations of a Theory of Monetary Policy.* Princeton, NJ: Princeton University Press.

Comment   Christina D. Romer

The premise of this chapter by Poole, Rasche, and Wheelock is brilliant. The Shadow Open Market Committee started business in 1973 as a self-appointed alternative to the official monetary policymaking committee in the United States. As such, their recommendations constitute a wonderful counterfactual to the policies that were actually followed. Like looking at the experiences of other countries in the 1970s (another great topic included in the conference), this counterfactual helps us to understand whether avoiding the Great Inflation was something that required knowledge not available at the time, or simply knowledge available but not used by American policymakers in the 1970s.

The SOMC's Economic Ideas

Poole, Rasche, and Wheelock begin their study with an extensive discussion of what members of the Shadow Open Market Committee (SOMC) believed about key economic relationships. This is, to my mind, the right place to start. I am a contributor to what Sargent (2002) has called the "Berkeley story" about the causes of the Great Inflation. This story emphasizes the crucial role of mistaken beliefs about how the economy operated in causing policymakers to take unfortunate policy actions. DeLong (1997) stressed the role of the Samuelson-Solow belief in an exploitable Phillips curve, along with a deep-seated fear of unemployment resulting from the trauma of the Great Depression, in leading both monetary and fiscal policy-

Christina D. Romer is the Class of 1957-Garff B. Wilson Professor of Economics at the University of California, Berkeley, former chair of the President's Council of Economic Advisers, and a research associate and codirector of the Monetary Economics Program at the National Bureau of Economic Research.

For acknowledgments, sources of research support, and disclosure of the author's material financial relationships, if any, please see http://www.nber.org/chapters/c9157.ack.

makers to err far too often on the side of overexpansion during the late 1960s and the 1970s.

David Romer and I (2002, 2004) expanded on DeLong's analysis by examining policy and ideas over a much longer period. We found that beliefs about fundamental economic relationships were the driving force for macroeconomic policy from the Great Depression to today. We found that the central beliefs were more complicated and nuanced than just a yes or no belief in a permanent trade-off. For example, for the 1970s, we showed that the Federal Reserve's failure to control inflation resulted from both a belief that the sustainable level of unemployment was very low and the view that inflation was relatively impervious to slack. This emphasis on the crucial role of mistaken economic ideas, particularly in the 1970s, has been shared by numerous other researchers, including Mayer (1998), Nelson (2005), and Hetzel (2008).

If bad ideas were the fundamental source of monetary policy mistakes in the 1970s, a natural way to evaluate the Shadow Open Market Committee is to ask if its members had better ideas. And, in some ways, they clearly did. Indeed, from the authors' description, the SOMC seemed to hold the three views that Romer and Romer (2004) found have been consistent across successful Federal Reserve chairs. First, the members believed in the natural rate hypothesis with a sensible estimate of normal unemployment; they did not think we could buy permanently lower unemployment with some more inflation. Moreover, the SOMC thought inflation was very costly. In this way, they hit our second key view, which is a strong belief that low inflation is beneficial to the economy. Perhaps most important, the authors show that the SOMC had a firm view that the economy responded to changes in the money supply; they had no doubt that inflation would fall if money growth were reduced. In this way, they escaped Arthur Burns's and G. William Miller's paralyzing view that inflation was caused by special factors and so monetary policy was powerless to counteract it (at least, at any reasonable cost).

Given that its members held some very sensible views, does it follow that the SOMC would have been better at monetary policymaking than the Federal Reserve? I am not at all sure. The reason for my skepticism is that the SOMC also held some other beliefs that may have countered or confounded their sensible ones. Most of these auxiliary beliefs center on operating procedures and monetary relationships. Reading the authors' chapter, I was struck by the overwhelming sense that 1970s monetarism would have been very sensible if it weren't for all this silly stuff about money. One of the core auxiliary beliefs was that money demand is stable. In addition, the SOMC seemed to be almost obsessed with the notion that the Federal Reserve could not use interest rates as a reliable guide for policy. For example, in March 1983, the SOMC declared: "Proposals to set targets for interest rates—real or nominal—would be destabilizing." The fear of interest rate targeting, combined with the over-optimism about the stability of money demand, might well have led the SOMC to erratic policy.

Finally, I can't resist saying a word about the SOMC's belief in the crucial importance of credibility and the usefulness of transparent, rules-based policy. Now, I am as big a fan of transparency in monetary policymaking as the next person. But, I feel overestimating the value of credibility is potentially very destructive. There is remarkably little evidence that credibility in monetary policymaking buys one much when it comes to lowering the costs of disinflation. In this context, I would cite the work of Ball (1994) and Ball and Sheridan (2005), which shows that other factors, such as labor market institutions, are far more important than credibility in determining the sacrifice ratio. Blind faith in the value of credibility may lead policymakers to fail to respond to genuine developments for fear of losing some hypothetical power.

Simulating a Gradualist Monetary-Base Rule

Besides discussing the SOMC's beliefs, the main thing the authors do is simulate the effects of a gradualist monetary base rule in a dynamic stochastic general equilibrium (DSGE) model. This rule says that the growth rate of the monetary base is dropped 1 percentage point per year until the desired growth rate is achieved. The authors use the narrative evidence from the SOMC policy statements to suggest that such a rule is a stylized version of what the SOMC was recommending in the 1970s and, indeed, throughout its whole existence. The model they use for the simulation is standard in most respects. The main bells and whistles involve the nitty-gritty of the monetary side of the model, such as an assumption about endogenous velocity and incorporation of the term structure of interest rates.

Implicitly, I think what we are supposed to get out of the simulation is the sense that such a monetary base rule would have worked better than the policies the Federal Reserve actually followed. The simulations suggest that gradualist monetary base targeting would have achieved low inflation with virtually no output costs. Since we actually experienced high inflation and high costs of disinflation, the SOMC rule clearly looks better.

Now, this is not how the authors frame their simulation. Rather than making an explicit comparison with actual policy or some other operating procedure, such as an interest rate rule, they focus on a horse race between a gradualist monetary base rule and a cold-turkey drop in the growth rate of the base to achieve the desired disinflation. In my view, this is a distraction. I do not think what we really care about is whether Paul Volcker should have acted more gradually. Rather, what we care about is a base rule versus a policy of fine-tuning or versus making gross mistakes concerning the level of monetary stimulus.

The focus on the horse race also leads the authors to make modeling choices that obscure some of the key issues. For example, they assume that there are no shocks to money demand. This is fine if one just cares about the relative success of one type of base rule versus another. But in evaluating the desirability of a base rule versus actual practice or an interest rate rule, assuming away money demand shocks comes painfully close to assuming the conclusion that a monetary base rule is desirable.

Likewise, the basic model, which includes a New Keynesian Phillips curve, is very forward-looking. The authors add the assumption that the stated policy rules are perfectly credible. These assumptions do not have big effects on the horse race the authors consider. But, for the implicit comparison to actual outcomes, they are surely very important. Credibility and forward-looking expectations practically ensure that any kind of a rule achieves disinflation with far less cost than a more ad hoc policy.

The SOMC's Actual Policy Recommendations

My comments so far are about the framework and assumptions the authors use for simulating the effects of a gradualist monetary base rule. It has taken as given that such a rule is a good proxy for what the Shadow Open Market Committee was recommending. In Romer and Romer (2012), David Romer and I take up that issue. Rather than using the narrative evidence on SOMC recommendations to suggest a stylized rule to be simulated, we look directly at those real-time recommendations. What money growth rate was the SOMC recommending at each meeting? Do these money growth rates appear to be moving policy in a desirable direction? Because the SOMC stopped consistently providing its recommendation for policy in terms of a growth rate of some monetary aggregate after 2001, we focus on the period 1973 to 2001.

It is important to be clear about the question we ask. We do not ask what would have happened if monetarists had been in charge of policy for the entire period we consider. I have no doubt that had we given Milton Friedman and Anna Schwartz free reign over monetary policy starting in 1973, macroeconomic history would have unfolded very differently. Indeed, many other features of the economy and policies might have been quite different had an effective monetarist regime been in place. But this regime did not occur, and so the records of the SOMC do not allow us to address this counterfactual.

Instead, we ask for each date in this period, what would have been likely to happen to policy in the short run if we had put monetarists in charge. It is reminiscent of the movie *Groundhog Day:* imagine each meeting is Anna Schwartz's first day as Federal Reserve chair. We can take the SOMC recommendations as an indication of the policies she would have followed in the short run.

The SOMC's policy recommendation at each meeting had two key features: the monetary concept used, and its recommended growth rate. In terms of the monetary concept, the authors are certainly correct that the monetary base was used most often. But, it was only used about two-thirds of the time. For most of the 1970s and for two brief periods in the 1980s, the committee stated its recommendation in terms of M1. And for two meetings in 1990 and 1991, it stated its recommendation in terms of M2. Thus, the notion that one should model the Shadow Open Market Committee as having a base rule is not obvious, especially for the period covered by this conference. More importantly, the fact that real-life monetary prescribers were clearly struggling with what concept to use indicates that the choice was difficult. It suggests that the relationship between monetary measures was not stable, and that the money demand and velocity shocks assumed away in the simulations were important.

Identifying the recommended money growth rate from the SOMC policy statements is usually straightforward. The main exceptions occur when the SOMC described policy in terms of a onetime correction and then a growth rate. These recommendations need to be converted to effective growth rates. In each case, we look only at what the SOMC was recommending for money growth over the next six months (until the next meeting) at an annual rate, since that was often the committee's central focus and since the committee consistently provided such recommendations.

Figure 1C.1 shows the recommended money growth rates of the SOMC. The markers are coded to show the concept being used (white circles for M1, black circles for the base, and white triangles for M2). We have made no attempt to standardize the measures. That is, we have not tried to guess how a recommendation of 6 percent base growth would translate into a recommendation for M1 growth. But, the few times when the SOMC says what a base growth rate corresponds to for M1 growth, the two are within a percentage point of each other. So, not standardizing may be fine.

Assessing the SOMC's Recommendations

The first thing to say about the SOMC's prescriptions is that one cannot help but notice how incredibly far they were from Milton Friedman's famous "k-percent" rule. Recommended money growth varied sharply—from a low of less than 1 percent annual growth to a high of over 9 percent. Now some of this extreme variation comes from the onetime corrections the SOMC sometimes included. The uncorrected rates are certainly smoother, but still highly variable. They fluctuate in a range of 4 to 8 percent, plus one recommendation of 2 percent growth.

There is also little change in the volatility of recommended growth rates over time. One might have expected the recommended rates to be particularly volatile in the 1970s, when the SOMC was reacting to often erratic Federal Reserve policy. However, consider the period from 1985 to 1997. This is the heart of the "great moderation," during which actual monetary policy was quite well-tempered. Even in this period of relatively low inflation and stable real growth, the money growth rate advocated by the SOMC fluctu-

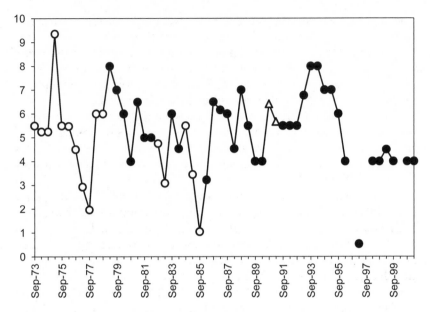

Fig. 1C.1   SOMC recommended money growth

Notes: The figure shows the money growth rate recommended by the SOMC. The color and shape of the marker shows the money concept being used: M1 is represented by white circles, the monetary base is represented by black circles, and M2 is represented by white triangles.

ated sharply. Only in the final few years of the sample are the recommendations stable.

We also look at how different the SOMC's recommended money growth was from actual money growth in the six months following each SOMC meeting. In calculating actual money growth, we are careful to use the same monetary concept as the SOMC. This difference (SOMC minus actual) is given in figure 1C.2. The figure also shows actual inflation in the six months following each SOMC meeting. The idea is to look at the difference between recommended and actual money growth in relation to inflation, to see if the SOMC seemed to be urging policy in the right direction.

Let me just go through the results episode by episode. (In Romer and Romer [2012] we also take a more systematic approach to the entire sample period.) For four of the first five meetings, the SOMC recommended slightly faster money growth than what actually occurred. I was quite surprised by this result. The first meeting of the Shadow Open Market Committee was in September 1973. Inflation was over 7 percent and the economic expansion had not yet peaked. It seems unlikely that the SOMC formed itself to argue that Arthur Burns was not being expansionary enough. My guess is that their early behavior is testimony to the fact that it is hard to use money growth targets as a reliable indicator for policy. At the very least, the first two and a half years of the committee do not

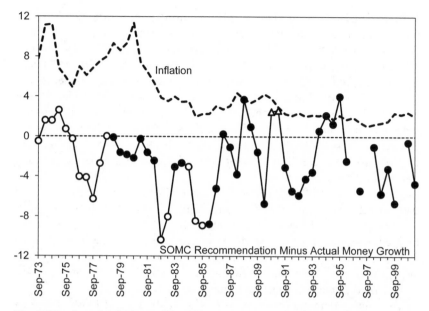

Fig. 1C.2   Actual inflation and the difference between SOMC and actual money growth

Notes: Actual inflation is measured as the percentage change at an annual rate in the price index for GDP in the two quarters following the SOMC meeting (from the first to third quarter for the March meeting and the third to first quarter for the September meeting). Actual money growth is calculated using the same concept as the SOMC was targeting. The change is for the six months following the meeting (from February to August for the March meeting and August to February for the September meeting). The color and shape of the marker shows the money concept being used: M1 is represented by white circles, the monetary base is represented by black circles, and M2 is represented by white triangles.

suggest that the SOMC would have been more successful in preserving nominal values.

To my mind, it is in the period 1976 to 1978 that the SOMC shines. This is the period when the Federal Reserve made its most blatant errors. It is sometimes hard to imagine just how close we came to avoiding the worst of the Great Inflation. By mid-1976, inflation had come down to just over 5 percent and real growth had recovered to robust levels. It is at this point that the Federal Reserve, I think because of misguided ideas, expanded recklessly. Notice how much lower money growth the SOMC was recommending. Proposed money growth rates were at times close to 5 percentage points below what actually happened. This is stunning suggestive evidence that the SOMC did, in this crucial period, seem to know substantially more than the Federal Reserve.

For the downward movement during the Volcker disinflation, the SOMC was essentially recommending policy similar to what the Federal Reserve actually did. There is a striking difference, however, coming out of the

1981 to 1982 recession. The SOMC recommended dramatically lower money growth in both September 1982 and March 1983 than the Federal Reserve actually created. The difference in September 1982 is a whopping 10 percentage points. By March 1983, the Shadow Open Market Committee was convinced that the Federal Reserve was losing its nerve and that inflation would return. The policy statement declared: "The current inflationary policy should end." In retrospect, given how well inflation behaved subsequently and the genuine risks to the world financial system caused by the sustained high interest rates, I believe few would argue that the 1981 to 1982 recession was not deep enough and did not last as long as it should have.

The record of the SOMC after the Volcker disinflation looks to me to be truly dismal. And remember, this is the time when the SOMC could chart its ideal course in a low-inflation, relatively stable economy. Look at the difference between what the SOMC was recommending in the period 1985 to 1986 and actual money growth. At a time when the inflation rate was down at approximately 2 percent, the SOMC was recommending money growth up to 9 percentage points below actual.

A similar phenomenon occurs in 1992 to 1993 and 1998 to 1999. In both cases, inflation was low, yet the SOMC recommended money growth roughly 5 percentage points below actual. The September 1998 recommendation is particularly interesting. Despite the August 1998 Russian financial crisis, the SOMC explicitly refused to respond to the international turmoil. The report for the September 14 meeting stated: "We urge this policy though we are aware of the risks in the world economy. . . . Stability of the U.S. economy should continue to be the Federal Reserve's primary goal."

Then, just to complete the sorry picture of the more recent era, look at 1994 to 1995. For some reason, the SOMC was proposing money growth considerably above what actual policy was producing. Inflation was still low—roughly 2 percent—and stable. As I recall that period, people were talking about the Clinton miracle and the robust expansion of the high-tech economy, not incipient recession and deflation. Overall, it appears that had the SOMC had its way in the period since the Volcker disinflation, the results might have been far less desirable than they actually were.

Besides looking at the twists and turns of what the SOMC was recommending, it is helpful to think about the overall thrust of their proposed policies. One cannot help but notice that the money growth the SOMC was recommending at each meeting over this twenty-five-year period was on average well below what actually occurred: the average difference over the full period is –2.4 percentage points. Now, given the inflation that occurred in the 1970s, it is tempting to take this difference in the overall thrust of policy to mean that the Shadow did indeed know better. And, as I have suggested, this interpretation is surely correct for a critical period in the late 1970s. But it seems to me that considering the twenty-five-year period as a whole, it is a sign that the SOMC might have known far less than the Federal Reserve. The Shadow Open Market Committee generally recommended money growth far below actual in a period when inflation was low and stable. Had the SOMC had its way in the period since the Volcker disinflation, the results most likely would not have been pretty.

Conclusion

So where does all of this leave us? I have to say, disappointed. I wanted to believe that the SOMC knew better. Certainly, given some of their ideas about basic economic relationships, they should have known better. But, in this case, the devil truly seems to have been in the details. The SOMC's attachment to certain operating procedures and assumptions led it to get the details severely wrong. If this analysis is correct, the SOMC's policy prescriptions would have led to superior macroeconomic performance than the Federal Reserve's only for a short, but admittedly very important, period. For the most part, the SOMC's recommendations would almost surely have led to less desirable macroeconomic outcomes. Or to put it in terms of Federal Reserve chairmen: I would have preferred the SOMC to Arthur Burns at his worst and certainly to G. William Miller, but give me Paul Volcker and Alan Greenspan any day.

References

Ball, Laurence. 1994. "What Determines the Sacrifice Ratio?" In *Monetary Policy,* edited by N. Gregory Mankiw, 155–82. Chicago: University of Chicago Press.

Ball, Laurence, and Niamh Sheridan. 2005. "Does Inflation Targeting Matter?" In *The Inflation-Targeting Debate,* edited by Ben S. Bernanke and Michael Woodford, 249–76. Chicago: University of Chicago Press.

DeLong, J. Bradford. 1997. "America's Peacetime Inflation: The 1970s." In *Reducing Inflation: Motivation and Strategy,* edited by Christina D. Romer and David H. Romer, 247–76. Chicago: University of Chicago Press.

Hetzel, Robert. 2008. *The Monetary Policy of the Federal Reserve: A History.* Cambridge: Cambridge University Press.

Mayer, Thomas. 1998. *Monetary Policy and the Great Inflation in the United States: The Federal Reserve and the Failure of Macroeconomic Policy, 1965–79.* Cheltenham, UK: Edward Elgar.

Nelson, Edward. 2005. "The Great Inflation of the Seventies: What Really Happened?" *Advances in Macroeconomics* 5 (2005): Article 3.

Romer, Christina D., and David H. Romer. 2002. "The Evolution of Economic Understanding and Postwar Stabilization Policy." In *Rethinking Stabilization Policy,* 11–78. Kansas City: Federal Reserve Bank of Kansas City.

———. 2004. "Choosing the Federal Reserve Chair: Lessons from History." *Journal of Economic Perspectives* 18:129–62.

————. 2012. "Monetarism in Real Time: Evidence from the Shadow Open Market Committee." University of California, Berkeley. Unpublished Paper.
Sargent, Thomas J. 2002. "Commentary: The Evolution of Economic Understanding and Postwar Stabilization Policy." In *Rethinking Stabilization Policy,* 79–94. Kansas City: Federal Reserve Bank of Kansas City.

Discussion

Matthew Shapiro began the discussion by claiming that the chapter had a rather self-congratulatory tone that came from running simulations of a model in which we know there is disconnected performance. He stressed that the authors should use the actual shock process that the model generates. Given the parameters, you can back out the shock process and show what history would look like with this policy and what the shocks would look like with the given equations. That way, it would be more consistent.

Robert King had a different interpretation of several of the figures in the chapter, notably the figure referring to the inflation targets of the period in question. He proposed that perhaps under the Paul Volcker and Alan Greenspan regimes, the Federal Reserve had a target inflation rate of 4 percent, while under the earlier period it was 0 percent. He felt it was improper to say that policy was optimal under the Federal Reserve and 4 percent off under the Shadow Open Market Committee (SOMC).

Bennett McCallum mentioned how Romer criticized the details of the SOMC's recommendations, and went further by saying that implicitly going along with that is a lack of attention to the dynamics. He advertised the policy rules he developed in the 1980s, which he felt were an attempt to write down in a dynamic and operational way what he thought the SOMC was promoting. Simulations he has made would indicate you would get pretty good performance with the policy the SOMC was arguing for. McCallum continued on by referring to comments made by Romer on how credibility was not important for reducing the sacrifice ratio (i.e., the trade-off between stabilizing inflation and maintaining sustainable employment or growth). He pointed out that reducing the sacrifice ratio is not necessary for successful policy, and even argued that most of the models used today for stabilization purposes do not have changing sacrifice ratios. Thus, a reduction might be attractive, but it is not at all necessary for good rules-based policy.

Alan Blinder referred to figures 1.5 and 1.6 in the chapter, and stressed that under either a gradualist or cold turkey approach to policy, the sacrifice ratio would be zero or infinity depending on how one wrote it. This left him with two deductions: either this model is totally at variance with reality, or Paul Volcker was probably the least credible head of the Federal Reserve in its history.

Andrew Levin referenced a paper he had written with Michael Bordo and Christopher Erceg that talked about credibility. Look at the convergence of Greece and Italy during the approach to monetary union, and Levin believed that experience looks very similar to the figures in the chapter presented here. There was credible disinflation, and everyone understood that they were converging to a monetary treaty. Output expanded, and the sacrifice ratio was probably close to zero. In the chapter presented here, the authors look back at US history. There are cases where having strong credibility is important. In the paper Levin referenced, it was shown that if you have imperfect credibility, then a gradualist policy is not the best. If you do something like Volcker, where you hit the rates hard to send a clear signal that the inflation objective has changed, you can reduce the sacrifice ratio, since the key issue is conveying to the public that things have changed so that they change their expectations.

Michael Woodford commented on the gradualist versus cold-turkey policies. Analyzing this under the assumption of immediate, perfect credibility is probably not the realistic way to analyze it. But assuming that one does that, is it really the case that it leads to superiority of the gradualist policy? If one actually assumes one can adopt a policy and have it be immediately credible, then it should be possible to immediately stop inflation without there being a required recession. The policy that would do this requires a onetime increase in the money supply and low money growth thereafter. You can announce that and have it be perfectly credible even while the onetime increase is occurring, and agents will perfectly anticipate lower money growth in the future. So, it is not actually true that a gradual process is optimal.

Benjamin Friedman returned to the comments of McCallum, noting that the idea of enhanced credibility of lower inflation in the future giving you an improved sacrifice ratio is a consequence of any model based on Calvo pricing, Taylor's overlapping contracts, Rotemberg quadratic adjustment costs, Leahy and Gertler Ss pricing, and so forth. McCallum added that the experiments being discussed here involve starting at a given point in time and assuming expectations are correct. Is this sensible dynamic analysis? One must look over a span of time. This all creates confusion between ex post and model-based sacrifice ratios. In reference to Woodford, McCallum did not believe you can just change policy and expect expectations to be rational immediately.

Alex Cukierman stated that stabilization and credibility must go together, and strongly disagreed with Romer's comments. The first element you need for stabilization is establishing credibility, since all the work involves changing expectations. If expectations do not capture ahead of time what the subsequent path will be, it does not mean they are not rational. It means there is uncertainty. When Volcker came into office, was he going to be strong or weak? Given this uncertainty, he had to prove himself and demonstrate after the failed policies of Chairmen Arthur Burns and G. William Miller. Was the recession needed to establish credibility?

Anna Schwartz stressed that Milton Friedman believed that the lessons of the Great Inflation would not be long-lasting, that inflations would recur because central banks would yield to the temptation to be overexpansive, and because they would be reluctant to tighten monetary policy. Her guess is that he would regard the recent performance of the Federal Reserve during this financial crisis as confirmation of his belief.

Allan Meltzer provided the group with a bit of history, stating that when Chairman Volcker came into office, he informed then-President Jimmy Carter that he would be tougher than his predecessors. Carter said that was what he wanted. Why did Carter and Congress change their minds? Inflation had become the biggest problem that the country had, and thus they supported Volcker. Volcker gave up the interest rate as the monetary policy instrument because he wanted markets to set the interest rate and did not want to be blamed for it. During a deep recession, he even enacted policy that raised the interest rate. This established his credibility as a tough central banker. What the public did not believe was that he would be able to stick to it when unemployment got high, and he showed that he would stick to it. In terms of the SOMC's influence, he said he was a practical monetarist and would not go to a rigid rule, but that he would get money growth and inflation under control.

The Supply-Shock Explanation of the Great Stagflation Revisited

Alan S. Blinder and Jeremy B. Rudd

Everything should be made as simple as possible, but
not simpler.
—Albert Einstein

2.1 Preamble

Between, say, the first OPEC shock and the early 1980s, economists developed what has been called "the supply-shock explanation" of what this conference calls the Great Inflation, that is, the period of high inflation seen in the United States (and elsewhere) between 1973 and 1982.[1] At the conceptual level, the supply-shock explanation can be succinctly summarized by four main propositions:

1. At any given moment, there is an underlying (or "core") inflation rate toward which the actual (or "headline") inflation rate tends to converge. This rate is determined by the fundamentals of aggregate demand and aggregate supply growth.

2. Many factors, including but not limited to monetary and fiscal policy, influence the growth rate of aggregate demand. On the supply side, the fundamental driving factor in the long run is the growth rate of productivity, but occasional abrupt restrictions in aggregate supply ("supply shocks") can dominate over short periods.

Alan S. Blinder is the Gordon S. Rentschler Memorial Professor of Economics at Princeton University and a research associate of the National Bureau of Economic Research. Jeremy B. Rudd is a senior economist at the Board of Governors of the Federal Reserve System.

This chapter was presented at the NBER conference on the Great Inflation, Woodstock, VT, September 2008. Blinder gratefully acknowledges research support from Princeton's Center for Economic Policy Studies. We also thank Olivier Blanchard, other conference participants, and two referees for useful suggestions. The opinions expressed here are our own, however, and do not necessarily reflect the views of any of the institutions with which we are affiliated. For acknowledgments, sources of research support, and disclosure of the authors' material financial relationships, if any, please see http://www.nber.org/chapters/c9160.ack.

1. For a short but comprehensive summary in an earlier NBER volume, see Blinder (1982, 262–64).

3. For empirical purposes, the core rate of inflation can be proxied by the rate of change of prices for all items other than food and energy.

4. The headline inflation rate can deviate markedly from the core rate over short periods. Rapid increases (or decreases) in food or energy prices, which are largely exogenous, can push inflation above (or below) the core rate for a while. There may be other special one-shot factors as well, such as the 1971 to 1974 Nixon wage-price controls.

This model, if you want to call it such, was applied by a number of scholars to explain the history of the Great Inflation with six additional propositions.[2]

5. The dramatic rise in inflation between 1972 and 1974 can be attributed to three major supply shocks—rising food prices, rising energy prices, and the end of the Nixon wage-price controls program—each of which can be conceptualized as requiring rapid adjustments of some *relative* prices. (Thus nominal rigidities play a central role in the story.)

6. The equally dramatic decline in inflation between 1974 and 1976 can be traced to the simple fact that the three above-named factors came to an end. In other words, double-digit inflation went away "by itself."

7. The state of aggregate demand thus had little to do with either the rise or fall of inflation between 1972 and 1976. This is not to say that aggregate-demand management (e.g., monetary policy) was irrelevant to the behavior of inflation over this period, but only that its effects were dwarfed by the effect of the supply shocks.

8. Specifically, while the rate of headline Consumer Price Index (CPI) inflation rose about 8 percentage points between 1977 and early 1980, the core rate may have risen by as little as 3 percentage points. The rest of the inflationary acceleration came from "special factors."

9. The initial impetus for rising inflation in 1978 came mainly from the food sector, with some help from mortgage interest rates.[3] The further increase into the double-digit range in 1979 mainly reflected soaring energy prices and, once again, rising mortgage rates. Finally, mortgage interest carried the ball almost by itself in early 1980.

10. The 1970s really were a break from recent history. Energy shocks appeared to be a product of the brave, new post-OPEC world.[4] Food shocks were not new. We had experienced them in the 1940s, but somehow managed to get away without any in the 1950s and 1960s.

2. Among the many who could be listed, see Gordon (1975), Phelps (1978), and Blinder (1979, 1982). The specific six points listed here follow Blinder (1982).

3. At the time, the mortgage interest rate was a direct component of the CPI. More on this in a later section.

4. However, Hamilton's (1983) subsequent work showed that this was not quite so.

These ten numbered points can be said to constitute the supply-shock explanation—or, more correctly, the special-factors explanation—of the Great Inflation. But before proceeding to analyze this explanation, two important preliminary points must be made.

First, the Great Inflation was in fact *two* distinct episodes, as figure 2.1—which plots headline and core inflation as measured by both the CPI (using current methodology) and the PCE price index—clearly shows.[5] There were sharp increases in inflation in 1973–1975 and then again in 1978–1980, but each was followed by a sharp *disinflation*. (And for later reference, it is worth noting that, in both episodes and by both measures, core inflation rose and fell *later* and *by smaller amounts* than headline inflation.) Any coherent explanation of the inflation of the 1970s must explain *both* the ups *and* the downs.

In addition, however, figure 2.1 displays a clear upward drift in core inflation, from under 2 percent in 1964, to around 4 percent by 1970, and then to about 6 percent by 1976—before it falls back to 4 percent or so after 1983. This upward drift, which is presumably explainable by the fundamental factors listed in point (2) in the previous list, constitutes an interesting and important macroeconomic episode in itself—and one that has certainly not gone unnoticed![6] But it is *not* the subject of this chapter. Had the upward drift in inflation from 2 percent to 6 percent (and then back down to 4 percent) been all that happened, no one would have dreamed of calling this episode the Great Inflation. Hence we focus squarely on the two big "inflation hills" that are so evident in the figure.

Second, the Great Inflation was really the Great *Stagflation.* Any coherent explanation must also explain the contemporaneous deep recessions. In particular, the economy did not merely experience *real output* declines over these two periods. *Unemployment* also rose sharply, implying that what was going on in each case was more than just a neoclassical drop in output in response, say, to the rise in the relative price of energy.

Why revisit this ancient explanation now? There are several reasons. First, all the data have been revised, and we have experienced nearly thirty additional years of macroeconomic history, including several more oil shocks. Some of this history looks quite different from the 1970s, which already

5. At the time of the conference, the core PCE price index was defined to exclude food, beverages, and energy goods and services. (The core CPI excludes food and energy only.) In the 2009 comprehensive revision to the national accounts, the Bureau of Economic Analysis modified the definition of core PCE prices so that food away from home was no longer excluded. This chapter uses the pre-revision definition of core PCE throughout. (The appendix gives definitions and sources for all series used in this chapter.)

6. Among these fundamental factors, we would count Vietnam War spending in the late 1960s, overexpansionary monetary policy, and the post-1973 productivity slowdown. According to Congressional Budget Office (CBO) estimates, the unemployment rate was at or below the NAIRU in every year from 1964 through 1974.

A. Current-methods CPI

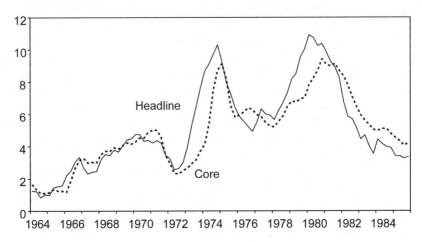

B. PCE price index

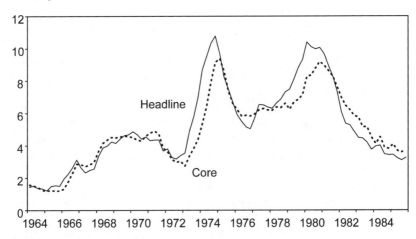

Fig. 2.1   Consumer price inflation, 1964–1985
Note: Four-quarter log differences.

provides sufficient reason to reexamine the supply-shock story. Second, both macroeconomic theory and the theory of stabilization policy have gone through several upheavals since 1980, during which (among other things) the canonical macro model has changed multiple times. Third, an extensive empirical and theoretical literature on supply shocks, partly spurred by Hamilton's (1983) important paper, has developed. Some of this literature disputes the supply-shock explanation. The purpose of this chapter is to reexamine the supply-shock explanation of the Great Stagflation in the light of these new facts, new models, and new econometric findings. Our central questions are: Do we need to rewrite the economic history of this period—and if so, how?

The analysis proceeds in four main steps. Section 2.2 outlines and slightly modernizes the basic conceptual framework (points [1] to [4] in the previous list) and reexamines it in the light of much new theory and many new empirical findings. Section 2.3 takes a fresh look at the evidence on the Great Inflation in the United States (points [5] to [10]), once again making use of new data, new theory, and new econometric findings. Section 2.4 then deals with a series of objections to the supply-shock explanation, some of which were raised before 1982, but most of which surfaced later. Finally, section 2.5 looks beyond the narrow historical confines of the 1972 to 1982 period, considering (albeit briefly) supply shocks both prior to and after the Great Stagflation. The main focus here is on why recent oil shocks seem to have had so little impact on either inflation or output.

Section 2.6 draws some conclusions. But we can end the suspense right now by stating that, at least in our judgment, the "old-fashioned" supply-shock explanation holds up quite well.

2.2   What Is the Supply-Shock Explanation of the Great Stagflation?

First we must define what we mean by a "supply shock." We begin, as is now conventional (but was not in 1973), by dividing the various influences on output and prices into two categories: factors that influence *aggregate supply* ("supply shocks") and factors that influence *aggregate demand* ("demand shocks"). Their respective hallmarks can be described in either of two ways.

1. Supply shocks affect the ability of firms to *produce* the gross domestic product, which means that they *directly* affect either the prices or quantities of factor inputs or the production technology. The resulting changes in output can be thought of as basically neoclassical in nature. On the other hand, demand shocks affect spending by the households, businesses, and governments that *purchase* the GDP. Naturally, any demand shock will have short-run Keynesian effects (e.g., result in changes in real output) if the economy has Keynesian properties, which it does.[7]

2. Supply shocks are events that, on impact, move the equilibrium price level and equilibrium real output in *opposite* directions (e.g., an adverse shock causes prices to go up and output to go down). Demand shocks are events that, on impact, move the equilibrium price level and equilibrium real

---

7. For this purpose, we define "Keynesian properties" as the presence of nominal rigidities plus some inertia in wage and price setting (whether from expectations or not) that makes this behavior at least somewhat backward-looking. We exclude purely forward-looking models with rational expectations. As is well-known, models in this latter class carry starkly different—and generally counterfactual—implications.

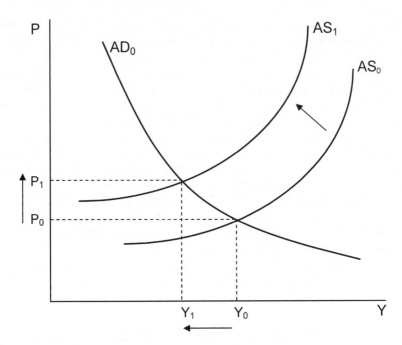

Fig. 2.2   Supply shocks in the AS/AD framework

output in the *same* direction (e.g., an expansionary demand shock pushes up both prices and output).

The second definition is exemplified by the standard aggregate supply and demand diagram (shown in figure 2.2) in which an upward-sloping aggregate supply curve shifts inward along a fixed aggregate demand curve, thereby simultaneously raising the equilibrium price level and reducing equilibrium output—a stagflationary outcome. The nonvertical aggregate supply curves AD_0 and AS_1, of course, embody some sort of nominal wage-price stickiness.

Either of the two definitions will suffice for our purposes. But it is important to note that some shocks have *both* supply-side *and* demand-side elements. A shock to the price of imported oil is, of course, the most prominent example. We will show later that neoclassical supply-side considerations alone cannot come close to explaining the magnitudes of the two recessions that occurred during the Great Stagflation. Rather, to explain these episodes empirically, the two big oil shocks must be viewed as having affected both aggregate supply and aggregate demand, with the aggregate demand effects notably larger.[8]

8. As detailed later in section 2.2.3, some demand-side influences amount to shifts of the AD curve, while others pertain to its slope (that is, to why demand is lower at a higher price level).

2.2.1 Three Types of Supply Shocks

To interpret the history of the 1970s and 1980s through the lens of the supply-shock model, it is important to distinguish among three different *types* of supply shocks, with the typology determined by the shocks' nature and timing. These three stylized types are not just theoretical constructs. Each has a clear historical counterpart in figure 2.3, which depicts the history of the *real* price of oil (in panel A) and the closely-related *real* consumer price of energy (in panel B) since 1965.

The first type of shock is *a transitory price spike* that gets reversed, leaving no permanent level effect—as exemplified in figure 2.3 by the behavior of real oil and energy prices following the second OPEC shock in 1979. Conceptually, we expect such a spike to cause a corresponding (but greatly muted) jump in headline inflation, which then reverses as the *inflationary* shock turns into a *deflationary* shock. If there is some pass-through from oil prices into core inflation, as there should be, then the latter should display a lagged, and even more muted, hump-shaped pattern.[9]

Figure 2.4 gives these qualitative points a quantitative dimension. To study pass-through empirically, we estimated a relatively standard backward-looking price-price Phillips curve model of US inflation on monthly data from January 1961 to December 1984. The basic specification takes the form

$$\pi_t = \alpha_0 + A(L)\pi_{t-1} + B(L)x_{t-1} + G(L)\zeta_{t-1} + \varepsilon_t,$$

where π_t is the inflation rate; x is the detrended unemployment rate, used here as a measure of slack; ζ is a supply-shock term; and ε is a stochastic error.[10] The supply-shock variable in our baseline specification (we tried several variants) is a weighted average change in relative food and energy prices, using smoothed personal consumption expenditures (PCE) shares as weights.[11] We take a six-month moving average of this weighted relative

---

9. The proportionate effect of an oil shock on consumer energy prices is much smaller than the percentage rise in oil prices, as can be seen from the two panels of figure 2.3. (For example, crude oil accounts for only a portion of the production and distribution costs of gasoline and heating oil.) The impact on headline inflation is further damped because energy accounts for a relatively small share of total consumption.

10. The number of monthly inflation lags used in the model was determined with the Akaike criterion, with twelve lags used as the default. Note, however, that we did not impose the "accelerationist" restriction $A(1) = 1$. The estimated model also includes additional terms to capture the impact of the Nixon wage-price controls—see section 2.3.1. (The appendix provides more details on this and other empirical specifications employed in the chapter; the calculations that underpin figures 2.4 through 2.6 are also described more fully in the appendix.)

11. Ideally, a CPI-based model would use CPI relative importance weights rather than PCE shares. Unfortunately, there are significant breaks in the relative importance weight series over time—notably in 1978, when the CPI moved from measuring prices faced by wage earners to prices faced by all urban consumers, and again after owner-occupied housing costs moved to a rental equivalence basis. In any event, whether weighting is used turns out to make little difference to the results.

A. Real oil price (2000 dollars)

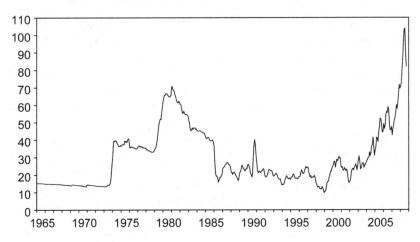

B. Real consumer price of energy (PCE-based, 2000=100)

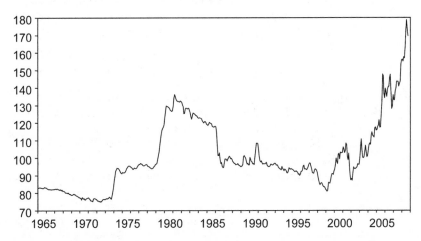

Fig. 2.3   Real oil and energy prices, 1965–2008

Notes: Series deflated by headline PCE price index; see appendix for data definitions. Last observation is September 2008.

price change variable, and use its first lag in the model (additional lags did not enter).

For this exercise, we treated the relative price of energy as exogenous, with panel A of figure 2.4 plotting the precise path of energy we assumed: relative energy prices rise by 35 percent (30 log points) over a period of twelve months and then return to where they started over the next twelve

A 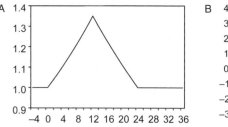   B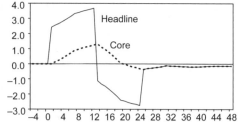

Fig. 2.4   Effect of a temporary spike in energy prices: *A*, level of real energy price; *B*, path of headline and core inflation (monthly percent change at annual rate)

months.[12] Panel B of the figure shows the simulated inflation results, which are just as expected. Headline inflation rises quickly and sharply by about 3 1/2 percentage points within a year, but then falls abruptly to *below* its preshock level (and below core inflation) as energy prices decline, before returning to normal. Core inflation moves less, more gradually, and with a lag, with a negligible impact on the core beyond eighteen months.

In terms of our supply-shock story, then, OPEC II should have first pushed headline inflation *above* core inflation, and then *below* it. For core inflation, the shock should have created a smaller rise in inflation that then "naturally" petered out, as in panel B of figure 2.4. The long-run effects on both headline and core should have been negligible. Thus, in this example, headline inflation first diverges from but then converges back to core inflation—a pattern that is evident in the real-world data shown in figure 2.1. Furthermore, core inflation itself should converge back to its preshock level, other things equal.[13]

The second type of supply shock, exemplified in figure 2.3 by OPEC I (1973 to 1974), is an *increase to a permanently higher relative price level.* Panel A of figure 2.5 shows how we entered this type of energy-price shock into our econometric model: the energy price is assumed to jump by 30 log points (35 percent) over two quarters and then to remain there forever. The speed of this simulated shock is not too different from what actually happened in 1973 and 1974: while the rise in oil prices took place over a period of about four months, the bulk of the pass-through to retail energy prices occurred over an eight-month period.

12. The actual OPEC II peak was spread out over a longer period: oil and especially energy prices did not return to their preshock levels until the collapse in oil prices in 1986. Note that this and the other two simulations assume a 30 log-point increase in relative *energy* (not oil) prices. Following OPEC I, real energy prices rose about 20 log points; the corresponding increase after OPEC II was 35 points, and the five-year net increase after the end of 2002 was around 45 points, so a 30 point increase is (in round terms) close to the average increase in log real energy prices over these three episodes.

13. Some of the "other things" that were not equal over this period include the back-to-back recessions of 1980 to 1982, which pushed core inflation down, and the large swing in food price inflation.

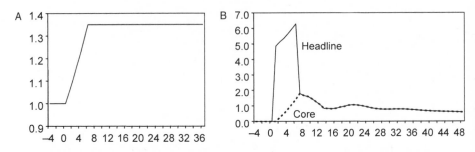

Fig. 2.5 Effect of a permanent jump in energy prices: *A*, level of real energy price;
B, path of headline and core inflation (monthly percent change at annual rate)

Panel B of figure 2.5 shows the simulated impact of the shock on head-line and core inflation. Headline inflation leaps quickly and dramatically (by about 6 percentage points), but then recedes just as quickly. After six months, the direct contribution of energy prices to headline inflation is zero. Core inflation moves up much more slowly and by much less. But the effects on core and headline inflation are essentially identical as soon as energy prices have finished moving up to their new higher level—and they both die out very slowly. So, in terms of the basic supply-shock story, a permanent increase in the *level* of energy prices should cause a quick burst of inflation that mostly, but not quite (because of pass-through to the core), disappears of its own accord. Once again, headline inflation quickly converges to core, but now core inflation remains persistently higher than it was before the shock. As is evident in figure 2.1, a similar pattern can be seen in actual US inflation during and after OPEC I.[14]

Writing in the 1980s or 1990s, our typology might have stopped there. But the first decade of the 2000s has taught us that we should perhaps consider a third type of supply shock; namely, a long-lasting *rise in the rate of energy price inflation,* as exemplified by the stunning run-up in the real prices of oil and energy from 2002 until mid-2008 (see figure 2.3). We entered this third type of shock into our model as a *permanent* rise from a zero rate of *relative* energy price increase to a rate of 6 percent per year, which cumulates to a 35 percent increase in the *level* of real energy prices over five years. (Panel A of figure 2.6 shows the first three years of the assumed real energy price path.) This hypothetical history is qualitatively similar to what actually occurred between 2002 and mid-2008, although the actual increase in real oil prices was, of course, followed by a spectacular decline.

Panel B of figure 2.6 shows the model simulation results. Headline infla-tion starts rising right away and continues to rise very gradually. Core infla-tion does the same, though with a short lag and to a smaller degree. But

---

14. It would be even more evident were it not for the effects that price controls had on the core. We discuss these in section 2.3.1.

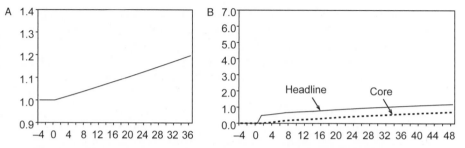

Fig. 2.6   Effect of a steady rise in energy prices: *A*, **level of real energy price;**
B, **path of headline and core inflation (monthly percent change at annual rate)**

notice that inflation keeps on rising as long as the higher energy inflation persists. Headline inflation now does *not* converge to core until real energy prices stop rising. Nor does the impact on core inflation fade away until that happens.[15]

2.2.2   Why Do We Need the Demand-Shock Piece?

The strictly neoclassical (that is, non-Keynesian) analysis of supply shocks is easy to explain, and even to calibrate. Consider a three-factor, constant-returns-to-scale production function for *gross* output, $Q = Q(K, L, E)$. Here, E denotes energy input, whose nominal price is P_E and whose relative price is $\rho = P_E/P$. Assume for the moment that energy is entirely imported, and that we are interested in real gross *domestic* product $Y = Q - \rho E$. As Bruno and Sachs (1985, 42–43) showed decades ago, optimal use of E implies a value-added production function of the form $Y = F(K, L; \rho)$, which is linearly homogeneous in K and L, in which the marginal products of K and L are the same as in $Q(.)$, and in which $F_\rho = -E$. Thus, a rise in the relative price of energy acts as a shift term akin to an adverse technology shock, and whose magnitude can be measured by the volume of energy use.

What does this framework imply about the size of the supply-side effects of the OPEC I and OPEC II shocks? Bruno and Sachs show that the elasticity of Y with respect to the real energy price, ρ, is $-s/(1 - s)$, where s is the energy share in *gross* output Q. Using national accounts data to compute the effects of higher prices of imported petroleum and products on real GDP, we find that the 1973–1974 oil shock implies a cumulative reduction in real GDP of 1.1 percent through the first quarter of 1975. Similarly, the OPEC II shock implies a real GDP reduction of 1.7 percent through the second quarter of 1980. (Details of these calculations are provided in the appendix.)

---

15. The estimated effect on core inflation from this third simulation is almost certainly higher than current reality. As we discuss in section 2.5, the pass-through of energy price shocks to core inflation appears to be much smaller now than in the 1970s and early 1980s, but the model used to generate these simulations is estimated through 1984.

But the actual decline in real GDP in the United States (relative to trend) was much larger in each case. For example, real GDP fell a little more than 3 percent between its 1973:Q4 peak and its 1975:Q1 trough, a five-quarter period during which normal (pre-1973) trend growth would have called for an increase of around 4.5 percent. Thus, in round numbers, we lost nearly 8 percent of GDP relative to trend.[16]

The period of the two oil shocks also saw large increases in the prices of other imported materials (in addition to oil). It is straightforward to extend the Bruno-Sachs framework to incorporate multiple imported inputs and to compute the real GDP effects of their price increases. Even with this extension, however, the impacts of the supply shocks are far smaller than the observed GDP declines. For 1973 to 1975, the supply-side reduction in real output from both higher oil and nonoil materials prices cumulates to 1.6 percent, while the corresponding estimate for the OPEC II period is 1.9 percent. (See the appendix for details.)

In addition, the pure neoclassical view does not provide any particular reason to think that *unemployment* should rise following an oil shock. In that framework, real wages and the rate of profit fall by enough to keep labor and capital fully employed. Put differently, a purely neoclassical oil shock reduces both actual and potential output equally, leading to no GDP gap (if the gap is measured correctly). In fact, however, the US unemployment rate soared from 4.8 percent in the second half of 1973 to almost 9 percent in the second quarter of 1975.

Both of these calculations suggest that something else was going on—probably something Keynesian on the demand side.[17]

2.2.3   The "Oil Tax"

That something is often called "the oil tax." The idea is simple: If imported energy, which mainly means imported oil, becomes more expensive, the real incomes of Americans decline just as if they were being taxed by a foreign entity. The "tax" hits harder the less elastic is the demand for energy, and we know that the short-run price elasticity is low. Using OPEC I as an example, the nominal import bill for petroleum rose by $21.4 billion through the end of 1974, which represented about 1.5 percent of 1973's GDP. If the marginal propensity to consume (MPC) was 0.9, this "tax" would have reduced nonoil consumption by almost 1.4 percent of GDP. If standard multiplier-accelerator effects created a peak multiplier of 1.5, the maximal hit to GDP would have been about 2 percent, or almost twice as large as the neoclassical supply-side

16. We obtain almost identical estimates of the cumulative GDP shortfall by using CBO's (ex post) measure of potential output.

17. Or, possibly, something "new-Keynesian" on the supply side (cf. Rotemberg and Woodford 1996).

effect.[18] Adding the two together would bring the total reduction in GDP to a touch above 3 percent, which is still far less than actually occurred.

These calculations encompass only imported oil. But there was also an internal redistribution within the United States, as purchasing power was transferred from energy users to energy producers. To the extent that the latter group—e.g., oil companies and their shareholders—had lower MPCs than the average consumer, aggregate demand would be reduced further. And there are yet more demand-side effects from an oil shock. For example:

1. In an unindexed tax system, which we had in 1973–1974, an upward shock to the price level leads to bracket creep, which amounts to a fiscal tightening. Inflation also raises the tax rates on capital since nominal interest rates and capital gains are taxed, and depreciation allowances are imputed on an historical-cost (nominal) basis.

2. To the extent that the Federal Reserve targets the nominal money supply, an upward shock to the price level reduces real balances, thereby inducing a monetary tightening. This channel was more relevant in 1973 than it is today, since the Fed now targets the federal funds rate.

3. A higher price level induces a negative wealth effect on consumer spending as both equity values and the real values of other financial assets decline.

4. The large change in relative input prices renders part of the capital stock obsolete, resulting in accelerated scrappage (see Baily 1981).[19]

5. The huge uncertainty induced by the oil shock (and subsequent recession) may lead investors and purchasers of consumer durables to "pause" while the uncertainty gets resolved (Bernanke 1983). In addition, until new, energy-efficient capital becomes available, firms may postpone their investment spending (Sims 1981).

6. Increased uncertainty may also induce consumers to increase precautionary saving (Kilian 2007a).

Point (2) in the previous list raises an important issue that we will return to several times in this chapter: the impact of a supply shock on real output and inflation depends critically on how the monetary authorities react. Monetary accommodation to mitigate the incipient recession will produce larger effects on inflation and smaller effects on output and employment. Monetary tightening to mitigate the increase in inflation will produce just

18. By comparison, Blinder (1979, 84–85) cited two econometric studies—Perry (1975) and Pierce and Enzler (1974)—that used an early version of the MPS (MIT = Penn = SSRC) model to attribute approximately a 3 percent decline in real GDP to OPEC I. We are aware of the continuing controversy over the size of the multiplier (see, e.g., Hall 2009). Naturally, using a smaller multiplier would make these effects smaller as well.

19. This is, strictly speaking, a supply-side effect. But it can also reduce demand by lowering equity values.

the opposite. This is one, though not the only, reason why responses to oil shocks vary both across countries and across time.

2.2.4   "Second-Round" Effects

Another important issue, related of course to monetary policy, is how much "second-round" inflation is induced by the "first-round" price-level effects of supply shocks—as, for example, higher energy costs creep into the prices of other goods and services and into wages.

Regarding the price channel, Nordhaus (2007, 223) recently used an input-output model to estimate that the long-run pass-through of energy costs into other consumer prices (which include airfares, apartment rents, and so on) is 80 percent as large as the direct effect of energy prices on the index. However, this estimate overstates the short- to medium-run effects of an energy-price shock. For example, airfares will react quickly to higher fuel costs, but the higher cost of the energy used to manufacture airplanes will probably not show up in airfares for years.[20] That said, there is still significant scope for sizable second-round price effects. Indeed, as might be expected, energy-intensive consumption goods and services posted relatively larger price increases following the first two oil shocks.[21] As evidence, the first two columns of table 2.1 report rank correlations between energy intensity and three-year price changes for various groupings of individual PCE components following OPEC I and OPEC II.[22] These correlations are similar whether one looks at total, core, nonenergy, or nontransportation components of PCE. (As is evident from the rightmost column of the table, however, similar correlations cannot be found during the most recent run-up in oil prices—a point to which we will return in section 2.5.)

One simple way to study the pass-through question is to examine the impacts of supply shocks on measures of *core* inflation, which by definition remove the mechanical impacts of energy and food prices on headline inflation. We did this earlier in figures 2.4 through 2.6, which showed the results of passing three different types of stylized supply shocks through

20. Moreover, it matters whether an estimate of this sort is based on crude or finished energy. Using the 1992 input-output accounts, we estimate that finished energy costs accounted for 3.4 percent of nonenergy PCE, while *crude* energy costs only accounted for 1.5 percent (these estimates include an imputation for the energy costs incurred in transporting and distributing consumption goods). For core PCE, the estimates are a little smaller (3 percent and 1.3 percent, respectively). That said, this still appears to be a reasonably large indirect effect given that the direct effect of finished energy on PCE prices (measured as the nominal share of energy goods and services in total consumption) was 5.5 percent in that year, and also given that crude energy price changes tend to be much larger than changes in finished energy prices.

21. In a more specialized context, Weinhagen (2006) finds evidence of significant pass-through of crude petroleum prices into the PPIs for plastics and organic chemicals over the period 1974 to 2003.

22. The rank correlation measure that we use is Kendall's "tau-b," which is more robust to the presence of ties across rankings. Energy intensities are estimated using data on total crude energy requirements from the 1972 and 1977 input-output tables. Price changes are December-over-December increases computed over the relevant periods.

Table 2.1   **Rank correlations between energy intensity and price change**

	Correlation with change in price from		
	1972 to 1975	1978 to 1981	2002 to 2007
1. All PCE components	0.308***	0.343***	0.048
2. Nonenergy PCE	0.256***	0.283***	−0.025
3. Nonenergy ex. transportation	0.270***	0.150*	−0.057
4. Core components	0.267***	0.326***	−0.036
5. Core ex. transportation	0.275***	0.193**	−0.072

***Significant at the 1 percent level.
**Significant at the 5 percent level.
*Significant at the 10 percent level.

a reduced-form price-price Phillips curve.[23] In this model, the effect of a sustained increase in relative energy prices yields, after one year, an indirect effect on core inflation roughly half as large as the direct effect on headline inflation. It is important to note that, in generating figures 2.4 through 2.6, the path of the unemployment rate was held constant. Hence, each simulation tacitly gives the second-round effects on core inflation *with an accommodating monetary policy* that prevents the supply shock from causing a slump. (More on this shortly.)

Figure 2.4 showed that the second-round effects of a temporary energy-price spike on core inflation, while notable, are entirely transitory—disappearing after about eighteen months. Thus core inflation displays a "blip" that vanishes by itself, without any need for the central bank to tighten—which can be thought of as justifying the policy decision to accommodate.

Figure 2.5, in which energy prices rise to a permanently higher plateau, shows another such blip, but one that does *not* disappear entirely of its own accord because of the presence of second-round effects. In this case, a central bank that does not want to see a persistent rise in core inflation would have to tighten.

Finally, figure 2.6 shows that persistently higher energy-price inflation will lead to persistently higher core inflation as well, although the magnitudes are small. (In the example, a 6 percentage point increase in energy-price inflation induces less than a 1 percentage point increase in core inflation after five years.) In this case, a monetary response may be appropriate.

23. No doubt, some of the effect of a supply shock in our price-price Phillips curves reflects the wage-price spiral—indeed, the textbook way to derive a price-price equation is by substituting a wage-price Phillips curve into a markup equation. In the case of food price pass-through, this channel is probably the main one at work. But, as suggested by the input-output analysis, energy is also an important intermediate input into consumer goods production. Hence, both channels are likely being captured by the coefficients on relative energy prices in our price-price models.

A second pass-through mechanism comes via expected inflation and wages. To illustrate the likely magnitudes and timing, we again consider a stylized supply shock—the 35 percent onetime jump in real energy prices shown in figure 2.5—in the context of an estimated wage-price model. The model consists of two equations, estimated on quarterly data from 1960:Q1 to 1985:Q4. The wage-price Phillips curve relates wage inflation (hourly compensation growth) to lagged headline CPI inflation, unemployment, and a long (40-quarter) moving average of trend productivity growth. The markup equation relates core CPI inflation to trend unit labor costs, unemployment, and several price-control terms explained later.

In contrast to the price-price Phillips curve discussed earlier, these models impose an accelerationist restriction: the coefficients on trend unit labor costs and lagged inflation in the markup equation are constrained to sum to one, and the coefficients in the wage equation are constrained so as to make the real consumption wage rise with trend productivity growth in a steady state. As a result, the implied pass-through of higher food and energy prices into core inflation is larger and more persistent than in the corresponding price-price model. (For more details, see the appendix.)

The response of this system to a jump in energy prices is shown in figure 2.7.[24] Qualitatively, the paths of headline and core inflation following the shock are similar to those from the earlier exercise: headline inflation spikes immediately but quickly recedes toward a core inflation rate that is persistently higher. Neither the magnitudes nor the exact dynamics are exactly the same, of course, because the mechanisms at work are different. In the wage-price system, higher energy prices raise headline inflation, which feeds into wage inflation. Rising wages, in turn, raise firms' costs, thus putting upward pressure on core inflation. By the end of the simulation period, real wages are rising at the same rate as before the energy price shock because the model constrains real wages to move in line with productivity. But nominal wage growth and consumer price inflation are persistently higher.

Finally, there is a countervailing force that offsets some of the "second-round" effects we have just estimated: each of the two oil shocks of the 1970s was associated with a deep recession. For example, the unemployment rate rose more than 4 percentage points in the recession that followed OPEC I. Such an increase in labor- and product-market slack puts significant *downward* pressure on core inflation. How much? In the simple pass-through model used for figure 2.5, each point-year of higher unemployment reduces core inflation by about 1/2 percentage point (on average) over the first year and by about 1/4 percentage point (on average) over the second year. Using this estimate, which is broadly consistent with many Phillips curves estimated by Gordon (1977, 1982, and others), the 4 percentage point run-up

24. Note that the time scale here is in quarters, in contrast to the monthly scale used in figures 2.4 through 2.6.

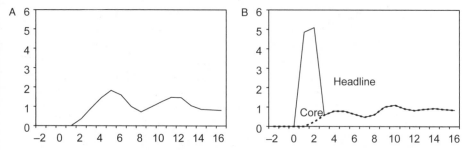

Fig. 2.7   Effect of a permanent jump in energy prices (quarterly wage-price system): *A*, **wage inflation (four-quarter percent change);** *B*, **path of headline and core inflation (percent change at annual rate)**

in unemployment would have been more than sufficient to offset the impact of OPEC I on core inflation.[25]

Of course, not all of the rise in unemployment that resulted from the 1973–1975 recession can be attributed to higher oil prices. Other supply shocks also hit the economy during this period, and there were significant swings in fiscal and monetary policy as well. Using a vector autoregression (VAR) model, Blanchard and Galí (2007) estimate that exogenous oil-price shocks were responsible for only about a third of the swing in real GDP.[26] If we impute one-third of the observed rise in unemployment to the oil shock, and feed this estimate into our model, we find very little offset from slack in the year following the shock, about a 50 percent offset in the second year, and a virtually complete offset by the end of the third year.

2.2.5   Lagging Perceptions of Productivity Growth

Almost everything we have discussed up to now was already on economists' radar screens by the late 1970s. But there is an additional inflationary channel that few people were talking about back then: the impact of lagging perceptions of productivity growth on inflation.

In principle, there is no reason why inflation and productivity growth should be systematically linked. According to simple economic theory, the trend growth rate of *real* wages should equal the trend growth rate of productivity (g), making the trend growth rate of *nominal* wages (w) equal to g plus the rate of inflation, π. If $w = g + \pi$, workers receive a constant share of national income *regardless of the inflation rate.* And in this frictionless and

25. However, virtually all of the first-year effect on core inflation would have remained because the unemployment rate rose relatively slowly at first.

26. Blanchard and Galí find that the shock accounts for roughly half of the reduction in *employment.* However, this overstates the effect of the shock on the *unemployment* rate, because Blanchard and Galí define employment as hours worked. In addition, our calculation is actually based on historical movements in an estimate of the unemployment *gap*, not the unemployment rate, to capture the fact that the rate of unemployment consistent with stable inflation (the NAIRU) was likely rising over this period. (See section 2.2.5.)

rational world, any decline in g would show up immediately as a decline in the growth rate of real wages, with no particular implications for inflation.

In practice, however, there are at least two *perceptual* channels through which a decline in productivity growth might boost inflation. The first stems from the possibility that a drop in the productivity growth rate is not promptly and fully reflected in real wage gains. If workers and firms are slow to recognize that the productivity growth rate has fallen, they may agree on real wage increases that are too high relative to actual increases in productivity. That would put upward pressure on unit labor costs, and hence on inflation. High real wages would also reduce employment demand and, therefore, tend to raise the level of unemployment consistent with stable inflation—the nonaccelerating inflation rate of unemployment (NAIRU).[27]

The second channel through which a productivity slowdown can raise inflation arises if policymakers fail to recognize it in time. If the central bank overestimates the growth rate of potential output—that is, if it fails to recognize that g has fallen—it will target a rate of aggregate demand growth that is too high, leading to increasing inflation. Furthermore, since the abovementioned mistakes by workers and firms will raise the NAIRU, policymakers may aim for a level of labor market slack that results in accelerating prices.

Arguably, both of these channels were at work during the Great Stagflation, especially the first episode. Productivity growth actually began to slow in the late 1960s as the expansion of the preceding decade came to an end. By the time of OPEC I, trend productivity growth had moved about a percentage point below the rate that had prevailed over the preceding twenty years. The failure of real wage growth to adjust downward can be seen in the behavior of labor's share of income over this period (figure 2.8). Labor's share started to move higher in the late 1960s and spiked during the 1969–1970 recession—a pattern typically seen during an economic downturn. But rather than moving back down, labor's share remained high over the 1970s and even appears to have trended upward slightly, since each successive cyclical peak was higher than the preceding one.

Regarding policy errors over the period, Orphanides (2003) has argued persuasively that contemporaneous estimates of the output gap (and, by extension, of the NAIRU) were far too optimistic. In addition, the natural rate of unemployment was itself drifting upward over the period, partly as a result of the increased entry of young baby boomers and women into the labor force. These demographic developments also appear to have eluded policymakers at the time. Besides resulting in an inflationary monetary pol-

---

27. In our empirical work, we control for changes in the NAIRU by detrending the unemployment rate with a band-pass filter. Staiger, Stock, and Watson (2001) argue that such a measure yields an unemployment gap that captures essentially all of the variation in labor-market slack that is relevant for inflation dynamics in a Phillips curve. In addition, they show that the resulting trend is suggestively (and negatively) correlated with low-frequency movements in US productivity growth.

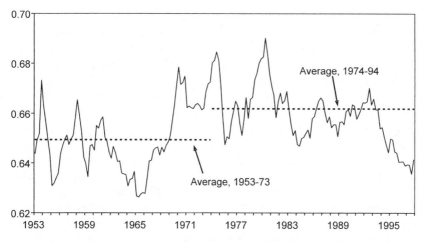

Fig. 2.8   Labor's share of income (nonfinancial corporate sector), 1953–1997
Note: Total compensation, nonfinancial corporate sector, divided by nominal nonfinancial corporate output.

icy, these misestimates of the output gap may have raised the perceived cost of bringing inflation under control. If policymakers see little reduction in inflation despite what they perceive to be a large margin of slack, they may erroneously conclude that the sacrifice ratio is higher than it really is.

In brief, when actual productivity decelerated in the early 1970s, sluggish adjustment of beliefs about productivity growth probably became a source of stagflation in its own right.

Blinder and Yellen (2001) and Ball and Moffitt (2001) turned this argument on its head to suggest that the opposite happened after the *speedup* in productivity growth in the mid-1990s—and that a surprising *disinflation* ensued. In support of this notion, figure 2.8 shows that labor's share fell to a thirty-year low over this period as real wage gains lagged far behind productivity growth.[28] In contrast to the experience of the 1970s, however, policymakers (specifically, Alan Greenspan) recognized the productivity acceleration early enough to prevent the Fed from running an inappropriately tight monetary policy.[29]

2.3   Reexamining the Evidence on the Great Inflation

The supply-shock "story" of the Great Inflation, which was summarized in points (5) through (10) of section 2.1, emphasizes four salient empirical observations:

28. Unfortunately, labor's share becomes harder to read after the late 1990s because of the surge in stock option exercises that occurred around that time.
29. See Blinder and Yellen (2001) and Meyer (2004).

1. The Great Inflation was actually *two* episodes of sharply higher inflation, *each of which was followed quickly by a disinflation*—a fact we emphasized in discussing figure 2.1. That inflation receded notably and quickly in the 1975 to 1977 period, and then again after 1980, is an important part of the story—one that is too often ignored.[30]

2. Blinder (1979, 1982) emphasized the strong *symmetry* apparent in the two inflation "hills" of figure 2.1. In each case, the graph provides circumstantial evidence that something—to wit, the supply shocks—"came and went."

3. Core inflation rose and fell, but by less than headline inflation in each direction. That observation is also consistent with the notion that each episode was dominated by food and/or energy shocks that then disappeared.[31]

4. Ignoring the two inflation "hills," core inflation rises from about 4 percent in the late 1960s and early 1970s to around 6 percent in the mid-to-late 1970s, but then ends up back at 4 percent in the mid-to-late 1980s.[32]

Let us now examine this story in more detail.

2.3.1 The Initial Shocks

The near-symmetry point (number [2] in the above list) is an important part of the supply-shock story. Table 2.2 displays three measures of consumer price inflation over the years 1972 to 1982: the current-methods CPI, the published PCE deflator, and the deflator for market-based PCE.[33] For each price measure, the table gives both headline and core inflation rates. The near symmetry of the rise and fall of inflation in the two episodes is apparent. In fact, these numbers correspond very closely to a similar table constructed by Blinder (1982, table 12.2, 265) from the data available then to make the same point.[34] Thus, our first conclusion is that *historical data revisions have not changed the basic story* of two nearly symmetrical episodes of rising and then falling inflation.[35]

---

30. For example, models generating "inflation bias" became popular in the 1980s. But they can explain only why inflation is too high, not the ups, and certainly not the downs. For an attempt, see Ireland (1999).

31. This is not meant to deny that the deep recessions that followed OPEC I and OPEC II brought both core and headline inflation down further. They did, just as strong aggregate demand pushed inflation a bit higher in 1977 and 1978.

32. From 1985 through 1990, core PCE inflation averaged 3.9 percent per year.

33. Market-based PCE is intended to capture market transactions for which actual prices are paid—with the exception of owner-occupied housing, which is included in market-based PCE. It is therefore more comparable to, though by no means identical to, the CPI than the standard PCE deflator. (As discussed in the appendix, we construct the market-based PCE deflator ourselves prior to 1997.) In the 1960s and 1970s, market-based goods and services represented about 90 percent of total nominal PCE and about 87 percent of the core; currently, the corresponding shares are 85 and 81 percent.

34. The only notable difference between these data and Blinder's is that the latter included the effects of mortgage interest rates (we discuss this influence later).

35. Blinder (1979, 1982) had to construct PCE minus food and energy on his own. Core PCE is now an official Bureau of Economic Analysis (BEA) series, and the vintage used here matches Blinder's original construction very closely.

Table 2.2   **Inflation rates in the United States, 1972–1982**

	Headline measures			Core measures		
	CPI	PCE	MPCE	CPI	PCE	MPCE
1972	3.0	3.4	3.0	2.6	3.1	2.5
1973	8.3	7.2	7.0	3.8	4.5	3.8
1974	10.9	11.4	11.2	9.4	9.6	8.9
1975	6.4	6.9	6.9	5.9	6.8	6.8
1976	4.9	5.2	5.5	6.4	6.0	6.6
1977	6.3	6.6	6.4	5.5	6.4	6.0
1978	7.8	7.6	7.1	6.8	6.8	6.1
1979	10.8	9.8	9.9	7.4	7.4	7.2
1980	10.9	10.6	10.5	10.0	9.6	9.3
1981	8.2	7.6	7.9	8.8	7.9	8.4
1982	5.1	5.0	4.8	6.6	6.0	5.9

Notes: Inflation rates computed as percent changes. The CPI data are expressed on a methodologically consistent basis, December over December. The MPCE index is a measure of market-based PCE prices (see the appendix for details). The PCE and MPCE inflation rates are Q4-over-Q4 changes.

Simply eyeballing these data suggests that one or more shocks pushed inflation up *and then disappeared.* In the first episode, the headline inflation rate jumped from about 3 percent in 1972 up to around 11 percent in 1974, and then fell back to about 5 percent by 1976. In the second, it rose from about 6 1/2 percent in 1977 to around 10 or 11 percent in 1979 and 1980, and then dropped back to 5 percent or so by 1982. But this is not an unobserved components exercise in which the econometrician must use statistical techniques to identify unseen shocks. The shocks were plainly visible, and we know precisely what they were: oil, food, and price controls. We take them up in turn.

The Oil Price Shocks of 1973–1974 and 1979–1981

Since the two OPEC shocks are well-known and have been studied extensively, we can be brief. Figure 2.9 displays the behavior of PCE energy inflation from 1968 to 1985.

The OPEC I shock, which resembled the jump to a higher plateau shown in figure 2.5, panel A, was kicked off by the so-called Arab oil embargo in October 1973, which roughly quadrupled the OPEC price of crude.[36] But given transportation costs and the blending of lower-price domestic crude (which then predominated) with imported oil, the composite US refiners' acquisition cost (RAC) "only" doubled. As one example of the retail price impact, the CPI for motor fuel rose 42 percent between September 1973 and May 1974, which is a 68 percent annual rate. At the macro level, energy *directly*

36. See Yergin (1993, chapters 29–30) for an historical account, and Adelman (1995, chapter 5) for a detailed analysis.

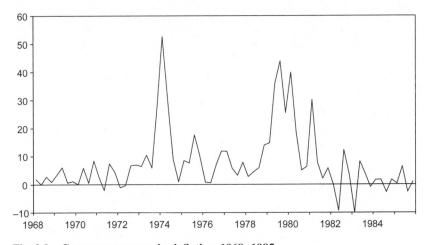

Fig. 2.9   Consumer energy price inflation, 1968–1985
Note: Annualized quarterly log differences of the energy component of the PCE deflator.

added 2 1/2 percentage points to the annualized PCE inflation rate during the last quarter of 1973 and the first two quarters of 1974. Then energy ceased being an engine of inflation as the real price of crude oil remained roughly flat from 1974 until late 1978 (see figure 2.3).

The OPEC II shock came when the 1978–1979 revolution in Iran, followed by the 1980 invasion of Iran by Iraq, sent crude prices skyrocketing again.[37] From 1978 to 1981, the composite RAC nearly tripled. But unlike OPEC I, OPEC II proved to be short-lived, looking much more like the price spike in panel A of figure 2.4 than the jump to a higher plateau in panel A of figure 2.5. The composite RAC fell from its 1981 peak ($35.24 per barrel) to a trough in 1986 ($14.55 per barrel) that was not much above its 1978 average ($12.46 per barrel). It did not persistently rise above $30 per barrel (in nominal terms) until 2004, and it only reattained its 1981 real price peak in late 2007.

Two points are worth emphasizing for later reference, especially in section 2.4, where we will examine the claims that inflationary monetary policy caused the oil shocks, rather than the other way around. First, it should be obvious that both OPEC shocks were set in motion by geopolitical events that cannot possibly be attributed to, say, money growth in the United States or even to world economic growth.[38]

Second, notice how sharply price increases are damped as we move up the stage-of-processing chain from crude oil prices to overall inflation. In the case of OPEC I, a 300 percent increase in crude prices led to a 100 percent increase in refiners' acquisition costs, and thence to a 45 percent (annual-

---

37. See Yergin (1993, chapters 33–34) and Adelman (1995, chapter 6).
38. This is not to deny that strong world growth helped OPEC make the price increases stick.

ized) increase in total retail energy prices, and finally to a 2 1/2 percentage point increase in overall inflation. If OPEC had, hypothetically, reacted by restoring the real value of its crude oil, it would have raised prices by another 2 1/2 percent. The subsequent reactions of overall US inflation would have amounted to rounding error. Thus, observers who fretted about the feedback loop from US inflation back to OPEC pricing (via the exchange rate, say) in both the 1970s and in 2006–2008 should have been thinking harder about magnitudes.

The Food Price Shocks of 1973–1974 and 1978–1980

We all remember the big oil shocks, but many economists seem to have forgotten that each of the two inflationary episodes also featured a sizable food-price shock. The two food shocks are apparent in figure 2.10. Since food has a much higher weight in the price indexes than energy, ignoring them constitutes a major omission.[39]

At the retail level, the 1973–1974 food-price shock corresponded pretty closely to the twenty-four calendar months of those two years. The CPI for food rose 20.1 percent from December 1972 to December 1973 and another 12.1 percent from December 1973 to December 1974. Compared to the 4.6 percent rate in the year preceding the shock or the 6.7 percent rate in the year following it, that represents a sharp though temporary burst of food inflation. In terms of their contribution to overall inflation, food prices added 4 1/2 percentage points to headline inflation in 1973, and a touch less than 3 percentage points in 1974 (and nothing directly to core inflation).[40]

What happened to cause this stunning turn of events? Seemingly everything—including corn blight, crop failures, and depleted inventories in many parts of the world (especially for grains), and the then-famous disappearance of the Peruvian anchovies.[41]

The 1978–1980 food shock was less dramatic, but it lasted longer and was far too large to ignore—even though most economists have managed to do so. The aforementioned food component of the CPI rose 11.4 percent in 1978, and 10.3 percent in both 1979 and 1980, before falling back to 4.4 percent in 1981. Food price inflation contributed 2 percentage points to overall inflation in 1978, and 1 3/4 percentage points in both 1979 and 1980.[42]

39. In December 1972, food was 22.5 percent of the CPI and 20.7 percent of the PCE deflator; energy was only 6 percent of the CPI and 6.5 percent of PCE.
40. The corresponding contribution of food prices to headline PCE price inflation was 3.1 percentage points in 1973 and 2.7 percentage points in 1974. Note that the core PCE deflator removes food *and* alcoholic beverages from the headline index; this is also the definition we use in discussing the contribution of "food" to headline PCE inflation.
41. See Bosworth and Lawrence (1982, 88–107) for a detailed discussion.
42. Food's relative importance in the CPI dropped in 1977 (to 17.7 percent of the overall index) with the introduction of the all-urban CPI-U. (Prior to this time, the published CPI only covered urban wage earners.) Food continued to represent about 20 percent of PCE; the corresponding contributions of food to PCE price inflation over the three years 1978 to 1980 were 2.1, 1.9, and 2.0 percentage points, respectively.

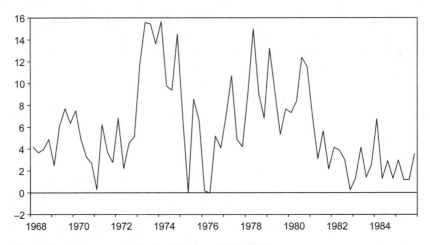

Fig. 2.10   Consumer food price inflation, 1968–1985

Note: Annualized quarterly log differences of the food and beverages component of the PCE deflator.

Weather and disease, of course, explained most of the food problems. Again, we are deeply skeptical that agricultural diseases, bad weather, and the hog cycle were lagged effects of monetary policy.

The End of Price Controls, 1973–1974

A third shock—the removal of wage and price controls in stages starting in 1973—also made an important contribution to the 1973–1974 burst of inflation, but was often ignored in the subsequent economic literature.[43] Unlike OPEC and the weather, the 1971–1974 price controls might conceivably be viewed as a lagged effect of earlier inflation. But other episodes of inflation *in peacetime,* both before and since, were *not* followed by controls. So we prefer to view the price controls more as a part of Richard Nixon's reelection campaign than as an endogenous response to past inflation.

Price controls were first put in place on August 15, 1971, starting with a short-term freeze. As measured by the fraction of the CPI that was subject to controls, they had their maximum effect in the period from September 1971 to April 1973. After that, they began to be dismantled in stages, and were completely removed by May 1974.[44] In particular, a large dose of decontrol came in February to May of 1974. Notice how well the timing of this decontrol aligns with the first hill in core inflation.

43. A major exception is the series of Phillips curve papers by Robert Gordon—see, for example, Gordon (1977, 1982). In addition, several studies of the effects of price controls appeared in the mid-1970s.

44. Their removal was briefly interrupted by "Freeze II" in the summer of 1973.

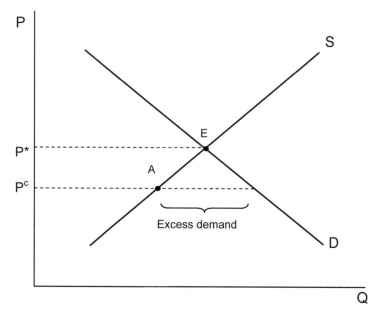

Fig. 2.11   Effect of price controls in a single market

It is obvious that removing price controls—thereby letting prices that were held artificially low bounce back to equilibrium levels—should result in a sudden burst of inflation that naturally peters out. In figure 2.11, which illustrates the effect of controls in a single market, the controlled price, P^C, is held below the equilibrium price, P^*, which forces the market to equilibrate at point A (with excess demand) rather than at point E. When controls are lifted, the market quickly moves from point A to point E. If the percentage price gap Δ ($\equiv P^*/P^C - 1$) is erased quickly, the item-specific inflation rate can be enormous.[45]

Blinder and Newton (1981) used this simple idea—together with a monthly time series that they constructed for the fraction of the CPI under price controls—to assess the impact of controls on US inflation in the 1970s. They fit wage-price systems with two different measures of aggregate demand, and then ran simulations that allowed them to estimate both the reduction in core inflation that resulted from the controls and the increase in inflation that occurred when the controls were lifted. They found that the maximum negative effect of price controls on the core price level came in February 1974; its

45. For example, if $\Delta = 0.07$ and the gap is closed in three months, the item-specific annualized inflation rate is 31 percent. Blinder and Newton (1981) estimated the typical value of Δ to range from 0.062 to 0.088, depending on the specification of their wage-price system. In our own replication of Blinder and Newton's work (discussed later), we obtain estimates for this parameter that range from 0.062 to 0.075, remarkably similar to their estimates.

Table 2.3   Contribution of price controls to core CPI inflation, 1973–1975

	Prepeak	Peak	Postpeak
A. Results from Blinder-Newton (1981)			
Actual data			
1. Inflation rate (*AR*)	5.90	12.72	7.84
2. Change in inflation		+6.82	−4.88
Estimated effect of controls, model 1			
3. Contribution to inflation	−1.34	5.12	0.28
4. Contribution to change in inflation		+6.46	−4.84
Estimated effect of controls, model 2			
5. Contribution to inflation	−1.82	2.17	−0.20
6. Contribution to change in inflation		+3.99	−2.37
B. Results from current data and model			
Actual data			
7. Inflation rate (*AR*)	3.94	10.00	5.58
8. Change in inflation		+6.06	−4.42
Estimated effect of controls			
9. Contribution to inflation	−1.73	2.73	0.77
10. Contribution to change in inflation		+4.45	−1.96

Notes: Dating of inflation peaks differs across Blinder-Newton results and results using current data; see text for details. Inflation rates from Blinder-Newton paper are average monthly percent changes at annual rates; rates using current data are annualized log differences. All contributions and changes are given in percentage points.

estimated magnitude was 3.1 or 4.2 percent, depending on the model used. In their first specification, the estimated contribution that controls made to reducing the price level dropped to zero by October 1974—implying that decontrol raised the annualized rate of core CPI inflation during the February to October of 1974 period by a stunning 4.6 percentage points. In their second specification, the estimated price level impact declined only to −2.2 percent by October, which implies a 3 percentage point contribution to annualized core inflation. In both cases, the estimated inflation impacts were negligible after October 1974.[46]

Panel A of table 2.3 reproduces results from Blinder and Newton (1981, table 4, 20). They observed that core CPI inflation reached a double-digit "peak" rate over the eight months from February to October 1974, with much lower inflation rates over the eight-month periods either immediately before or immediately after. Specifically, in the CPI data that were available to Blinder and Newton at the time, the run-up in core inflation from the prepeak period to the peak was 6.8 percentage points, and the subsequent decline from peak to postpeak was 4.9 percentage points (line 2 in the table). According to their first model, lifting price controls accounted for virtually

46. However, the first model found roughly a zero long-run effect on the price level, while the second found that price controls permanently reduced the price level by about 2.4 percent.

the *entire* swing in core inflation (see line 4 of the table); in their second model, controls accounted for about half (line 6).

To take a fresh look at this old finding, we used the Blinder-Newton time series for the fraction of the CPI under controls in a monthly price-price Phillips curve model fit to the current-methods core CPI. (The appendix provides details on the model's specification.) The current-methods CPI suggests a slightly different dating for the inflation peak, so we considered a nine-month peak period from February to November of 1974, with nine-month pre- and postpeak periods defined symmetrically.

Panel B of table 2.3 summarizes our updated results. First, as can be seen from line 8 of the table, our revised definition of the peak inflation period implies a pre- and postpeak swing that is not too different from what Blinder and Newton obtained with their dating.[47] Second, the estimated contribution of controls to the swing in core inflation that we find (line 10) implies that controls account for more than two-thirds of the increase in core CPI inflation and nearly half of its subsequent decline—magnitudes that are roughly comparable to what Blinder and Newton found with their second specification. Our estimate of the depressing effect of controls on inflation in the "prepeak" period is also very close to Blinder and Newton's.[48]

These updated results verify that price controls made significant contributions to both sides of the first inflation "hill." And they show that anyone who tries to explain the rise and fall of *core* inflation over the 1972 to 1975 period *without* paying careful attention to price controls is missing something very important.

The Mismeasurement of Homeownership Costs, 1979–1980

Our last important special factor during the Great Inflation was not a shock at all, but rather a measurement problem. We mention it briefly here only for completeness.

Prior to January 1983, the nominal mortgage interest rate was among the prices included in the CPI, and it had a large weight. Since the nominal mortgage rate, R, depends inter alia on expected inflation, $R = r + \pi^e$, and since π^e surely reacts to π, this odd treatment created a dynamic feedback loop within the measurement system: any increase (decrease) in π would raise (lower) R, which would in turn feed back into yet-higher (lower) measured π. When mortgage rates fluctuated a lot, as they did in the late 1970s and early 1980s, this quirk induced a great deal of volatility in measured

47. The levels and changes in inflation given in lines 7 and 8 of the table differ from Blinder and Newton's for three reasons: we use a current-methods CPI, we use a slightly longer peak period, and we compute the inflation rate as an annualized log change.

48. As noted, Blinder and Newton's first specification implied that controls left the price level 0.2 percent higher in the long run (defined as the estimated impact in December 1975), while their second specification yielded a long-run reduction in the price level of 2.4 percent. Our updated model implies a long-run reduction in the price level of 0.7 percent, which is within Blinder and Newton's range of estimates.

inflation, which is why the Bureau of Labor Statistics (BLS) changed its procedure for measuring the price of owner-occupied housing services in 1983. Specifically, Blinder (1982, 273) showed that mortgage interest costs added about 2 1/2 percentage points to CPI inflation in both 1979 and 1980.

Since we use the current-methods CPI here, this measurement problem disappears. Indeed, that is the main reason why the data shown in figure 2.1 display a smaller inflation "hill" in 1978–1980 than the data showed in real time.[49]

2.3.2   The Pass-Through of Food and Energy Shocks into Core Inflation

One key question about supply shocks is how they filter into other prices (including wages), thereby inducing "second-round" effects. In section 2.2, we used an estimated price-price Phillips curve (described in the appendix) to show how some highly stylized energy shocks would pass through into core inflation. We now perform that same exercise using the time series on *actual* food and energy shocks during the 1973 to 1980 period. The counterfactual question to which we seek an answer is this: How different would the Great Inflation (1972 to 1982) have been if the food and energy shocks had never occurred?

To do so, we compare a baseline path for core inflation, obtained by inputting the actual behavior of food and energy prices, with a counterfactual path in which food and energy prices grow steadily at 4 percent and 3 percent per annum, respectively. We perform the simulations separately for current-methods core CPI inflation (figure 2.12) and market-based core PCE inflation (figure 2.13). In each figure, the upper panel plots actual inflation together with the baseline and counterfactual paths, while the lower panel shows the difference between the two paths (that is, the estimated contribution of food and energy price pass-through to core inflation).

In the 1973 to 1974 episode, the simulations indicate that pass-through of food and energy prices added about 2 1/2 percentage points to core CPI inflation and about 1 1/2 percentage points to core market-based PCE inflation.[50] And in both cases, core inflation remained above its preshock level after the supply shocks dissipated, precisely as suggested by figure 2.5. In the 1978 to 1980 episode, the simulations imply that pass-through of the supply shocks contributed about 2 percentage points to the *increase* in core inflation by either measure.

A second way to estimate pass-through is to simulate a two-equation

---

49. Consistent with Blinder's (1982) calculation, the difference in annualized inflation rates between the officially published CPI-U and an experimental CPI that uses a rental-equivalence approach to recalculate the owner-occupied housing component of the index (the CPI-U-X1) is 2 1/4 percentage points over the two-year period from May 1978 to May 1980. (On a twelve-month-change basis, the differential reaches a peak of 3 1/4 percentage points in June 1980.)

50. The difference between the two estimates mainly reflects the fact that the CPI for food rose faster than the PCE-based measure of food price inflation. Food prices also receive a slightly smaller coefficient in the PCE model.

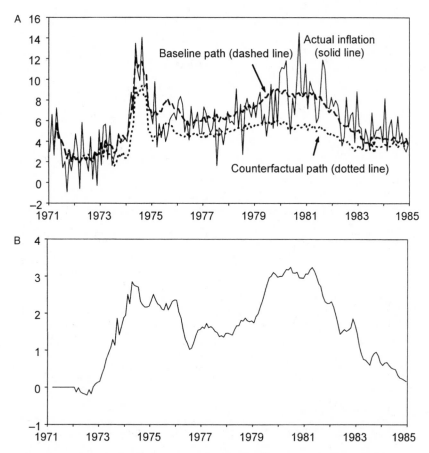

Fig. 2.12   Effects of supply shocks on core CPI inflation: *A*, **baseline and counterfactual core CPI inflation;** *B*, **difference between baseline and counterfactual paths**
Note: Inflation rates expressed as annualized monthly log differences.

wage-price system. As the first step, we estimate a wage-price Phillips curve in which wage inflation depends on *headline* price inflation, generate fitted values using *actual* food and energy inflation, and compare this to the fitted values that obtain under the *counterfactual* path for food and energy inflation. The results are shown in the upper panel of figure 2.14; as can be seen, wage inflation would have been roughly flat over much of this period had headline inflation not been boosted by the food and energy price shocks.

As was shown in the stylized example in section 2.2.4, the lower unit labor costs that result from less wage inflation lead to lower core price inflation as well. This in turn puts additional downward pressure on wage inflation, leading to further reductions in core inflation, and so on. These familiar

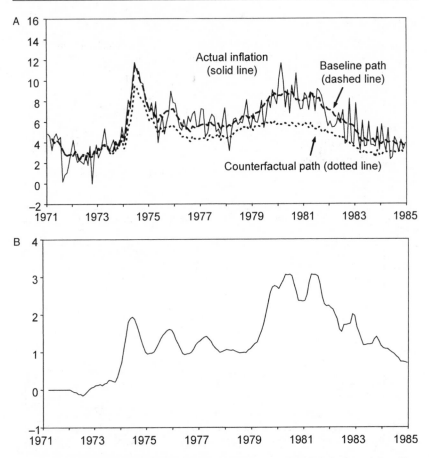

Fig. 2.13   Effects of supply shocks on core market-based PCE inflation: *A*, baseline and counterfactual core market-based PCE inflation; *B*, difference between baseline and counterfactual paths

Note: Inflation rates expressed as annualized monthly log differences.

wage-price interactions are captured by a two-equation system consisting of the aforementioned wage-price Phillips curve and a markup equation relating core CPI inflation to unit labor cost growth.[51] The results are shown in the lower panel of figure 2.14, which plots *actual* core CPI inflation against two simulated paths from the full wage-price system. The two simulations differ in their assumptions about food and energy prices. As can be seen in the figure, the model implies a comparably large pass-through of food and energy prices into core inflation, despite the fact that these shocks now affect the core *only* to the extent that they feed into wages.

51. We also considered a version of the model that used the market-based PCE price index; the results were essentially similar. (Details of both models' specifications are in the appendix.)

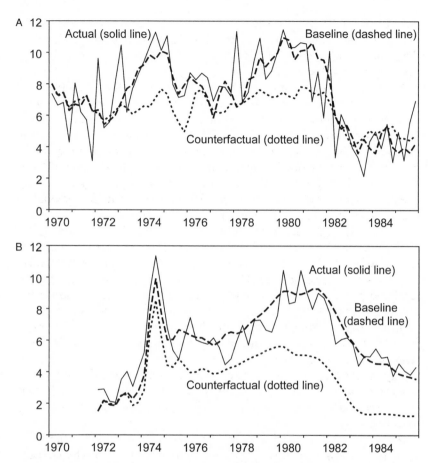

Fig. 2.14   Supply shocks and wage-price dynamics: *A*, nonfarm business compensation inflation from wage-price equation; *B*, core CPI inflation from wage-price system
Note: Inflation rates expressed as annualized quarterly log differences.

2.3.3   The Effect of the Business Cycle

As we have mentioned repeatedly, oil and food shocks are expected to be contractionary as well as inflationary. But by how much? And by how much would we expect the resulting recessions to mitigate the inflationary consequences of the shocks?

To obtain quantitative answers, we use a small structural VAR model to estimate how much of the increase in unemployment that followed the energy and food shocks can be attributed to them. Our baseline VAR includes core PCE inflation, the unemployment rate, the weighted sum of relative (to core) food and energy price inflation, and the federal funds rate, with the variables ordered so that inflation is at the top of the ordering and the federal funds rate is at the bottom.[52] We also consider an augmented system in which commodity price inflation (measured by the log change in the crude Producer Price Index, or PPI) is included after the food and energy price term and before the funds rate.

To assess the contribution of the supply shocks to the 1973–1975 and 1980–1982 recessions, we utilize a standard variance decomposition technique to apportion actual movements in the unemployment rate into a baseline path (the forecast implied by the VAR with all shocks set to zero) and the contributions of each stochastic shock. The contributions of the shocks, of course, reflect the full dynamic structure of the VAR. For example, one key way in which a positive shock to food and energy price inflation raises unemployment is through its effect on the federal funds rate (higher inflation results in a higher funds rate, which reduces activity).[53]

The results from the two VAR models for the 1973–1975 and 1980–1982 recessions are shown in figures 2.15 and 2.16, respectively. For each specification, the figure shows the baseline forecast for the unemployment rate along with the estimated effects of the food and energy shocks in the left-hand panels and the combined effects of the commodity, food, and energy shocks in the right-hand panels. Taken together, these figures show that the models attribute a significant share of the increases in unemployment to the supply shocks that occurred in both recessions. But they also remind us that the effects are long delayed. In the 1973 to 1975 episode, the supply shocks only start to have appreciable effects on the unemployment rate after the end of 1974. Similarly, the supply shocks make a relatively small contribution to unemployment in the first year of the 1980–1982 downturns.

One important implication of this familiar lag pattern is that the recessions that followed each supply shock came *after* most of the inflation damage was already done. While the two recessions no doubt played roles in the downsides of each inflation hill in figure 2.1 (and thereafter), they played little role in limiting the upsides.[54] Thus, since our focus is on explaining the two hills, the offset from economic slack is small enough to be ignored.

On this point, our results are consistent with the work of Blanchard and Galí (2007), who use a VAR model in which oil prices are replaced by a

52. Specifically, the food and energy term is defined as the difference between headline and core PCE inflation. It is straightforward to demonstrate that this equals the weighted sum of *relative* food and energy inflation, where the relatives are expressed in terms of core inflation and the weights are the shares of food and energy in the total index.

53. Full details on the VAR specifications can be found in the appendix.

54. For the 1973–1975 recession, this conclusion is strengthened by the observation that the NAIRU was likely increasing rapidly over much or all of this period. For example, our simple estimate of trend unemployment rises nearly a percentage point from the end of 1973 to the end of 1975. (Note that the trend continues to rise—albeit at a slower rate—until the start of the 1980s.)

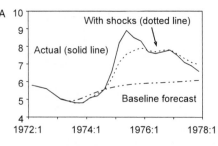
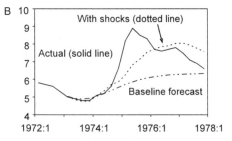

Fig. 2.15   Contribution of supply shocks to unemployment rate increase, 1973–1975 recession: *A*, food and energy price shocks only; *B*, food, energy, and crude PPI shocks

Note: Level of unemployment rate in percent.

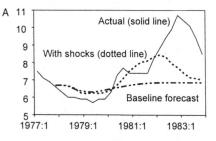
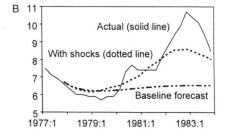

Fig. 2.16   Contribution of supply shocks to unemployment rate increase, 1980–1982 recessions: *A*, food and energy price shocks only; *B*, food, energy, and crude PPI shocks

Note: Level of unemployment rate in percent.

broader measure of crude materials prices to consider the contributions of materials price shocks to output fluctuations. For the 1973–1975 recession, they find that these shocks account for about half of the swing in real GDP, with the biggest contribution coming at roughly the same time as the trough in output—which is comparable to the effect that we find in our baseline VAR (see panel A of figure 2.15). For the back-to-back recessions of 1980–1982, the Blanchard-Galí model attributes a larger fraction (perhaps two-thirds) of the swing in output to materials price shocks. But actual output falls faster in 1980 than their model predicts, with the most rapid predicted declines in output occurring in 1981. Once again, this seems consistent with our finding of only a small effect.

2.3.4   Putting the Pieces Together

Table 2.4 is a rough—and deliberately impressionistic—summary of the findings of this long section. It puts together the estimated contributions to *headline* inflation of the two energy shocks, the two food shocks, their pass-through into core inflation, and the end of price controls. In coming up with these numbers, we roughly average our findings both over the two

Table 2.4   **Approximate impacts of special factors on the two inflation "hills" (in percentage points)**

Special factor	1973–1974 episode	1978–1980 episode
Energy prices	1½	2
Food prices	2½	1½
Pass-through of food and energy prices[a]	1½	1½
End of price controls[a]	2	0
Total	7½	5
Memo: Actual rise in inflation	6	4

[a]Adjusted for core inflation's weight in overall inflation.

different price indexes (CPI and PCE) and over time—and we stick to round numbers. Thus we view the first of the two inflation "hills" as rising from about 4 percent to about 10 percent and the second as rising from a bit over 6 percent to a bit over 10 percent (see figure 2.1).

The basic finding is dramatic, although it should come as no surprise at this point. For each of the two inflation hills shown in figure 2.1, the special factors account for *more than 100 percent* of the rise (and subsequent fall) of headline inflation—that is, the supply-shock explanation, with no role for aggregate demand, actually overexplains the Great Inflation.

But since we have emphasized that the Great Inflation was really the Great *Stagflation,* we also note that the numbers underlying figure 2.15 imply that roughly 60 percent of the run-up in unemployment in the 1973–1975 recession, and roughly 45 percent of the run-up in the back-to-back recessions of 1980–1982, can be attributed to the supply shocks.

2.4   Arguments against the Supply-Shock Explanation

Four related sets of arguments have been raised against the supply-shock explanation of the Great Stagflation. Each evokes, in its own way, shadows of the classical dichotomy: that real phenomena cannot affect inflation. But since they are subtly different, we take each one up in turn.

2.4.1   Relative Price Shocks Cannot Affect Absolute Prices

The simplest argument, which was raised immediately after OPEC I, holds that it is logically fallacious to believe that a change in a relative price can be a source of generalized inflation. Instead, a rise in the relative price of energy (P_E/P) should be effectuated by some combination of higher nominal prices for energy products (P_E) and lower nominal prices for a variety of other things (call these P_O, for "other" prices). There is no reason for the overall price level, $P = \omega P_E + (1 - \omega)P_O$, to rise unless the money supply does. As Milton Friedman (1975) asked at the time in a much-quoted *Newsweek* column, "Why should the *average* level of all prices be affected significantly by changes in the prices of some things relative to others?"[55]

This attitude, of course, reflects pre-Keynesian thinking. Ever since the Keynesian revolution, most (but not all) economists have believed in pervasive nominal price and wage rigidities, so that relative price increases can and do lead to a higher price level—as, for example, when P_E rises and P_O does not fall. Furthermore, if one of the sticky nominal prices is the nominal wage, then real wages will get stuck too high for a while, causing unemployment.

We find it remarkable that the classical dichotomy still has such a hold on the minds of economists. Indeed, as recently as 2006, Ball made much the same argument in a different context—namely, that globalization cannot possibly affect inflation because it is fundamentally a series of *real* events. A similar view underpins Barsky and Kilian's (2002) attempt to rewrite the history of the Great Inflation. They argue that oil price shocks can affect "gross output price measures such as the CPI, but not necessarily the price of value added" (such as the GDP price index). We have already studied one counterargument: the wage-price spiral provides an obvious channel through which higher food and energy prices can affect domestic output prices, even if food and energy are both imported.[56]

One way to conceptualize this debate is to recognize that, with sticky wages and prices, the causation between inflation and relative-price changes undoubtedly runs in both directions. On the one hand, since some prices are stickier than others, an inflationary demand shock will induce changes in relative prices. On the other hand, a supply shock that requires a large change in some relative price(s) can be a source of overall inflation because other prices do not fall easily. The empirical question then becomes, which channel is quantitatively more important in practice? We think the answer is obvious, especially for the years of the Great Inflation.

Taylor (1981) noticed years ago that inflation increased in the late 1960s with low relative price variability, but then increased much more in the 1970s with high relative price variability. He attributed the first increase to demand shocks and the second to supply shocks—precisely as we do. Based on his econometric investigation, he concluded that the data suggest "a causal ordering in which relative price variability (due to *exogenous* supply shocks) is the main reason for variability in the overall inflation rate" (69, emphasis added).

55. In the next sentence (which is never quoted) Friedman provided a partial answer: "Thanks to delays in adjustment, the rapid rises in oil and food prices may have temporarily raised the rate of inflation somewhat" (114). As with so many "strong monetarist" positions, the question boils down to one of degree, not direction.

56. See Blanchard (2002). In addition, the proposition that intermediate price increases (such as a rise in the price of oil) can have no effect on a value-added deflator only holds true under perfect competition, as Rotemberg and Woodford (1996) discuss.

Fourteen years later, focusing on the importance of the skewness rather than the variance (of relative price changes) in a menu-cost model of price stickiness, Ball and Mankiw (1995) argued for causation running from higher skewness (e.g., very large increases in a few prices) to higher average inflation.[57] They pointed in particular to the extreme skewness of relative price changes in the years 1973 to 1974, 1979 to 1980, and 1986 (their sample ended in 1989). To Ball and Mankiw (1995, 190), "the explanation for these episodes is obvious: OPEC. . . . The direction of causation is clear: *exogenous* events in the Middle East induced skewness in the distribution of relative prices, which led to changes in the U.S. inflation rate" (emphasis again added). This seems obvious to us, too, and we fail to see why some economists are so intent on denying the obvious.

2.4.2 "Inflation Is Always and Everywhere a Monetary Phenomenon."

Friedman's famous dictum holds that an economy does not produce rising inflation without an increase in the growth rate of the money supply. And, indeed, he and his disciples emphasized this point in arguing for a tightening of monetary policy at the time of OPEC I. In this view, supply shocks could not have been the main culprit explaining the surge in inflation. It must have been excessive money growth.

This is neither the time nor the place to document and discuss the profound disconnect between inflation and *measured* money growth since the 1970s. The literature on this issue is vast, but not much of it is recent because the issue was resolved years ago. However, one should not read too much into this dismissal of "the Ms": after all, "money growth" and "monetary policy" are not synonymous. We would certainly never claim that a central bank's reactions have nothing to do with the propagation of the inflationary impact of a supply shock.

2.4.3 The Fed's Reactions Make Supply Shocks Contractionary

Indeed, it has long been recognized that the central bank's reaction function exerts a strong—some might even say determinative—influence on the inflationary consequences of any shock, whether it comes from the demand or the supply side.[58] Refer back to the aggregate supply and demand diagram in figure 2.2—which, we now assume, depicts what happens when the central bank holds the money supply constant. A more accommodative monetary policy, designed to cushion the impact on output, would shift the aggregate demand curve outward, causing more inflation. A tighter monetary policy,

---

57. Not everyone agreed with their interpretation. For example, Balke and Wynne (2000) suggested that an alternative theoretical model with flexible prices and suitably distributed technology shocks could give rise to a similar relation, while Bryan and Cecchetti (1999) argued that the statistical correlation between mean inflation and skewness is biased upward in small samples.

58. Some early papers on this subject, as it pertains to oil shocks, include Gordon (1975), Phelps (1978), and Blinder (1981).

designed to limit the inflationary consequences of the supply shock, would shift the aggregate demand curve inward, causing a larger output decline. This is simple stuff that every Economics 101 student learns (or should learn).

Bernanke, Gertler, and Watson (1997) accept the notion that oil shocks are inflationary, but they dispute the idea that they are recessionary per se. Instead, they use VAR-based evidence to argue that it is the central bank's reactions—to wit, tightening monetary policy to fight inflation—that causes the ensuing recessions. In their words, "the endogenous monetary policy response can account for a very substantial portion (in some cases, nearly all) of the depressing effects of oil shocks on the real economy" (94).

In some sense, we have no need to dispute their proposition. After all, Bernanke, Gertler, and Watson (1997) agree that exogenous adverse oil shocks lead to both higher inflation and slower real growth; they just attribute the latter to the Fed's monetary policy response rather than to OPEC directly. And we noted earlier that the pure neoclassical effects of oil shocks are far too small to explain actual events; large demand-side effects are necessary to explain the ensuing recessions.

However, the Bernanke, Gertler, and Watson (1997) analysis of the two big oil shocks has been criticized by Hamilton and Herrera (2004) on a couple of grounds. First, Hamilton and Herrera argue that the Bernanke-Gertler-Watson conclusions are based on unrealistic counterfactual assumptions (e.g., very large changes in monetary policy) whose effects are unlikely to be captured well by a VAR estimated on historical data. Second, they argue that Bernanke, Gertler, and Watson's estimated real effects of oil shocks are too small; alternative estimates imply that oil shocks continue to have contractionary effects of their own, even after controlling for monetary policy.[59]

And there are other entrants in this debate. Leduc and Sill (2004) use a calibrated model to argue that roughly 40 percent of the observed drop in output after an oil shock is attributable to the monetary policy response, while Carlstrom and Fuerst (2006) use an alternative theoretical framework to conclude that a smaller amount (perhaps none) of the drop in output is due to monetary policy. After reviewing the literature, Kilian (2007a, 25) concludes that "how much the Fed's endogenous response to higher oil prices contributed to the subsequent economic declines still remains unresolved."

Stepping back from the detail, the central empirical question here is the degree to which the contractionary effects of the supply shocks were exacerbated or mitigated by tighter or looser monetary policy. To investigate this issue, we reprise the structural VAR models that we used earlier in section 2.3.3. In these models, a significant portion of the increase in the federal funds rate that follows an inflationary supply shock is offset by the subse-

---

59. In their reply to Hamilton and Herrera, Bernanke, Gertler, and Watson (2004) consider an alternative model and find that the response of monetary policy to an oil shock still accounts for roughly half of the shock's real impact. This is less than their original estimate, though still economically significant.

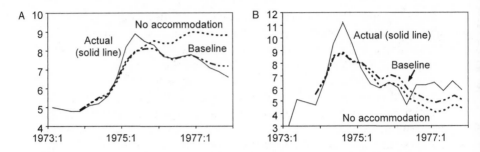

Fig. 2.17   Contribution of policy accommodation to unemployment and inflation, 1973–1975 recession: *A*, unemployment rate (percent); *B*, core PCE inflation (percent, annual rate)

quent rise in unemployment, as increasing slack induces an easing of monetary policy. We therefore consider a counterfactual specification in which the policy rate is constrained *not* to respond to unemployment. We focus on our four-variable VAR, since this model attributes relatively more of the increase in unemployment over the 1973–1975 recession to the supply shocks.[60]

Figure 2.17 depicts the responses of unemployment and core inflation under the two specifications following a sequence of supply shocks like those seen in 1973–1974. As is evident from panel A, the Fed's accommodation of the shock (defined here as the reduction in the federal funds rate that the VAR attributes to the unemployment increase that results from the shock) has a large effect on the path of unemployment. Importantly, however, most of the impact on the unemployment rate comes some time *after* the recession because of the long lags between changes in the funds rate and changes in unemployment. Panel B shows the effects on core inflation under the two alternatives; accommodating the shock results in a core inflation rate that is nearly 3/4 percentage point higher by the end of the simulation period.[61]

2.4.4   Monetary Policy, Not Supply Shocks, Caused the Great Inflation

Notice that the Bernanke, Gertler, and Watson (1997) critique does not dispute the idea that exogenous increases in the price of oil set in motion reactions, including those of the Fed, that resulted in both inflation and recession. Their quarrel is only with the notion that higher oil prices

---

60. The VAR system becomes very unstable when the response of the federal funds rate to unemployment is shut off. We therefore detrend the unemployment rate before including it in the VAR. However, we add the trend back in figure 2.17 in order to make the simulated series comparable to the actual unemployment rate.

61. We would not want to push these results too hard. As our discussion of Bernanke, Gertler, and Watson (1997) makes clear, there are important econometric issues associated with an experiment of this sort. For example, our "no accommodation" scenario implies a federal funds rate that is on average more than 200 basis points higher than the baseline over the entire simulation period. At best, then, this exercise should be viewed as suggesting a likely order of magnitude for the effect of monetary accommodation following the 1973–1974 shocks.

per se, rather than tighter monetary policy, caused the recessions that followed OPEC I and OPEC II.

The final version of the monetary-policy criticism of the supply-shock explanation of the Great Inflation goes a step further—a step too far, in our view. This criticism has been expressed in at least three different ways. What they have in common is that each lays the blame for the Great Inflation squarely at monetary policy's door. In its strongest form—which we consider first—the criticism argues that the jumps in oil prices in 1973–1974 and again in 1979–1980 were not really "exogenous," but rather were largely reactions to previous inflationary monetary policies.

Barsky and Kilian (2002)

In the Barsky-Kilian (2002) variant, expansionary monetary policies in the United States and other countries led *both* to the aggregate inflation we observed in the 1970s and 1980s *and* to increases in world commodity prices—including the price of oil. In words that evoke what Friedman and other monetarists were saying at the time, they claim that "in the 1970s the rise in oil prices . . . was in significant measure a response to macroeconomic forces, ultimately driven by monetary conditions" (139).

We would never claim that the state of world demand, of which a nontrivial share emanates from the United States, is irrelevant to OPEC's ability to push through price increases *and make them stick*. So there must be *some* causal link from prior US monetary policy to oil prices. The dispute is about magnitudes. Like Taylor (1981), Ball and Mankiw (1995), Gordon (in various papers), and many other observers, we cannot help thinking that geopolitical factors were far more important in October 1973 than the state of world aggregate demand, which in any case fell sharply in 1974. In particular, should we ignore the fact that OPEC I came right after the Yom Kippur War? (Just a coincidence?) Or that OPEC's oil output fell rather than rose after the shock—suggesting that it was supply rather than demand driven?

Indeed, a close reading of the history of the period suggests that the main effect of the OPEC I production cuts, which were neither exceptionally large nor long-lasting, was to create significant uncertainties about oil supply, which induced a surge in precautionary demand for oil.[62] Similarly, the rise in prices associated with the second OPEC shock appears to have been driven more by fear of future shortages than by *actual* reductions in supply.[63] But from a macroeconomic perspective, these are nevertheless "exogenous" shocks inasmuch as they were sparked by political or other events, and not (mainly) by an overheated world economy.

To obtain explicit quantitative evidence regarding the nature of the two oil shocks, we adapt Kilian's (2007b) model of the oil market. Kilian uses a

62. See Adelman (1995, 110–18) and Yergin (1993, 613–17).
63. Adelman (1995, 167–78); Yergin (1993, chapter 33).

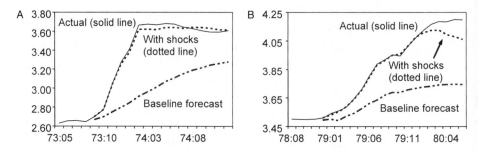

Fig. 2.18   Contribution of oil-specific demand shocks to log real oil price:
A, OPEC I shock; *B*, OPEC II shock

VAR with measures of oil production, aggregate commodity demand, and the real oil price to identify three types of shocks: shocks to general commodity demand (including for oil), shocks to oil supply, and shocks to oil demand specifically. In line with our preceding discussion, he identifies the last shock with exogenous shifts in precautionary oil demand or shifts in expectations about future oil supply.

We implemented a version of Kilian's empirical framework and used it to consider the contribution of oil-specific demand shocks to the OPEC I and OPEC II price increases.[64] We find that large shocks of this type did in fact hit the oil market around these two periods. Moreover, we can use the same technique applied in figures 2.15 and 2.16 to decompose the actual movement in oil prices into a baseline forecast and the contribution of the oil-market-specific shocks. This is done in figure 2.18 for the OPEC I and OPEC II periods. As is evident from the figure—and as one would expect given the historical evidence just cited—these shocks account for most of the run-up in real oil prices seen around these episodes.

What about the broader rise in commodity prices that Barsky and Kilian (2002) point to as evidence of a money-fueled boom? It is true that a number of observers at the time blamed higher commodity prices on rapid world economic growth in 1972 and 1973.[65] But the effects of the increase in demand were exacerbated by supply-side factors, most notably underinvestment in capacity by primary producers that resulted from price controls and low rates of return in these industries. In addition, some have attributed the emergence of a "shortage mentality" to the first oil shock, as uncertainty about supplies of other raw materials led to precautionary stockbuilding. Finally, year-to-year movements in commodity prices in the 1970s do not appear to correlate well with movements in world money supply or reserves.[66]

---

64. Once again, a detailed description of the model is in the appendix.
65. See chapter 4 of the 1976 *Report of the National Commission on Supplies and Shortages,* from which most of this discussion is taken.
66. See Bosworth and Lawrence (1982, chapter 4), who also discuss the role of stockbuilding of commodities in the face of perceived supply problems.

DeLong (1997)

DeLong (1997) also blames the Great Inflation on faulty monetary policy, but in a different way. He argues that trend inflation was rising well before the supply shocks hit because (a) the Fed was trying to exploit what it saw as a nonvertical Phillips curve, and (b) policymakers still remembered (and were terrified of) the Great Depression. The latter factor, in particular, made them fearful of using higher unemployment to fight inflation. In DeLong's view, this situation made a burst of inflation inevitable. The food and energy shocks played only subsidiary roles, creating transitory swings in inflation around a trend that was rising for other reasons.[67]

As noted at the outset, the gradual buildup of inflation during the 1960s is beyond the scope of this chapter. But there is obviously a kernel of truth in DeLong's argument. After all, figure 2.1 shows that inflation did rise in the 1965 to 1970 period, long before OPEC I and higher oil prices. Indeed, following a rapid acceleration in prices from 1965 to 1968, there was a modest upward trend in the core inflation rate from 1968 until about 1976 or 1977. It is also true that, prior to 1972, most economists viewed the empirical Phillips curve as nonvertical even though the theoretical long-run Phillips curve should be vertical à la Friedman and Phelps.

But a more balanced view of this early inflation would recognize a few other pertinent factors. One was the strong influence of Vietnam War spending on chronic excess demand in the late 1960s—an inflationary *fiscal* (not monetary) policy. Second, we should remember that this loose fiscal policy was subsequently reversed by the 1968 income-tax surcharge *and a tightening of monetary policy*—both of which were explicitly rationalized as anti-inflationary measures. These actions show that the authorities were not paralyzed by fear of higher unemployment.[68] Third, the pre-1973 inflation was dwarfed by what came after. Had inflation remained below 5 percent, as it did prior to 1973, we would never have had a conference on the Great Inflation. As we have argued at length in this chapter, something very different happened after 1972. Fourth, the sharp reflation of the US economy in 1972, using both expansionary monetary and fiscal policy, was almost certainly designed to assist Richard Nixon's reelection campaign, as were the wage-price controls that reduced inflation in 1971–1973 but then raised it in 1973–1974.[69] Bad memories of Nixon's defeat in the 1960 election were probably more relevant to the macroeconomic policies of 1971–1972 than were bad memories of the Great

67. DeLong (1997, 268–70) argues that the supply shocks had no effect on wages, and so did not enter trend inflation. But the results in section 2.3.2 from our wage-price models suggest that this claim is incorrect.

68. Nor were they sufficiently paralyzed by fears of an economic downturn to prevent the 1973–1975 recession from being exceptionally long and severe.

69. For details on the behavior and impact of fiscal and monetary policy over this period, including quantitative estimates, see Blinder (1979, 29–35, 141–46, and 179–94).

Depression.[70] Finally, the breakdown of the Bretton Woods system in 1972–1973 ended one traditional aspect of monetary discipline.

In sum, to attribute the Great Inflation to unemployment-phobic central bankers trying to exploit what they thought was a downward-sloping Phillips curve seems to be a grotesque exaggeration of a much more complex reality.

Cecchetti et al. (2007)

Although they reject any mono-causal explanation, Cecchetti et al. (2007) also argue that underlying inflation picked up before 1972 because of insufficient concern about inflation by monetary policymakers combined with a reluctance to use unemployment as a remedy. Their work uses cross-country evidence; and given the striking similarity in timing of the Great Inflation in many countries, they are rightly skeptical of country-specific explanations. One might think such an attitude would have led Cecchetti et al. straight to the supply-shock explanation; after all, the oil and food shocks of 1972–1974 were worldwide phenomena.[71] But they actually downplay the importance of supply shocks because their data-driven dating of the Great Inflation places the start date in the late 1960s. We have already argued that the evidence for this dating is not very persuasive.[72]

2.5   Energy and Food Shocks before and after the Great Stagflation

If food and energy shocks are so critical to understanding the Great Stagflation, why didn't the United States experience them either before or after the 1973 to 1982 period? And if so, why didn't they have similarly dramatic effects? Let's start, briefly, with the period before 1973, and then go on to the period after 1982.

Regarding oil shocks, OPEC I seemed to be something new, if not indeed something sui generis, at the time. As Nordhaus (2007) emphasized, it truly was a "shock" to Americans in every sense of the word. But Hamilton (1983) subsequently showed that OPEC I was not as unique as it seemed at the time. The US economy had not only experienced oil shocks before, it had reacted to them similarly.

Regarding food shocks, Blinder (1982) showed that we had indeed experienced two sharp inflationary food-price shocks in the 1940s. The unusual

70. For evidence from the horse's mouth, see Nixon (1962, 309–11). Also see Abrams (2006) for summaries of relevant conversations between Nixon and then-Fed chairman Arthur Burns. All that said, it must be admitted that Richard Nixon and Arthur Burns were not the only advocates of expansionary monetary and fiscal policies in 1972.

71. The title of Bruno and Sachs's famous 1985 book was *Economics of Worldwide Stagflation.*

72. To be clear, we are *not* advancing a mono-causal explanation of US inflation from 1965 to 1982. Monetary and fiscal policy, for example, clearly mattered. Our point is that the two big hills in figure 2.1 are *mainly* attributable to special factors (supply shocks and price controls).

period was the placid years from 1952 through 1972, when CPI food price inflation exceeded 5 percent only once in twenty-one years.[73] And, of course, the United States did experience a sharp surge of inflation when World War II price controls were lifted in 1946.

The period after 1982 is more puzzling; and it is, of course, the subject of more recent research. While the United States has experienced several oil-price shocks, both positive and negative, since 1982, none of them seems to have had such dramatic effects on either output or inflation as the supply shocks of the 1970s and early 1980s. Hooker (1996, 2002), Blanchard and Galí (2007), and Nordhaus (2007), among others, present econometric evidence that the more recent oil shocks had smaller macroeconomic effects than the earlier ones. The basic stylized facts from this research seem to be that the positive response of core inflation has diminished sharply over time and the negative responses of real GDP and employment have nearly vanished.[74] Why might that be?

One reason is obvious: Thanks largely to an array of market reactions to higher energy prices after OPEC I and II, the United States and other industrialized countries are now far less energy intensive than they were in 1973. In the case of the United States, the energy content of GDP has fallen dramatically since 1973, and is now about half of what it was then. This dramatic change is depicted in figure 2.19, which shows the number of BTUs (British thermal units) consumed (in thousands) per dollar of real GDP annually from 1950 to 2007. The rate of decline of this measure of energy intensity picks up after OPEC I and slows in the mid-1980s with the cartel's collapse and attendant drop in oil prices, though the series has continued to trend down since then. By itself, this halving of the US economy's energy intensity would reduce the macroeconomic impacts of oil shocks by about 50 percent—with the reductions roughly equal for prices and quantities.

However, Hooker (2002) finds that pass-through from oil prices to other prices has diminished to negligible proportions over time, which is about twice the change that can be explained by energy's shrinking share. Furthermore, he cannot link the smaller pass-through to the reductions in energy's share. In fact, this is a very general result, and can be extended to Phillips curve models that use share-weighted relative energy prices in lieu of oil prices. Moreover, as the rightmost column of table 2.1 shows, repeating our input-output exercise for the five-year period 2002–2007 reveals essentially no positive relationship between the energy intensity of consumption goods and their price change over this period. So there must be more to the story.

73. See Blinder (1982, tables 12.7 and 12.8, 277). After the Great Stagflation ended, we once again lived in a food-shock-free era until 2008. From December 2007 to September 2008, the food component of the CPI rose at a 7.5 percent annual rate. But even that was only about 3 percentage points above overall CPI inflation and about 5 percentage points above core.

74. For example, Nordhaus's (2007, table 2, 224) descriptive regression for output shows the coefficient of the oil-shock variable falling from –0.50 in the 1960 to 1980 sample to –0.19 over 1970 to 1990, and to –0.06 over 1980 to 2000.

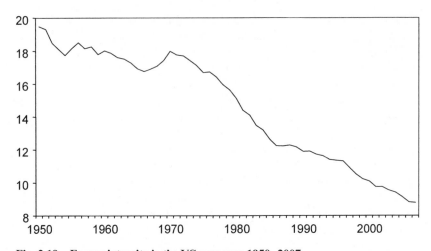

Fig. 2.19   Energy intensity in the US economy, 1950–2007
Source: Energy Information Administration, *Annual Energy Review 2007,* table 1.5.

A fascinating paper by Nordhaus (2007) explores three possibilities. The first is that the more gradual nature of the 2002–2008 oil price increases weakened their effects. While huge in total, the rolling oil shock of 2002–2008 is far smaller than either OPEC I or OPEC II *when viewed on an annualized basis*—just 0.7 percent of GDP per annum (through the second quarter of 2006, when Nordhaus's study ends) versus roughly 2 percent of GDP per annum for both OPEC I and II (see table 3 on page 227 of his paper). More gradual oil price increases are easier to cope with.

Nordhaus also finds modest evidence that wages have absorbed more of the recent oil shocks than was true in the 1970s. Greater wage flexibility makes the responses to an oil shock more neoclassical and less Keynesian—and therefore smaller.

Perhaps most important, Nordhaus uses econometric Taylor rules to estimate that the Federal Reserve responded more to *headline* inflation until 1980 but more to *core* inflation afterward. If so, the work of Bernanke, Gertler, and Watson (1997) would predict substantially smaller contractionary effects following the more recent oil shocks because of the limited effect that oil shocks now appear to have on core inflation. And remember that the empirical puzzle is at least somewhat greater for the real effects of oil shocks than for the effects on nonenergy inflation, even though both have diminished a great deal.[75]

75. Hooker (2002) also points out that it is difficult to use the Bernanke, Gertler, and Watson (1997) idea to explain the empirically observed instability in the US Phillips curve. Bernanke, Gertler, and Watson find—and Hooker confirms—that policy appears to respond *less* aggressively to oil price shocks in recent years (this is, of course, consistent with Nordhaus's finding). But that makes it difficult to attribute the reduced pass-through of oil prices into the core to less-accommodative monetary policy.

Blanchard and Galí (2007) also adduce some modest evidence in favor of greater wage flexibility in recent years.[76] But their more speculative hypothesis is that the anti-inflation credibility of monetary policy has increased since the 1970s, which would reduce both the inflationary impacts and the output losses from an oil shock, presumably by limiting the reaction of inflation expectations. Blanchard and Galí (2007) do find smaller recent impacts on expected inflation, but they warn that, "The model we have developed is too primitive in many dimensions, and its quantitative implications must be taken with caution" (65–66).[77]

Kilian (2007a) adds two other empirically appealing ideas to the list, both connected with international trade. First, the changed structure of the US automobile industry since 1973—arguably itself a reaction to the OPEC shocks—means that Americans no longer turn only to imports when they seek smaller, more fuel-efficient vehicles.[78] So domestic aggregate demand falls by less after an oil shock than it formerly did. The domestic auto industry, which is of course especially vulnerable to higher gasoline prices, is also a much smaller share of the economy now than in the 1970s.

Second, the rolling 2002–2008 oil shock seems to have been driven by strong global demand for industrial output, not by supply or demand shocks specific to the oil market. While rising oil prices still constitute an "oil shock" to oil-importing nations like the United States, the recent shock came accompanied by stronger export performance, which cushioned the blow to aggregate demand.

In sum, the search for an explanation of why oil shocks have smaller impacts now than they did in the 1970s has not come up empty. Rather, it has turned up a long list of factors, no one of which appears to be dominant. But each may play some role. Alas, reality is sometimes complicated, as Einstein understood.

2.6   Conclusion

Blinder (1979, 1982), Gordon (1982), and others concluded decades ago that the two OPEC shocks, the two roughly contemporaneous food price shocks, and the removal of wage-price controls in 1973–1974 played starring roles in the macroeconomic events that constituted the Great Stagflation. Money and aggregate demand were, by comparison, bit players. This supply-shock explanation, which we summarized in the ten points in the Preamble, was never intended to exclude influences from the demand side,

76. They consider six countries but concentrate on the United States—a point that Blanchard emphasized in his discussion.

77. In particular, the treatment of inflation expectations is both critical to credibility issues like this and hard to adjudicate empirically.

78. The SUV craze clearly represented some back-sliding in this regard, and the auto industry is now paying the price.

whether monetary or fiscal. But it did take the empirical view that, compared to the powerful special factors that were at work, conventional demand-side influences were minor during the years from 1973 to 1982.[79]

More than a quarter century has now passed since Blinder's 1982 paper was published. How well has the supply-shock explanation held up to the accumulation of new data, new theories, and new econometric evidence since then? Our answer is: for the most part, pretty well.

New data: The passage of time has changed the historical data that Blinder and others studied at the time. But we have shown in this chapter that data revisions, while altering the precise numbers, do not change the basic story of the period in any important ways. Whether simply tabulating data or making more complicated econometric estimates, the events of 1973 to 1982 look much the same with current data as they did with earlier data vintages.[80] A far bigger change to our interpretation of this period comes from Hamilton (1983) and subsequent work, which has taught us that OPEC I was not the first oil shock.

But the experience since 1982 *has* been different, and far more benign, than what OPEC I and II led us to expect. While there were no food shocks between the late 1970s and 2007, the quarter century from 1982 to 2007 did witness several sizable oil shocks, both positive and negative. And compared to the experience of the 1970s, these shocks seem to have packed far less punch, on both inflation and output. Why?

New developments in the economy: First, and most obviously, the US economy became far less energy-intensive after the big oil-price shocks of the 1970s and early 1980s. That adjustment alone should have reduced the impact of an oil shock by half. Second, and related, the US automobile industry has downsized, both relative to GDP and in the type of cars it produces. Third, it is easier for the economy to adjust to more gradual shocks, such as the one we experienced from 2002 until mid-2008. Fourth, while the OPEC I and II shocks received plenty of help from food prices, other commodity prices, and wage-price controls, the recent rolling oil shock took place during (and to some extent because of) a worldwide boom. A fifth set of reasons stems from changes in monetary policy: the Fed came to focus more on core inflation and, perhaps, gained anti-inflation credibility that now helps keep expected inflation under control. Finally, and also conjecturally, the United States and other industrial economies may now be more flexible, and hence better able to handle oil shocks, than they were in the 1970s.

New theoretical or empirical analyses: Notice that none of the factors on this list calls for a revisionist history of the 1970s. In particular, not much on the list suggests that new economic theories or new econometric findings

---

79. We exclude from this statement the demand-side impacts of the supply shocks, which we have discussed extensively.

80. The main exception is that mortgage interest rates have been removed from the CPI.

have undermined the conventional wisdom on the supply-shock explanation circa 1982.[81] Rather, this list of candidate explanations—some of which are clear facts, and others of which are conjectures—suggests that economies, like organisms, adapt to difficulties. The US economy changed in a variety of ways that made the impact of oil shocks smaller in the 1990s and 2000s than in the 1970s and early 1980s.

If that is correct, the supply-shock explanation of stagflation remains *qualitatively* relevant today, but is less important *quantitatively* than it used to be. Thus with luck and sensible policy, the food and energy shocks that pummeled the US economy in the first two or three quarters of 2008 need not have the devastating effects that the supply shocks of the 1970s and early 1980s did.[82] Contrary to a popular misconception, we are *not* condemned to repeat history.

Appendix

This appendix gives the definitions and sources for the data series that we employ, describes the specification of our empirical models, and details the calculations that underpin figures 2.4 through 2.6, the Bruno-Sachs estimates from section 2.2.2, and the input/output-based calculations from section 2.2.4.

Data Definitions and Sources

All standard data from the National Income and Product Accounts (NIPAs) were downloaded from the Bureau of Economic Analysis (BEA) website; all published CPI, PPI, and employment data were downloaded from the Bureau of Labor Statistics (BLS) website (both accessed on December 6, 2007, with the data in figure 2.3 updated through the third quarter of 2008 with data accessed on November 25, 2008).[83]

Market-based PCE prices: Official data for the market-based PCE price index (headline and core) are published from 1997 to the present. To extend the market-based series back prior to 1997, we use a Fisher aggregation

81. One possible exception is the role of monetary-policy credibility in controlling inflation expectations, which did not receive much attention before 1980, and which may or may not be quantitatively important.

82. At the time of the conference (late September 2008), the energy shock was reversing and food price inflation appeared to be cresting. But the financial panic that followed the failure of Lehman Brothers was about to move into high gear. It got much worse, and a sharp drop in output ensued in 2008:Q4 and 2009:Q1. But most observers—at least so far—attribute those sharp output declines to the financial crisis, not to the oil shock.

83. The core PCE and market-based PCE price indexes that are used in this chapter are therefore constructed according to the definitions that were in place prior to the 2009 comprehensive revision to the NIPAs.

routine that replicates the procedure followed by the BEA in constructing the NIPAs. We then use detailed PCE data from the NIPAs to strip out the prices of nonmarket PCE components from the published indexes, where our definition of "nonmarket" mimics the BEA's. (As a check, we compared the monthly changes in our constructed index to the corresponding changes in the official series; the correlation between the two series was nearly perfect.)

Current-methods CPI: A research series that puts the CPI on a methodologically consistent basis over the period 1978 to the present (the CPI-U-RS) is available from the BLS, while an experimental CPI that uses a rental-equivalence approach to recalculate the owner-occupied housing component of the index (the CPI-U-X1) extends from 1967 to 1983. Our current-methods CPI is constructed as follows.

1957 to 1966: Published CPI-U less 0.2 percentage point per year
1967 to 1977: CPI-U-X1 less 0.2 percentage point per year
1978 to present: CPI-U-RS (the published CPI-U is used in the most recent period)

The 0.2 percentage point adjustment controls for the effect of lower-level geometric means aggregation, which was introduced in 1999. In addition, we subtract additional small amounts (0.1 percentage point per year for the headline CPI and 0.12 percentage point per year for the core) in 1987–1989 and 1996–1997 to control for the effect of expenditure-weight updates, which the BLS do not consider to be methodological changes. The various splices are done on a not seasonally adjusted (NSA) basis; the resulting index is seasonally adjusted with seasonal factors that are obtained from the published or rental-equivalence series, depending on the period involved.

In addition, research series for the food and energy components of the CPI are available from 1978 to the present. We splice these to the published indexes prior to 1978, making an additional subtraction of 0.3 percentage point per year to the published food index in order to capture the effect of methodological changes that are specific to this component. (For the calculations in section 2.3.1, we use published detail on energy and food because current-methods data are not available for the detailed components of the CPI.)

CPI relative importance weights: Published values for the CPI relative importance weights are available for December of most years. Where necessary, these are interpolated using the same dynamic updating formula that is employed in constructing the published index.

Oil prices: The nominal oil price that is shown in figure 2.3 and used in the VARs and oil-market models is a spliced series that combines the PPI for crude petroleum (domestic production) and the RAC for imported crude oil.

The PPI for crude petroleum extends back to 1947. However, this series is affected by price controls in the early 1970s, and is therefore an imperfect measure of the world oil price. The RAC for imported and domestic crude oil extends back to 1968 on an annual basis, with published monthly data available starting in 1974. (These data are available from the Department of Energy's Energy Information Administration website.) In addition, the 1975 *Economic Report of the President* contains monthly data for the domestic and composite RAC for November and December of 1973, and monthly data for the imported RAC starting in September of 1973.

We therefore use the imported RAC when it is available, and extend it back before September of 1973 by splicing it to the PPI. On an annual-average basis, the log change in the resulting spliced series is 124 log points from 1970 to 1974, compared with 144 log points for the imported RAC; there is similar congruence with the domestic RAC.

World oil production: World crude oil production (thousands of barrels per day) from the *Oil and Gas Journal,* downloaded from the Haver Analytics database. These data are available monthly from 1970 to the present.

Energy intensity: Energy consumption in thousands of BTUs per dollar of real GDP, from table 1.5 of the Energy Information Administration's *Annual Energy Review 2007.*

G7 industrial production: Organization for Economic Cooperation and Development (OECD) industrial production for the G7 economies, downloaded from the Haver Analytics database. These data are available monthly from 1961 to the present.

Labor income share: Ratio of compensation of employees to gross value added, nonfinancial business sector (from the NIPAs).

Hourly compensation, nonfarm sector; output per hour, nonfarm sector: Published indexes from the BLS Productivity and Costs release.

Detailed Descriptions of Empirical Specifications

Price-control models: The model used in section 2.3 to estimate the effect of price controls on core CPI inflation is a standard price-price Phillips curve with additional terms to capture the impact of the controls. The basic specification takes the form

$$\pi_t = \alpha_0 + A(L)\pi_{t-1} + B(L)x_{t-1} + G(L)\zeta_{t-1} + \varepsilon_t$$

where π_t is the inflation rate (defined as an annualized log difference), x is a measure of slack, ζ is a supply-shock term, and ε is a stochastic error. Slack is defined as the detrended unemployment rate; the trend is defined as the low-frequency component obtained from a band-pass filter with the filter width and cutoffs set equal to the values used by Staiger, Stock, and Watson (2001) and with an autoregressive integrated moving average (ARIMA) model used for endpoint padding. The number of inflation lags was determined with the Akaike criterion, with twelve lags used as the default; note, however, that we do not impose the "accelerationist" restriction $A(1) = 1$. The models are estimated at the monthly frequency from January 1961 to March 1979.

Two additional terms are added to the model in order to capture the effect of price controls. The first is the relative importance of controlled prices, λ_t, which is taken from Blinder and Newton (1981). The second term is a set of variables that are intended to capture the "catch-up" effect that occurs when the controls are lifted. In the original Blinder-Newton paper, this term was defined as

$$(1 - \lambda_t) g \sum_{j=0}^{R} v_j \delta_{t-j},$$

where δ_t is the fraction of the CPI that is decontrolled in month t. This is in turn defined as

$$\begin{aligned}\delta_t &= \lambda_{t-1} - \lambda_t \\ \delta_t &= 0\end{aligned} \quad \text{if} \quad \begin{aligned}\lambda_t &\leq \lambda_{t-1} \\ \lambda_t &> \lambda_{t-1}\end{aligned}.$$

(This condition is modified so as to ensure that δ_t is only positive or zero; in particular, δ_t is set to zero from May 1973 to August 1973—when "Freeze II" resulted in a temporary increase in the fraction of the CPI that was subject to controls—and $\delta_{1973:09}$ is set equal to $\lambda_{1973:05} - \lambda_{1973:09}$.) The v_j terms are lag coefficients, while the g parameter is a measure of the "disequilibrium gap"—the percent difference between the representative industry's actual and desired price—when the controls are lifted; it can be obtained implicitly under the assumption that the sum of the v_j coefficients equals one.

In the original Blinder-Newton work, the v_j were constrained to lie along a (linear) polynomial—an assumption that is less satisfactory in the current data. We therefore implement the model by defining an alternative set of terms

$$D_0 = (1 - \lambda_t) \delta_t$$
$$D_1 = (1 - \lambda_t) \delta_{t-1}$$
$$\vdots$$
$$D_i = (1 - \lambda_t) \delta_{t-i},$$

with as many consecutive D_i terms added (starting with D_0) as are statistically significant. The full model for estimation is therefore given by

$$\pi_t = \alpha_0 + \alpha_1 \lambda_t + A(L)\pi_{t-1} + B(L)x_{t-1} + G(L)\zeta_{t-1} + \sum_{i=0}^{R} \theta_i D_i + u_t.$$

Note that the sum of the θ coefficients (suitably scaled to reflect inflation's being expressed at an annual rate) yields an estimate of the disequilibrium gap g. The core CPI model used to generate the results in the text has fifteen lags of the dependent variable, three lags of the unemployment gap, and the contemporaneous value and five lags of the D_i terms.

The supply-shock terms ζ_t in our baseline specification are defined with reference to a weighted change in relative food and energy prices, $\tilde{\omega}_t(\pi_t^s - \pi_t)$, where π_t^s is food or energy inflation, π_t is core inflation, and $\bar{\omega}_t$ is the twelve-month average share of nominal food or energy expenditures in total nominal PCE.[84] We then take a six-month moving average of the weighted relative price changes, and use their first lag in the model (additional lags did not enter).

As noted in the text, we examined the robustness of these results along a number of dimensions. First, we tried using a different measure of aggregate demand pressure—the rate of capacity utilization in manufacturing—in our Phillips curves; while this alternative demand indicator was only borderline significant (with p-values around 15 percent), using it had only a small effect on our results. Second, we experimented with alternative specifications for the model's relative energy and food price terms; this typically implied a slightly *larger* contribution of controls to the pre- and postpeak swing in core inflation. We also fit similar price-price models for the market-based core PCE price index (the specification of this model is described later), and fit a wage-price system for the CPI (again described later); once again, the estimated relative impact of controls on inflation was similar. Finally, we note that the model used for this exercise is estimated through the beginning of 1979, which maximizes its ability to track actual inflation in the dynamic simulations. If we instead extend the sample period to December 1984 (to include the second set of supply shocks and the Volcker disinflation period), which requires a few minor changes to the model's specification (see the next section), the resulting dynamic simulations slightly overpredict inflation over a portion of the postpeak period. As a result, the model attributes only a little more than a third of the postpeak decline in inflation to price controls; however, the estimated contribution of controls to the *increase* in inflation is found to be around 85 percent, which is somewhat larger than our baseline estimate.

Price-price Phillips curves: The price-price Phillips curves used in section 2.3.2 to compute the pass-through of the food and energy price shocks into core inflation are variants of the price control model. Specifically, for the core CPI model we extend the estimation period of the price control model to the end of 1984; this requires a minor adjustment to the specification (we drop all but the contemporaneous value and first lag of the unemployment gap, as the remaining terms are not statistically significant).[85]

---

84. As noted in the text, a CPI-based model would ideally use CPI relative importance weights rather than PCE shares. There are, however, significant breaks in the relative importance weight series over time—notably in 1978, when the CPI moved from measuring prices faced by wage earners to prices faced by all urban consumers, and again after owner-occupied housing costs moved to a rental equivalence basis. In any case, whether weighting is used turns out to make little difference to the results.

85. Index rounding is quite severe for the CPI prior to the mid-1960s (this is why month-to-month inflation rates often manifest a sawtooth pattern with flat "peaks" in the early part of the sample). We therefore checked that our models' tracking performance was robust to this property of the data by considering an estimation period that started in 1965 (it was).

For the core market-based PCE deflator, we construct a similar price-price model in which inflation is related to fifteen lags of the dependent variable (lag length was again determined by the Akaike criterion), six lags of the unemployment gap, one lag each of the relative food and energy price terms (defined in a parallel fashion to the terms used in the core CPI equation), the fraction of the CPI under price controls (we do not have a corresponding estimate of the fraction of the PCE deflator subject to controls), and the contemporaneous value and six lags of the price control catch-up term. Dynamic simulations of the resulting specifications do a reasonably good job tracking actual core CPI and core market-based PCE price inflation over the estimation period.

The resulting core CPI model is also used to generate the stylized supply shocks shown in figures 2.4 through 2.6.

Wage-price systems: We estimate a wage equation in which nonfarm hourly compensation growth (expressed as an annualized log-difference) is related to eight lags of the headline (current-methods) CPI, the unemployment rate, and a 40-quarter moving average of trend productivity growth. Trend productivity growth is obtained by regressing productivity growth on a constant and a dummy variable set equal to one starting in 1974:Q1 (the estimation period for this productivity equation is 1950 to 1994).[86] All data are quarterly, and the wage and markup equations are estimated from 1960:Q1 to 1985:Q4.

The markup equation relates core (current-methods) CPI inflation to four of its lags, the contemporaneous value and one lag of trend unit labor costs, the unemployment gap, the fraction of the CPI subject to controls, and the contemporaneous value and one lag of the price control catch-up term (defined on a quarterly basis).[87]

To obtain the estimates shown in figure 2.14, we set food and energy price inflation equal to the values indicated in the text. The CPI relative importance weights for food were set to 0.225 through 1977 and then to 0.180 from 1978-forward; the corresponding weights for energy were 0.06 and 0.085.[88]

In contrast to the price-price Phillips curves that we employ, these models impose an accelerationist restriction in which the coefficients of the wage equation are constrained such that the real consumption wage rises with trend productivity growth in a steady state, and the coefficients on trend unit labor costs and lagged inflation in the markup equation are constrained to

86. We also experimented with using the low-frequency component of productivity growth from a band-pass filter. The results were similar, though a moving average of this latter measure was not always significant in every estimation period we considered.

87. We obtained similar results from a model that used PCE price inflation in the wage equation and a markup equation for the market-based core PCE deflator. (To stimulate this alternative system, we assumed that the path of relative nonmarket price inflation was equal to its actual path in both cases.)

88. The relative importance weights for food and energy in the CPI shift in 1978 when the index moves from a wage-earners basis to an all-urban-consumers basis.

sum to one. (Unlike the price-price case, the data do not reject this restriction for the wage-price system.) As a result, the implied pass-through of higher food and energy prices into core inflation is larger and more persistent than what is implied from the corresponding price-price model. We also experimented with models that relaxed the accelerationist condition for the price markup equation; while the results were closer to those obtained from the price-price model, this alternative wage-price system underpredicts core inflation somewhat by the end of the simulation period.

Oil-market model (Kilian 2007b): The oil-market model is a three-variable recursive VAR in oil production growth, aggregate commodity demand, and the real oil price (with that ordering). We define oil production growth as the log-difference of world crude oil production from the *Oil and Gas Journal,* and use the log real oil price shown in figure 2.3.

For his measure of aggregate commodity demand, Kilian (2007b) uses an index of shipping prices that he constructs himself. The reason for using this index, as opposed to a measure of industrial-country production, is that Kilian seeks to capture the recent contribution to world commodity demand from emerging-market economies like China. Over the period we are concerned with (the 1970s and early 1980s), this factor is less important. In addition, in the early 1970s Kilian's index appears to be largely based on shipping costs for grains; these are probably unduly affected by the food price increases that occurred during this period. We therefore use OECD industrial production for the G7 economies as our commodity-demand proxy (in the VAR, this variable is expressed as a log-deviation from a cubic trend fit from January 1961 to June 2007).

The VAR is estimated using monthly data from February 1971 to December 1987. (Note that the impulse responses from our specification appear qualitatively similar to what Kilian obtains from his system.)

Structural VAR model: We fit two recursive VAR specifications. The first is a four-lag, four-variable VAR in core PCE inflation (defined as an annualized log-difference), the unemployment rate, weighted relative food and energy price inflation (computed as the difference between headline and core PCE inflation), and the federal funds rate. The second model uses two lags and five variables—the first three variables just listed, the annualized log change in the Producer Price Index for crude materials, and the federal funds rate. (This is also their ordering in the VAR.) The data are quarterly, and the sample extends from 1959 (this is dictated by the availability of the core PCE deflator) to the end of 1985.

Our use of retail food and energy prices, rather than, say, oil prices, is motivated by two considerations. First, as discussed in section 2.2.2, the direct impact of higher oil (and food) prices on production is most likely second-order. The important recessionary impacts of the shocks come from their effects on aggregate demand, and these are best measured by retail prices (e.g., consumer energy prices rather than oil prices). Second, the impact of oil shocks on real activity and inflation appears to have diminished since the early 1980s. We therefore choose to end the model's estimation period around that time. And since we are constrained by the availability of the core inflation series, which only starts in the late 1950s, degrees of freedom are at a premium. Hence, a more parsimonious specification is preferable, and the specification we consider allows food and energy prices to enter in as economical a fashion as possible.

Detailed Descriptions of Calculations

Stylized supply-shock examples (figures 2.4 to 2.6): We use the price-price Phillips curves for the core CPI estimated over the extended sample (1961 to 1984) to calibrate the effect of an increase in the relative price of energy. We set the share of energy in consumption (which is used to weight the relative energy price term) equal to its 1973–2007 average of 0.063. To compute headline inflation, we note that the change in the headline CPI equals the change in the core CPI plus ω times the change in energy prices relative to the core, where ω denotes the relative importance weight of energy in the total CPI. We set this equal to its 1973–2007 average of 0.081.

Neoclassical effect of supply shocks (Bruno-Sachs): To implement the Bruno-Sachs calculations in section 2.2, we require a measure of gross output and its deflator, the share of (imported) energy in gross output, and the price of imported energy. We use NIPA data on imported petroleum and products (nominal values and prices), and compute nominal gross output as nominal GDP plus oil imports. We use a Tornqvist aggregation formula to compute the gross output deflator (specifically, we combine the imported oil and GDP deflators according to the formula). Each quarter's change in the real price of imported oil (the log difference in the oil import deflator less the log difference in the computed gross output deflator) is then multiplied by $-s/(1-s)$, where s is the share of imported oil in gross output. (Note that each share s at time t is computed as an average of the shares in quarters t and $t-1$.) This gives the quarter-by-quarter effects on value added (GDP) of changes in the real price of oil, which are then cumulated over a specified period to yield the estimated overall impact on real GDP of the change in imported oil prices.

As noted in the text, the Bruno-Sachs analysis can be extended to include imported materials inputs more generally. This is done in our calculation by using NIPA data on imports of petroleum and products along with data on imports of nonoil materials (nominal values and prices). For these calculations, we modify the definition of gross output accordingly (that is, we define it as GDP plus oil imports plus imports of nonoil materials).

Input-output estimates of energy intensity: We used the eighty-five-item 1972 and 1977 commodity-by-commodity total requirements tables from the input-output accounts, along with the corresponding PCE bridge tables (which provide estimates of the commodity content of the detailed components of PCE) to construct estimates of the crude energy content of individual PCE components. We define crude energy as coal and crude petroleum and natural gas (commodity codes 7 and 8). The bridge tables were inputted by hand from various issues of the *Survey of Current Business,* while the 1972 and 1977 total requirements tables were downloaded from the BEA website.

For the 2002–2007 calculation that is referred to in section 2.5, we use the 1992 total requirements table and PCE bridge table; both of these were obtained from the BEA website.

References

Abrams, Burton A. 2006. "How Richard Nixon Pressured Arthur Burns: Evidence from the Nixon Tapes." *Journal of Economic Perspectives* 20:177–88.
Adelman, M. A. 1995. *The Genie out of the Bottle: World Oil since 1970.* Cambridge, MA: MIT Press.
Baily, Martin Neil. 1981. "Productivity and the Services of Labor." *Brookings Papers on Economic Activity* 1:1–50. Washington, DC: Brookings Institution.
Balke, Nathan S., and Mark A. Wynne. 2000. "An Equilibrium Analysis of Relative Price Changes and Aggregate Inflation." *Journal of Monetary Economics* 45:269–92.
Ball, Laurence. 2006. "Has Globalization Changed Inflation?" NBER Working Paper no. 12687. Cambridge, MA: National Bureau of Economic Research, November.
Ball, Laurence, and N. Gregory Mankiw. 1995. "Relative-Price Changes as Aggregate Supply Shocks." *Quarterly Journal of Economics* 110:161–93.
Ball, Laurence, and Robert Moffitt. 2001. "Productivity Growth and the Phillips Curve." In *The Roaring Nineties: Can Full Employment Be Sustained?,* edited by Alan Krueger and Robert Solow, 61–90. New York: Russell Sage Foundation and Century Foundation Press.
Barsky, Robert B., and Lutz Kilian. 2002. "Do We Really Know That Oil Caused the Great Stagflation? A Monetary Alternative." In *NBER Macroeconomics Annual 2001,* edited by Ben S. Bernanke and Kenneth Rogoff, 137–83. Cambridge, MA: MIT Press.
Bernanke, Ben S. 1983. "Irreversibility, Uncertainty, and Cyclical Investment." *Quarterly Journal of Economics* 98:85–106.
Bernanke, Ben S., Mark Gertler, and Mark Watson. 1997. "Systematic Monetary Policy and the Effects of Oil Price Shocks." *Brookings Papers on Economic Activity* 1:91–142. Washington, DC: Brookings Institution.
———. 2004. "Oil Shocks and Aggregate Macroeconomic Behavior: The Role of Monetary Policy (Reply)." *Journal of Money, Credit, and Banking* 36:287–91.
Blanchard, Olivier J. 2002. "Comment on 'Do We Really Know That Oil Caused the Great Stagflation? A Monetary Alternative.'" In *NBER Macroeconomics Annual 2001,* edited by Ben S. Bernanke and Kenneth Rogoff, 183–92. Cambridge, MA: MIT Press.
Blanchard, Olivier J., and Jordi Galí. 2007. "The Macroeconomic Effects of Oil Shocks: Why Are the 2000s So Different from the 1970s?" NBER Working Paper no. 13368. Cambridge, MA: National Bureau of Economic Research, September.

Blinder, Alan S. 1979. *Economic Policy and the Great Stagflation.* New York: Academic Press.

———. 1981. "Monetary Accommodation of Supply Shocks under Rational Expectations." *Journal of Money, Credit, and Banking* 13:425–38.

———. 1982. "The Anatomy of Double-Digit Inflation in the 1970s." In *Inflation: Causes and Effects,* edited by Robert E. Hall, 261–82. Chicago: University of Chicago Press.

Blinder, Alan S., and William J. Newton. 1981. "The 1971–1974 Controls Program and the Price Level: An Econometric Post-Mortem." *Journal of Monetary Economics* 8:1–23.

Blinder, Alan S., and Janet L. Yellen. 2001. "The Fabulous Decade: Macroeconomic Lessons from the 1990s." In *The Roaring Nineties: Can Full Employment Be Sustained?,* edited by Alan Krueger and Robert Solow, 91–156. New York: Russell Sage Foundation and Century Foundation Press.

Bosworth, Barry P., and Robert Z. Lawrence. 1982. *Commodity Prices and the New Inflation.* Washington, DC: Brookings Institution.

Bruno, Michael, and Jeffrey D. Sachs. 1985. *Economics of Worldwide Stagflation.* Cambridge, MA: Harvard University Press.

Bryan, Michael F., and Stephen G. Cecchetti. 1999. "Inflation and the Distribution of Price Changes." *The Review of Economics and Statistics* 81:188–96.

Carlstrom, Charles T., and Timothy S. Fuerst. 2006. "Oil Prices, Monetary Policy, and Counterfactual Experiments." *Journal of Money, Credit, and Banking* 38:1945–58.

Cecchetti, Stephen G., Peter Hooper, Bruce C. Kasman, Kermit L. Schoenholtz, and Mark W. Watson. 2007. "Understanding the Evolving Inflation Process." US Monetary Policy Forum Working Paper, July.

DeLong, J. Bradford. 1997. "America's Peacetime Inflation: The 1970s." In *Reducing Inflation: Motivation and Strategy,* edited by Christina D. Romer and David H. Romer, 247–80. Chicago: University of Chicago Press.

Friedman, Milton. 1975. "Perspective on Inflation." In *There's No Such Thing as a Free Lunch,* 113–15. LaSalle, IL: Open Court. (Reprint of June 24, 1974 *Newsweek* article.)

Gordon, Robert J. 1975. "Alternative Responses of Policy to External Supply Shocks." *Brookings Papers on Economic Activity* 1:183–204. Washington, DC: Brookings Institution.

———. 1977. "Can the Inflation of the 1970s Be Explained?" *Brookings Papers on Economic Activity* 1:765–78. Washington, DC: Brookings Institution.

———. 1982. "Price Inertia and Policy Ineffectiveness in the United States, 1890–1980." *Journal of Political Economy* 90:1087–117.

Hall, Robert E. 2009. "By How Much Does GDP Rise if the Government Buys More Output?" *Brookings Papers on Economic Activity* 2:183–231. Washington, DC: Brookings Institution.

Hamilton, James D. 1983. "Oil and the Macroeconomy since World War II." *Journal of Political Economy* 91:228–48.

Hamilton, James D., and Ana Maria Herrera. 2004. "Oil Shocks and Aggregate Macroeconomic Behavior: The Role of Monetary Policy (Comment)." *Journal of Money, Credit, and Banking* 36:265–86.

Hooker, Mark A. 1996. "What Happened to the Oil Price-Macroeconomy Relationship?" *Journal of Monetary Economics* 38:195–213.

———. 2002. "Are Oil Shocks Inflationary? Asymmetric and Nonlinear Specifications versus Changes in Regime." *Journal of Money, Credit, and Banking* 34:540–61.

Ireland, Peter N. 1999. "Does the Time-Consistency Problem Explain the Behavior of Inflation in the United States?" *Journal of Monetary Economics* 44:279–91.

Kilian, Lutz. 2007a. "The Economic Effects of Energy Price Shocks." Unpublished Manuscript. University of Michigan, October.

———. 2007b. "Not All Oil Shocks Are Alike: Disentangling Demand and Supply Shocks in the Crude Oil Market." Unpublished Manuscript. University of Michigan, November.

Leduc, Sylvain, and Keith Sill. 2004. "A Quantitative Analysis of Oil-Price Shocks, Systematic Monetary Policy, and Economic Downturns." *Journal of Monetary Economics* 51:781–808.

Meyer, Laurence H. 2004. *A Term at the Fed: An Insider's View.* New York: HarperCollins.

Nixon, Richard M. 1962. *Six Crises.* Garden City, NJ: Doubleday and Company.

Nordhaus, William D. 2007. "Who's Afraid of a Big Bad Oil Shock?" *Brookings Papers on Economic Activity* 2:219–40. Washington, DC: Brookings Institution.

Orphanides, Athanasios. 2003. "The Quest for Prosperity without Inflation." *Journal of Monetary Economics* 50:633–63.

Perry, George L. 1975. "The United States." In *Higher Oil Prices and the World Economy: The Adjustment Problem,* edited by Edward R. Fried and Charles L. Schultze, 71–104. Washington, DC: Brookings Institution.

Phelps, Edmund S. 1978. "Commodity-Supply Shock and Full-Employment Monetary Policy." *Journal of Money, Credit, and Banking* 10:206–21.

Pierce, James L., and Jared J. Enzler. 1974. "The Effects of External Inflationary Shocks." *Brookings Papers on Economic Activity* 1:13–54. Washington, DC: Brookings Institution.

Rotemberg, Julio J., and Michael Woodford. 1996. "Imperfect Competition and the Effects of Energy Price Increases on Economic Activity." *Journal of Money, Credit, and Banking* 28:549–77.

Sims, Christopher. 1981. In: "General Discussion." *Brookings Papers on Economic Activity* 1:64. Washington, DC: Brookings Institution.

Staiger, Douglas, James H. Stock, and Mark W. Watson. 2001. "Prices, Wages, and the US NAIRU in the 1990s." In *The Roaring Nineties: Can Full Employment Be Sustained?,* edited by Alan Krueger and Robert Solow, 3–60. New York: Russell Sage Foundation and Century Foundation Press.

Taylor, John B. 1981. "On the Relation between the Variability of Inflation and the Average Inflation Rate." *Carnegie-Rochester Conference Series on Public Policy* 15:57–85.

US National Commission on Supplies and Shortages. 1976. *Government and the Nation's Resources.* Washington, DC: US Government Printing Office, December.

Weinhagen, Jonathan C. 2006. "Price Transmission: From Crude Petroleum to Plastics Products." *Monthly Labor Review* (December):34–43.

Yergin, Daniel. 1993. *The Prize: The Epic Quest for Oil, Money, and Power.* New York: Touchstone.

Discussion

Vitor Gaspar began by stressing the importance of downward inflexibility of prices, citing the empirical evidence using micro price data. Relative price adjustment happens through price declines all of the time. His second

remark was in reference to the authors using the term "exogenous disturbance" to describe movements in economic variables. In economic models,
equilibrium price changes happen because of technology, preference, institutions, and so forth. One must remember that price- and wage-setting are
endogenous.

Martin Feldstein posed the question of what policy should have been in
1980 to 1981 under the Blinder and Rudd view of the world.

Matthew Shapiro compared this chapter to previous work by Robert Barsky and Lutz Kilian. In their work, it was a sticky price story, and you see
incipient inflation coming from monetary, and possibly fiscal, expansion.
This goes back to the guns and butter problems of the 1960s, culminating
with the clash of Bretton Woods. These are all indicator variables, and move
in well in advance of OPEC. With reference to another Kilian paper, he further goes on to point out that aggregate demand pressure is largely coming
from money, but also from fiscal policy pushing up commodity prices quite
broadly. Shapiro believed it has something to do with the combination of
the President Lyndon Johnson administration and the collapse of Bretton
Woods. What really puzzled him, however, is how the authors refer to the
demise of price controls as a supply shock. Christina Romer continued,
stressing that the end of price controls is just a lagged demand shock. She
pointed out that there were big positive, monetary policy shocks before both
oil price run-ups in the 1970s. The closest thing that the economy came to
in terms of an exogenous monetary expansion is Chairman Arthur Burns
in the 1970s.

William Poole looked back at the long history of significant changes in the
inflation rate, and clearly there are large changes in relative prices that occur.
The prices that move the most are for those goods with inelastic supply.
Therefore, the leading edge of a breakout in inflation is from the goods
that are inelastically supplied, like food and energy. Regulated prices, like
electricity, do not move. We should resort to the microeconomic viewpoint
to see how inflation is created in the economy.

Edward Nelson challenged the authors to create a graph of M2 along with
inflation two years later to get a perspective of the relationship between monetary policy and inflation and the role of money growth. While he agreed
that the Federal Reserve did not accommodate these oil shocks, he felt it
preaccommodated the oil shocks because if you have large enough nominal
spending or momentum for nominal spending and expansionary policy,
then you do not have the downward price pressure during a relative price
shock because you expect the aggregate price level to rise. The political pressure story for actions of the Federal Reserve in 1972 tends to look past the
enthusiasm for monetary expansion on economic grounds that were present.
One should look at the work of Athanasios Orphanides and the role of the
output gap. Chairman Arthur Burns had the unorthodox view that when
you imposed price controls, that lowered inflation expectations.

Andrew Levin felt like the chapter said that the story was bad luck and that there was not much that monetary policy could do. One reason Levin is not comfortable with this is the cross-country evidence, particularly in Germany and Japan. The effects of the 1979 oil shock were much smaller and more transitory for these other countries relative to the United States, much like what we have seen over the past few years. This made him think that the monetary policy regime is critical. Lars Svensson agreed with Levin, noting the response to inflation was very different in other countries.

Robert King suggested that the authors supplement their work with measures of inflation expectations. Looking at long-term nominal interest rates gives guides on what agents are thinking about. Supply shocks being followed by high inflation in the 1970s had to be associated with the underlying monetary regime and expectations. This could be explained by differences in credibility.

Blinder began the rebuttal by stressing that he and Rudd are not pushing the idea that monetary policy was completely irrelevant, and referenced the two humps in inflation in the 1970s as the reason that the Great Inflation is called the Great Inflation. Was policy loose? In reference to Feldstein's question, Blinder had no answer because it depends on how urgent you think it is to bring inflation down. Was inflation going to fall anyway? How fast, and to what level? Where did they want it to go? All the answers to these questions lead to different policy prescriptions. In reference to price controls as supply shocks, the authors are aware it is not a supply shock, but they also find no evidence that it is a lagged aggregate demand shock. There are many episodes when inflation went up and no one put on price controls during peacetime. Finally, was it all bad luck? Blinder thought it could partially be bad luck. The two humps in inflation were largely bad luck, but better monetary policy might have made them less steep. The United States could have enacted centralized wage bargaining like Germany, but this was not an option given the atomistic labor market in the United States. There was a lot of literature in the 1970s and 1980s about the differential responses across countries to the oil-price shocks. While they had broad similarities, the details were different and some can be explained by wage setting.

Rudd concluded the discussion. First, he felt that monetary policy was not the story to be told. If you look at the history, the commodity price shocks were a big deal. There were lots of government studies done that identified a couple of things. In 1972 to 1973, there was a surge in world demand that might have led to some increase in the commodity prices, but that was exacerbated by a lot of supply-side elements. Price controls led to chronic underinvestment, and return to capital were too low. There was a shortage mentality, and third world countries took advantage of these shortage mentalities with other materials, which all led to panic hoarding. In reference to the Kilian vector autoregressions that Shapiro referred to, Rudd felt they underscored something really important and nuanced that was going on in the oil market. It was an exogenous shock, not necessarily a supply disruption, that was oil-market specific. It led to panic that bid up prices. None of this has anything to do with monetary policy as much. Nelson made a valid point, but some work by Blinder was unable to find an econometric link between monetary aggregates and inflation. Lastly, was the Federal Reserve too accommodating? Real money balances fell during the first big shock. There was a deep recession, but perhaps it was not deep enough? The United States came close to a depression in the early 1980s. Institutions just began working better during and after Chairman Volcker, but some of it came at a cost that was large for the economy.

II

New Monetary Policy Explanations

3

The Great Inflation Drift

Marvin Goodfriend and Robert G. King

3.1 Introduction

Between 1952 and 1965, the annual average US inflation rate ranged between 0 and 4 percent. Over the next fifteen years, it rose systematically and substantially, twice peaking above 10 percent in 1975 and 1980.

What economic forces led to this increase? Any explanation of inflation dynamics must involve an understanding of how a central bank interacts with the private economy and the real shocks that hit it. We use two basic ideas about Federal Reserve behavior—that the US central bank, like others around the world, was concerned with smoothing the path of short-term nominal interest rates and with maintaining a relatively small output gap—

Marvin Goodfriend holds the Friends of Allan Meltzer Professorship in Economics at Carnegie Mellon University and is a research associate of the National Bureau of Economic Research. Robert G. King is professor of economics at Boston University, an advisor in the Research Department of the Federal Reserve Bank of Richmond, and a research associate of the National Bureau of Economic Research.

The chapter was prepared for the Great Inflation conference sponsored by the National Bureau of Economic Research in Woodstock, Vermont, September 25–27, 2008. The chapter benefitted from preliminary presentations at the June 2007 Kiel Symposium on the Phillips Curve and the Natural Rate of Unemployment, the June 2008 North American Econometric Society Summer Meetings, and a July 2008 seminar at the Federal Reserve Bank of New York. The ideas were developed initially in a paper prepared for the November 2004 Carnegie Rochester Policy Conference. This chapter also benefitted from presentations at Cornell University, the Federal Reserve Bank of Kansas City, the Institute for International Economic Studies at Stockholm University, and the Swedish Riksbank. We thank Susanto Basu for providing us with a time series on aggregate technical change; Torsten Persson, Mathias Trabandt, and Michael Woodford for valuable discussions on related matters; Michael Siemer for research assistance; and Lars Svensson for discussing our paper at the conference. Goodfriend thanks the Gailliot Center for Public Policy at the Tepper School of Business for financial support. For acknowledgments, sources of research support, and disclosure of the authors' material financial relationships, if any, please see http://www.nber.org/chapters/c9168.ack.

to explain why a time-varying inflation trend would have become part of the US inflation process during this period and, more specifically, why there would have been a rise in trend inflation.

In adopting this approach, we focus on implications of these two basic ideas about central bank behavior and abstain from incorporating other forces that arguably may be very important for the Great Inflation in the United States and other countries. We combine these central banking assumptions with three postulates about the interaction of the central bank and the macroeconomy. First, we assume that there is a Phillips curve that is vertical in the long run and that the central bank understands this structural feature of the economy as well as the level of capacity output at each point in time. Our analysis utilizes a simple New Keynesian form of the Phillips curve modified to allow for a time-varying inflation trend. Second, we assume that private agents understand the nature of the central bank's decision rules and the consequences that they have for the inflation process. Third, we assume that the central bank adopts fully credible policy rules. Other accounts of the rise of inflation in the United States highlight departures from these assumptions and, indeed, our prior investigation of the Volcker disinflation stressed the role of imperfect credibility and private sector learning during that episode.[1]

In constructing our model and interpreting history, we thus view the US central bank as typically giving prominence to two objectives, stabilization of economic activity and avoidance of large period-to-period changes in short-term interest rates. We portray the Federal Reserve as maintaining these objectives in the face of real developments that affected the level of output and the level of the real interest rate, thus making inflation variable. We show that a very simple modern macroeconomic model, which we take as embodying key elements in many contemporary models, makes the prediction that inflation contains a "stochastic trend component" in the language of modern time series econometrics. Thus, the upward drift in US inflation from 1966 through 1979 arises as a consequence of a series of adverse real shocks hitting the macroeconomy and the central bank allowing inflation to randomly walk upward. This viewpoint explains, in one sense, how there could come to be no "nominal anchor" for US monetary policy by August 1979 when Paul Volcker became chairman of the Federal Reserve Board.

Since our model has a very simple form for trend inflation and since this form is one that has been long used to forecast inflation (Nelson and Schwert 1977) and has recently been found to be quite successful vis-à-vis competitors (Stock and Watson 2007), we are able to produce a detailed link between our theory and empirical work on inflation.

We also see the inflation process as at times more complicated than our simple trend model, during intervals in which there is inflation-fighting by

1. Goodfriend and King (2005).

the central bank, and we discuss these in detail later. The idea that there are episodic components of inflation that are not described by the stochastic trend model, during which there are forecastable linkages between inflation and real activity, also accords with further recent empirical work by Stock and Watson (2008). We see the Great Inflation as a low frequency variation, overlain by these business cycle components, although we do not provide a theory that fully integrates the trend and cycle. That said, our theory does link the inflation trend to underlying real developments in the macroeconomy, as we discuss further below. We illustrate these linkages by considering how the inflation trend responds to changes in productivity growth as measured by Basu, Fernald, and Kimball (2006). More generally, our theory emphasizes the link between innovations in the inflation trend and innovations to the natural rate of interest, which opens the door for fluctuations in saving and investment to drive the inflation trend within a richer dynamic model.

The organization of the chapter is as follows. In section 3.2, we describe the components of the model. In section 3.3, we discuss monetary policy and motivate the inclination of central banks to pursue what we call "business as usual"—the stabilization of output at capacity and a continuity of the short-term nominal interest rate. In section 3.4, we derive equilibrium outcomes and show how "business as usual" gives rise to a stochastic inflation trend. In section 3.5, we discuss how alternative central bank operating rules could bring about "business as usual" outcomes. In section 3.6, we list the empirical implications of our hypothesis, and then turn in section 3.7 to a detailed evaluation of the Great Inflation from the perspective of our model. Among other things, we describe episodes during the Great Inflation that appear to require an integrated model of the business cycle and inflation trends. A final section provides a brief conclusion.

3.2   Model Components

We work with a simple linear model that incorporates five components from modern macroeconomics: New Keynesian pricing, a real business cycle core, a Fisher equation, an Euler equation, and the term structure of interest rates.

3.2.1   New Keynesian Pricing

New Keynesian macroeconomics has developed a battery of models to explain price setting by forward-looking firms. The simplest of these models, embedding price adjustment opportunities along the lines of Calvo (1983), leads to a "new Keynesian pricing" equation that links inflation (π_t) and real output (y_t),

$$(1) \qquad \pi_t = \beta E_t \pi_{t+1} + h(y_t - y_t^*).$$

In this expression, y_t^* is a measure of capacity output, so that $y_t - y_t^*$ is a measure of the output gap, and $E_t\pi_{t+1}$ is the expected inflation rate. The parameter h can be related to structural features such as the frequency of price adjustment, the elasticity of marginal cost with respect to output, and so forth.

As has been much stressed in the recent literature,[2] the New Keynesian approach indicates that the relevant measure of capacity output is the level of output that would prevail if nominal prices were flexible. That is, it is a level of output that can be modeled along the lines of real business cycle analysis and that therefore is expected to fluctuate through time in response to a range of macroeconomic shocks, including productivity, government expenditures, tax rates, and energy prices.

We use a version of this model due to Woodford (2008) that allows for time-varying trend inflation, so that the inflation dynamics are written as

$$(2) \qquad \pi_t = \overline{\pi}_t + \beta E_t[\pi_{t+1} - \overline{\pi}_{t+1}] + h(y_t - y_t^*),$$

where $\overline{\pi}_t$ is a time-varying trend rate of inflation, which satisfies

$$(3) \qquad \overline{\pi}_t = \lim_{k \to \infty} E_t\pi_{t+k}.$$

That is, $\overline{\pi}_t$ is the stochastic trend rate of inflation in the sense of Beveridge and Nelson (1981).

This specification of New Keynesian pricing exhibits a short-run Phillips curve relationship, so that a monetary stimulus raises both inflation and real variables such as output and employment, if there are no changes in expected inflation.[3] But, at the same time, there is no long-run Phillips curve relationship, so that a permanent increase in money growth and in inflation has no quantitatively significant effect on employment or output.

3.2.2 The Real Business Cycle Core

The model has a "real business cycle core," in which macroeconomic activity would respond to a variety of real shocks in the absence of nominal frictions. Such a component is critical, we believe, on both the short-run and long-run fronts. Quarter-to-quarter, there are many changes in current and prospective real conditions that are important for output and the real interest rate. In the longer term, the evolution of economic activity is dominated by growth in productivity.

To model the RBC core of the economy, we assume that "capacity output growth" evolves according to

---

2. See Goodfriend and King (1997), Goodfriend (2002), and Woodford (2003).

3. As originally presented in our November 2004 Carnegie Rochester paper, the results relating trend inflation variability to interest-rate smoothing and output stabilization (which are derived in section 3.4) also hold for two alternative specifications: a Phillips curve derived from Calvo (1983) with $\beta = 1$ and a Phillips curve with structural inflation persistence in the style of Fuhrer and Moore (1995) that involves no long-run trade-off between inflation and output. See the appendix.

(4) $$\Delta y_t^* = \rho \Delta y_{t-1}^* + v_t,$$

which is a simple difference stationary stochastic process of the form estimated by Nelson and Plosser (1982), which allows for shocks to the level of economic activity and also to the expected growth rate.[4] (We use the notation Δ to denote such differences throughout the chapter: $\Delta x_t = x_t - x_{t-1}$ for any variable x.) This simple specification cannot adequately capture the changes in trend productivity growth that we believe to have occurred over the postwar period, but it has the desirable property that it does let us approximate the comovement of output and the real interest rate in response to permanent shocks to the level of productivity within a more fully articulated model.

3.2.3   The Fisher Equation

There is a Fisherian relationship in the model that links the nominal interest rate (R_t) to the real interest rate (r_t) and expected inflation $(E_t\pi_{t+1})$. Such a specification is critical to understanding the evolution of the nominal interest rate in the United States and other countries. The Fisher equation is

(5) $$R_t = r_t + E_t\pi_{t+1}.$$

In our study, this linkage will play a key role.

3.2.4   The Euler Equation

There is a transmission mechanism between real interest rates and real economic activity that includes additional expectational elements, because optimizing theories of consumption and investment suggest the importance of this feature and because both consumption and investment appear to be substantially influenced by expectations in the US economy. Expectations are important determinants of aggregate demand and output in a model with Keynesian features, such as ours. According to modern consumption theory, the expected growth rate of consumption should be related to the real interest rate, which we write as

(6) $$r_t = \sigma(E_t y_{t+1} - y_t) + r,$$

where $r > 0$ represents positive time preference. The "natural rate of interest" is defined as

(7) $$r_t^* = \sigma(E_t y_{t+1}^* - y_t^*) + r.$$

The capacity output process implies that the "natural rate of interest" evolves as

(8) $$r_t^* = \sigma\rho\Delta y_t^* + r,$$

---

4. Our model does not distinguish between consumption and investment, a key aspect of RBC models.

so that we have built in a positive comovement of the real interest rate and output growth present in studies of real business cycle (RBC) models with stochastic productivity trends.

3.2.5   The Term Structure of Interest Rates

The model contains the expectations theory of the term structure. While it has been criticized as an incomplete description of long-term yields, we think that the expectations theory nevertheless contains the essential features of bond-pricing for our purposes. In our model, we include specifications of the real and nominal returns on a long-term discount bond; that is, one with L periods to maturity. The first specification governs the real term structure,

$$(9) \qquad r_{Lt} = \frac{1}{L} \sum_{j=0}^{L-1} E_t r_{t+j} + (r_L - r) = \sigma \frac{1}{L} (E_t y_{t+L} - y_t) + r_L,$$

and the second specification governs the nominal term structure,

$$(10) \qquad R_{Lt} = \frac{1}{L} \sum_{j=0}^{L-1} E_t R_{t+j} = r_{Lt} + \frac{1}{L} \sum_{j=1}^{L} E_t \pi_{t+j}.$$

It is important to stress that longer-term yields reflect permanent variations, as these are dominant in such an expected future average. Accordingly, we will frequently employ the idea that variations in long-term nominal yields are dominated by "expected inflation trends."

3.3   Monetary Policy

We must specify the objectives of monetary policy in order to close the model. In this regard, Section 2A of the Federal Reserve Act says that "The Board of Governors of the Federal Reserve System and the Federal Open Market Committee shall maintain long run growth of the monetary and credit aggregates commensurate with the economy's long run potential to increase production, so as to promote effectively the goals of maximum employment, stable prices, and moderate long-term interest rates." In terms of our model, we translate the abovementioned goals into an "output gap stabilization objective" $y_t = y_t^*$, and "a low inflation objective" $\pi_t = \pi \approx 0$, noting that the low inflation objective takes care of the low long-term interest rate objective.

Interestingly enough, the title of the original Federal Reserve Act of 1913 emphasized a different set of objectives: "to furnish an elastic currency, to afford a means of rediscounting commercial paper, and to establish a more effective supervision of banking in the United States." At the time, the United States was on the gold standard, which itself maintained price stability, and the Federal Reserve was set up to provide financial stability. This it did, by improving banking supervision and by smoothing short-term interest rates. The period between the Civil War and the founding of the Federal Reserve was marked by a number of recessions associated with sudden, sharp, and sustained spikes in short-term interest rates. Interest rate spikes of over 10 percentage points occurred on eight occasions, four of which were associated with major banking panics in 1873, 1884, 1893, and 1907. By providing currency and bank reserves through its discount window or by buying securities in the open market, the Fed introduced a degree of continuity into short-term nominal interest rates and eliminated the kind of interest rate spikes seen earlier. Between 1890 and 1910, the three-month nominal rate was quickly mean-reverting and highly seasonal. By contrast, between 1920 and 1933, the three-month nominal rate was close to a random walk.[5]

"Continuity of the short rate" quickly became and has remained a routine feature of monetary policy. Short rate continuity is today reflected in the Fed's use of an interest rate policy instrument rather than a bank reserves policy instrument, and in the fact that the Fed likes to prepare markets for federal funds rate target changes. Interest rate continuity is reinforced by the fact that maintaining a given policy stance often means keeping the federal funds rate target fixed for months at a time.[6] Interest rate continuity is not mentioned explicitly, or even implicitly anymore, as an objective of the Federal Reserve partly because it is so widely accepted, and partly because until 1994 the Federal Reserve deliberately obscured its management of short-term interest rates to deflect public criticism for high interest rates produced periodically to control inflation.[7] Nevertheless, the Federal Reserve maintains a degree of short rate continuity as a matter of routine practice. The "interest rate continuity objective" in our model is an attenuation by the central bank of one-period-ahead forecast errors in the short-term nominal interest rate, $R_t - E_{t-1}R_t$.

To sum up, we think of the central bank as having three fundamental objectives: output gap stabilization, interest rate continuity, and low inflation. In retrospect, the lesson of the Great Moderation period following the Volcker disinflation of the early 1980s was that monetary policy best stabilizes the output gap and maintains low and stable interest rates by putting a priority on price stability. However, that lesson had not yet been learned during the Great Inflation. Our contention is that the failure of monetary policy in the Great Inflation was due, in part, to the inclination of central banks (including the Federal Reserve) to put stabilization of the output gap and continuity of the short-term interest rate ahead of price stability. This was understandable. Prior to the Great Inflation, inflation in the United States was relatively low. Protracted inflation had never before been a problem in the United States in peacetime. The importance of monetary policy

---

5. See Mankiw, Miron, and Weil (1987).
6. See Goodfriend (1991), Meltzer (2003), and Poole (1991).
7. Goodfriend (2003) and Meltzer (2003).

for inflation and inflation expectations was not then recognized fully. Later, the Fed lacked confidence that tight monetary policy could bring inflation down at any politically acceptable cost. We denote "business as usual" as the inclination of central banks to pursue output gap stabilization and interest rate continuity. We work out the implications of business-as-usual monetary policy for understanding the Great Inflation in the balance of the chapter.

3.4   Equilibrium Outcomes with "Business as Usual"

In this section we characterize the equilibrium behavior of inflation, output, and interest rates in a macromodel that combines New Keynesian pricing, the real business cycle core, the Fisher equation, the Euler equation, the term structure of interest rates, and business-as-usual monetary policy. The macroeconomic model that we develop gives rise to a time-varying trend rate of inflation, a "stochastic trend" component to inflation in the language of modern time series econometrics.

3.4.1   Trend Inflation Variability

To analyze the evolution of trend inflation, we begin by noting that the "law of iterated expectations" implies that

(11) $$\bar{\pi}_t = E_t \bar{\pi}_{t+1}$$

since $E_t \bar{\pi}_{t+1} = E_t[\lim_{k \to \infty} E_{t+1} \pi_{t+1+k}] = [\lim_{k \to \infty} E_t \pi_{t+1+k}] = \bar{\pi}_t$. This is a useful observation, as it allows us to write (2) as

(12) $$\pi_t = (1 - \beta)\bar{\pi}_t + \beta E_t \pi_{t+1} + h(y_t - y_t^*).$$

Hence, with a fixed or slowly evolving inflation trend, inflation at each point in time should resemble that under (1). For example, inflation should depend importantly on expected future output gaps, as stressed in much recent literature,

(13) $$\pi_t = \bar{\pi}_t + h \sum_{j=0}^{\infty} \beta^j E_t (y_{t+j} - y_{t+j}^*).$$

Thus, as one looks across various periods of high and low inflation, the general level of inflation would be fully explained by the trend.

To explore the origins of the inflation trend, suppose that the central bank fully stabilizes the output gap as part of its business-as-usual practices. Zero output gaps at all dates imply that

(14) $$\pi_t - \bar{\pi}_t = \beta(E_t \pi_{t+1} - E_t \bar{\pi}_{t+1})$$

mechanically from (2). However, since $\bar{\pi}_t = E_t \bar{\pi}_{t+1}$, this condition is equivalently that

(15) $$\pi_t = E_t \pi_{t+1} = \bar{\pi}_t.$$

A striking feature of this simple model is that inflation is *only* the stochastic trend. (We add a transitory component in section 3.7.1.) The simple model serves to stress that output stabilization delivers a stochastic trend in inflation.

Further, a well-known property of stochastic trends is that their changes are unpredictable, so that our inflation trend evolves according to

$$(16) \qquad \bar{\pi}_t = \bar{\pi}_{t-1} + \varepsilon_t,$$

with ε_t being a random shock—to be determined later—with the property that $E_{t-1}\varepsilon_t = 0$. In terms of the model characteristics that we stressed earlier, we note that the absence of a long-run trade-off means that a zero output gap is consistent with stochastically evolving trend inflation. Of course, zero trend inflation, or any other constant inflation trend, would imply a zero output gap. This would be the special case in which ε_t was always zero.

3.4.2   Innovations to the Inflation Trend

According to the previous derivation, output gap stabilization makes trend inflation variability possible. The variability of innovations to trend inflation, however, is governed by the other half of "business as usual," the degree of interest rate continuity. To see why, define the central bank's "interest rate continuity" parameter ϕ, where $0 < \phi < 1$ so that the degree of continuity increases with ϕ. Full stabilization of the output gap implies that $r_t = r_t^* = \sigma\rho\Delta y_t^* + r$ according to (8). We can write the consequences for the one-period-ahead forecast error for the nominal interest rate in terms of the forecast error in the natural rate of interest as

$$(17) \qquad R_t = E_{t-1}R_t + (1-\phi)(r_t^* - E_{t-1}r_t^*).$$

The Fisher equation (5) then implies that

$$(18) \qquad E_t\pi_{t+1} - E_{t-1}\pi_{t+1} = -\phi(r_t^* - E_{t-1}r_t^*).$$

Hence, the innovation ε_t in the stochastic inflation trend evolves as

$$(19) \qquad \varepsilon_t = \phi\sigma\rho v_t,$$

where $\sigma\rho v_t$ is the forecast error in the natural rate of interest, and ϕ controls the influence of shocks to capacity output v_t on trend inflation. In this basic model, ε_t is also the innovation to the inflation rate itself, although that need not be the case. (See the appendix.) Without any interest rate continuity ($\phi = 0$), there are no innovations to trend inflation and nominal interest rate forecast errors fully reflect forecast errors in the natural rate of interest. In this case trend inflation is constant over time at a level determined by historical conditions. With full interest rate continuity ($\phi = 1$), one-period-ahead nominal interest rate forecast errors are eliminated completely, since the ε_t

innovation to expected inflation is the negative of the $\sigma\rho\nu_t$ innovation to the natural interest rate.

As long as "business as usual" pursues some degree of interest rate continuity, trend inflation should rise in periods when the natural interest rate is surprisingly low. For example, surprisingly low productivity growth typically lowers real interest rates in real business cycle models, as it does here according to equations (4) and (8). In a richer dynamic model, many different kinds of shocks would produce innovations in the natural interest rate working through saving and investment: according to our theory, such shocks would also contribute to the variability of trend inflation.

In ways that are reminiscent of Goodfriend (1987) and Broadbent and Barro (1997), the central bank's concern for smoothing the nominal interest rate produces nonstationarity in a nominal variable. However, in our context this nominal variable is the inflation rate rather than the price level. With output always at capacity and short-term nominal interest rate forecast errors at least somewhat attenuated, the central bank gives up control of long-run inflation, allowing trend inflation to evolve through time as a random walk.

3.4.3   Comovement of Short-Term Interest and Inflation

Under the inflation process derived earlier, the effect of a real interest rate innovation on the path of the nominal interest rate is given by

(20)
$$E_t R_{t+j} - E_{t-1} R_{t+j}$$
$$= [E_t r^*_{t+j} - E_{t-1} r^*_{t+j}] + [E_t \pi_{t+j} - E_{t-1} \pi_{t+j}]$$
$$= [\rho^j - \phi]\rho\sigma\nu_t$$

for $j = 0,1,2,3,\ldots$ and $0 < \rho < 1$, with the coefficient $[\rho^j - \phi]\rho\sigma$ combining both real rate and expected inflation effects.

With full interest rate continuity ($\phi = 1$) a surprise increase in the current real interest rate is matched by an offsetting decrease in trend inflation, which leaves the current nominal short-term interest rate unchanged. Future nominal short rates then move gradually lower as the real natural interest rate returns asymptotically to its steady state r and the nominal interest rate moves permanently lower by $\rho\sigma\nu_t$. With partial interest rate continuity ($0 < \phi < 1$), a rise in the real rate can lead nearby nominal rates to rise while far away nominal rates fall.[8]

---

8. Gurkaynak, Sack, and Swanson (2005) find empirical support for this possibility with regard to US monetary policy in the period from 1990 to 2002. They report that forward rates at the short end of the yield curve increase following a surprise tightening of the federal funds rate (and decrease following a surprise easing). At longer horizons, however, they report that forward rates actually move in the direction opposite to that of the policy surprise; that is, a surprise policy tightening actually causes long-term forward rates to fall.

3.4.4   Term Structure Implications

The nominal long-bond rate would reflect the inflation effects more promptly than the short-bond rate. According to (10), the response of the L period long rate is

$$(21) \qquad R_{Lt} - E_{t-1}R_{Lt} = \frac{1}{L} \sum_{j=0}^{L-1} [E_t R_{t+j} - E_{t-1}R_{t+j}]$$

$$(22) \qquad = \frac{1}{L} \sum_{j=0}^{L-1} \{[E_t r^*_{t+j} - E_{t-1}r^*_{t+j}] + [E_t \pi_{t+j} - E_{t-1}\pi_{t+j}]\}$$

$$= \frac{1}{L} \sum_{j=0}^{L-1} [\rho^j - \phi]\rho\sigma v_t = \left[\frac{1}{L}\frac{1-\rho^L}{1-\rho} - \phi\right]\rho\sigma v_t.$$

The long-term interest rate would be a better indicator of movements in trend inflation than the short-term interest rate, with $R_{Lt} - E_{t-1}R_{Lt}$ approximately $-\phi\rho\sigma v_t = \bar{\pi}_t - \bar{\pi}_{t-1}$ for very long-term instruments.

3.5   Implementing "Business as Usual"

The consequences for inflation, output, and interest rates of "business as usual" were characterized in section 3.4 without saying anything about how the central bank's priorities for output gap stabilization and interest rate continuity could be implemented. We have four objectives in this section. First, we want to understand how business-as-usual priorities might be implemented with an interest rate rule. Second, we want to understand implementation in terms of a money growth rule. Third, we want to explain how a central bank, unaware of the effect of its business-as-usual priorities on trend inflation, could produce inadvertently the rational expectations equilibrium characterized in section 3.4. Fourth, we want to indicate how business-as-usual practices are susceptible to sudden, severe inflation surges capable of subordinating output gap stability and interest rate continuity to a priority for stabilizing inflation.

3.5.1   Implementation with an Interest Rate Rule

The interest rate rule

$$(23) \qquad R_t = \bar{\pi}_t + r^*_t + \Omega(\pi_t - \bar{\pi}_t)$$

can deliver business-as-usual outcomes under the "Taylor principle" condition $\Omega > 0$, as follows. The rule says that the central bank adjusts its nominal interest rate policy instrument R_t so that the real interest rate $R_t - \bar{\pi}_t$ responds to the gap between actual inflation and what is, in effect, a time-varying inflation target $\bar{\pi}_t$. In addition, the central bank adjusts $R_t - \bar{\pi}_t$ one-for-one with fluctuations in the natural real rate of interest r^*_t.

We start by describing how this rule might work practically in response to a change in economic conditions. Suppose a negative shock to capacity output $v_t < 0$ in equation (4) causes r_t^* to fall in equation (8). In order to implement interest rate continuity and attenuate the incipient fall in R_t, the central bank must increase $\bar{\pi}_t$ somewhat. The required increase in $\bar{\pi}_t$ will vary from $\sigma\rho v_t$ to zero as the central bank's interest-rate-continuity parameter ϕ varies from unity to zero. The increase in $\bar{\pi}_t$ makes the inflation gap negative at the initial π_t. If the response coefficient Ω is sufficiently large, so that $R_t - \bar{\pi}_t$ is very sensitive to the inflation gap, then equilibrium interest rate policy will push π_t arbitrarily close to $\bar{\pi}_t$. In fact, in this case the central bank responds to deviations of inflation from its time-varying inflation target sufficiently aggressively that these never take place. Instead, equilibrium inflation π_t jumps immediately and permanently by $\bar{\pi}_t - E_{t-1}\bar{\pi}_t = -\phi\sigma\rho v_t$. It follows from (23) that $R_t - \bar{\pi}_t = r_t^*$. Since inflation is a random walk in this case, $E_t\pi_{t+1} = \bar{\pi}_t$, we have that $R_t - E_t\pi_{t+1} = r_t^*$ and the real interest rate shadows perfectly the underlying natural real rate of interest so that $y_t = y_t^*$ and the output gap is stabilized fully.

Interest rate rule (23) is consistent with a unique, stable rational expectations equilibrium that we described earlier. Formally, combining interest rate rule (23) and Fisher equation (5), using the fact that $\bar{\pi}_t = E_t\bar{\pi}_{t+1}$, we find that $E_t\pi_{t+1} - E_t\bar{\pi}_{t+1} = \Omega(\pi_t - \bar{\pi}_t)$. Then, the stable forward-looking solution is $\pi_t = \bar{\pi}_t$, the business-as-usual equilibrium we derived in section 3.4.

3.5.2   Implementation with a Money Growth Rule

The money growth rule

(24) $$\Delta m_t^S = (\alpha - \phi\sigma\rho)v_t + \alpha\rho\Delta y_{t-1}^* + \pi_{t-1}$$

delivers business-as-usual objectives in a model that includes equations (2) through (7) augmented to include money demand function $\Delta m_t^D = \alpha\Delta y_t + \pi_t$, money growth rule (24), and a money market equilibrium condition $\Delta m_t^D = \Delta m_t^S$.

Suppose initially that the central bank wishes only to stabilize the output gap and sets $\phi = 0$. To do so, the central bank would move the current money stock with αv_t so that money market clearing makes current aggregate demand y_t conform to movements in capacity output y_t^* at the going inflation rate. To stabilize the output gap in the future, the central bank must make future money growth conform to future movements in money demand at capacity output and initial trend inflation. The required future money growth is reflected in the $\alpha\rho\Delta y_{t-1}^*$ term in (24). Future money growth would mirror the return of capacity output to its long-run growth path scaled by the income elasticity of money demand, α. In this case, the nominal interest rate would shadow the real natural rate associated with the shock v_t. Monetary policy would stabilize the output gap fully and perpetuate the initial inflation trend.

If the central bank also seeks to implement interest rate continuity with

$0 < \phi < 1$, it must attenuate one-period-ahead forecast errors in the nominal interest rate by making expected inflation covary negatively with the shock to capacity output v_t. The central bank can do this by promising to make future money growth covary negatively with v_t. Consider a negative shock to v_t. Seeing higher money growth coming, firms expect inflation to rise, and higher expected inflation stabilizes the short nominal rate against the negative shock to the real rate. Let the money growth rule continue to make y_t conform to y_t^* as discussed earlier. In this equilibrium, firms pass higher expected inflation through one-for-one to current inflation. The pass-through shows up as the $-\phi\sigma\rho v_t$ term in (24), which reflects the natural real interest rate innovation, $\sigma\rho v_t$, multiplied by the central bank's interest-rate-continuity parameter ϕ. This term reflects the effect of higher π_t on current money demand that the central bank must accommodate to continue to stabilize y_t at y_t^*. The lagged π_{t-1} term present in the money growth rule is there so that money growth in period $t + 1$ and thereafter perpetuates the elevated period t inflation trend required to stabilize the output gap.

3.5.3   How "Business as Usual" Creates Inflation Drift

Is it possible that a central bank in pursuit of output gap stabilization and interest rate continuity could push an economy unknowingly into the equilibrium with stochastic trend inflation characterized in section 3.4? This is an important question to ask because there is little evidence that central banks, during the Great Inflation, thought of themselves as managing inflation expectations deliberately with either an interest rate rule or a money growth rule to implement business-as-usual objectives. We answer the question in the affirmative below, showing how the public's rational expectations drive the stochastic trend in inflation, which the central bank happily accommodates in the pursuit of its business-as-usual priorities.

To understand how business-as-usual monetary policy inadvertently puts a stochastic trend in the inflation rate, imagine that initially the inflation rate is low and stable and is expected to remain so at $E\hat\pi$. Imagine also that the economy is subject to shocks to capacity output. Initially, suppose that the sole objective of monetary policy is to stabilize the output gap; that is, $\phi = 0$. In this case, the central bank would not distinguish between nominal and real interest rates; it would regard its management of the short-term *nominal* rate as equivalent to management of the short-term *real* interest rate. With no continuity restrictions, the central bank would move R_t so that $R_t - E\hat\pi = r_t^*$ at all times. For instance, the central bank would respond to a negative v_t shock to capacity output by matching the initial fall in the real natural rate r_t^* with its nominal interest rate policy instrument R_t, and shadowing the real natural rate as it moved back gradually to its steady state level r, according to equations (4) and (8). If the central bank focused exclusively on stabilizing the output gap, there would be no reason for inflation to be destabilized. Inflation, inflation expectations, and trend inflation all would remain firmly anchored at $E\hat{\pi}$. The long-term interest rate would remain firmly anchored as well.

However, matters change if the central bank pursues a degree of interest-rate continuity, $0 < \phi < 1$, in addition to stabilizing the output gap. Now the central bank would attenuate somewhat the initial response of R_t to v_t. For instance, the central bank would respond to a negative v_t shock with an attenuated cut in R_t so that $R_t - E\hat{\pi} > r_t^*$. Interest continuity thereby would push current aggregate demand below current capacity output. To stabilize the output gap, the central bank would compensate for the insufficient contemporaneous interest rate cut by steering the interest rate somewhat *below* real natural interest rates in the future. Doing that, however, would push future aggregate demand *above* the path of future capacity output.

All this presumes that inflation, expected inflation, and trend inflation remain anchored at $E\hat{\pi}$. But there is a problem: steering future real interest rates below real natural rates pushes future aggregate demand above capacity output. New Keynesian pricing implies that the prospect of negative expected future output gaps would elevate future inflation. Hence, we would no longer have a rational expectations equilibrium. The public would catch on to the fact that a negative shock to capacity output would be followed by higher inflation. Rationally expected future inflation would rise with negative shocks to capacity output.

But this is not the end of the story. Elevated expected inflation $E_t\pi_{t+1}$ in response to $v_t < 0$ would deepen the contemporaneous real interest rate cut $r_t = R_t - E_t\pi_{t+1} < R_t - E\hat{\pi}$, for any given degree of interest-rate continuity ϕ. A deeper real rate cut, in turn, would allow the central bank to steer interest-rate policy closer to real natural rates in the future. In the limit, the economy converges to a rational expectations equilibrium response in which expected inflation would rise enough to push the current real interest rate all the way down to the current real natural interest rate. At this point, the central bank would stabilize the output gap fully because its nominal interest rate instrument (adjusted for elevated expected inflation) would perfectly shadow the natural real interest rate. Moreover, with the output gap stabilized fully, actual and expected rates of inflation would rise initially, identically, and permanently in response to a shock to capacity output. So, we see how the central bank's commitment to business-as-usual priorities and the public's incentive to form expectations of inflation rationally push the economy into the equilibrium with stochastic trend inflation characterized in section 3.4.

3.6   Empirical Implications of "Business as Usual"

Our model of business-as-usual monetary policy has the following empirical implications that we put to work in section 3.7 to help understand the Great Inflation:

1. Inflation is a random walk with a transitory component.

2. The random walk in inflation is driven by innovations to the natural interest rate, which are produced by shocks to the growth of capacity output in our model.

3. The variance of the permanent shock to inflation is directly related to the degree of interest-rate continuity pursued by the central bank and the variance and autocorrelation of shocks to the natural interest rate; it is inversely related to the intertemporal elasticity of substitution in consumption.

4. Short-term interest-rate continuity puts a random walk component in the long-term interest rate.

5. Real interest rate and inflation rate innovations are negatively correlated due to interest-rate smoothing.

6. Long-term interest rates lead short-term interest rates.

7. The powerful incentive for a central bank to pursue business-as-usual priorities when inflation is well behaved means that *low* inflation should inherit a stochastic trend from shocks to capacity output, though the variance of the stochastic trend may be small.

We also see the Great Inflation as overlain with "inflation fighting episodes" in which the Federal Reserve sought to restrain inflation by reducing real output. We do not specify a model that determines when the Fed sought to contain inflation, but our theory of trend inflation nevertheless makes predictions about the connections between business-as-usual monetary policy and episodes of inflation fighting. The connections that we see are:

8. A prolonged series of particularly severe, cumulative negative shocks to the growth of capacity output should be associated with (a) sharply rising inflation, (b) rising long-term interest rates, and (c) rising short-term interest rates that lag the rise in long-term rates. The rise in trend inflation could trigger a shift of priorities from "business as usual" to "inflation fighting."

9. "Inflation fighting" that makes progress against inflation should precipitate a recession if there is imperfect credibility. However, a return to "business as usual" would reverse the gains against inflation quickly in the presence of ongoing negative shocks to capacity output. Episodes of "inflation fighting" would thereby contribute to the variability of the stochastic inflation trend.

10. The marginal predictive content of the output gap for inflation should deteriorate in a period of low and stable inflation relative to a period of high and variable inflation because "business as usual" predominates in the former period and the latter period is apt to contain episodes of "inflation fighting."

3.7   Understanding the Great Inflation

We draw on a variety of evidence to understand the Great Inflation in terms of our business-as-usual model of monetary policy. First, we show that the statistical time-series model of US inflation identified and estimated by Stock and Watson (2007) is predicted by our model. Second, we use a measure of aggregate technology change for the United States constructed by Basu, Fernald, and Kimball (2006), together with Romer and Romer (1989) inflation-fighting dates, and time series for inflation and the term structure of interest rates, to show that these data behave as predicted by our model preceding periods when the Federal Reserve made "inflation fighting" a priority. Third, we emphasize that the attachment to "business as usual" predicts the "stop and go" character of monetary policy during the Great Inflation documented and studied by Shapiro (1994), in which the gains against inflation achieved during periods of fighting inflation were short-lived. Fourth, we explain why our model of monetary policy predicts the post-Great Inflation deterioration of predictive content of the output gap for inflation found by Atkeson and Ohanian (2001) and confirmed by Stock and Watson (2007).

3.7.1   A Statistical Time-Series Model of US Inflation

In their 2007 study of the statistical behavior of US inflation from the 1950s to 2004, Stock and Watson find that a "univariate inflation process is well described by an unobserved component trend-cycle model with stochastic volatility or, equivalently, an integrated moving average [IMA] process with time-varying parameters."[9] They report that the model explains a variety of recent forecasting puzzles and begins to explain some multivariate inflation forecasting puzzles as well. Their statistical model is implied by our business-as-usual model of monetary policy as follows.

In section 3.4, we utilized the New Keynesian pricing equation (2) without a shock term to highlight the random walk implication of our model: $\pi_t = \bar{\pi}_t$ and $\bar{\pi}_t = \bar{\pi}_{t-1} + \varepsilon_t$. However, standard practice is to add a white noise shock to the inflation equation, say η_t. Then, since η_t is unforecastable, the inflation solution becomes $\pi_t = \bar{\pi}_t + \eta_t$, where $\bar{\pi}_t = \bar{\pi}_{t-1} + \varepsilon_t$ under business-as-usual assumptions of output at capacity and interest-rate continuity.

In purely statistical terms, the Stock and Watson findings of a unit root in π_t, with negative first-order autocorrelations, and generally small higher-order autocorrelations of $\Delta\pi_t$, suggest that the inflation process is well described by the IMA (1, 1) process

(25) $$\Delta\pi_t = (1 - \Lambda B)a_t,$$

---

9. Stock and Watson (2007, 3).

where Λ is positive, a_t is serially uncorrelated with mean zero and variance σ_a^2, and B is a backshift operator.

Stock and Watson point out that the IMA(1, 1) statistical model is observationally equivalent to an unobserved components model in which π_t has a stochastic trend τ_t and a serially uncorrelated disturbance η_t:

(26) $\pi_t = \tau_t + \eta_t$, η_t serially uncorrelated $(0, \sigma_\eta^2)$

(27) $\tau_t = \tau_{t-1} + \varepsilon_t$, ε_t serially uncorrelated $(0, \sigma_\varepsilon^2)$,

where cov $(\eta_t, \varepsilon_j) = 0$ for all j.

Thus, our theoretical model implies the statistical model of inflation developed by Stock and Watson, and we can interpret aspects of their statistical analysis from the perspective of our model.

Stock and Watson report IMA(1, 1) parameters and the implied unobservable components parameters, as well as a variety of other statistics estimated using quarterly US inflation data from the 1950s to 2004 for a variety of inflation indexes. Broadly speaking, the findings are similar for all the indexes. For our purposes, the main findings are these: (a) inflation is driven by a random walk component τ_t plus a transitory component η_t; (b) a time-varying estimate of the standard deviation of the permanent innovation $\sigma_{\varepsilon,t}$ is 0.5 (percentage points at an annual rate) in the 1950s through the mid-1960s, rises sharply to a peak of 1.4 in the mid-1970s, falls gradually back below 0.5 by the mid-1980s, and settles below 0.2 after the mid-1990s; (c) a time-varying estimate of the standard deviation of the transitory innovation $\sigma_{\eta,t}$ is around 0.5 from the 1950s to 2004.

From this statistical perspective, the Great Inflation is a story about the "Great Inflation Drift" in the sense that the elevated variance of inflation during the great inflation period is entirely due to large increases in the variance of the innovation of the stochastic trend component driving inflation. Importantly, Stock and Watson point out that although the estimated variance of the permanent innovation in inflation diminished in statistical and economic importance since the mid-1980s, the confidence intervals for the largest AR root continue to include one, so that there is evidence of continuing trend variability for inflation.

Stock and Watson's statistical model of the inflation process supports three empirical predictions of our model listed in section 3.6. First, US inflation is characterized parsimoniously, and consistently, as a random walk with a transitory component. This is in keeping with our view that "business as usual" has been the predominant mode of monetary policy behavior, and that it induces a stochastic trend in inflation in the presence of shocks to capacity output. Second, the increased variability of inflation during the Great Inflation shows up as an increase in the variability of the innovation in the stochastic trend component, as our model of monetary policy predicts.

Third, inflation through 2004 still contains a small stochastic trend, which our model predicts should reflect the Federal Reserve's inclination to pursue business-as-usual priorities for output gap stabilization and continuity of the short rate when inflation is low.

3.7.2   From "Business as Usual" to "Fighting Inflation"

Our model suggests that business-as-usual monetary policy can be sustained indefinitely with low and reasonably stable inflation if the shocks to capacity output are small, especially if the central bank implements relatively little interest rate continuity so that ϕ is not too large. Nevertheless, business as usual exposes inflation to considerable variability if shocks to capacity output become large and happen to cumulate in one direction or another for a period of time. The public can tolerate a considerable range of inflation drift as long as it is relatively gradual and "orderly." As an operational matter, the central bank can continue to pursue business-as-usual objectives effectively as long as trend inflation does not drift too violently. However, a particularly severe series of cumulative negative shocks to capacity output has the potential to drive inflation, expected inflation, trend inflation, and the long-term interest rate all suddenly and sharply higher, even if all had been well-behaved for years. If inflation drifts upward too far, too fast in a "disorderly" manner, then business as usual may become unsustainable. The public may demand that inflation be contained and the central bank may be unable to execute stabilization policy effectively in the absence of a nominal anchor.

When such developments cause output gap stability and interest-rate continuity to be subordinated to containing inflation, the central bank is forced to switch from business as usual to fighting inflation. The central bank fights inflation by raising its nominal interest rate policy instrument above expected inflation in order to elevate longer-term real interest rates according to (9) to depress aggregate demand below capacity. According to New Keynesian pricing, given the expected rate of inflation, the central bank must sustain an output gap in order to make progress against inflation.[10] Once inflation is stabilized, even without much (if any) reduction, pressure builds quickly for the central bank to revert to business as usual in order to close the output gap and stabilize interest rates again. Thus, our business-as-usual model of monetary policy predicts that a period of large, cumulative negative shocks to capacity output is likely to precipitate a cycling of monetary policy priorities with upward inflation drift interrupted periodically but temporarily by deliberately contractionary monetary policy. We explore this idea next, although it goes beyond the implications of our theory.

---

10. Goodfriend and King (2005) analyze the mechanics of fighting inflation in a closely related model.

3.7.3   Factors Precipitating Inflation Fighting

Romer and Romer (1989) document that the Federal Reserve tightened monetary policy decisively to fight inflation on six occasions since World War II. These episodes began respectively in October 1947, September 1955, December 1968, April 1974, August 1978, and October 1979. Only two significant increases in unemployment were not preceded by Fed action to fight inflation. One occurred in 1954 after the Korean War and the second occurred in 1961, after the Fed tightened monetary policy to improve the international balance of payments. The two earliest Romer dates were part of a series of Fed policy actions through the mid-1960s that kept inflation relatively low on average. We are interested in the remaining four Romer dates, those that occurred during the Great Inflation.

We interpret Romer dates as instances when the Federal Reserve switched from business as usual to fighting inflation. Our model predicts that periods of business as usual preceding Romer dates should exhibit (a) sharply rising inflation, (b) a sequence of severe cumulative negative shocks to the growth of capacity output, (c) rising long-term interest rates, and (d) rising short-term interest rates lagging long rates. To check whether the Romer dates are precipitated as predicted, we employ an annual time-series measure of technological progress in the United States constructed by Basu, Fernald, and Kimball (2006, BFK series) that controls for aggregation effects, varying utilization of capital and labor, nonconstant returns, and imperfect competition. We utilize the BFK series in conjunction with data on inflation and the term structure of interest rates, all shown in figures 3.1 through 3.5 at the end of the chapter, to check whether the evidence supports the predictions of our model for each of the Romer dates in the Great Inflation. As discussed later, the evidence is broadly consistent with the predictions of our model.

December 1968

Inflation averaged about 1.5 percent at an annual rate in the first half of the 1960s, and surged at the start of the Great Inflation in 1965 to around 3 percent in 1966. Inflation stabilized briefly in the first half of 1967 after the Federal Reserve tightened monetary policy briefly, but surged again to around 4.5 percent by the first Romer date of the Great Inflation in December 1968. A number of explanations have been offered to explain the start of the Great Inflation: for example, excessive Federal spending to finance the Vietnam buildup, insufficient Federal Reserve independence, and a willingness to tolerate higher inflation in the belief that it might bring unemployment down according to the Phillips curve.[11] Our interest, however, is to check whether the December 1968 switch to fighting inflation is preceded, in addition to the sharp rise in inflation, by the three other factors

---

11. For instance, see Meltzer (2005) and references contained therein.

identified by our business-as-usual model of monetary policy. As predicted, BFK technology growth slows sharply from 1964 to 1969. The ten-year government bond rate moved up from 4 percent in 1966 to nearly 6 percent in 1968, indicating that 2 percentage points of the inflation surge prior to December 1968 was regarded as permanent. Finally, starting at 4 percent at the end of 1966, the federal funds rate clearly lagged the ten-year rate rise prior to December 1968.

April 1974

Inflation rose sharply from around 3 percent in mid-1973 to nearly 10 percent by the April 1974 Romer date, exacerbated by the first oil shock and the relaxation of price controls. Again, BFK technology growth slows sharply in the period preceding the 1974 Romer date. The ten-year bond rate moved up from about 6 percent in late 1972 to around 7.5 percent in April 1974, reversing the decline achieved during the previous period of inflation fighting beginning in December 1968, indicating that only 2 percentage points of the surge in inflation was then regarded as permanent. Finally, starting from around 4 percent in late 1972, the federal funds rate briefly lagged the ten-year rate on the way up, but passed the bond rate in 1973 and reached around 10 percent by April 1974.

August 1978

In early 1977, inflation settled at around 6 percent as a result of the inflation fighting begun in April 1974. Inflation began to move up once more in 1978, however, rising to around 7 percent by the August 1978 Romer date. Once more, BFK technology growth slows sharply in the period preceding the Romer date. The ten-year bond rate fell back to around 7.5 percent in mid-1977 as a result of the inflation fighting begun in April 1974. The ten-year rate then rose sharply by around 1 percentage point to around 8.5 percent by the 1978 Romer date, indicating that 1 percentage point of the upward inflation drift was regarded as permanent. Finally, starting from around 5 percent in mid-1977, the federal funds rate lagged the rising long rate, but again caught up around the Romer date.

October 1979

The period from August 1978 to the Romer date of October 1979 saw inflation surge from 7 percent to around 9.5 percent. And again, as predicted by our model, BFK technology growth in 1979 was surprisingly weak, lengthening the period of surprisingly slow growth of technology that preceded the August 1978 Romer date. The ten-year rate moved up by another 1 percentage point to October 1979, indicating that 1 percentage point of the inflation surge was regarded as permanent. In this case, however, starting roughly in line with the ten-year rate in August 1979, the federal funds rate actually led the long rate up as part of the inflation-fighting policy actions undertaken in the wake of the August 1978 Romer date. Then, on the October 1979 Romer date the Fed moved the federal funds rate sharply higher than the long-term interest rate to 13.5 percent.

3.7.4   Stop-and-Go Monetary Policy

Looking at the record before and after Romer dates, there is a recurrent pattern highlighted previously by Shapiro (1994). It is clear that the Romer dates initiate periods of inflation fighting in that they are all preceded by sharply higher inflation and followed by sharply higher short-term interest rates engineered by the Fed relative to long-term interest rates. Nevertheless, within two or three years inflation is no lower than when the period of "inflation fighting" began, indicating that these inflation-fighting episodes were meant only to contain inflation temporarily or that they were aborted attempts at reducing the inflation rate. For instance, the pattern is evident with respect to the inflation-fighting periods initiated by the December 1968 and April 1974 Romer dates. The Fed initiated recessions in 1970 and 1973 to 1975 as part of its inflation-fighting actions. And these recessions brought down inflation, trend inflation, and long bond rates. However, these gains were reversed within a few years.

Our model of monetary policy predicts that stop-and-go policy should be an integral part of a period of protracted inflation driven by recurring cumulative negative shocks to technology such as we saw during the Great Inflation. According to the model, business-as-usual priorities exposed the US economy to upward inflation drift due to unexpectedly slow growth of technology during the Great Inflation years. On a few occasions, a series of especially large negative shocks to technology growth pushed inflation, expected inflation, and long-term interest rates up sharply and precipitated a period of inflation fighting. The model predicts that inflation, inflation expectations, and long-term interest rates could be brought down *only* by creating a protracted recession; that is, by creating an output gap of enough size and duration to induce a disinflation in line with New Keynesian pricing. Thus, the model predicts that the stabilization of inflation would create pressure for monetary policy to end the accompanying recession and return to business as usual. The return to business as usual would expose the economy once more to upward inflation drift in the presence of unexpectedly slow growth of technology. Our view, then, is that the Fed's attachment to business-as-usual priorities, in conjunction with negative productivity growth shocks, is central to understanding the tremendous output and employment volatility during the Great Inflation.

3.7.5   Predictive Content of the Output Gap for Inflation

A striking statistical finding emphasized by Atkeson and Ohanian (2001) and confirmed by Stock and Watson (2007) is that the marginal predictive content of output-gap variables for inflation has deteriorated dramatically since 1984. Specifically, Atkeson and Ohanian compare the accuracy of inflation forecasts augmented with three different output-gap variables to a naive forecast that at any date inflation will be the same over the next year as it has been over the last year. They find that none of the forecasts is more accurate than the naive forecast, which is essentially a random walk forecast of inflation. Stock and Watson (2007) investigate the marginal predictive content of output-gap variables for inflation in more detail by augmenting a benchmark univariate forecasting model with a variety of measures and specifications of gap variables, and by comparing the marginal predictive content of the gap variables for two sample periods—a Great Inflation sample period from 1970 to 1983, and a Great Moderation sample period from 1984 to 2004.

Stock and Watson report that the relative performance of gap forecasts deteriorated substantially from the first period to the second. For example, during the 1970 to 1983 period at the four-quarter horizon, an inflation forecast augmented with an unemployment rate gap outperformed a univariate inflation autoregression benchmark with a relative mean square forecast error of 0.88. But during the 1984 to 2004 period it performed worse than the benchmark, with a relative mean squared forecast error (MSFE) of 1.48. Stock and Watson report that the change in relative performance is even larger at the eight-quarter horizon. The deterioration of output-gap forecasts is found for all activity predictors examined. The poor performance of gap variables is not simply a consequence of failing to allow for a time-varying nonaccelerating inflation rate of unemployment (NAIRU) or time-varying potential GDP. Finally, Stock and Watson report that the Atkeson and Ohanian naive (random walk) forecast substantially improves upon the abovementioned forecasts at the four- and eight-quarter horizons in the 1984 to 2004 period, but not at shorter horizons and not in the first period.

We regard the changing informativeness of the output gap for future inflation as important evidence in support of our business-as-usual model of monetary policy. Given the central bank's incentive to pursue business-as-usual priorities when inflation is low and stable, and to allow inflation to drift around, we would have expected the output gap to have much less predictive content for inflation during the Great Moderation than during the Great Inflation. Even though business as usual was also the predominant mode of Federal Reserve behavior during the Great Inflation, the Fed was then forced into fighting inflation on four Romer-date occasions. The output gap had great predictive content for inflation during the inflation fighting episodes because the Fed then deliberately created output gaps to contain inflation and bring it down. Thus, on the basis of our theoretical model one would not be surprised to learn that the Great Inflation sample period displays predictive content of output gaps for inflation far in excess of that evident during the Great Moderation.

3.8   Conclusion

The Great Inflation in the United States can be characterized statistically as a period in which a highly-volatile stochastic inflation trend exhibited fifteen years of predominantly positive innovations. We showed that a simple textbook macroeconomic model implies that a stochastic inflation trend arises if the central bank seeks to maintain output at a capacity level that varies through time, and also places weight on continuity of the short-term interest rate. Both of these features were, we believe, important components of Federal Reserve behavior. In our model, rising inflation results from a combination of bad policy and bad luck. The presence of stochastic trend inflation results from bad policy, which perpetuates inflation shocks. Our model identifies the relevant shocks as those that reduce the growth of capacity output and the natural real interest rate. We emphasized the effect of shocks to productivity growth on capacity output, but other real factors are relevant for the evolution of capacity output, including shifts in distortionary taxes and regulations. We found evidence of bad luck in that productivity growth was indeed surprisingly and especially slow during episodes of sharply rising inflation during the period.[12]

One reason for studying the Great Inflation is to prevent its recurrence. Our interpretation of the period suggests that a preoccupation with short-term interest rates and with maintaining output at capacity would, in the presence of adverse shocks to the growth of capacity output, combine to produce another period of inflation drift with similarly adverse consequences for employment and output.

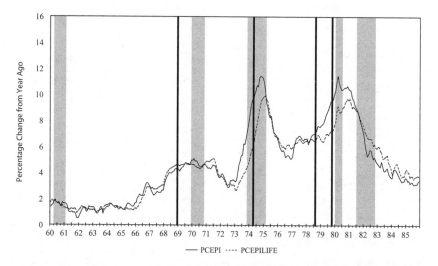

Fig. 3.1   Personal consumption expenditures chain-type price index (PCEPI) and consumption expenditures chain-type price index less food and energy (PCEPILIFE)
Notes: Vertical lines indicate "Romer dates." Shaded areas indicate NBER recessions. Dates are under First Month of Year; tick marks are every three months.

12. Other theories of the origin and nature of the Great Inflation would also suggest a link between real slowdowns and rising trend inflation (see, e.g., Orphanides 2003). An important task of future research is to distinguish empirically between competing theories.

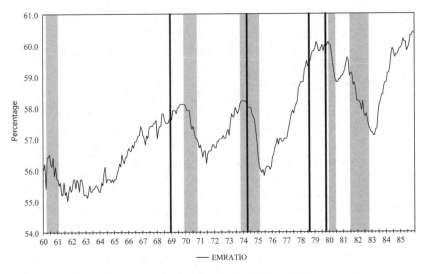

Fig. 3.2   Civilian employment-population ratio (EMRATIO)

Notes: Vertical lines indicate "Romer dates." Shaded areas indicate NBER recessions. Dates are under First Month of Year; tick marks are every three months.

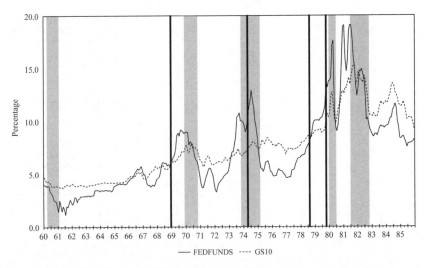

Fig. 3.3   Effective Federal funds rate (FEDFUNDS) and Ten-year Treasury constant maturity rate (GS10)

Notes: Vertical lines indicate "Romer dates." Shaded areas indicate NBER recessions. Dates are under First Month of Year; tick marks are every three months.

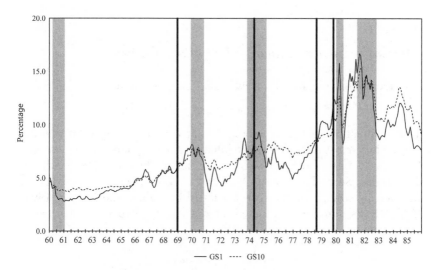

Fig. 3.4   One-year Treasury constant maturity rate (GS1) and Ten-year Treasury constant maturity rate (GS10)

Notes: Vertical lines indicate "Romer dates." Shaded areas indicate NBER recessions. Dates are under First Month of Year; tick marks are every three months.

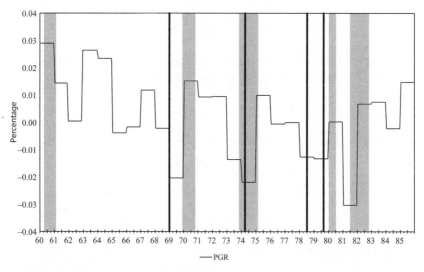

Fig. 3.5   Productivity growth rate (PGR)

Notes: Vertical lines indicate "Romer dates." Shaded areas indicate NBER recessions. Dates are under First Month of Year; tick marks are every three months.

Appendix
Alternative Specifications of the Phillips Curve

Consider modifying the New Keynesian Phillips curve to

$$\pi_t = (1 - \theta) E_t \pi_{t+1} + \theta \pi_{t-1} + h(y_t - y_t^*).$$

This formulation nests two popular Phillips curve specifications that display no long-run trade-off between inflation and output relative to capacity. First, with $\theta = 0$, there is a Phillips curve implied by Calvo (1983) with no discounting. Second, with $0 < \theta < 1$, there is a Phillips curve with structural inflation persistence of the sort developed by Fuhrer and Moore (1995). Under the assumption that there is no output gap, we can rewrite the previous equation as

$$\pi_{t+1} = \frac{1}{1 - \theta} \pi_t - \frac{1}{1 - \theta} \pi_{t-1} + \xi_{t+1},$$

where ξ_{t+1} is a random shock with the property that $E_t \xi_{t+1} = 0$. Subtracting π_t from both sides and lagging the result by a period implies the following first-difference, first-order autoregressive process for the evolution of inflation

$$\pi_t - \pi_{t-1} = \frac{\theta}{1 - \theta}(\pi_{t-1} - \pi_{t-2}) + \xi_t,$$

which has a stable rational expectations solution if $\theta < 1/2$. The forecast revisions for changes in inflation are given by

$$E_t \Delta \pi_{t+j} - E_{t-1} \Delta \pi_{t+j} = \left(\frac{\theta}{1 - \theta} \right)^j \xi_t,$$

and those for the levels of inflation are

$$E_t \pi_{t+j} - E_{t-1} \pi_{t+j} = \left[\sum_{h=0}^{j} \left(\frac{\theta}{1 - \theta} \right)^h \right] \xi_t$$

$$= \frac{1 - \theta}{1 - 2\theta} \left[1 - \left(\frac{\theta}{1 - \theta} \right)^{j+1} \right] \xi_t.$$

Thus, the inflation trend evolves as

$$\bar{\pi}_t = \bar{\pi}_{t-1} + \lim_{j \to \infty} \{ E_t \pi_{t+j} - E_{t-1} \pi_{t+j} \}$$

$$= \bar{\pi}_{t-1} - \frac{1 - \theta}{1 - 2\theta} \xi_t.$$

We continue to assume there is no output gap so that the actual real interest rate evolves as the natural interest rate according to equation (8) in the text. Then, we use the Fisher equation (5) to decompose the one-period-ahead forecast error in the short-term nominal interest rate as

$$R_t - E_{t-1}R_t = (r_t^* - E_{t-1}r_t^*) + (E_t\pi_{t+1} - E_{t-1}\pi_{t+1}).$$

Using the "continuity of the short rate" policy rule (17),

$$R_t - E_{t-1}R_t = (1 - \phi)(r_t^* - E_{t-1}r_t^*),$$

and the Phillips curve formulation with no output gap given at the start of the appendix, we write

$$\xi_t = -\phi(1 - \theta)(r_t^* - E_{t-1}r_t^*).$$

Finally, we use equations (4) and (8) to express the inflation innovation in terms of the shock to capacity output growth

$$\xi_t = -\phi(1 - \theta)\sigma\rho v_t.$$

There are two points to be made about the formulation of the Phillips curve given in this appendix. First, it allows for a time-varying inflation trend when $\theta = 0$ even though a trend does not enter directly into the specification of the Phillips curve. Inflation is only the stochastic trend in this case, as in the model studied in the body of the chapter. Second, with structural inflation persistence ($0 < \theta < 1/2$), there is potentially much greater variability of trend inflation in response to natural interest rate shocks than implied by the specification of the Phillips curve given in section 3.2. However, in this case the inflation rate converges gradually over time to the new inflation trend after a shock because inflation evolves thoeretically as a first-difference, first-order autoregressive process. It is worth noting that this latter theory of inflation is inconsistent with Stock and Watson's (2007) finding that actual inflation is best modeled statistically as a first-difference, first-order moving average process. Of course, actual inflation time series may contain a first-difference autoregressive component that is hard to identify statistically in the data.

References

Atkeson, Andrew, and Lee E. Ohanian. 2001. "Are Phillips Curves Useful for Forecasting Inflation?" *Federal Reserve Bank of Minneapolis Quarterly Review* (Winter):2–11. http://www.mpls.frb.org/research/qr/qr2511.html.
Basu, Susanto, John G. Fernald, and Miles Kimball. 2006. "Are Technology Improvements Contractionary?" *American Economic Review* 96 (5):1418–48.
Beveridge, Stephen, and Charles R. Nelson. 1981. "A New Approach to Decomposition of Economic Time Series into Permanent and Transitory Components with Particular Attention to Measurement of the Business Cycle." *Journal of Monetary Economics* 7:151–74.

Board of Governors of the Federal Reserve. 1970–1979. Federal Reserve Act. http://www.federalreserve.gov/aboutthefed/section2a.htm.

Broadbent, Ben, and Robert J. Barro. 1997. "Central Bank Preferences and Macroeconomic Equilibrium." *Journal of Monetary Economics* 39 (1): 17–43.

Calvo, G. A. 1983. "Staggered Prices in a Utility Maximizing Framework." *Journal of Monetary Economics* 12:383–98.

Fuhrer, Jeffrey C., and George R. Moore. 1995. "Inflation Persistence." *Quarterly Journal of Economics* 110:127–59.

Goodfriend, Marvin. 1987. "Interest Rate Smoothing and Price Level Trend-Stationarity." *Journal of Monetary Economics* 19:335–48.

———. 1991. "Interest Rates and the Conduct of Monetary Policy." *Carnegie-Rochester Conference Series on Public Policy* 34:7–30.

———. 2002. "Monetary Policy in the New Neoclassical Synthesis: A Primer." *International Finance* 5:165–92. (Reprinted in 2004 in Federal Reserve Bank of Richmond *Economic Quarterly* 90(3): 21–45.)

———. 2003. "Book Review." In *A History of the Federal Reserve Volume I: 1913–1951,* by Allan H. Meltzer. Federal Reserve Bank of Minneapolis, *The Region* 17 (December): 82–89.

Goodfriend, Marvin, and Robert G. King. 1997. "The New Neoclassical Synthesis and the Role of Monetary Policy." In *NBER Macroeconomics Annual 1997,* edited by B. S. Bernanke and J. J. Rotemberg, 231–82. Cambridge, MA: MIT Press.

———. 2005. "The Incredible Volcker Disinflation." *Journal of Monetary Economics* 52:981–1015.

Gurkaynak, Refet S., Brian Sack, and Eric Swanson. 2005. "The Sensitivity of Long-Term Interest Rates to Economic News: Evidence and Implications for Macroeconomic Models." *American Economic Review* 95 (1): 425–36.

Mankiw, N. G., Jeffrey Miron, and David Weil. 1987. "The Adjustment of Expectations to a Change in Regime: A Study of the Founding of the Federal Reserve." *American Economic Review* 77:358–71.

Meltzer, Allan. 2003. *A History of the Federal Reserve Volume 1:1913–1951.* Chicago: University of Chicago Press.

———. 2005. "Origins of the Great Inflation." In Conference on Reflections on Monetary Policy 25 Years after October 1979, October. *Federal Reserve Bank of St. Louis Review,* March–April, part 2, 145–75.

Nelson, Charles R., and Charles I. Plosser. 1982. "Trends and Random Walks in Macroeconomic Time Series." *Journal of Monetary Economics* 10:139–62.

Nelson, Charles R., and G. William Schwert. 1977. "Short-Term Interest Rates as Predictors of Inflation: On Testing the Hypothesis That the Real Rate of Interest Is Constant." *American Economic Review* 67:478–86.

Orphanides, Athanasios. 2003. "The Quest for Prosperity Without Inflation." *Journal of Monetary Economics* 50:633–63.

Poole, William. 1991. "Interest Rates and the Conduct of Monetary Policy: A Comment." *Carnegie-Rochester Conference Series on Public Policy* 34:31–40.

Romer, Christina D., and David H. Romer. 1989. "Does Monetary Policy Matter? A New Test in the Spirit of Friedman and Schwartz." In *NBER Macroeconomics Annual 1989,* edited by O. J. Blanchard and S. Fisher, 121–69. Cambridge, MA: MIT Press.

Shapiro, Matthew D. 1994. "Federal Reserve Policy: Cause and Effect." In *Monetary Policy,* edited by N. Gregory Mankiw, 307–34. Chicago: University of Chicago Press.

Stock, James W., and Mark W. Watson. 2007. "Why Has Inflation Become Harder to Forecast?" *Journal of Money, Credit, and Banking* 29 (1 suppl.): 3–33.

———. 2008. "Phillips Curve Inflation Forecasts." Paper presented at Federal Reserve Bank of Boston Conference, May.
Woodford, Michael. 2003. *Interest and Prices: Foundations of a Theory of Monetary Policy.* Princeton, NJ: Princeton University Press.
———. 2008. "How Important is Money in the Conduct of Monetary Policy?" *The Journal of Money, Credit, and Banking* 40 (8): 1561–98.

Comment   Lars E. O. Svensson

Introduction

Goodfriend and King's chapter provides an interesting explanation of the Great Inflation. It starts with the assumption that the Fed objectives were to stabilize the output gap and maintain "continuity of the interest rate" and then presents a model where inflation becomes a stochastic trend. In particular, inflation increases with negative innovations in potential-output growth. Fed monetary policy is seen as switching between business as usual and inflation fighting.

Model

There is a New Keynesian Phillips curve,

$$\pi_t - \bar{\pi}_t = \beta E_t(\pi_{t+1} - \bar{\pi}_{t+1}) + h(y_t - y_t^*),$$

where $\bar{\pi}_t$ denotes an inflation trend that is assumed to follow a random walk (martingale),

$$\bar{\pi}_t = E_t \bar{\pi}_{t+1}.$$

There is an aggregate-demand relation that relates the output gap between output, y_t, and potential output, y_t^*, to the real interest-rate gap between the real interest rate, r_t, and the natural interest rate, r_t^*,

$$y_t - y_t^* = E_t(y_{t+1} - y_{t+1}^*) - \frac{1}{\sigma}(r_t - r_t^*),$$

where σ is the reciprocal of the intertemporal elasticity of substitution. Potential-output growth follows an AR(1) process,

Lars E. O. Svensson is deputy governor of Sveriges Riksbank, the central bank of Sweden; affiliated professor at the Institute for International Economic Studies, Stockholm University; a research fellow of the Centre for Economic Policy Research; and a research associate of the National Bureau of Economic Research.

A first version of this comment was presented at the Great Inflation Conference sponsored by the NBER in Woodstock, Vermont, September 25–27, 2008. I thank Mathias Trabant for help with this comment. For acknowledgments, sources of research support, and disclosure of the author's material financial relationships, if any, please see http://www.nber.org /chapters/c9169.ack.

$$\Delta y_t^* = \rho \Delta y_{t-1}^* + v_t,$$

where v_t is a shock with zero mean. This implies that the natural interest rate follows

$$r_t^* - r = \sigma E_t \Delta y_{t+1}^* = \sigma \rho \Delta y_t^* = \rho(r_{t-1}^* - r) + \sigma \rho v_t.$$

The nominal interest rate, R_t, is given by the Fisher equation,

$$R_t = r_t + E_t \pi_{t+1}.$$

It is assumed that the model is known by the Fed and the private sector and that the Fed's monetary policy is both known by the private sector and fully credible. The authors examine rational-expectations equilibria with fully credible policies.

The Fed's monetary policy is characterized by output-gap stabilization and "continuity of the short rate" rather than low inflation. "Continuity" here actually means "predictability."

A first question is why monetary policy is not modeled as a loss function that is minimized, such as

$$L_t = (\pi_t - \pi_t^*)^2 + \lambda(y_t - y_t^*)^2 + \mu(R_t - E_{t-1}R_t)^2.$$

Could the Great Inflation then be explained by high weights on output-gap stabilization and interest-rate predictability, that is, high λ and μ, and a drifting inflation target π_t^*?

A second question is why have the authors chosen interest-rate *predictability*, focusing on $R_t - E_t R_{t-1}$, rather than the more traditional interest-rate *smoothing*, focusing on $R_t - R_{t-1}$? The more standard loss function with interest-rate smoothing would be

$$L_t = (\pi_t - \pi_t^*)^2 + \lambda(y_t - y_t^*)^2 + \mu(R_t - R_{t-1})^2.$$

Does it matter whether the Fed focuses on predictability or smoothing of the short rate? Yes, it does, because smoothing will have to be state-dependent to be equivalent to predictability. In any case, a study of the Federal Open Market Committee's (FOMC's) transcript might reveal whether the Fed was emphasizing predictability or smoothing.

Equilibria with Zero Output Gaps

The authors focus on equilibria with zero output gaps, $y_t - y_t^* = 0$. Thus, by the Phillips curve, inflation is equal to trend inflation

$$\pi_t = \bar{\pi}_t = E_t \pi_{t+1} = E_t \bar{\pi}_{t+1}.$$

By the aggregate-demand relation, the real rate is equal to the natural rate,

$$r_t = r_t^*,$$

and, by the Fisher equation, the nominal rate is equal to the natural rate plus trend inflation,

$$R_t = r_t^* + \bar{\pi}_t.$$

What, then, is equilibrium trend inflation? Consider innovations, $R_t - E_{t-1}R_t$, in the nominal rate and use $E_{t-1}\bar{\pi}_t = \bar{\pi}_{t-1}$ in the Fisher equation to get

$$R_t - E_{t-1}R_t = r_t^* - E_{t-1}r_t^* + \bar{\pi}_t - \bar{\pi}_{t-1}.$$

Now, assume a given degree of predictability of the short rate ϕ, $0 \leq \phi \leq 1$, relative to the forecast error of the natural rate,

$$R_t - E_t R_{t-1} = (1 - \phi)(r_t^* - E_{t-1}r_t^*).$$

Setting these two expressions for the innovation in the nominal rate equal to one another leads to the equilibrium innovation in trend inflation,

$$\bar{\pi}_t - E_{t-1}\bar{\pi}_t = -\phi(r_t^* - E_{t-1}r_t^*) = -\phi\sigma\rho v_t.$$

Since trend inflation is a random walk, the equilibrium trend inflation is determined as

(1) $$\bar{\pi}_t = \bar{\pi}_{t-1} - \phi\sigma\rho v_t.$$

Thus, trend inflation increases with negative potential-output growth innovations, more when there is high predictability of the short rate (when ϕ is large). This is the authors' main result and the basis for their interpretation of the Great Inflation.

The innovation in the natural interest rate and the potential-output growth innovation are related and proportional,

$$r_t^* - E_{t-1}r_t^* = \sigma\rho(\Delta y_t^* - E_{t-1}\Delta y_t^*) = \sigma\rho v_t.$$

Hence, we understand the main result directly from the Fisher equation, $R_t = r_t^* + \bar{\pi}_t$. If the nominal rate is more predictable, innovations in trend inflation have to cancel innovations in the neutral rate.

Implementation

How should we interpret trend inflation? One interpretation is that the Fed sets and announces an inflation target according to (1). Trend inflation then becomes a predetermined variable. We can then assume that the Fed follows an interest-rate rule given by

(2) $$R_t = \bar{\pi}_t + r_t^* + \Omega(\pi_t - \bar{\pi}_t).$$

If we choose the coefficient Ω to be positive and sufficiently large, the above equilibrium will be unique. In equilibrium, the third term in (2) will be zero. But exactly how would the Fed implement this?

There is a simultaneity problem in implementing (2) in that π_t is a forward-looking variable and R_t and π_t will be simultaneously determined. The instrument rule (2) is what, in previous research, I have called an "implicit instrument rule." One can imagine that R_t and π_t are determined by some iteration during the announcement day; that is, when the Fed announces an R_t, the private sector responds with a π_t, the Fed responds with a new R_t, and so on, until the economy has converged on the equilibrium R_t and π_t before the end of the day. Obviously, this is not how monetary policy is implemented.

Another way for the Fed to implement the equilibrium would be to predict the equilibrium π_t, and set R_t accordingly. The Fed might predict π_t to depend linearly on the two predetermined variables r_t^* and $\bar{\pi}_t$ and satisfy

$$\pi_t = g_1 r_t^* + g_2 \bar{\pi}_t = \bar{\pi}_t,$$

that is, that the coefficients g_1 and g_2 satisfy $g_1 = 0$ and $g_2 = 1$. Substituting this prediction of π_t into the instrument rule implies

$$R_t = \bar{\pi}_t + r_t^* + \Omega(g_1 r_t^* + g_2 \bar{\pi}_t - \bar{\pi}_t) = \bar{\pi}_t + r_t^*.$$

This is a different instrument rule, which in previous research I have called an "explicit instrument rule," where the nominal rate only depends on predetermined variables. But this variant of the instrument rule has different determinacy properties. In this case, the predetermined variables are all exogenous, which means the nominal rate becomes exogenous. Then, in this model, there is indeterminacy and no unique equilibrium.

The authors assume that there is money, m_t, and a money demand,

$$\Delta m_t = \alpha \Delta y_t + \pi_t,$$

and that the Fed follows the money-supply rule

$$\Delta m_t = \alpha \Delta y_t^* - \phi \sigma \rho v_t + \alpha \rho \Delta y_{t-1}^* + \pi_{t-1}.$$

This implies

$$\alpha \Delta (y_t - y_t^*) + \Delta \pi_t = -\phi \sigma \rho v_t,$$

so if the output gap is zero the inflation innovation is consistent with (1). But is this equilibrium unique? And is $\bar{\pi}_t$ still determined by the Fed and predetermined?

In the section "How 'Business as Usual' Creates Inflation Drift," is the central bank implementing monetary policy without explicitly setting $\bar{\pi}_t$? Is $\bar{\pi}_t$ determined/inferred by the private sector? Is it a forward-looking variable? Is the equilibrium then unique?

Generally, for determinacy, "out-of-equilibrium" behavior by the policymaker must be specified, as discussed in some detail in Svensson and Woodford (2005). Earlier, the instrument rule (2) is an out-of-equilibrium commitment, in the sense that it specifies how the Fed would set the nominal interest rate if the inflation rate would deviate from the equilibrium level $\bar{\pi}_t$. However, the fact that the instrument rule is implicit implies that it has some implementation problems. Svensson and Woodford (2005) discuss out-of-equilibrium commitments that do not have such problems.

Concluding Comments and Questions

If the Fed has specific objectives, why not specify a loss function and optimal policy for this loss function (under commitment or discretion)? The assumptions of a known model, credible policies, and rational expectations seem rather strong for the Great Inflation period. Nevertheless, that a major explanation for the Great Inflation could be a small weight on inflation stabilization and a drifting inflation target does not seem so far-fetched.

In the model presented, is trend inflation a predetermined inflation target determined by the Fed or a forward-looking variable determined by the private sector? It is not clear (at least not to me) that there is determinacy if trend inflation is not a predetermined variable. The eigenvalue configuration of the system needs to be clarified. A unit root is OK for a predetermined variable but not for a forward-looking variable. The assumption that trend inflation is a random walk seems to imply that the variable has a unit root, which means that it cannot be a forward-looking variable determined by the private sector.

Generally, explicit out-of-equilibrium behavior by the Fed may be needed to ensure equilibrium. This is the case as shown earlier when trend inflation is a predetermined variable. But if the Fed's behavior is described by an implicit instrument rule, a simultaneity problem makes the implementation problematic.

Reference

Svensson, Lars E. O., and Michael Woodford. 2005. "Implementing Optimal Policy through Inflation-Forecast Targeting." In *The Inflation-Targeting Debate,* edited by Ben S. Bernanke and Michael Woodford, 19–83. Chicago: University of Chicago Press.

Discusion

Olivier Blanchard started the questions: What if interest is moving rather than predictable? What if the Federal Reserve, instead of computing the output gap using the natural rate, adjusted it slowly to movements in the natural rate, thus being behind the curve? When the natural rate goes down, it takes a while to adjust.

Andrew Levin was concerned that the magnitude of the inflation drift generated from this model is of the order of 1 to 2 percent, and there has to be some other mechanism generating such a drift given that movements in the natural rate of interest are not sufficient from results using models at the Federal Reserve.

Michael Woodford proclaimed that this chapter has an example of a model that attributes increases in inflation to negative supply shocks. The way it happens here is different from conventional wisdom. The typical view is that you have a shock that lowers potential GDP, and it is likely that the central bank is not willing to lower output as much as potential is falling, and secondly is not willing to raise interest rates as much as it would need to in order to lower output. Therefore, inflation rises. In the model shown here, the central bank wants to be sure it lowers output as much, as potential has gone down and the problem is that it is not willing to cut interest rates in equilibrium as much to keep inflation stable, and thus in order to avoid cutting nominal interest rates it raises long-run inflation expectations so it can cut output as much as it wants without cutting nominal interest rates. Isn't this unintuitive?

Athanasios Orphanides was puzzled about the motivation of the interest-rate continuity objective. Is it the desire to avoid surprising markets when changing interest rates? Can't the central bank, rather than change interest rates today, just announce they will change rates tomorrow? Or is there a deeper explanation? Lars Svensson disagreed, because such an announcement would cause surprise in the markets. But this is what Orphanides was puzzled by. Is it continuity of the short rate, or does it include forward rates?

Christina Romer wanted to know how well the predictions of this model performed. She and Matthew Shapiro remember that the Romer-Romer policy dates were not predictable for inflation, but they were predictable for interest rates. This could be a problem for this chapter. Romer thinks the reason the dates are predictable for interest rates is that there is a recognition lag, and the Federal Reserve has often started moving down the path of monetary tightening before it was recorded in the minutes that they were tightening policy. The second issue Romer raised was with regards to symmetry. If there are positive shocks to potential output, does that mean there should be periods of deflation in the 1950s, 1960s, and late 1990s?

Robert King provided the rebuttal. First, he thanked Orphanides for providing an earlier review of a paper that contained the chapter presented here as an exercise. They were encouraged to work more on it. The objective of this chapter from the authors' points of view was to start understanding the preconditions to the Volcker disinflation. Why did inflation run up? Calvo pricing was used, but with imperfect credibility, and thus one can trace out the real output costs associated with imperfect credibility. Also, the use of long-term interest rates was useful to gauge the sense that there was sluggish adjustment of long-term inflation expectations in that time interval. As Blanchard pointed out, a major feature of the time period was the higher level of long-term interest rates. The previous paper Orphanides reviewed had started here and tried to move forward, and relied heavy on historical documents. King also addressed the inflation process in the model, pointing out that the authors wanted inflation to have a random walk, which is possible under Calvo pricing when output is at capacity. Some portion of a random walk in inflation is essential. The authors were intrigued by the fact that long-term interest rates are stationary, yet inflation has a random walk component. The simple model provided here can do that. Svensson wanted the authors to be more precise on how inflation is a martingale process, yet the Calvo model itself with the assumption of output at capacity generates a martingale, and innovations can be anything. King admits Woodford is correct in that the model is unorthodox in terms of Federal Reserve response, yet Woodford assumed that the Federal Reserve would act as it always had. Orphanides questioned the interest-rate continuity factor, and King interpreted it as a postulate for many things, including (not surprisingly) the markets. Lastly, in reference to comments by Romer, one element of the Romer-Romer dates that sticks out to King is that every time there is a disinflation attempt described by a Romer-Romer date, inflation is higher than it was at the onset of the disinflation about two to three years later. This is why agents might have been skeptical about Volcker when forming expectations. Lastly, the model should be symmetric in its reactions.

4

Falling Behind the Curve
A Positive Analysis of
Stop-Start Monetary Policies
and the Great Inflation

Andrew Levin and John B. Taylor

4.1 Introduction

US consumer price inflation, which had been stable at around 1 percent in the late 1950s and early 1960s, reached double-digit levels by the late 1970s. This bout of inflation is commonly referred to as the Great Inflation and has been viewed as one of the most dramatic failures of US monetary policy since the founding of the Federal Reserve. Many analysts and commentators have sought to identify the primary causes of the Great Inflation; indeed, understanding its sources might help minimize the likelihood of a recurrence.

Of course, the US economy was buffeted by a wide range of shocks over this period, including changes in fiscal policy during the late 1960s, a downward shift in structural productivity growth around 1970, wage and price controls in the early 1970s, and the Organization of the Petroleum Exporting Countries (OPEC) oil price hikes in 1973 and 1979. Moreover, some

Andrew Levin is an economist at and special adviser to the Board of Governors of the Federal Reserve System. John B. Taylor is the Mary and Robert Raymond Professor of Economics at Stanford University, the George P. Shultz Senior Fellow in Economics at the Hoover Institution, and a research associate of the National Bureau of Economic Research.

This is the revised version of a manuscript prepared for the September 2008 NBER conference on the Great Inflation. We appreciate comments and suggestions from the organizers, Michael Bordo and Athanasios Orphanides, and from other participants in the conference. This chapter also has benefited greatly from invaluable conversations with Bill English, Chris Erceg, Dale Henderson, Bob Hetzel, Brian Madigan, Ben McCallum, Edward Nelson, and David Small, and from the excellent research assistance of Kathleen Easterbrook. The views expressed in this paper are solely those of the authors, and do not necessarily reflect the views of the Board of Governors of the Federal Reserve System or anyone else associated with the Federal Reserve System. For acknowledgments, sources of research support, and disclosure of the authors' material financial relationships, if any, please see http://www.nber.org/chapters/c9170.ack.

of those shocks had substantial short-term effects on inflation outcomes and contributed to an elevated level of uncertainty about the near-term inflation outlook. Nonetheless, as Meltzer (2010b) emphasizes, a coherent explanation of the Great Inflation must account for the sources of the *persistent upward drift in inflation* over an extended period of about a decade and a half.

In this chapter, we document the evolution of long-run inflation expectations and we model the stance of US monetary policy over the period from 1960 to 1980. We use this evidence to distinguish among various explanations of the Great Inflation and draw lessons for the future. Despite the remarkable breadth of the existing literature, relatively scant attention has been paid to the behavior of long-run inflation expectations over this period. Furthermore, most of the empirical studies have represented the conduct of monetary policy over the entire Great Inflation period using a linear reaction function with a fixed intercept, thereby assuming time-invariant values for the implicit inflation objective as well as for the equilibrium short-term real interest rate.

We begin by considering several distinct measures of long-run inflation expectations, which indicate that such expectations rose markedly during the late 1960s, remained elevated at that plateau through the mid-1970s, and then rose at an alarming pace from 1977 until mid-1980. Next, we gauge the stance of monetary policy in terms of the ex ante short-term real interest rate; that is, the federal funds rate less the Livingston Survey of one-year-ahead expected inflation. We then proceed to analyze the behavior of real interest rates and show that the course of monetary policy during the Great Inflation period can be represented as a series of stop-start episodes that occurred in 1968 to 1970, 1974 to 1976, and 1979 to 1980. In each case, policy tightening induced a contraction in economic activity, but that stance of policy was not maintained long enough to induce a sustained decline in the inflation rate.

The remainder of the chapter is organized as follows. Section 4.2 documents the evolution of long-run inflation expectations. Section 4.3 models the stance of monetary policy. Section 4.4 draws implications and section 4.5 concludes.

4.2   The Evolution of Inflation Expectations

In this section, we characterize three stylized facts regarding the evolution of long-run inflation expectations over the Great Inflation period.

Stylized Fact 1: The Great Inflation started in the mid-1960s. The classic measure of short-run inflation expectations is the Livingston Survey of one-year-ahead projections of consumer price inflation. As recounted by Croushore (1997), this survey of business economists was initiated by Joseph Livingston in 1946 and is now conducted by the Federal Reserve

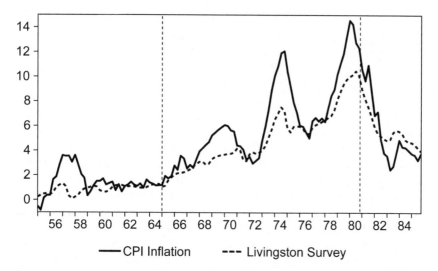

Fig. 4.1   Actual inflation and short-run inflation expectations, 1955–1985

Note: The solid line depicts the realized four-quarter-average CPI inflation rate, and the dashed line depicts the median response to the Livingston Survey regarding expected inflation over the year ahead.

Bank of Philadelphia, which began providing support for the survey in the late 1970s and assumed full responsibility in 1989. Since its inception, the survey has been conducted in May and December of each year, shortly after the release of the preceding month's Consumer Price Index (CPI).[1] There have generally been about fifty respondents to each survey, including professional forecasters, chief economists of financial institutions and nonfinancial corporations, and a few academic and government economists.[2] Over the years, the Livingston Survey has received widespread attention in the business press and has been analyzed in numerous research papers.[3]

As shown in figure 4.1, the Livingston Survey indicates that short-run inflation expectations were stable at about 1 percent from 1956 until 1964, even though actual CPI inflation exhibited substantial variation over this period. An inflation rate of around 1 percent was viewed as broadly consistent with the Federal Reserve's mandate under the Employment Act of 1946,

---

1. Given this timing of the survey, the horizon of the inflation projections is not exactly one year but alternates between ten and fourteen months—this modest degree of variation in the forecast horizon can be relevant for certain types of statistical tests but is not crucial for any of the analysis presented in this chapter.

2. In the mid-1990s, the sample of respondents included economists from nonfinancial businesses (30 percent), financial institutions (50 percent), academic institutions (13 percent), and other organizations including government agencies, labor unions, and insurance companies (8 percent). For further discussion, see Croushore (1997).

3. A comprehensive bibliography is available online at http://www.philadelphiafed.org.

which established the objectives of "maximum employment, production, and purchasing power" for all federal agencies.[4]

In 1956 to 1957, for example, realized CPI inflation reached a peak of nearly 4 percent, but one-year-ahead inflation expectations remained well-anchored, reflecting the private sector's confidence that the stance of monetary policy was consistent with inflation returning to around 1 percent within a year. In effect, business economists and professional forecasters did not expect these inflation fluctuations to be very persistent, but instead anticipated that inflation would subside quite quickly. Indeed, the firm anchoring of inflation expectations during the late 1950s and early 1960s may have contributed to the relatively low persistence of actual inflation over this period.[5]

Starting in 1965, however, a sharply different pattern of expectations formation becomes evident in the Livingston Survey: short-run inflation expectations began rising in parallel with actual inflation and reached about 4 percent by 1970, indicating that forecasters anticipated that the upswing in actual inflation would *not* be purely transitory. Moreover, by 1971 and 1972, short-run inflation expectations were virtually identical to actual CPI inflation, consistent with the view that policymakers would allow inflation to stay at around 4 percent rather than taking any decisive action to return to an environment of price stability.

A large empirical literature has made note of the persistent negative forecast errors that were associated with survey measures of inflation expectations from the mid-1960s through the late 1970s. For an environment with stable linear inflation dynamics, such results might be interpreted as pointing to the "irrationality" of survey respondents. In contrast, persistent forecast errors are associated with the *optimal* forecast in a Markov regime-switching environment where the current state is not directly observed by private agents (cf. Evans and Wachtel 1993).[6]

Yields on Treasury securities provide additional confirmation that inflation expectations began to shift markedly around 1965. In particular, Gürkaynak, Sack, and Wright (2007) employed the methodology of Nelson and Siegel (1987) and Svensson (1994) to fit daily data on the entire term structure of bond yields since 1961, thereby obtaining a smoothed yield curve that can be used to compute forward interest rates at each date. During the 1960s and early 1970s, the seven-year bond was the longest matu-

4. The Employment Act of 1946 also established the Joint Economic Committee (JEC), which subsequently stated that the act "provides a tried and successful institutional framework for the coordination of economic policies to the end of maximizing employment and production within a framework of price stability and growth" (*JEC Report,* March 1966, 2) A year later, the JEC indicated that "[p]rices rose too rapidly in 1966 and are in danger of doing so again in 1967" (*JEC Report,* March 1967, 18)

5. For further discussion, see Bordo and Schwartz (1999), Sargent (1999), Levin and Piger (2004), and Benati (2008).

6. Ang, Bekaert, and Wei (2007) provide further evidence on the efficiency of survey-based inflation forecasts.

rity issue that was auctioned regularly by the US Treasury, and hence for this period Gürkaynak, Sack, and Wright (2007) constructed daily series of one-year forward nominal interest rates for horizons up to six years ahead. Henceforth, we refer to the six-year-ahead forward interest rate as the "far-ahead forward rate"; it should be noted, however, that we have conducted sensitivity analysis that confirms that all of our conclusions are robust to the use of forward rates at even longer horizons (which are available starting in the early 1970s).

To make inferences from far-forward nominal interest rates regarding the evolution of long-run inflation expectations, we assume that the far-forward real short-term interest rate has a constant value of 2 percent and that the term premium has a constant value of 1 percent. The constancy of the far-forward real interest rate is consistent with the view that the real economy would be expected to converge to its balanced growth path over a seven-year horizon, and the value of 2 percent for the equilibrium short-term real interest rate is the same as embedded in the Taylor (1993) rule. Of course, investors might well perceive the equilibrium real interest rate as time-varying, especially in response to a persistent shift in productivity growth like the one that occurred during the 1970s. Indeed, a long literature has documented the extent to which term premiums vary over time, reflecting movements in the perceived distribution of returns as well as in the market price of risk. Nonetheless, as discussed further later, the variations in the far-forward real interest rate and in the term premium appear to be fairly small compared with the marked shifts in expected inflation that occurred during the Great Inflation, so that this measure of long-run inflation expectations can be very useful, at least as a rough gauge.

As depicted by the solid line in figure 4.2, this measure indicates that long-run inflation expectations were quite stable from 1961 until early 1965 at a rate just above 1 percent, consistent with the implications from the Livingston Survey. In effect, this evidence confirms that during the early 1960s inflation expectations were firmly anchored at a level broadly consistent with the Federal Reserve's mandate of price stability.

In 1965, however, this measure exhibits a fairly dramatic kink: far-forward inflation expectations began to drift upward steadily, reaching a peak of about 4.5 percent in 1970, and then remained in the range of 3.5 to 4.5 percent over the next several years. Again, this pattern is consistent with the implications of the Livingston Survey—not only that inflation expectations drifted upward during 1965 to 1970, but that these expectations remained at an elevated plateau during the early 1970s.

Importantly, these findings regarding the early stages of the Great Inflation are not sensitive to alternative assumptions about the determination of real interest rates or term premium. For example, a recent study by Ang, Bekaert, and Wei (2008) also provides a measure of long-run expected inflation implied by a no-arbitrage factor model of the term structure. Their

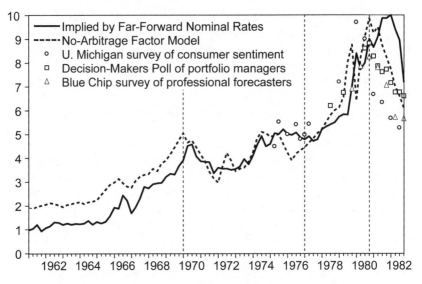

Fig. 4.2   The evolution of long-run inflation expectations, 1961–1982

Notes: The solid line depicts the forward rate of expected inflation six years ahead, using nominal forward rates computed by Gürkaynak, Sack, and Wright (2007) and subtracting a constant far-forward real rate of 2 percent and a constant term premium of 1 percent. The dashed line depicts the five-year expected inflation rate from the no-arbitrage factor model of Ang, Bekaert, and Wei (2008). The three survey measures of long-run inflation expectations are defined in the notes to table 4.1.

analytical framework utilizes latent factors and allows for Markov switching among four different regimes, and was estimated using data over the period 1952:2 to 2004:4 for CPI inflation and zero-coupon Treasury yields at four maturities (1, 4, 12, and 20 quarters).

As shown by the dashed line in figure 4.2, the five-year average expected inflation rate produced by the no-arbitrage factor model of Ang, Bekaert, and Wei (2008) moves largely in parallel with the measure implied by far-forward nominal interest rates. During the early 1960s, the no-arbitrage measure is nearly a percentage point higher than the measure based on far-forward rates, because the factor model implies that the real interest rate and the inflation risk premium were a bit below their historical averages during this period. (Of course, that implication might change if the Livingston Survey were incorporated into the estimation procedure.) More broadly, however, the factor model underscores the findings noted earlier: inflation expectations were relatively low and stable during the early 1960s, began rising steadily in 1965, and reached a peak of about 5 percent by 1970.

Moreover, while no direct surveys of long-run inflation expectations were conducted during this period, the view that the Great Inflation started around 1965 is certainly corroborated by the general tenor of media reports,

November 1965

"Latest paddle at the Washington woodshed"

November 1966

"Could stand some escalation."

February 1969

"He keeps getting bigger and bigger all the time."

December 1969

"Signals—hut... hut?"

Fig. 4.3   Perspectives on the early years

Sources: Upper left, Edward Kuekes, *Cleveland Plain Dealer,* reprinted in *New York Times* (*NYT*) on November 28, 1965; *upper-right,* Don Hesse, *St. Louis Globe-Democrat,* reprinted in *NYT* on November 27, 1966; *lower-left,* Bil Canfield, *Newark Evening News,* reprinted in *NYT* on February 2, 1969; lower-right, Bil Canfield, *Newark Evening News,* reprinted in *NYT* on December 7, 1969.

congressional hearings, and academic conferences through the remainder of the decade. Indeed, as shown in figure 4.3, editorial cartoons provide contemporary evidence of widespread public concerns about the upward drift in inflation from 1965 to 1969.

In summary, the evidence from the Livingston Survey and from bond yield data demonstrates conclusively that the roots of the Great Inflation can be traced back to around 1965. This conclusion is consistent with the broad assessment of DeLong (1997), who argued that the Great Inflation began well before 1970.

Stylized Fact 2: Long-run inflation expectations remained at a plateau of about 4 to 5 percent during the first half of the 1970s and shifted upward rapidly over the remainder of the decade. In the mid- to late 1970s, several surveys of inflation expectations began to include questions regarding respondents' expectations at longer horizons. In spring 1975, for example, the University of Michigan's survey of consumer sentiment started asking occasionally about the expected average CPI inflation rate over the next five to ten years. In mid-1978, Richard Hoey's "Decision-Makers Poll" of institutional portfolio managers started including an occasional question about the expected average CPI inflation rate over the coming decade.[7] And in fall 1979, Blue Chip Economic Indicators began asking about the longer-run outlook in its survey of professional forecasters, including a question about the expected ten-year average inflation rate for the gross national product (GNP) deflator.[8]

Table 4.1 reports the median value of the long-run inflation projections from each of these three surveys over the period from 1975 through the end of 1980; these survey results are also plotted in figure 4.2. Although the timing of the surveys is quite uneven over this period, the results can be directly compared in 1979 and 1980, and the degree of consistency in long-run inflation expectations across the three groups of respondents—households, institutional portfolio managers, and professional forecasters—seems particularly remarkable in light of the volatility of actual inflation over this period.

Moreover, as shown in figure 4.2, these survey-based measures of long-run inflation expectations line up quite closely with the two indicators derived from the term structure of nominal interest rates, further bolstering our confidence that these measures serve as useful gauges of the evolution of long-run inflation expectations.

The Michigan survey indicates that household expectations regarding the longer-run inflation outlook stayed in the range of 4.5 to 5.5 percent from mid-1975 until early 1977, a range that is very similar to that of the two expectations measures derived from bond yield data and to the levels of these two measures at the beginning of the decade. Evidently, long-run inflation expectations had remained around this plateau since about 1970; that is, policymakers were not successful in bringing down long-run inflation

7. The Decision-Makers Poll was initiated when Richard B. Hoey was employed at Bache, Halsey, Stuart, & Shields, and he continued to conduct the survey when he moved to Warburg, Paribus, & Becker, then to Drexel, Burnham, Lambert, and finally to Barclays de Zoete Wedd Research. The number of respondents varied between 175 and 500 and included chief investment officers, corporate financial officers, bond and stock portfolio managers, industry analysts, and economists. Although the survey was originally disseminated via proprietary newsletters, Holland (1984) received permission to publish the median survey responses for long-run inflation expectations; see also *Economic Report of the President* (1985, chapter 1), Havrilesky (1988), and Darin and Hetzel (1995).

8. Although Blue Chip Economic Indicators is a proprietary survey, the median responses for long-run inflation expectations are publicly available for 1979 to 1991 and can be downloaded from http://www.philadelphiafed.org.

Table 4.1   **Surveys of long-run inflation expectations, 1975–1980**

	Michigan survey (households)	Decision-Makers Poll (portfolio managers)	Blue Chip survey (professional forecasters)
1975			
Q2	4.5	—	—
Q3	5.5	—	—
1976			
Q1	5.0	—	—
Q3	5.4	—	—
Q4	4.8	—	—
1977			
Q1	5.0	—	—
Q2	5.4	—	—
1978			
Q3	—	6.2	—
1979			
Q1	7.2	—	—
Q2	—	6.8	—
Q4	—	—	6.9
1980			
Q1	9.7	—	—
Q2	—	—	7.9
Q3	9.0	8.6	—
Q4	—	8.8	8.3

Notes: This table reports the median of respondents' projections for three surveys: the University of Michigan survey of consumer sentiment asked about average CPI inflation over the next five to ten years; the Decision-Makers Poll survey of institutional portfolio managers asked about average CPI inflation over the next ten years; and the Blue Chip Economic Indicators survey of professional forecasters asked about the average GNP price inflation rate over the next ten years.

expectations but did at least manage to avoid any marked upward shift over the period through early 1977.

Starting in mid-1977, however, long-run inflation expectations began rising at an alarming pace. The Michigan survey indicates that these expectations rose sharply from 5 percent in early 1977 to around 7 percent by early 1979 and to more than 9 percent by early 1980. The results of the Decision-Makers Poll are very similar, with long-run inflation expectations rising from about 6 percent in mid-1978 to about 7 percent in mid-1979 and to nearly 9 percent by 1980. Again, these trajectories are very close to those of the two indicators derived from term structure data, which rose from 5 percent in early 1977 to about 8.5 percent by early 1980.

Stylized Fact 3: Long-run inflation expectations did not begin to ebb until late 1980. Long-run inflation expectations did not start shifting downward until late 1980. This characteristic is apparent from the two indicators derived from term structure data as well as from the survey-based measures. In the Decision-Makers survey, for example, long-run inflation expectations rose from 6 3/4 percent in mid-1979 to about 8 1/2 percent in mid-1980, and then peaked at about 8 3/4 percent that October; indeed, this measure did not return to around 6 3/4 percent until spring 1982. Similarly, the Blue Chip survey measure of long-run inflation expectations was around 7 percent in fall 1979—the first time that this question was included in the survey—but rose to about 8 percent in spring 1980 and peaked at 8 1/4 percent in fall 1980.

The absence of any noticeable decline—and indeed, perhaps even a further pickup—of long-run inflation expectations in 1980 appears to have reflected continuing skepticism about the prospects for making lasting progress on the inflation front. Editorial cartoons, such as those shown in figure 4.4, can provide a distinct perspective regarding that skepticism. In particular, the broad tenor of editorial cartoons in early 1980 was essentially unchanged from a year earlier, exhibiting only limited confidence that policymakers would take decisive steps to reverse the upward drift in inflation.

In October 1979, about two months after Paul Volcker was appointed chairman of the Board of Governors, the Federal Reserve switched operating procedures, resulting in an unprecedented jump in the federal funds rate and other short-term interest rates. At least initially, the switch in operating procedures may have appeared to be aimed primarily at stemming the upward spiral of actual and expected inflation rather than at bringing the inflation rate down. For example, Volcker told the Joint Economic Committee in February 1980 that those policy measures signaled "unwillingness to finance an accelerating rate of inflation" (Volcker 1980, 77)

Given that a shift in monetary policy tends to affect aggregate demand and inflation with "long and variable lags" (Friedman 1961, 464), it would have been reasonable to anticipate that several quarters might pass before seeing clear evidence of the impact of the October 1979 policy measures. Nevertheless, the Carter administration was apparently reluctant to wait that long, perhaps in part because of the approaching presidential primaries and a general election later in the year.[9] As the administration later explained, "Early in 1980, there were few signs of recession. If anything, activity seemed to be picking up. . . . By early March, there was fear that inflationary pressures . . . were mounting . . . and that without some additional action, these would . . . lead to an explosion of prices" (*Economic Report of the President,* January 1981, 160–61).

In mid-March 1980, President Carter issued an executive order authorizing the Federal Reserve to impose controls on the growth of credit. President Carter explained the rationale as follows: "The traditional tools used by the

9. As noted by Schreft (1990), Senator Edward Kennedy—Carter's major opponent for the Democratic Party nomination—gave a campaign speech in January 1980 describing inflation as "out of control." Moreover, contemporary newspaper accounts indicated that Carter's advisers "hoped that the anti-inflation program [announced in March] would be accepted by the public, thus giving the President an advantage over the other contenders for the Democratic nomination." (Schreft 1990, 35)

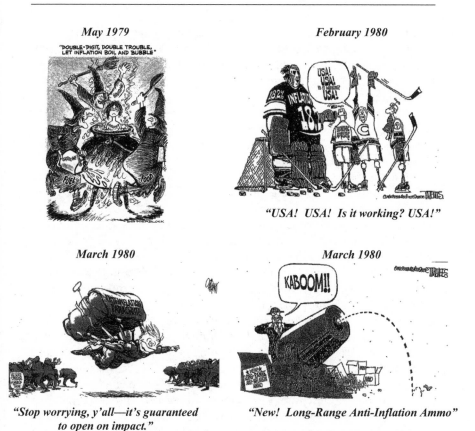

Fig. 4.4   **Perspectives on the final years of the Great Inflation (1979–1980)**
Sources: upper-left, A 1979 Herblock Cartoon, copyright by The Herb Block Foundation; *upper-right and lower-right,* Tim Menees, copyright (c), *Pittsburgh Post-Gazette,* 2012; *lower-left,* Pat Oliphant, (c) 1980 Universal Uclick, reprinted with permission, all rights reserved.

Federal Reserve to control money and credit expansion are a basic part of the fight on inflation. But in present circumstances, those tools need to be reinforced so that effective restraint can be achieved in ways that spread the burden reasonably and fairly" (Carter 1980, 7–8). Using that authority, the Federal Reserve initiated the Credit Restraint Program (CRP), a set of measures that included voluntary restraints for a wide range of financial institutions as well as the imposition of reserve requirements for all lenders (not just commercial banks) on increases in certain types of consumer credit.[10]

10. Schreft (1990, 35–38) provides a detailed description of the CRP, which also included four other measures: an increase in the marginal reserve requirement on managed liabilities of large banks; a special deposit requirement on additions to the managed liabilities held by nonmember banks; a special deposit requirement on any additional assets held by money market mutual funds; and a surcharge on the discount window borrowings of large banks.

Although the CRP was not expected to have a major impact on consumer behavior, incoming data during spring 1980 revealed sharp declines in credit aggregates, retail sales, and business spending. Even though the credit controls were eased substantially during May, "the economy was so weak by late June that the controls were nonbinding" (Schreft 1990, 43). The Federal Reserve announced the phaseout of the CRP in early July, less than four months after the credit controls were imposed.

After the sharp drop in economic activity during the second quarter of 1980, economists generally anticipated that the contraction would continue through the end of the year and would be nearly as severe as the 1974 to 1975 recession. Under the Federal Reserve's operating procedures, however, broad monetary aggregates recovered quickly during late spring and summer, and relatively accommodative monetary conditions apparently contributed to an unexpectedly brisk pace of economic recovery. For example, M1 (which had grown at an annual rate of about 7.5 percent from October 1979 through February 1980 and then dropped sharply during March and April) exhibited a robust growth rate of about 15 percent from June through September 1980. Meanwhile, the federal funds rate (which was around 13 percent during fall 1979 and winter 1980) dropped to around 9 percent in spring 1980 and remained at that level through September. Over the same period, core CPI inflation was also running at an annual rate of about 9 percent, and the short-term inflation expectations in the Livingston Survey remained close to 10 percent—about the same level as in late 1979.

Thus, looking at the entire period from October 1979 through September 1980, the evolution of monetary and credit conditions likely contributed to the variability of real economic activity but did not succeed in bringing down actual or expected inflation. In contrast, long-term inflation expectations finally began to recede after the Volcker Fed maintained its disinflationary policy during 1981 and 1982 despite the sharp contraction in economic activity.

4.3   An Empirical Model of Monetary Policy during the Great Inflation

In this section, we gauge the stance of monetary policy in terms of the ex ante short-term real interest rate—that is, the federal funds rate less the Livingston Survey of one-year-ahead expected inflation—and we formulate an empirical model of the evolution of monetary policy during the Great Inflation period. A number of previous studies (including Clarida, Galí, and Gertler 1998 and Taylor 1999) have focused on interest rate rules with fixed coefficients and have shown that monetary policy did not satisfy the Taylor principle over this period; that is, the federal funds rate was not raised by more than one-for-one in response to movements in actual inflation as would be implied by the Taylor (1993) rule. Here we extend that earlier analysis by allowing for discrete shifts in the intercept of the policy rule. This approach is useful in accounting for the possibility of occasional upward shifts in the

Federal Reserve's implicit inflation objective—as suggested by the evidence on long-run inflation expectations—and provides a representation for the stop-start pattern of policy tightening and easing that we discussed in the previous section.

To see this, let

(1) $$r_t = \bar{r} + \gamma_\pi (\pi_t - \pi^*) + \gamma_y (y_t - y_t^*),$$

where r_t is the short-term real interest rate, π_t is the actual inflation rate, π^* is the central bank's objective for the inflation rate, and $y_t - y_t^*$ is the output gap. If the slope coefficients $\gamma_\pi = \gamma_y = 0.5$, then the real interest rate should be raised by 50 basis points in response to a 1 percentage point increase in the inflation rate relative to target or the output gap. We assume that $\bar{r} = 2$ is the steady-state value of the real interest rate. We now proceed to show that by permitting simple shifts in the implicit inflation objective π^*, equation (1) provides a good fit of the real interest rate during the Great Inflation. We first must describe how we measure the other variables in the equation.

4.3.1   Measuring the Real Interest Rate

When inflation is fairly inertial, the current inflation rate may provide a reasonable estimate for expected inflation going forward. In such a situation the real interest rate can be computed by subtracting the current inflation rate from the nominal rate. In that case, equation (1) can be written with the nominal rate on the left-hand side and the inflation rate added to the right-hand side, yielding the Taylor rule. But if inflation is more variable—as in the Great Inflation period—it is necessary to get a better measure of inflation expectations. For this purpose, we use the Livingston Survey of one-year-ahead CPI inflation projections. An advantage of this measure is that it was available nearly two decades prior to the onset of the Great Inflation. Accordingly, our analysis focuses on the real federal funds rate at a quarterly frequency, computed by subtracting the Livingston Survey measure from the quarterly average of the nominal federal funds rate.[11]

4.3.2   Measuring the Output Gap and the Inflation Rate

As emphasized by Orphanides (2002, 2003), the use of real-time estimates of the output gap—as opposed to retrospective estimates constructed at a much later date—can have crucial implications in making assessments of the stance of monetary policy, especially because the difference between real-time versus retrospective estimates of the output gap may be quite large during periods in which there are substantial shifts in trend productivity growth or the natural unemployment rate.

There are no extant records from the 1960s or 1970s regarding real-time

---

11. The Livingston Survey is conducted semiannually, in May and November; thus, we use linear interpolation to obtain a quarterly time series of one-year-ahead inflation expectations.

Federal Reserve staff estimates of potential output or the output gap. Thus, following Orphanides (2002, 2003), one approach is to utilize the real-time assessments of potential output and the output gap that were constructed by the Council of Economic Advisors (CEA) and published annually in the *Economic Report of the President (ERP)*. And during the late 1960s, those estimates may well serve as a useful real-time proxy for the assessments that would have been relevant for policymakers at that time. Unfortunately, however, as the CEA estimates became increasingly politicized during the 1970s, neither economic analysts nor policymakers continued paying serious attention to these estimates.

Therefore, following the approach of Cecchetti et al. (2007), we construct another proxy for the real-time output gap by applying a one-sided Hodrick-Prescott (HP) filter to each vintage of real GNP drawn from the Philadelphia Fed's real-time data set, using a smoothing parameter of 1,600.[12] While the Hodrick-Prescott method was not available in the 1970s, it corresponds well with less formal procedures economic analysts use to assess trends.[13]

As shown in figure 4.5, the HP filtered series for the real-time output gap is very similar to the CEA series during the late 1960s, but the two measures diverge quite dramatically starting in 1970. In particular, from 1966 to 1969, both series imply that the output gap was fairly close to zero—roughly 5 percentage points below the Congressional Budget Office's (CBO's) most recent retrospective estimate, which we henceforth refer to as the "true" output gap. In contrast, the CEA estimates indicate a dramatic widening of the output gap through the mid-1970s; indeed, the trough of about –15 percent during 1975 suggests that the magnitude of slack in the economy was approaching that of the Great Depression—an implication that underscores the pitfalls of using the CEA series as a real-time measure of the output gap. In contrast, the HP filtered measure remains only a few percentage points below the "true" output gap through the early 1970s, reaching a trough of about –6 percent in early 1975 before recovering sharply and then remaining positive from 1976 through 1979.

We measure actual inflation using the realized four-quarter average CPI inflation rate at each date; that is, the same definition of inflation as in the Livingston Survey projections. For this measure of inflation, there is no distinction between real-time versus revised vintages of data, because the CPI is not subject to revision.

4.3.3   Discrete Shifts in the Implicit Inflation Objective

Now consider the inflation objective, π^*. Of course, policymakers did not have an explicit inflation goal during the 1960s and 1970s. As an empiri-

---

12. We have confirmed that the results are virtually identical for alternative values of the smoothing parameter.

13. Nikolsko-Rzhevskyy and Papell (2009) analyze the implications of alternative proxies for the real-time output gap based on linear and quadratic detrending procedures.

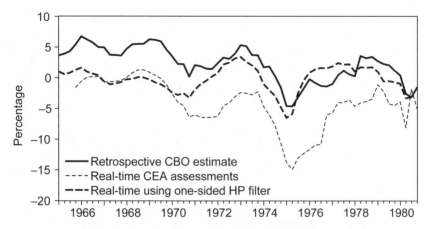

Fig. 4.5   Real-time versus final assessments of the output gap

Notes: This figure depicts three estimates of the output gap over the period 1965:1 through 1980:4. The solid line depicts the retrospective estimates of the CBO, using all data available through 2007. The short-dashed line depicts the contemporaneous estimates of the CEA, published annually in the *Economic Report of the President.* The long-dashed line depicts the estimate obtained by applying a one-sided Hodrick-Prescott filter to each vintage of real GNP taken from the Federal Reserve Bank of Philadelphia's real-time data set.

cal matter, however, discrete shifts in the implicit inflation objective can be detected by testing for structural breaks in the regression intercept for equation (1).

Figure 4.6 provides a graphical depiction of these structural breaks by comparing the evolution of the short-term real interest rate with prescriptions of the Taylor (1993) rule, using three alternative values of the implicit inflation goal: 1 percent, 5 percent, and 8 percent. This figure highlights a sequence of three stop-start episodes that appear to have occurred in 1968 to 1970, 1974 to 1976, and 1979 to 1980.

In each of those episodes, the stance of monetary policy evolved in three distinct stages: (1) policy remained passive while inflation begins to pick up; (2) policy shifted to a contractionary stance once the inflation rate exceeded a particular threshold, where the value of the threshold depended on the previous inflation peak; and (3) contracting economic activity caused the policy tightening to stop before inflation converged back to its initial rate. While the stance of monetary policy followed a roughly similar stop-start pattern in each case, it should be noted that the underlying reasons for that pattern differ across the three episodes: in 1970 and in 1976, policymakers intentionally shifted to a more accommodative stance, whereas the 1979 to 1980 episode occurred during a period in which the Federal Reserve employed a reserves-oriented operating procedure to control money supply growth while the federal funds rate evolved endogenously.

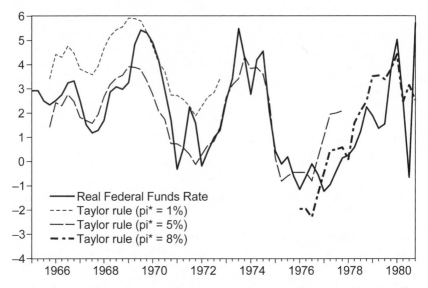

Fig. 4.6   Three episodes of start-stop monetary policy, 1965–1980

Notes: The solid line depicts the ex ante real federal funds rate, using the Livingston Survey as the measure of expected inflation. The other lines depict prescriptions of the Taylor (1993) rule for three specifications of the inflation objective: 1 percent (short-dashed), 5 percent (long-dashed), and 8 percent (dash-dotted).

4.3.4   Regression Analysis

The graphical implications of figure 4.6 are confirmed by regression analysis of a policy rule that incorporates interest-rate smoothing and that allows for discrete shifts in the regression intercept, using quarterly data for the period 1965q4 to 1980q3. The regression equation has the following form:

$$(2) \qquad FFR_t = c_0 + \rho FFR_{t-1} + (1 - \rho)$$
$$[\alpha(PI4CPI_t - \delta_1 DUM70_t - \delta_2 DUM76_t) + \beta YGAP_t],$$

where FFR is the federal funds rate, PI4CPI is the four-quarter-average CPI inflation rate, YGAP is the one-sided HP-filter estimate of output gap, DUM70 equals 1 for $t \geq$ 1970q2 and 0 otherwise, and DUM76 equals 1 for $t \geq$ 1976q1 and 0 otherwise.[14] It should be noted that the first dummy variable allows for the possibility of a shift in the implicit inflation objec-

14. This reaction function is specified in terms of the contemporaneous values for the CPI inflation rate and the one-sided HP-filtered output gap, consistent with policymakers' careful monitoring of the latest data releases and other economic news. An alternative approach would be to specify the reaction function solely in terms of lagged values of the output gap, thereby implying that policymakers had no current-quarter information about real economic activity. Both hypotheses can be nested in a single policy reaction function; the regression results for that nested specification (not shown here) confirm that the contemporaneous output gap is statistically significant while the coefficient on the lagged output gap is close to zero.

Table 4.2   **Regression evidence on start-stop monetary policies during the Great Inflation**

Variable	Coefficient	Std. error	t-statistic
OLS estimation without shifts in intercept			
c_0	0.15	0.39	0.37
ρ	0.83	0.11	7.54
α	1.07	0.34	3.08
β	1.82	1.33	1.36
OLS estimation allowing for intercept shifts			
c_0	0.40	0.36	1.11
ρ	0.61	0.10	5.89
α	1.41	0.20	7.08
β	1.24	0.38	3.30
δ_1	1.94	0.49	3.97
δ_2	2.10	0.53	3.93
IV estimation allowing for intercept shifts			
c_0	0.31	0.37	0.84
ρ	0.70	0.12	5.81
α	1.48	0.28	5.21
β	1.53	0.62	2.44
δ_1	2.05	0.62	3.30
δ_2	2.21	0.68	3.26

Notes: The upper and middle panels report the results of ordinary-least squares (OLS) estimation of equation (2), and the lower panel indicates the results of instrumental variable (IV) estimation, where the instruments include a constant, DUM70, DUM76, the lagged values of PI4CPI and YGAP, and two lagged values of RFFE.

tive when Arthur Burns became Federal Reserve chairman, and the second dummy variable allows for another shift that occurred at the onset of the election year of 1976.

As shown in the top panel of table 4.2, the regression results in the absence of intercept shifts (that is, imposing the restriction $\delta_1 = \delta_2 = 0$) are very similar to those reported in earlier studies. In particular, the estimated policy rule exhibits a very high degree of interest-rate smoothing ($\rho = 0.83$) and a fairly aggressive response to the output gap ($\beta = 1.85$). Moreover, the coefficient on inflation is very close to unity, confirming that policy did not satisfy the Taylor principle during this period; that is, the stance of policy was not tightened sufficiently to stabilize inflation around a constant objective.

Now consider allowing for shifts in the regression intercept in 1970q2 and 1976q1. From the middle panel of table 4.2, it is evident that these dummy variables are highly significant, with t-statistics exceeding 4, and the estimated coefficients δ_1 and δ_2 indicate that the Fed's implicit inflation objective rose by about 2 percentage points at each of these dates. Indeed, while these two breakdates have been treated as known a priori (based on the key points in Burns' tenure as Federal Reserve chairman), the significance levels are so high that breaks close to these two dates would be confirmed even by procedures that test for the presence of structural breaks at an unknown set of dates and that tend to exhibit substantially lower empirical power. Moreover, once we account for these two shifts in the implicit inflation objective, the coefficient on inflation in the policy rule is significantly greater than unity. The statistical significance of this coefficient mainly reflects the relatively tight stance of monetary policy in 1974 and 1975 that was aimed at preventing the deterioration in the near-term inflation outlook from becoming embedded in longer-run inflation expectations.

Of course, given that the output gap and inflation rate are endogenously determined, ordinary least squares (OLS) regression only yields consistent estimates of the policy rule coefficients under a specific set of identifying assumptions, namely, that these two explanatory variables do not respond contemporaneously to adjustments in the federal funds rate.[15] Thus, it is helpful to perform sensitivity analysis via instrumental variables (IV) estimation, which does not require those identifying assumptions. As shown in the bottom panel of table 4.2, the IV estimates are essentially the same as the OLS estimates, but the standard errors are somewhat higher and hence the confidence intervals are correspondingly somewhat wider.

4.4   Assessing Some Prominent Explanations for the Great Inflation

What are the implications of these stylized facts about inflation expectations and the evolving stance of monetary policy? In our view, these facts raise serious doubts about most of the prominent explanations of the Great Inflation, point to an alternative explanation, and suggest a way to prevent reoccurrences in the future.

4.4.1   Faulty Economic Theories

The evidence in sections 4.2 and 4.3 is not consistent with the view that changes in economic theory were the primary source of swings in trend inflation—an interpretation that has previously been emphasized by one of us (Taylor 1997).[16] While the rise in actual and expected inflation during the second half of the 1960s—the height of the period when many economists supported the notion of a stable long-run Phillips curve—may suggest that economic theory had a significant impact on actual policy over that period, the rapid surge in inflation during the second half of the 1970s (by which point most economists had concluded that there was no long-run Phillips curve trade-off) raises strong doubts about such an explanation for the Great Inflation.

15. These identifying assumptions are frequently employed in structural vector autoregression (VAR) analysis of monetary policy shocks; cf. Christiano, Eichenbaum, and Evans (1999) and Hetzel (2008, 276) for further discussion.

16. See also Romer and Romer (2002a, 2002b, 2004).

Our assessment of the limited role of faulty economic theories in the Great Inflation is consistent with the narrative analysis of Meltzer (2005, 2010a, 2010b). In particular, Federal Reserve Chairman William McChesney Martin Jr. was a pragmatist who "did not find economic models useful and . . . gave most attention to market data and market participants, not economists," while Burns was "an empirical economist who disdained deductive models," and most other Federal Open Market Committee (FOMC) members "were not ideologues or slavish adherents to a particular theory."[17] Meltzer also notes that the problem of inflation "was not new in 1965, and it was not new to Martin."[18] Indeed, Martin had been successful in ending two previous surges of inflation during the 1950s, and as discussed further later, the policy tightening that Martin initiated in 1969 presumably would have resulted in substantial disinflation if it had been maintained beyond the end of his term in January 1970.

4.4.2 Aggregate Supply Shocks

Over the past several decades, a number of studies have attributed the Great Inflation to the influence of adverse aggregate supply shocks (cf. Blinder 1982; Hetzel 1998; Mayer 1998; and Ireland 2007). According to this hypothesis, Federal Reserve policies systematically translated transitory shocks to the *price level* into persistent upward shifts in the *inflation rate*. Nonetheless, the evidence in section 4.2 on the evolution of inflation expectations is not consistent with the view that aggregate supply shocks were at the roots of the Great Inflation. First, the Livingston Survey and bond yield data indicate that inflation expectations started rising during the late 1960s, well before the onset of sharp increases in the prices of oil and other commodities.[19] Second, longer-run inflation expectations remained at around 4 to 5 percent from 1970 through 1975, despite the oil price shock triggered by the OPEC embargo in mid-1973. Third, longer-run inflation expectations spiraled upward from 1976 through mid-1979, a period when energy and commodity prices were relatively stable.

Moreover, the evidence in section 4.3 indicates that the Federal Reserve's response to the first OPEC oil shock was broadly in line with the prescriptions of the Taylor rule with an inflation goal of 5 percent. Actual consumer inflation jumped up nearly 9 percentage points from 1972Q4 through 1974Q4, reflecting the winding down of wage and price controls as well as the transitory effects of the OPEC oil price shock. The FOMC responded by tightening the stance of policy, and the federal funds rate rose from about 6 percent in January 1973 to 10 percent by autumn and to 12 percent in

17. Meltzer (2010b, chapter 7, 11).
18. Meltzer (2010a, chapter 3, 149).
19. Indeed, the analysis of Barsky and Kilian (2001) indicates that the OPEC oil price hike of 1973 was not an exogenous shock but instead was induced by the accommodative stance of monetary policy over preceding years.

mid-1974. Indeed, this policy tightening (which was criticized by numerous observers at the time) may have damped the response of inflation expectations to the oil price shock. In particular, one-year-ahead projections in the Livingston Survey rose about 3 percentage points, and the longer-run inflation expectations of bond investors appear to have moved up by around a percentage point or so.

4.4.3   Natural Rate Misperceptions

Some analysts have argued that policymakers' misperceptions of potential output growth and the natural unemployment rate were the primary reason that the stance of monetary policy was excessively accommodative in the late 1960s and the 1970s.[20] Our analysis indicates that such misperceptions may well have contributed to short-term inflation pressures over this period but cannot explain the evolution of longer-run inflation expectations and hence do not provide a complete account of the causes of the Great Inflation.

From an analytical perspective, policymakers' misperceptions of natural rates tend to induce persistent errors in the setting of the policy instrument, which in turn causes inflation to deviate from the longer-run goal. Nevertheless, such policy mistakes and the associated inflation outcomes should be *transitory,* as long as the inflation goal itself remains fixed and credible. In particular, the private sector should anticipate that policymakers will gradually revise their natural rate estimates in response to incoming information—including inflation outcomes that are persistently higher than expected—and hence that the stance of monetary policy will subsequently be adjusted to bring the inflation rate back to the specified goal. Thus, in the absence of any other considerations, this hypothesis implies that the private sector's longer-run inflation expectations should remain stable even if actual inflation is elevated due to policymakers' natural rate misperceptions.

In contrast, as we have seen in section 4.2, longer-run inflation expectations did indeed shift up markedly during the Great Inflation. In effect, by 1970, investors appear to have lost confidence that policymakers would take sufficient actions—even over a horizon of five or ten years—to bring inflation back to the level of about 1 to 2 percent that had prevailed during the mid-1950s and early 1960s. As for the late 1970s, surveys of consumers and professional forecasters as well as Treasury bond data indicate that inflation expectations became completely unhinged. In contrast, longer-run inflation expectations remained fairly stable at around 4 to 5 percent during the first half of the 1970s—precisely the period over which Orphanides (2002) concluded that policymakers' natural rate misperceptions were particularly large.

Although narrative evidence is inherently subject to alternative interpretations, our reading of that evidence appears to be consistent with Meltzer

20. See Orphanides (2002, 2003).

(2005, 2010a, 2010b) in casting doubt on the degree to which natural rate misperceptions played a fundamental role in explaining the Great Inflation. The following points are noteworthy.

Martin served as Federal Reserve chairman from April 1951 through January 1970. When inflation began rising in 1965 to 1968, Martin delayed tightening mainly due to concerns about coordination with anticipated adjustments in fiscal policy, particularly the expectation—supported by the analysis of Federal Reserve staff and of the Council of Economic Advisors—that the tax surcharge that was finally enacted in May 1968 would curtail aggregate demand and induce a significant decline in inflation.[21] Nonetheless, Martin recognized the pitfalls of having kept monetary policy on hold, noting in December 1967: "The horse of inflation is out of the barn and already well down the road. We cannot return the horse to the barn . . . but we can prevent it from trotting too fast."[22] In 1969, after it became clear that the tax surcharge had not restrained aggregate demand or inflation, the Federal Reserve moved decisively to tighten the stance of policy. In a front-page interview with *The New York Times,* Martin stated:

> It appears that the Federal Reserve was overly optimistic in anticipating immediate benefits from fiscal constraint . . . but now we mean business in stopping inflation. . . . A credibility gap exists in the business and financial community as to whether the Federal Reserve will push restraint hard enough to check inflation. The Board means to do so and is unanimous on that point. (*New York Times,* February 27, 1969, 1)

The funds rate rose from 6 percent in early January to around 9 percent by June—that is, the ex ante real funds rate increased from a roughly neutral value of about 2 percent to a very tight level of around 5 percent—and the Federal Reserve maintained that stance of policy through the end of Martin's term in January 1970.[23] Following the appointment of Arthur Burns to succeed Martin in February 1970, however, the Federal Reserve reversed course.[24] As a consequence, the funds rate declined about 4 percentage points over the course of the year, even though trend inflation and inflation expectations had not turned downward.

By the mid-1970s, policymakers were well aware of the difficulties in estimating potential output and the natural unemployment rate. For ex-

21. See the discussion in Bremner (2004, 251–56). Meltzer (2010a) notes that as of late spring 1968, the Federal Reserve and the Administration had similar macroeconomic forecasts in which "inflation would fall gradually to about 2.5 percent by mid-1969" (chapter 4, 49).

22. FOMC Minutes, December 12, 1967, 98.

23. Martin filled the remainder of his predecessor's term as Federal Reserve governor from 1950 to 1956 and was then appointed to a full fourteen-year term on February 1, 1956. Because no Federal Reserve governor may serve more than one full term, January 31, 1970 also marked the conclusion of Martin's final four-year term as Federal Reserve chairman.

24. Maisel (1973) described the discussion at Burn's first FOMC meeting on February 10, 1970 as "the most bitter debate I experienced in my entire service on the FOMC" (250). See also Meltzer (2010b, chapter 6).

ample, in testimony to the Joint Economic Committee in February 1976, Burns "firmly rejected the idea that anyone could give an accurate numerical value for full employment. Any number was both unreliable and subject to change."[25] Similarly, at the May 1978 FOMC meeting, Federal Reserve staff indicated that estimating the natural rate of unemployment was "a very difficult problem," and committee members referred to a wide range of estimates.[26]

In summary, the narrative evidence confirms that natural rate misperceptions did not play a significant role during the onset of the Great Inflation (1965–1970) and were not the key factor driving the surge in actual and expected inflation during the late 1970s.

4.4.4   Misperceptions of the Sacrifice Ratio

A number of studies have emphasized the extent to which policymakers' misperceptions of the sacrifice ratio may have played a key role in the Great Inflation.[27] Indeed, the narrative evidence suggests that concerns about the prohibitive cost of disinflation may well have contributed to the marked shift in the stance of monetary policy during 1970. According to the minutes of a Federal Reserve Board meeting in November 1970, Chairman Burns stated that "the Federal Reserve could not do anything about [union wage pressures] except to impose monetary restraint, and he did not believe the country was willing to accept for any long period an unemployment rate in the area of 6 percent. Therefore, he believed that the Federal Reserve should not take on the responsibility for attempting to accomplish by itself, under its existing powers, a reduction in the rate of inflation to, say, 2 percent."[28]

Nevertheless, our evidence does *not* support the view that the ultimate magnitude of the Great Inflation can be attributed to misperceptions of the sacrifice ratio. In particular, a monetary policymaker with strong concerns about the sacrifice ratio would perceive the cost of reversing an upward shift in inflation expectations as prohibitively high and hence would rationally decide to keep inflation expectations anchored as firmly as possible. In contrast, as we have seen, the actual stance of monetary policy was highly accommodative during the final two years of Burns' chairmanship—with the ex ante real federal funds rate remaining at or below zero—even though consumer inflation was rising rapidly toward double-digit levels. Under Chairman Miller, the Federal Reserve shifted to a roughly neutral stance of policy but did not place any substantial downward pressure on inflation. As a result, longer-run inflation expectations (which had remained reasonably stable until 1977) picked up markedly by mid-1979.

---

25. Meltzer (2010b, chapter 7, 120).
26. Meeting Transcript, FOMC, May 16, 1978, 6. For further details of this discussion, see Meltzer (2010b, chapter 7, 71).
27. See Sargent (1999); Primiceri (2006); Sargent, Williams, and Zha (2006); among others.
28. Hetzel (1998) gives this excerpt from the minutes of the Federal Reserve Board meeting on November 16, 1970.

4.4.5   Time Inconsistency Problems

Some analysts have argued that the Great Inflation resulted from time inconsistency problems in the conduct of monetary policy.[29] In particular, under the assumption that the central bank cannot make credible commitments regarding the path of policy, the policymaker's incentive to produce inflationary outcomes is an increasing function of the natural rate of unemployment. Thus, at least in principle, an upward trend in the natural rate of unemployment during the 1960s and 1970s could have induced the coincident upward trend in inflation.

The evidence in sections 4.2 and 4.3 contradicts this hypothesis. First, actual and expected inflation moved up during the late 1960s, that is, *before* policymakers were even aware that the natural unemployment rate had shifted upwards. Second, longer-run inflation expectations remained at a plateau of about 4 to 5 percent from 1970 to 1975, whereas econometric analysis indicates that the natural unemployment rate continued rising steadily throughout the 1970s as a consequence of demographic shifts and technological factors. Finally, this hypothesis does not provide any motivation for the sequence of stop-start episodes that occurred over the course of the Great Inflation.

4.4.6   Political Factors

If all these explanations seem inconsistent with our data, then what factors generated the recurring sequence of stop-start policies and the corresponding upward drift of longer-run inflation expectations? We think the most plausible explanation is a combination of periodic political pressures on the Federal Reserve and a lack of clear guidelines that would have helped policymakers to resist those pressures.

One well-known example of such political pressure is the instance when President Johnson took Federal Reserve Chairman Martin "out to the woodshed" in December 1965, shortly after the Federal Reserve Board approved an increase in the discount rate.[30] Transcripts of President Nixon's office recordings have revealed the pressures faced by Chairman Burns in the early 1970s.[31] A variety of documents have underscored the political pressures on the Federal Reserve during the early years of the Carter Administration.[32]

29. See Kydland and Prescott (1977), Barro and Gordon (1983), and Ireland (1999), among others. For a contrary view, see Beyer and Farmer (2007).

30. A first-hand account of this episode is given in Califano (1991, 108–10). Further background is provided by Bremner (2004, 209–11).

31. See Abrams (2006). For example, shortly after announcing Burns' nomination as Federal Reserve chairman, Nixon had a private conversation with Burns and told him, "I know there's the myth of the autonomous Fed." Burns (1979) also highlighted these pressures: "My conclusion that it is illusory to expect central banks to put an end to the inflation that now afflicts the industrial economies does not mean that central banks are incapable of stabilizing actions; it simply means that their practical capacity for curbing an inflation that is driven by political forces is very limited" (29).

32. See Kettl (1986), Biven (2002), Weise (2008), and Meltzer (2010b).

In contrast, the conduct of monetary policy became relatively well-insulated from political pressures after the Great Inflation.[33] The clarification of Federal Reserve accountability that came with the introduction of regular monetary policy reports and testimony under the Full Employment and Balanced Growth Act (1978) likely helped defuse some of the political pressures on the Federal Reserve. And in the early 1980s, President Reagan voiced consistent strong support for Chairman Volcker's policies, thereby initiating a pattern of acknowledging the Federal Reserve's operational independence that was generally followed by subsequent administrations. Perhaps most importantly, by the late 1970s the general public became acutely familiar with the high costs of inflation, and that awareness has provided the ongoing foundation for monetary policies aimed at fostering price stability along with maximum sustainable employment.[34]

4.4.7   Lessons for the Future

If political factors are the primary explanation for the Great Inflation, then what actions might be taken to reduce the likelihood of a recurrence? Our analysis suggests that simple rules can be valuable in providing transparent benchmarks for the conduct of monetary policy. For example, the Taylor (1993) rule specifies a quantitative inflation objective of 2 percent and prescribes adjustments to the stance of policy that would be expected to foster the achievement of that objective over time. Moreover, this rule is specified in terms of the current inflation rate and output gap, thereby avoiding the pitfalls of relying on any given model for generating macroeconomic forecasts.

On occasion, of course, policymakers might find compelling reasons to modify, adjust, or depart from the prescriptions of any simple rule, but in those circumstances, transparency and credibility might well call for clear communication about the rationale for that policy strategy. For example, while the Taylor rule embeds a constant value of the equilibrium short-term real funds rate, denoted as r^*, economic theories and empirical evidence suggest that r^* may move gradually and persistently in response to a shift in the trend rate of total factor productivity growth. Thus, under circumstances of elevated uncertainty about trend productivity growth, there could be significant benefits from monitoring statistical and model-based indicators of r^*.

33. Some legislative measures in the mid-to-late 1970s gave an early sign of this trend. The Federal Reserve's monetary policy deliberations were specifically exempted from the requirements of the Government in the Sunshine Act (1975), and these deliberations were also exempted from the General Accounting Office (GAO) audits that were instituted under the Federal Banking Agency Audit Act (1978).

34. Meltzer (2010a) notes that in Gallup polls from 1978 to 1982, more than 50 percent of respondents listed inflation and the high cost of living as the *most important problem* facing the country.

4.5   Conclusion

In this chapter, we have characterized the evolution of long-run inflation expectations and the stance of monetary policy over the period from 1965 to 1980, and we have employed this evidence to distinguish among various competing explanations regarding the causes of the Great Inflation.

Using survey-based measures and financial market data, we have shown that long-run inflation expectations rose markedly from 1965 to 1969, remained elevated but stable through the mid-1970s, and then deteriorated at an alarming pace from 1977 to 1980. We have also shown that the course of monetary policy over this period is well represented by a sequence of stop-start episodes that occurred in 1968 to 1970, 1974 to 1976, and 1979 to 1980. In each case, belated policy tightening induced a contraction in economic activity, but that stance of policy was not sustained long enough to bring inflation back to previous levels.

Finally, we have shown that several prominent explanations of the Great Inflation do not stand up to the evidence and that the most plausible explanation is a combination of periodic political pressures on the Federal Reserve and a lack of clear guidelines that would have helped policymakers to resist those pressures. This analysis suggests that the risk of a recurrence of the Great Inflation—as well as other costly policy choices—could be addressed through the use of simple rules as benchmarks for the conduct of monetary policy.

References

Abrams, Burton A. 2006. "How Richard Nixon Pressured Arthur Burns: Evidence from the Nixon Tapes." *Journal of Economic Perspectives* 20 (4): 177–88.

Ang, Andrew, Geert Bekaert, and Min Wei. 2007. "Do Macro Variables, Asset Markets, or Surveys Forecast Inflation Better?" *Journal of Monetary Economics* 54:1163–212.

———. 2008. "The Term Structure of Real Rates and Expected Inflation." *Journal of Finance* 63 (2): 797–849.

Barro, Robert J., and David B. Gordon. 1983. "A Positive Theory of Monetary Policy in a Natural Rate Model." *Journal of Political Economy* 91:589–610.

Barsky, Robert, and Lutz Kilian. 2001. "Do We Really Know Oil Caused the Great Stagflation? A Monetary Alternative." In *NBER Macroeconomics Annual 2001,* edited by Ben S. Bernanke and Kenneth Rogoff, 137–82. Cambridge, MA: MIT Press.

Benati, Luca. 2008. "Investigating Inflation Persistence across Monetary Regimes." *Quarterly Journal of Economics* 123:1005–60.

Beyer, A., and R. Farmer. 2007. "Natural Rate Doubts." *Journal of Economic Dynamics and Control* 31:797–825.

Biven, W. Carl. 2002. *Jimmy Carter's Economy: Policy in an Age of Limits.* Chapel Hill: University of North Carolina Press.

Blinder, Alan S. 1982. "The Anatomy of Double-Digit Inflation in the 1970s." In *Inflation: Causes and Effects,* edited by Robert E. Hall, 261–82. Chicago: University of Chicago Press.

Bordo, M., and A. Schwartz. 1999. "Under What Circumstances, Past and Present, Have International Rescues of Countries in Financial Distress Been Successful?" *Journal of International Money and Finance* 18:683–708.

Bremner, Robert. 2004. *Chairman of the Fed: William McChesney Martin, Jr. and the Creation of the Modern American Financial System.* New Haven, CT: Yale University Press.

Burns, Arthur F. 1979. "The Anguish of Central Banking." Per Jacobsson Lecture, Sava Centar Complex, Belgrade, Yugoslavia, September 30.

Califano, Joseph A. 1991. *The Triumph and Tragedy of Lyndon Johnson: The White House Years.* New York: Simon & Schuster.

Carter, James. 1980. Text of the President's Address on Economic Policy at the White House, March 14, 1980. In US Congress, Joint Economic Committee, *Hearings on the President's New Anti-Inflation Program,* 96th Congress, 2nd Session, 7–8. Washington, DC: Government Printing Office.

Cecchetti, Stephen, Peter Hooper, Bruce Kasmin, Kermit Schoenholtz, and Mark Watson. 2007. *Understanding the Evolving Inflation Process.* US Monetary Policy Forum Report. http://www.princeton.edu/~mwatson/papers/USMPF_Report _July_2007.pdf.

Christiano, Lawrence, Martin Eichenbaum, and Charles Evans. 1999. "Monetary Policy Shocks: What Have We Learned and to What End?" In *Handbook of Macroeconomics,* edited by J. B. Taylor and M. Woodford, 66–145. Amsterdam: Elsevier Press.

Clarida, Richard, Jordi Galí, and Mark Gertler. 1998. "Monetary Policy Rules in Practice: Some International Evidence." *European Economic Review* 42:1033–67.

Croushore, Dean. 1997. "The Livingston Survey: Still Useful after All These Years." *Business Review,* Federal Reserve Bank of Philadelphia, March/April.

Darin, Robert, and Robert Hetzel. 1995. "An Empirical Measure of the Real Rate of Interest." *Economic Quarterly, Federal Reserve Bank of Richmond* Winter:17–47.

DeLong, J. Bradford. 1997. "America's Peacetime Inflation: The 1970s." In *Reducing Inflation: Motivation and Strategy,* edited by Christina Romer and David Romer, 247–76. Chicago: University of Chicago Press.

Economic Report of the President. 1981. Washington, DC: US Government Printing Office.

———. 1985. Washington, DC: US Government Printing Office.

Evans, M. D., and P. Wachtel. 1993. "Inflation Regimes and the Sources of Inflation Uncertainty." *Journal of Money, Credit and Banking* 25:475–511.

Friedman, Milton. 1961. "The Lag in Effect of Monetary Policy." *Journal of Political Economy* 69:447–66.

Gürkaynak, Refet S., Brian Sack, and Jonathan H. Wright. 2007. "The US Treasury Yield Curve: 1961 to the Present." *Journal of Monetary Economics* 24:2291–304.

Havrilesky, Thomas. 1988. "New Evidence on Expected Long-Term Real Interest Rates." *Journal of Forensic Economics* 1:19–23.

Hetzel, Robert L. 1998. "Arthur Burns and Inflation." *Federal Reserve Bank of Richmond Economic Quarterly* 84:21–44.

———. 2008. *The Monetary Policy of the Federal Reserve: A History.* Cambridge: Cambridge University Press.

Holland, A. Steven. 1984. "Real Interest Rates: What accounts for their recent rise?" *Economic Review, Federal Reserve Bank of St. Louis* December: 18–29.

Ireland, Peter N. 1999. "Does the Time-Consistency Problem Explain the Behavior of Inflation in the United States?" *Journal of Monetary Economics* 44:279–91.

———. 2007. "Changes in the Federal Reserve's Inflation Target: Causes and Consequences." *Journal of Money, Credit and Banking* 39:1851–82.

Kettl, Donald F. 1986. *Leadership at the Fed.* New Haven, CT: Yale University Press.

Kydland, Finn E., and Edward C. Prescott. 1977. "Rules Rather Than Discretion: The Inconsistency of Optimal Plans." *Journal of Political Economy* 85 (3): 473–92.

Levin, Andrew, and Jeremy Piger. 2004. "Is Inflation Persistence Intrinsic in Industrial Economies?" European Central Bank Working Paper no. 334.

Maisel, Sherman J. 1973. *Managing the Dollar.* New York: Norton.

Mayer, Thomas. 1998. *Monetary Policy and the Great Inflation in the United States: The Federal Reserve and the Failure of Macroeconomic Policy, 1965–79.* Cheltenham, UK: Edward Elgar Press.

Meltzer, Allan H. 2005. "Origins of the Great Inflation." *Federal Reserve Bank of St. Louis Review* 87 (2, part 2): 145–75.

———. 2010a. *A History of the Federal Reserve, Volume 2, Book 1, 1951–1969.* Chicago: University of Chicago Press.

———. 2010b. *A History of the Federal Reserve, Volume 2, Book 2, 1970–1986.* Chicago: University of Chicago Press.

Nelson, Charles, and Andrew Siegel. 1987. "Parsimonious Modeling of Yield Curves." *Journal of Business* 60 (4): 473–89.

Nikolsko-Rzhevskyy, Alex, and David H. Papell. 2009. "Taylor Rules and the Great Inflation: Lessons from the 1970s for the Road Ahead for the Fed." Manuscript, University of Houston.

Orphanides, Athanasios. 2002. "Monetary Policy Rules and the Great Inflation." *American Economic Review* 92:115–20.

———. 2003. "Historical Monetary Policy Analysis and the Taylor Rule." *Journal of Monetary Economics* 50:983–1022.

Primiceri, Giorgio E. 2006. "Why Inflation Rose and Fell: Policymakers' Beliefs and US Postwar Stabilization Policy." *Quarterly Journal of Economics* 121:867–901.

Romer, Christina D., and David H. Romer. 2002a. "The Evolution of Economic Understanding and Postwar Stabilization Policy." In *Rethinking Stabilization Policy,* 11–78. Kansas City: Federal Reserve Bank of Kansas City.

———. 2002b. "A Rehabilitation of Monetary Policy in the 1950s." *American Economic Review* 92:121–27.

———. 2004. "Choosing the Federal Reserve Chair: Lessons from History." *Journal of Economic Perspectives* 18:129–62.

Sargent, Thomas. 1999. *The Conquest of American Inflation.* Princeton, NJ: Princeton University Press.

Sargent, Thomas, Noah Williams, and Tao Zha. 2006. "Shocks and Government Beliefs: The Rise and Fall of American Inflation." *American Economic Review* 96:1193–224.

Schreft, Stacey. 1990. "Credit Controls: 1980." *Economic Review, Federal Reserve Bank of Richmond* November/December:25–55.

Svensson, Lars. 1994. "Estimating and Interpreting Forward Rates: Sweden 1992–94." NBER Working Paper no. 4871. Cambridge, MA: National Bureau of Economic Research, September.

Taylor, John B. 1993. "Discretion versus Policy Rules in Practice." *Carnegie-Rochester Conference Series on Public Policy* 39:195–214.

———. 1997. "Comment: America's Peacetime Inflation." In *Reducing Inflation: Motivation and Strategy,* edited by Christina Romer and David Romer, chapter 6. Chicago: University of Chicago Press.

———. 1999. "A Historical Analysis of Monetary Policy Rules." In *Monetary Policy Rules,* edited by John B. Taylor, chapter 7. Chicago: University of Chicago Press.

Volcker, Paul. 1980. Remarks before the US Congress. Joint Economic Committee, *Hearing on the 1980 Economic Report of the President,* 96th Congress, 2nd session, Part I, 77. Washington, DC: Government Printing Office.

Weise, Charles L. 2008. "Political Constraints on Monetary Policy during the Great Inflation." MPRA Paper no. 8694. University of Munich.

Comment   Bennett T. McCallum

I enjoyed this chapter by Andrew Levin and John Taylor very much. I started studying economics in the early to mid-1960s, about the time that Levin and Taylor date the beginning of the Great Inflation, and moved into monetary economics as the inflation progressed. I recall discussing Volcker's announcement of October 6, 1979 with Allan Meltzer during a visit to Carnegie-Mellon just a week or so later. And I recall a telephone conversation with Marvin Goodfriend (at the Richmond Fed) during the summer of 1981 at a time at which the Federal Reserve was trying to decide whether to let the M1 growth rate climb back into its official target range, after finally getting it down to about 2 percent per annum.

Anyhow, the account given by Levin and Taylor rings true. More specifically, I think they are correct to redate the Great Inflation (GI) away from the "1970s" label, although I believe most of us have understood that to be the case, with the label used just as a shorthand. They date the episode as 1965 to 1980. A look at the data (see table 4C.1) shows that M1 growth rates were significantly higher after 1964 than before, so their start date seems about right.[1] Stating that the GI "ended in late 1980" seems a bit inadequate, however. The interest easing in spring 1980 came about after the imposition of credit controls, against the Fed's wishes, which precipitated a truly sharp fall in output. To me it was the tight money over the first two-thirds of 1981 that was crucial—the tightness shows up, by the way, in M1 growth figures when "adjusted" values used by the Fed at the time are taken into account. (Mine come from Broaddus and Goodfriend 1984.)

Bennett T. McCallum is the H. J. Heinz Professor of Economics at Carnegie Mellon University and a research associate of the National Bureau of Economic Research.

Prepared for presentation at the NBER conference on the Great Inflation, September 25–27, 2008, in Woodstock, Vermont. For acknowledgments, sources of research support, and disclosure of the author's material financial relationships, if any, please see http://www.nber.org/chapters/c9171.ack.

1. It is also the case, though not documented here, that monetary base growth rates show a distinct increase around 1964.

Table 4C.1   Selected statistics, percentages (average or changes)

Year or average over	CPI infl. Dec. to Dec.	Fed funds rate	"Real" funds rate	M1 growth rate	Adj. M1 growth: AB&MG (1984)	Unemployment rate
1960–1964	1.2	2.9	1.7	2.8		5.7
1965–1969	3.9	5.4	1.5	5.0		3.8
1970–1974	6.7	7.1	0.4	6.1		5.4
1975	6.9	5.8	−1.1	4.7		8.5
1976	4.9	5.0	0.1	6.7	5.8	7.7
1977	6.7	5.5	−1.2	8.0	7.9	7.1
1978	9.0	7.9	−1.1	8.0	7.2	6.1
1979	13.3	11.2	−2.1	6.9	6.8	5.8
1980	12.5	13.4	0.9	7.0	6.9	7.1
1981	8.9	16.4	7.5	6.9	2.4	7.6
1982	3.8	12.3	8.5	8.7	9.0	9.7
1983	3.8	9.1	5.3	9.8	10.3	9.6
1984	3.9	10.2	6.3	5.8	5.2	7.5
1985–1989	3.7	7.8	4.1	7.7		6.2

Source: McCallum (2008). "AB&MG (1984)" refers to Broaddus and Goodfriend (1984) in the reference list.

In this chapter, Levin and Taylor make two analytical claims that will be contested by some participants. First, they dispute the idea that the GI can be attributed to mismeasurement of the output gap. Second, by arguing that there was not a single regime in place during the relevant years, they in effect deny the idea—associated with Clarida, Galí, and Gertler (2000) and Taylor (1999)—that the problem was "instability" resulting from an interest rate rule that does not satisfy the Taylor principle. Here I think that their "shifting inflation target" hypothesis could perhaps be represented as one hyper-rule that does fail to satisfy the Taylor principle. In that case, the conclusion (as is now fairly well known) is that the difficulty is the non-learnability of either of the two stable rational expectations (RE) solutions (McCallum 2003).

A major feature of the Levin and Taylor analysis is their figure 4.6, which is a Taylor-rule type of diagram, with differing inflation targets for different periods, and with the rule expressed as a real-rate rule (using the Livingston measure for expected inflation). My reading of this plot shows actual rates being fairly consistent with a Taylor rule with target inflation $\pi^* = 5$ over 1966 to 1975 (except for 1969 to 1970) and with $\pi^* = 8$ over 1977 to 1980. That is slightly different from their stop-start episodes, but is also different from a maintained Taylor rule with $\pi^* = 1$ or 2 percent, and more different at the end of 1965 to 1980. I do not disagree basically with their characterization of policy, except that I would give even more emphasis to the idea that the Fed was simply not taking responsibility for inflation control. Of course, there were many academics in the 1960s (and early 1970s) who thought of several other topics, rather than monetary policy, when discussing inflation.

Levin and Taylor's use of real-rate versions of the Taylor rule is useful, but does not give a drastically different conclusion than a nominal-rate comparison between rule and actual values, as in Taylor (1999). This type of comparison continues, I believe, to be valuable. In that regard, it is interesting to compare the messages of four different rules discussed in McCallum (2000). These rules are as follows:

(1) $$R_t = \bar{r} + \Delta p_t^a + 0.5(\Delta p_t^a - \pi^*) + 0.5\tilde{y}_{t-1}$$

(2) $$\Delta b_t = \Delta x^* - \Delta v_t^a + 0.5(\Delta x^* - \Delta x_{t-1})$$

(3) $$R_t = \bar{r} + \Delta p_t^a - 0.5(\Delta x^* - \Delta x_{t-1})$$

(4) $$\Delta b_t = \Delta x^* - \Delta v_t^a - 0.5h_{t-1}.$$

The data used reflects annualized percentages, 1960:Q1 to 1998:Q4. The variables are: R = FFR, x = log GDP, y = log real GDP (linked), $p = x - y$, $v = x - m$, Δp_t^a = average of past four quarters, Δv_t^a = average of past sixteen quarters, $\tilde{y}_t$ is Hodrick-Prescott cycle component, $\pi^* = 2$, $\bar{r} = 2$, $\Delta x^* = 5$, h in (4) is the composite target defined in (1) (see figure 4C.1). Here the picture

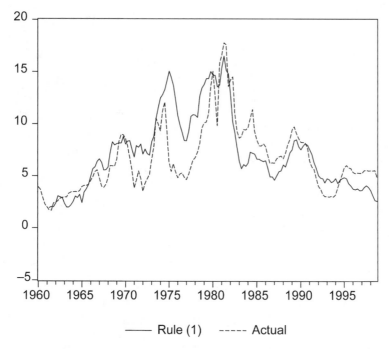

Fig. 4C.1   US interest rates, actual and implied by rule (1)

suggests that the federal funds rate was below the Taylor-rule prescription for almost every quarter during 1966 to 1980, much of the time by 300 basis points. Some critics of this historical approach complain that the rule (1) plot does not show the values that would have been obtained if the rule had been followed. That is true; to predict these would require adoption of a specific model and a simulation. But the plot clearly indicates that actual policy was such as to permit inflation.

Next, let's look at an analogous plot for rule (2), figure 4C.2, with a base-growth instrument and nominal GDP growth target. Here actual base growth is higher than specified by the rule continuously over 1961 to 1980. Units are comparable, so the message is even stronger.

In the next graph, figure 4C.3, I use the base-growth instrument and the Taylor-style target variable. Again the plot's message is stronger than with rule (1) while the rule's instrument setting is less choppy.

In figure 4C.4, we consider the interest rate instrument and Δx_t target variable. This rule would not have signaled inflationary policy over 1972 to 1974.

In the foregoing four-way comparison, the clearest signals come from the two rules with base-growth instruments. Is it counterintuitive that the instrument variable would appear more important than the target variable? My interpretation is that different instruments require different auxiliary

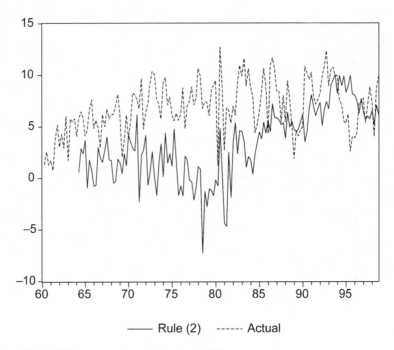

Fig. 4C.2   US base growth, actual and rule (2)

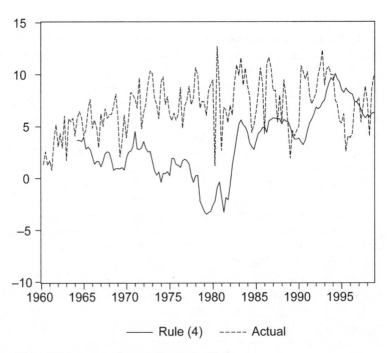

Fig. 4C.3   US base growth, actual and rule (4)

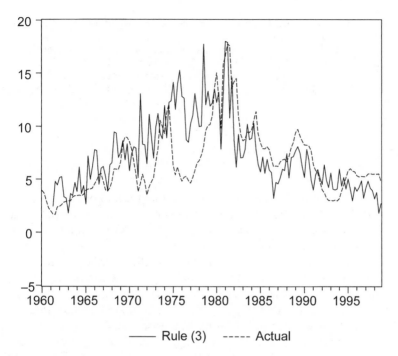

—— Rule (3)   ----- Actual

Fig. 4C.4   US interest rate, actual and rule (3)

assumptions: a constant value for $\bar{r}$ in R_t rules as compared with use of Δv_t^a as an implicit forecast of future Δv_t in Δb_t rules.

In any event, three of these four rules would have called for considerably tighter monetary policy over the period studied and the fourth (rule 3) would have called for tighter policy most of the time. Accordingly, the results of this examination are certainly consistent with Levin and Taylor's punch line, namely, that "the risk of a recurrence of the Great Inflation—as well as other costly policy choices—could be addressed through the use of simple rules as benchmarks for the conduct of monetary policy."

References

Broaddus, A., and M. Goodfriend. 1984. "Base Drift and the Longer Run M1 Growth Rate: Experience from a Decade of Monetary Targeting." *Federal Reserve Bank of Richmond Economic Review* 70:3–14.

Clarida, R., J. Galí, and M. Gertler. 2000. "Monetary Policy Rules and Macroeconomic Stability: Evidence and Some Theory." *Quarterly Journal of Economics* 115 (1): 147–80.

McCallum, B. T. 2000. "Alternative Monetary Policy Rules: A Comparison with Historical Settings for the United States, the United Kingdom, and Japan." *Federal Reserve Bank of Richmond Economic Quarterly* 86 (1): 49–79.

———. 2003. "Multiple-Solution Indeterminacies in Monetary Policy Analysis." *Journal of Monetary Economics* 50 (5): 1153–75.

———. 2008. "Monetarism." In *The Concise Encyclopedia of Economics,* 2nd ed., edited by D. R. Henderson, 350–53. Indianapolis: Liberty Fund, Inc.

Taylor, J. B. 1999. "A Historical Analysis of Monetary Policy Rules." In *Monetary Policy Rules,* edited by J. B. Taylor, 319–348. Chicago: University of Chicago Press.

Discussion

Christina Romer felt the need to emphasize that the authors are rediscovering the wheel of the Great Inflation starting in 1965. Any story that stresses money or ideas cites the 1960s as the onset of the Great Inflation. Romer also took issue with the role of credibility and unanchoring of expectations. There is a mystery of why inflation expectations did not take off until 1976 or 1977. In 1974 and 1975, Chairman Arthur Burns ran tight monetary policy in a recession, so it makes sense that people's expectations did not become unhinged. Romer's last point dealt with the natural rate mismeasurement. The natural rate was computed wrong for a reason. It was a symptom of the bad ideas, most importantly the idea that monetary policy was not effective. Matthew Shapiro added that one of the reasons the gap estimates were so crazy and were often ignored by some at the Federal Reserve was due to the atmospherics. Chairman Burns often referred to estimates as the "so-called natural rate."

Edward Nelson was not sympathetic to the idea that Chairman Burns was much better than Chairman G. William Miller. The idea that Chairman Miller should be held responsible for the period 1978 to 1979 is premised on the idea that monetary policy works on inflation immediately, which is not how the process is seen in inflation-targeting regimes. Both Burns and Miller attributed poor inflation outcomes in the late 1970s to special factors such as exchange rate depreciation. The idea that monetary policy loosened dramatically under Miller is just unfounded. On the contrary, he raised nominal and real interest rates quite a bit. If you believe that monetary policy actions take over a year to have a substantial effect on inflation, then you can blame the rise in inflation in 1978 to 1979 on Chairman Burns, not Chairman Miller, and you can attribute the decline in inflation from 1980 onward partially to the actions of Chairman Miller.

Jeremy Rudd made two small points. First, if you look at the statistical properties of the Livingston Survey, inflation expectations take off in 1972. If you do a regression of changes in the survey expectations on changes in actual inflation and its lags, however, there is no relationship between these variables from 1964 to 1972. Inflation expectations do trend up, but it is not until the end of 1972 that there begins to be a recognizable relationship between inflation expectations and actual inflation. Rudd's second point involved defending the Council of Economic Advisors series on the natural rate of unemployment. What they were computing is exactly what people at the time were thinking about and using for policy. In 1978, there was an article in the Federal Reserve Bulletin about the prospects for inflation and it argues that the productivity slowdown is a level phenomenon related to inflation and unemployment was currently at 5 3/4 percent and approaching full employment. Most current measures say the economy was 2 percent below the nonaccelerating inflation rate of unemployment (NAIRU) at the point. In terms of the 15 percent output gap measured at the time, researchers used an Okun's law coefficient of 3, and most people kept that in mind too long. Lastly, the authors cannot use the one-sided Hodrick-Prescott filter since the technique did not exist at the time.

John Williams echoed a comment made by McCallum, claiming that the history of Chairman Paul Volcker was puzzling. In March of 1980 the interest rate was cut, and the credit controls were put into place. The GDP fell at an 8 percent annual rate. By December of 1980, the Federal Funds rate was up near 20 percent. But the Federal Reserve was cutting rates when GDP was falling. In terms of Regulation Q and disintermediation, Williams cited work from the Federal Reserve Bank of Dallas that estimated an IS equation relating output growth to the Federal Funds rate and Regulation Q variables. From their point of view, the fact that Regulation Q was binding meant monetary policy had large effects on output.

Allan Meltzer discussed three issues. First, he was interested in seeing evidence that Chairman Burns resigned, since he wanted a Democrat to reappoint him. Second, the idea of Chairman Miller having an inflation target of 8 percent seemed mind-boggling to Meltzer, since Miller did not think in those terms. Third, to give Miller credit for the 1980 decline in inflation, one must remember that the relative price shock had gone through and so even if the Federal Reserve did nothing but continue its current policies, the measured rate of inflation should have come down because the charts show that the relative price shock ended. Chairman Volcker did have to renew the policy. It is interesting to compare what actually happened to what was predicted. James Tobin thought it would take ten years with output growth of −10 percent to bring inflation down. But these were all Brookings Institution estimates, and no one else ever believed it. Tobin was a practical monetarist. But the public was supportive of the idea that inflation should end, and thousands of people cut up their credit cards when they thought the credit controls were going to be severe. It all took two years to settle down, not ten.

Athanasios Orphanides referred to his own work where he showed that policy from the mid-1960s to the late 1970s using the classic Taylor rule with a 2 percent inflation target and the real-time output gap predicts a policy very similar to what actually happened, and he found this very distressing. In 1975, specifically, the Council of Economic Advisors knew that their estimates were badly measured and were already working on revising the methodology in order to fix the estimates. The Taylor rule prescription for 1975 was to be much lower than the actual policy rate, so actual policy was more optimal. The same strand of literature also points out that if you use a Taylor rule and remove the output gap from the equation, then policy would have performed much better in the 1970s. Orphanides stressed that this is exactly what the authors are doing when they use the one-sided HP filter, because you are just using white noise in place of the output gap. Regarding the reliability and political sensitivity of output gap measures, there was something terrible that happened to economists starting in the late 1960s. The productivity slowdown, depending on when you date it, threw off all of the estimates of the natural rate, so there is a period of one-sided misperceptions that make output gap policies look bad. Would things have been better if the Federal Reserve had used something else? In 1980, the Council of Economic Advisors stopped producing potential output estimates, so the Federal Reserve had to produce their own. You can track the misperceptions embedded in Federal Reserve Board staff estimates from 1980 onward, and they are sizable for many years. In fact, the same people who were computing these estimates at the Council of Economic Advisors were computing them at the Federal Reserve Board, so it was all the same methodology. In terms of historical appearance of the potential output measure in Federal Reserve Board documents, within three months of estimates being presented at the Council of Economic Advisors in the late 1960s, those estimates showed up in the appendix of a Federal Reserve Board document that soon developed into what is now known as the Green Book.

Christopher Sims had two broad comments. First, he felt it was a mistake to look at the fact that inflation expectations began to increase in 1964 and to use some single mechanism to explain the single uptick. Giorgio Primaceri has the most plausible explanation in Sims's view, but what it comes down to is there were different mechanisms at play at different times. In the beginning, there was the experience of the 1950s and Korean War Inflation, which ended by themselves. But then there was too much reliance on Phillips curve misestimates and bad ideas. How does fiscal theory play a role? Sims then went on to proclaim that policy reaction functions with exogenous inflation targets do not explain anything. If target inflation rates shift around, a model that explains Federal Reserve behavior has to explain why target rates are moving around. If you put into your system a policy reaction function with an inflation target and do not have an explanation of that inflation target anywhere in your system, you have just given up on explaining monetary policy.

Levin began his comments by emphasizing that when you refer to the "Great Inflation of the 1970s" as has become commonplace, it seems more plausible to attribute all of the inflation to energy shocks. There were pressures long before those shocks. The same goes for the ending of the Great

Inflation. It is still a mystery, from the credit controls, the lack of coordination, and so forth. It's as if the Federal Reserve was full of a bunch of comedians. What kind of inflation control were they trying to implement? Levin then segued into Sims's comments, agreeing that there were lots of factors at play, like Regulation Q. It hit the economy very hard, the Federal Reserve was reluctant to tighten, and it created political pressures that took away a lot of independence from the Federal Reserve. In reference to McCallum, Levin felt there were two key phases to the Great Inflation. Long-run inflation expectations started at around 1 percent from 1965 to 1970, and then jumped up to 5 percent. They were stable there until 1976, and then there was another 4 percent deterioration to 9 percent. What went wrong on the jumps? Was it confidence, or lack thereof, in the Federal Reserve chairman? Levin was in agreement with Nelson that it was not all Chairman Miller's fault, since he was in office for such a short period of time. In the end, Levin believed that the lack of an explicit inflation target for a central bank can be a big problem, and in order to have good policy you need clear objectives.

5

Monetary Policy Mistakes and the Evolution of Inflation Expectations

Athanasios Orphanides and John C. Williams

> In monetary policy central bankers have a potent means for fostering stability in the general price level. By training, if not also by temperament, they are inclined to lay great stress on price stability. . . . And yet, despite their antipathy to inflation and the powerful weapons they could yield against it, central bankers have failed so utterly in this mission in recent years. In this paradox lies the anguish of central banking.
> —Arthur Burns (1979, 7)

5.1 Introduction

Numerous explanations have been put forward for the causes of the Great Inflation of the late 1960s and 1970s in the United States. But one explanation that may be the most worrisome for the future is that policy mistakes made by otherwise well-informed and well-intentioned policymakers, free of institutional and political constraints, were responsible for these outcomes. The epigraph quoted from the 1979 Per Jacobsson Lecture delivered by Arthur Burns shortly after the end of his tenure as chairman of the Federal Reserve exemplifies this concern. In this chapter, we provide a historical account of the Great Inflation and subsequent evolution of the economy in the United States using an estimated model with a benevolent and sophisticated policymaker. We examine how the economy would have fared if the Federal Reserve had applied modern optimal control techniques—of the type recommended by many academic researchers today—to reach its policy decisions from the middle of the 1960s on.[1]

Athanasios Orphanides is former governor of the Central Bank of Cyprus. John C. Williams is president and chief executive officer of the Federal Reserve Bank of San Francisco.

We thank Nick Bloom, Bob Hall, Seppo Honkapohja, Andy Levin, John Taylor, Bharat Trehan, and participants at the NBER conference on the Great Inflation and other presentations for helpful comments and suggestions. We also thank Justin Weidner for excellent research assistance. The opinions expressed are those of the authors and do not necessarily reflect the views of the Federal Reserve Bank of San Francisco or the Board of Governors of the Federal Reserve System. For acknowledgments, sources of research support, and disclosure of the authors' material financial relationships, if any, please see http://www.nber.org/chapters/c9176.ack.

1. Optimal control methods were first developed in the 1960s and have gained popularity in the academic literature during the past ten years. See Svensson and Woodford (2003); Woodford (2003); Giannoni and Woodford (2005), and Svensson and Tetlow (2005), for modern derivations and applications of optimal control techniques to monetary policy. See Levin and Williams (2003) and Orphanides and Williams (2008, 2009) for analysis of the optimal control approach to realistic degrees of uncertainty.

We then compare the resulting simulated outcomes to those obtained under alternative monetary policy strategies designed to be robust to model misspecification.

The main thesis of this chapter is that the modern optimal control approach to monetary policy is prone to inviting policy errors that lead to instability in inflation and inflation expectations like those that occurred during the Great Inflation, while alternative robust policy strategies could have been more effective at stabilizing inflation and unemployment. Our reading of the narrative evidence highlights three critical factors that contributed to the unmooring of inflation expectations and the resulting runaway inflation of the Great Inflation. First, policymakers placed a high priority on stabilizing real economic activity relative to price stability. Second, they severely overestimated the productive capacity of the economy during the critical period of 1965 to 1975. In particular, contemporaneous measures of the unemployment rate corresponding to full employment were significantly lower than retrospective estimates. Third, they were overly confident of their understanding of the precise linkage between measures of utilization gaps and inflation. The modern optimal control approach is not designed to protect against any of these factors.

This chapter provides a "stress test" of optimal control policies and other policy strategies to see how they would have fared in times of particular macroeconomic turmoil and when the central bank faced imperfect information. The 1960s and 1970s provide an ideal laboratory for such an experiment. The US economy was buffeted by large shocks, providing severe stress to the economy, and the realized macroeconomic performance was abysmal. Our analysis is related to that of Orphanides (2002) and Orphanides and Williams (2005a), who show that a strong response to flawed measures of economic slack can help explain the very high inflation and unemployment that developed during the 1960s and 1970s and that policies that reacted less aggressively to slack would have been more effective at stabilizing both inflation and unemployment during that period. The contribution of the current chapter is to analyze the stabilization properties of optimal control policies and alternative policy approaches using counterfactual simulations of the US economy over the past several decades. In so doing, we aim to use the experiences of the past to glean lessons for the design of robust monetary policy for the future.

Our model respects the natural rate hypothesis and shares key features with modern models used for monetary policy analysis. We investigate what would have happened over history had policymakers implemented state-of-the-art optimal control methods under the assumption of rational expectations. We focus on the difficulties associated with anchoring inflation expectations when policymakers attempt to maintain a high degree of employment stability relative to price stability in an environment where the central bank has imperfect information about the economy. The estimated model confirms the presence of adverse supply shocks and natural rate misperceptions during the 1970s, which caused policy to become overly expansionary. However, we find that these shocks alone cannot account for the Great Inflation experience.

Using counterfactual simulations, we show that in the absence of informational imperfections, following the optimal control policy during the 1960s and 1970s would have maintained reasonably well-anchored inflation expectations and succeeded in achieving a relatively high degree of economic and price stability. Under these assumptions, monetary policy could have offset the shocks that buffeted the economy during this period.

However, our model simulations also show that informational imperfections, such as policymakers' misperceptions of the natural rate of unemployment, significantly reduce the effectiveness of this approach to policy. The presence of imperfect knowledge amplifies the effects of the underlying shocks, and optimal control monetary policies designed assuming complete information would have failed to keep inflation expectations well anchored. Indeed, optimal control policies would have avoided the Great Inflation only if the weight given to stabilizing the real economy were relatively modest—with the best results achieved if the most weight were placed on stabilizing prices.

We also examine an alternative policy strategy that could have been more robust and avoided this experience, even in the presence of supply shocks and natural rate misperceptions. We show that such a strategy would have been very effective at stabilizing inflation and economic activity, despite the large shocks of the 1970s. A striking result is that this policy rule yields simulated outcomes close to the realized behavior of the economy during the Great Moderation starting in the mid-1980s, suggesting that the actual practice of monetary policy during this period changed in ways that incorporated the key properties of the robust monetary policy rule.

The remainder of the chapter is organized as follows. Section 5.2 examines the narrative evidence of policymakers' views on the natural rate of unemployment and the importance of stabilizing economic activity during the 1960s and 1970s. Our model of the US economy and its estimation are described in section 5.3. Section 5.4 describes the optimal control monetary policy and its implementation in the model simulations. The models of expectations formation and the simulation methods are described in sections 5.5 and 5.6, respectively. Section 5.7 examines the performance of the optimal control policy using counterfactual model simulations. Section 5.8 analyzes the performance of a simple robust monetary policy rule, and section 5.9 concludes.

5.2   A Narrative History

In this section, we examine the narrative evidence regarding the views of policymakers regarding the natural rate of unemployment and the role of stabilizing real activity at "full employment" before, during, and after the Great Inflation.[2] We use this narrative evidence to inform the specification of monetary policy in the model simulations reported in the subsequent sections of the chapter.

To set the stage for later events, it is useful to recall the evolution of the policy debate in the post-World War II period. In the Employment Act of 1946, Congress declared that "it is the continuing policy and responsibility of the Federal Government to use all practicable means . . . to promote maximum employment, production and purchasing power" (quoted in Council of Economic Advisers, 1966, 170).[3] Until the 1960s, policymakers interpreted the Employment Act of 1946 to be a broad mandate to protect price stability, that is, to promote "purchasing power" and growth and to dampen business cycle fluctuations. In congressional testimony in August 1957, for example, Federal Reserve Chairman William McChesney Martin stated that "[t]he objective of the System is always the same—to promote monetary and credit conditions that will foster sustained economic growth together with stability in the value of the dollar." To this end, he stressed the importance of price stability: "Price stability is essential to sustainable growth. Inflation fosters maladjustments" (Martin 1957, 8).

During the 1960s, an increasing number of economists argued that fiscal and monetary policy should play a more active role in managing aggregate demand with the goal of achieving and maintaining full employment. In 1961, the incoming Council of Economic Advisers (CEA) adopted what became known as the "New Economics," which was highlighted in the 1962 *Economic Report of the President* (Council of Economic Advisers 1962). The new strategy was eloquently summarized by Walter Heller, who, according to *Time,* as "Chief Economic Adviser of the Kennedy Council, presided over the birth of the New Economics as a practical policy" (*Time* 1965, 67A). Heller said:

> The promise of modern economic policy, managed with an eye to maintaining prosperity, subduing inflation, and raising the quality of life, is indeed great. And although we have made no startling conceptual breakthroughs in economics in recent years, we *have,* more effectively than ever before, harnessed the existing economics—the economics that has been taught in the nation's college classrooms for some twenty years—to the purposes of prosperity, stability, and growth. (Heller 1966, 116, emphasis in the original)

---

2. See, Mayer (1999), Meltzer (2003), and Hetzel (2008a), among others, for detailed histories of Federal Reserve policy during this period.

3. Chapter 7 of the 1966 *Economic Report of the President* was devoted to the twenty years of experience with the act since it became law on February 20, 1946. This edition of the report, published in early 1966, provides a useful snapshot of policy thinking at the start of the Great Inflation.

A key aspect of the New Economics was a heightened focus on achieving a desired *level* of economic activity, as measured by the unemployment rate or the level of GDP, rather than the less demanding goal of economic expansion. This focus on achieving the economy's potential level of activity necessitated the measurement of potential output and the unemployment rate corresponding to full employment. Arthur Okun, chairman of the CEA in the late 1960s, later summarized the implications of the new strategy for economic policy as follows:

> The revised strategy emphasized, as the standard for judging economic performance, whether the economy was living up to its potential rather than merely whether it was advancing. Ideally, total demand should be in balance with the nation's supply capabilities. When the balance is achieved, there is neither the waste of idle resources nor the strain of inflationary pressure. The nation is then actually producing its potential output. (Okun 1970, 40)

Okun explained that the New Economics reflected a "shift in emphasis from the achievement of expansion to the realization of potential" (41) and explained how this implied greater policy activism:

> [T]he focus on the gap between potential and actual output provided a new scale for the evaluation of economic performance, replacing the dichotomized business cycle standard which viewed expansion as satisfactory and recession as unsatisfactory. This new scale of evaluation, in turn, led to greater activism in economic policy: As long as the economy was not realizing its potential, improvement was needed and government had a responsibility to promote it. (41)

The shift in emphasis toward more explicit targets for employment and the level of economic activity was not intended to downplay the need to preserve price stability. The twin policy objectives of full employment and price stability were stressed repeatedly, starting with the very first study that provided the quantitative definitions of full employment that would shape policy throughout the 1960s: "The full employment goal must be understood as striving for maximum production without inflation pressure" (Okun 1962, 82).

The New Economics also emphasized the importance of monetary policy in achieving these goals. Indeed, the essence of monetary policy was seen in a rather conventional manner not inconsistent with current views. According to the 1962 *Economic Report of the President:* "The proper degree of 'tightness' or 'easiness' of monetary policy . . . depend[s] on the state of the domestic economy, on the fiscal policies of the Government, and on the international economic position. When the economy is in recession or beset by high unemployment and excess capacity, monetary policy should clearly be expansionary. . . . When demand is threatening to outrun the economy's production potential, monetary policy should be restrictive" (CEA 1962,

85). As this quote makes clear, such a policy depends crucially on measuring the economy's capacity accurately.

The critical test for the New Economics would begin in 1965, when the economy was nearing what was perceived at the time to be full employment. The apparent success of economic policy up to that point was the topic of the cover story of the December 1965 *Time* magazine. The story noted that "[e]conomists have descended in force from their ivory towers and now sit confidently at the elbow of almost every important leader in Government and business, where they are increasingly called upon to forecast, plan and decide" (65). Indeed, Okun later remarked, "The high-water mark of the economists' prestige in Washington was probably reached late in 1965" (1970, 59).

Although the New Economics held sway at the CEA and at many academic institutions, Federal Reserve Chairman Martin remained skeptical that policymakers would ever possess the precise knowledge of the economy demanded by the policies of the New Economics. Although Martin's attitude was interpreted by some as a mistrust of economists, it would be more accurate to describe his views as reflecting a mistrust of the fine-tuning approach advocated by some economists who were gaining influence at the time. As Sherman Maisel, an economist who joined the Board of Governors in 1965, later recounted: "The press frequently reported Martin's dismay over the number of economists appointed to the Board. He felt that the economy was too complex to explain in detail; intuition would be lost and false leads followed if too much stress were put on measurement" (Maisel 1973, 114). Nonetheless, by 1965, the center of gravity at the Federal Reserve was shifting away from what we would describe as Martin's robust policy approach toward a fine-tuning approach that sought to achieve a quantitative full-employment goal as well as price stability.

By July 1965 the unemployment rate had fallen to about 4.5 percent and the balance of payments was deteriorating. Martin believed that policy needed to be tightened to restrain inflationary pressures. During the second half of 1965, he attempted to forge a consensus at the Federal Reserve toward policy tightening. But the Council of Economic Advisers and like-minded economists at the Federal Reserve argued against such a preemptive move. In their view, a 4 percent unemployment rate corresponded to full employment. Therefore, the economy was operating below its full-employment level and inflationary pressures were unlikely to emerge.[4]

---

4. The CEA (1962) put the unemployment rate corresponding to full employment at 4 percent. The 1962 *Economic Report of the President* indicated that "in the existing economic circumstances, an unemployment rate of about 4 percent is a reasonable and prudent full employment target for stabilization policy" (46). Although this goal of a 4 percent unemployment rate may appear overly ambitious in retrospect, it did not appear so at the time. Indeed, many considered the 4 percent goal for the unemployment rate insufficiently ambitious. For them, 4 percent was seen to be an interim goal, with the ultimate objective being even lower unemployment.

Martin postponed proposing a policy tightening until December 1965, when, despite significant opposition from members of the Board of Governors, he felt it was no longer prudent to wait. On December 3, 1965, the Federal Reserve Board increased the discount rate from 4.0 to 4.5 percent, with four members of the board voting in favor of and three voting against the rate hike. The published announcement explained: "With slack in manpower and productive capacity now reduced to narrow proportions, with the economy closer to full potential than at any time in nearly a decade . . . it was felt that excessive additions to money and credit availability in an effort to hold present levels of interest rates would spill over into further price increases. Such price rises would endanger the sustainable nature of the present business expansion" (Board of Governors of the Federal Reserve System 1965, 1,668). Governors Robertson, Mitchell, and Maisel dissented from the discount rate action "on the ground that it was at least premature in the absence of more compelling evidence of inflationary dangers" (Board of Governors of the Federal Reserve System 1965, 1,668).

In remarks that were delivered a few days later, on December 8, Chairman Martin had an opportunity to explain his reasoning for the rate hike:

> The Federal Reserve, in all its actions, aims always at the same goal: to help the economy move forward at the fastest sustainable pace. We reach our destination most rapidly as well as more assuredly when we travel at maximum *safe* speed—and this speed cannot be the same under all conditions and at all times. . . .
>
> To me, the effective time to act against inflationary pressures is when they are in the development stage—before they have become full-blown and the damage has been done. Precautionary measures are more likely to be effective than remedial action: the old proverb that an ounce of prevention is worth a pound of cure applies to monetary policy as well as to anything else. . . .
>
> [S]o long as inflation is merely a threat rather than a reality, it is enough to prevent the pace of economic expansion from accelerating dangerously. But once that pace has become unsustainably fast, then it becomes necessary to reduce the speed, and once such a reduction is started, there is no assurance it can be stopped in time to avoid an actual downswing. (Martin 1965, emphasis in original)

The discount rate increase prompted a bruising congressional hearing the following week, on December 13–14, 1965. The hearing, "Recent Federal Reserve Action and Economic Policy Coordination" (US Congress 1966) served as a forum for criticizing Chairman Martin for tightening policy. It provides an invaluable glimpse into the policy debate at the time and highlights the crucial role that perceptions about full employment had acquired. Martin represented the majority view and Governors Mitchell and Maisel, who opposed the tightening, represented the dissenting view at the hearing on December 13, 1965. At the hearing, it was confirmed that a crucial reason for the disagreement on the tightening was a disagreement about the risks to the inflation outlook. Furthermore, details emerged as to the assessments of the chairman and dissenting members of the board regarding what constituted full employment.

The discussion centered on whether a 4 percent unemployment rate was the appropriate definition of full employment. Martin remarked, "As long as unemployment of manpower and plant capacity was greater than could be considered acceptable or normal, we had every reason to lean on the side of monetary stimulus." Senator Jacob Javits asked, "Do you consider a 4 percent unemployment acceptable and normal and is that the basis for your decision?" (US Congress 1966, 116). Noting that this is a long-standing debate among experts, Martin replied that, although the Federal Reserve Board would want "as low a level as it is possible to have," he did not know what the right level ought to be. Responding to subsequent questions he added, "We [the Board of Governors] have never addressed ourselves to a definitive discussion of the 3 or 4 or 5 percent." But he admitted that in making the policy decision the board deemed that "we were approaching a state of full employment" (116–17). The unemployment rate had fallen to 4.2 percent in November 1965.

Those arguing against a policy tightening pointed to the fact that unemployment was still above 4 percent and therefore inflationary pressures should be absent, despite the fact that inflation, as measured by the Consumer Price Index, had been edging up for some time. In his prepared statement at the hearing, Governor Mitchell explained that the challenge to policy at the end of 1965 was to "ease the economy onto a steady growth path at full employment," adding, "I believe this can be done with reasonably stable prices" (US Congress 1966, 21). But, with the unemployment rate exceeding 4 percent, he disagreed that a policy tightening was necessary. "[T]he evidence on prices does not, in my view, now call for more monetary restraint than is already being applied" (22). The crux of his argument evolved around the definition of full employment: "Those who regard 4 percent unemployment . . . as the approximate total of the frictionally unemployed . . . may feel that we have achieved our employment goals and that any further progress in reducing unemployment cannot come from aggregate demand. . . . I am not yet ready to agree that there is no further room for compression of the unemployment rate" (22–23).

Indeed, Governor Maisel argued that 4 percent may have been too high a target for the unemployment rate. He explained that he disagreed with the policy decision because he felt that policy tightening was premature. In his prepared remarks, he noted, "Raising the discount rate would be interpreted as a view by the Board that because full employment increases inflationary problems, restrictive monetary policy must be invoked at its mere approach" (31). Asked about his views on full employment, in the light of the various efforts to reduce frictional unemployment he replied, "My assumption is that the retraining enables us to say that 4 percent unemployment was only an interim goal. . . . As a result 4 percent might have been a proper goal five years ago. . . . Now we need to think of these retraining programs you have cited and see what our present goal should be. Should it be 3 percent or what?" (181). The view that the interim goal for unemployment could perhaps be adjusted downwards was also shared by the Council of Economic Advisers. As noted in the *Economic Report of the President* published in early 1966, "The unemployment rate has now virtually reached the interim target and is projected to fall below 4 percent in 1966. There is strong evidence that the conditions originally set for lowering the target are in fact being met, and that the economy can operate efficiently at lower unemployment rates" (CEA 1966, 75).

This debate centered on estimates of the unemployment rate consistent with price stability and the proper policy response to movements in inflation and unemployment. Importantly, the participants did not possess fundamentally divergent views of the inflation process. Indeed, both sides used a relatively conventional understanding of the process of inflation and the effect of "gaps" on inflation. In particular, policymakers clearly believed that they had the power to control inflation through monetary policy. The 1966 *Economic Report of the President* provides a view of inflation that relates well to models used today:

> As a first approximation, the classical law of supply and demand leads one to expect that the change in the price level will depend mainly on the size of the gap between capacity and actual output. The more production falls short of potential—i.e., the greater is excess productive capacity—the further prices should drop. Conversely, when demand outruns aggregate supply, the imbalance should raise prices. . . .
>
> Expectations and attitudes also affect price changes. An economy accustomed to price stability is less vulnerable to inflation." (CEA 1966, 63–65)

Note the explicit recognition of the role of expectations in the determination of inflation.[5]

Even when inflation got noticeably higher in the second half of the 1960s, the mistaken belief that the full-employment unemployment rate was very low continued to distort policy decisions, exacerbating inflationary pres-

---

5. To be sure, there are differences between the reasoning in the 1960s and modern models. One important difference is that the models of the New Economics era typically implied a long-term trade-off between inflation and unemployment, whereas modern models such as ours typically respect the natural rate hypothesis. But this difference is not key for explaining the Great Inflation in our view. As explained by Modigliani and Papademos (1975), in both types of models, there exists a rate of unemployment (the nonaccelerating inflation rate of unemployment, or NAIRU) that is consistent with the policymaker's definition of reasonable price stability. In our model, this corresponds to the natural rate of unemployment. What is critical is that in both types of models, misperceptions about the NAIRU (or natural rate) have inflationary consequences under the optimal control approach to policy.

sures. Although the rise in inflation during 1966 and thereafter vindicated Martin's position, this evidence proved insufficient to stem the tide toward greater fine-tuning with an emphasis on achieving what was believed to be full employment. Later, Herbert Stein went so far as to call the belief that the natural rate of unemployment was 4 percent "the most serious error of the Nixon CEA" (Stein 1996, 19). As he explained, "fascinated by the idea of "the natural rate of unemployment," which we thought to be 4 percent, we thought it necessary only to let the unemployment rate rise slightly above that to hold down inflation" (19–20). The resulting policy actions would have been the "optimum feasible path," except that they built upon a fatally flawed view of the productive capacity of the economy. Instead of restoring stability, they led to further increases in inflation.

The inflation rate rose from below 2 percent in the early 1960s to over 5 percent by 1970. Figure 5.1 shows the four-quarter average of the US inflation rate, measured by the GDP price deflator, from 1955 to 2003. (Note that throughout this chapter, unless otherwise indicated, the figures show the four-quarter moving average of the inflation rate to reduce the visual clutter caused by quarterly volatility in this series.) For comparison, the horizontal line shows the 2 percent inflation target that we assume reflects the policymaker's price stability objective for our counterfactual simulations reported in later sections. The inflation rate was around this level before the Great Inflation and returned once again to this level in the last decade

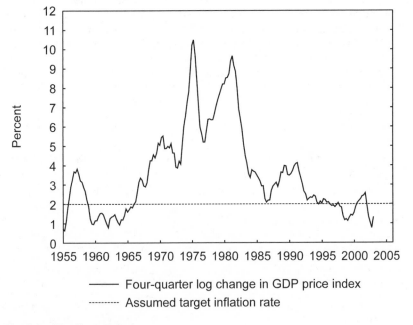

Fig. 5.1   The Great Inflation

of our sample. Inflation expectations became unmoored during the Great Inflation (see Levin and Taylor [this volume] for further discussion of the evidence on inflation expectations) and only in the 1990s did they become anchored again. By the beginning of the 1980s, survey measures of long-run inflation expectations had risen to over 8 percent.

Under Arthur Burns, who became Fed chairman in 1970, the Federal Reserve continued the activist bent with even greater force (Hetzel 1998; Orphanides 2003). The high degree of confidence that economists had regarding their ability to measure the capacity of the economy and to gauge inflationary pressures is nicely illustrated by the staff briefing to the Board of Governors from August 1970 presented by John Charles Partee (who become a governor in 1976): "there is substantial underutilization of resources, as evidenced by a 5 percent unemployment rate and an operating rate in manufacturing estimated at well under 80 percent of capacity. In these circumstances, there is virtually no risk that economic recovery over the year ahead would add to the inflationary problem through stimulation of excess—or even robust—demand in product or labor markets" (Board of Governors 1970, 19).

In his "Anguish" lecture (1979), Burns admitted that the Federal Reserve was slow to recognize the upward drift in the natural rate of unemployment, thus adding to inflation (Burns 1979). Figure 5.2 plots real-time estimates of the natural rate of unemployment and a retrospective measure of the natural

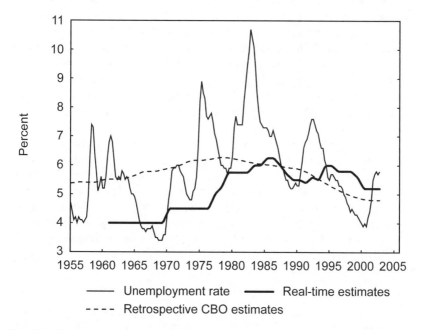

Fig. 5.2   Estimates of the natural rate of unemployment

rate equal to the Congressional Budget Office (CBO) estimates available at the time that this chapter was written. The actual unemployment rate is plotted as well. The real-time series for the natural rate is taken from Orphanides and Williams (2005a), extended to include more recent data. These real-time estimates were constructed drawing on a number of sources (see Orphanides and Williams [2002] for details). As seen in the figure, differences between real-time estimates of the natural rate of unemployment and current retrospective estimates were especially large and persistent during the second half of the 1960s and the 1970s. The mean absolute difference between the real-time and current estimates was 1.2 percentage points over this period. But such natural rate "misperceptions" are not merely a historical curiosity, with the mean absolute difference between the two measures equaling 0.6 percentage points over the period of 1980 to 2003.[6]

The overly optimistic estimates of the economy's capacity was of particular importance in light of the high value placed on achieving full employment relative to price stability. Despite the upward trend in inflation since 1965, the Federal Reserve remained focused on stabilizing real activity, with the hope that inflationary pressures would subside. At the May 1975 meeting of the Federal Open Market Committee (FOMC), the board staff argued that "there is such a large amount of slack in the economy now that real growth would have to exceed our projection by a wide margin, and for an extended period, before excess aggregate demand once again emerged as a significant problem" (Board of Governors of the Federal Reserve 1975, 26). Furthermore, "[s]imulations using the econometric model suggested that a considerably faster rate of expansion could be stimulated without having a significant effect on the rate of increase in prices—that a considerably more rapid rate of increase in real GNP would still be consistent with a further winding down of inflationary pressures" (27). The inflation rate in fact did come down from its 1975 peak of about 10 percent over the next few years, but bottomed out above 5 percent, well in excess of conventional views of price stability.

Monetary policy moved away from the policy activism of the earlier period and toward an approach focused more on inflation stabilization only after Paul Volcker became chairman in 1979. Volcker eschewed the fine-tuning approach and concentrated instead on the goal of price stability, seeing this as the only way to effectively reanchor inflation expectations and restore broader stability to the economy (Goodfriend and King 2005; Hetzel 2008b; Lindsey, Orphanides, and Rasche 2005; Orphanides and Williams 2005a). He explained his rationale in his first Humphrey-Hawkins testimony on February 19, 1980.

---

6. Note that this measure of natural rate misperceptions does not take into account uncertainty regarding the CBO's estimates of the natural rate. Instead, it merely measures changes in the estimates that reflect changes in methodology and the effects of new data.

In the past, at critical junctures for economic stabilization policy, we have usually been more preoccupied with the possibility of near-term weakness in economic activity or other objectives than with the implications of our actions for future inflation. To some degree, that has been true even during the long period of expansion since 1975. As a consequence, fiscal and monetary policies alike too often have been prematurely or excessively stimulative or insufficiently restrictive. The result has been our now chronic inflationary problem, with a growing conviction on the part of many that this process is likely to continue. Anticipations of higher prices themselves help speed the inflationary process. . . .

The broad objective of policy must be to break that ominous pattern. That is why dealing with inflation has properly been elevated to a position of high national priority. Success will require that policy be consistently and persistently oriented to that end. Vacillation and procrastination, out of fears of recession or otherwise, would run grave risks. Amid the present uncertainties, stimulative policies could well be misdirected in the short run. More importantly, far from assuring more growth over time, by aggravating the inflationary process and psychology, they would threaten more instability and unemployment. (Volcker 1980, 2–3)

5.3   An Estimated Model of the US Economy

We now turn to the evaluation of alternative monetary policy strategies. We use counterfactual simulations of the estimated quarterly model of the US economy described in Orphanides and Williams (2008). The specification of the model is motivated by the recent literature on micro-founded models incorporating some inertia in inflation and output (see Woodford [2003] for a fuller discussion). The main difference from other monetary policy models is that the unemployment gap is substituted for the output gap in the model to facilitate estimation using real-time data. The two concepts are closely related in practice by Okun's law, and the key properties of the model are largely unaffected by this choice.

5.3.1   The Model

The structural model consists of two equations that describe the behavior of the unemployment rate and the inflation rate and equations describing the time-series properties of the exogenous shocks. To close the model, the short-term interest rate is set by the central bank, as described in the next section.

The "IS curve" equation is motivated by the Euler equation for consumption with adjustment costs or habit:

(1) $$u_t = \phi_u u_{t+1}^e + (1 - \phi_u)u_{t-1} + \alpha_u(i_t^e - \pi_{t+1}^e - r^*) + v_t,$$

(2) $$v_t = \rho_v v_{t-1} + e_{v,t}, \, e_v \sim N(0, \sigma_{e_v}^2).$$

Equation (1) relates the unemployment rate, u_t, to the unemployment rate expected in the next period, one lag of the unemployment rate, and the difference between the expected ex ante real interest rate—equal to the difference between the expected nominal short-term interest rate, i_t^e, and the expected inflation rate in the following period, π_{t+1}^e—and the natural rate of interest, r^*. The unemployment rate is subject to a shock, v_t, that is assumed to follow an AR(1) (autoregression) process with innovation variance $\sigma_{e_v}^2$. The AR(1) specification for the shock is based on the evidence of serial correlation in the residuals of the estimated unemployment equation, as discussed later.

The "Phillips curve" equation is motivated by the New Keynesian Phillips curve with indexation:

$$(3) \qquad \pi_t = \phi_\pi \pi_{t+1}^e + (1 - \phi_\pi)\pi_{t-1} + \alpha_\pi(u_t - u_t^*) + e_{\pi,t}, e_\pi \sim N(0, \sigma_{e_\pi^*}^2).$$

It relates inflation, π_t—measured as the annualized percent change in the gross national product (GNP) or gross domestic product (GDP) price index, depending on the period—during quarter t to lagged inflation, expected future inflation, and the difference between the unemployment rate, u_t, and the natural rate of unemployment, u_t^*, during the current quarter. The parameter ϕ_π measures the importance of expected inflation on the determination of inflation, while $(1 - \phi_\pi)$ captures the effects of inflation indexation. The "markup" shock, $e_{\pi,t}$, is assumed to be a white noise disturbance with variance $\sigma_{e_\pi}^2$.

We model the low frequency behavior of the natural rate of unemployment as an exogenous AR(1) process independent of all other variables:

$$(4) \qquad u_t^* = (1 - \rho_{u^*})\overline{u}^* + \rho_{u^*}u_{t-1}^* + e_{u^*,t}, e_{u^*} \sim N(0, \sigma_{e_u^*}^2).$$

We assume this process is stationary based on the finding using the standard augmented Dickey-Fuller test that one can reject the null of nonstationarity of the unemployment rate over 1950 to 2003 at the 5 percent level.

5.3.2   Model Estimation and Calibration

The investment/savings (IS) curve and Phillips curve equations are estimated using forecasts from the Survey of Professional Forecasters (SPF) as proxies for the expectations that appear in the equations.[7] Expectations are assumed to be formed in the previous quarter; that is, the expectations affecting inflation and unemployment in period t are those collected in quarter

---

7. Specifically, the mean forecasts of the unemployment rate and the three-month Treasury bill rate are used. The inflation forecasts are constructed using the annualized log difference of the GNP or GDP price deflator, taken from the reported forecasts of real and nominal GNP or GDP. The survey is currently maintained by the Federal Reserve Bank of Philadelphia. See Croushore (1993) and Croushore and Stark (2001) for details on the survey methodology.

$t-1$. This matches the informational structure in many theoretical models (see Woodford 2003 and Giannoni and Woodford 2005). To match the inflation and unemployment data as closely as possible with these forecasts, the first announced estimates of these series are used. These are obtained from the Real-Time Data Set for Macroeconomists maintained by the Federal Reserve Bank of Philadelphia. In estimating the inflation equation, the CBO (2001) estimates of the natural rate of unemployment are used as proxies for the true values over time. The data sample used for estimating the model runs from 1968:Q4 to 2004:Q2, where the starting date is the first sample point in the SPF.[8]

Estimation results are reported in equations (5) through (7), with standard errors indicated in parentheses. The IS curve equation is estimated using least squares with AR(1) residuals. Unrestricted estimation of the IS curve equation yields a point estimate for ϕ_u of 0.39, with a standard error of 0.15. This estimate is below the lower bound of 0.5 implied by theory; however, the null hypothesis of a value of 0.5 is not rejected by the data.[9] Thus the restriction $\phi_u = 0.5$ is imposed in estimating the remaining parameters of the equation. Note that the estimated equation also includes a constant term (not shown) that provides an estimate of the natural real interest rate, which is assumed to be constant:

(5) $$u_t = 0.5u_{t+1}^e + 0.5u_{t-1} + \underset{(0.022)}{0.056}(i_t^e - \pi_{t+1}^e - r^*) + v_t,$$

(6) $$v_t = \underset{(0.085)}{0.513}v_{t-1} + e_{v,t}, \hat{\sigma}_{e_v} = 0.30,$$

(7) $$\pi_t = 0.5\pi_{t+1}^e + 0.5\pi_{t-1} - \underset{(0.087)}{0.294}(u_t - u_t^*) + e_{\pi,t}, \hat{\sigma}_{e_\pi} = 1.35.$$

Unrestricted estimation of the Phillips curve equation yields a point estimate for ϕ_π of 0.51, just barely above the lower bound implied by theory.[10] For symmetry with the treatment of the IS curve, the restriction $\phi_\pi = 0.5$ is imposed and the remaining parameters are estimated using ordinary least squares (OLS). The estimated residuals for this equation show no signs of serial correlation in the price equation, consistent with the assumption of the model.

We do not estimate the model of the natural rate of unemployment; instead, we set the autocorrelation parameter, ρ_{r^*}, to 0.99 and set the unconditional mean to the sample average of the unemployment rate.

8. Expectations for the Treasury bill rate were not collected in the first few years of the sample. When these are not available, the expectations of the three-month rate implied by the slope of the term structure under the expectations hypothesis are used.

9. This finding is consistent with the results reported in Giannoni and Woodford (2005) who, in a similar model, find that the corresponding coefficient is constrained to be at its theoretical lower bound.

10. For comparison, Giannoni and Woodford (2005) find that the corresponding coefficient is constrained to be at its theoretical lower bound of 0.5.

5.4   Monetary Policy

We focus on two alternative approaches to monetary policy. The first is the optimal control approach. The second is a simple monetary policy rule that is closely related to nominal income growth targeting. In both cases, the policy instrument is the nominal short-term interest rate. We assume that the central bank observes all variables from previous periods when making the current-period policy decision. We further assume that policy is conducted under commitment.

5.4.1   Optimal Control Monetary Policy

It is important to make clear from the start that we make no claim that the Federal Reserve set policy according to the mechanical optimal control algorithms we describe in this chapter during the 1960s and 1970s. Indeed, the development of formal quantitative monetary policy evaluation exercises was still in its infancy at that time. The Federal Reserve Board staff first completed an ambitious project using optimal control in the mid-1970s (Kalchbrenner and Tinsley 1976). Although Federal Reserve Governor Henry Wallich (1976) stated that "[t]he use of optimal control techniques in planning for economic stabilization is approaching the policy stage," in fact, this project was never integrated with the policy process at the Federal Reserve during this period.[11] We would argue that the optimal control approach resembles the spirit of fine-tuning practiced by policymakers at that time. In any case, our goal is to evaluate the performance of such an optimal control strategy under the conditions that existed in the 1960s and 1970s.

The optimal control approach stipulates that the policy instrument is chosen to minimize the central bank's loss function given the constraints imposed by the central bank's model. We construct the optimal control policy rule, as is typical in the literature, assuming that the policymaker knows the true parameters of the structural model and assumes all agents use rational expectations. The parameters of the optimal control policy are computed assuming the central bank knows the natural rate of unemployment.[12] Note that for the optimal control policy, as well as the simple monetary policy rules described later, we use lagged information in the determination of the interest rate, reflecting the lagged release of data.

We assume that the central bank's objective is to minimize a loss equal to the weighted sum of the unconditional variances of the inflation rate, the

11. Nonetheless, it is worth noting that the loss function in Kalchbrenner and Tinsley (1976) penalized an unemployment rate above 4.8 percent and an inflation rate above 2.5 percent. This target for the unemployment rate is consistent with our analysis of real-time estimates of the natural rate of unemployment used in the model simulations in this chapter. The 2.5 percent inflation target is somewhat higher than the 2 percent inflation target we assume in our model simulations.
12. See, for example, Sargent's (2007) description of the optimal policy approach.

difference between the unemployment rate and the natural rate of unemployment, and the first-difference of the nominal federal funds rate:

$$(8) \qquad \mathcal{L} = \text{Var}(\pi - 2) + \lambda\text{Var}(u - u^*) + v\text{Var}(\Delta(i)),$$

where $\text{Var}(x)$ denotes the unconditional variance of variable x. We assume an inflation target of 2 percent. In the following, we consider different values of the parameters of the loss function.[13]

The optimal control policy is described by a set of equations that describes the first-order optimality condition for monetary policy and the behavior of the Lagrange multipliers associated with the constraints on the optimization problem implied by the structural equations of the model economy. Because we are interested in describing the setting of interest rates in a potentially misspecified model, it is useful to represent the optimal control policy by an equation that relates the policy instrument to macroeconomic variables, rather than in terms of Lagrange multipliers that are model-specific. There are infinitely many such representations. In the following, we focus on one representation of the optimal control policy, denoted as the "OC" policy. In the OC policy, the current interest rate depends on three lags of the inflation rate, the difference between the unemployment rate and the central bank's estimate of the natural rate of unemployment, and the difference between the nominal interest rate and the natural rate of interest. The OC representation yields a determinate rational expectations equilibrium in our model. We find that including three lags of these variables is sufficient to very closely mimic the optimal control outcome, assuming the central bank observes the natural rate of unemployment.[14]

As discussed previously, during much of the 1960s and 1970s, policy-makers placed a great deal of weight on the stabilization of real activity. We represent such preferences with values of $\lambda = 16$ and $v = 1$. In that case, the OC policy is given by the following equation:

$$(9) \qquad i_t = 1.16 i_{t-1} - 0.05 i_{t-2} - 0.21 i_{t-3}$$
$$+ 0.23\pi_{t-1} - 0.07\pi_{t-2} + 0.05\pi_{t-3}$$
$$- 3.70(u_{t-1} - \hat{u}^*_{t-1}) + 2.81(u_{t-2} - \hat{u}^*_{t-1}) - 0.15(u_{t-3} - \hat{u}^*_{t-1}),$$

plus a constant reflecting the constant natural rate of interest and inflation target, where $\hat{u}^*_t$ denotes the central bank's estimate of the natural rate of unemployment.

In the following, we also examine the performance of the OC policy

---

13. Based on an Okun's law type relationship, the variance of the unemployment gap is about one-fourth that of the output gap, so a choice of $\lambda = 4$ corresponds to equal weights on inflation and output gap variability.

14. In deriving the OC policy, we use the innovation processes from the estimated model and set the innovation standard deviation of the natural rate of unemployment to 0.07. See Orphanides and Williams (2009) for details.

derived for alternative values of λ. The resulting OC policy for $\lambda = 4$ and $v = 1$ is given by the following equation:

$$(10) \qquad i_t = 1.17 i_{t-1} + 0.02 i_{t-2} - 0.28 i_{t-3}$$
$$+ 0.18 \pi_{t-1} + 0.03 \pi_{t-2} + 0.01 \pi_{t-3}$$
$$- 2.47 (u_{t-1} - \hat{u}^*_{t-1}) + 2.11 (u_{t-2} - \hat{u}^*_{t-1}) - 0.33 (u_{t-3} - \hat{u}^*_{t-1}).$$

Compared to the OC policy derived with $\lambda = 16$, this policy is characterized by a stronger response to inflation and a much smaller response to the unemployment rate. Finally, the OC policy derived for $\lambda = 0$ and $v = 1$ is given by:

$$(11) \qquad i_t = 1.12 i_{t-1} + 0.13 i_{t-2} - 0.34 i_{t-3}$$
$$+ 0.17 \pi_{t-1} + 0.09 \pi_{t-2} - 0.01 \pi_{t-3}$$
$$- 1.63 (u_{t-1} - \hat{u}^*_{t-1}) + 1.53 (u_{t-2} - \hat{u}^*_{t-1}) - 0.38 (u_{t-3} - \hat{u}^*_{t-1}).$$

As expected, this policy is characterized by a stronger response to inflation and a much smaller response to the unemployment rate than the OC policy derived for $\lambda = 4$.

5.4.2   Central Bank Natural Rate Estimates

As seen in these equations, a key input into the setting of OC policies is the central bank's estimate of the natural rate of unemployment. In deriving the OC policy, we assume that the central bank knows the true structure of the economy, including the value of the natural rate of unemployment. In the model simulations, however, we also examine alternative assumptions regarding the central bank's knowledge of the natural rate. One alternative is that the central bank's estimates of the natural rate follow the historical pattern of the real-time estimates reported in figure 5.2. We refer to this case as "historical natural rate misperceptions." A second alternative is that the central bank estimates the natural rate based on the Kalman filter applied to the Phillips curve equation for inflation. We refer to this case as "Kalman filter estimates." In each case, we assume that the true values of the natural rate of unemployment follow the current CBO estimates shown in figure 5.2.

In the case of Kalman filter estimation of the natural rate of unemployment, we assume that the central bank uses an appropriate Kalman filter consistent with the data. In particular, the central bank's real-time Kalman filter estimate of the natural rate of unemployment, $\hat{u}^*_t$, is given by

$$(12) \qquad \hat{u}^*_t = a_1 \hat{u}^*_{t-1} + a_2 \left(u^*_t - \frac{e_{\pi,t}}{\alpha_\pi} \right),$$

where a_1 and a_2 are the Kalman gain parameters. The term within the parentheses is the current-period "shock" to inflation that incorporates the effects of the transitory inflation disturbance and the deviation of the natural rate of unemployment from its unconditional mean, scaled in units of the unemployment rate. Note that the central bank only observes this "surprise" and not the decomposition into its two components.

The optimal values of the gain parameters depend on the variances of the various shocks in the model. Based on a calibrated Kalman filter model, we assume that the central bank uses the following values: $a_1 = 0.982$ and $a_2 = 0.008$ (see Orphanides and Williams [2009] for the derivation of these values). We assume that the central bank starts the simulation with the value of 4 percent, consistent with the evidence from real-time estimates reported earlier.

5.5   Expectations and Simulation Methods

We assume that private agents and, in some cases, the central bank form expectations using an estimated reduced-form forecasting model. Specifically, following Orphanides and Williams (2005b), we posit that private agents engage in perpetual learning; that is, they reestimate their forecasting model using a constant-gain least squares algorithm that weights recent data more heavily than past data. (See Sargent [1999]; Cogley and Sargent [2001]; and Evans and Honkapohja [2001] for related treatments of learning.) This approach to modeling learning allows for the possible presence of time variation in the economy, including the natural rates of interest and unemployment. It also implies that agents' estimates are always subject to sampling variation—that is, the estimates do not eventually converge to fixed values.

Private agents forecast inflation, the unemployment rate, and the short-term interest rate using an unrestricted vector autoregression (VAR) model containing three lags of these three variables and a constant. Note that we assume that private agents do not observe or estimate the natural rate of unemployment directly in forming expectations. The effects of time variation in the natural rate on forecasts are reflected in the forecasting VAR by the lags of the interest rate, inflation rate, and unemployment rate. As discussed in Orphanides and Williams (2008), this VAR forecasting model provides accurate forecasts in model simulations.

At the end of each period, agents update their estimates of their forecasting model using data through the current period. Let Y_t denote the 1×3 vector consisting of the inflation rate, the unemployment rate, and the interest rate, each measured at time t: $Y_t = (\pi_t, u_t, i_t)$. Further, let X_t be the 10×1 vector of regressors in the forecast model: $X_t = (1, \pi_{t-1}, u_{t-1}, i_{t-1}, \ldots, \pi_{t-3}, u_{t-3}, i_{t-3})$. Also, let c_t be the 10×3 vector of coefficients of the forecasting model. Using data through period t, the coefficients of the forecasting model can be written in recursive form as follows:

(13) $c_t = c_{t-1} + \kappa R_t^{-1} X_t (Y_t - X_t' c_{t-1})$,

(14) $R_t = R_{t-1} + \kappa (X_t X_t' - R_{t-1})$,

where κ is the gain. Agents construct the multiperiod forecasts that appear in the inflation and unemployment equations in the model using the estimated VAR.

The matrix R_t may not be full rank at times. To circumvent this problem, in each period of the model simulations, we check the rank of R_t. If it is less than full rank, we assume that agents apply a standard ridge regression (Hoerl and Kennard 1970), where R_t is replaced by $R_t + 0.00001 * I(10)$ and $I(10)$ is a 10×10 identity matrix.

5.5.1 Calibrating the Learning Rate

A key parameter in the learning model is the private-agent updating parameter, κ. Estimates of this parameter tend to be imprecise and sensitive to model specification, but tend to lie between 0 and 0.04.[15] We take 0.02 to be a reasonable benchmark value for κ.

5.6   Model Simulations

We examine a set of alternative counterfactual simulations to investigate the implications of alternative monetary policy frameworks on macroeconomic developments over the past forty years. We start our simulations in the first quarter of 1966, which corresponds to what we and many observers consider to be the beginning of the Great Inflation in the United States.

5.6.1   Initial Conditions

The state variables of the model economy with learning are as follows: the current and lagged values of the inflation rate, the federal funds rate, the unemployment rate, the true natural rate of unemployment, the real-time estimate of the natural rate, the shocks to the structural equations, and the matrices c and R for the forecasting model. We initialize the c and R matrices using the values implied by the reduced-form solution of the model under rational expectations for the stipulated monetary policy rule. In so doing, we are implicitly assuming that the initial conditions for the agents' learning model are consistent with the policy rule in place. That is, we assume that at the start of the simulation, expectations are well aligned with the monetary policy regime under consideration. Over time, expectations then evolve as described earlier. This assumption implies that the initial conditions for these state variables are different across the counterfactual simulations. As

15. See Sheridan (2003), Orphanides and Williams (2005a), Branch and Evans (2006), and Milani (2007).

a result, the simulated paths will often differ significantly from the historical patterns.

To compute the history of equation residuals, we first compute the implied forecasts from our forecasting model of inflation, the unemployment rate, and the federal funds rate over the period 1966 to 2003. We treat the forecasts generated by the learning model as the true data for agents' expectations and then compute tracking residuals; that is, the values of the historical residuals for the equations for the unemployment rate, the inflation rate, and the natural rate of unemployment. Thus, given these residuals and the historical path for the nominal interest rate, the model's predictions will exactly match the historical paths for all endogenous variables. We then conduct counterfactual experiments in which we modify assumptions regarding monetary policy, but do not change the paths for the equation residuals for unemployment, inflation, and the natural rate of unemployment, which we assume are exogenous. Each counterfactual simulation starts in the first quarter of 1966 and ends in the fourth quarter of 2003.

5.7   Performance of Optimal Control Policies

If the Federal Reserve had accurate estimates of the natural rate of unemployment, then the OC policy derived assuming a moderately large weight on unemployment stabilization would have avoided the Great Inflation. Figure 5.3 shows the simulated paths for key variables assuming that the Fed follows the OC policy derived under $\lambda = 16$ and $v = 1$. The left column of the figure shows the outcomes assuming the Fed knew the true values of the natural rate of unemployment. Inflation would have been somewhat volatile during the 1970s, reflecting the effects of the large shocks hitting the economy at the time, but the deviation of the four-quarter inflation rate from target would not have exceeded 3 percentage points during that period.

In the absence of natural rate misperceptions, inflation expectations would have remained reasonably contained during the 1970s. The middle left panel shows the simulated four-quarter-ahead inflation expectations under the OC policy. For comparison, the figure also shows the corresponding SPF inflation forecasts, which rose dramatically in the 1970s.[16] As seen in figure 5.3, the OC policy acts to raise the unemployment rate up to the natural rate by 1967 and holds the unemployment rate moderately above the natural rate through most of the 1970s, offsetting the inflationary effects of the supply shocks of that period. These policy actions help stabilize inflation and inflation expectations and avoid the need of a disinflationary policy at the end of the decade.

---

16. For this figure and those that follow, the SPF three-quarter-ahead inflation forecast is substituted for the four-quarter-ahead forecast in the periods when the latter is missing from the survey.

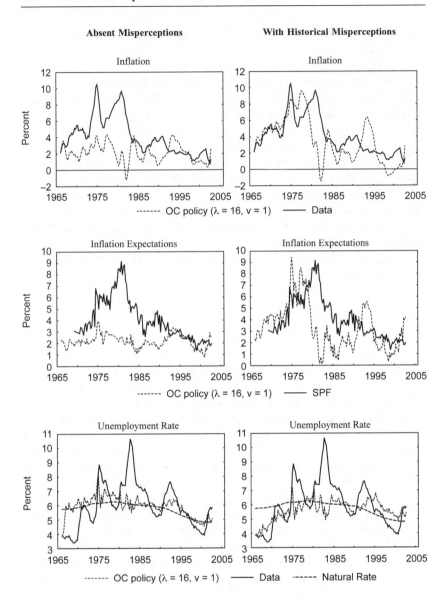

Fig. 5.3   Counterfactual simulations under OC policy with λ = 16

According to our model simulation, this same OC policy performs dismally in the face of the historical natural rate misperceptions, leading to a Great Inflation outcome in the 1970s. The panels in the right column of figure 5.3 show the outcomes when the Fed uses the historical real-time natural rate estimates. The simulated path of inflation during the 1970s is similar to that seen in the actual data. But, unlike the actual data, the high volatility of inflation continues through to the end of the sample. Owing to the low real-time estimate of the natural rate of unemployment, in this simulation the Fed does not act to raise unemployment during the latter part of the 1960s and early 1970s, as seen in the right panel of figure 5.3. This extended period of easy policy leads to a sustained rise in inflation and inflation expectations. By the time the supply shocks of the 1970s strike, inflation expectations are completely untethered from the assumed 2 percent target.

Could the high inflation of the late 1970s have been mitigated by following an optimal control policy predicated on placing a much lower weight on unemployment stabilization? Orphanides and Williams (2008, 2009) show that "robust optimal control" policies derived assuming downward biased values of λ and v can be robust to imperfect knowledge of the type studied in this chapter. We examine the effectiveness of such an approach by evaluating the performance of the OC policies derived assuming alternative weights on unemployment in the central bank loss of 4 and 0.

The OC policy derived assuming $\lambda = 4$ avoids the worst of the Great Inflation during the 1970s, even with natural rate misperceptions. The left column in figure 5.4 shows the simulation results when the natural rate is known by the Fed. The results are similar to the case of the OC policy derived assuming $\lambda = 16$. In the case of natural rate misperceptions, monetary policy is too easy during the late 1960s and early 1970s and, as a result, inflation and inflation expectations trend upwards. But, the rise in inflation during this period is not as extreme as seen in the actual data.

In the absence of natural rate misperceptions, the OC policy that places no weight on unemployment stabilization, $\lambda = 0$, is effective at stabilizing inflation during the 1970s (and indeed for the entire sample period). The left column panels in figure 5.5 show the simulated paths of inflation, inflation expectations, and unemployment under this policy in the case of no natural rate misperceptions. Under this policy, fluctuations in inflation and inflation expectations are far more muted than under the OC policy derived assuming $\lambda = 4$ or 16. This greater stabilization of inflation comes at the cost of only somewhat greater variability in the unemployment rate.

With the historical natural rate misperceptions, the OC policy derived with a zero weight placed on the stabilization of unemployment in the loss function avoids the Great Inflation, but still allows some inflation volatility to develop. The panels in the right column of figure 5.5 show the simulated paths of inflation, inflation expectations, and unemployment under this policy in the case of historical natural rate misperceptions. Given the incorrect low estimate of the natural rate of unemployment at the start of the simulation, this policy keeps unemployment too low for too long. As a result, in the simulation, the inflation rate rises and inflation expectations become untethered. Note that the policy error does not stem from a concern for stabilizing unemployment for its own good, but instead reflects the importance of deviations of unemployment from its natural rate for the

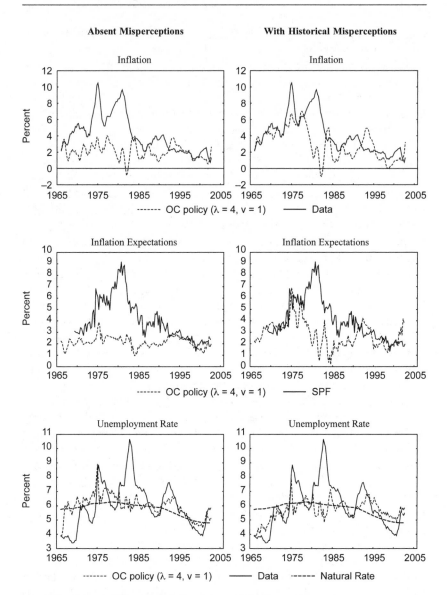

Fig. 5.4   **Counterfactual simulations under OC policy with λ = 4**

future path of inflation. With inflation reaching 6 percent by mid-decade, policy acts aggressively to bring inflation back down to target by the end of the 1970s and a major stagflation is averted.

Table 5.1 quantifies the performance of the various OC policies during the late 1960s and 1970s. The first three columns report the root mean squared differences of the inflation rate from its target value of 2 percent,

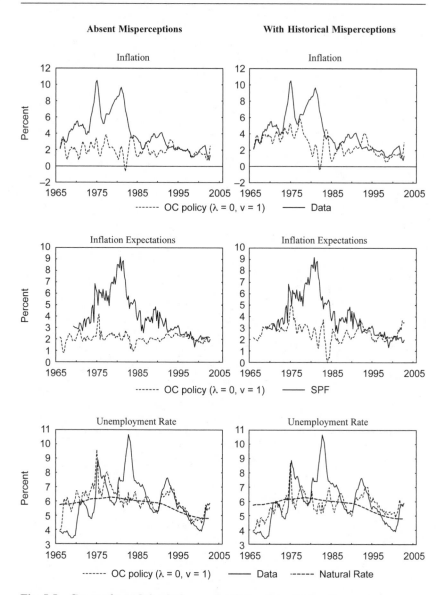

Fig. 5.5   Counterfactual simulations under OC policy with λ = 0

the unemployment rate from its natural rate, and the first difference of the short-term interest rate, respectively. The final three columns report the implied values of the central bank loss for three different values of λ, the weight placed on the squared deviations of the unemployment rate from the natural rate. Table 5.2 reports the same set of statistics for the full sample of 1966 to 2003.

Table 5.1   Loss comparison (1966–1979)

	RMSD			Loss $\mathcal{L}$		
	$\pi - 2$	$u - u^*$	Δi	$\lambda = 0$	$\lambda = 4$	$\lambda = 16$
Historical data	4.2	1.5	0.7	18.2	27.8	56.5
No misperceptions						
OC ($\lambda = 0$)	1.4	1.0	0.8	2.7	6.5	17.9
OC ($\lambda = 4$)	1.4	0.8	1.0	3.1	5.6	13.0
OC ($\lambda = 16$)	1.5	0.7	1.5	4.5	6.3	11.4
Historical misperceptions						
OC ($\lambda = 0$)	2.3	1.0	0.6	5.6	9.3	20.3
OC ($\lambda = 4$)	3.2	1.0	0.9	10.9	14.9	27.1
OC ($\lambda = 16$)	4.7	1.1	1.3	24.0	28.9	43.4
Kalman filter						
OC ($\lambda = 0$)	2.0	0.9	0.7	4.4	8.0	18.6
OC ($\lambda = 4$)	2.6	0.9	0.9	7.6	11.2	22.9
OC ($\lambda = 16$)	3.7	1.0	1.3	15.3	19.3	31.2
Robust policy rule	1.5	0.9	1.4	4.3	7.6	17.4

Note: RMSD = root mean squared differences.

Table 5.2   Loss comparison (1966–2003)

	RMSD			Loss $\mathcal{L}$		
	$\pi - 2$	$u - u^*$	Δi	$\lambda = 0$	$\lambda = 4$	$\lambda = 16$
Historical data	3.3	1.4	1.0	11.6	19.6	43.8
No misperceptions						
OC ($\lambda = 0$)	1.2	0.7	0.6	2.0	4.0	10.0
OC ($\lambda = 4$)	1.3	0.6	0.9	2.5	3.8	7.7
OC ($\lambda = 16$)	1.5	0.5	1.2	3.7	4.6	7.3
Historical misperceptions						
OC ($\lambda = 0$)	1.7	0.8	0.6	3.4	5.7	12.9
OC ($\lambda = 4$)	2.3	0.8	0.8	6.0	8.4	15.5
OC ($\lambda = 16$)	3.3	0.8	1.2	12.4	14.9	22.5
Kalman filter						
OC ($\lambda = 0$)	1.6	0.8	0.6	2.9	5.3	12.6
OC ($\lambda = 4$)	2.0	0.8	0.8	4.8	7.0	13.9
OC ($\lambda = 16$)	2.7	0.8	1.2	8.8	11.1	18.0
Robust policy rule	1.3	0.8	1.0	2.7	5.2	12.6

The first row of table 5.1 reports key summary statistics for the actual data over the period of the Great Inflation from 1966 to 1979. Corresponding results for the full sample are reported in table 5.2. Rows two through four of each table report the simulated outcomes under OC policies in the case of no natural rate misperceptions. All three of these policies yield fluctuations in inflation and the unemployment rate over 1966 to 1979 that are broadly comparable to those experienced during the period of the Great Moderation and nothing like the horrible performance that actually occurred during the Great Inflation.

The magnitude of simulated inflation fluctuations under the OC policies with historical natural rate misperceptions depends crucially on the weight placed on unemployment stabilization in the objective function. Rows five through seven of tables 5.1 and 5.2 report the results for OC policies with historical natural rate misperceptions. The policy designed assuming no weight on unemployment stabilization performs the best of the three, even if the true value of λ is 16. The OC policy designed for $\lambda = 16$ yields much larger central bank losses over this period.

Interestingly, given the presence of natural rate misperceptions, the OC policies derived with a nonnegligible weight on stabilizing unemployment yield much greater inflation variability in the final twenty years of our sample than is seen in the data. Although these policies describe the Great Inflation period reasonably well, they do not match the experience since the disinflation of the early 1980s. In contrast, the OC policy derived assuming no weight on unemployment stabilization does a much better job of describing inflation during the latter part of the sample.

The performance of OC policies is significantly improved if the central bank uses an appropriate Kalman filter to estimate the natural rate of unemployment, rather than using the historical estimates. Rows eight through ten of tables 5.1 and 5.2 report the summary statistics in the case of Kalman filter estimation of natural rates. The simulated outcomes lie between those of the two cases previously considered of no misperceptions and historical misperceptions. As in the case of historical misperceptions, the OC policy designed for no weight on unemployment stabilization performs the best. We also experimented with alternative values of the Kalman gain (not shown). A higher gain applied to the inflation surprise, a_2, implies a quicker adjustment of the central bank's estimate of the natural rate from 4 percent toward its true value of roughly 6 percent early in the sample. As a result, the OC policies using higher gains perform somewhat better than the results reported in tables 5.1 and 5.2. Conversely, a lower value of a_2 than our benchmark value implies worse performance during this period than reported.

In summary, this analysis suggests that a benevolent policymaker striving to achieve full employment and price stability using modern optimal control methods could well have made policy decisions during the 1960s and 1970s that would have led to unmoored inflation expectations and highly volatile inflation. The magnitude of these problems depends on the weight that the policymaker places on the stabilization of real activity. Only if that weight is relatively small or if the policymaker has excellent information about the economy does the optimal control policy perform reasonably well in terms of stabilizing inflation and unemployment.

5.8   Performance of a Simple Policy Rule

We now examine the performance of an alternative monetary policy rule that has proven to be robust to various forms of model uncertainty in other contexts (see Tetlow 2006 and Orphanides and Williams 2008, 2009). The rule was proposed by Orphanides and Williams (2007) and takes the form:

$$(15) \qquad i_t = i_{t-1} + \theta_\pi(\overline{\pi}^e_{t+3} - \pi^*) + \theta_{\Delta u}(u_{t-1} - u_{t-2}).$$

A key feature of this policy is the absence of any measures of natural rates in the determination of policy. This policy rule is related to the elastic price standard proposed by Hall (1984), whereby the central bank aims to maintain a stipulated relationship between the forecast of the unemployment rate and the price level. It is also closely related to the first difference of a modified Taylor-type policy rule in which the forecast of the price level is substituted for the forecast of the inflation rate.

We choose the parameters of these simple rules to minimize the central bank loss for $\lambda = 4$ and $v = 1$, under the assumptions of rational expectations and constant natural rates.[17] The resulting optimized simple rule is given by:

$$(16) \qquad i_t = i_{t-1} + 1.74(\overline{\pi}^e_{t+3} - \pi^*) - 1.19(u_{t-1} - u_{t-2}).$$

This is the same rule as analyzed in Orphanides and Williams (2008, 2009), where it was shown to be effective at stabilizing inflation and unemployment in model simulations with imperfect knowledge.

According to the model simulation, if the Fed had followed this simple rule over the past forty years, inflation would have been relatively stable and the Great Inflation would never have occurred. Figure 5.6 compares the simulated paths of inflation, inflation expectations, the real interest rate, and the unemployment rate under this simple robust policy rule to the actual data. Because this simple policy rule does not respond to the natural rate of unemployment, the simulations are invariant to the assumed path of central bank natural rate estimates. Inflation does fluctuate a bit during the 1970s, reflecting the large shocks of that period, but the deviations from target are short-lived. The simulated path for inflation is very stable since the mid-1980s.

This simple policy rule is extremely effective at keeping inflation expectations well anchored. Although the inflation rate itself fluctuates under the simple policy rule, inflation is expected to return to near its target rate of 2 percent within one year. As discussed in Orphanides and Williams (2008), the anchoring of inflation expectations is key to the success of this rule in stabilizing inflation and unemployment. A striking result is that this simple rule does better at stabilizing inflation and inflation expectations than the

---

17. If we allow for time-varying natural rates that are *known by all agents,* the optimized parameters of this simple rule under rational expectations are nearly unchanged. The relative performance of this policy is also unaffected.

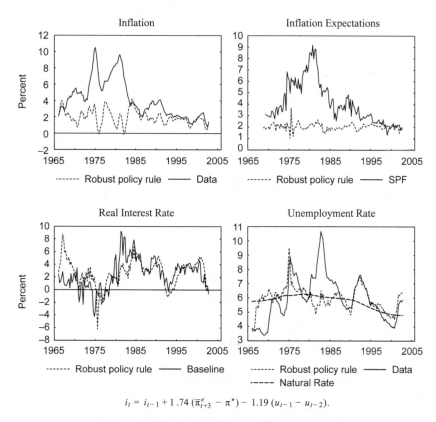

$$i_t = i_{t-1} + 1.74 \, (\overline{\pi}^e_{t+3} - \pi^*) - 1.19 \, (u_{t-1} - u_{t-2}).$$

Fig. 5.6   Counterfactual simulations under robust simple policy rule ($\lambda = 4$)

OC policy derived for $\lambda = 0$. The anchoring of inflation expectations implies that the gap between the unemployment rate and the natural rate is considerably smaller throughout the sample than in the actual data.

Interestingly, the simulated behavior of inflation, inflation expectations, and unemployment over the latter part of our sample is very close to that of the actual data. This finding suggests that the actual policy framework during this period may not have been very different from that prescribed by this robust simple rule.

The simple robust policy rule performs as well as or better than the best OC policy where the central bank uses the Kalman filter to estimate the natural rate of unemployment. The final rows of tables 5.1 and 5.2 report the summary statistics for the robust policy rule. This holds for any of the three values of the central bank loss considered here.

The anchoring of long-run inflation expectations under the simple robust policy rule is illustrated by the small variance in the simulated path for inflation expectations over the next ten years. The thin solid line in figure 5.7

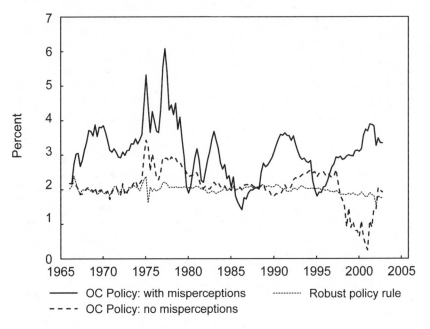

Fig. 5.7   Simulations of ten-year inflation expectations

shows the simulated path for ten-year inflation expectations when monetary policy follows the simple robust policy rule. This line fluctuates very little over the entire sample. By comparison, surveys of ten-year Consumer Price Index inflation expectations (not shown) reached around 8 percent at the start of the 1980s, and then gradually fell to around 2.5 percent in the late 1990s. Since that time, these long-run inflation expectations have fluctuated very little.

In contrast, the OC policy derived assuming $\lambda = 16$ does a poor job of anchoring long-run inflation expectations. The thick solid line in the chart shows the path of ten-year inflation expectations under the OC policy optimized for $\lambda = 16$ and assuming historical natural rate misperceptions. This line fluctuates considerably over the sample, reflecting the relatively poor anchoring of inflation expectations under this regime. The dashed line shows the corresponding outcomes under the OC policy optimized for $\lambda = 16$ and assuming no natural rate misperceptions. Not surprisingly, long-run inflation expectations are generally reasonably well anchored in this case. However, even in this case, there are extended episodes during the 1970s and early 2000s when long-run inflation expectations fluctuate significantly.

5.9   Conclusion

Our narrative account and counterfactual simulations squarely attribute the Great Inflation to policy actions that were viewed by many at the time to reflect the latest advances in macroeconomics as embodied in the New Economics. The fine-tuning approach to monetary policy, with its emphasis on stabilizing the level of real activity, might have succeeded in stabilizing the economy if policymakers had possessed accurate real-time assessments of the natural rate of unemployment. In the event, they did not and they failed to account for their imperfect information regarding the economy's potential and the effects of these misperceptions on the evolution of inflation expectations and inflation. Price and economic stability were only restored after the Federal Reserve, under Chairman Volcker, refocused policy on establishing and maintaining price stability.

This chapter shows that, even if the Federal Reserve had applied modern optimal control techniques in conducting monetary policy, it would not have been more effective at stabilizing inflation during the 1970s owing to the presence of realistic informational imperfections such as misperceptions of the natural rate of unemployment. Such optimal control policies would likely have failed to keep inflation expectations well anchored, resulting in highly volatile inflation. An optimal control policy would have succeeded only if the weight placed on stabilizing the real economy were relatively modest—with the best results achieved if virtually all the weight were placed on stabilizing prices. Finally, we show that a strategy of following a simple first-difference policy rule would have been more successful than optimal control policies in maintaining price stability and employment stability in the presence of realistic informational imperfections. In addition, this policy rule yields simulated outcomes close to the realized behavior of the economy during the Great Moderation starting in the mid-1980s, suggesting that the actual practice of monetary policy during this period changed in ways that incorporated the key properties of the robust monetary policy rule.

References

Board of Governors of the Federal Reserve System. 1965. "Federal Reserve Policy Actions." *Federal Reserve Bulletin* December:1667–68.
———. 1970. "Minutes of Action for the Meeting of Federal Open Market Committee." August 18.
———. 1975. "FOMC Memorandum of Discussion." May.
Branch, William A., and George W. Evans. 2006. "A Simple Recursive Forecasting Model." *Economics Letters* 91:158–66.
Burns, Arthur. 1979. "The Anguish of Central Banking." The 1979 Per Jacobsson Lecture, Belgrade, September 30.
Cogley, Timothy, and Thomas Sargent. 2001. "Evolving Post-World War II US Inflation Dynamics." In *NBER Macroeconomics Annual 2001*, edited by B. S. Bernanke and K. S. Rogoff, 331–73. Cambridge, MA: MIT Press.
Congressional Budget Office. 2001. *CBO's Method for Estimating Potential Output: An Update.* Washington, DC: Government Printing Office, August.

Council of Economic Advisers. 1962. *Economic Report of the President.* Washington, DC: US Government Printing Office.

———. 1966. *Economic Report of the President.* Washington, DC: US Government Printing Office.

Croushore, Dean. 1993. "Introducing: The Survey of Professional Forecasters." *Federal Reserve Bank of Philadelphia Business Review* November/December:3–13.

Croushore, Dean, and Tom Stark. 2001. "A Real-Time Data Set for Macroeconomists." *Journal of Econometrics* 105:111–30.

Evans, George, and Seppo Honkapohja. 2001. *Learning and Expectations in Macroeconomics.* Princeton, NJ: Princeton University Press.

Giannoni, Marc P., and Michael Woodford. 2005. "Optimal Inflation Targeting Rules." In *The Inflation Targeting Debate,* edited by B. S. Bernanke and M. Woodford, 93–162. Chicago: University of Chicago Press.

Goodfriend, Marvin, and Robert G. King. 2005. "The Incredible Volcker Disinflation." *Journal of Monetary Economics* 52 (5): 981–1015.

Hall, Robert E. 1984. "Monetary Strategy with an Elastic Price Standard." *Price Stability and Public Policy: A Symposium Sponsored by the Federal Reserve Bank of Kansas City,* 137–59. Kansas City: Federal Reserve Bank of Kansas City.

Heller, Walter W. 1966. *New Dimensions of Political Economy.* Cambridge, MA: Harvard University.

Hetzel, Robert. 1998. "Arthur Burns and Inflation." *Federal Reserve Bank of Richmond, Economic Quarterly* 84 (Winter): 21–44.

———. 2008a. *The Monetary Policy of the Federal Reserve: A History.* Cambridge, MA: Cambridge University Press.

———. 2008b. "What is the Monetary Standard, Or, How Did the Volcker-Greenspan Fed Tame Inflation?" *Federal Reserve Bank of Richmond Economic Quarterly* 94 (Spring): 147–71.

Hoerl, A. E., and R. W. Kennard. 1970. "Ridge Regression: Biased Estimation of Nonorthogonal Problems." *Tecnometrics* 12:69–82.

Kalchbrenner, J. H., and Peter A. Tinsley. 1976. "On the Use of Feedback Control in the Design of Aggregate Monetary Policy." *American Economic Review* 66 (2): 349–55.

Levin, Andrew T., and John C. Williams. 2003. "Robust Monetary Policy with Competing Reference Models." *Journal of Monetary Economics* 50:945–75.

Lindsey, David E., Athanasios Orphanides, and Robert H. Rasche. 2005. "The Reform of 1979: How It Happened and Why." In *Reflections on Monetary Policy 25 Years After October 1979, Federal Reserve Bank of St. Louis Review* 87 (March/April): 187–235.

Maisel, Sherman J. 1973. *Managing the Dollar.* New York: Norton.

Martin, William M. 1957. "Statement before the Committee of Finance, United States Senate." August 13.

———. 1965. "Remarks before the 59th Annual Meeting of the Life Insurance Association of America." New York, December 8.

Mayer, Thomas. 1999. *Monetary Policy and the Great Inflation in the United States: The Federal Reserve and the Failure of Macroeconomic Policy, 1965–1979.* Cheltenham, UK: Edward Elgar.

Meltzer, Allan H. 2003. *A History of the Federal Reserve: Volume 1.* Chicago: University of Chicago Press.

Milani, Fabio. 2007. "Expectations, Learning, and Macroeconomic Persistence." *Journal of Monetary Economics* 54:2065–82.

Modigliani, Franco, and Lucas Papademos. 1975. "Targets for Monetary Policy in the Coming Year." *Brookings Papers for Economic Activity* 1:141–63.

Okun, Arthur. 1962. "Potential Output: Its Measurement and Significance." In *American Statistical Association 1962 Proceedings of the Business and Economic Section,* 98–104. Washington, DC: American Statistical Association.

———. 1970. *The Political Economy of Prosperity.* Washington, DC: Brookings Institution.

Orphanides, Athanasios. 2002. "Monetary Policy Rules and the Great Inflation." *American Economic Review* 92 (2): 115–20.

———. 2003. "The Quest for Prosperity without Inflation." *Journal of Monetary Economics* 50 (3): 633–63.

Orphanides, Athanasios, and John C. Williams. 2002. "Robust Monetary Policy Rules with Unknown Natural Rates." *Brookings Papers on Economic Activity* 2 (2002): 63–118.

———. 2005a. "The Decline of Activist Stabilization Policy: Natural Rate Misperceptions, Learning, and Expectations." *Journal of Economic Dynamics and Control* 29 (11): 1927–50.

———. 2005b. "Imperfect Knowledge, Inflation Expectations and Monetary Policy." In *The Inflation Targeting Debate,* edited by Ben Bernanke and Michael Woodford, 201–34. Chicago: University of Chicago Press.

———. 2007. "Inflation Targeting under Imperfect Knowledge." In *Monetary Policy under Inflation Targeting,* edited by Frederic Mishkin and Klaus Schmidt-Hebbel, 77–123. Santiago: Central Bank of Chile.

———. 2008. "Learning, Expectations Formation, and the Pitfalls of Optimal Control Monetary Policy." *Journal of Monetary Economics* 55:S80–S96.

———. 2009. "Imperfect Knowledge and the Pitfalls of Optimal Control Monetary Policy." In *Central Banking, Analysis and Economic Policies: Monetary Policy under Uncertainty and Learning,* edited by Carl Walsh and Klaus Schmidt-Hebbel, 115–44. Santiago: Central Bank of Chile.

Sargent, Thomas J. 1999. *The Conquest of American Inflation.* Princeton, NJ: Princeton University Press.

———. 2007. "Evolution and Intelligent Design." Draft of presidential address to the American Economic Association. New York University, September.

Sheridan, Niamh. 2003. "Forming Inflation Expectations." Working Paper. Johns Hopkins University, April.

Stein, Herbert. 1996. "A Successful Accident: Recollections and Speculations about the CEA." *Journal of Economic Perspectives* 10 (3): 3–21.

Svensson, Lars E. O., and Robert Tetlow. 2005. "Optimum Policy Projections." *International Journal of Central Banking* 1:177–207.

Svensson, Lars E. O., and Michael Woodford. 2003. "Optimal Indicators for Monetary Policy." *Journal of Monetary Economics* 46:229–56.

Tetlow, Robert J. 2006. "Real-Time Model Uncertainty in the United States: 'Robust' Policies Put to the Test." Finance and Economics Discussion Series Working Paper. Federal Reserve Board, May 22.

Time. 1965. "We Are All Keynesian Now." December 31.

United States Congress. 1966. *Recent Federal Reserve Action and Economic Policy Coordination.* Hearings before the Joint Economic Committee, Part 1, December 13 and 14, 1965. Washington, DC: Government Printing Office.

Volcker, Paul A. 1980. "Statement before the Committee on Banking, Finance and Urban Affairs, House of Representatives." February 19.

Wallich, Henry C. 1976. "Discussion." *American Economic Review* 66 (2): 356–59.

Woodford, Michael. 2003. *Interest and Prices: Foundations of a Theory of Monetary Policy.* Princeton, NJ: Princeton University Press.

Comment   Seppo Honkapohja

Great Inflation and Imperfect Knowledge

There have been numerous attempts to explain and understand the period of rapid inflation in the United States in the second half of the 1960s and in the 1970s. The papers in this conference are welcome additions to this literature. One prominent set of arguments by one or both of the authors of this chapter has as its starting point the idea that monetary policy in this period was misguided because of imperfect knowledge about the Phillips curve and the natural rate of unemployment (or productivity growth). Monetary policy was not sufficiently tight because the estimates of the natural rate of unemployment were too low, so that higher actual unemployment was thought to indicate slack in the economy.[1]

Explanations of the Great Inflation that are based on imperfect knowledge and misperceptions by policymakers and/or private agents can be usefully formulated in terms of a learning model rather than a model relying on a rational expectations equilibrium (REE). There are already many learning models of the Great Inflation. The seminal contribution is the book by Sargent (1999) and an important subsequent paper is Cho, Williams, and Sargent (2002). Tom Sargent has recently proposed somewhat different explanations of the Great Inflation in some other papers, see, for example, Cogley and Sargent (2005) and Sargent, Williams, and Zha (2006). Other important papers using learning models of the Great Inflation include Bullard and Eusepi (2005), Orphanides and Williams (2005a, 2005b), and Primiceri (2006).

This chapter by Orphanides and Williams focuses on a further aspect of the discussion about monetary policy during the Great Inflation. The basic idea is to consider a counterfactual experiment. It is asked whether the Great Inflation could have been avoided if monetary policy had been based on optimal policy by a benevolent policymaker in an REE but ignoring misperceptions of the natural rate of unemployment.

This is an important question as it provides new perspectives on the practical usefulness of optimal monetary policy frameworks. I am happy to com-

Seppo Honkapohja is a member of the board of the Bank of Finland.

For acknowledgments, sources of research support, and disclosure of the author's material financial relationships, if any, please see http://www.nber.org/chapters/c9177.ack.

1. See, for example, Orphanides (2002), Orphanides (2003a, 2003b), and Orphanides and Williams (2002).

ment on the very nice chapter. My discussion has three parts. First, I provide some remarks outlining the basic ideas of learning models and suggest that the literature previously cited divides into two main strands. Second, I try to provide some intuition for the obtained results from the viewpoint of what we know about properties of learning models of monetary policy. Third, I make some comments and questions about the analysis.

Basic Ideas in Learning Models

Models of adaptive learning have three important building blocks.[2] The starting point in the learning approach is the assumption that agents and policymakers have imperfect knowledge and try to learn (i.e., improve their knowledge over time as new data becomes available). The beliefs of economic agents are formulated in terms of models with parameters, which are estimated from existing data. Expectations of the agents in any period are based on the estimated model and the parameters of the model are updated over time using standard econometric techniques. In any period these expectations feed into decisions by the agents and consequently to actual outcomes.

Because economic outcomes depend on the forecasts, the economy is seen as a self-referential model. If the forecasting models of the agents are compatible with an REE, then learning dynamics may converge over time to the REE of interest. The REE is then a fixed point of the dynamical system describing learning and the economy. This convergence takes place provided the economy satisfies an expectational stability criterion. Recently, ideas of learning have been widely applied in models of economic policy, and the literature on learning and monetary policy is growing rapidly.[3] A useful implication of this literature is that good policy facilitates convergence of learning by private agents.

The basic models with learning rely on some fairly strong assumptions. These are (a) the functional form of agents' forecasting models is correctly specified relative to the REE of interest, (b) agents accurately observe all relevant variables, and (c) the economic environment is perceived to be fairly stationary. There are papers that relax one or more of these assumptions.[4]

Relaxing assumption (a) leads to models with asymptotic misspecification and some of the papers on the Great Inflation in the aforementioned literature indeed consider learning dynamics with misspecified beliefs. The resulting dynamics can then exhibit occasional rapid movements known

2. Evans and Honkapohja (2001) provide a treatise on the analysis of adaptive learning and its implications in macroeconomics. Sargent (2008) and Evans and Honkapohja (2009b) are recent surveys of the field.

3. For surveys of the literature see Evans and Honkapohja (2009a), Bullard (2006), and Evans and Honkapohja (2003a).

4. The literature has also explored other ways of relaxing the basic setting. One avenue is based on the assumption that agents entertain multiple forecasting models and make the most use of models that have performed well in the past.

as escape dynamics. Sargent (1999) and Cho, Williams, and Sargent (2002) are studies of these escape dynamics. If instead assumption (b) and/or (c) is relaxed, perpetual learning dynamics evolve near an REE after a transition period, provided the expectational stability condition is satisfied. The second strand of the literature on learning and the Great Inflation takes this approach and focuses on so-called perpetual (constant-gain) learning. The earlier work by Orphanides and Williams as well as the current chapter use standard persistent learning dynamics, not escape dynamics in modeling the Great Inflation.

Understanding the Main Results

I focus on the analytical part of the chapter, which is a counterfactual exercise based on an estimated model (though there are also elements of calibration in the model formulation). The main idea of the chapter is to assess the performance of two types of policies using the 1970s experience as a "testing ground." One set of policies are based on optimal control in an REE while the other type of policies employ a simple first-difference rule and assume that the economy evolves in accordance with learning dynamics. One can take either a positive or a normative view about the comparisons. According to the former, a good model should be able to explain the Great Inflation and the subsequent period, while according to the latter it is useful to find a policy rule that would have avoided the Great Inflation.

The main results in the chapter are, first, that a policy rule based on optimal control when agents are assumed to have rational expectations does not anchor inflation expectations if in fact private agents are learning and there are misperceptions about the natural rate of unemployment. There is also a corollary to this result: the optimal rule with all weight on inflation (the policymaker is an "inflation nutter") delivers anchoring of inflation expectations in the 1960 to 1970s. The second main result of the chapter is that there is an alternative simple "first-difference" policy rule that would have worked well in the sense that the Great Inflation would not have occurred under that rule. The latter rule also has good empirical performance in the subsequent period.

The estimated model has only three equations but there are lagged variables. It is then difficult to formulate a good intuition for these results. Let me try to provide some intuition by looking at the properties of the rules and how these kinds of rules perform in somewhat simpler New Keynesian models.

Starting with the basic optimal rule, there are three important properties: (a) interest-rate inertia; (b) the response to (lagged) inflation is fairly weak, certainly weaker than to unemployment gaps; and (c) unemployment gaps are defined with respect to estimated natural rate, which deviates a lot from the true rate (see figure 5.2 in the chapter). Property (a) is conducive to determinacy and learning-stability, but (b) suggests the possibility of big fluctuations and combining it with (c), it is evident that poor anchoring of inflation can be the outcome.

Considering the optimal control policy rule of an inflation nutter, it is evident that the weight of unemployment in the rule is smaller than in the basic case. This also means that estimated natural rate plays a small role in the rule, which contributes to the anchoring of inflation, and inflation expectations indeed remain anchored. More generally, figure 5.2 shows a lot of variation in the real-time estimates of the natural rate in the 1970s, so that imprecise knowledge about natural rate is the underlying reason for nonanchoring in the base case. These considerations confirm that the imprecise estimation of the natural rate of unemployment is central for these results in the chapter.

Let me next discuss the preferred optimal simple rule proposed in the chapter. According to this rule, the change in interest rate responds strongly to deviations of inflation (expectations) from the inflation target and to changes in observable unemployment. The preferred rule can be thought of as a version of a price-level targeting rule with a time-varying price level target. Let me write the rule in general terms as

$$i_t = i_{t-1} + \theta_\pi (\overline{\pi}^e_{t+3} - \pi^*) + \theta_{\Delta u}(u_{t-1} - u_{t-2}).$$

Here π^* is a target for inflation. For the inflation term in the rule we have

$$\overline{\pi}^e_{t+3} - \pi^* = \overline{p}^e_{t+3} - \overline{p}^*_{t+3} - (\overline{p}^e_{t+2} - \overline{p}^*_{t+2}),$$

where $\overline{p}^*_{t+3} = \overline{p}^*_{t+2} + \pi^*$. This means that the rule is a differenced version of a "price-level Taylor rule"

$$i_t = \theta_\pi (\overline{p}^e_{t+3} - \overline{p}^*_{t+3}) + \theta_{\Delta u} u_{t-1} + K,$$

which incorporates a moving price-level target. It is known that in the standard New Keynesian model price level rules tend to keep inflation under control and contribute to stability, including learning-stability, provided the E-stability condition is satisfied. See, for example, Evans and Honkapohja (2006, 2013). It should also be noted that this preferred rule does not depend on the estimated natural rate. This also helps with anchoring of inflation.

Further Comments and Questions

In this last section, I want to make further comments and note some questions.

First, the focus on the chosen form of the optimal control rule is potentially problematic. It is well-known that in the standard New Keynesian model a similar "fundamentals-based" formulation runs into problems with determinacy and learning-stability. This problem is alleviated if an interest-rate smoothing motive is postulated (see Duffy and Xiao 2007). Moreover, in standard New Keynesian models there can be problems of stability under constant gain learning with backward-looking (or "operational") form of such rules (see Evans and Honkapohja 2009c). It would be worthwhile to check whether the E-stability condition fails for the optimal control rule.

The chapter suggests that policy should be based on the simple first-difference instrument rule rather than optimal control rules. This argument is limited, since it would be worthwhile to also explore the performance of more robust implementations of optimal policy than the just fundamentals-based rule. Some alternative optimal rules worthy of comparison would be the expectations-based optimal rules proposed in Evans and Honkapohja (2003b), Evans and Honkapohja (2006), and Preston (2008), as well as the optimal rules that are obtained if the policymakers know learning rules of private agents (see Gaspar, Smets, and Vestin 2006; Molnar and Santoro 2010). The performance of these optimal policy frameworks ought to be compared with the performance of the first-difference rule preferred by the authors.

I am also a little bit puzzled about the main empirical conclusion of the chapter. According to the results, the Great Inflation could have arisen because either (a) best-practice policy under rational expectations was employed when private agents were in fact learning, or (b) the policy objective put too much weight on unemployment stabilization when in fact REE prevailed in the inflationary episode. The chapter does not sufficiently contrast these alternatives as a positive empirical conclusion. Looking at the narrative discussion in section 5.2, my guess is that the authors would favor the suggestion (a). The highly variable natural rate in the Great Inflation episode (see figure 5.2 of the chapter) and other structural changes in the 1970s suggest that expectations may not have been rational. However, the discussion in section 5.2 also focuses a lot on the importance of measuring the natural rate of unemployment and, in the period beginning in the 1990s, the empirical performance of the OC policy with very small weight on unemployment is roughly comparable to that of the simple robust rule (compare figures 5.5 and 5.6). Could this period be viewed as a case for assessing more generally relative merits of the REE and learning approaches?

References

Bullard, J. 2006. "The Learnability Criterion and Monetary Policy." *Federal Reserve Bank of St. Louis Review* 88:203–17.
Bullard, J., and S. Eusepi. 2005. "Did the Great Inflation Occur Despite Policymaker Commitment to a Taylor Rule?" *Review of Economic Dynamics* 8:324–59.
Cho, I.-K., N. Williams, and T. J. Sargent. 2002. "Escaping Nash Inflation." *Review of Economic Studies* 69:1–40.
Cogley, T., and T. J. Sargent. 2005. "The Conquest of US Inflation: Learning and Robustness to Model Uncertainty." *Review of Economic Dynamics* 8:528–63.
Duffy, J., and W. Xiao. 2007. "The Value of Interest Rate Stabilization Policies When Agents are Learning." *Journal of Money, Credit, and Banking* 39:2041–56.
Evans, G. W., and S. Honkapohja. 2001. *Learning and Expectations in Macroeconomics.* Princeton, NJ: Princeton University Press.
———. 2003a. "Adaptive Learning and Monetary Policy Design." *Journal of Money, Credit, and Banking* 35:1045–72.

————. 2003b. "Expectations and the Stability Problem for Optimal Monetary Policies." *Review of Economic Studies* 70:807–24.

————. 2006. "Monetary Policy, Expectations and Commitment." *Scandinavian Journal of Economics* 108:15–38.

————. 2009a. "Expectations, Learning and Monetary Policy: An Overview of Recent Research." In *Monetary Policy under Uncertainty and Learning,* K. Schmidt-Hebbel and C. E. Walsh, 27–76. Santiago: Central Bank of Chile.

————. 2009b. "Learning and Macroeconomics." *Annual Review of Economics* 1:421–51.

————. 2009c. "Robust Learning Stability with Operational Monetary Policy Rules." In *Monetary Policy under Uncertainty and Learning,* K. Schmidt-Hebbel and C. E. Walsh, 145–70. Santiago: Central Bank of Chile.

————. 2013. "Learning as a Rational Foundation for Macroeconomics and Finance." In *Rethinking Expectations: The Way Forward for Macroeconomics,* edited by R. Frydman and E. S. Phelps, chapter 2. Princeton, NJ: Princeton University Press.

Gaspar, V., F. Smets, and D. Vestin. 2006. "Adaptive Learning, Persistence and Optimal Monetary Policy." *Journal of the European Economic Association* 4:376–85.

Molnar, K., and S. Santoro. 2010. "Optimal Monetary Policy When Agents Are Learning." Norges Bank Working Paper 2010/8.

Orphanides, A. 2002. "Monetary Policy Rules and the Great Inflation." *American Economic Review, Papers and Proceedings* 92:115–20.

————. 2003a. "Monetary Policy Evaluation with Noisy Information." *Journal of Monetary Economics* 50:605–31.

————. 2003b. "The Quest for Prosperity Without Inflation." *Journal of Monetary Economics* 50:633–63.

Orphanides, A., and J. C. Williams. 2002. "Robust Monetary Policy with Unknown Natural Rates." *Brookings Papers on Economic Activity* 2:63–118.

————. 2005a. "The Decline of Activist Stabilization Policy: Natural Rate Misperceptions, Learning and Expectations." *Journal of Economic Dynamics and Control* 29:1927–50.

————. 2005b. "Imperfect Knowledge, Inflation Expectations, and Monetary Policy." In *The Inflation-Targeting Debate,* edited by B. Bernanke and M. Woodford, 201–34. Chicago: University of Chicago Press.

Preston, B. 2008. "Adaptive Learning, Forecast-Based Instrument Rules and Monetary Policy." *Journal of Economic Dynamics and Control* 32:3661–81.

Primiceri, G. E. 2006. "Why Inflation Rose and Fell: Policy-Makers' Beliefs and US Postwar Stabilization Policy." *Quarterly Journal of Economics* 121:867–901.

Sargent, T. J. 1999. *The Conquest of American Inflation.* Princeton, NJ: Princeton University Press.

————. 2008. "Evolution and Intelligent Design." *American Economic Review* 98:5–37.

Sargent, T. J., N. Williams, and T. Zha. 2006. "Shocks and Government Beliefs: The Rise and Fall of American Inflation." *American Economic Review* 96:1193–224.

Discussion

Christopher Sims had technical comments. Constant gain learning is easier to analyze in a theoretical model than in one with constant parameter change, but there is no excuse in this empirical exercise to use it instead of a Kalman filter with an explicit model for parameter change. The Kalman filter distinguishes between periods when there is a lot to be learned about parameters and when there is not, and there could be a different historical pattern derived from it. It does not discount mechanically, but according to how the explanatory variables move. Sims then moved to Honkapohja's discussion on the research of Thomas Sargent, clearing up the issue that Sargent's early work is at complete odds with his later work. Early on, Sargent felt that this entire issue dealt with escape dynamics, whereas later on he contradicts that. In the end, it might be econometrics is to blame for bad policy. In order to get bad policy, you need to have people stuck on theories that are bad. Using this flawed theory, people were estimating rich econometric models, but they should have known that the theory was not working. Everyone was stuck on the two equation models, and that was the problem.

Lars Svensson liked the chapter, but felt it had a big inconsistency. The authors seem to perform optimal control without optimal filtering. If the state of the economy is unobservable, optimal control also means optimal filtering, in that you estimate the underlying state of the economy. In this chapter, the natural rate is unobservable. A rational policymaker would conduct optimal policy and also try to estimate the natural rate. In this type of linear model, to estimate the natural rate is to use a Kalman filter and update priors of the natural rate, which might lead to a huge misperception. If inflation takes off, then the modeler should realize they have the wrong idea about the natural rate and the Kalman filter provides the weights one can put on their indicators. Svensson thought this was a problem with much of Orphanides, work, in that he does not take into account whether misperceptions are the best unbiased estimates of the relevant states or not. It might be interesting to see this experiment when the policymaker has the chance to update his or her estimate of the natural rate given the realization of inflation and output, and it might lead to strikingly different results. Svensson also stressed that the techniques to do all of this were known in the 1970s. There was an ambitious optimal control problem being done at the Federal Reserve Board that Chairman Burns did away with. That was being done with backward-looking variables, and Svensson and Michael Woodford have done work on the same problem using forward-looking variables. The algorithm is easily obtainable. What is being done here is an approximation to that problem.

Andrew Levin felt this chapter did not identify what went wrong during the Great Inflation. With regards to 1965 to 1969, Chairman Martin made it clear that his highest concerns were eliminating inflation pressures and keeping orderly financial markets. Levin had a difficult time finding any quotes where Chairman Martin refers to natural unemployment rates or an output gap. The FOMC tightened in 1969 knowing that a recession might be the cost of such tightening. Therefore, for the authors to place a weight of 16 on stabilizing the output gap in their loss function is not plausible from 1965 to 1969. But that was just stage one, and Chairman Martin ended that stage by admitting he felt he failed to control inflation. Stage two was 1976 to 1980. The figure that the authors provide in their chapter shows inflation expectations coming down in 1976, and by 1980 they are around 2.5 to 3 percent. Levin cited his work with John Taylor as evidence that this did not happen, thus it cannot be a natural rate misperception that led to the spike in inflation expectations that was actually realized.

Otmar Issing admitted he has a learned a lot from the work of Orphanides. To him, this chapter left the lasting message that policymakers do not know as much as they used to think they did. Could this happen in 2008, or 2020? Every policymaker should have the warning sign about pretense of knowledge. The more policymakers think they know, the more dangerous their actions become. Take Walter Heller, for example. He was the chairman of a group of economists that came to Germany in the 1950s, a group that made strong recommendations for extremely expansionary policy. Issing admired the German people for respecting the opinions of Heller, yet rejecting them. Heller came back later and admitted he had been wrong and praised German economic policy. It is not that the policymakers were ignoring the recommendations—they were aware of the risks of being wrong.

Vitor Gaspar suggested the Mark Twain quote: "It ain't what you don't know that gets you into trouble. It's what you know for sure that just ain't so." Gaspar felt the authors provided a marvelous illustration of the fundamental insight of Milton Friedman, in that when you design optimal/feasible policy, you have to take account of what you do and cannot possibly know. The simple rule here seems to be a good illustration of just that.

Bennett McCallum felt Levin's comments had merit. Yet even if this study does not really speak to Martin's behavior and is not completely historically correct, it provides a nice cautionary tale. It emphasized the kind of pressures that were there historically and continue to be there. The only reservation McCallum had about the chapter was the estimated model. The trouble is that without the constraints on lagged and expected future variables with weights of 0.5, where do you go? Half of the parameters are not estimated. If you leave them all free, you will not get nearly as nice of results. Can one really take the results seriously then? Would you tell an undergraduate student that this is a full-blown estimated macroeconomic model?

Seppo Honkapohja agreed with Sims's comments on Sargent's literature, and adds that he thinks there is still a misperception element at play. One could also go and say there are multiple models being learned about, and that policymakers chose the wrong model.

Benjamin Friedman paralleled some of Sims's comments, and thought that much of the conversation was remarkably like sermon-speak—that is, there is a certain scripture or certain religious figures that indicate anything that you think is good you attribute as an interpretation of something that religious figure believed in. The notion that writing down an interest rate reaction function with a term in the deviation of inflation from something and a term in the change of the unemployment rate, and deriving the values of that, does not strike Friedman as something that Milton Friedman advocated. If there are figures in the profession whom we all admire, it does not mean we can attribute any policy we see as good policy to that person.

Williams began the response with comments directed toward Sims and Svensson. In a previous paper with Orphanides, the authors did do policy evaluation using unconditional moments and the standard monetary policy using the optimal Kalman filter. This was optimal policy using rational expectations. When you add in the learning, you show that with learning and the combination of mistakes, policymakers want to put more weight on output in their reaction function. Williams himself admits he does not know the deep parameters of the Kalman filter. In fact, the chapter presented here has a section on the optimal Kalman filter, and the authors admit they want to work on that next.

Orphanides continued the response by emphasizing the criticisms people make about the real-time natural estimates used here. Orphanides strongly believed that these are the estimates that policymakers would have used had they had sophisticated models at the time, referencing previous comments made by Rudd on the methodology being used at the time and how similar it is to what is used now. From the mid-1970s onward, the real-time estimates being used are those the Congressional Budget Office was using. If one tries to do this in a Kalman filter, what are the signal-to-noise ratios you assume? What are the parameters of the model? Orphanides felt the model here is very close to what happened in real time and reflects the best efforts of the profession. It is not a new concept, as was pointed out by Svensson. Optimal control was something the Federal Reserve had been working on, and William Poole probably remembers it. With regards to Friedman's remarks, Orphanides acknowledged he is a great admirer of the work of Milton Friedman, but to interpret Milton Friedman's policy teaching as one that necessarily uses money growth numbers seems like an extremely narrow viewpoint. A much deeper lesson from Orphanides's perspective that we can take from Milton Friedman is that one should always respect the limits of knowledge, the ability of using economic models for stabilization purposes, and the idea of measuring something that is "natural." If you actually estimate these beasts, why do optimal control? To continue, what kind of policy would approximate the lesson of Milton Friedman? Orphanides was convinced it would be some sort of difference rule. This is not different from the kind that Knut Wicksell proposed after he defined what the "natural rate" was. Afterwards comes the question about implementation of such a rule. To respond to McCallum, Orphanides referenced a previous paper in the *Journal of Money, Credit, and Banking* where he and Williams estimated a model with free parameters, and that works quite well in terms of estimation. What the authors wanted to do here was restrict parameters to bring the model as close as possible to modern New Keynesian models that respects the limits that the forward-backward hybrid combination can have on the parameters. If we do not hold the weights at 0.5, then the estimated parameters are far out of bounds. This worried McCallum, but Orphanides thought that the New Keynesian model was a good tool. Orphanides rejected Levin's views on the attempt to reconstruct history, which is not what the authors were trying to do. The authors do not believe chairmen Martin and Burns followed the recommendations of the Federal Reserve Board staff at the time. What the authors attempted to do is ask the following question: Suppose they did follow the recommendation of an optimal control policy using modern techniques—would they have avoided the big mistakes? The answer this chapter provides is no, because of the misperceptions. The basic lesson is that because of learning and misperceptions that result in over-expansionary policy, one would not be able to control inflation. It is key that in order to understand the Great Inflation, one needs to realize the economic profession's obsession with the ability to stabilize both the real side of the economy and inflation. Even with the very best models, we have failed. In other papers, Orphanides and Williams have tried to match history, but misperceptions always create mistakes. In reference to Sims and constant gain learning, the authors used constant gain learning as a parable for how actual people in the economy, as opposed to the hypothesized rational expectations agents, might be using past data to form expectations. The authors tried to capture the evolution of the expectations formation process that results from suspicion that things might be changing. Orphanides admitted that they could have time variation in parameters, and then they would have a Kalman filter giving an optimal way to shift the parameters. In the end, the authors wanted to approximate James Stock and Mark Watson. They are good at forecasting, and how do they change their vector autoregressions?

III

Other Countries' Perspectives

6

Opting Out of the Great Inflation
German Monetary Policy after the
Breakdown of Bretton Woods

Andreas Beyer, Vitor Gaspar, Christina Gerberding, and
Otmar Issing

6.1 Introduction

In the second half of the twentieth century, the German Bundesbank established its reputation as one of the most successful central banks in the world. Along with the Swiss National Bank, the Bundesbank was the first central bank to announce and pursue a strategy based on monetary targets after the breakdown of Bretton Woods. In this chapter, we relate the Bundesbank success in maintaining price stability and in anchoring inflation expectations to its strategy. We examine the strategy as it was presented, refined, and communicated by the Bundesbank itself. Our goal is to provide a historical account of the conduct of monetary policy, focusing especially on the first ten years of monetary targeting, from 1975

Andreas Beyer is principal economist at the European Central Bank. Vitor Gaspar is special adviser at the Bank of Portugal. Christina Gerberding is a senior economist in the Monetary Policy and Analysis Division at Deutsche Bundesbank. Otmar Issing is honorary professor and president of the Center for Financial Studies at the University of Frankfurt.

Chapter prepared for the National Bureau of Economic Research, the Great Inflation conference, Woodstock, Vermont, September 25–27, 2008. The views expressed in this chapter do not necessarily reflect those of the European Central Bank (ECB) or the Eurosystem. We thank Edward Nelson and Athanasios Orphanides for sharing their real-time output gap data with us. Furthermore, we thank our discussant Benjamin Friedman for his challenging and thought-provoking comments. We are also grateful to Michael Bordo, Vitor Constancio, Gabriel Fagan, Dieter Gerdesmeier, Alfred Guender, Lars Jonung, Athanasios Orphanides, Werner Roeger, Franz Seitz, Ulf Söderström, Lars Svensson, Guntram Wolff, Andreas Worms, and Charles Wyplosz for insightful discussions and their valuable suggestions. We also wish to thank participants of a seminar held by the Eurosystem's MPC and participants of the NBER conference at Woodstock for their comments that helped improve an earlier draft of this chapter. Last but not least we would like to express our gratitude to Aurelie Therace for her efficient help in preparing the final manuscript. For acknowledgments, sources of research support, and disclosure of the authors' material financial relationships, if any, please see http://www.nber.org/chapters/c9158.ack.

until the middle of the 1980s, when price stability was virtually reached in Germany.

According to the Bundesbank Act of 1957, the objective of monetary policy was to safeguard the currency. This formulation left open whether the focus should be on stabilizing the external or the internal value of the currency, and indeed, the potential conflict between these two goals was not well understood by those involved until well into the 1960s. However, after the breakdown of the Bretton Woods system, the emphasis shifted decidedly toward the goal of domestic price stability.[1] Hence, it was clear from the beginning that the monetary targets were intermediate targets. They were instrumental to achieving price stability. Helmut Schlesinger (1988, 6)—as quoted in von Hagen (1995, 108)—made the point crystal clear:

> [T]he Bundesbank has never, since 1975, conducted a rigid policy geared at the money supply alone; all available information about financial markets and the development of the economy must be analyzed regularly. . . . Furthermore, the Bundesbank had to check the consistency of her original monetary targets with the ultimate policy goals.

Moreover, the Bundesbank's operational framework for monetary policy implementation implied that the first step in the transmission mechanism was the control over a money market interest rate. Thus, in this chapter, we characterize the Bundesbank's monetary policy strategy through an interest rate rule in the tradition of Taylor (1993, 1999), modified to take account of the implications of monetary targeting for the Bundesbank's interest rate decisions. The issue has already been repeatedly considered in the literature (e.g. Clarida, Galí, and Gertler 1998; Gerberding, Seitz, and Worms 2005).

The central role of monetary policy in anchoring inflation and inflation expectations was recognized as crucial by the Bundesbank early on. Such concern is transparent in the mechanics of the derivation of the monetary target. From this viewpoint, central banking practice progressed ahead of theory's emphasis on credibility and reputation (as developed later in the work of Kydland and Prescott 1977; Barro and Gordon 1983a, 1983b).

In the last fifteen years, the new neoclassical synthesis and New Keynesian models became the workhorse for the theory of monetary policymaking (see Woodford [2003] and Galí [2008] for authoritative, book-length surveys).[2] These models rely on a Real Business Cycle (RBC) core. They add on price setting by monopolistic competitive firms subject to some constraint or cost on price changes, leading to nominal stickiness. Another key feature is that economic agents form expectations in a forward-looking way, taking into

---

1. For a detailed discussion, see Neumann (1999, 294).

2. These models have also been actively used in policymaking institutions. Prominent examples are the ECB, the Board of Governors, and the International Monetary Fund (IMF). Relevant references are Smets and Wouters (2003, 2007); Coenen, Christoffel, and Warne (2008); Christiano, Motto, and Rostagno (2008); Erceg, Guerrieri, and Gust (2006); Edge, Kiley, and Laforte (2007); and Bayoumi et al. (2004).

account what they know about the central bank's reaction function. Hence, despite their well-known limitations, these models provide a natural environment to discuss commitment, credibility, and reputation (see, for example, Gaspar and Kashyap 2007).

Building on the modified loss function approach (pioneered by Rogoff 1985), we will show in this chapter how focusing on money growth helps to bring the conduct of monetary policy closer to optimal policy under commitment (thereby improving on the outcome under discretion). It does so by inducing a persistent, history-dependent response of policy rates to deviations of inflation and output from target. Therefore, it allows us to rationalize monetary targeting as a commitment device (here we follow the lead of Söderström 2005).

Inevitably, such stylized story does not do full justice to monetary targeting as practiced by the Bundesbank. Nevertheless, it does, in our view, help to interpret the historical evidence. Specifically, our stylized story suggests one mechanism through which monetary targeting provided a means to anchor inflation and inflation expectations. We derive an interest rate rule corresponding to this set-up and confront it with real-time data. We find that the interest rate rule implied by our model of monetary targeting captures the Bundesbank's monetary policy actions well. We compare the policy pursued in Germany with those conducted by the Fed and the Bank of England.

The chapter is organized as follows. In section 6.2 we provide an overview of the relative performance of German monetary policy as compared with other industrialized countries. In section 6.3 we briefly describe institutions and history of monetary policy in Germany in the relevant period. We elucidate the concept of "pragmatic monetarism" and clarify the crucial role of the explicit derivation of the monetary target. In section 6.4 we introduce a simple macroeconomic framework based on the standard New Keynesian model. We derive a role for monetary targeting as a commitment device. We obtain the instrument rule implied by our framework. In section 6.5 we estimate an interest rate rule, inspired by our theoretical analysis, using real time German data and compare the results with estimates for the United States and the United Kingdom. In section 6.6 we conclude.

6.2   Brief Overview of Inflation Developments in Selected Industrial Countries in the Period 1959 to 1998

In the second half of the twentieth century, the German Bundesbank acquired a strong reputation for maintaining lower inflation rates than many other countries could. In this section we will look at the relevant stylized facts and put them into historical context, in particular from a monetary policy perspective. From a global view, the second half of the twentieth century was marked by three periods: the system of Bretton Woods (which lasted until 1973), followed by the period of the Great Inflation until the end of the 1970s, and subsequently by the period of Great Moderation from the early to mid-1980s onwards.

6.2.1   Rise and Fall of the Bretton Woods Regime

The first part of the post–World War II period was marked by the Bretton Woods International Monetary Regime. The beginning of this stage is characterized by the transition to a regime of convertibility—for current account transactions—by most Western European Countries in December 1958. It involved the fixing of a par value for each currency in terms of gold. The framers of the system intended to reconcile the positive aspects of the classical gold standard (for example, exchange rate stability, intense international trade) with autonomous national macroeconomic policies. The idea was that currency convertibility would be expected only for current account transactions (capital controls were accepted) and that exchange rates would be fixed but adjustable (in the face of fundamental disequilibria). According to Garber (1993, 461): "The collapse of the Bretton Woods system of fixed exchange rates was one of the most accurately and generally predicted of major economic events." The intuition is that there are intrinsic elements of internal tension in any gold exchange standard. Bordo (1993) categorizes the problems under the heading adjustment, liquidity, and confidence. One aspect is known as the Triffin (1960) dilemma. The system relied on the convertibility of the US dollar into gold. On the other hand, it required the availability of US dollars as liquidity. The latter required US balance of payment deficits, thereby undermining (the former) convertibility of the US dollar. The most symbolic moment was, perhaps, the suspension of the convertibility of the dollar into gold, in August 1971. The system then collapsed completely into a system of generalized floating in 1973. With the collapse of the last operational link to gold, the age of a commodity standard was over.

According to a very well-known folk theorem of international monetary economics, fixed exchange rates, freedom of movement of financial capital, and autonomous monetary policy constitute an impossible trinity. As mentioned earlier, the Bretton Woods regime allowed for capital controls. Nevertheless, over time, in the context of full convertibility for current account transactions, the effectiveness of capital controls was gradually diminishing. The Bundesbank was vividly aware of the constraint that participation in the Bretton Woods systems imposed on its ability to pursue domestic price stability. During the period 1959 to 1973 the deutsche mark (DM) was revalued three times against the US dollar (1961, 1969, and 1971).[3]

6.2.2   The Stylized Facts

In the period 1960 to 1998, German inflation, measured in accordance with the Consumer Price Index (CPI), was, on average, 3.1 percent per year

---

3. There were also short episodes of floating.

(with a standard deviation of 1.8 percentage points). During this period German inflation was the lowest and most stable, as recorded internationally (see table 6.1, which reports the average numbers of key macroeconomic variables for the G7 countries and Switzerland over that period). Only Switzerland came close with an average inflation rate of 3.3 percent (and a standard deviation of 2.3 percentage points). These results compare with the United States, which recorded an inflation rate of 4.4 percent, on average per year, with a standard deviation of 2.9 percentage points. Across the G7 countries inflation was highest and most volatile in Italy with, respectively, 7.4 percent and 5.4 percentage points for annual inflation and for its standard deviation. After the full period the DM had retained about 30 percent of its original value, compared with less than 20 percent for the US dollar, the Canadian dollar, and the Japanese yen, about 13 percent for the French franc, about 8.5 percent for the pound sterling, and only about 6 percent for the Italian lira.

It is interesting (and instructive) to recall that during the 1960s, in the context of the Bretton Woods system, inflation was actually slightly higher in Germany than in the United States. Specifically, the ten-year average was 2.4 percent in Germany, while it was 2.3 percent in the United States (Canada was very close, with an inflation rate of 2.5 percent). Nevertheless, in the United Kingdom, France, and Italy inflation was on average above 3 percent and in Japan above 5 percent. However, using an average for the 1960s can be misleading. In the last years of the 1960s, the rise in consumer prices was accelerating in the United States with inflation at 2.8 percent in 1967, 4.2 percent in 1968, 5.4 percent in 1969, and 5.9 percent in 1970. The corresponding numbers for Germany were 1.6, 1.6, 1.9, and 3.4 percent.

The differences between the inflation rates in Germany and the other G7 countries were most marked at the start of the period of floating exchange rates. In fact, in the period 1974 to 1982 prices increased by 46 percent in Germany (with an average annual rate of 4.8 percent). In the same period of eight years, prices almost doubled in the United States (with an annual average inflation rate of 9 percent). The differences persisted in the subsequent disinflation. In the longer period 1974 to 1989 (the year of the fall of the Berlin Wall), prices increased by 72 percent in Germany (with an average annual rate of 3.5 percent) and by 181 percent in the United States (corresponding to an annual average rate of 6.7 percent). It is also worth noting that only in Germany and Switzerland did inflation peak at single-digit levels in the 1970s and the 1980s. Italy and the United Kingdom recorded two-digit ten-year averages in the 1970s. Italy did so in the 1980s as well (see figure 6.1). Table 6.1 shows that the same comparison also applies to the volatility of inflation.[4]

Germany's favorable performance applies also to the behavior of nominal interest rates. In figure 6.2 we show the averages of short-term (three months)

---

4. With some qualification for the case of Canada.

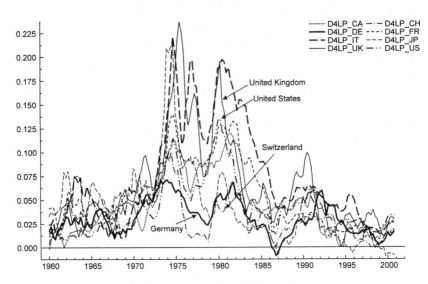

Fig. 6.1   Inflation in G7 countries and Switzerland

and long-term (ten years) interest rates during the 1970s. Evidently, German interest rates were then at the lower end of the interest-rate spectrum.

Regarding the behavior of real variables, however, it is worth noting that they did not diverge significantly among industrialized countries during the same period. Figure 6.3 shows that in the 1970s, there was no obvious trade-off between real GDP growth rates and inflation across countries.

6.2.3   Explanations of the Great Inflation

To avoid the accusation of omitting important facts, let us refer briefly to the most widespread explanation of the Great Inflation. According to Bruno and Sachs (1985), the key factor behind the acceleration of prices was the oil price shocks.[5] Bruno and Sachs (1985) state: "A clear and central villain of the piece is the historically unprecedented rise in commodity prices (mainly food and oil) in 1973–74 and again in 1979–80 that not coincidentally accompanied the two great bursts of stagflation" (7). The traditional explanation emphasizes supply shocks and the subsequent demand response. Supply shocks play the role of the initial exogenous impulse followed by endogenous adjustment of the private sector and policy authorities. Barsky and Kilian (2002, 2004) offer an alternative reading of the facts. According to their account, oil prices, and other commodity prices, should be seen as responding to global supply and demand factors. Specifically, the authors account for the increase in oil prices in 1973 as a delayed adjustment

---

5. Other related references would be Samuelson (1974), Gordon (1975), Blinder (1979), Darby (1982), and Hamilton (1983).

Table 6.1   Selected macroeconomic indicators for G7 and Switzerland, 1960–1998

	Canada		Switzerland		Germany		France		Italy		Japan		United Kingdom		United States	
	mean	s.d.	mean	s.d.	mean	s.d.	mean	s.d.	mean	s.d.	mean	s.d.	mean	s.d.	mean	s.d.
CPI % p.a.	4.5	3.1	3.3	2.3	3.1	1.8	5.3	3.6	7.4	5.4	4.4	4.0	6.5	4.8	4.4	2.9
real GDP % p.a.	3.6	2.1	2.3	2.6	2.7	2.0	3.3	1.9	3.4	2.9	4.5	4.0	2.4	1.9	3.4	2.0
real cons. % p.a.	3.2	2.4	2.6	2.4	3.3	2.8	3.0	2.1	3.7	2.6	4.4	3.7	2.1	2.6	2.9	2.3
Empl. % p.a.	2.2	1.6	0.7	1.9	0.2	1.2	0.6	0.8	0.1	1.2	1.0	0.8	0.3	1.4	1.8	1.3
Unemp. % p.a.	7.7	2.4			5.4	3.6	6.5	3.9	8.2	2.7	2.2	0.9	6.3	3.4	6.0	1.5
RL	8.5	2.6	4.6	1.1	7.1	1.5	8.3	2.9	10.4	4.2	6.0	2.3	9.4	2.9	7.4	2.5
RS	7.2	3.5			5.3	2.3	7.7	3.4	11.7	4.4	6.0	3.0	8.3	3.2	6.0	2.7

Notes: s.d. = standard deviation; p.a. = per annum; RL = level of long-term interest rate; RS = level of short-term interest rate.

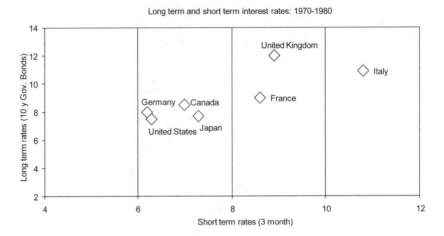

Fig. 6.2   Average nominal interest rates in the 1970s

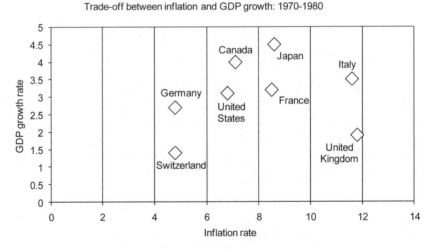

Fig. 6.3   Average inflation and real growth rates in the 1970s

to consistent demand pressure persisting since the late 1960s. The adjustment was delayed because during the 1960s oil prices were regulated through long-term contracts between oil producers and oil companies. In a situation of clear excess demand at the going price, conditions were ripe for the Organization of the Petroleum Exporting Countries (OPEC) to renege on its contractual agreements with oil companies leading to much higher oil prices. From such a viewpoint, it seems plausible that broad upward trends in commodity prices, the collapse of Bretton Woods, and the collapse of the oil market regime were all driven by excess demand growth in the late

1960s and the early 1970s. This would be compatible, following Barsky and Kilian, with a broad monetary account of the Great Inflation. Despite our obvious sympathy for such an account, investigating it is beyond the scope of this chapter.

Still, the fact that inflation in the United States and other member countries of the Bretton Woods system accelerated well before the first hike in oil prices supports the hypothesis that demand shocks (among them, increases in government spending) in conjunction with accommodative monetary policy prepared the ground for the inflationary surges of the 1970s. Furthermore, figure 6.1 suggests that it was the response to the oil price shocks of the 1970s that made most of the difference. The Bundesbank did not manage to avoid price acceleration completely (CPI inflation averaged 4.8 percent during the 1970s) but performed much better than most of all other industrialized countries.[6] The remainder of the chapter is thus devoted to the question: How did Germany manage to opt out of the Great Inflation?

6.3   Sound Money and Price Stability in Germany

6.3.1   The Legacy of the Bundesbank and Stability-Oriented Monetary Policy

On December 31, 1998, together with all national central banks joining the European Monetary Union (EMU), the Deutsche Bundesbank ended its life as a central bank responsible for conducting monetary policy for its currency. Combining this period with the term of its predecessor, the Bank deutscher Länder, the overall period coincides with the existence of the DM.[7]

The DM developed—together with the Swiss franc—into the most stable currency in the world after 1945, and the Bundesbank achieved a reputation as a model of a solid, successful central bank. This left a legacy reaching beyond its existence as a central bank responsible for a national currency. The statute of the European Central Bank (ECB), enshrined in the Maastricht Treaty, reflects this fact very well. But it is also fair to say that, in addition, the Bundesbank's track record influenced the world of central banking on a global scale.

This worldwide attention was heavily influenced by the fact that Germany (again together with Switzerland) avoided the Great Inflation of the 1970s. What explains the superior performance compared to most other countries? In this subsection, we will examine the historical, cultural, and institutional

---

6. The differences would be even more striking if one would consider a wider sample of industrialized countries (see, for example, Frenkel and Goldstein [1999] who consider twenty-three countries).

7. To be precise: the bank deutscher Länder was established on March 1, 1948. The DM became the currency of (then) West Germany on June 21, 1948. The Bundesbank replaced its predecessor on July 26, 1957.

background. In the next subsection, we will develop a theoretical model that formalizes the Bundesbank's strategy, and in section 6.5, we will characterize quantitatively the conduct of monetary policy by the Bundesbank.

To explain Germany's post–World War II monetary history one has to go back to 1948 and even beyond. The institutional foundation was laid in 1948 by law of the allies—West Germany did not yet exist as a state—which gave the Bank deutscher Länder (Bank of the German States) independence from any political authorities.[8] When a few months later the DM was introduced, this institution was entrusted with preserving the stability of the new currency.

The currency reform in cooperation with the simultaneous economic reforms of Ludwig Ehrhard laid the foundations of (West) Germany's economic success, the so-called "Wirtschaftswunder" (economic miracle).

As a consequence, most Germans for the first time in their lives enjoyed a stable currency. This experience had a deep impact on the mind of the German people. The mark, initially (1873) created as a currency based on gold, had ended its existence in the hyperinflation of 1923 that destroyed Germany's civil society.[9] The successor of the mark, the reichsmark, created in 1924, ended its short life with the currency reform of 1948. People had again lost most of their wealth invested in nominal assets. No wonder that a strong aversion against inflation and a desire for monetary stability became deeply entrenched in the minds of the German people![10] It became so entrenched in Germans' expectations, habits, and customs that it deserved the special expression "stability culture." It is interesting to stress the virtuous interaction between Germany's stability culture and the independence of the Bundesbank.

A particular historical episode illustrates it emphatically. The German Constitution of 1949 required the government to prepare the Deutsche Bundesbank law. It was no secret that then-chancellor Konrad Adenauer was not a friend of an independent central bank. However, his clash with the central bank in May 1956 when he criticized in public the increase of the discount rate (from 4.5 to 5.5 percent)—"the guillotine will hit ordinary citizens"—had already demonstrated to what extent the media and the public, at large, were behind the independence of the central bank from political interference. As a consequence, he lost the battle against the minister of the economy Ludwig Erhard. In the end, the Bundesbank law of 1957 in section 12 stated explicitly that: "In exercising the powers conferred on it by

8. De jure the Allied Bank Commission could interfere, but never made any use of this prerogative. See Buchheim (1999).
9. Stefan Zweig (1970), a writer, claims in his memoirs of that time that the experience of this total loss of the value of the currency more than anything else made Germans "ripe for Hitler" (359).
10. It was interesting to see that in the days before the Berlin Wall fell demonstrators in the streets of Leipzig carried posters saying: "If the D-Mark is not coming to us we will come to the D-Mark." So this desire for stability had also affected the mind of East Germans.

this Act, [the Bundesbank] is independent of instructions from the Federal Government." Together with the mandate in section 3 of "safeguarding the currency" the Bundesbank Act established the institutional fundament for a stability-oriented monetary policy.

Notwithstanding the fact that this law could have been changed at any time by a simple majority of the legislative body and insofar seemed to be based on shaky legal ground, the reputation of the Bundesbank became such that there was never any serious initiative to change the law. The status of the Bundesbank and the support for its stability-oriented monetary policy were firmly grounded on (and, in turn, reinforced) by the "stability culture" (see Issing 1993).

At the time of the ratification of the Bundesbank Act there were not only hardly any independent central banks in the world, it is even difficult to find any serious discussion in the literature on the issue of an appropriate institutional arrangement for a central bank. Interest in this topic was mainly triggered by the experience of the Great Inflation in the 1970s and the increasingly obvious failures of monetary policy in many countries. First publications discussed credibility issues (Barro and Gordon) and the time inconsistency problem (Kydland and Prescott). The outcome of monetary policy depending on the statute—here the degree of independence of the central bank—commanded broader attention only in the 1990s, with a paper by Alesina and Summers.[11]

Since then, the number of publications on central bank independence has exploded, discussing all aspects ranging from defining independence to measuring its degree to designing optimal contracts for central bankers. Is it wrong to say that the good performance of the Bundesbank, not least in the 1970s, has contributed to, if not triggered, this branch of research?

This interest in the topic and the result by more and more research papers also supported the claim to give independence to the new central bank that was yet to be founded, the European Central Bank. One should not forget that some of the countries signing the Maastricht Treaty at that time (1992) still had not given independence to their own national central banks. Since then "independence" of the central bank has become a model also on a global scale.

In a nutshell, the message stemming from experience and theory is: institutions matter! The outcome of monetary policy is heavily dependent on the institutional design of the central bank.

Another aspect of great importance pertained to the exchange rate regime (see previous section for a brief reference to the Bretton Woods system and some selected references to the relevant literature). For many years, the Bundesbank was in favor of a fixed exchange rate of the DM against the

---

11. See Alesina and Summers (1990). An early paper by Bade and Parkin (1980) was widely ignored and not even published.

US dollar. It even argued against the appreciation of the DM in 1961. The law of the "uneasy triangle" had been more or less forgotten (Issing 2006). However, towards the end of the 1960s, it became increasingly apparent that the fixed exchange rate was a constraint for conducting a monetary policy geared toward a domestic goal, namely price stability (Richter 1999; von Hagen 1999). In a regime of a fixed exchange rate and free capital flows, money growth becomes endogenous and any attempt to withstand the import of inflation is finally self-defeating.

The Bundesbank experienced a period of excessive money growth driven by interventions buying US dollars. In the late 1960s and early 1970s, the external component of money creation was sometimes even higher than the growth of the monetary base, implying that the internal contribution of money creation was negative. The consequences of this constellation for the institutional design of monetary policy were far-reaching: the Bundesbank, notwithstanding its independence from political interference, equipped with all the necessary instruments, was powerless with respect to pursuing a domestic goal since the exchange rate was fixed and capital flowed freely across borders. This fundamentally changed when in March 1973 Germany let its currency float against the US dollar. The Bundesbank, relieved from its obligation to intervene in the exchange market, could now consider conducting a monetary policy to safeguard the internal stability of its money (i.e., maintaining price stability).

In 1973, the Bundesbank declared the fight against inflation to be the principal goal of its monetary policy[12] and, in line with this, had already started to slow down inflation (which had peaked at almost 8 percent in mid-1973) when in October 1973, the first oil crisis broke out. The rise in oil prices thwarted the efforts of the Bundesbank while real output started to decline at the same time. Being confronted with such a situation, the Bundesbank attempted to keep monetary expansion within strict limits in order to avoid possible spillover effects into the wage and price-setting. In doing so, it did, however, not commit itself to any clear strategy and quantification.[13] Instead, the Bundesbank mainly tried to influence the behavior of market participants by means of "moral suasion." However, the social partners more or less ignored the signals given by the Bundesbank and agreed on high increases in nominal wages in 1974, trying to compensate for the loss in real disposable income. As a consequence, unemployment increased and inflation went up.

---

12. See Deutsche Bundesbank (1974, 1975) pages 42 and 1, respectively. At the same time, the Bundesbank never completely ignored other, secondary objectives, such as the stabilization of the business cycle and the stabilization of the external value of the currency. For more detailed accounts on the weights given to (domestic) price stability versus other goals during the period in question, see von Hagen (1999) and Baltensperger (1999).

13. In fact, the Bundesbank tried to ensure that "monetary expansion was not too great but not too small either." See Deutsche Bundesbank (1974), *Annual Report* (AR), especially p. 17.

Against this experience, the idea of adopting a formal quantitative target for money growth that would provide a nominal anchor for inflation and inflation expectations rapidly gained ground. As it happened, this period coincided with the "monetarist counterrevolution." The leading monetarists Milton Friedman, Karl Brunner, and Alan Meltzer claimed that central banks should abstain from any attempt to fine-tune the economy and should instead follow a strategy of monetary targeting. (A floating exchange rate was a necessary condition for controlling the money supply.) These ideas in principle found positive reactions in Germany (Richter 1999; von Hagen 1999). The Bundesbank discussed this approach internally and with leading proponents. Helmut Schlesinger, member of the Executive Board and chief economist, had an intensive exchange of views, not least when participating in the intellectually influential Konstanz Seminar founded by Karl Brunner in 1970.[14] The rejection of fine-tuning and the medium-term orientation of monetary policy implied by monetary targeting was also strongly supported by the German Council of Economic Experts (1974).

However, in spite of the Bundesbank being the first central bank in the world to adopt a monetary target (for the year 1975), the honeymoon with leading monetarists came soon to an end. This process had already started when the Bundesbank declared its move to the new strategy "an experiment," stressed that it would not (and, in the short run, could not) control the monetary base, and over many years missed its monetary target.

The Bundesbank interpreted its approach as a kind of "pragmatic monetarism" and kept to this strategy until 1998 (see Baltensperger 1999; Issing 2005; and also Neumann 1997, 1999). Not surprisingly, this attitude was heavily criticized, especially by Karl Brunner (1983). However, in its monetary policy practice, the strategy served the Bundesbank well in defending the stability of its currency—if not in absolute terms it did at least (together with the Swiss National Bank) substantially better than most other central banks.

6.3.2   The Conduct of Policy under Monetary Targeting

Derivation of the Money Growth Target

The choice of a monetary target in 1974 undoubtedly signaled a fundamental regime shift.[15] Not only was it a clear break with the past but also a decision to discard alternative approaches to monetary policy.[16] There were

---

14. See Fratianni and von Hagen (2001). The authors give a comprehensive survey on subjects discussed and persons attending. The seminar still continues and was chaired for many years by the leading German monetarist Manfred Neumann.

15. Parts of this section are taken from Issing (2005).

16. It must be recognized that the start of monetary targeting was characterized by a high degree of uncertainty. After all, Germany had just come out of the Bretton Woods "adjustable peg" system in which many topics were seen as irrelevant.

two main arguments in favor of providing a quantified guidepost for the future rate of monetary expansion. First and foremost was the intention of controlling inflation through the control of monetary expansion. Second, the Bundesbank tried to provide guidance to agents' (especially wage bargainers') expectations through the announcement of a quantified objective for monetary growth.[17] Therefore, with its new strategy, the Bundesbank clearly signaled its responsibility for the control of inflation. At the same time, the Bundesbank expressed its view that while monetary policy by maintaining price stability in the longer run would exert a positive impact on economic growth, the fostering of the economy's growth potential should be considered a task of fiscal and structural policies, while employment was a responsibility of the social partners conducting wage negotiations.

Although the formulation of the new strategy was heavily influenced by the ideas of the leading monetarists, the implementation of monetary targeting in Germany deviated from the theoretical blueprint in a number of ways. One important difference was that Bundesbank did not formulate its targets in terms of the monetary base, but in terms of a broadly defined monetary aggregate, the central bank money stock (defined as currency in circulation plus the required minimum reserves on domestic deposits calculated at constant reserve ratios with base January 1974).[18] Second the Bundesbank did not attempt to control the money stock directly, but followed an indirect approach of influencing money demand by varying key money market rates and bank reserves (two-stage implementation procedure). Third, the Bundesbank made it clear from the beginning that it could not and would not promise to reach the monetary target with any degree of precision. Accordingly, in this period, the new regime of monetary targeting was in many respects an experiment.

From the outset, the Bundesbank recognized the importance of adopting a simple, transparent, and at the same time comprehensible method for the derivation of the annual monetary targets.[19] The analytical background for the derivation formula was provided by the quantity theory of money. Starting from the quantity *identity,* one gets that average money growth, $\Delta \bar{m}$, and average inflation, $\Delta \bar{p}$, will fulfill the identity:

$$(1) \qquad \Delta \bar{m}_t + \Delta \bar{v}_t \equiv \Delta \bar{p}_t + \Delta \bar{y}_t,$$

where p, m, y, and v are the (logs of the) price level, the money stock, real income, and the income velocity of money, respectively, and the bars denote long-run average values. Taking the velocity trend and the long-run average

17. See Schlesinger (1983) on this issue.
18. The ratios were 16.6 percent for sight deposits, 12.4 percent for time deposits, and 8.1 percent for savings deposits. After the mid-1980s, the heavy weight on currency increasingly proved to be a disadvantage, and when setting the target for 1988, the Bundesbank switched to the money stock M3. See Deutsche Bundesbank (1995, 81).
19. See also Issing (1997) for the following considerations.

rate of real output growth to be exogenous, it follows from (1) that trend inflation can be pinned down by controlling the trend rate of money growth:

$$(2) \qquad \Delta \bar{p}_t = \Delta \bar{m}_t - \Delta \bar{y}_t + \Delta \bar{v}_t.$$

Based on this reasoning, the Bundesbank derived the target for *average* money growth in year t, Δm_t^*, from the sum of the (maximum) rise in prices it was willing to tolerate, Δp_t^*, the predicted growth in potential output, $E_{t-1} \Delta y_t^*$, and the expected trend rate of change in velocity, $E_{t-1} \Delta v_t^*$:

$$(3) \qquad \Delta m_t^* = \Delta p_t^* + E_{t-1}(\Delta y_t^*) - E_{t-1}(\Delta v_t^*),$$

where the deltas now represent year-on-year changes, and E_{t-1} denotes expectations at the end of year $t - 1$. The target rate for average (year-on-year) money growth was then translated into a target rate for money growth in the course of the year (see table 6.2 and Neumann 1997, 180).

The approach reflected the insight that monetary growth consistent with this derivation would create the appropriate conditions for real growth in line with price stability. While these basic relationships were uncontested over medium to longer-term horizons, the Bundesbank was fully aware of the fact that they might not strictly apply over the shorter term. On a month-to-month or quarter-to-quarter basis and even beyond, the basic relationship between the money stock and the overall domestic price level was often obscured by a variety of other factors. Any attempt to strictly tie money growth to its desired path in the short term might have led to disturbing volatility in interest and exchange rates, thus imposing unnecessary adjustment costs on the economy. Accordingly, the Bundesbank repeatedly pointed to the medium-term nature of its strategy and explained that it was prepared to tolerate short-term deviations from the target path if that seemed advisable or acceptable in terms of the overriding goal of price stability.

From 1975 to 1978: The Learning Phase

First experiences with monetary targets were not particularly encouraging. Between 1975 and 1978, the quantitative targets were clearly (and in 1978 considerably) overshot (see table 6.2). The sharp increase in interest rates that had taken place immediately after the end of the Bretton Woods system was almost completely reversed in 1974 and 1975, and real short-term interest rates were kept rather low until the beginning of 1979 (see figure 6.6, panel A). Clarida and Gertler (1997) interpret this as evidence "that the Bundesbank's commitment to fight inflation waned somewhat during the period between the two major oil shocks." Von Hagen (1999) argues that following the first oil price shock, short-term employment-related goals gained prominence. In the Bundesbank's own reading, the loosening was mainly motivated by two considerations that, in hindsight, turned out to be partly based on misjudgments. First, policymakers apparently overestimated the extent to which the currency appreciation would dampen real activity and

Table 6.2   Monetary targets and their implementation (in percentage)

Year	Target: Growth of central bank money stock (1975–1987) or money stock M3 (from 1988)			Actual money growth		Target achieved	Inflation rate (CPI)[d]
	In the course of the year[a]	Annual average	Midyear review	In the course of the year	Annual average		
1975	8			10.1 (9.5)	7.8	No	5.9
1976		8		(9.0)	9.2	No	4.2
1977	(6–7)[b]	8		(9.5)	9.0	No	3.8
1978	(5–7)[b]	8		(12.1)	11.4	No	2.7
1979	6–9		Lower limit	6.3	9.1	Yes	4.1
1980	5–8	(6)	Lower half	4.9	4.8	Yes	5.4
1981	4–7	(5–5.5)	Lower half	3.5	4.4	Yes	6.3
1982	4–7	(4.75)	Upper half	6.0	4.9	Yes	5.3
1983	4–7		Upper half	7.0	7.3	Yes	3.4
1984	4–6	(5)		4.6	4.8	Yes	2.3
1985	3–5	(4.5)		4.5	4.6	Yes	2.2
1986	3.5–5.5	(4.5)		7.7	6.4	No	−0.2
1987	3–6			8.1	8.1	No	0.3
1988	3–6			6.7	6.3	No	1.2
1989	About 5	(Just under 5)		4.7	5.7	Yes	2.8
1990	4–6	(About 5)		5.6	4.3	Yes	2.7
1991	4–6	(5.25)	3–5	5.2	4.6	Yes	3.6
1992	3.5–5.5	(5–5.25)		9.4	8.1	No	4.0
1993	4.5–6.5	(6)		7.4	7.8	No	3.6
1994	4–6	(5.5)		5.7	9.0	Yes	2.7
1995	4–6	(5.75)		2.1	0.6	No	1.8
1996	4–7	(5.5)		8.1	7.5	No	1.4
1997[c]	3.5–6.5			4.7	6.2	Yes	1.9
1998[c]	3–6			5.5	4.4	Yes[c]	1.0
Mean				6.6	6.5		3.0

[a]Between the fourth quarter of the previous year and the fourth quarter of the current year; 1975: Dec. 1974 to Dec. 1975.
[b]According to Annual Reports for 1977 and 1978.
[c]Embedded in a two-year orientation for 1997/1998 of about 5 percent per year.
[d]From 1995, all-German figures.

inflation. The second misjudgment concerned the depth of the 1975 recession, which in hindsight, turned out to have been greatly overestimated (see Gerberding, Seitz, and Worms 2004).[20]

Nevertheless, the Bundesbank was able to slow down inflation from the high levels before to 2.7 percent in 1978. During this period the Bundesbank gained valuable insights into the new regime and introduced a number of technical modifications (see table 6.2). These experiences helped the Bundes-

20. See Bundesbank, AR 1975 and 1976.

bank to enhance the monetary targeting concept from its experimental stage into a fully-fledged strategy. As a consequence, at the end of 1978, the potential-oriented monetary targeting strategy had been established and had proven its value. Therefore, the Bundesbank was well prepared when the German economy entered especially troubled waters.

From 1979 to 1985: The Strategy Bears Fruit

The economic situation in 1978 was broadly seen as rather comfortable. German real GDP had grown by around 3 percent, accompanied by high levels of employment growth and falling unemployment. The situation was, however, less positive in terms of monetary growth and inflation. Monetary growth had overshot its target and there were signs of acceleration in the rate of inflation, which in 1978 stood, on average, at 2.7 percent. Furthermore, in 1979, the sharp increase in oil prices associated with the second oil price shock hit the German economy. The resulting massive increase in import prices, especially energy prices, augmented by a weakening of the exchange rate, brought about a turnaround in Germany's current account position, leading to a current account deficit in 1979 for the first time in many years.

At the same time, government fiscal policy was clearly expansionary. Thus, fiscal policy rendered the central bank's task even more difficult. Moreover, the European Monetary System (EMS), an exchange rate regime defining the exchange rates of participating currencies in terms of central rates against the ECU, had begun rather quietly in March 1979, but subsequently faced tensions and the need to adjust parities from as early as September 1979.

It was obvious from the beginning that the direct effect of the oil price shock on consumer prices could not be prevented by monetary policy. At the same time, the Bundesbank had carefully analyzed the lessons of the first oil price shock. Against this experience, in 1979 the Governing Council of the Bundesbank was well aware of the threat that the oil price increase could translate again into sustained increases in inflation brought about by second-round effects in wage- and price-setting.[21] In responding to these challenges, the Bundesbank took decisive action. The discount rate was increased in steps from 3 percent at the start of 1979 to reach 7.5 percent in May 1980. In parallel, the Lombard rate was increased from its initial level of 3.5 percent to 9.5 percent in May 1980, and in February 1981 (as a special Lombard) to as much as 12 percent, the normal Lombard window being closed.[22] By subsequently reducing the monetary targets from 1979 onwards, the Bundesbank sent out a clear signal for restoring price stability.

Not until the second half of 1981 did the growth rates for the monetary base begin to come down. Toward the end of 1981, there were increasingly

---

21. See Schlesinger (1980) on this point.
22. See Baltensperger (1999) for a more detailed description of this period, the monetary targets, and their realizations.

clear signs of an easing of price and wage pressures. The DM regained confidence in the foreign exchange markets and strengthened again, not only within the EMS but also in relation to the US dollar. The external adjustment process was promoted through a slowdown in domestic demand and the current account position improved noticeably. Furthermore, through the "monetary warning," the government became aware of the unsustainability of its deficit policy. From then on, budget consolidation was increasingly recognized as being an urgent task.

The subsequent years 1982 to 1985 can be regarded as a phase of monetary relaxation and normalization. The Bundesbank's monetary policy was focused on bringing down inflation and restoring the stability of the currency, and it proved able to realize this aim throughout the period. The benchmark figure for the tolerated rate of inflation (which, until 1984, was termed the "unavoidable" rate of price increase) was gradually reduced from 3.5 percent in 1982 to 2 percent in 1985. At the same time, actual inflation fell steadily from an annual average rate of 5.2 percent in 1982 to 2.0 percent in 1985. When price stability was virtually reached in the middle of the 1980s, the Bundesbank changed over from the concept of an "unavoidable" rate of inflation to a medium-term price norm or price assumption of no more than 2 percent (see table 6.3).

The Last Test: German Reunification

Given the stability-oriented monetary policy strategy and the developments just described it is far from surprising that, at the end of the 1980s, the Bundesbank was one of the most respected central banks in the world. At the beginning of the 1990s, it was about to face an important historical test, in the form of German reunification.

The DM was introduced in the eastern Länder on June 1, 1990. Curiously, the introduction of the currency preceded political unification (October 3, 1990). The extension of the territorial scope of monetary policy clearly led to a significant increase in uncertainty. Specifically, the operation entailed an increase in money supply of the order of 15 percent of West German money stock. This number compared with about 10 percent, which would have been appropriate on the basis of estimates of the relative size of the former German Democratic Republic's (GDR's) GDP at market prices. Moreover, there were additional factors challenging the conduct of the Bundesbank's stability-oriented policy. In fact, German reunification led to a massive expansion of aggregate expenditure in Germany, including sizable general government deficits. As a consequence inflation rose quickly, with price increases (in West Germany) exceeding 4 percent in the second half of 1991.

How could the Bundesbank under these circumstances maintain price stability over the medium term? How could it preserve credibility?

The Bundesbank decided to stick to its tried and tested framework, including the normative rate of 2 percent for inflation. This option implied that the

Table 6.3   **Numerical inputs for the derivation of the money growth targets (average annual changes in percentage)**

Period	Medium-term price assumption[a]	Expected growth of potential output	Expected change in — Capacity utilization	Expected change in — Trend velocity (−)	Envisaged increase in money stock	Target[b]	Sources
1975	No explicit derivation by single factors					+8	MR Dec. 1974
1976	+4/+5	+2	+2.5	−1	+8		AR 1976, MR Jan. 1976
1977	+3.5[c]/+4[d]	+3	+2	−1	+8	(6–7)	AR 1976, MR Jan. 1977
1978	+3/+3.5	+3	+		+8	(5–7)	AR 1977, MR Jan. 1978
1979	+	+3	+	+		6–9	MR Jan. 1979
1980	+4	+3		−1	(+6)	5–8	AR 1979, MR Dec. 1979
1981	+3.5/+4	+2.5		−1	+5/+5.5	4–7	AR 1980, MR Dec. 1980
1982	+3.5[c]	+1.5/+2		0	(+4.75)	4–7	AR 1981, MR Dec. 1981
1983	+3.5	+1.5/+2				4–7	MR Dec. 1982
1984	+3	+2			+5	4–6	AR 1983, MR Dec. 1983
1985	+2	Over 2	+		+4.5	3–5	MR Dec. 1984
1986	+2[c]	+2.5			+4.5	3.5–5.5	MR Jan. 1986
1987	+2	+2.5				3–6	MR Jan. 1987
1988	+2	+2		+.5		3–6	MR Feb. 1988
1989	+2	+2/+2.5		+.5	5	about 5	MR Dec. 1988
1990	+2	+2.5		+.5	about 5	4–6	MR Dec. 1989
1991[e]	+2	+2.5 (+2.25)[e]		+.5		4–6 (3–5)[e]	AR 90, MR July 1991
1992	+2	+2.75		+.5		3.5–5.5	MR Dec. 1991
1993	+2	+3		+1	+6	4.5–6.5	MR Dec. 1992
1994	+2	+2.5		+1	+5.5	4–6	MR Jan. 1994
1995	+2	+2.75		+1	+5.75	4–6	MR Jan. 1995
1996	+2	+2.5		+1	+5.5	4–7	MR Jan. 1996
1997	+1.5/+2	+2.25		+1	+5	3.5–6.5	MR Jan. 1997
1998	+1.5/+2	+2		+1	+5	3–6	MR Jan. 1998

[a]Before 1985: unavoidable increase in prices.
[b]Targets referred to central bank money stock (defined as currency in circulation plus required minimum reserves on domestic deposits calculated at constant reserve ratios with base January 1974) until 1987 and the broad money stock M3 thereafter.
[c]Explicit reference to GDP deflator.
[d]Explicit reference to Consumer Price Index.
[e]Downward correction of target range in midyear review.

Bundesbank was, for a short time, prepared to accept monetary expansion above the announced target. Again, the money growth targets proved to be highly beneficial in terms of anchoring inflation expectations, even though it was not easy to derive an adequate money growth target for reunited Germany (see Issing et al. 2005, 3). The Bundesbank abided by its well-proven strategy right up to the beginning of EMU in January 1999. While some technical features of the strategy (e.g., the exact definition of the target variable) were changed over time, its major elements—the explicit derivation of the annual money growth targets from medium-term macroeconomic benchmark figures, the flexible implementation that included temporary departures from the medium-term rule, and the two-stage implementation procedure—stayed intact. In this respect, the Bundesbank's approach certainly stands out by reason of its consistency and remarkable continuity.

Lessons

What are the lessons that can be drawn? Why was Germany better able to counter the inflationary shocks of the 1970s than most other countries? Several key aspects emerge from this brief review of German monetary policy after the end of the Bretton Woods system. To begin with, the Bundesbank was the first central bank to announce a monetary target and thus to undertake a strategy of commitment, transparently communicated to the public.[23] Moreover, when announcing the money growth targets, the Bundesbank disclosed the most important guiding principles behind its decisions, such as the maximum rise in prices that would be tolerated by the central bank and its estimate of potential output growth. By doing so, the Bundesbank fostered transparency and provided an anchor for medium-term inflation expectations. In retrospect, against the background of the more recent debate about the merits of an intensive communication policy, these elements of the Bundesbank's strategy appear very modern indeed.

After the initial years of experimentation, the strategy had proven its value in the baptism of fire of 1979 and the early 1980s. In doing so, it had managed to establish credibility which, in turn, had started to set in motion a virtuous circle. Still, one may well ask—and indeed, it has often been asked—how the Bundesbank was able to get away with its practice of deviating time and again from the announced targets while at the same time preserving its reputation as a bulwark of monetary stability.[24] After all, even if one excludes the years 1975 to 1978, the targets were missed seven out of twenty times (see figure 6.4).

As explained by Issing (1997, 71), the target misses were rarely of a completely involuntary nature, but mostly constituted deliberate monetary policy decisions. Yet it was exactly in those situations that the monetary targets had an especially valuable disciplining effect because once a target was missed the decision makers were put under pressure to justify the outcome in terms of the ultimate aim of safeguarding the currency. Similarly, Schlesinger (2002) argues that the targets imposed discipline on the decision makers by forcing them to explain their decisions and to persuade the public that failure to meet the intermediate target did not jeopardize the final goal of policy. Finally, according to Neumann (2006, 14), "the Bundesbank was the first central bank that provided the public (or at least, an elite audi-

23. See Issing (1992, 291).
24. See Neumann (2006, 14).

1975-1987: Targets for the central bank money stock   1988-1998: Targets for the money stock M3

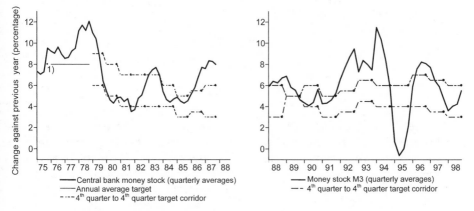

———Central bank money stock (quarterly averages)
———Annual average target
- - - - 4th quarter to 4th quarter target corridor

———Money stock M3 (quarterly averages)
— - — 4th quarter to 4th quarter target corridor

1) Point target for December 1974 to December 1975

Fig. 6.4   Money growth targets 1975–1998

ence), with an intelligible numerical framework that facilitated the evaluation of its policy course from the outside." Viewed from this perspective, the money growth targets represented a movement away from purely discretionary policy toward a more rule-based behavior. The Bundesbank itself has sometimes designated its strategy as constrained or disciplined discretion; Neumann (1997) talks of "rule-based discretion."

6.4   Monetary Targeting as a Commitment Device

As explained in the previous section, the Bundesbank did not attempt to control the money stock directly, but followed an indirect management procedure that worked via influencing conditions in the money market. Hence, on a basic level, the Bundesbank's approach may be described as setting the short-term interest rate so as to achieve the rate of money growth that was viewed as consistent with the attainment of the final goal, price stability. In this section, we present a model that formalizes this approach and enables us to compare the implied interest rate rule with other interest rate rules proposed in the academic literature (such as the Taylor rule and its many variants).

Taylor (1999) and more recently, Orphanides (2003) and Kilponen and Leitemo (2008) have discussed the implications of targeting money growth for a central bank that sets the short-term interest rate. Although we know from the previous section that the Bundesbank's practice of monetary targeting differed from the monetarist blueprint in a number of ways, it is still instructive to consider the simple case of a "pure" or "strict" money growth rule first. Under strict money growth targeting, the central bank is required to find the short-term interest rate, i_t, which sets the growth rate of money equal to the prespecified target:

(4)
$$\Delta m_t = \Delta m_t^*$$

subject to a money demand relation that relates real money holdings to output and the interest rate:[25]

(5)
$$(m_t - p_t) = \eta_y \cdot y_t - \eta_i \cdot i_t + \varepsilon_t^{md}$$

where ε_t^{md} captures short-run dynamics and shocks to money demand. Taking first differences, the growth rate of money is related to the inflation rate, the change in the nominal interest rate, and the growth rate of output through

(5a)
$$\Delta m_t = \pi_t + \eta_y \Delta y_t - \eta_i \Delta i_t + \Delta \varepsilon_t^{md}.$$

Given the money demand relation (5), equilibrium velocity can be written as

(6)
$$v_t^* = -((m_t - p_t)^* - y_t^*), \text{ where}$$

$$(m_t - p_t)^* - y_t^* = (\eta_y - 1)y_t^* + \eta_i \cdot i_t^* + \varepsilon_t^{v*}$$

$$\Rightarrow v_t^* = (1 - \eta_y)y_t^* - \eta_i \cdot i_t^* - \varepsilon_t^{v*}$$

and equilibrium changes in velocity

(6a)
$$\Delta v_t^* = (1 - \eta_y)\Delta y_t^* - \eta_i \cdot \Delta i_t^* - \Delta \varepsilon_t^{v*}$$

are represented by a function of potential output growth and of changes in the steady-state level of the nominal interest rate (if there are any). We define the velocity shock ε_t^{v*} as a shock to *equilibrium* money demand. We interpret ε_t^{v*} as a portfolio shock that can be observed by the central bank due to its institutional knowledge.

As discussed in the previous section, a central bank with the objective of controlling long-run average inflation will set the money growth target equal to the "acceptable" rate of inflation, π_t^*, adjusted for the predicted growth rate of potential output and the expected trend rate of change in velocity (which is exactly what the Bundesbank did):

(7)
$$\Delta m_t^* = \pi_t^* + E_t \Delta y_t^* - E_t \Delta v_t^*.$$

Note that in contrast to equation (3), we now assume that the money growth targets are based on current-period expectations of Δy_t^* and Δv_t^*, which presupposes that the money growth targets are regularly updated to

---

25. Such a money demand equation can be derived from the optimization problem of a household who values money holdings in its utility function that is separable in real balances and consumption goods (see Woodford 2003).

take account of revisions in the estimates of potential output growth and the trend change in velocity.[26] From (6a) the formula for the money growth target can be reformulated as:

(7a) $$\Delta m_t^* = \pi_t^* + \eta_y E_t \Delta y_t^* + \Delta \varepsilon_t^{v*},$$

where we abstract from changes in the nominal equilibrium interest rate (as the Bundesbank did).[27]

Combining (5a) and (7a), the deviation of money growth from target can now be expressed as:

(8) $$\Delta m_t - \Delta m_t^* = \pi_t - \pi_t^* + \eta_y(\Delta y_t - E_t \Delta y_t^*) - \eta_i \Delta i_t + \{\Delta \varepsilon_t^{md} - \Delta \varepsilon_t^{v*}\}.$$

Using the equality of actual money growth with target (equation [4]) entails:

(9) $$\pi_t - \pi_t^* + \eta_y(\Delta y_t - E_t \Delta y_t^*) - \eta_i \Delta i_t + \{\Delta \varepsilon_t^{md} - \Delta \varepsilon_t^{v*}\} = 0.$$

Solving for the nominal interest rate, (9) can be transformed into an instrument rule of the form:

(10) $$i_t = i_{t-1} + \frac{1}{\eta_i}(\pi_t - \pi_t^*) + \frac{\eta_y}{\eta_i}(\Delta y_t - E_t \Delta y_t^*) + \frac{1}{\eta_i}\{\Delta \varepsilon_t^{md} - \Delta \varepsilon_t^{v*}\}.$$

According to (10), money growth targeting implies an interest rate reaction to the lagged interest rate, to the deviation of inflation from target, to the deviation of actual output growth from (the central bank's estimate of) potential output growth (which is equivalent to the change in the output gap), and to the difference between the "true" money demand shock $\Delta \varepsilon_t^{md}$, and the portfolio shock observed by the central bank, $\Delta \varepsilon_t^{v*}$. As pointed out by Orphanides (2003), the interest rate rule implied by (strict) money growth targeting thus belongs to the class of "natural-growth targeting rules," which do not rely on estimates of the natural rate of interest and output and thus "stay clear of the pitfalls known to plague the natural-rate-gap-based policy approach" (990). Notice, however, that in order to be a meaningful specification, which would be suitable for characterizing the practical implementation of monetary policy, the money demand shocks in (10) should have reasonable properties. We will discuss this issue in more detail in section 6.5, where we present our empirical results.

However, as discussed in the previous section, the Bundesbank did not adhere to a strict version of the Friedman rule, but instead pursued a strategy of "pragmatic monetarism." Most importantly, the assumption that the central bank hits the money growth target each period that underlies equation (4) is at odds with the Bundesbank's acclaimed medium-

---

26. As regards the Bundesbank, the fact that the targets were usually formulated as a corridor of 2 or 3 percentage points (see table 6.3) provided flexibility for adjustments to changes in the underlying estimates. In addition, there was a regular midyear review of the targets.

27. See Gerberding, Seitz, and Worms (2007, 5).

term orientation and the fact that it tolerated short-term deviations from target.

In order to capture these features of the Bundesbank's monetary policy strategy, we choose a framework that allows us to interpret a monetary target as a commitment device. Specifically, we assume that policymakers at the Bundesbank were aware of the pitfalls of discretionary policy and used monetary targeting as a device to get closer to the optimal (but time-inconsistent) commitment solution. More formally, we assume that the Bundesbank council optimized the setting of the policy instrument(s) with respect to a standard objective function, modified to include an additional money growth target:[28]

$$(11) \qquad E_0 \sum_{t=0}^{\infty} \beta^t [(\pi_t - \pi_t^*)^2 + \hat{\lambda}_x x_t^2 + \hat{\lambda}_i (i_t - i_t^*)^2 + \hat{\lambda}_m (\Delta m_t - \Delta m_t^*)^2],$$

where β is the discount factor, x_t is the output gap defined as the gap between actual output, y_t, and potential output, y_t^*, and $\hat{\lambda}_x$, $\hat{\lambda}_i$, and $\hat{\lambda}_m$ are the relative weights attached to the output, interest rate, and money growth terms.

The use of a modified loss function to attenuate the pitfalls associated with discretionary monetary policy was pioneered by Rogoff (1985). More recently, several authors have analyzed the properties of monetary policy strategies based on modified loss functions in the context of forward-looking New Keynesian-type models. There are many variants of modified loss functions, including price-level targeting (Svensson 1999; Vestin 2006; Røisland 2006; and Gaspar, Smets, and Vestin 2007); average inflation targeting (Nessén and Vestin 2005); interest-rate smoothing (Woodford 1999); nominal income growth targeting (Jensen 2002); and speed limit targeting (Walsh 2003).

For our purposes, the most closely related contribution in the literature is Söderström (2005), who analyzes the implications of delegating a loss function to the central bank, which deviates from society's true loss function by an additional money growth target. As shown by Söderström, this modification can be beneficial for a central bank acting under discretion since the money growth target introduces interest rate inertia and history dependence into interest rate decisions, both of which are features of the optimal commitment policy. In Söderström's baseline simulations, a money growth target closes about 80 percent of the gap between discretionary policy and the optimal policy under precommitment. This result is more remarkable given the fact that it is obtained in the context of a standard New Keynesian model where money growth is neither useful as an indicator of future inflation nor of output growth, and where

---

28. In the loss function (11), we have abstracted from the complications arising from a gap between the efficient and the natural level of output, but one should keep in mind that with a positive value of x*, the optimal discretionary policy suffers from an average inflation bias as well as a stabilization bias (see Woodford 2003, 469).

money plays no direct role in the transmission mechanism of monetary policy.

Nevertheless, our objective differs from Söderström's. Specifically, we want to derive the interest rate rule characterizing optimal discretionary policy under the modified loss function (11). In our reading, this loss function captures some relevant dimensions of the Bundesbank's approach of pragmatic monetarism. Most importantly, it accounts for misses of the monetary target in the context of a strategy where monetary growth is *always* important for monetary policymaking. Hence, we expect the interest rate rule implied by this loss function to provide a useful starting point for the empirical analysis undertaken in section 6.5.

In order to derive the interest rate rule implied by the modified loss function (11), we need a model of the underlying structural relationships between the target variables. To keep the analysis as simple as possible, we assume that these relationships are adequately captured by the standard New Keynesian model, which, despite its well-known limitations, is the workhorse in the theory of monetary policymaking.

Specifically, we use the baseline version of the model, which consists of an aggregate supply and an aggregate demand equation, augmented by the simple money demand relation (5):[29]

$$\text{(12)} \qquad \pi_t - \pi_t^* = \beta(E_t\pi_{t+1} - \pi_{t+1}^*) + \kappa x_t + u_t^\pi$$

$$\text{(13)} \qquad x_t = E_t x_{t+1} - \varphi(i_t - E_t\pi_{t+1} - r_t^n)$$

$$\text{(5)} \qquad (m_t - p_t) = \eta_y \cdot y_t - \eta_i \cdot i_t + \varepsilon_t^{md},$$

where u_t^π is a cost-push shock and r_t^π is a natural-rate shock. For simplicity's sake, we assume that both are independent and identically distributed (i.i.d.). Combining equation (5) with the definition of the money growth target from equation (7a) yields:

$$\text{(14)} \qquad \Delta m_t - \Delta m_t^* = \pi_t - \pi_t^* + \eta_y(\Delta y_t - \Delta y_t^*) - \eta_i \Delta i_t + \{\Delta\varepsilon_t^{md} - \Delta\varepsilon_t^{v*}\}$$

$$= \pi_t - \pi_t^* + \eta_y \Delta x_t - \eta_i \Delta i_t + \Delta\varepsilon_t,$$

where $\varepsilon_t = \varepsilon_t^{md} - \varepsilon_t^{v*}$ and we have again assumed that the money growth target is regularly updated to take account of observed portfolio shifts and of revisions in the central bank's estimates of potential output growth. Alternatively, the shock variable in (14) would have to be modified to include shocks to potential output growth.[30]

Clearly, the model misses some important elements for understanding

---

29. For details on the model, see Woodford (2007, 6).

30. Loss function (11) assumes that output is targeted at the natural rate, which is a time-varying variable. If output-gap targeting is feasible, the value of the natural rate must be known (or, in real-life terms, a good estimate is available). Therefore, y_t^n can, in principle, also serve as an input for the (time-varying) money growth target (see Jensen 2002, 948).

monetary policymaking, such as the role of financial factors in the transmission mechanism. Nevertheless, it does provide a simple and workable framework to discuss the key issues of commitment, credibility, and reputation (see, e.g., Gaspar and Kashyap 2007).

We are now in a position to derive the interest rate rule implied by the modified period loss function (11) subject to the underlying model composed of equations (12), (13), and (14). Formally, the solution can be found by minimizing the Lagrangian expression:

$$
(15) \quad L_t = E_t \begin{bmatrix} (\pi_t - \pi_t^*)^2 + \hat{\lambda}_x x_t^2 + \hat{\lambda}_i(i_t - i_t^*)^2 + \hat{\lambda}_m(\Delta m_t - \Delta m_t^*)^2 \\ +\beta(\pi_{t+1} - \pi_{t+1}^*)^2 + \beta\hat{\lambda}_x x_{t+1}^2 + \beta\hat{\lambda}_i(i_{t+1} - i_{t+1}^*)^2 + \beta\hat{\lambda}_m(\Delta m_{t+1} - \Delta m_{t+1}^*)^2 + \beta^2 ... \\ +\phi_{1,t}(\beta(E_t\pi_{t+1} - \pi_{t+1}^*) + \kappa x_t + u_t^\pi - (\pi_t - \pi_t^*)) \\ +\phi_{2,t}(E_t x_{t+1} - \varphi(i_t - E_t\pi_{t+1} - r_t^n) - x_t) \\ +\phi_{3,t}(\pi_t - \pi_t^* + \eta_y\Delta x_t - \eta_i\Delta i_t + \Delta\varepsilon_t - (\Delta m_t - \Delta m_t^*)) \\ +\beta\phi_{1,t+1}(\beta(E_{t+1}\pi_{t+2} - \pi_{t+2}^*) + \kappa x_{t+1} + u_{t+1}^\pi - (\pi_{t+1} - \pi_{t+1}^*)) \\ +\beta\phi_{2,t+1}(E_{t+1}x_{t+2} - \varphi(i_{t+1} - E_{t+1}\pi_{t+2} - r_{t+1}^n) - x_{t+1}) \\ +\beta\phi_{3,t+1}(\pi_{t+1} - \pi_{t+1}^* + \eta_y\Delta x_{t+1} - \eta_i\Delta i_{t+1} + \Delta\varepsilon_{t+1} - (\Delta m_{t+1} - \Delta m_{t+1}^*)) + ... \end{bmatrix}
$$

with respect to the paths of each of the four endogenous variables, π_t, x_t, Δm_t, and i_t. The derivation is complicated by the fact that the money growth target introduces lagged values of the endogenous variables into the state vector. In any stationary equilibrium therefore, the expected values of the endogenous variables will depend on their own lagged values.[31] In general, analytical solutions to this kind of problem are not available, but Söderlind (1999) and Dennis (2007) have developed algorithms that provide numerical solutions. While we do not want to take that route here, it is possible to gain important insights into the nature of the policy problem by considering the analytical solution to the much simpler static version of the problem.[32] Hence, in what follows we assume that when taking interest rate decisions, the Bundesbank Council was concerned only with minimizing the current period loss function, taking private sector expectations as given. In this case, (15) reduces to:

$$
(15a) \quad L_t = E_t \begin{bmatrix} (\pi_t - \pi_t^*)^2 + \hat{\lambda}_x x_t^2 + \hat{\lambda}_i(i_t - i_t^*)^2 + \hat{\lambda}_m(\Delta m_t - \Delta m_t^*)^2 \\ +\phi_{1,t}(\beta(E_t\pi_{t+1} - \pi_{t+1}^*) + \kappa x_t + u_t^\pi - (\pi_t - \pi_t^*)) \\ +\phi_{2,t}(E_t x_{t+1} - \varphi(i_t - E_t\pi_{t+1} - r_t^n) - x_t) \\ +\phi_{3,t}(\pi_t - \pi_t^* + \eta_y\Delta x_t - \eta_i\Delta i_t + \Delta\varepsilon_t - (\Delta m_t - \Delta m_t^*)) \end{bmatrix}
$$

---

31. See Clarida, Galí, and Gertler (1999, 1692, fn 74), or Walsh (2003).
32. For a similar approach, see Guender and Oh (2006).

and the first-order conditions are:

(16a) $$\frac{\partial L}{\partial(\pi_t - \pi_t^*)} = 2(\pi_t - \pi_t^*) - \phi_{1,t} + \phi_{3,t} = 0 \qquad \text{for all } t$$

(16b) $$\frac{\partial L}{\partial x_t} = 2\hat{\lambda}_x x_t + \phi_{1,t}\kappa - \phi_{2,t} + \phi_{3,t}\eta_y = 0 \qquad \text{for all } t$$

(16c) $$\frac{\partial L}{\partial i_t} = 2\hat{\lambda}_i(i_t - i_t^*) - \phi_{2,t}\varphi - \phi_{3,t}\eta_i = 0 \qquad \text{for all } t$$

(16d) $$\frac{\partial L}{\partial(\Delta m_t - \Delta m_t^*)} = 2\hat{\lambda}_m(\Delta m_t - \Delta m_t^*) - \phi_{3,t} = 0 \qquad \text{for all } t.$$

Solving for the Lagrangian multipliers and inserting the solutions into (16c) yields:

(17) $$\hat{\lambda}_i(i_t - i_t^*) - \varphi\hat{\lambda}_x x_t - \varphi\kappa(\pi_t - \pi_t^*) - (\varphi\kappa + \varphi\eta_y + \eta_i)\hat{\lambda}_m(\Delta m_t - \Delta m_t^*) = 0,$$

which can be transformed into an (implicit) instrument rule of the form:

(18) $$i_t = i_t^* + \frac{\lambda_x \varphi}{\lambda_i} x_t + \frac{\kappa\varphi}{\lambda_i}(\pi_t - \pi_t^*) + \frac{\lambda_m \varphi}{\lambda_i}\left(\kappa + \frac{\eta_i}{\varphi} + \eta_y\right)(\Delta m_t - \Delta m_t^*).$$

Equation (18) reproduces the well-known result that the implicit interest rule under discretion takes the form of a standard Taylor rule. However, the inclusion of a money growth term in the loss function implies an additional interest rate response to deviations of money growth from target. Interestingly, the Euler equations ("targeting rules") derived by Dennis (2007) for the case of fully optimal discretionary policy take essentially the same form as equation (18). This suggests that the functional form of the policy rule (18) is not specific to the simple one-period optimization problem considered here, but carries over to the much more complex intertemporal optimization problem.[33] Note, however, that in order to apply the Dennis algorithm to the problem described by equation (15), the model has to be extended to include the first difference of the interest rate in the vector of endogenous variables.[34] As a consequence, under fully optimal discretionary policy, the current interest rate will be a function of the first difference of the interest rate as well as of all the variables included in equation (18).

In order to test whether the Bundesbank attached any weight to its money growth targets (relative to other potential targets), we could stop the analysis here and estimate equation (18) directly. This is the route taken by most empirical studies, such as Clarida, Galí, and Gertler (1998). However, in

33. See Dennis (2007, equation [25]).
34. The model is closed by including the definition of the additional variable, $\Delta i_t = i_t - i_{t-1}$, among the model equations. See Dennis (2007, Technical Appendix).

order to make the policy rule implied by the modified loss function (11) more directly comparable with other types of simple interest rate rules, we do not follow this approach here, but instead repeat the earlier exercise and eliminate the money growth term from equation (18). The process of elimination of money growth deviations from the policy rule mimics the steps we have taken earlier for the case of pure money growth targeting. To simplify the procedure, we first rewrite equation (18) as:

$$(19) \qquad i_t = i_t^* + \frac{\Gamma_2}{\Gamma_1} x_t + \frac{\Gamma_3}{\Gamma_1} (\pi_t - \pi_t^*) + \frac{\Gamma_4}{\Gamma_1} (\Delta m_t - \Delta m_t^*)$$

with $\Gamma_1 = \hat{\lambda}_i$, $\Gamma_2 = \hat{\lambda}_x \varphi$, $\Gamma_3 = \varphi \kappa$, $\Gamma_4 = \hat{\lambda}_m (\varphi \kappa + \eta_i + \varphi \eta_y)$, and then use equation (14) to substitute out the money growth term:

$$(20) \quad i_t = i_t^* + \frac{\Gamma_2}{\Gamma_1} x_t + \frac{\Gamma_3}{\Gamma_1} (\pi_t - \pi_t^*) + \frac{\Gamma_4}{\Gamma_1} (\pi_t - \pi_t^* + \eta_y \Delta x_t - \eta_i \Delta i_t + \Delta \varepsilon_t).$$

Finally, solving for i_t, we get:

$$
\begin{aligned}
(21) \qquad i_t = {} & \frac{\Gamma_1}{(\Gamma_1 + \Gamma_4 \eta_i)} i_t^* + \frac{\Gamma_2}{(\Gamma_1 + \Gamma_4 \eta_i)} x_t \\
& + \frac{(\Gamma_3 + \Gamma_4)}{(\Gamma_1 + \Gamma_4 \eta_i)} (\pi_t - \pi_t^*) + \frac{\Gamma_4 \eta_y}{(\Gamma_1 + \Gamma_4 \eta_i)} \Delta x_t \\
& + \frac{\Gamma_4}{(\Gamma_1 + \Gamma_4 \eta_i)} \Delta \varepsilon_t + \frac{\Gamma_4 \eta_i}{(\Gamma_1 + \Gamma_4 \eta_i)} i_{t-1}.
\end{aligned}
$$

According to (21), the interest rate rule of a central bank that targets money growth differs from a standard Taylor rule in that it implies a response to the deviation of actual output *growth* from potential output *growth* (which is equivalent to targeting the *change* in the output gap) as well as a response to the lagged interest rate and to the difference between the "true" money demand shock and the portfolio shock observed by the central bank. As shown by Giannoni and Woodford (2003), responding to the lagged interest rate (interest rate inertia) and to the change rather than the level of the output gap (history dependence) are both features of the optimal commitment policy. Equation (21) therefore nicely illustrates the argument put forth by Söderström (2005) that money growth targeting may play a useful role in overcoming the stabilization bias of discretionary policy. The response to money demand shocks implied by equation (21) is usually viewed as a major drawback of monetary targeting. However, it cannot be established a priori how serious this problem is when the central bank takes into account portfolio shifts when implementing monetary targeting (as routinely practiced by the Bundesbank). In section 6.5 we attempt to look at the relevant empirical evidence.

Equation (21) is the basis for the interest rate rule that we will estimate in the next section.[35] As before, the intuition presented is predicated on some restrictions on the behavior of the error term in the money demand equation. We will further discuss the issue in section 6.5.

6.5   The Conduct of Monetary Policy and Monetary Policy Rules

In this section, our goal is to provide a systematic comparison of policy rules followed in Germany, the United States, and the United Kingdom. To allow for a fair comparison, our aim was to use model specifications for each of the three countries that are as similar as possible regarding the dynamic structure and the corresponding variables. In order to provide a more precise characterization of systematic differences in the conduct of monetary policy, we estimate and compare interest rate reaction functions. The specification of the estimated reaction functions is based on the interest rate rule derived in the previous section, which includes the elements of a standard Taylor rule as well as the features implied by including a money growth target in the loss function.

6.5.1   Brief Reference to the Literature

There is a voluminous literature about monetary policy reaction functions, especially as regards the United States. According to the established view, there was a regime shift around October 1979 (the start of the Volcker disinflation).[36] The broad strand of the empirical literature sees the main difference between the pre-Volcker period and the Volcker-Greenspan period as pertaining to the interest response to an increase in inflation (or expected inflation). Specifically, the claim is that the coefficient measuring the interest rate response to inflation was significantly below unity during the pre-Volcker period and significantly above unity in the later period. An inflation coefficient below unity corresponds to accommodative monetary policy as real interest rates decline in response to an inflation increase (see, e.g., Clarida, Galí, and Gertler 1998, 2000 or Lubik and Schorfheide 2004). In other words, before 1979 US monetary policy does not comply with the Taylor principle. Characterization of monetary policy in the interim period, between 1979 and 1982, is difficult as it seems dominated by transition dynamics induced by the Fed's monetary experiment. Moreover, the Fed's policy response to economic slack also seems difficult to pin down. Orphanides (2003, 2004) goes as far as to argue that the key distinction does not involve the response to expected inflation, but rather the response

35. In the above mentioned simple model we do not consider lags in monetary transmission. In the empirical results we will see that forecast inflation performs better than current inflation. Transmission lags can rationalize such a result (see comments in section 6.5).

36. See Beyer and Farmer (2007) for an econometric investigation and Gaspar, Smets, and Vestin (2006) for an analytical narrative drawing on the documentary evidence provided in Lindsey, Orphanides, and Rasche (2005).

to policymakers' real-time perceptions of real activity (excess demand). Using real-time data to reestimate the Fed's policy rule, he finds that, prior to Volcker's appointment, policy was too responsive to perceived output gaps. Specifically, loose monetary policy was a consequence of responding strongly to overestimations of economic slack. More recent papers (Boivin 2006; Kim and Nelson 2006; Partouche 2007) using a time-varying coefficients framework find important, but gradual, changes in the Fed's response to both inflation and real activity, not properly accounted for by the typical split-sample approach.

6.5.2   A Comparison of Empirically Estimated Policy Rules

As a starting point for a comparative analysis of German and US monetary policy reaction functions during the Great Inflation, it is useful to take another look at the relative inflation performance of the two countries from the mid-1960s to the early 1980s. According to figure 6.5, the upsurge of inflation in Germany in the early 1970s was stopped by quick disinflation, which preceded the Volcker disinflation by about six years. Still, the dating of the regime shift is not as straightforward for Germany as it is for the United States, where the appointment of Paul Volcker as chairman provides an obvious date for a structural break. Two potential candidates are the breakdown of the Bretton Woods system in March 1973 and/or the official start of the monetary targeting regime in 1975:Q1.[37] However, most studies on the Bundesbank's reaction function, including Clarida, Galí, and Gertler (1998) and Gerberding, Seitz, and Worms (2005, 2007), choose an even later date, namely 1979:Q1, as the starting point of their analysis. The reason for doing so can best be understood by comparing the behavior of real interest rates and inflation during the period in question.

As shown in figure 6.6, pre-1979 the US real rate steadily declines as inflation rises, becoming persistently negative during most of the 1970s. In late 1979, the real rate rose sharply, leading to a subsequent decline in inflation. This observation provides the rationale for the analysis in Beyer and Farmer (2007). They argue that the source of the inflation build-up in the 1970s was a downward drift in the real interest rate that was translated into a simultaneous increase in unemployment and inflation by passive Fed policy. For Germany, the picture is different. Real interest rates rose sharply after the breakdown of the Bretton Woods system in March 1973. Moreover, real interest rates were (almost) always significantly positive throughout the period. Nevertheless, the early increase in real interest rates was almost completely reversed in 1974 and 1975 and the real rate was kept rather low until the beginning of 1979 (data: inflation measured by

---

37. The Bundesbank had already established an internal monetary target for its own orientation for the year 1974 (see Dudler 1980, 299), so 1974:Q1 may be considered another potential breakpoint.

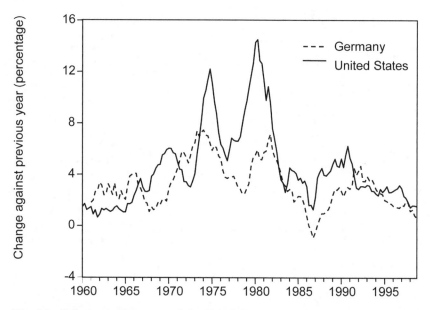

Fig. 6.5   Inflation in Germany and the United States (consumer prices, quarterly data)

CPI inflation against previous quarter, real rates calculated by subtracting period $t + 1$ inflation from three-month money market rates, three-quarter centered moving averages). Overall, however, the visual comparison between the conduct of monetary policy in Germany and the United States in the 1970s suggests loose monetary policy in the latter country, but not in Germany.

In the remainder of this section, our aim is to characterize differences in monetary policy in terms of differences in the estimated monetary policy reaction functions. In order to be better able to capture empirical regularities, we extend the interest rate rule derived in the previous section (equation [21]) in two directions. First, the theoretical model of section 6.4 was silent on the frequency of the data, but it is usually taken to describe regularities observed in quarterly data and in quarterly rates of change. However, when applying the model to the Bundesbank's monetary policy, we have to take account of the fact that the Bundesbank's money growth targets were annual targets that referred to money growth over the previous four quarters. Hence, in the empirical application of equation (21), we extend the time horizon of the inflation and output growth variables to annual (four-quarter) rates of change. Second, we allow for forward-looking behavior on part of the policymakers; that is, we allow them to focus on expected rather than current inflation. This modification of equation (21) can be rationalized by lags in the transmission of monetary policy impulses that are not accounted for

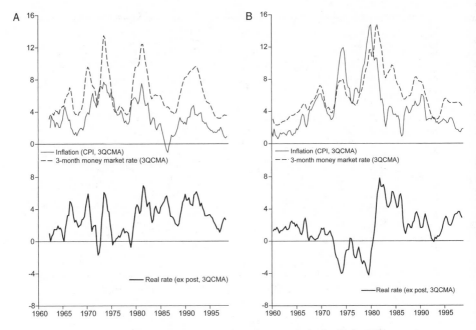

Fig. 6.6   Interest rates and inflation: *A*, in Germany; *B*, in the United States

in the baseline New Keynesian model.[38] Third, in order to capture interest rate dynamics not accounted for by the first lag of the interest rate, we also included the second lag of the interest rate among the endogenous variables. Hence, we start from a specification of the following form:

$$(22) \quad i_t = (1 - \rho_1 - \rho_2) \left(\begin{array}{l} \alpha + \beta E((\pi^a_{t+n} - \pi^*)|\Omega_t) + \gamma_1 E((y_t - y^*_t)|\Omega_t) \\ + \gamma_2 E(\Delta_4(y_t - y^*_t)|\Omega_t) + \dfrac{\gamma_2}{\eta_y}(\Delta_4 \varepsilon^{md}_t - \Delta_4 \varepsilon^{y*}_t) \end{array} \right)$$
$$+ \rho_1 i_{t-1} + \rho_2 i_{t-2} + u_t$$

where $E(\pi^a_{t+n}|\Omega_t)$ is policymakers' inflation forecast for period $t + n$ formed in t on the basis of the information available at time t, π^a denotes annual inflation, $E((y_t - y^*_t)|\Omega_t)$ is policymakers' estimate of the current output gap, again formed on the basis of information available at the time, u_t is an error term, and Δ_4 denotes changes over the previous four quarters. An important issue is the method used to generate the forecasts of inflation, the output gap, and the output growth gap. Unfortunately, as regards the Bundesbank, real-time forecasts of these variables over the relevant time horizons and at

38. Strictly speaking, this argument is valid only for the part of the interest rate response to inflation that derives directly from the inflation stabilization objective in the loss function (11). Therefore, we also estimated specifications of the interest rate reaction function that allow for a response to current as well as expected future inflation. However, not surprisingly, in these exercises one of the two terms usually drops out.

the appropriate frequency do not exist. Therefore, we follow the method first proposed by McCallum (1976) and proxy the unobserved forecasts by the corresponding realizations (see Clarida, Galí, and Gertler 1998). Hence, the error term u_t is a linear combination of the forecast errors and the exogenous disturbance term. In order to keep the forecast errors as small as possible, we use the initial (unrevised) figures on inflation and output as well as the first available estimates of the output gap.[39] To avoid endogeneity problems, these variables are instrumented by a vector of variables I_t, which were part of policymakers' real-time information sets and that are orthogonal to the error term u_t (for details on the instrument sets, see tables 6.4 through 6.6).

Finally, for empirical tractability, the model requires a sufficiently stable empirical money demand function. Reviewing the empirical literature on money demand, we are confident that this condition is fulfilled as there is broad evidence for the existence of sufficiently stable cointegrated money demand models. In conventional cointegrated money demand models, money is usually explained by output (e.g., GDP, serving as a scale variable), and one or more suitable interest rate variables that represent own rates and opportunity costs for holding money. Derivations of actual money from the long-run money demand relationship $(m - m^*)$ are then interpreted as stationary (i.e., transitory) money demand shocks, corresponding to the *level* of ε_t in equation (21). For example, Beyer (1998) finds a stable cointegrated long-run money demand function for German M3 over the sample period 1975 to 1994 with stationary money demand shocks. The standard deviation of their first differences is 4.6 percent, compared with a standard deviation of 3.5 percent for the year-on-year growth rate of money. Similarly, Baba, Hendry, and Starr (1992) find a stable long-run money demand function for US M1 for the sample period 1960 to 1988 and likewise see Hendry and Ericsson (1991b) for UK M1 over the sample 1963 to 1989.[40] Hence we believe that the empirical model (22) is a valid approximation for empirically estimating our modified theoretical Taylor rule (21).

We first report our findings for Germany, which are summarized in table 6.4. The estimates are based on the real-time data set described in Gerberding, Seitz, and Worms (2004). In order to compare the conduct of monetary policy in Germany before and after the collapse of Bretton Woods, the data set was extended backwards to 1965 so that it now covers the sample period 1965 to 1998.[41] As formal tests for structural break do not yield unambiguous

39. See Gerberding, Seitz, and Worms (2005, 279).
40. Using annual data Hendry and Ericsson (1991a) find a stable long-run money demand function for US M1 over the sample period 1878 to 1970.
41. The first vintage of Bundesbank estimates of potential output that we were able to reconstruct dates from April 1972 (Bundesbank, AR 1971). In order to go back beyond this date, we proxied the unavailable "true" real-time data by the estimates dating from April 1972. We think this justifiable since there are no indications of major revisions during the time span 1965 to 1972. For instance, the estimates of the German output gap in the 1960s published by the Organization for Economic Cooperation and Development (OECD) in April 1970 (see OECD 1970) are very similar to the estimates that we reconstructed from the April 1972 vintages of Bundesbank data on actual and potential output.

Table 6.4   Estimates of the extended reaction function, inflation forward-looking (from t to $t + 4$), change in output gap from $t - 4$ to t, real-time data

Estimation equation

$$i_t = (1 - \rho_1 - \rho_2) \left(\begin{array}{c} \alpha + \beta E(\pi^a_{t+4} | \Omega_t) + \gamma_1 E((y_t - y_t^*) | \Omega_t) \\ + \gamma_2 E(\Delta_4(y_t - y_t^*) | \Omega_t \end{array} \right) + \rho_1 i_{t-1} + \rho_2 i_{t-2} + u_t$$

	β	γ1	γ2	ρ1	ρ2	$\bar{R}^2$	SEE	J-stat (p-values)
			Germany's "great" inflation					
1965:Q1–1973:Q1	0.52***	0.44***	—	0.72***	–0.12*	0.71	1.09	0.64
	(0.09)	(0.08)		(0.07)	(0.06)			
1965:Q1–1974:Q4	0.69***	0.51***	—	0.72***	–0.17*	0.76	1.41	0.55
	(0.15)	(0.13)		(0.12)	(0.09)			
1965:Q1–1978:Q4	1.05***	0.52***	—	0.62***	–0.04	0.81	1.21	0.79
	(0.24)	(0.07)		(0.14)	(0.11)			
			Post-Bretton Woods/monetary targeting					
1973:Q2–1998:Q4	0.82***	0.58**	1.39**	1.02***	–0.09	0.92	0.81	0.63
	(0.30)	(0.25)	(0.66)	(0.05)	(0.06)			
1975:Q1–1998:Q4	1.70***	0.06	0.75***	1.05***	–0.21***	0.92	0.69	0.59
	(0.22)	(0.13)	(0.23)	(0.06)	(0.05)			
1979:Q1–1998:Q4	1.89***	0.05	0.74***	0.98***	–0.17***	0.94	0.64	0.89
	(0.19)	(0.10)	(0.24)	(0.07)	(0.05)			

Notes: Estimation method: generalized method of moments (GMM); heteroskedasticity and autocorrelation-consistent (HAC)-robust standard errors in parentheses. R^2: adjusted coefficient of determination. SEE: standard error of the regression. J-stat: p-value of the J-statistic on the validity of overidentifying restrictions. Left-hand side variable: three-month money market rate (end of quarter). Right-hand side variables: inflation gap according to CPI; output gap with Bundesbank's own estimates of production potential. For further details on the data see Gerberding, Seitz, and Worms (2004). The instrument set includes contemporary values of the inflation variable (CPI over previous year in percent) and a commodity price variable (change of Hamburg Archive of World Economics [HWWA] index of commodity prices in DM over previous quarter in percent), as well as up to three lags of each explanatory variable, the commodity price variable, and a money growth variable (change in the Bundesbank's respective monetary target variable over previous year in percent). Pretesting suggests that this instrument structure is sufficient.
***Significant at the 1 percent level.
**Significant at the 5 percent level.
*Significant at the 10 percent level.

results, we present estimates for three different break points, with the Bretton Woods/premonetary targeting samples ending in 1973:Q1, 1974:Q4, and 1978:Q4, respectively. In table 6.4, we only report results for a forward-looking specification of the reaction function where the horizon of the infla-tion forecast variable has been set to four quarters. However, in order to check the robustness of the results to changes in the horizon of the inflation vari-able, we conducted the exercise for different horizons of the inflation forecast, reaching from $n = 0$ to $n = 4$, and found that the results were qualitatively the same.[42] Our estimations also established that the term $(\Delta_4 \varepsilon_t^{md} - \Delta_4 \varepsilon_t^{v*})$ does

42. Results available from authors on request.

not play a major econometric role. In theory, this term is unobservable. Point estimates and standard errors of regressors in model (22) remain virtually unaffected whether an empirical proxy of that term is included or not. However, as part of a money demand shock this error variable has interesting policy implications, which we will discuss further below (see table 6.6).

The analysis yields a number of interesting results. First, we find that the coefficient β, which captures the interest rate response to inflation, is significantly below one before the introduction of monetary targeting (i.e., for the sample periods 1965:Q1 to 1973:Q1 and 1965:Q1 to 1974:Q4, respectively), but significantly above one afterwards (i.e., for the samples starting in 1975:Q1 and later). Note, however, that the standard error of the inflation coefficient and of the equation is lowest for the (arguably more stable) 1979 to 1998 period. From this, we conclude that the Bundesbank respected the Taylor principle (responded to a rise in expected inflation in a stabilizing way) right from the beginning of the monetary targeting regime. This contrasts with empirical estimates of standard Taylor rules for the United States over the 1970s. Second, the response to the perceived output gap, γ_1, is significantly positive, with point estimates about 0.5 in the Bretton Woods/premonetary targeting subsamples. By contrast, it is close to zero and insignificant under monetary targeting. If one follows Orphanides (2003), the lack of response to real-time estimates of the output gap, which at the time were heavily biased downwards in most countries, may also have been an important reason for Germany's superior inflation performance after the regime shift. Third, the coefficient on the output growth gap, which is insignificant before the introduction of monetary targeting, becomes highly significant afterwards. According to our theoretical model, this is an important feature that distinguishes the Bundesbank's policy under monetary targeting from a purely discretionary approach. Hence, we interpret this result as evidence that the money growth targets did bring the Bundesbank policy closer to the (otherwise not feasible) optimal commitment solution. Fourth, we find a significant degree of interest rate inertia, captured by ρ, in all subsample periods, with point estimates of about 0.6 before and about 0.8 after the regime change. The high degree of inertia after the regime shift is in accordance with the predictions of the theoretical model as well as with the Bundesbank's often professed preference for conducting policy with a steady hand ("Politik der ruhigen Hand").[43]

Table 6.5 present the results for a very similar formulation for the United States. We use the three months' Treasury Bill (T-Bill) rate as a short-term interest rate. Regarding the explanatory variables, inflation is again measured by year-on-year changes in CPI. For the output gap, $(y_t - y_t^*)$, we use the real-time perceptions of the US output gap reconstructed by Orphanides (2003). We report results for annual changes in the output gap as well as for

43. In Gerberding, Seitz, and Worms (2007), we show that for the sample period 1979:Q1 to 1998:Q4, this result is robust to the inclusion of an AR(1) model for the error term.

Table 6.5 The United States: Estimates of the extended reaction function, inflation forward-looking y-o-y (from $t-3$ to $t+1$). A, using real-time inflation forecast; B, using realized data.

	β	γ1	γ2	ρ1	Const.	$\bar{R}^2$	SEE	J-stat (11dof) (p-values)
	A. Estimation equation							
	$i_t = (1-\rho_1)(\alpha + \beta E_t(\pi^a_{t+1}|\Omega_t) + \gamma_1 E_t((y_t - y^*_t)|\Omega_t) + \gamma_2 E_t(\Delta_j(y_t - y^*_t)|\Omega_t)) + \rho_1 i_{t-1} + u_t$							
1970:Q1–1979:Q2	1.100***	0.367***	0.064	0.592***	0.009***	0.86	0.006	0.11*34
j = 1	(0.114)	(0.072)	(0.053)	(0.098)	(0.003)			(>10%)
1970:Q1–1979:Q2	1.023***	0.390***	−0.013	0.545***	0.012***	0.87	0.006	0.15*34
j = 4	(0.128)	(0.098)	(0.026)	(0.109)	(0.004)			(>10%)
1983:Q1–1998:Q4	3.499***	0.926***	0.512***	0.912***	−0.004**	0.93	0.004	0.15*60
j = 1	(1.150)	(0.418)	(0.183)	(0.028)	(0.002)			(>10%)
1983:Q1–1998:Q4	2.721***	0.458***	0.122***	0.89***	−0.003	0.96	0.003	0.17*60
j = 4	(0.609)	(0.161)	(0.035)	(0.029)	(0.002)			(>10%)
	B. Estimation equation							
	$i_t = (1-\rho_1)(\alpha + \beta E_t(\pi^a_{t+1}|\Omega_t) + \gamma_1 E_t((y_t - y^*_t)|\Omega_t) + \gamma_2 E_t(\Delta_j(y_t - y^*_t)|\Omega_t)) + \rho_1 i_{t-1} + u_t$							
1970:Q1–1979:Q2	0.619***	0.195***	0.095	0.458***	0.018***	0.87	0.006	0.22*34
j = 1	(0.030)	(0.040)	(0.059)	(0.064)	(0.001)			(>10%)
1970:Q1–1979:Q2	0.591***	0.206**	0.014	0.493***	0.018***	0.86	0.006	0.22*34
j = 4	(0.033)	(0.084)	(0.028)	(0.108)	(0.002)			(>10%)
1983:Q1–1998:Q4	2.73*	1.406	0.419***	0.960***	−0.002*	0.94	0.004	0.15*60
j = 1	(1.506)	(1.035)	(0.076)	(0.025)	(0.001)			(>10%)
1983:Q1–1998:Q4	2.040***	0.475**	0.149***	0.89***	−0.002	0.96	0.003	0.17*60
j = 4	(0.540)	(0.221)	(0.027)	(0.029)	(0.002)			(>10%)

Notes: Estimation method: GMM; HAC-robust standard errors in parentheses. R^2: adjusted coefficient of determination. SEE: standard error of the regression. *J*-stat: *p*-value of the *J*-statistic on the validity of overidentifying restrictions. Left-hand side variable: 3-month T-Bill rate. Right-hand side variables: Green Book inflation forecasts (y-o-y CPI); output gap; and y-o-y changes in the output gap. For further details on the output gap data see Orphanides (2003, 996). The instrument set includes up to 3 lags of i, π, $(x - x^*)$. Extending the set of instruments by including changes of commodity prices as well as three lags of nominal money growth M2 (y-o-y) does not change the results qualitatively.

***Significant at the 1 percent level.

**Significant at the 5 percent level.

*Significant at the 10 percent level.

its quarterly changes. Notice that for the United States we normalize the inflation target π^* at zero. For the forward-looking element, we use inflation expectations one period ahead that are formed at period t. In panel A of table 6.5, we use real-time inflation forecasts based on Green Book data (as in Orphanides 2003, 2004), whereas in panel B we use the lead of revised inflation data. For interest-rate smoothing we restricted ourselves to reporting the case of one lag only.[44]

For analyzing the United States we follow the strategy that is common in the empirical literature and estimate over samples that correspond to the chairmanships of Burns–Miller and Volcker–Greenspan. Using quarterly data, we consider the period 1970:Q1 to 1979:Q2 "the Burns-Miller period" and the period 1983:Q1 to 1998:Q4 "the Volcker-Greenspan period". The omitted interim period is characterized by transitional dynamics and does not yield useful estimates.

We are able to reproduce a number of well-known findings. First, for real-time inflation forecast data (see panel A) we can replicate Orphanides's (2003) findings with a Taylor coefficient greater than unity also in the Burns-Miller period, whereas for revised inflation data (panel B) the Taylor coefficient on inflation is significantly below unity in the Burns-Miller period and significantly above one in the Volcker-Greenspan period. Second, the coefficient on the lagged interest rate is much larger in the latter period (becoming close to one). Third, and focusing on formulation with the annual measure of the change in the output gap, the coefficient on the output gap is always significant, at the 5 percent level, except for the Volcker–Greenspan period in case of quarterly changes of the output gap (see panel B, third row). Regarding the history dependence of monetary policy, we find significant differences between the United States and Germany. For the United States the coefficients for both quarterly or annual changes in the output gap are insignificant during the 1970s. Conversely, it is highly significant during the 1980s and 1990s whereas for Germany it is significant throughout the entire post-Bretton Woods sample period. The comparison of the models for Germany and the United States between table 6.4 and table 6.5 therefore suggests that the conduct of monetary policy in the United States and Germany differed during the 1970s, but after 1983, US monetary policy approached the practice that the Bundesbank followed since 1975.

Turning to the case of the United Kingdom, already from eyeballing figures 6.1 through 6.3 one would expect, with respect to Germany but to a lesser extent also to the United States, very different empirical results for any estimated Taylor rule. Compared to the United States and Germany, inflation in the United Kingdom peaked highest and interest rates during the 1970s were at a much higher level, whereas growth performance was

---

44. We also estimated the models with two lags and got very similar quantitative and the same qualitative results compared to the one lag-only specification.

comparatively much weaker than in the United States or Germany. In order to explain the United Kingdom three-month T-bill rate, we use the real-time perceptions of the UK output gap reconstructed by Nelson and Nikolov (2003). For future inflation we use revised data, analogue to table 6.5, panel B, for the United States. The results in table 6.6 confirm our priors. Interest rates in the 1970s appear to follow a near-unit root process. Neither output nor inflation gap are remotely significant. This changes only later in the 1980s and 1990s, when the output gap remains insignificant but the Taylor coefficient on inflation is estimated rather tightly at 1.5.

6.5.3   The Role of Money Demand Shocks

As pointed out in the previous subsection, dealing with the term $(\Delta_4 \varepsilon_t^{md} - \Delta_4 \varepsilon_t^{v*})$ has interesting policy implications. The term represents those (exogenous) changes in money demand that are not identified and accounted for by the central bank. Ignoring this term in the empirical model implies an assumption that the central bank—in our case the Bundesbank—did not make systematic mistakes in identifying shocks to money demand. Under this assumption, the variable $(\Delta_4 \varepsilon_t^{md} - \Delta_4 \varepsilon_t^{v*})$ will be a white noise (or at least stationary) process that can be subsumed as, say, $\tilde{u}_t$, into the error term of equation (22). However, we are aware that our framework also has testable implications for the Bundesbank's response to unidentified disturbances to money demand.[45] Specifically, we would expect to find that policy was tightened in response to an increase in this variable and vice versa. Unfortunately, since we do not have reliable information on the magnitude of the portfolio shocks observed by the Bundesbank, in real time, ε_t^{v*}, we cannot test this hypothesis directly. However, as a robustness check, we conducted an alternative test that is based on the assumption that the Bundesbank was able to identify a fraction δ of the "true" money demand shock so that $\varepsilon_t^{v*} = \delta \varepsilon_t^{md}$ holds. Under this assumption, we can rewrite equation (22) as:

$$(22a) \quad i_t = (1 - \rho_1 - \rho_2) \left(\begin{array}{l} \alpha + \beta E((\pi_{t+n}^a - \pi^*)|\Omega_t) + \gamma_1 E((y_t - y_t^*)|\Omega_t) \\ + \gamma_2 E(\Delta_4(y_t - y_t^*)|\Omega_t) + \dfrac{\gamma_2}{\eta_y}(1 - \delta)\Delta_4 \varepsilon_t^{md} \end{array} \right)$$
$$+ \rho_1 i_{t-1} + \rho_2 i_{t-2} + u_t,$$

where δ denotes the fraction of the true money demand shock that the Bundesbank was able to identify. In the special case when $\delta = 1$, the Bundesbank could identify all shocks as portfolio shocks, whereas if $\delta = 0$ the shock to money demand remained unreduced. Using the residuals from the money demand model of Beyer (1998) to estimate equation (22a), we find that the coefficient δ is highly significant, with a point estimate of

---

45. We thank our discussant, Benjamin Friedman, for bringing this important point to our attention.

Table 6.6   The United Kingdom: Estimates of the extended reaction function, inflation forward-looking y-o-y (from $t-3$ to $t+1$)

Estimation equation

$$i_t = (1 - \rho_1)(\alpha + \beta E_t(\pi^a_{t+1}|\Omega_t) + \gamma_1 E_t((y_t - y^*_t)|\Omega_t) + \gamma_2 E_t(\Delta_j(y_t - y^*_t)|\Omega_t)) + \rho_1 i_{t-1} + u_t$$

	β	$\gamma 1$	$\gamma 2$	$\rho 1$	Const.	$\bar{R}^2$	SEE	J-stat (11dof) (p-values)
1970:Q1–1979:Q2 $j=1$	−0.10 (0.463)	0.007 (0.34)	0.02 (0.05)	0.869*** (0.10)	0.015*** (0.005)	0.73	0.015	0.24*35 (>10%)
1970:Q1–1979:Q2 $j=4$	0.058 (0.33)	−0.02 (0.37)	0.07 (0.083)	0.827*** (0.081)	0.016** (0.006)	0.74	0.014	0.23*35 (>10%)
1983:Q1–1996:Q1 $j=1$	1.531*** (0.14)	−0.32 (0.28)	−0.09 (0.095)	0.70*** (0.071)	0.002 (0.002)	0.92	0.0078	0.16*53 (>10%)
1983:Q1–1996:Q1 $j=4$	1.526*** (0.156)	−0.20 (0.299)	−0.02 (0.081)	0.72*** (0.069)	0.004 (0.003)	0.92	0.0079	0.16*53 (>10%)

Notes: Estimation method: GMM; HAC-robust standard errors in parentheses. R^2: adjusted coefficient of determination. SEE: standard error of the regression. J-stat: p-value of the J-statistic on the validity of overidentifying restrictions. Left-hand side variable: 3-month T-Bill rate. Right-hand side variables: inflation (y-o-y CPI); output gap; and y-o-y changes in the output gap. For further details on the output gap data see Nelson and Nikolov (2003). The instrument set includes up to 3 lags of i, π, $(x-x^*)$, and changes of commodity prices as well as three lags of nominal money growth "money + quasi-money" (y-o-y).

***Significant at the 1 percent level.

**Significant at the 5 percent level.

*Significant at the 10 percent level.

0.77.[46] On the other hand, the fact that our estimate of δ is also significantly different from one suggests that the Bundesbank did react to shocks to money demand, which it was unable to identify in real time. Specifically, when money growth increased as a consequence of a nonidentified disturbance to money demand, the Bundesbank would tighten policy, in contrast with what would be the case under perfect information. This empirical finding is in line with the testable implication from the theoretical model presented in the previous section. Nevertheless, the relatively high value of δ suggests that the Bundesbank was able to identify most money demand disturbances in real time. Hence, it responded to such shocks in a much more muted way, thereby limiting the volatility of policy rates.

6.5.4   Summary

To sum up, the empirical results for Germany, the United States, and the United Kingdom suggest that monetary policy in the three countries was conducted very differently in the 1970s. For Germany and the United States, estimating a Taylor rule for that period produces reasonable results but reveals different policy strategies. Money as a commitment device has worked well for Germany and is reflected by a significant coefficient in changes of the output gap variable. For the United States we do not find any similar history dependence in the data for the 1970s, but we do find it for the Volcker–Greenspan period in the 1980s and 1990s. By sharp contrast, monetary policy in the United Kingdom has been very different both with respect to the United States and Germany. Our empirical findings do not allow for any Taylor-type characterization of UK monetary policy in the 1970s and only very vaguely for the 1980s and 1990s.

6.6   Conclusion

In this chapter we examine an important episode in European monetary history. We investigate the conduct of monetary policy in Germany in the 1970s and the 1980s. It was during this period that the Bundesbank acquired its credibility and reputation as a bulwark against inflation. Our goal was to illustrate how the monetary growth targeting strategy, followed by the Bundesbank since 1975, contributed to this success. We wanted, as much as possible, to examine the strategy as conceived, communicated, and refined by the Bundesbank itself. Naturally we are not able to do full justice to the Bundesbank's approach. We can only present a simplified (stylized) view of the conduct of monetary policy in that period.

Nevertheless, we think that by focusing on anchoring inflation and inflation expectations, we capture a fundamental aspect of the interaction between monetary policy and the behavior of economic agents. Using a

---

46. Results available from Andreas Beyer on request.

standard New Keynesian model and a modified loss function (incorporating money growth deviations) we are able to explain the role of money growth targeting as a commitment device. Under some mild conditions regarding the existence of a stable money demand function that are fulfilled (at least for Germany) for the time period under consideration, we are able to derive a role for money as a commitment device that succeeds even in the context of the New Keynesian model (in which money plays no active role).

The operation of monetary growth targeting as a commitment device is compatible with target misses, even repeatedly. In the modified loss function framework monetary growth targeting is permanently relevant and imposes structure on the monetary policy reaction function. Nevertheless, given that monetary deviations from target have to be traded off against other arguments in the loss function, frequent deviations from target cannot be excluded. In practice, the Bundesbank had to account for the determinants of observed deviations and explain how, in the end, it would deliver on the final goal of price level stability.

A standard objection to monetary targeting is that it induces unwarranted volatility in policy rates in response to unidentified disturbances to money demand. In the context of our theoretical model, it is the case that the central bank will tighten in response to nonobserved positive shocks to money demand. Empirically, we find this holds true for the Bundesbank. Nevertheless, empirical evidence shows that money demand was stable in Germany during the period. Moreover, the Bundesbank appears to have been able to take into account most special factors in real time. Hence, the response of policy to money demand disturbances was much attenuated, limiting the relevance of this concern for the historical performance of the Bundesbank.

Issing in his Stone Lecture (Issing et al. 2005, 50ff.) affirms:

> The Bundesbank missed its target roughly half of the time. . . . This does not mean, however, that the Bundesbank did not take monetary targets seriously. On the contrary, money growth targets were regarded as constituting the basis for a rules-oriented approach to monetary policy. Announcing a monetary target implied a commitment by the Bundesbank towards the public. Deviations of money growth from the target had always to be justified. Even if it is true that the reputation of the Bundesbank ultimately was achieved by its success in fulfilling its mandate to safeguard the stability of its currency, its final goal, current policy continuously had to be justified in the context of its pre-announced strategy. In this sense, the strategy contributed to the transparency, the accountability and the credibility of Bundesbank's policy.

From our theoretical framework we derive an interest rate rule. Using real-time data, we find that it closely approximates the monetary policy, as it was conducted by the Bundesbank, in the period of 1975 to 1998. The main finding is that the Bundesbank response to the output growth gap was highly significant. Such a response is a characteristic of the conduct of monetary policy under commitment. It is also robust policy against problems in the measurement of the level of potential output in real time. A similar response to the growth gap was not present in the reaction function of the Federal Reserve System during the Burns-Miller period. It does become significant, for the United States, in the later Volcker-Greenspan period. We were able to characterize systematic monetary policy for Germany and the United States. Our empirical findings suggest a much less stable approach in the United Kingdom.

References

Alesina, A., and L. Summers. 1990. "Central Bank Independence and Macro-economic Performance." Discussion Paper. Harvard University.

Baba, Y., D. F. Hendry, and R. M. Starr. 1992. "The Demand for M1 in the USA, 1960–1988." *Review of Economic Studies* 59 (1): 25–61.

Bade, R., and M. Parkin. 1980. "Central Bank Laws and Monetary Policy." Discussion Paper. University of Ontario.

Baltensperger, E. 1999. "Monetary Policy under Conditions of Increasing Integration (1979–96)." In *Fifty Years of the Deutsche Mark—Central Bank and the Currency in Germany since 1948,* edited by Deutsche Bundesbank, 419–523. Oxford: Oxford University Press.

Barro, R. J., and D. B. Gordon. 1983a. "A Positive Theory of Monetary Policy in a Natural Rate Model." *Journal of Political Economy* 91:589–610.

———. 1983b. "Rules, Discretion and Reputation in a Model of Monetary Policy." *Journal of Monetary Economics* 12:101–21.

Barsky, R. B., and L. Kilian. 2002. "Do We Really Know That Oil Caused the Great Stagflation? A Monetary Alternative." In *NBER Macroeconomic Annual 2001,* edited by Ben S. Bernanke and Kenneth Rogoff, 137–83. Cambridge, MA: MIT Press.

———. 2004. "Oil and the Macroeconomy since the 1970s." *Journal of Economic Perspectives* 18 (4): 115–34.

Bayoumi, T., H. Faruqee, B. Hunt, D. Laxton, J. Lee, A. Rebucci, I. Tchakarov, and P. D. Karam. 2004. "GEM: A New International Macroeconomic Model." IMF Occasional Papers no. 239. Washington, DC: International Monetary Fund.

Beyer, A. 1998. "Modelling Money Demand in Germany." *Journal of Applied Econometrics* 13 (1): 57–76.

Beyer, A., and R. Farmer. 2007. "Natural Rate Doubts." *Journal of Economic Dynamics and Control* 31:797–825.

Blinder, A. 1979. *Economic Policy and the Great Stagflation.* New York: Academic Press.

Boivin, J. 2006. "Has US Monetary Policy Changed? Evidence from Drifting Coefficients and Real-Time Data." *Journal of Money, Credit and Banking* 38 (5): 1149–73.

Bordo, M. 1993. "The Bretton Woods International Monetary System: A Historical Overview." In *A Retrospective on the Bretton Woods System,* edited by M. Bordo and B. Eichengreen, 3–98. Chicago: University of Chicago Press.

Brunner, K. 1983. "Has Monetarism Failed?" *Cato Journal* 3 (1): 23–62.

Bruno, M., and J. Sachs. 1985. *Economics of Worldwide Stagflation.* Cambridge, MA: Harvard University Press.

Buchheim, C. 1999. "The Establishment of the Bank Deutscher Länder and the West German Currency Reform." In *Fifty Years of the Deutsche Mark—Central Bank and the Currency in Germany since 1948,* edited by Deutsche Bundesbank, 55–100. Oxford: Oxford University Press.

Clarida, R., and M. Gertler. 1997. "How the Bundesbank Conducts Monetary Policy." In *Reducing Inflation: Motivation and Strategy,* edited by C. Romer and D. Romer, 363–412. Chicago: University of Chicago Press.

Clarida, R., J. Galí, and M. Gertler. 1998. "Monetary Policy Rules in Practice: Some International Evidence." *European Economic Review* 42:1033–67.

———. 1999. "The Science of Monetary Policy." *Journal of Economic Literature* 37:1661–707.

———. 2000. "Monetary Policy Rules and Macroeconomic Stability: Evidence and Some Theory." *Quarterly Journal of Economics* 115:147–80.

Coenen, C., K. Christoffel, and A. Warne. 2008. "The New Area Wide Model of the Euro Area: A Micro Founded Open Economy Model for Forecasting and Policy Analyses." ECB Working Paper Series, no. 944, October. Frankfurt: European Central Bank.

Darby, M. R. 1982. "The Price of Oil and World Inflation and Recession." *American Economic Review* 72 (4): 738–51.

Dennis, R. 2007. "Optimal Policy in Rational Expectations Models: New Solution Algorithms." *Macroeconomic Dynamics* 11 (01): 31–55.

Deutsche Bundesbank. Various years. *Annual Report.*

Dudler, H.-J. 1980. "Examination of Witnesses: Hermann-Josef Dudler, Testimony, November 10, 1980." In *Treasury and Civil Service Committee, Monetary Policy Volume II: Minutes of Evidence,* 297–307. London: Her Majesty's Stationery Office, 1981.

Edge, R. M., M. T. Kiley, and J.-P. Laforte. 2007. "Documentation of the Research and Statistics Divisions Estimated DSGE Model of the US Economy: 2006 Version." Federal Reserve Board Discussion Paper 2007-53.

Erceg, C., L. Guerrieri, and C. Gust. 2006. "SIGMA: A New Open Economy Model for Policy Analysis." *International Journal of Central Banking* 2 (1): 1–50.

Fratianni, M., and J. von Hagen. 2001. "The Konstanz Seminar on Monetary Theory and Policy." *European Journal of Political Economy* 17:641–64.

Frenkel, J., and M. Goldstein. 1999. "The International Role of the Deutsche Mark." In *Fifty Years of the Deutsche Mark: Central Bank and Currency in Germany since 1948,* edited by Deutsche Bundesbank, 685–730. Oxford: Oxford University Press.

Galí, J. 2008. *Monetary Policy, Inflation and the Business Cycle: An Introduction to the New Keynesian Framework.* Princeton, NJ: Princeton University Press.

Garber, P. 1993. "The Collapse of the Bretton Woods Fixed Exchange Rate System." In *A Retrospective on the Bretton Woods System,* edited by M. Bordo and B. Eichengreen, 461–94. Chicago: University of Chicago Press.

Gaspar, V., and A. Kashyap. 2007. "Stability First: Reflections Inspired by Otmar Issing's Success as the ECB's Chief Economist." In *Monetary Policy: A Journey from Theory to Practice,* 86–118. Frankfurt: European Central Bank.

Gaspar, V., F. Smets, and D. Vestin. 2006. "Monetary Policy over Time." *Macroeconomic Dynamics* 10 (02): 207–29.

———. 2007. "Is Time Ripe for Price Level Path Stability?" ECB Working Paper Series, no. 818. Frankfurt: European Central Bank.

Gerberding, C., F. Seitz, and A. Worms. 2004. "How the Bundesbank Really Conducted Monetary Policy: An Analysis Based on Real-Time Data." Deutsche Bundesbank Discussion Paper Series 1, no. 25/2004.

———. 2005. "How the Bundesbank Really Conducted Monetary Policy." *North American Journal of Economics and Finance* 16:277–92.

———. 2007. "Money-Based Interest Rules, Lessons from German Data." Deutsche Bundesbank Discussion Paper Series 1, no. 06/2007.

German Council of Economic Experts. 1974. "Full Employment for Tomorrow." Stuttgart.

Giannoni, M. P., and M. Woodford. 2003. "How Forward-Looking Is Optimal Monetary Policy?" *Journal of Money, Credit, and Banking* 35 (6, Part 2): 1425–69.

Gordon, R. 1975. "Alternative Responses to External Supply Shocks." *Brookings Papers on Economic Activity* 1:183–206. Washington, DC: Brookings Institution.

Guender, A. V., and D. Y. Oh. 2006. "Price Stability through Price-level Targeting or Inflation Targeting? A Tale of Two Experiments." *Journal of Economics and Business* 58 (5–6): 373–91.

Hamilton, J. 1983. "Oil and the Macroeconomy since World War II." *Journal of Political Economy* 91 (2): 228–48.

Hendry, D. F., and N. R. Ericsson. 1991a. "An Econometric Analysis of UK Money Demand in 'Monetary Trends in the United States and the United Kingdom' by Milton Friedman and Anna J. Schwartz." *American Economic Review* 81 (1): 8–38.

———. 1991b. "Modelling the Demand for Narrow Money in the United Kingdom and the United States." *European Economic Review* 35 (4): 33–86.

Issing, O. 1992. "Theoretical and Empirical Foundations of the Deutsche Bundesbank's Monetary Targeting." *Intereconomics* 27:289–300.

———. 1993. "Central Bank Independence and Monetary Stability." The Institute of Economic Affairs, Occasional Paper 89, London.

———. 1997. "Monetary Targeting in Germany: The Stability of Monetary Policy and of the Monetary System." *Journal of Monetary Economics* 39 (1): 67–79.

———. 2005. "Why did the Great Inflation Not Happen in Germany?" *Federal Reserve Bank of St. Louis Review* March/April:329–36.

———. 2006. "Europe's Hard Fix: The Euro Area." *International Economics and Economic Policy* 3 (3–4): 181–96.

Issing, O., V. Gaspar, O. Tristani, and D. Vestin. 2005. *Imperfect Knowledge and Monetary Policy (The Stone Lectures in Economics)*. Cambridge: Cambridge University Press.

Jensen, H. 2002. "Targeting Nominal Income Growth or Inflation?" *American Economic Review* 92:928–56.

Kilponen, J., and K. Leitemo. 2008. "Model Uncertainty and Delegation: A Case for Friedman's k-Percent Money Growth Rule?" *Journal of Money, Credit, and Banking* 40 (3): 547–56.

Kim, C., and C. Nelson. 2006. "Estimation of a Forward-Looking Monetary Policy Rule: A Time-Varying Parameter Model Using Ex-Post Data." *Journal of Monetary Economics* 53:1949–66.

Kydland, F., and E. Prescott. 1977. "Rules Rather Than Discretion: The Inconsistency of Optimal Plans." *Journal of Political Economy* 85:473–91.

Lindsey, D., A. Orphanides, and R. Rasche. 2005. "The Reform of October 1979: How It Happened and Why." Finance and Economics Discussion Paper, Federal Reserve Board.

Lubik, T. A., and F. Schorfheide. 2004. "Testing for Indeterminacy: An Application to US Monetary Policy." *American Economic Review* 94 (1): 190–217.

McCallum, B. 1976. "Rational Expectations and the Estimation of Econometric Models: An Alternative Procedure." *International Economic Review* 17:484–90.

Nelson, E., and K. Nikolov. 2003. "UK Inflation in the 1970s and 1980s: The Role of Output Gap Mismeasurement." *Journal of Economics and Business* 55 (4): 353–70.

Nessén, M., and D. Vestin. 2005. "Average Inflation Targeting." *Journal of Money, Credit, and Banking* 37:837–63.

Neumann, M. J. M. 1997. "Monetary Targeting in Germany." In *Towards More Effective Monetary Policy,* edited by I. Kuroda, 176–98. Wilmington, MA: Hampshire Press.

———. 1999. "Monetary Stability: Threat and Proven Response." In *Fifty Years of the Deutsche Mark: Central Bank and Currency in Germany since 1948,* edited by Deutsche Bundesbank, 269–306. Oxford: Oxford University Press.

———. 2006. "Pre-commitment and Guidance—Lessons from the Bundesbank's History." In *Monetary Policy—A Journey from Theory to Practice,* edited by European Central Bank, 5–13. Frankfurt.

Organization for Economic Cooperation and Development. 1970. *Economic Survey of Germany.* Paris: OECD, April.

Orphanides, A. 2003. "Historical Monetary Policy Analysis and the Taylor Rule." *Journal of Monetary Economics* 50:983–1022.

———. 2004. "Monetary Policy Rules, Macroeconomic Stability and Inflation: A View from the Trenches." *Journal of Money, Credit, and Banking* 36:151–57.

Partouche, H. 2007. "Time-Varying Coefficients in a GMM Framework: Estimation of a Forward Looking Taylor Rule for the Federal Reserve." Banque de France Working Paper no. 177, September.

Richter, R. 1999. "German Monetary Policy as Reflected in the Academic Debate." In *Fifty Years of the Deutsche Mark—Central Bank and the Currency in Germany since 1948,* edited by Deutsche Bundesbank, 525–71. Oxford: Oxford University Press.

Rogoff, K. 1985. "The Optimal Degree of Commitment to an Intermediate Monetary Target." *Quarterly Journal of Economics* 100 (4): 1169–89.

Røisland, Øistein. 2006. "Inflation Inertia and the Optimal Hybrid Inflation/Price Level Target." *Journal of Money, Credit, and Banking* 38 (8): 2247–51.

Samuelson, P. 1974. "Worldwide Stagflation." In *Collected Scientific Papers,* vol. 4, no. 268, 1977a, edited by H. Nagatani and K. Crowley, 801–07. Cambridge, MA: MIT Press.

Schlesinger, H. 1980. "Central Bank Policy: Keeping the Reign Tight." *Wirtschafts Woche, 1980* 34 (5): 77–80.

———. 1983. "The Setting of Monetary Objectives in Germany." In *Central Bank Views of Monetary Targeting,* edited by P. Meek, 6–17. New York: Federal Reserve Bank of New York.

———. 1988. "The Strategy of the German Bundesbank." In *Transformations of the Monetary Policy of the German Bundesbank, Kredit und Kapital Supplement 10,* edited by W. Ehrlicher and D. B. Simmert, 3–20. Berlin: Duncker & Humblot.

———. 2002. "The Bundesbank and Its Money Supply." In *Exogeneity and Endogeneity—The Money Supply in the History of Economic Thought and in Modern Policy,* edited by B. Scheffold, 137–59. Marburg: Metropolis Verlag.

Smets, F., and R. Wouters. 2003. "An Estimated Stochastic Dynamic General Equilibrium Model of the Euro Area." *Journal of European Economic Association* 1 (5): 1123–75.

———. 2007. "Shocks and Frictions in US Business Cycles: A Bayesian DSGE Approach." *American Economic Review* 97 (3): 586–607.

Söderlind, P. 1999. "Solution and Estimation of RE Macromodels with Optimal Policy." *European Economic Review Papers and Proceedings* 43:813–23.

Söderström, U. 2005. "Targeting Inflation with a Role for Money." *Economica* 72:577–96.

Svensson, L. E. O. 1999. "Price Level Targeting vs. Inflation Targeting: A Free Lunch?" *Journal of Money, Credit, and Banking* 31:277–95.

Taylor, J. 1993. "Discretion versus Policy Rules in Practice." *Carnegie-Rochester Conference Series on Public Policy* 39:195–214.

———. 1999. "A Historical Analysis of Monetary Policy Rules." In *Monetary Policy Rules,* edited by John. B. Taylor, 319–48. Chicago: University of Chicago Press.

Triffin, R. 1960. *Gold and the Dollar Crisis.* New Haven, CT: Yale University Press.

Vestin, David. 2006. "Price-Level versus Inflation Targeting." *Journal of Monetary Economics* 53:1361–76.

von Hagen, J. 1995. "Inflation and Monetary Targeting in Germany." In *Inflation Targets,* edited by Leonard Leidermann and Lars Svensson, 107–21. Washington, DC: Center for Economic and Policy Research (CEPR).

———. 1999. "A New Approach to Monetary Policy (1971–78)." In *Fifty Years of the Deutsche Mark: Central Bank and Currency in Germany since 1948,* edited by Deutsche Bundesbank, 403–38. Oxford: Oxford University Press.

Walsh, Carl E. 2003. "Speed Limit Policies: The Output Gap and Optimal Monetary Policy." *American Economic Review* 93 (1): 265–78.

Woodford, M. 1999. "Optimal Monetary Policy Inertia." NBER Working Paper no. 7261. Cambridge, MA: National Bureau of Economic Research.

———. 2003. *Interest and Prices: Foundations of a Theory of Monetary Policy.* Princeton, NJ: Princeton University Press.

———. 2007. "How Important Is Money in the Conduct of Monetary Policy?" Paper prepared for the Conference in Honor of Ernst Baltensperger. Bern, June 8.

Zweig, S. 1970. *Yesterday's World—Memories of a European.* Frankfurt: Fisher Taschenbuch Verlag.

Comment   Benjamin M. Friedman

In 2003, Milton Friedman famously concluded, "The use of quantity of money as a target has not been a success."[1] The object of this chapter by Beyer, Gaspar, Gerberding, and Issing is to present a counterexample to Friedman's proposition. The specific example the authors suggest is German monetary policy during the 1970s and 1980s. As the title suggests, the chapter reminds us that Germany, more so than most other countries (and certainly more so than the United States), avoided what became the high and chronic price inflation of those years. The chapter's central argument, which the authors advance through a combination of historical narrative, formal analysis, and empirical evidence, is that the key to Germany's suc-

Benjamin M. Friedman is the William Joseph Maier Professor of Political Economy at Harvard University and a research associate of the National Bureau of Economic Research.

I am grateful to Igor Barenboim for research assistance and helpful discussions. For acknowledgments, sources of research support, and disclosure of the author's material financial relationships, if any, please see http://www.nber.org/chapters/c9159.ack.

1. *Financial Times,* June 7, 2003, 12.

cess in this regard was the Bundesbank's adoption of numerical targets for money growth—exactly the policy strategy that Friedman later concluded had been unsuccessful.

It seems difficult to argue with the proposition that the German economy successfully avoided the worst of the 1970s to early 1980s inflation. As the authors' narrative nicely shows, German consumer price inflation topped out at about 7 percent in 1974 and at about the same rate again in 1982. In the United States, inflation on that basis went to 11 percent in 1974 and 13 percent in 1981. The experience in the United Kingdom was even worse.

The question, therefore, for purposes of providing a counterexample to Friedman's proposition, is what role the Bundesbank's money-targeting strategy played in achieving that success. The authors focus on the experience beginning in 1975, when the bank first announced a target for growth of the "central bank money stock." As is well known, the bank often failed to achieve its target. During the thirteen years when the target was for the central bank money stock—1975 to 1987, which is also when Germany's inflation experience differed most from that of other Western industrialized countries—the bank achieved its target in seven years but failed to do so in six. From 1988 through 1998, when the target was instead the M3 money stock (and also when inflation in Germany was not all that different from what other industrialized countries had), the bank achieved its target in six years and missed in five. Especially for the years in which the target was for central bank money, which is presumably more readily controllable than the more endogenous M3, this record naturally calls into question just how hard the Bundesbank was trying to achieve its money growth targets and, therefore, how much importance to assign them in accounting for Germany's relative success in containing inflation.

This chapter, like many of Otmar Issing's valuable contributions over the years, verbally narrates the history of Bundesbank monetary policy in a way that places the bank's money growth targets at the center of the story. Still, economists, like other social scientists, are trained not to accept, in the absence of other supporting evidence, the first-person accounts of government officials (and others too) who explain for the public record what they and their colleagues did and why. The chapter therefore also proceeds to more formal, empirically-based analysis.

The bulk of the empirical analysis that the authors carry out, however, does not constitute a test of the question at hand. Their empirical tests are mostly uninformative about what role the Bundesbank's money growth targets played in its actual monetary policymaking. They therefore have little or no light to shed on what contribution a policy strategy based on money growth targets made, or might have made, to Germany's inflation experience.

It is easiest to see why this is the case by considering the argument in a simplified form that parallels the more cumbersome formulations in the chapter. The authors work with a standard three-equation representation of the economy consisting of an aggregate demand function,

(1) $$x = f[i - (p - p_{-1})],$$

a Phillips curve, or aggregate supply relation,

(2) $$p = g(x) + \mu,$$

and a money demand function,

(3) $$m - p = h(x, i) + \varepsilon,$$

where the variables have the conventional symbols and μ and ε are disturbance terms. (The authors' equivalent equations are slightly more complicated, involving expectations in the usual way, and the rate of change rather than the level of prices; but these differences do not matter for understanding why the tests for which they present results do not bear on the Bundesbank's use of money growth targets or not. The authors do write their aggregate demand function as here, without any disturbance term, but this also does not matter.)

Using the standard quantity relation, the authors then posit that the Bundesbank established its target for money growth as (approximately) the sum of the targeted growth in output and prices. Again simplifying by ignoring the difference between levels and changes,

(4) $$m^* = j(x^*, p^*).$$

The gap between actual and targeted money is therefore

(5) $$m - m^* = p + h(x, i) + \varepsilon - j(x^*, p^*).$$

Rearranging, we have

(5′) $$m - m^* = k[(x - x^*), (p - p^*), i] + \varepsilon,$$

which is a simplified form of the authors' equation (8).

What, then, did the Bundesbank do? According to the authors, "the primary objective of the Bundesbank council was to minimize deviations of inflation and money growth from target, while also seeking to stabilize output and the interest rate around their respective steady-state values." Hence, the bank's objective—expressed here for a single period, again for simplicity's sake—was to minimize

(6) $$E\{V[(p - p^*)^2, (x - x^*)^2, (i - i_{-1})^2, (m - m^*)^2]\},$$

which is a simplified form of the authors' equation (11). Differentiating this objective with respect to the policy instrument i would then lead to a policy reaction function of the familiar augmented Taylor-rule form

(7) $$i = F[(p - p^*), (x - x^*), i_{-1}, (m - m^*)],$$

that is, a standard Taylor rule augmented by not only the interest-rate smoothing term but also the money targeting term.

As the authors point out, other researchers have estimated policy reaction functions of this general form for the Bundesbank, as well as many other central banks.[2] The test for the role of money targets in the setting of the policy interest rate then turns on the estimated coefficient on the $(m - m^*)$ term. (I have followed this procedure too. In a 1996 paper with Kenneth Kuttner, for example, we found a statistically significant response of the US federal funds rate to the deviation of M1 from target during 1981 to 1986 and to the deviation of M2 from target during 1980 to 1986, and on that basis we concluded that the Federal Reserve's monetary policy actually was targeting money growth, at least in part, during those years.[3])

Here, however, the authors take a different approach. By substituting the money demand function for m and the quantity relation for m^*, they eliminate both variables from the policy reaction function to get

$$(7') \qquad\qquad i = G[(p - p^*), (x - x^*), i_{-1}, \varepsilon],$$

where the coefficients on the first three terms are combinations of the coefficients in equations (1), (2), and (3), and ε is again the disturbance to the money demand equation. This is a simplified form of the authors' equation (10).

At first glance, this policy reaction function, (7'), may look like merely the familiar Taylor-rule function with interest-rate smoothing added—hence the term in i_{-1}—but without any reference to money growth targeting. But the two are not the same. The coefficients are different from the rule that would have resulted from simply differentiating a version of the objective in (6) from which the term in $(m - m^*)$ has been excluded. Because none of the coefficients would differ in sign, however, in the absence of very sharp priors on the magnitudes of the underlying structural values, it would be impossible to test the difference between the reaction function with and without money growth targeting on that basis alone. Fortunately, however, there is another difference. The reaction function derived from minimizing (6), the objective incorporating money growth targeting, also includes the money demand function disturbance, ε. The test for the presence of money growth targeting is therefore a test of the significance of the expected positive coefficient on ε.

What renders most of the authors' empirical tests for money growth targeting in this chapter uninformative about the Bundesbank's use (or nonuse) of money growth targets is that, instead of going ahead and estimating their equivalent of the interest rate reaction function as they have derived it—here the simplified (7'), in the chapter, their equation (10)—in all of

---

2. The most familiar example, which the authors also cite, is Clarida, Galí, and Gertler (1998).
3. See Friedman and Kuttner (1996).

the regressions that they show in the chapter they delete ε, the disturbance from the money demand function. Hence what they are estimating is merely a relationship between the policy interest rate and the variables that would be in a Taylor-rule reaction function (with interest-rate smoothing) anyway, with no specifically anchored reference to money growth targeting.

Their argument for excluding the money demand disturbance is that the central bank, for good reasons, wanted to accommodate movements in money growth that had nothing to do with output or prices and instead represented pure portfolio shifts. This argument may sound sensible as a matter of good monetary policy practice, but here its implications are deeply subversive of what the authors are trying to achieve. If the central bank knows the money demand function and is able to predict in advance the disturbance term and adjust its money growth target to allow for it, then what it is actually targeting is simply a combination of the variables, other than the interest rate itself, that appear on the right-hand side of the money demand function—in the authors' model, meaning output and prices. On this rendering, money growth targeting is not just observationally equivalent to following the usual Taylor rule, it is conceptually and functionally equivalent. In other words, under this procedure, the money growth target has no substantive content whatever, and the central bank never need pay attention to actual observations of realized money growth. Whether policymakers think they are targeting money growth along with prices and output or merely think they are targeting prices and output makes no difference.

And, of course, functional equivalence implies observational equivalence: the authors' estimates of the associated reaction function, with both m and m^* substituted out, *and with ε excluded*, provide no information about what role, if any, money growth targeting actually played in the Bundesbank's setting of the policy interest rate.

In the version of the chapter that the authors presented at the conference, they appeared to recognize this problem, although they did not articulate it in any clear way. What they instead emphasized, and continue to emphasize in the revised version of the chapter published in this volume, is that the equation they estimate—their equation (10) without the $\Delta\varepsilon$ term—has a particular functional form that is more complex than the simplified version I have shown here for illustrative purposes. According to the authors, "the interest rate rule of a central bank that targets money growth differs from a standard Taylor rule in that it implies a response to the deviation of actual output growth from potential output growth (which is equivalent to targeting the change in the output gap), as well as an additional response to the lagged interest rate and to money demand shocks." But the response to lagged interest rates is a reflection of interest-rate smoothing, not money growth targeting. And in their empirical tests, they omit the money demand shocks. They are therefore left arguing that the presence in their estimated equation of a term in *the change of* the output gap, in addition to the level of the output gap, is evidence of money growth targeting.

This argument is not persuasive. More than half a century ago, A. W. Phillips (the same Phillips who later invented what we now call the Phillips curve) showed that adding the change in a targeted variable to the policymaker's reaction function would deliver improved results in a wide variety of dynamic systems.[4] (In addition, Phillips showed that, in some cases, adding the integral of the targeted variable to the reaction function also might result in further improvement.) Phillips would surely have been startled to be told that he was somehow advocating money growth targets—nearly a decade before the publication of Friedman and Schwartz's history, indeed, even before publication of Friedman's seminal "Restatement" of the quantity theory of money.[5] Conversely, surely most advocates of money targeting, in the decades since then, would be reluctant to accept that, all along, all they were suggesting was merely that the central bank include an additional term—in output!—in its interest rate setting rule.

The omission of the $\Delta \varepsilon$ term from the estimated form of the authors' equation (10) is, of course, remediable. The authors kindly shared their data with me, and so I did this myself in advance of the conference. Because the authors did not include $\Delta \varepsilon$ in their estimated equation, they had no need for an empirical estimate of the disturbance to money demand and therefore no need to bother estimating a money demand function. After a minimum of experimentation with the German data, which I had never used before, I settled on this specification:

(8) $\Delta m - \Delta p = a + b_1 \Delta x + b_2 \Delta i + b_3 (\Delta m - \Delta p)_{-1} + b_4 (\Delta m - \Delta p)_{-2}.$

The results, with $\bar{R}^2 = .86$ for 1972 to 1997, were not bad (see table 6C.1). I then subtracted the fitted from the actual value of m to derive the ε series I needed to estimate the authors' interest rate reaction function (10).

The results were not encouraging (see table 6C.2). The $\Delta \varepsilon$ term was significant for the 1977–1987 sample, though not for 1987–1997, nor for the full 1977–1997 sample. But the sign in each case was negative. In other words, the larger the realized disturbance to money demand, the *lower* the Bundesbank set the interest rate. If the estimated equation included actual money growth, this is what one would hope to see: for given observed money growth, the more that growth represents merely the disturbance to money demand the less the central bank should react to it. But the point is that the authors' interest rate reaction function does *not* include actual money or money growth, and so what is being estimated is *not* the response to the money demand disturbance given observed money growth. One can imagine policymakers' simply ignoring this component of money growth (if they are

---

4. See Phillips (1954).
5. See Friedman and Schwartz (1963) and Friedman (1956).

Table 6C.1   **Estimates of money demand function**

Dependent variable $\Delta m - \Delta p$	
Sample	1972–1997
Dependent variable lag 1	1.32 (0.08)***
Dependent variable lag 2	–0.44 (0.08)***
Δx	0.02 (0.04)
Δi	–0.38 (0.13)***
R^2	0.86

***Significant at the 1 percent level.

Table 6C.2   **Estimates of equation (10) including $\Delta\varepsilon$**

	Dependent variable i		
Sample	1977–1997	1977–1987	1987–1997
$\pi - \pi^*$	1.87 (0.34)***	1.96 (0.12)***	–0.49 (1.05)
x	–0.05 (0.23)	–1.73 (0.20)***	1.72 (0.61)***
Δx	1.95 (0.73)***	–1.89 (0.30)	–1.18 (0.47)**
$\Delta\varepsilon$	–0.32 (0.32)	–1.51 (0.22)***	–0.54 (0.33)
ρ_1	1.01 (0.06)***	1.13 (0.11)***	1.68 (0.09)***
ρ_2	–0.11 (0.07)	–0.39 (0.11)***	–0.55 (0.05)***
R^2	0.93	0.77	0.96
J-stat.	0.14	0.18	0.22

***Significant at the 1 percent level.
**Significant at the 5 percent level.

able to identify it) along the lines of the authors' explanation for why they excluded the money demand disturbance from their estimated equation in the first place. To repeat, that logic makes money growth targeting conceptually, functionally, and observationally equivalent to following a Taylor rule with no reference to money growth targets at all. But there is no reason that this component of money growth should enter the interest rate reaction function with a negative sign. And, indeed, the indicated sign in the authors' derivation of equation (10) is positive.

In the postconference revision published in this volume, the authors report that they then tried the same exercise, relying on the residuals from a money demand equation that Beyer had estimated some years earlier, and found a significant positive coefficient.[6] This regression (which they do not show) is potentially informative about the Bundesbank's use of money growth targets. Given the contrast to the negative coefficient that I found, however, the result is at best fragile. It hinges not just on whether Beyer's money

6. See Beyer (1998).

demand function is superior to the one I used—which would not be at all surprising—but whether the corresponding residuals were (approximately) the residuals on which the Bundesbank relied in real time.

With this one exception, then, the tests that the authors carry out in this chapter are uninformative about the role that money growth targets played in German monetary policy during the years in question (and my attempt to redo their empirical analysis in a way that could have been informative proved unfruitful). This does not necessarily mean, of course, that money growth targets did not play a role. As Clarida, Galí, and Gertler (1998), among others, have shown, estimating an interest rate reaction function like (7) instead of the equivalent to (7′)—that is, before substituting out m and m^*—does indicate a positive response of i to $(m - m^*)$. (I confirmed this as well, again using the authors' data set.) But that alternative form of analysis is not what this chapter does. And, in any case, the finding of a significant response of i to $(m - m^*)$ is not the same as showing that that response was important to the success of German monetary policy in containing inflation.

I would like to conclude by returning to where this discussion began: that it seems difficult to argue with the proposition that German monetary policy in the 1970s and early 1980s was a success. What criterion should we use for judging success in this example? To be sure, Germany did experience significantly less inflation than other Western industrialized countries during this period. But is that all that matters?

Years ago, not long before the beginning of the period under examination in this chapter, a familiar and interesting question was why European unemployment rates, and the German unemployment rate in particular, were always so much lower than ours in the United States. Several decades later, after the period under study here had ended—and right up until the 2007 to 2009 financial crisis hit—an equally familiar and interesting question was why European unemployment rates, including Germany's, were always so much *higher* than ours. Importantly, the difference was not that the average US unemployment rate had declined; ours remained more or less what it had been. Rather, most European countries' average unemployment rates, including Germany's, became far higher. As a result, the productive capacity of Germany and other European countries remained for decades well below what it would otherwise have been. As Laurence Ball, for example, has shown, the anti-inflationary policies of the 1970s and early 1980s, tried out in the context of European labor market institutions, were an important part of how that transition from low average unemployment to high average unemployment, with consequent loss of productive capacity, happened.[7] Instead of focusing only on inflation rates, maybe assessments of whether German monetary policy was really a success should take such matters into account as well.

7. See Ball (1997).

References

Ball, Laurence M. 1997. "Disinflation and the NAIRU." In *Reducing Inflation: Motivation and Strategy,* edited by Christina Romer and David Romer, 167–92. Chicago: University of Chicago Press.

Beyer, Andreas. 1998. "Modelling Money Demand in Germany." *Journal of Applied Econometrics* 13:57–76.

Clarida, Richard, Jordi Galí, and Mark Gertler. 1998. "Monetary Rules in Practice: Some International Evidence." *European Economic Review* 42:1033–67.

Friedman, Benjamin M., and Kenneth N. Kuttner. 1996. "A Price Target for US Monetary Policy? Lessons from the Experience with Money Growth Targets." *Brookings Papers on Economic Activity* 1:77–146. Washington, DC: Brookings Institution.

Friedman, Milton. 1956. "The Quantity Theory of Money—A Restatement." In *Studies in the Quantity Theory of Money,* edited by M. Friedman, Section I. Chicago: University of Chicago Press.

Friedman, Milton, and Anna Jacobson Schwartz. 1963. *A Monetary History of the United States, 1867–1960.* Princeton, NJ: Princeton University Press.

Phillips, A. W. 1954. "Stabilization Policy in a Closed Economy." *Economic Journal* 64:290–323.

Discussion

The discussion began with Allan Meltzer questioning why Germany had lower inflation that the United States. First, as Issing pointed out, there was political support for attacking inflation rather than economic stabilization. President Richard Nixon used to say that no one ever lost an election because of inflation. Second, and very importantly, the Bundesbank had strategies that aimed specifically at sustaining a low inflation rate. The Federal Reserve was dominated by a Phillips curve that was not well estimated, and people that relied on it forgot that most of the points used to estimate it came from the time of the gold standard. Third, the Bundesbank made a commitment that the public believed that they and the Swiss National Bank were the dominant anti-inflationists. This is critical, and the political part is missing from most of our models of US policy. Optimal monetary policy is not possible unless the Congress and the Federal Reserve are willing to go along with it. The Congress had a mandate that it sent to the Federal Reserve to perform. The chairman of the Federal Reserve is aware of this and frightened of Congress.

Lars Svensson thought of the Bundesbank's legacy as its commitment to price stability, and not to monetary targeting as the authors suggest. There is conflict between achieving the inflation target and the money growth target. Issing and his colleagues chose an inflation target, and in the end Svensson believed that money is more of a smokescreen. The Bundesbank was thus just an early flexible inflation targeter. On a more technical note, Svensson referenced the model and how putting money growth into the central bank loss function is not very attractive; rather, one should use a lagged state variable. Nominal interest-rate smoothing does the same thing, and you do not need money in the loss functions to make the discretion equilibrium closer to the commitment equilibrium.

Athanasios Orphanides followed up on Svensson's comments in agreeing that money growth targeting proved a very successful framework for avoiding inflation. It avoided relying on utilization gaps and instead focused on stabilizing the growth rate of the economy. It is very close to nominal income targeting. The basic lesson that it provided was to not let policymakers perform gapist policy. The main question Orphanides posed was about the role of independence of the central bank in delivering different outcomes in Germany versus the United States at the time. In 1957, both central banks recognized that the objective of policy should be price stability because this would be how the central bank would achieve maximum sustainable growth in the economy. Starting from the same initial conditions, the story unfolds much differently.

Michael Woodford thought the chapter provided interesting evidence that the approach to policymaking that the Bundesbank was using had characteristics of what simple theoretical models would suggest as good policy. Yet, Woodford wondered if this proves that putting a stabilization objective for money growth in the loss functions for the central bank is the most practical way of achieving those benefits. Svensson had suggested using lagged interest rates, and another alternative is using a loss function that tries to stabilize the rate of change in the output gap. This makes discretionary policy look more like optimal policy and brings about results that are clearly a feature of Bundesbank policy. Woodford was not convinced that the only way to cure the suboptimal features of discretionary minimization of a New Keynesian loss function was to have discretionary minimization of some other loss function. One could simply design other procedures, most notably inflation targeting, and implement optimal policy with these.

John Crow did not believe money was important for the Bundesbank, and stressed it was mostly about the politics of the time. The central bank is in charge of money, and money does matter, which he stressed in reference to work at the Bank of Canada. The fact was that they needed to move to target prices straight away. Money demand responds faster to interest rates than to inflation. The path is the demand for money, then money, then the real economy, then inflation. Crow also questioned Issing about how the ambiguous response to inflation targeting of the Bundesbank and even the European Central Bank was not just political, but also technical.

Christina Romer asked why Germany opted into optimal policy rather than opting out like the United States? In the crucial period being looked at, German inflation went from 1 percent to 7 percent. It was at 5 percent even before the oil shock. So why did they make the mistakes in the late

1960s and seem to fix it in the 1970s? Is it in fact that they had bought into some of the same bad ideas of the United States but learned something the United States did not learn?

Issing began the rebuttal, claiming that the statements of Svensson were unfair. The Bundesbank was in conflict with strict monetarist ideas, and he thought the money had a crucial role. What they were doing might not be completely transparent, and it was probably inflation targeting in disguise. Issing agreed with Orphanides's story about avoiding the gapist policies. While stabilization gaps and real-time data were all instruments available to the bank, they did not rely on them. As a final point, to model monetary policy, which is neither strict money targeting, a Taylor rule, or inflation targeting, is a very ambitious approach. One can always improve on policy, but none of this says money does not matter. The political story is important, yet it is the job of the central bank to control money so that inflation does not get out of control.

Vitor Gaspar concluded with two points. First, in reference to McCallum, the authors will work on spelling out the argument that estimating instrument rules with money growth directly in them is not desirable. Lastly, there is confusion in this debate because there are many ways to explain inertia in a policy rule. The authors felt the beauty of their approach was that it was more compatible with the language of the Bundesbank at the time and was a description of what it actually did.

7

Great Inflation and Central Bank Independence in Japan

Takatoshi Ito

7.1 Introduction

The Bank of Japan (BOJ) was born in 1882, only after the new Meiji government experimented unsuccessfully with transplanting the national banking system (without a central bank) from the United States. The government, after some unpleasant inflation under the national banking system, decided to adopt the central banking system modeled after the Belgium central bank. During more than 125 years of its uninterrupted history, the Bank of Japan saw three episodes of high inflation, defined by more than 20 percent of Consumer Price Index (CPI) inflation rate: (a) 1917 to 1919, the World War I years; (b) 1945 to 1949, immediately after the end of World War II; and (c) 1973 to 1974, the first oil crisis.[1] See table 7.1 for details. The

Takatoshi Ito is dean of and professor in the Graduate School of Public Policy at the University of Tokyo, a faculty fellow of the Centre for Economic Policy Research (CEPR), and a research associate of the Tokyo Center for Economic Research (TCER) and of the National Bureau of Economic Research.

This chapter was written for the conference on the Great Inflation. The author is grateful to comments on earlier versions by editors, a discussant, anonymous referees, Michael Bordo, Frederic Mishkin, and Athanasios Orphanides. The author has also benefited from detailed comments by Shigenori Shiratsuka, Masato Shizume, and other participants of a seminar at the Bank of Japan in July 2009. In addition, the author is grateful to many economists and executives, currently and in the past, of the Bank of Japan over the past three decades. Any remaining errors are those of the author. For acknowledgments, sources of research support, and disclosure of the author's material financial relationships, if any, please see http://www.nber.org/chapters/c9166.ack.

1. This can be taken as support to a view that, in the very long run, monetary discipline has been maintained in Japan since the 1880s, except for a few episodes. A more direct test of monetary neutrality in the long run was carried out by Oi, Shiratsuka, and Shirota (2004).

Table 7.1   Three episodes of high inflation

	CPI (%)	WPI (%)
Episode I		
1917	22.7	25.8
1918	34.6	31.0
1919	33.0	22.5
Episode II		
1945	n/a	51.1
1946	n/a	364.5
1947	n/a	195.9
1948	83.0	165.6
1949	31.7	63.3
Episode III		
1974	23.3	31.4

Source: See Ito (1997). n/a = not available.
Note: Author's calculation.

first episode reflected the export boom during World War I.[2] The second episode, when prices increased more than 200 times in a few years, was a result of the devastation of productive capacity and deficit financing cum monetization, which followed the end of World War II. So the 1973 to 1974 episode was the only example of high inflation unrelated to a war in which Japan was involved.

The main focus of this chapter is to examine the third episode of high inflation, when the CPI inflation rate remained above 10 percent from May 1973 to September 1975, with a spike up to 23 percent in 1974. (The inflation rate is defined as the percentage increase of CPI over the same month of the preceding year.)

It is commonly argued that the oil crisis was the culprit to blame for the 1973 to 1975 high inflation. However, the inflation rate already reached 10 percent several months before the Middle East crisis, which occurred in October 1973.[3] The oil crisis only aggravated, though very badly, an inflationary spiral that was already in progress.

Reasons for the great inflation of 1973 to 1974 are the following: first, in late 1972, the Bank of Japan underestimated the strength of the economy and potential of prices to rise quickly. Second, there was a strong resistance against yen revaluation/appreciation. This was particularly true between December 1971, when the Smithsonian Agreement was reached, and Feb-

2. Shizume (2002) examines monetary policy in the interwar period, using the Taylor rule. He concludes that monetary policy was amplifying rather than mitigating domestic cycles due to consideration of the stability of the exchange rate, throughout the periods under the gold standard, 1897 to 1913 and 1930 to 1931; and managed exchange rate regime, 1913 to 1929; and after 1932.

3. Seminal work that pointed out that monetary easing, or excess liquidity, existed before the oil price jump of October 1973 were Komiya (1976; 1988, ch. 8) and Komiya and Yasui (1984).

ruary 1973, when the yen was finally floated. The pressure for appreciation prompted interventions by the monetary authorities in terms of selling yen, which added yen liquidity to the market, promoting inflation. Politicians also voiced their dislike of yen appreciation, and some of them were calling for stopping yen appreciation at any cost. The bank lowered the official discount rate (ODR)—that was the policy rate then—in June 1972, when recovery in output had already become obvious. Third, Mr. Kakuei Tanaka became prime minister (PM) in July 1972, advocating large fiscal spending. There was strong pressure from his government to keep the interest rate from rising. It was a regular practice in the 1960s and 1970s that any interest rate change was subject to preliminary discussion with and a tacit approval of the government and prime minister, before actually being decided in the Policy Board (in charge of monetary policy). The Monetary Policy Committee was not functioning as an independent decision-making body at all. (Details of pressure from politicians will be explained in later sections.)

With political pressure, it was not until April 1973 that the ODR was raised. By that time, the CPI inflation rate was exceeding 9 percent. The first three (out of five) interest rate hikes in 1973 were too little and too late. By the time of the oil price hike of October 1973, the fight against inflation had already been lost. Both headline and core CPI inflation rates rose above 20 percent by the beginning of 1974.

A panic-like chaos resulting from high inflation in 1974 finally convinced the bank and politicians to apply strong tightening.[4] The ODR was raised from 4.25 percent to 9 percent, in five steps, in 1973. However, the interest rate level stayed well *below* the inflation rate throughout this episode. The real interest rate, measured by the difference between ODR and CPI headline inflation rate, was on average minus 5.6 percent in 1973, and minus 14.1 percent in 1974.[5] Disinflation in 1974 was accompanied by a sharp output decline, a great sacrifice. The negative growth rate of 1974 was the first since 1950.

There are three possible hypotheses to explain the bank's soft stance toward inflation. The first hypothesis is that the Bank of Japan did not know that the inflationary pressure was building in the economy. Examination of a memoir (Nakagawa 1981) and the bank historical archives (Bank of Japan 1986) reveal that this was probably not the case. The second hypothesis is that the Bank of Japan knew that the inflationary risk was rising, but did not seek tightening in time because of a fear of being turned down. The third hypothesis is that although the Bank of Japan knew of the risk and

---

4. Wholesalers were believed to have bought and hoarded goods. Consumers also bought in bulk to guard themselves from future inflation. These actions shrank supply quickly and contributed to further price increases. One widely reported story was that toilet paper would be missing from store shelves, so consumers, in a panic, rushed to supermarkets to purchase toilet paper—clearing the store selves, indeed.

5. Even when the overnight call rate was used instead of ODR, the real interest rate was minus 4.4 percent in 1973 and minus 10.6 percent in 1974.

attempted to tighten, the tightening proposal was rejected by the government. The relationship with the government (especially prime ministers, as well as finance ministers) in 1972 to 1973 holds a clue. A close examination of the events reveals that the truth is somewhere between the second and third hypothesis.

After the 1973 to 1974 episode of high inflation that was widely attributed, in part, to a mistake of the Bank of Japan, one might think that the Bank of Japan would have been discredited. On the contrary, the bank came out of the episode with a stronger voice. The bank argued that if its recommendation to tighten monetary policy was to be overruled, the tragic experiences of 1972 to 1973 would be repeated. With this logic, the Bank of Japan obtained de facto independence. The ODR was raised much earlier in 1979 to 1980, the second oil crisis, than in 1973. Even more remarkable here was that the ODR was raised during the months of a budget debate in the Diet—between January and March—which up to that time was politically inconceivable.[6] The real interest rate remained positive in 1979 to 1980, in contrast to being hugely negative in 1973 to 1974. The real interest rate measured by the difference between the ODR and CPI headline inflation rate was on average 1 percent in 1979 and 0.4 percent in 1980, while the real interest rate of the call rate was 2.2 percent in 1979 and 3.2 percent in 1980. As a result, even with sharp oil price increases in 1979 to 1980, the inflation rate in Japan remained moderate, peaking at 8.7 percent.

The rest of this chapter is organized as follows. The next section reviews the 120-year history of inflation in Japan. Section 7.3 describes the economic events and political developments as well as monetary policy actions, which resulted in the Great Inflation of 1972 to 1974. The monetary policy during this period is considered to be a mistake.[7] Section 7.4 describes why the Bank of Japan gained monetarist rhetoric and de facto independence after the mistake of 1972 to 1973. Section 7.5 reviews no-inflation experience during the second oil crisis, 1978 to 1980. Section 7.6 will be devoted to some econometric analysis to substantiate the arguments in the preceding sections. Section 7.7 concludes the chapter.

7.2   Great Inflation of 1973 to 1974

7.2.1   Transition from the Bretton Woods to Free Floating

The collapse of the Bretton Woods regime in August 1971 suddenly freed the Bank of Japan from conducting monetary policy solely to maintain the balance of payments by controlling domestic demands. Theoretically the

---

6. The reason for the hesitation of ODR changes during the budget process was that it would make budget assumptions outdated, while a budget bill could not be changed easily.
7. See Ito (1992, 125–27) for an earlier description of the "mistake."

exchange rate could move freely to adjust imports and exports, and the Bank of Japan could concentrate its policy objectives to domestic prices. But, this did not happen, at least not until February 1973.

After some chaotic trading in the yen/dollar market and gradual appreciation of the yen after the collapse of the Bretton Woods regime, the G10 countries agreed in December 1971 to a new parity with a narrow band with fluctuation plus/minus 2.25 percent. The yen had appreciated gradually from 360 yen to 315 yen per dollar by the mid-December 1971. Under the Smithsonian Agreement of December 18, 1971, the central rate for the yen/dollar rate was determined, after tough negotiation, to be 308 yen/dollar, a 16.88 percent revaluation (according to the International Monetary Fund [IMF] definition) from the Bretton Woods rate of 360 yen/dollar.

The Smithsonian rate of 308 yen/dollar was regarded by many in Japan as a dangerously appreciated yen level. The export industries, particularly shipbuilding, were considered to be vulnerable. Guarding against further appreciation became a new national objective. As the yen had stuck at the most appreciated level (ceiling) of the Smithsonian band in 1972, monetary policy and fiscal policy were conducted to stimulate the domestic economy so that imports would increase and the trade surpluses would come down. Even if inflation would result from increasing domestic demand, that would not be a problem, politicians insisted. Political pressure to keep monetary policy relaxed was strong, but no dissenting voice from the Bank of Japan was heard in public.

7.2.2   The "Mistake": Overview

Movements of the inflation rates—CPI and Wholesale Price Index (WPI)—and the interest rates—ODR and call rate—from 1971 to 1975 are shown in figure 7.1, where inflation variables are defined as a change over the same month of one year earlier. Table 7.2 shows industrial production, M2 growth rate, and yen/dollar rate, as well as CPI and WPI inflation. There were little cautionary signs of inflation until the summer of 1972, the CPI inflation rate being at around 5 percent, and slightly declining, and the WPI inflation rate close to zero. However, the WPI started to increase in the summer of 1972, and quickly reached 5 percent, the level of CPI inflation rate, by November 1972. The sharp increase in the WPI was considered to be an indication of future inflation in the CPI.

In June 1972, the interest rate was cut to stimulate the economy. According to Nakagawa (1981), this rate cut was first planned in April, but delayed for political reasons. This will be explained in detail later. By the time of implementation, it was way behind the curve, since the WPI inflation rate started to increase and industrial production started to show signs of recovery.

The WPI inflation rate continued to accelerate, and reached 11 percent by April 1973, while the CPI inflation rate reached 9.4 percent by April 1973. In

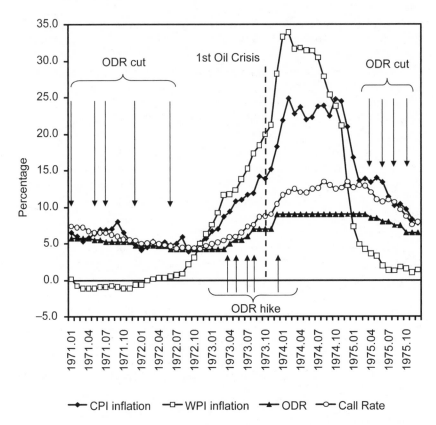

Fig. 7.1 **Great Inflation of 1973–1974**

April 1973, the Bank of Japan raised its policy interest rate (ODR) for the first time since the collapse of the Bretton Woods system.

Because the inflation rate rose sharply and exceeded 10 percent by summer 1973 and there were some signs already a year earlier, the interest rate cut of June 1972 was a "mistake."[8] By the same reasoning, the absence of

8. Hetzel (1999) provides the overview of Japanese monetary policy during the period from 1970 to 1998. He argues that the Bank of Japan had little room to make decisions until the fixed exchange rate was abandoned. It is true that under the Bretton Woods regime (which ended in August 1971), there could not be totally autonomous monetary policy—independent from the US monetary policy—but since substantial capital controls were in place, the interest rate could be deviated from the United States. However, Japanese monetary policy could not be totally autonomous due to the balance of payment (BOP) constraints (see Ito 1992, ch. 5). In sum, monetary policy had a room to maneuver due to capital controls, but there was an overall BOP constraint. After August 1971, there were substantial policy options, including how much appreciation and fluctuation of the yen to be tolerated, how much inflation rate to be tolerated, how much capital liberalization to be allowed. Before the Smithsonian Agreement—an attempt to fix the exchange rates at new rates with wider bands—the major countries were struggling with how much appreciation vis-à-vis the US dollar was to be tolerated, and Japan was not an exception. The Smithsonian Agreement, December 1971, was a result of

Table 7.2   Prices and money prior to Great Inflation

	CPI inflation	WPI inflation	Industrial Production	M2 growth	Yen/dollar rate	Monetary policy action
1972.01			1.3	25.1	312.23	
1972.02			3.0	25.3	304.98	
1972.03			3.9	26.1	302.44	
1972.04			3.8	26.2	303.56	
1972.05	5.2	0.4	8.3	25.5	304.44	
1972.06	4.8	4.1	-0.6	26.6	303.68	Interest rate cut
1972.07	5.0	4.5	0.0	27.1	301.11	
1972.08	5.9	5.3	0.2	26.4	301.10	The yen/dollar
1972.09	3.9	5.0	0.4	26.9	301.10	rate virtually
1972.10	4.4	3.2	10.6	27.8	301.10	fixed
1972.11	5.1	5.0	11.4	28.5	301.10	
1972.12	5.7	6.3	14.7	26.5	301.23	
1973.01	6.7	7.6	17.1	26.1	301.96	
1973.02	7.0	9.3	16.9	26.8	279.48	
1973.03	8.7	11.6	16.5	26.9	265.26	
1973.04	9.4	11.8	16.9	27.3	265.52	Interest rate hike

Inflation acceleration ← Output expands rapidly ← Money growth had remained high

monetary tightening until the CPI inflation rate was near 10 percent in April 1973 showed that the bank was too slow to respond. Reasons for this mistake based on political economy are presented in the following.

Figure 7.1 also shows that after the Middle East Crisis of October 1973, both the CPI and WPI inflation rates increased sharply. The WPI inflation rate rose to near 35 percent, and the CPI near 25 percent by spring 1974. This was the greatest peacetime inflation for Japan. Due to a very high inflation rate, wages rose sharply in 1974 as well as 1973, in order to compensate for an increase in living costs. Companies were enjoying profits from the demand stimulation of 1972 and 1973 (until the oil price shock, starting in October 1973). The inflation spiral was in place from mid-1973 to 1974. Oil prices tripled from July 1973 to January 1974, with the selective embargo by the Oil Producing Exporting Countries (OPEC). The sharp increase in imported oil prices aggravated the already high and increasing inflation rate.

While the CPI inflation rate above 20 percent was very high, the industrial production growth rate turned negative in 1974, as shown in figure 7.2. The real GDP growth rate became negative for the first time since 1955, when

---

hard negotiation groping for new constellation of fixed exchange rates. Japan accepted more than 16 percent appreciation, but probably that was too little. Since there was a wide band, theoretically, monetary policy had room to maneuver under the Smithsonian regime. However, the yen had stuck at the ceiling, before Japan decided to abandon the Smithsonian regime in February 1973, one month ahead of European countries. Hence, including the choice of abandoning the Smithsonian regime, there were policy choices between December 1971 and February 1973. It was certainly true that monetary policy was freed from US monetary policy after February 1973.

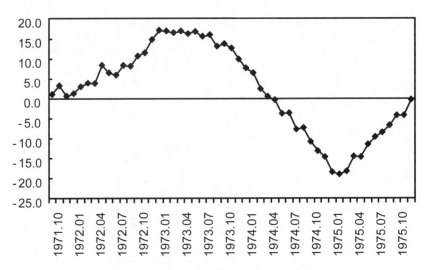

Fig. 7.2   Industrial Production growth rate ($y - y$), 1971–1975

GDP statistics became available. Table 7.3 shows GDP changes, quarter-to-quarter annualized rates, and year-on-year growth rates. Table 7.4 shows the GDP growth rates. The year 1974 was typical of stagflation—a very high inflation rate with negative growth in output.

Table 7.3 and vertical lines in figure 7.1 show the timing of the monetary policy actions. The interest rate (ODR) was raised five times in the nine-month period starting in April 1973. However, there was no action in 1974. Obvious questions are why tightening did not come earlier and why there was not more tightening in 1974. We will answer these questions later.

Figure 7.3 shows movements of the CPI headline, CPI core (excluding fresh food), and CPI core-core (excluding food and energy-related). Since all three CPIs move together, it shows the role of energy was relatively small, in the run-up to the high inflation period of 1974. There is a maximum 5 percent point difference between core and core-core, which is roughly the contribution of energy prices.

Negative growth in 1974 and quite depressed wage increase in 1975 were the reason that the inflation rate came down in the second half of 1974 and throughout 1975. The WPI inflation rate fell below 5 percent in the spring of 1975, and by the end of 1975, the CPI inflation rate fell below 10 percent. The great inflation of 1973 to 1974 was over, with a heavy sacrifice in output activities in 1974.

7.2.3   Why Easing Went Too Far: The Mistake of June 1972

As explained before, the necessity of lowering the ODR by 50 basis points on June 24, 1972, is highly questionable since the output had shown signs of recovery, and prices, particularly the WPI, also showed the sign of recovery.

Table 7.3   **Growth rates, 1971–1975, quarter-to-quarter and year-to-year**

	q-to-q	y-to-y	
1971-I	**0.9**	**4.8**	ODR cut; monetary easing
1971-II	**1.6**	**4.5**	
1971-III	**1.2**	**3.7**	
1971-IV	**0.9**	**4.6**	
1972-I	**3.3**	**7.5**	
1972-II	**1.9**	**7.3**	
1972-III	2.1	8.8	
1972-IV	2.5	9.8	
1973-I	3.3	10.3	
1973-II	**0.9**	**9.3**	ODR hike; monetary tightening
1973-III	**0.3**	**7.6**	
1973-IV	**1.2**	**5.6**	
1974-I	−3.4	−1.7	
1974-II	0.7	−0.9	
1974-III	1.3	−0.2	
1974-IV	−0.5	−2.0	
1975-I	0.1	1.5	
1975-II	**2.2**	**3.4**	ODR cut; monetary easing
1975-III	**1.1**	**3.0**	
1975-IV	**1.1**	**4.3**	

Table 7.4   **Monetary policy actions and critical questions**

	Official discount rate (%)	
	1970–1975	
Date yyyy.mm.dd	Change	New level
1970.10.28	−0.25	6.00
1971.01.20	−0.25	5.75
1971.05.08	−0.25	5.50
1971.07.28	−0.25	5.25
1971.12.29	−0.50	4.75
1972.06.24[a]	−0.50	4.25
1973.04.02[b]	**0.75**	**5.00**
1973.05.30[b]	**0.50**	**5.50**
1973.07.02	**0.50**	**6.00**
1973.08.29	**1.00**	**7.00**
1973.12.22	**2.00**	**9.00**
1975.04.16	−0.50	8.50
1975.06.07	−0.50	8.00
1975.08.13	−0.50	7.50
1975.10.24	−1.00	6.50

[a]Was this necessary?
[b]Was this too late?

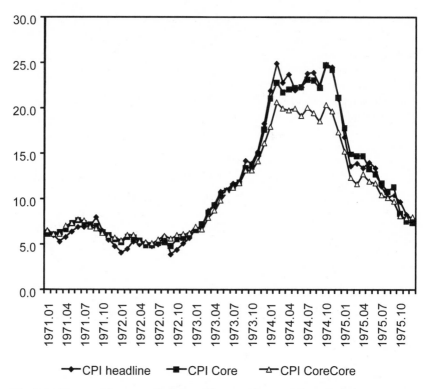

Fig. 7.3   Energy prices contributed to only a small part of Great Inflation

Bank of Japan (1986) and Nakagawa (1981), a former bank senior official, describes what really went on behind the scene over this period.

In April 1972, lowering the ODR was considered as a part of an anti-yen appreciation package of the government. Inside the BOJ, opinions were divided into two camps, one favoring lowering the ODR and the other considering the rate cut unnecessary. Governor Sasaki maintained to the press that it was not necessary. On May 10, Governor Sasaki met Prime Minister Sato, and the Governor was asked to consider lowering the ODR. On May 11, Governor Sasaki mentioned that the ODR would be lowered on the condition that the bank deposit rates would be lowered. Inside the bank, the proposal by the governor to lower the rate, although with one technical condition, was considered to be a surprise turnaround of his position. (See BOJ [1986, 381] for events on May 10 and 11.)

It took more than a month to decide on the deposit rate, because the Ministry of Posts and Communication, which oversaw the Postal Saving System, was opposed to the deposit rate cut. Finally, on June 23, the postal saving deposit rates were lowered, and the bank decided to lower the ODR.

This episode reveals three problems. First, the governor apparently was persuaded by the prime minister on the interest rate decision. Second, as all the private-sector interest rates were effectively linked to ODR, the ODR decision should seep into the system automatically. However, bank deposit taking and postal saving deposit taking competed for household deposits. Thus, the Ministry of Posts and Communication could effectively block the timely implementation. Third, between the government plan of April and the actual implementation, two months had passed. The wisdom of lowering the interest rate should have been reassessed by the Bank of Japan as well as by the government in June.

Nakagawa (1981) regrets that the bank (including himself) had not been courageous enough to scrap the plan for the interest rate cut, since between April and June, economic activity picked up considerably. He, however, thinks that once the political process forcing the Postal Saving System to lower the deposit rate had gone through the cycle, it was difficult to scrap it (Nakagawa 1981).

7.2.4   Why Tightening Did Not Come Earlier

With the government and the Bank of Japan pressing for domestic demand stimulation—again to avoid appreciation of the yen—in the first half of 1972, the wish was granted. In the second half of 1972, the economy was growing full steam. The GDP growth rate was increasing in the 9 to 10 percent range in the second half of 1972, and rose above 10 percent in 1973 (recall table 7.3); industrial production was increasing in the 10 to 15 percent range from mid-1972 to the end of 1972. The CPI inflation rate was above 5.7 percent and WPI inflation rate was 6.3 percent in December 1972. It seems very natural that the Bank of Japan would react to raise the interest rate as early as October 1972, and as late as December 1972. Why was the ODR not raised until April 1973?

The simple answer for a delayed reaction to inflation signals was again actual and potential political pressure. The economy indeed became strong and inflation pressure mounted by the end of 1972. The ODR was not raised until April 1973.

The government decided to have a fiscal expansion package for the 1972 fiscal year budget (April 1972 to March 1973) under Prime Minister Sato. The 1973 fiscal year was also intended to maintain fiscal stimulus. On July 7, 1972, Mr. Tanaka became prime minister. He won the presidency of the Liberal Democratic Party—hence automatically guaranteed to become prime minister—on the platform of "Reconstruction of the Japanese Archipelago"—large public works to build a network of road and railroad infrastructure. He announced an additional fiscal spending program in August. In October a supplementary budget and a second additional plan for a fiscal investment program was announced. He was very popular among the voters. It was clear that he would be opposed to the rate hike. The Bank of Japan felt that it would not be possible to seek a rate hike. On

November 9, PM Tanaka reiterated a strong opposition to yen revaluation (BOJ 1986, 403)

On November 13, the House of Representatives was dissolved, and on December 11, 1972, the general election took place. According to Bank of Japan (1986) and Nakagawa (1981), the Ministry of Finance told the Bank of Japan not to consider even the appearance of a policy change during the election period.

Right after the election, the budget discussion started in the Diet and the budget debate and votes continued until March 13, 1973. Traditionally no monetary policy changes were made during the budget process, because that would affect the assumption of the budget. This time, tradition was kept.

On February 14, 1973, the yen was floated (earlier than the European currencies) as a result of heavy pressure for yen appreciation. In March 1973, currency speculation became widespread among the European currencies, resulting in free floating (the end of the Smithsonian).

When the budget process was over, and the fixed-exchange rate fetter was broken, the Bank of Japan got an approval for a rate hike. On March 31, 1973, the approval was given (and implemented two days later) in a chat between the finance minister and governor in the corridor of the Diet (BOJ 1986).

Eight months of selecting a prospending prime minister, the dissolution of the Diet, and the budget process in the Diet explains the tardy implementation of the rate hike. There was an explicit approval of inflation if it would contribute to keep the nominal exchange rate within the approved range under the Smithsonian rate. On August 9, 1972, Ministry of International Trade and Industry (MITI) Minister Nakasone mentioned that he preferred domestic inflation to yen appreciation (BOJ 1986, 401). He said, "Japan is forced to choose between another yen revaluation and adjustment inflation. I think another yen revaluation should be definitely avoided; hence the economic activities should be stimulated." The inflation to avoid appreciation was named "adjustment inflation." Indeed, one way to achieve real exchange rate appreciation—which may be required to prevent the trade surplus from increasing—is inflation. Of course, inflation carries high costs of adjustment and distortions, and is an inferior policy compared to appreciation of the nominal exchange rate. However, this view was not shared among politicians at the time.

The step of the April 1973 rate hike, 75 basis points, was unusually high, probably reflecting the fact that the bank was behind the curve. Three other rate hikes—May 30 (+0.50), July 2 (+0.50), Aug 29 (+1.00)—followed in a hurry (recall table 7.4 and figure 7.2). However, the inflation rate continued rising. With the news of the Middle East War breaking out on October 6, 1973, the inflation rate was already at a dangerously high level, with the CPI at 15 percent and the WPI at 20 percent. Inflation rates shot up after October—some direct result of increasing oil prices, and some indirect, but immediate, effects of speculative inventory hoarding and panic buying. The Bank of Japan decided to raise ODR by 200 basis points on December 22, to put maximum pressure against inflation.

The real interest rate remained negative from October 1972 until mid-1975. The period from October 1972 to mid-1974 is characterized as widening the gap (more negative interest rate) and accelerating growth—a clear sign of being behind the curve. The real interest rate remained negative until mid-1975. Tightening was too little, too late throughout 1973.

A crucial question is whether the Bank of Japan knew of the danger of postponing the rate hike and if so, whether the bank sought after the rate hike even with risk of clashing with the government. The Bank of Japan (1986, 409–11) described the inside thinking at the time. As the pace of inflation picked up, the Bank of Japan decided to push for the ODR hike in February 1973. The yen was floated on February 14 and appreciated substantially. This removed one constraint on monetary policy. However, this produced a political push for stimulus. Again, it was still in the budget process, which was the politically sensitive time of the year to change the interest rate, so that the Bank of Japan tried to raise the reserve ratio rather than the interest rate. The increase in the reserve ratio was decided on March 2, and implemented on March 16. The Policy Board chair noted, "The economy recently has become more active; prices are rising high; and corporate investment has become strong, . . . in order to restrain the lending of financial institutions and manage aggregate demand appropriately, . . . the reserve ratio was decided to be raised, upon approval of the Minister of Finance" (110–11). The budget bill was passed in the House of Representatives on March 13, and Prime Minister Tanaka admitted on March 16 the need for a policy switch to monetary tightening and fiscal adjustment for restraining aggregate demand. This gave an approval for a policy action toward tightening. The ODR hike was decided on March 31 (Saturday) and implemented on April 2, "in order to restraint aggregate demand." In addition, quantitative restraint on lending from city banks was strengthened.

There is not much of a trace of a struggle between the bank and the government prior to February 1973, reading through Bank of Japan (1986). The bank was probably too self-restrained, or gave up on fighting against the Ministry of Finance as well as inflation.

7.2.5 Political Economy

Let us recap the Great Inflation episode. There were two kinds of major mistakes committed in 1972 and 1973: too much easing, especially the June 1972 rate cut; and too little and too late tightening that started in April 1973. Possible reasons for the mistake are as follows:

1. Was the Bank of Japan targeting price stability?
2. Did the Bank of Japan fail to forecast the inflation rate pick up?

3. Did the government put pressure on the Bank of Japan to stimulate the economy?

4. Did the Bank of Japan have courage to disagree?

Answers in short are as follows based on the documents that examined the decision making of the 1970s.

1. No, the Bank of Japan did not put price stability as priority number one.

2. Yes, the Bank of Japan knew prices were rising.

3. Yes, the Bank of Japan was under pressure from the government to lower and keep low the interest rate, and could not resist the pressure.

4. No, the Bank of Japan did not fight back.

Let us elaborate on these points in the following subsections.

Lack of Clear Policy Objective under the Managed Float

Recall that the average inflation rate in Japan during the 1960s was 1.3 percent measured in WPI and 5.7 percent measured in CPI, and the economy did fine, growing at more than 10 percent a year and with current account remaining surplus. Thus, it is not surprising that policymakers in 1971 and 1972 were not alarmed by the CPI inflation rate at around 6 percent, especially when the WPI inflation rate was at around 0 percent. The ODR was lowered four times between October 1970 and July 1971, in the hope of stimulating domestic demand further and averting an appreciation of the yen. These actions were under the Bretton Woods regime, and quite understandable, if maintaining the exchange rate regime was the superior objective.

After the Bretton Woods regime collapsed, the government and the Bank of Japan decided to resist pressure for strong yen appreciation pressure by heavy intervention. However, they underestimated the strength of the Japanese manufacturing industries. By putting a policy objective to moderate yen appreciation, inflation was tolerated.

Lack of Political Independence

The Bank of Japan Law in the 1970s (until 1998) did not give the bank a policy objective of price stability or legal independence from the Ministry of Finance. The objective of the bank in the law was to "maximize the potential of the economy," and the bank policy was under the direction of the minister of finance. On the other hand, the interest rate was supposed to be decided by the Policy Board (in charge of monetary policy) of the Bank of Japan that includes appointments from outside the bank. Theoretically, the Policy Board can make interest rate decisions that may be opposed by the government. The government has the power to replace Policy Board members as well as the governor. In reality, the bank senior executives sought after a tacit prior approval from the government over interest rate decisions, and the Policy Board had become just an automatic approving body of the bank executives. Getting approval of the interest rate changes was tricky. It often depended on the relationship between the governor and the minister of finance, or between the governor and the prime minister

Later in 1998, the Bank of Japan Law was revised. Cargill, Hutchison, and Ito (1997, 2001) describes the history and legal details of the Bank of Japan laws, with a comparison of scores of legal independence between the old and new laws.

What could the central bank have done in the absence of independence? Without independence, the governor could be replaced at the will of the government, and so could members of the Policy Board. It was tradition that the change in monetary policy had to be negotiated with the Ministry of Finance (and prime minister), although by law the Policy Board at the Bank of Japan could decide on its own power. Even lowering the interest rate was difficult because the Ministry of Posts and Telecommunications tended to oppose lowering the deposit rate. Increasing the interest rate, of course, was much harder. Could the governor put his job on the line to disagree with the government? Maybe that was not the Japanese style.

7.3   Monetarist Rhetoric for Independence

One lesson that the Bank of Japan learned from the mistake of creating high inflation in 1973 and 1974 was to enhance de factor independence. To develop more theoretical underpinning for controlling inflation was one lesson, and to assert the danger of inflation, when met with pressure from the government, was another. If the future inflation can be credibly warned with some indicators, that would be persuasive.

The Bank of Japan published a study in 1975 on the importance of monetary aggregate, M2+CDs, in predicting future inflation and output, and announced a new monetary policy procedure in 1978.[9] Beginning in July 1978, the Bank of Japan made it a regular procedure to announce a "forecast" of the growth rate of the average outstanding balance of money (M2+CDs) relative to the same period in the previous year, at the beginning of the quarter. For example, the forecast for monetary growth in the first quarter of 1985 over the first quarter of 1984 was announced at the beginning of the first quarter of 1985. There are two important features for this procedure. First, the forecast included the will of the Bank of Japan: "[T]he policy actions of the Bank of Japan itself are included in the determination of these forecasts, and in this sense the forecasts represent increases in the money supply that the Bank of Japan is willing to permit" (Suzuki

9. See Bank of Japan, (1975, 1988) for their description of the procedure and assessments.

1987, 331)[10] Second, three quarters out of four were already history in the announced annual growth rate. The forecast represents an average of three quarters' realized monetary growth and the current quarter's projected monetary growth. Therefore, the will to change in money is concentrated on the current quarter.

If the monetary growth rate is an indicator for warning future inflation, monetarism rhetoric can be used in the debate against those who argue otherwise. Although the Bank of Japan did not seem to actively use the monetarism rhetoric against political pressure, the monetary indicator may have contributed to confidence among the bank economists internally.

At the time, a monetarist thinking had a strong influence among central bank researchers as well as academics. The Bank of Japan must have thought that there was a high correlation between M2 + CDs and future nominal GNP, and that it could relatively easily control M2 + CDs via monetary policy instruments. Thus, using M2 + CDs as an intermediate target, the bank could target low inflation rate and full-employment output at the same time.

The new procedure had rhetoric of distinct monetarism flavor. In fact, Milton Friedman (1985b) praised that the Bank of Japan followed monetarist rule that he had advocated.[11] By keeping the monetary growth rate steady, say at k percent, then output would be stabilized and the inflation rate would be kept low (near k percent). The Bank of Japan has been the least monetarist central bank in its rhetoric, and the most monetarist in its policy. It has also achieved the best results. However, Suzuki (1985) was more cautious. He branded the Japanese monetary policy of the time as "eclectic gradualism," which is a position between Keynesian fine-tuning and a monetarist k percent-growth rule.

A decade later, Suzuki (1985) observed that the money-supply growth rate was gradually reduced, and so was the nominal-GNP growth rate—but without interfering with the real-GNP growth rate; moreover, fluctuations in the money supply have decreased.[12] This means that the gradual decrease in the money-supply growth rate reduced inflation without reducing economic growth; that is, no trade-off between inflation and potential growth.

Was the successful Bank of Japan policy a k percent rule? According to Ito (1989, 1992), the Bank of Japan did not practice the k percent-growth rule preached by monetarists in the following details of implementation. If the k percent rule had been implemented, then higher-than-forecasted growth in money should have been followed by lower-than-trend growth in

10. See Ito (1989) for more detailed descriptions and examination of the Bank of Japan "forecasts" of monetary aggregate growth rates.

11. Milton Friedman (1985a) was very critical of the Federal Reserve under Chairman Paul Volcker in its implementation of the 1979 policy to target the growth rate of monetary aggregate (M1) in an attempt to fight inflation.

12. See also Cargill, Hutchison, and Ito (1997, ch. 3) for the updated discussion.

money, to maintain the long-run growth rate of k percent by offsetting the upward deviation.

However, it was found that when the actual monetary growth rate deviated from its forecast rate, the target rate of the following period (quarter) was most likely to be adjusted toward the actual growth rate. That is, if the actual growth rate was higher than the target rate in quarter T, the target rate of quarter $T + 1$ was higher than the target rate in quarter T. In addition, the target was unbiased in the sense that the mean of the forecast error was zero—the "forecasts" were rational expectations.

The observed facts are not consistent with monetarist practice. If the k percent rule had been taken seriously, the target rate for quarter $T + 1$ should move in the opposite direction of the deviation so that k percent growth in the money stock could be maintained in the long run. That is, if the actual rate was higher than the target rate in quarter T, then the target rate of quarter $T + 1$ should be *lower* than the target rate in quarter T, in order to compensate for the unexpected increase (see Ito 1989).

Thus, despite praise from monetarists, the monetary policy of the Bank of Japan cannot be judged to have been practicing monetarism as defined by the k percent rule. However, the fact that the inflation rate was brought down gradually without affecting the trend growth rate was praised as a successful implementation of monetary policy with monetary aggregate emphasis (see Suzuki 1985, 1987). It is conceivable that the monetary growth emphasis from 1978 to the mid-1980s gave some weapon of rhetoric in fighting against pressure from the government (see Ito 1992, chapter 5).

The emphasis on monetary growth rate was more or less terminated after 1987, when the monetary aggregate growth rate became much higher than forecasts consistently, most likely from the instability of money demand due to rapid financial liberalization at the time.

7.4   No Great Inflation from 1979 to 1980

7.4.1   Overview

Another oil crisis came at the end of the 1970s. If the oil crisis was a culprit of the Great Inflation earlier, which I have refuted already, the same would happen. If the second oil crisis was managed—and indeed it was the case, shown following—that would strengthen the case that the Bank of Japan made a mistake the first time.

Figure 7.4 shows the interest rates (ODR and call rate) as well as the inflation rates (CPI and WPI) for the period from January 1976 to December 1980. The CPI inflation rate had fallen slowly to the 5 percent level by the end of 1979. The economy was back to normal from 1978 to the beginning of 1979. The economy showed the sign of a boom by the end of 1978. The dollar had a confidence crisis in mid-1978. The dollar decline (yen rise)

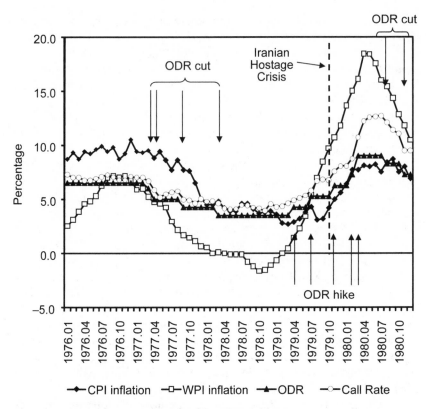

Fig. 7.4   Inflation during second oil crisis of 1979–1980

occurred for several months, but reversed after October 1978. This time, expansionary monetary policy was not taken. The WPI started to rise in the spring of 1979. This time, WPI movement was noted as a good forward indicator of CPI inflation. Although the CPI inflation rate was still stable at the 3 percent range, the ODR was hiked in April 17, 1979, and again in July 24, 1979, as shown in table 7.5. The WPI continued to rise, although CPI was still lagging behind during the summer of 1979. The oil prices started to rise in the summer, and accelerated further after the hostage crisis at the US Embassy in Iran in October 1979.

As the CPI inflation rate started to rise after October 1979, the Bank of Japan decided to raise the ODR further. The ODR was hiked again in November 2, 1979. The inflation rate continued to rise quickly.

The Bank of Japan sought and obtained an approval from the government to raise the policy interest rate, ODR, again in February and March of 1980. This was the first time that the Bank of Japan was able to raise the interest rate during the budget process. The bank could not respond quickly due to the moratorium during the budget process during the Great Inflation

Table 7.5   Official discount rate (%), 1976–1980

Date yyyy.mm.dd	Change	New level
1977.03.12	–0.50	6.00
1977.04.19	–1.00	5.00
1977.09.05	–0.75	4.25
1978.03.16	–0.75	3.50
1979.04.17	**0.75**	**4.25**
1979.07.24	**1.00**	**5.25**
1979.11.02	**1.00**	**6.25**
1980.02.19	**1.00**	**7.25**[a]
1980.03.19	**1.75**	**9.00**[a]
1980.08.20	–0.75	8.25
1980.11.06	–1.00	7.25

[a]ODR increase during budget process.

episode, as described in the preceding section. Thus, the fact it was achieved brought tremendous joy to the Bank of Japan policymakers. The reason that the bank persuaded politicians and the Ministry of Finance was due to the high inflation experience of 1973 and 1974. The bank convinced the ministry and politicians of the importance of timely monetary policy actions. Many scholars, including Cargill, Hutchison, and Ito (1997), describe that the Bank of Japan achieved a de facto independence from the government by 1979.

The CPI inflation rate was kept under 10 percent a year, and the real interest rate (call minus CPI inflation rate) remained positive. The effects of the second oil crisis were over by the end of 1980.

7.4.2   Quick Start of Tightening: April, July, and November 1979

In January 1979, the governor mentioned that no more relaxing of monetary policy would come, and the policy stance was changed to "neutral." In March 1979, OPEC raised oil prices by more than 10 percent. The WPI started to increase sharply from January to March.

With the first sign of the WPI increase, the bank sought to raise the interest rate (Nakagawa 1981, 111–26). First, on March 20, Governor Morinaga mentioned that the Bank of Japan switched to a cautionary stance. In early April, Governor Morinaga told Prime Minister Ohira and the finance minister that the Bank of Japan wanted to raise ODR. They were in favor, but some other cabinet members were not in favor. Prime Minister Ohira understood the Bank of Japan position. The ODR hike was decided on April 16 (and implemented on April 17).

Nakagawa (1981, 116–26) also mentioned that the bank understood that early actions were needed due to lags in the monetary policy process. The WPI rose sharply from March to May 1979, mainly due to energy prices.

Businesses complained of monetary tightening, arguing that monetary policy was ineffective against imported inflation. The Bank of Japan rebutted that the imported price increase would raise the CPI eventually and it would start the process of inflationary spiral, and that real activity was strong. In addition, Germany raised the interest rate at the end of March. The lessons of the 1972 to 1974 episode must have been learned and applied here.

The Economic Planning Agency disagreed with the Bank of Japan judgment, saying there were differences between the first oil crisis and 1979: the labor market was soft, money supply growth rate was lower, corporations were cautious, the utilization rate was lower, the exchange rate was floating, and the government was cautious. The Bank of Japan rebutted that it was worse due to a large amount of government bonds that had been issued between 1973 and 1979, the yen had depreciated, and oil prices began to rise early.

In July 1979, another ODR hike was realized. Nakagawa (1981, 126–34) explained this hike as follows. The OPEC raised the oil prices in July. At the Tokyo summit, restraining demand was agreed. Governor Morinaga met PM Ohira the day before flying to the Bank for International Settlements (BIS) meeting, proposed a rate hike, and got a nod immediately. Business activity was considered to be strong. The government, especially the Ministry of Finance, was cautious, and argued that the timing could be August or September. However, Governor Morinaga had gotten a nod from the prime minister on its personal relationship, and won the debate against the ministries.

The government still insisted that "in order to suppress aggregate demand" was an inappropriate reason for the rate hike. The Bank of Japan explained the action: "[D]emand-supply became tight. . . . Money supply continues to increase and money tightening is not felt. Hence, in order to avoid making imported inflation into home-made inflation, it is absolutely necessary to raise the official discount rate" (Nakagawa 1981, 129). Upon agreement between the Ministry of Finance and the Bank of Japan, it was decided that the ODR be raised on July 23, and implemented July 24.

The ODR was further raised in November 1979. The WPI continued to rise (a large jump in September), the yen depreciated (223 yen/dollar at the end of September and 240 yen/dollar in October). The House of Representatives election took place on October 7. The Liberal Democratic Party lost many seats. Mr Ohira remained as Prime Minister, but only after a fierce fight and split voting in the House of Representatives (the so-called forty-day fight). The government was in chaos. The BOJ determined to raise ODR early, and this time there was no objection from the Ministry of Finance, but the bank waited until the next PM was to be determined (since there was no precedent of changing ODR during a general election or before a new cabinet was formed). The BOJ decided to raise ODR on November 1 and implemented it on November 2.

7.4.3   Interest Rate Hike in February and March 1980

After the November 2 ODR hike, inflation worries continued. On November 4, 1979 the Iranian hostage crisis (the US Embassy was attacked and diplomats were taken hostage and were not released until January 1981) occurred, and the oil market conditions continued to tighten. On December 27, Afghanistan was invaded by the Soviets. As the political events multiplied, the oil prices continued to rise.

Domestic output activity was increasing, and steel and utilities prices were rising. In February 1980, the WPI inflation rate was near 20 percent. In view of these developments, newly appointed Governor Maekawa decided to raise the interest rate. However, this was the time of the budget process in the Diet. The interest rate hike was opposed by the Ministry of Finance on grounds of timing. I conjecture that the BOJ argued against the Ministry of Finance with the logic that the missed opportunity would result in a repeat of the high inflation of 1973 and 1974.

Governor Maekawa met Prime Minister Ohira in early February and requested an ODR hike. Prime Minister Ohira promised a reply within a week. Prime Minister Ohira gave a go-ahead in the replay. On February 18, 1980, it was decided to raise ODR by 1 percent, and was implemented a day later.

On March 18, the ODR was hiked again by 175 basis points. Between February and March, it was observed that the CPI started to rise sharply. The government also changed the priority toward fighting inflation. In the United States, the interest rate was raised to near 20 percent to fight inflation in early 1980.[13]

In the end, Japan fared well in the second oil crisis. The CPI inflation rate never reached 10 percent, and the real interest rate measured by call rate over the CPI inflation rate remained positive. The worst of inflation was over by the summer of 1980, and the ODR was lowered in August and November 1980. By the end of 1980, the WPI inflation rate came down to 10 percent, and the CPI inflation rate decelerated to 7 percent.

"Lessons" of 1973 and 1974 were fully utilized by the BOJ to persuade the Ministry of Finance and the Prime Minister for early actions on monetary tightening. Raising ODR twice during the budget process was a strong indication that the BOJ had achieved de facto independence. However, still it relied on the understanding of the prime minister, and the trust between governor and the prime minister, rather than a legal framework. Credibility and de facto independence seemed to be subject to who was governor and who was prime minister. This precarious relationship would continue until the revision of the Bank of Japan Law in 1998.

---

13. Paul Volcker took over as chairman of the Federal Reserve Board in 1979 to fight inflation with a determined manner.

7.5   Econometric Analysis

7.5.1   Purpose

In the narrative, it was established that the Bank of Japan made a mistake prior to and during the first oil crisis, while the bank skillfully managed the second oil crisis. In this section, econometric analysis will be employed to quantify this narrative. A modified Taylor rule equation during the period when the Bank of Japan was considered to be successful will be estimated, and the fitted values with estimated coefficients from the well-run period will be applied to the presumed-mistake periods.[14]

The Taylor rule (and its variants) should be used with care when it is used as more than a description of the response function of the central bank or for normative interpretations.[15] If it is to be used in the normative spin, it is absolutely important to find a time period when conduct and consequences of monetary policy conduct are impeccable.

In Japan's case, after the mistake of 1972 to 1974, the Bank of Japan gained de facto independence by reminding the government of the sorry episode in 1972 and 1973.[16] The Bank of Japan successfully lowered the inflation rate from 10 percent in 1975 to 2 percent in the early 1980s.[17] Once the inflation rate was brought down to a level near 2 percent, the monetary policy entered a happy state of maintaining a low and stable inflation rate. Monetary policy during the economic boom toward the end of the 1980s was a bit controversial in retrospect, because it allowed an asset price bubble to form, which later burst. However, in the sense of CPI price stability, the second half of the 1980s had a good performance. In the 1990s, there was some question raised by several authors whether loosening of monetary policy after the bubble burst (1991 and 1992) was quick enough to prevent a sharp decline in output after 1993.[18] However, the Bank of Japan had controlled the interest rate in an attempt to stabilize inflation and output until the financial system fell into a serious crisis, with some failure of medium-size regional bank, and the official discount rate being lowered to 0.5 percent in September 1995. Soon after the interest rate was lowered to 0.5 percent in September 1995, the Bank of Japan lost its grip on infla-

---

14. For Taylor rule, see Clarida, Galí, and Gertler (1999) and Taylor (1999), to name a few. See Jinushi, Kuroki, and Miyao (2000); Kuttner and Posen (2004); and Ahearne et al. (2002) for application of the Taylor rule to the Japanese case.

15. Taylor (2009, FAQ section) insists that the Taylor rule is normative from the beginning. Others, including Orphanides (2003a, 2003b, 2003c); Clarida, Galí, and Gertler (1998, 1999); and Ito and Mishkin (2006) are rather cautious on the normative interpretation.

16. See Cargill, Hutchison, and Ito (1997) for such an interpretation.

17. See, for example, Friedman (1985b) and Ito (1992, ch. 5).

18. See Ahearne (2002); Clouse et al. (2000); Ito and Mishkin (2006); Jinushi, Kuroki, and Miyao (2000); Kuttner and Posen (2004) for the discussion of Japan's monetary policy in the early to mid-1990s.

tion, partly due to the zero bound of the nominal interest rate and partly due to near deflation.

With the abovementioned discussions in mind, I take the period from January 1982 to December 1995 as a benchmark period that can be regarded as a successful period in CPI inflation stability. The benchmark Taylor rule will be estimated for this period.

Several provisos should be mentioned at this point. First, the policy rate was the official discount rate (ODR), and many market interest rates were tied to the ODR. Second, there were monetary policy measures other than the policy rate. The so-called "window guidance"—constraints on bank lending by moral suasion—was playing a major role. The reserve requirement was also used. Hence, the interest rate was not the only variable that represented monetary policy. Third, many market infrastructures and economic structures went through changes during the 1970s and 1980s. Financial liberalization particularly progressed in the second half of the 1980s. Attempts are made to take into account these issues, but treatment is admittedly far from perfect.

After examining the estimated coefficients and the deviations of fitted value from actual value within the sample, the out-of-sample backcasting will be conducted to see whether the Bank of Japan would have behaved differently in the 1970s. In particular, the mistake of monetary policy creating the Great Inflation of 1972 to 1974 will be examined in light of the estimated Taylor rule of 1982 to 1995. This exercise will answer the following question: Suppose that the Bank of Japan in 1972 to 1974 (the "mistake" years) had reacted to macro variables in the manner they had in 1982 to 1995. How much would the counterfactual interest rate have been hiked compared to the actual interest rate? If it could be shown that the counterfactual interest rate would have been much higher than actual, then the prudent Bank of Japan à la 1982 to 1995 would have mitigated the inflation problem in 1972 to 1974.

The typical Taylor rule equation is as follows:

$$i_t = r^f + \pi_t + \beta_\pi \cdot (\pi_t - \pi^*) + \beta_y \cdot (y_t - y^*),$$

where i_t denotes the nominal policy interest rate, r^f the natural real interest rate, π^* the target inflation rate, π_t is the inflation rate, and $y_t - y^*$ is the output gap. In the original Taylor (1993), both β were assumed to be 0.5, and r^f and π^* were both assumed to be 2. Here, as in the literature, β will be estimated using data in the benchmark period. In the implementation of estimating this equation, the following specification is used:

$$i_t - \pi_t = r^f + \beta_\pi \cdot (\pi_t - \pi^*) + \beta_y \cdot (y_t - y^*) + \varepsilon_y.$$

The left-hand side becomes the real interest rate at time t. There are several departures from the usual Taylor rule regression in the literature. First, since the decision making is done on a monthly basis (rarely two policy rate changes in the same month), a monthly model is highly recommended. The GDP gap will not be available on the monthly basis, so that the industrial production will be used as a measure of output. The industrial production gap will be defined and used in place of GDP. Second, efforts will be made to obtain data that were available at the time of decision making, although the data used in the regression are not exactly the real time data. Third, since the equilibrium real rate r^f is difficult to calculate, the equilibrium nominal rate is to be estimated as a constant term of the regression model.

7.5.2   Data

Several variables have to be carefully defined for the Taylor-rule type econometric application. First, the output gap (output deviation from its potential) and inflation gap (inflation deviation from its target) have to be defined in the spirit of "real-time data"—that is, data that were known at the time the policy was decided. The importance of using real-time data is particularly emphasized by Orphanides (2003a, 2003b, 2003c). For example, use of the original data at time t should be used instead of later revisions, including base year change or preliminary to final. Second, any detrending, or estimating and taking out potential output, should be carried out with the data only up to time t. Third, since data collection and data disclosure takes time, at the time of monetary policy decision in month t, available data of Industrial Production and CPI are not those of month t, but either month $t - 1$ or even $t - 2$.[19] Although official data may be available only for $t - 2$, various other economic variables can be used to guess what would be announced later.[20] So, we assume that the data that the Bank of Japan knows at month t would be Industrial Production and CPI of month $t - 1$.

Because we attempt to build a monthly model, GDP cannot be used as a variable for output gap. In place of GDP, Industrial Production will be used. The base year of Industrial Production is changed every five years. If we had picked up data from the present database, it would be a series of current estimation methods, and different from the variable that was known at the time of decision making in the 1970s to the 1990s. Therefore, the original Industrial Production data set is collected from historical series that were available at the time of decision making.[21] For the output gap

19. The Policy Board Meetings (in charge of monetary policy decisions) became regularly scheduled meetings (with the meeting dates preannounced) under the revised Bank of Japan Law, which took effect in April 1998. Earlier, monetary policy meetings were called upon when needed. However, we assume that even without a prescheduled meeting, the bank staff makes the decision to call a meeting or not at least every month.

20. The CPI of month t becomes available in month $t + 2$. One option is to use the CPI inflation rate on the right-hand side of the variable of two months ago. However, with information of CPI of Tokyo Area, which is announced in month $t + 1$, one can guess the national CPI with some accuracy before their disclosure. Therefore, the CPI on the right-hand side is the inflation rate of $t + 1$.

21. Admittedly, this is not "genuine" real-time data, since original documents, such as every issue of the *Monthly Report* of the Bank of Japan, are not checked against the old database. The minutes of the monetary policy meetings were not kept before 1998.

$y_t - y^*$, a deviation of the Industrial Production from its linear trend, which is known at time t, is used.[22] Obviously the future path of industrial production is not known, and the trend must be estimated using only the past date at the time of decision making. The industrial production gap was estimated from January 1971 to December 2008.

For the inflation measure (π), the year-on-year change of headline CPI is used.[23] The base year of the CPI and weights of goods and services in the consumption basket are revised every five years in Japan. As CPI of a new base year becomes available, the Bank of Japan and the government starts using the new CPI for their decision making. The real-time CPI is constructed by choosing the headline CPI of the base year that was in place.[24]

The target inflation rate is also difficult to determine. The inflation rate during the 1960s was much higher than the later period. It is assumed that the target inflation rate, π^* was 4 percent from January 1971 to December 1977. As the Bank of Japan became serious in lowering the inflation rate in 1978 by adopting the monetary aggregate "forecast" (see Ito 1989), it is assumed that the target rate was gradually (1/24 percentage point a month) lowered from 4 percent in December 1977 to 2 percent by December 1981. The target inflation rate was again lowered gradually from 2 percent in December 1992 to 1 percent in December 1998, and has stayed at 1 percent since then.

7.5.3   Estimation

Based on the previous discussion, the equation to be estimated is the following:

22. The output gap is the residual in the log-linear trend regression using data of the preceding ten years $[t - 119, t]$. Extract the residual at t. By multiplying by 100, the percentage deviation from the trend line is stored. Then, repeat the procedure (i.e., rolling regression) from January 1971 to December 2008.

23. The headline inflation was most often mentioned in the 1970s, 1980s, and 1990s. When the exit condition from quantitative easing was mentioned in March 2001, it was defined in the CPI (excluding fresh food, but including energy prices). Since the 2000s are not a period for analysis in this chapter, the headline CPI is used throughout. Otherwise the inflation rate to be analyzed should be switched from headline inflation to CPI, excluding food, of May 2001 with the change in the base year as well. Another potential adjustment that is ignored in this chapter is the introduction of consumption tax (a form of value added tax, or VAT) in April 1989 and tax rate increase in April 1997. When the 3 percent consumption tax was introduced in April 1989, some of excise and other indirect taxes were abolished, so that the net effect on the consumer prices were much less than 3 percent. Ito and Mishkin (2006) argued that the year-on-year inflation rate due to consumption tax was 1.3 percent for April 1989 to March 1990, and 1.6 percent for April 1997 to March 1998. However, no adjustment is made in this chapter for consumption tax increases, on the assumption that the Bank of Japan was alert on inflation even due to the consumption tax increases, as inflation due to consumption tax increases may trigger second round inflation.

24. As in Industrial Production, what we collected from old base-year CPI may not be genuine real-time CPI. Original documents at the time of monetary policy board meeting were not checked against our data. Minutes were not kept, and often the meeting was called suddenly. In this sense, what we call real-time data here are what we believe to the best approximation of the real-time data.

Table 7.6   **Monthly Taylor rule, 1982–1995**

	Equation (1): Sample: 1982M01 1995M12			
	Coefficient	Std. error	t-statistic	Prob.
C	3.723	0.130	28.54	0.000
$\pi_t - \pi_t^*$	0.336	0.165	2.03	0.044
$y_t - y_t^*$	0.127	0.021	5.97	0.000
R^2	0.366	Mean dependent var.		3.333851

(1) $$i_t - \pi_{t-1} = c + \beta_\pi \cdot (\pi_{t-1} - \pi_t^*) + \beta_y \cdot (y_{t-1} - y_t^*) + \varepsilon_t,$$

where the constant term c will be interpreted as the long-run real interest rate. The inflation and industrial production are lagged once due to observation lag for the central bank. Since the inflation rate is defined as year-on-year, there will be serial correlation in the residuals. generalized methods of moments (GMM) is used to estimate equation (1).[25]

The sample period of estimation is from January 1982 to December 1995. The choice of this time period is discussed earlier in this section.

Table 7.6 shows the estimation results. Both inflation gap and output gap have statistically significant estimates with correct sign. The magnitude of coefficients are smaller than the original Taylor assumption of 0.5. If the inflation rate rises 1 percentage point, the nominal interest rate rises 1.34 percentage points, since the "real" interest rate responds by 0.34 percentage point. If the output gap moves positively (overheating) by 1 percentage point, then the nominal interest rate rises by 0.127 percent, assuming no change in the inflation rate.

Figure 7.5 shows the actual and fitted values in the sample period, and their difference, the residual of the equation. Assuming that the fitted value can be interpreted as a desirable path, the figure suggests the following interpretation: the monetary policy was too tight (actual > fitted) in 1985 and 1986, while the monetary policy was too loose in 1988 and 1989. The two years of 1988 and 1989 are known to be the last stage of the real estate bubble. Several authors have suggested that the Bank of Japan made a mistake in these years by allowing the bubble to form, thus the asset prices should have been included in deciding monetary policy. (See Okina and Shiratsuka 2002, 2004). However, as figure 7.5 suggests, even a plain CPI Taylor rule would have flagged loose monetary policy as being too loose in these two years.

---

25. For the instruments, c, $\pi_{t-2} - \pi^*$, $y_{t-2} - y^*$, $dyen_{t-1}$, $doil_{t-1}$ are used, where $dyen_t$ is the year-on-year change of the yen/dollar rate in month t and $doil_t$ is the year-on-year change of the oil prices in month t.

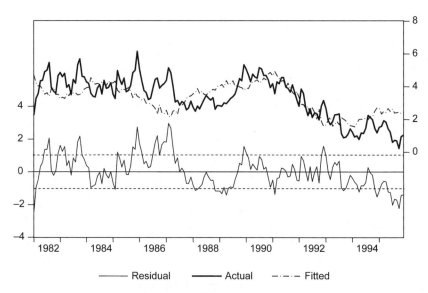

Fig. 7.5   Actual value, fitted value, and residual: call $- \pi_{t-1}$

7.5.4   Out of Sample Backcasting

Now that we have reasonable estimates of the modified Taylor rule for the period in which the monetary policy can be regarded as desirable on average, we can evaluate the monetary policy of other periods in question. We are particularly interested in the "mistake" in the early 1970s, when the inflation rate rose above 20 percent. Using the estimated coefficients of table 7.6, and then plugging in the data of 1972, we obtain the counterfactual call rate during the period in question.[26] Figure 7.6 shows the actual and counterfactual nominal call rate. Obviously, the counterfactual nominal rate (i.e., the desirable call rate) would have been much higher than the actual call rate. The desirable interest rate would have been around 36 percent when the actual rate was 12 percent. This exercise shows numerically what we have already established in the narrative. In the year after the collapse of the Bretton Woods system, monetary policy made a mistake. When the first oil crisis came, the inflation rate was already high. With the additional shock of oil price increases, the inflation rate rose sharply, exceeding 20 percent. The magnitude of the mistake was more than 20 percentage points in the call rate.

One should be careful in interpreting these findings. The path of the counterfactual call rate is not a desirable path. If the desirable path of 1972 had

26. One obtains counterfactual "real" interest rate by the procedure, and then by adding the inflation rate, the counterfactual nominal interest rate is obtained.

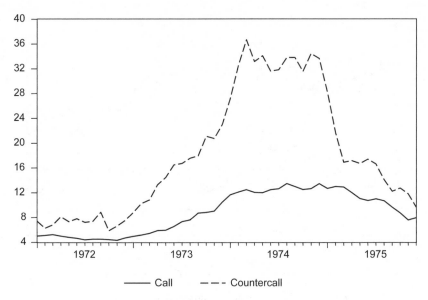

Fig. 7.6   Counterfactual 1972–1975

been implemented, then the actual inflation rate would have been lower, so that the interest rate in 1973 would not have been so high. The desirable rate should be interpreted as the rate that, given the actual history up to $t-1$, would have been the desirable call rate in month t.

Figure 7.7 shows the similarly generated desirable rate for the period of 1978 to 1982, the period that encompasses the second oil crisis. This shows that the counterfactual interest rate was not much different (up to 1.5 percentage points) from the actual rate in 1979 to 1980, the oil crisis years. This confirms the narrative that the second oil crisis was handled much better than the first one.

7.6   Concluding Remarks

This chapter investigated the great inflation of Japan, 1973 to 1974, when the CPI inflation rate reached almost 30 percent a year, and the WPI inflation rate higher than that. The period coincided with the first oil crisis. Close examinations revealed that easing in 1971 and 1972 went too far, stimulating the economy too much, and tightening in 1973 came too little, too late. The CPI inflation rate was already above 10 percent when the Middle East War broke out in October 1973. The oil price increase and the sense of panic for not obtaining the energy resources caused further increases in prices.

The reasons for too much easing and too little tightening from 1971 to 1973 include several political economy reasons as well as economic

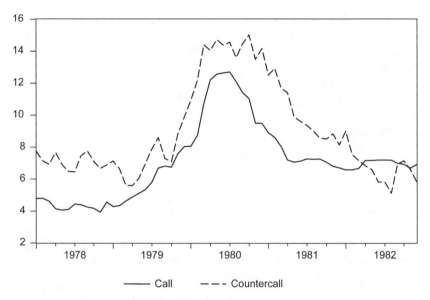

Call ——— **Countercall** — — -

Fig. 7.7   Counterfactual 1978–1982

reasons. First, too much attention and efforts were devoted to prevent the yen appreciation under the Smithsonian regime. Some politicians openly voiced preference to inflation over nominal appreciation of the yen. Second, the Bank of Japan was not independent from the government. The prime minister exerted pressure on the bank to lower the interest rate or to prevent the interest rate hike. The timing of implementation was also influenced by the political agenda and schedule. It was commonly thought that the interest rate could not be changed during the budget discussion in the Diet; that is, December to March. Third, the Bank of Japan did not fight the government enough to push for the right decisions. Self-restraints were applied not to cause conflict against the Ministry of Finance.

The second oil crisis was handled much better than the great inflation experience. The CPI remained lower than 10 percent, and the real interest rate was kept positive. The interest rate was raised as soon as the WPI started to increase in 1978. The ODR was raised even when the budget was still being discussed in the Diet. The bank gained de facto independence using the logic that without swift actions, the mistake of high inflation would be repeated. Prime Minister Ohira was also quite respectful to Governor Maekawa for the bank's judgment and decisions.

The modified (monthly) Taylor rule was specified and estimated using the data of the period from January 1982 to December 1995, a period of relative success in achieving low and stable inflation rate. Then the estimate coefficients of the equation were applied to the data of the mistake period, 1972 to 1975. The desirable interest rate would have been some 20 percentage points higher than the actual rate. When the same procedure was applied to the second oil crisis period, 1978 to 1982, then it was shown that the desirable rate would not have been much different from the actual rate. The exercise confirms the conclusion of the narrative. The roots of the Great Inflation can be found well before the onset of the first oil crisis, which took place in October 1973. The modeling analysis implies that the interest rate was way too low before and after October 1973.

References

Ahearne, Alan, Joseph Gagnon, Jane Haltmaier, and Steve Kamin. 2002. "Preventing Deflation: Lessons from Japan's Experience in the 1990s." Board of Governors of the Federal Reserve System, International Finance Discussion Papers, no. 729.
Bank of Japan. 1975. "On the Importance of Money Supply in Japan." [In Japanese.] *Monthly Review, Research and Statistics Bureau* July:1–11.
———. 1986. *Nihon Ginko Hyakunenshi [One-Hundred Year History of the Bank of Japan,* volume 6]. Tokyo: Bank of Japan.
———. 1988. "On the Recent Behavior of the Money Supply." [In Japanese.] *Monthly Review, Research and Statistics Bureau* February (1988): 1–24.
Cargill, Thomas F., Michael M. Hutchison, and Takatoshi Ito. 1997. *The Political Economy of Japanese Monetary Policy.* Cambridge, MA: MIT Press.
———. 2001. *Financial Policy and Central Banking in Japan.* Cambridge, MA: MIT Press.
Clarida, Richard, Jordi Galí, and Mark Gertler. 1998. "Monetary Policy Rules in Practice: Some International Evidence." *European Economic Review* 42:1033–67.
———. 1999. "The Science of Monetary Policy: A New-Keynesian Perspective." *Journal of Economic Literature* 37:1661–707.
Clouse, James, Dale Henderson, Athanasios Orphanides, David Small, Peter Orphanides, and Peter Tinsley. 2000. "Monetary Policy When the Nominal Short-Term Interest Rate is Zero." Finance and Economics Discussion Series, 2000-51. Washington, DC: Board of Governors of the Federal Reserve System.
Friedman, Milton. 1985a. "The Fed's Monetarism Was Never Anything But Rhetoric." Letters to the Editor, *Wall Street Journal,* December 18.
———. 1985b. "Monetarism in Rhetoric and in Practice." In *Monetary Policy in Our Times,* edited by Albert Ando, Hidekazu Eguchi, Roger Farmer, and Yoshio Suzuki, 15–28. Cambridge, MA: MIT Press.
Hetzel, Robert L. 1999. "Japanese Monetary Policy: A Quantity Theory Perspective." *Federal Reserve Bank of Richmond Economic Quarterly* 85 (Winter): 1–25.
Ito, Takatoshi. 1989. "Is the Bank of Japan a Closet Monetarism? Monetary Targeting in Japan, 1978–1988." NBER Working Paper no. 2879. Cambridge, MA: National Bureau of Economic Research.
———. 1992. *The Japanese Economy.* Cambridge, MA: MIT Press.
———. 1997. "The Long-Run Purchasing Power Parity for the Yen: Historical Overview." *Journal of the Japanese and International Economies* 11:502–21.

Ito, Takatoshi, and Frederic S. Mishkin. 2006. "Two Decades of Japanese Monetary Policy and the Deflation Problem." In *Monetary Policy with Very Low Inflation in the Pacific Rim,* edited by T. Ito and A. Rose, 131–93. Chicago: University of Chicago Press.

Jinushi, Toshiki, Yoshihiro Kuroki, and Ryuzo Miyao. 2000. "Monetary Policy in Japan since the Late 1980s: Delayed Policy Actions and Some Explanations." In *Japan's Financial Crisis and Its Parallels to US Experience,* edited by Mikitani and Posen, 115–48. Washington, DC: Institute for International Economics.

Komiya, Ryutaro. 1976. "Reasons for Inflation in 1973–74." [Original in Japanese: "The Showa 48–49 Inflation on Genin."] University of Tokyo, *Keizaigaku Ronshu* 42 (1): 2–40.

———. 1988. *The Japanese Economy: Trade, Industry, and Government.* Tokyo: University of Tokyo Press.

Komiya, Ryutaro, and Kazuo Yasui. 1984. "Japan's Macroeconomic Performance since the First Oil Crisis: Review and Appraisal." *Carnegie-Rochester Conference Series on Public Policy* 20:69–114.

Kuttner, Kenneth N., and Adam S. Posen. 2004. "The Difficulty of Discerning What's Too Tight: Taylor Rules and Japanese Monetary Policy." *North American Journal of Economics and Finance* 15:53–74.

Nakagawa, Yukitsugu. 1981. *On Monetary Policy: Personal Experience at the Bank of Japan.* [Original in Japanese: *Taikenteki Kinyu Seisaku Ron: Nichigin no Mado kara.*] Tokyo: Nihon Keizai Shinbunsha.

Oi, Hiroyuki, Shigenori Shiratsuka, and Toyoichiro Shirota. 2004. "On Long-Run Monetary Neutrality in Japan." Institute for Monetary and Economic Studies, Bank of Japan, *Monetary and Ecnomic Studies* 22 (3): 79–113.

Okina, Kunio, and Shigenori Shiratsuka. 2002. "Asset Price Bubbles, Price Stability, and Monetary Policy: Japan's Experience." Bank of Japan, *Monetary and Economic Studies* October:35–76.

———. 2004. "Policy Commitment and Expectation Formation: Japan's Experience under Zero Interest Rates." *North American Journal of Economics and Finance* 15:75–100.

Orphanides, Athanasios. 2003a. "Historical Monetary Policy Analysis and the Taylor Rule." *Journal of Monetary Economics* 50:983–1022.

———. 2003b. "Monetary Policy Evaluation with Noisy Information." *Journal of Monetary Economics* 50:605–31.

———. 2003c. "The Quest for Prosperity without Inflation." *Journal of Monetary Economics* 50:633–63.

Shizume, Masato. 2002. "Economic Developments and Monetary Policy Responses in Interwar Japan: Evaluation Based on the Taylor Rule." Bank of Japan, *Monetary and Economic Studies* 20 (3): 77–116.

Suzuki, Yoshio. 1985. "Japan's Monetary Policy over the Past 10 Years." Bank of Japan, *Monetary and Economic Studies* 3 (2): 1–10.

———, ed. 1987. *The Japanese Financial System.* Clarendon: Oxford University Press.

Taylor, John B. 1993. "Discretion versus Policy Rules in Practice." *Carnegie-Rochester Conference Series on Public Policy* 39:195–214.

———. 1999. "A Historical Analysis of Monetary Policy Rules." In *Monetary Policy Rules,* edited by J. B. Taylor, 319–44. Chicago: University of Chicago Press.

———. 2009. *Getting off Track: How Government Actions and Interventions Caused, Prolonged, and Worsened the Financial Crisis.* Stanford: Hoover Press.

Comment   Frederic S. Mishkin

Takatoshi Ito has written a very interesting and useful account of the Great Inflation of 1973 to 1974 in Japan and the role that the Bank of Japan played in generating it. The story he tells is that the Bank of Japan initially eased monetary policy too far in 1972 in the face of a stronger economy by lowering the official discount rate (ODR), its policy interest rate, and then did not tighten monetary policy sufficiently by raising the ODR in 1973 to contain rapidly rising inflation. The result was that in the aftermath of the oil-price shock that sharply raised energy prices toward the end of 1973, CPI inflation shot up to a peak of over 20 percent in 1974, well above what other advanced countries were experiencing.

In contrast, when the second oil-price shock struck in 1979, the rise in inflation was very moderate, staying below 10 percent, well below what countries like the United States experienced. In contrast to the 1973 to 1974 episode, the Bank of Japan did not pursue easy monetary policy before the second oil-price shock and started hiking the ODR before the oil-price shock hit in response to a strong economy. Then with the oil-price shock that again sharply raised energy prices in the fall of 1979, the Bank of Japan tightened monetary policy aggressively by raising the ODR, thereby ensuring that another Great Inflation did not occur.

Ito's chapter also explains why the Bank of Japan had such different policies in these two episodes that led to such different outcomes. He documents that the Bank of Japan eased monetary policy in 1972 because it underestimated the strength of the economy, but more importantly because it wanted to lower interest rates to prevent the yen from appreciating. The Bank of Japan was then slow to raise the ODR in 1973 because of political pressure from the Ministry of Finance and the prime minister. Then when it began to raise the ODR after the first oil-price shock occurred, it had gotten behind the curve and instead of real interest rising as inflation rose, it fell dramatically. The result was the Great Inflation of 1973 to 1974.

In contrast, the Bank of Japan seemed to learn a lesson from the Great Inflation episode and was able to tighten monetary policy even before the second oil-price shock hit, and then it raised interest rates aggressively once the second oil-price shock occurred because the Bank of Japan had obtained de facto independence and was now focused on achieving price stability.

Ito's account of Japanese monetary policy during the 1970s is important

Frederic S. Mishkin is the Alfred Lerner Professor of Banking and Financial Institutions at the Graduate School of Business, Columbia University, and a research associate of the National Bureau of Economic Reserarch

The views expressed here are my own and are not necessarily those of Columbia University or the National Bureau of Economic Research. For acknowledgments, sources of research support, and disclosure of the author's material financial relationships, if any, please see http://www.nber.org/chapters/c9167.ack.

because it provides several key lessons about how monetary policy should be conducted to control inflation. Here I want to discuss four general lessons for monetary policy that I derive from his analysis: (a) oil-price shocks that sharply raise energy prices do not necessarily lead to great inflations; (b) an excessive focus on stabilizing the foreign exchange rate can have high costs; (c) a key source of the time-inconsistency problem is the political process, and so central bank independence is important; and (d) communication strategy is an important element of inflation control.

Oil-Price Shocks That Sharply Raise Energy Prices Do Not Necessarily Lead to Great Inflations

A common view that has been expressed about the Great Inflation in the United States is that the oil-price shocks of 1973 and 1979 played an important role in producing the very high inflation rates during this period. Ito's chapter shows that the importance of oil-price shocks in inflation outcomes is much less than this view might indicate. What the Japanese experience shows is that oil-price shocks that sharply raise energy prices do not lead to high inflation unless the monetary authorities are willing to tolerate high inflation and thus have little credibility as inflation fighters. Ito's account illustrates that the Bank of Japan (BOJ) was not focused on controlling inflation before the first oil-price shock hit. It had eased monetary policy earlier, despite a strengthening economy and rising inflation, and then was reluctant to tighten monetary policy when the oil-price shock hit.

Given this monetary policy stance, it is no surprise that monetary policy credibility to control inflation was very low when the oil-price shock struck. In such an environment, a sharp rise in energy prices would lead to a sharp rise in inflation expectations, which would add to the direct effects of the oil-price rise on inflation, thus causing inflation to sharply accelerate. Indeed, the fact that Japan's inflation rate rose more rapidly in response to the rise in energy prices than occurred in other advanced economies is well explained by the particularly low credibility of the BOJ.

Ito's evidence from his estimates of a Japanese Taylor rule drives this point home. Using a Taylor rule whose parameters were estimated over the low and stable inflation period from 1982 to 1995, he finds that the policy interest rate should have been far higher than it actually was during the Great Inflation episode, given the actual outcomes on inflation and the output gap. Indeed, he finds that the magnitude of the monetary policy mistake was huge: 20 percentage points. Although drawing conclusions from estimated Taylor rules has some tricky elements, the magnitude of estimates of the deviation from his estimated Taylor rule is so large that it clearly demonstrates Ito's point that monetary policy was far too easy during the Great Inflation period and must be seen as the reason why inflation went to such high levels.

In contrast, by 1979, the Bank of Japan, with support from the Japanese prime minister, made a much stronger commitment to achieving price stability. They displayed this both with rhetoric (which will be discussed later) and through actions. The BOJ tightened monetary policy before the second oil-price shock to contain inflation, and then when the oil-price shock occurred, raised interest rates aggressively. With stronger credibility as an inflation fighter, the response of expected inflation to the rise in energy prices was muted, and the result was that the rise in inflation was quite limited.

The conclusion from the Japanese inflation experience with these two oil-price shocks is an important one. Clearly, oil-price shocks that sharply raise energy prices do not necessarily lead to great inflations. If the monetary authority has credibility to keep inflation under control, then sharp rises in energy prices do not produce very high inflation. This illustrates why it is so important for central banks to have a clear-cut commitment to price stability: such a commitment, along with actions consistent with it, produces far better inflation outcomes. We saw this principle operating in the United States during the most recent oil-price shock that caused energy prices to surge in 2008. Despite the oil-price shock, core inflation rose very little, even when the Federal Reserve was lowering interest rates to cope with the contractionary shock resulting from the financial crisis that began during the summer of 2007. Not only does a commitment to and credibility for inflation control have the benefit of producing better inflation outcomes, but it also provides the monetary authorities with increased flexibility to use monetary policy to respond to negative aggregate demand shocks.

Excessive Focus on Stabilizing the Foreign Exchange Rate Is a Mistake

Ito's chapter points out that a major reason why monetary policy was too easy during the first oil-price shock episode was because the Japanese government and the BOJ did not want to allow the yen to appreciate further. The result was a surge in inflation. The focus on the exchange rate therefore led to an undesirable inflation outcome.

An excessive focus on the exchange rate can also cause monetary policy to be too tight when the economy is hit by a contractionary shock. One striking example occurred in Chile in 1998, when the Chilean central bank was reluctant to ease monetary policy and let the exchange rate depreciate in order to cushion the effects of substantial negative terms of trade shock (Mishkin and Savastano 2000). Instead, the central bank raised interest rates and even narrowed the exchange rate band. The excessive focus on the stabilizing the exchange rate thus lead to contractionary monetary policy when it needed expansionary to offset the contractionary effects of the negative terms of trade shock. The result was that inflation fell below the Banco Central de Chile's inflation objective and the economy went into a recession.

The lesson from the Japanese, as well as the Chilean, experience indicates that an excessive focus on the exchange rate can lead to poor monetary policy outcomes. Excessive focus on stabilizing exchange rates can lead to serious monetary policy mistakes.

A Key Source of the Time-Inconsistency Problems Is the Political Process, so Central Bank Independence Is Important

The classic model of time-inconsistency in monetary policy, Barro and Gordon (1983), has central banks deviating from the optimal plan and pursuing inflationary monetary policy because the central bank is aiming for an unemployment target below the natural rate. Because central banks can avoid falling into the time-inconsistency trap by just recognizing that it exists, doubts have been whether the time-inconsistency is an important problem for monetary policy.

The story that Ito tells about the Great Inflation period in Japan indicates that political pressure on the BOJ was an important reason why it decided to ease monetary policy in 1972 before the first oil-price shock and then did not tighten monetary policy when it was needed in 1973. As discussed in the chapter, Prime Minister Sato met with Governor Sasaki of the BOJ in May of 1972 and pressured him to lower the policy rate to prevent an appreciation of the yen. Then, when Prime Minister Tanaka came into power with a goal of pursuing large public work projects, he was opposed to interest rate hikes. In addition, the BOJ felt that it could not raise interest rates during the budget process and so delayed raising the policy rate until April of 1973. Ito tells us that the Bank of Japan was unable to resist political pressure to keep interest rates low.

The Japanese experience provides support for the view that it is the political process that leads to the time-inconsistency problem and overly expansionary monetary policy. Hence, there is still a strong case for the time-inconsistency problem to be an important source of overly expansionary monetary policy that leads to high inflation. This evidence provides support for a position that I have argued elsewhere (Mishkin 2000): the source of the time-inconsistency problem is likely to be in the poltical process and not inside the central bank itself.

Ito argues that the reason why political pressure was so effective during the Great Inflation period was that the BOJ had very little independence at the time. The governor of the BOJ could be replaced at the will of the government and there was a tradition that any change in monetary policy had to be negotiated with the Ministry of Finance and the prime minister. The Great Inflation episode thus provides a strong case for central bank independence to alleviate the time-inconsistency problem.

Ito does make the claim that the better performance of the BOJ during the second oil-price shock was due to the Bank of Japan having been given de facto independence. I am somewhat skeptical that this is the best way to describe what in fact had occurred. There was no change in the Bank of Japan Act and it was not until 1998 that a new Bank of Japan Act granted the BOJ substantially more independence. What enabled the BOJ to pursue tighter monetary policy was the support that Prime Minister Ohira gave to the BOJ to pursue this policy. In one sense we could think of this support as increasing the BOJ's independence to pursue the monetary policy that it thought was necessary, but the ability of the BOJ to conduct this policy was still dependent on personalities. A different prime minister might not have been as supportive of the BOJ, and in that case the BOJ's "independence" would have evaporated.

Communication Strategy Is an Important Element of Inflation Control

The chapter also discusses the BOJ's use of monetarist rhetoric to provide a better theoretical underpinning for inflation control after the Great Inflation episode in 1978. Specifically, the BOJ had turned to announcing a "forecast" of the growth rate of the money supply (M2 + CDs). It is not clear how important this monetarist rhetoric was in helping the BOJ to resist political pressure and thereby enhance its ability to pursue an independent monetary policy to control inflation. Furthermore, as Ito points out, the BOJ did not engage in a monetarist k percent rule along monetarist lines. However, the increased focus of the BOJ on rhetoric to emphasize the importance of controlling inflation might have helped its case with politicians to focus on inflation control. What is clear is that the government was much more supportive of BOJ monetary policy tightening to control inflation in the 1979 to 1980 period. There is a good case to be made that the BOJ's communication strategy helped it to pursue anti-inflationary monetary policy with much success during this period. The Japanese experience in that period was supportive of an important principle of monetary policymaking, which is that communication strategy is an important element of inflation control.

Conclusion

Takatoshi Ito's chapter on the Japanese monetary policy and the Great Inflation is well worth reading. It provides an important service because it teaches us valuable lessons that are applicable to how monetary policy should be conducted, not only in Japan, but also everywhere else.

References

Barro, Robert J., and David B. Gordon. 1983. "A Positive Theory of Monetary Policy in a Natural Rate Model." *Journal of Political Economy* 91 (4): 589–610.
Mishkin, Frederic S. 2000. "What Should Central Banks Do?" *Federal Reserve Bank of St. Louis Review* 82 (6): 1–13.
Mishkin, Frederic S., and Miguel Savastano. 2001. "Monetary Policy Strategies for Latin America." *Journal of Development Economics* 66 (2): 415–44.

The Great Inflation in the United States and the United Kingdom
Reconciling Policy Decisions and Data Outcomes

Riccardo DiCecio and Edward Nelson

8.1 Introduction

In this chapter we study the Great Inflation in both the United States and the United Kingdom. Our concentration on more than one country reflects our view that a sound explanation should account for the experience of the Great Inflation both in the United States and beyond. We emphasize further that an explanation for the Great Inflation should be consistent with both the data and what we know about the views that guided policymakers.

Figure 8.1 plots four-quarter inflation for the United Kingdom using the Retail Price Index (RPI), and four-quarter US inflation using the Consumer Price Index (CPI). The peaks in inflation in the mid-1970s and 1980 are over 20 percent in the United Kingdom, far higher than the corresponding US peaks. On the other hand, the ups and downs do resemble those in the United States; if we plotted the UK series alone and removed the numbering from

Riccardo DiCecio is an economist and special assistant to the president of the Federal Reserve Bank of St. Louis. Edward Nelson is chief of the Monetary Studies Section of the Federal Reserve Board.

An earlier version of this chapter was presented at the NBER Great Inflation conference, Woodstock, Vermont, September 25–27, 2008. We thank Frank Smets and Rafael Wouters for providing the estimation code for Smets and Wouters (2007). We are grateful to Michael Bordo and Athanasios Orphanides (the conference organizers and volume editors), Matthew Shapiro (our discussant), and conference and preconference attendees for comments on the previous versions of this chapter. We are also indebted to Leon Berkelmans, Christopher Erceg, Jesper Lindé, Andrew Levin, Christopher Neely, Ricardo Nunes, Christina Romer, David Wheelock, seminar participants at the Federal Reserve Board, and an anonymous referee for many useful suggestions. Charles Gascon, Luke Shimek, and Faith Weller provided research assistance. The views expressed in this chapter are those of the authors and should not be interpreted as those of the Federal Reserve Bank of St. Louis, the Federal Reserve System, or the Board of Governors. For acknowledgments, sources of research support, and disclosure of the authors' material financial relationships, if any, please see http://www.nber.org/chapters/c9172.ack.

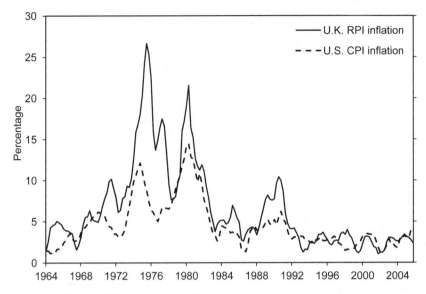

Fig. 8.1   UK and US four-quarter inflation rates

the vertical axis, the figure might easily be mistaken at first glance for a depiction of US inflation. This suggests that US and UK inflation share a basic common explanation. But, for reasons discussed later, the most standard rationalizations for the coincidence of inflation across economies—those that emphasize trading and exchange rate linkages—are not very appealing when it comes to explaining the similarities in the US and UK inflation experiences. Instead of appealing to common shocks or to exchange rate regime, we explain the similarity of US and UK inflation by appealing to the common *doctrines* underlying policy decisions. In particular, the flawed approach to inflation analysis, which dominated UK policymaking for several postwar decades, became very influential in the United States in the 1970s.

In the course of our chapter, we establish the following about the Great Inflation of the 1970s:

1. Nonmonetary approaches to inflation analysis and control dominated pre-1979 policymaking in the United Kingdom.

2. US policymakers adopted this framework from the early 1970s, and so believed that inflation was a nonmonetary phenomenon, in a sense made precise later in the chapter. This implied a belief that cost-push forces could produce inflation in the long run, even without monetary accommodation.

3. The nonmonetary view of inflation was held consistently by Federal Reserve Chairman Arthur Burns from late 1970 until his departure in 1978, and adhered to by other senior policymakers during Burns' tenure and in 1978 to 1979.

4. As a corollary, 1970s inflation outcomes did not reflect policymakers' use of a Phillips curve model (with or without the "vertical in the long run" property).

We use "Great Inflation of the 1970s" rather than "Great Inflation" deliberately because our account stresses the influence of UK ideas on 1970 to 1979 US policymaking, and not on US policy in both the 1960s and 1970s. For the United States, we do not find it useful to categorize the 1960s as part of the same inflation epoch as that of the 1970s. To do so is to gloss over the very significant segment of US policymaking in 1969 to 1970, in which both policy decisions and the principles guiding them were largely modern and appropriate (i.e., natural rate/long-run-vertical Phillips curve ideas had been rapidly incorporated into policy thinking; and the monetary authorities deliberately made real interest rates positive in order to move from an excess aggregate demand position, to a zero or temporarily negative output gap, so as to remove inflationary pressure). The key to understanding 1970s policymaking in the United States is an appreciation of the fact that, instead of continuing the 1969 to 1970 framework, US policy thinking "went British," with cost-push ideas becoming dominant at the most senior policy levels from late 1970. As Milton Friedman (1979b) observed, "Ever since the founding of the colonies in the New World, Britain has been a major source of our economic and political thought" (56). The Great Inflation period is another example of this influence, as the predominant US policy thinking during the 1970s was patterned on a UK precedent.

In section 8.2 we discuss why we emphasize doctrine in studying the Great Inflation. Then in sections 8.3 and 8.4 we document the common themes in UK and US policymaking. We go on to illustrate in section 8.5 some of our points about UK policymaking doctrine in the 1970s through an examination of the monetary policy shock realizations implied by a version of the Smets and Wouters (2007) model estimated on UK data. We also critically consider more benign interpretations of UK monetary policy decisions during the 1970s. Section 8.6 concludes.

8.2   Why We Emphasize Doctrine

With the benefit of hindsight, the discussions of the Great Inflation in such 1990s contributions as Taylor (1992), McCallum (1995), and DeLong (1997) can be seen as a backlash against the mechanical application of an "as-if" approach to analyzing past policy episodes. A common practice in studying US inflation data had been to take for granted that policymakers knew the correct model of private economic behavior (i.e., the specification of IS [investment/saving] and Phillips curves). Likewise, the "as-if" approach viewed data outcomes as the result of policymakers' optimization of their objective function, conditional on their correct specification of private behavior (which appeared as constraints in the policymaker optimization problem). Applications to the Great Inflation of the time-consistency or conservative-central-banker hypotheses can be thought of as quintessential examples of the "as-if" approach. These stories attribute to policymakers' knowledge of the economy's structure, and characterize high inflation as a conscious choice by policymakers—a choice following from their assumed preference for a positive output gap target.

The as-if assumption is not appropriate for the study of policymakers' choices, even though it is valuable for the modeling of choices by private agents. Recognition of this point has naturally been followed by the greater integration into the study of the Great Inflation of nonquantitative information, including the record of policymakers' stated views of the economy. Such an approach has been pursued by Romer and Romer (2002, 2004), Orphanides (2003), and others in the study of US 1970s policymaking, and is continued in this chapter. The emphasis that this approach gives to the importance of policymakers' views also brings the study of the Great Inflation onto the same footing as the study of other episodes in monetary history. For example, Romer and Romer (2004) observe that examination of the ideas driving policymaking was an important element of Friedman and Schwartz's (1963) study of the Great Depression,[1] while the analysis of inflation targeting by Bernanke et al. (1999) makes extensive use of policymakers' statements.

The emphasis on policymakers' misconceptions about economic behavior has further antecedents in the 1970s discussions of the Great Inflation in both the United States and the United Kingdom. Friedman (1972, 13) argued that "the erratic and destabilizing monetary policy has largely resulted from the acceptance of erroneous economic theories." In that connection, Friedman attributed cost-push views regarding inflation to Federal Reserve Chairman Arthur Burns. In the United Kingdom, Robbins (1973) likewise blamed policy mistakes on cost-push views, which, he argued, meant that the United Kingdom was suffering from a "crisis of intellectual error . . . due largely to misconceptions prevalent even at high expert levels" (17). Finally, Laidler (1979, 899) judged that the United Kingdom's inflation performance reflected the use of "erroneous economics" in policy formation.

It is one thing to attribute the policy decisions underlying the Great Inflation to policymakers' erroneous views about economic behavior; it is another to take a stand on the specific theoretical errors that were the main source of Great Inflation policies. Romer (2005) groups a number of candidate explanations for the Great Inflation under the umbrella of the "ideas hypothesis." The arguments made in the aforementioned studies by Taylor (1992), McCallum (1995), and DeLong (1997) all fall under that umbrella; specifically,

---

1. Meltzer (2003) also traces Great Depression-era monetary policy decisions to Federal Reserve doctrine, which he argues was constant across the 1920s and 1930s.

all three studies conjecture that 1970s policymakers believed in a long-run Phillips curve trade-off. While sharing these authors' rejection of the time-consistency story, we further reject their appeal to a trade-off explanation. We believe that an important element of a good positive-economics explanation for the Great Inflation is recognition that inflation was not *consciously* created by policymakers. This is a much-neglected feature of the Great Inflation. Any story of the Great Inflation that appeals *either* to time-consistency arguments *or* to monetary policy exploitation of a Phillips curve equation is, at its core, claiming that policymakers *deliberately* injected inflation into the economy. This claim flies in the face of the evidence that 1970s policymakers believed that inflation was not a monetary phenomenon. Policymakers in the 1970s had a modern view of the costs of inflation, but lacked a modern view of their power to determine the inflation rate through monetary policy. An approach that attempts to be realistic about the considerations driving 1970s monetary policy decisions must take this fact into account.

8.2.1 Sources

Gorodnichenko and Shapiro (2007, 1152) observe that the absence of electronic versions of Arthur Burns's public statements is an obstacle to a comprehensive analysis of the information in those statements. This observation is valid for the textual analysis that Gorodnichenko and Shapiro apply to statements, which requires the entirety of the statements (i.e., the population); it is also a legitimate concern if the aim is to discern Burns's model of the economy, as this again ideally involves studying the population of statements, and certainly requires a large and representative sample. Large samples of Burns's statements have been covered by the separate analyses of Burns's views on the economy in Romer and Romer (2002, 2004), Hetzel (1998), Christiano and Gust (2000), Orphanides (2003), and Nelson (2005), with much nonoverlapping material across papers. One aim of this chapter is to reconcile our characterization of Burns's views with these studies. But in obtaining the characterization we give, we make use of a large sample of Burns's statements that includes many not cited in the earlier studies. One reason why we are able to undertake this task is that there has been a major improvement in the electronic availability of Federal Reserve chairmen's statements through the Federal Reserve Bank of St. Louis's FRASER archival database. This database contains speeches and opening statements to Congress made by Chairman Burns, including the substantial number not included in the selection in Burns (1978). At the time of writing, the database did not include the question-and-answer portion of congressional testimony, but we draw on these by consulting the relevant hardcopy transcripts.

In the United Kingdom, central bank independence did not exist prior to 1997. Monetary policy decisions were made by the Treasury, and so by the executive branch of the government. Nelson (2005, 2009) characterizes the economic doctrine of pre-1997 UK governments by collecting and reconciling public statements on economic matters given by leading policymakers. In this chapter, on the other hand, we look at a source not previously consulted—namely, the UK Treasury's *Economic Progress Report,* a monthly analysis of economic conditions that began publication in January 1970. In the following section, we set out the doctrine revealed by analysis of this policy publication.

8.3 Official UK Doctrine on Inflation during the 1970s

This section outlines the doctrine underlying policymaking in the United Kingdom during the 1970s. The documentation of UK Treasury views provided here shows that there were several aspects of UK official doctrine on inflation held consistently over 1970 to 1979 (not all completely independent propositions, but listed separately for ease of our documentation following):

1. Monetary policy can be a source of inflation, by producing excess aggregate demand.
2. Pure cost-push inflation (i.e., sustained inflation in the absence of excess demand) can occur.
3. It follows from (1) that monetary restraint (e.g., monetary policy designed to remove the excess of nominal spending growth over potential output growth in the long run) is a necessary element of inflation control.
4. But from (2), monetary restraint is not *sufficient* for inflation control, even in the long run.
5. There is a first-difference or speed-limit term driving inflation dynamics, irrespective of the sign of the output gap.
6. There is no long-run trade-off between inflation and the output gap (or equivalently, no long-run trade-off between inflation and unemployment in relation to its natural rate).

We now document each of these points using the Treasury's *Economic Progress Report* (referred to henceforth as *EPR*).

1. Excess demand can add to inflation:
The UK Treasury recognized that "excess total demand" could be a source of inflation (*EPR,* July 1978, 4) and this was one reason "to avoid overheating the economy" (*EPR,* November 1977, 1).

2. Inflation can be a purely cost-push phenomenon:
A pure cost-push of inflation holds that inflation does not depend on the output gap when the output gap is negative, and that inflation accordingly can be driven by cost-push forces on a sustained basis even in the absence of monetary accommodation.[2] This view was prevalent in UK policy circles

2. For discussions of "purely cost-push" views of inflation that support the definition of that view that we use here, see Newbery and Atkinson (1972, 474) and Humphrey (1976, 10). Humphrey further notes, in line with the argument presented here, that, until the 1970s, the pure cost-push view was "[m]ore influential in the United Kingdom and the United States."

in the 1960s,[3] and it continued to dominate UK policy thinking during the 1970s. For example, the Treasury argued that the postwar period in the United Kingdom had "led to a general realization that inflation could not be simply identified with excess total demand" (*EPR,* July 1978, 4). Its own analysis of inflation emphasized nonmonetary factors. For example, a 1968 Treasury analysis in the publication *Economic Trends* observed,

> The retail price index rose by about 1/2 per cent in June. . . . The increase in June was largely the result of higher prices for fresh fruit and the reintroduction of prescription charges, which were only partially offset by lower potato prices. (H. M. Treasury, "The Economic Situation," in *Economic Trends,* August 1968, vii)

An analysis like this might be appropriate for analyzing erratic monthly movements in the price level, but the Treasury carried it over to the analysis of longer-term inflation movements. And in explaining inflation movements at a level deeper than referring to movements in specific components of the price index, the Treasury appeared satisfied to appeal to the relation between prices and costs:

> The main factor sustaining this continuing high rate of price increase has been the rapid advance in wage costs. (*EPR,* November 1970, 6)

> The factors underlying the rise of prices have, however, changed. The initial acceleration was mainly a result of the effects of devaluation on import prices. . . . Since last autumn, however, a different pattern has emerged. . . . [T]here has been a very marked rise in costs resulting mainly from the fast rise in money wages. (*EPR,* January 1971, 6.)

> A higher level of pay settlements was much the most important factor in the faster rise of costs and prices during 1970. (*EPR,* May 1971, 5)

> The slow rise in the prices of basic materials and fuel in recent months has, however, been more than offset by the strong rate of increase in wage costs, which have become the dominant influence on price rises. (*EPR,* June 1975, 6)

The prevalence of cost-push explanations for inflation at the official level across the 1970s indicates that exogenous cost shocks were not being cited simply to account for short-run movements in inflation, but for sustained movements too. This reflected the UK Treasury's uncritical acceptance of the notion that "the phenomenon of persistent inflation reflected a cost-push—and specifically wage-push—progress, associated with modern collective bargaining procedures (*EPR,* July 1978, 4).

3. Monetary restraint is a necessary element of inflation control:
The Treasury did accept that monetary restraint could contribute to avoiding inflation that arose from positive output gaps. Consequently, it

---

3. See Nelson and Nikolov (2004) and Nelson (2009) for discussion.

referred to 1977 policy developments with the observation, "Firm control of the main monetary aggregates continued to be an important feature of policy" (*EPR*, April 1978, 5).

4. Monetary restraint is not sufficient for inflation control:

But the UK authorities thought that a negative output gap did not remove inflationary pressure. Persistent inflation alongside negative output gaps— which UK policymakers thought was the state of affairs prevailing during most of the 1970s—therefore appeared to justify the use of nonmonetary instruments against inflation. The Treasury credited incomes policy with lowering inflation: "Current pay policy appears to have been successful in avoiding an inflationary 'pay explosion'" (*EPR*, April 1978, 5). The incomes policy that the Treasury praised in 1978 was the latest in a long line of official postwar attempts to control or manipulate directly the course of wages and prices in the United Kingdom, an approach to inflation control suggested by the cost-push view of inflation.[4]

5. There is a speed-limit term driving inflation dynamics:

The UK Treasury did concede a role for demand in determining inflation when the output gap was negative, but this concession was limited to an influence of the *change* in the output gap on inflation (not of the gap level, as in Phillips curve analysis). For example, in 1967 the Treasury observed,

> If over any period the projected rate of *increase* in output is faster than that of potential output, the pressure of demand will *rise* and this is normally likely to result in a feedback through the economy on the rate of increase of wage rates. (H. M. Treasury, "Econometric Research for Short-Term Forecasting," *Economic Trends*, February 1967, x, emphasis added)

In the 1970s, the Treasury again allowed a gap-growth-rate term as a possible influence on inflation:

> The index of retail prices has shown a much smaller monthly increase recently . . . reflecting some slowing down in the growth of domestic costs and possibly the falling pressure of demand. (*EPR*, November 1975, 7)

The Treasury thus saw only a deteriorating output gap, not a constant negative output gap level, as capable of removing inflationary pressure.

6. There is no long-run trade-off between inflation and the output gap:

The UK Treasury did not embrace the trade-off view of inflation associated with a permanently negatively sloped Phillips curve.[5] It viewed the whole postwar period as witnessing "persistence of inflation even during

---

4. Parkin (1976) catalogues and critiques the nonmonetary measures against inflation taken by UK policymakers during the period from 1951 to 1972.

5. To be precise, here we mean a curve that is negatively sloped when a scatter of unemployment and inflation is considered.

the downturn and 'trough' phases of the business cycle" (*EPR,* July 1978, 4), thereby defying simple Phillips curve analysis. This did *not* lead the Treasury to adopt modern expectational Phillips curve analysis before the late 1970s, but *did* lead it to reject the view that eliminating inflation and restoring a zero output gap (from its perceived negative value) were incompatible goals. Thus in 1975, the Treasury observed, "A sharp reduction in the rate of inflation is now an overriding priority for the nation and a precondition for a reduction of unemployment" (*EPR,* August 1975, 1). It later added, "Failure to control inflation will put all these objectives at risk" (*EPR,* July 1976, 3).

8.3.1   The Change in Official Doctrine (1979)

In 1979, following the election of the Thatcher government, the Treasury noted that the newly introduced policy framework "represent[ed] a complete change of attitude towards the way in which the economy works" (*EPR,* June 1979, 1); in particular, inflation was now accepted as being a monetary phenomenon, and incomes policies were abandoned. Consistent with this framework, the Treasury attributed the decline in inflation in 1982 to "a low pressure of demand" (*EPR,* November 1982, 10). Its perspective on the pressure of demand that had prevailed during the 1970s changed too; the Treasury observed that the "underlying growth in productivity in most countries seems to have fallen since the early 1970s" (*EPR,* October 1979, 1), and, in parallel with US developments described in Orphanides (2003), the UK authorities revised down their estimates of potential output for the 1970s.[6] With more realistic estimates of potential output, previous output/inflation combinations were now seen as much more compatible with a monetary explanation for inflation.

8.3.2   International Factors: Bretton Woods

Where does Bretton Woods fit into the UK experience? Cecchetti et al. (2007) note that the Great Inflation outside the United States is often routinely explained by appealing to the transmission of US inflation via the Bretton Woods mechanism. The breakdown of Bretton Woods is also often similarly cited as a source of world inflation. Some studies of the United Kingdom, such as Benati (2004), do use Bretton Woods as a means of classifying different UK monetary policy regimes.[7] Here we explain why we emphasize flaws in domestic policy thinking rather than the changing status of Bretton Woods as the source of the United Kingdom's Great Inflation.

The United Kingdom had a fixed exchange rate until June 1972, with no changes in its dollar exchange value between 1967 and 1971. It would nevertheless be inappropriate to conclude that Bretton Woods was a constraint

---

6. See Nelson and Nikolov (2004) for details on output gap mismeasurement in the United Kingdom during the 1970s, and the subsequent official revisions.

7. For other recent discussions of whether Bretton Woods was responsible for the spread of the Great Inflation, see Bordo and Eichengreen (2008) and Romer (2005).

whose disappearance produced the United Kingdom's Great Inflation, and whose pre-1972 presence prevented UK economic doctrines from determining UK monetary policy. On the contrary, extensive foreign exchange controls gave UK policymakers substantial scope to vary domestic interest rates for reasons other than the exchange rate constraint.

It is difficult to pinpoint an instance in which the fixed exchange rate policy in itself dictated a tighter monetary policy in the United Kingdom in the 1960s and 1970s. A policy tightening in 1966 did coincide with a foreign exchange crisis, but also coincided with a perceived positive output gap, which in its own right would justify a tightening. When a foreign exchange crisis in 1967 coincided with a perceived negative output gap, devaluation was permitted; for the rest of the 1960s, the balance-of-payments constraint was perceived as a restriction on the allocation of output across sectors rather than on demand in aggregate. And there was no conflict between exchange rate policy and demand management in 1970 and 1971: interest rates were cut, and never raised, in both years; this monetary expansion was desired by the authorities for domestic reasons; and the balance of payments surpluses that occurred were consistent with the aim of stimulating the UK economy. When a conflict between the UK authorities's expansion of demand and their exchange rate obligations did arise in 1972, the conflict was resolved not by imposition of the external constraint on monetary policy decisions, but by floating of the pound sterling.

8.3.3 International Factors: The Influence of Overseas Experience

As the preceding discussion implies, we assign little importance to structural economic forces, as opposed to common policymaking doctrine, in accounting for similarities in inflation rates across countries during the 1970s. This assignment, as well as our emphasis on the United Kingdom as the originator of doctrine, matches up with an assessment made on one occasion by Milton Friedman (1979a, 35–36):

> I do not believe there is any such thing as world inflation; there is only inflation in individual nations. Given a floating exchange rate system, there need be no relationship between the inflation [rate] in one country and another. . . . [T]here is a common element, namely the force of ideas. . . . Countries all over the world are experiencing inflation because countries all over the world have been affected by the socialist and Keynesian sets of ideas that have emanated very largely from Great Britain.

But this account has so far left unanswered the question of why UK policymakers were guided by an erroneous doctrine for so long. If, as we argue, UK policymakers were mistaken in regarding inflation as a cost-push phenomenon, why did they not realize their error earlier? In particular, why didn't low inflation in countries like Germany make UK policymakers wake up to the need to use monetary policy as the central weapon against inflation, and to abandon their reliance on price and wage control measures?[8]

The answer is that UK policymakers and many leading UK commentators rationalized other countries' experiences in two ways. The first rationalization was the position that inflation in other countries may well reflect excess demand problems in those countries, but that the UK inflation problem actually *was* a cost-push problem. For example, a 1970 news report of a bulletin by the UK's influential National Institute of Economic and Social Research said, "In most other European countries, it is argued, inflation is caused by increasing consumer demands. In Britain, by contrast, inflation appears to be the result of the sharp rises in wages."[9] The second rationalization attributed low inflation in Germany to nonmonetary factors, such as the incomes policies allegedly implied by Germany's "social market" framework.

Many prominent outside commentators on the UK economy accepted or reinforced the view that UK inflation was cost-push in nature. For example, in 1970, the Organization for Economic Cooperation and Development (OECD) Secretary General Emile van Lennep said, "Inflation has been accelerating in the United Kingdom despite the fact that demand pressure has been falling for several years."[10] Later, Blinder (1979, 74) observed, "From what I have heard about the UK economy, not even the most dedicated data miner can detect an effect of demand on inflation." Blinder added that it "may indeed be empirically valid" to treat unemployment as exerting no influence on UK wage determination (1979, 75).

8.3.4 Summing Up the 1970s Doctrine

Our characterization of UK policymakers' views of inflation can be summarized by a modified Phillips curve such as:[11]

(1)
$$\pi_t = b + \alpha D_t (y_t - y_t^*) + \delta \Delta (y_t - y_t^*) + E_t \pi_{t+1} + \xi_t.$$

Here π_t is quarterly inflation, b is a constant, $y_t - y_t^*$ is the output gap (i.e., the log of the ratio of output to potential output), Δ is the first-difference operator, and ξ_t is a cost-push process that is highly persistent and undergoes shifts in mean. The parameters α and δ are strictly positive, while D_t is an indicator function that depends on the sign of the output gap: $D_t = 1.0$ for $y_t > y_t^*$, but $D_t = 0$ for $y_t < y_t^*$. The presence of this term implies that if equation (1) is a valid description of inflation behavior, the output gap level

---

8. Beyer et al. (2009) provide further comparison of German and UK monetary policies during the 1970s.

9. *Kansas City Star,* August 26, 1970.

10. Quoted in *Daily Telegraph* (London), November 11, 1970.

11. Nelson (2009) justifies this equation on the basis of a different set of UK policymaker statements from that used here. The representation is also similar to the equation that Friedman and Schwartz (1982) use to characterize cost-push views of inflation.

matters for inflation only when there is positive excess demand; excess supply (i.e., a negative output gap) fails to withdraw inflationary pressure. We will find that equation (1) is *not* in fact a valid description of inflation determination in the United Kingdom, and that the post-1979 policymakers were therefore correct to reject it. Nevertheless, UK policymakers' adherence to a view of inflation captured by equation (1) takes us far in understanding UK policy decisions during the 1970s. We take this point up in section 8.5. Prior to that, we demonstrate that the erroneous views about inflation that were prevalent in the United Kingdom did not remain a source of error special to UK policy circles. On the contrary, these views were adopted during the 1970s by the principal policymakers in the United States.

8.4   Official US Doctrine on Inflation during the 1970s

As we discuss in detail in appendix A, in 1969 and 1970 US policymakers had fairly orthodox views of inflation, most notably expressed in their endorsement of a modern Phillips curve. That is, policymakers believed that inflation was elastic with respect to demand pressure in all regions, and that the Phillips curve became vertical in the long run. This position appears to have been that of Arthur Burns upon becoming Federal Reserve chairman in early 1970, and similar views were held by several key Nixon administration personnel. But both Burns and other senior policymakers rapidly changed their view of the inflation process in favor of a predominantly nonmonetary approach.[12] We contend that Burns's views throughout the period from late 1970 to his departure as chairman in early 1978, as well as those of other major officials in 1970 to 1978 and into 1979, are well captured by equation (1) and the accompanying propositions (1) through (6) given earlier. As we will see, Burns and other Federal Reserve Board figures explicitly appealed to the UK experience as a forerunner of the US experience. Let us review the doctrinal items (1) through (6) of section 8.3 once more, this time using them to describe US doctrine.

1. Excess demand can add to inflation:
Chairman Burns accepted that "policies that create excess aggregate demand . . . lead ultimately to galloping inflation" (July 30, 1974, testimony to Banking and Currency Committee, House of Representations, in Burns 1978, 170). Accordingly, for inflation arising from excess demand, "the raging fires of inflation will eventually burn themselves out" if the boom was

---

12. Romer and Romer (2002) contend that Burns entered office already holding cost-push views of inflation. For the contrary argument that Burns underwent a change shortly after taking office, see Nelson (2005). There is no disagreement across these accounts on the importance of nonmonetary views in Burns's thinking from late 1970 to late 1973, and both sources provide considerable documentation. Accordingly, our documentation here focuses on the more contentious and less documented question of what were Burns's views from 1974 to 1978.

wound back by official restriction of demand (Burns, August 6, 1974, 17).[13] Burns accepted that excess demand conditions had been created in the late 1960s and in 1973; accordingly, the "current inflation began in the middle 1960s" (August 21, 1974, 6) with "the underlying inflationary trend caused by lax financial policies" (July 27, 1976, 671), while 1973 had again seen an "overheating of the economy" (September 20, 1974, 4). More generally, Burns observed that "we also know that when the money supply grows excessively, inflation will be generated" (July 26, 1977, testimony, in Banking, Finance and Urban Affairs Committee, House of Representatives 1977b, 99). This proposition, he noted, was especially relevant to the medium term: "excessive monetary growth will eventually result in more rapid inflation" (September 25, 1975, testimony, in Budget Committee, US Senate, 1975b, 177). Therefore, "[i]f we create money at a more rapid rate than we have been doing, sooner or later that money will go to work and express itself in higher prices" (July 29, 1975, testimony, in Joint Economic Committee 1975, 158).

Burns's successor as Federal Reserve chairman, G. William Miller, shared this perspective, contending, "If the Fed takes the restraint off and lets the money be printed, then, sure, there could be lower interest rates for a while, but then there would be a terrible inflation—and disaster."[14]

2. Inflation can be a purely cost-push phenomenon:

Federal Reserve officials during the 1970s also believed, however, that exogenous cost-push forces (the ξ_t term in equation [1]) could produce sustained inflation without monetary accommodation. The experience of the United Kingdom was invoked as an empirical example of this phenomenon. For example, an unsigned article in the *Federal Reserve Bulletin* of October 1970 stated,

> The United Kingdom provides the clearest example among the industrialized countries of inflation that is primarily of the cost-push variety. The British economy is clearly operating below its productive potential. . . . Yet labor costs have been rising rapidly. (Board of Governors 1970, 749.)

Around this time, Chairman Burns came to the view that the US economy had inherited the cost-push characteristics perceived as relevant to the United Kingdom. By mid-1975, when asked if he expected wages to respond to fundamentals, Burns said, "I hope you're right about the behavior of wages. That's the way things should work, but they haven't worked that way in recent years in this country or in Canada or in Great Britain" (May 1,

---

13. References given in the text with a date and page number but no other bibliographical information are from Chairman Burns's statements and speeches as given in the *Federal Reserve Bulletin* or in the Federal Reserve Bank of St. Louis' FRASER archive of Burns's public statements (available at http://fraser.stlouisfed.org/historicaldocs/statements/). More information on these statements is given chronologically in appendix B.

14. Quoted in the *New York Times*, July 4, 1978.

1975, testimony, in Banking, Housing and Urban Affairs Committee, US Senate 1975, 194).

Burns cited wage-push as a major source of inflationary pressure: "I do think that our trade unions at the present time have excessive market power. I also think that some of our legislation has been conducive to increases in wages and, therefore, to higher inflation rates" (September 4, 1975, testimony, in Agriculture and Forestry Committee, US Senate 1975, 16). Thanks to labor union behavior, wage-push pressures would exist even in the absence of wage-increasing legislation: "inflation has not come to an end. . . . One of the most important sources it is coming from and will continue to come from is the increase in wages" (July 29, 1975, testimony, in Joint Economic Committee 1975, 152). In 1977 Burns claimed: "in the last analysis the wage increases that take place are fundamental to the rate of inflation" (November 9, 1977, testimony, in Banking, Housing and Urban Affairs Committee, US Senate 1977, 30).

However, Burns also cited firms as originators of cost-push pressure: "my impression is that many of our business corporations are no longer paying attention to factors on the demand side in the same way they did in earlier years" (October 2, 1975, testimony, in Budget Committee, House of Representatives 1975, 78). Prices in particular sectors were also autonomous contributors to inflation, a key example being food prices: "concern about the effects of rising food prices on the overall rate of inflation is clearly warranted" (September 4, 1975, testimony, in Agriculture and Forestry Committee, US Senate 1975, 3). Burns had a parallel concern about import prices: "If the dollar depreciates in foreign exchange markets, that releases forces that tend to raise our price level" (July 26, 1977, testimony, in Banking, Finance and Urban Affairs Committee, House of Representatives, 1977b, 70). Any of these factors could aggravate domestic cost-push forces, Burns argued: "Nowadays, inflation from almost any source tends to be built into wages and thus to aggravate the wage-price spiral" (September 4, 1975, testimony, in Agriculture and Forestry Committee, US Senate 1975, 4). He summed up: "inflation has become, as you correctly point out, a complex phenomenon. I deplore some of the price increases that are taking place . . . I think, sometimes, that we are moving into a cost-plus economy, and that is a disturbing development" (September 25, 1975, testimony, in Budget Committee, US Senate 1975b, 168). The great importance Burns attributed to cost-push factors came out in August 1974 when he stated that only about 3 to 3.5 percentage points of the United States' annual rate of inflation of 12 percent in the first half of 1974 could be attributed to money growth (August 21, 1974, testimony, in Committee on the Budget, US Senate 1974, 238).

Burns's cost-push views were so entrenched that they obscured his interpretation of the Fisher relation between expected inflation and nominal interest rates. He did recognize that the Fisher relation was fundamental: "Over the long run, the rate of inflation is the dominant influence on interest rates" (September 25, 1975, testimony, in Budget Committee, US Senate, 1975b, 166). But since Burns believed that the wage-price controls introduced in August 1971 had directly reduced inflationary expectations, he felt that nominal interest rates could fall without implying a loosening of monetary policy. In a speech in November 1971, Burns said that "the freeze has been extremely effective," adding, "[i]nterest rates have come down substantially as the inflationary premium has been squeezed out" (November 11, 1971, 2). This viewpoint allowed Burns to interpret cuts in interest rates by the Federal Reserve not as force-fed monetary stimulation, but as responses to falling private inflationary expectations: "Interest rates are still falling, and yesterday's decline in the Federal Reserve discount rate recognizes that" (November 11, 1971, 3).

3. Monetary policy is a necessary part of inflation control:
Burns accepted quantity-theory logic in the sense that he realized that the Federal Reserve could be a dominant influence on nominal spending growth ($\Delta m + \Delta v$) over longer periods. He accordingly accepted that a necessary condition for price stability was for the Federal Reserve to provide nominal income growth rates that were not persistently excessive in relation to long-run growth in potential output (Δy^*). Thus he observed in 1975 that existing monetary growth rates, "while appropriate in the present environment, could not be maintained indefinitely without running a serious risk of releasing new inflationary pressures" (May 1, 1975, testimony, in Banking, Housing and Urban Affairs Committee, US Senate 1975, 172). Burns saw the Federal Reserve as concerned with "bringing the long-run growth of the monetary aggregates down to rates compatible with general price stability" (July 29, 1977, testimony, in Banking, Finance and Urban Affairs Committee, House of Representatives, 1977a, 68). Likewise, a downward money growth path was "absolutely *necessary* if President Carter's publicly announced goal of reducing the pace of inflation by two percentage points by the end of 1979 is to be achieved" (May 3, 1977, 467, emphasis added). We italicize "necessary" because using it instead of "necessary and sufficient" distinguishes Burns's nonmonetary view of inflation from the standard, monetary view. Monetary policy, in Burns's conception, was a necessary instrument for securing price stability because monetary policy actions were required to prevent the emergence of positive output gaps. Thus, when an excess-demand problem was perceived as having emerged in 1973, Burns observed that "classical tools of economic stabilization—that is, general monetary and fiscal policies— can be more helpful at such a time" (February 26, 1974, statement, in Joint Economic Committee 1974, 720).[15]

---

15. Burns therefore recognized, in line with equation (1), that excess demand pressure could be superimposed on cost-push factors as a source of inflation, and acknowledged that an excess demand problem had emerged in 1973. Burns's 1974 statements on the need for demand restraint thus do not constitute a repudiation of his cost-push views of inflation (though for a contrary interpretation, see Romer and Romer 2004, 141).

4. Monetary policy is not sufficient for inflation control:

Burns believed that monetary policy was not sufficient for inflation control. To cast the issue in quantity-equation terms, for $\Delta m + \Delta v$ to secure dependable control of inflation (π), inflation should be endogenous and continuously related to aggregate demand. In those circumstances, actions on $\Delta m + \Delta v$ ultimately bear down on π alone, leaving Δy to be pinned down by the exogenous rate of potential output growth Δy^*. This was not, however, Burns's position; rather, he saw π as insensitive to aggregate demand over a large range, as it is in equation (1), implying that aggregate demand control cannot by itself secure inflation control.

In the following exchange Burns explicitly denied that one could speak of a specific noninflationary growth rate of money, or equivalently, a specific monetary policy that could deliver price stability:

> Mr. Neal: [W]hat would have happened had the money growth rate been consistent with price stability?

> Dr. Burns: I don't know that I or anyone else could ever answer that question, because we would be dealing with an imaginative reconstruction of the past. In any such reconstruction of the past, you would certainly have to specify the character of fiscal policy in the country. You would have to specify the labor policies pursued by the Government and by the trade unions and by business firms. You would have to specify pricing policies. Then you might get some approach to a meaningful answer. . . . But I don't think you would learn a thing merely by asking what would have happened if monetary policy had kept the rate of growth of the money supply at a level that is consistent with general price stability. (July 27, 1976, question and answer session, in Banking, Currency and Housing Committee, House of Representatives 1976, 28)

Reflecting his judgment that monetary policy actions were insufficient for inflation control, Burns contended that incomes policy was needed, a recommendation he repeated emphatically even after the abolition of wage-price controls in April 1974. For example, in August 1974, Burns said that "monetary policy should not be relied upon exclusively" and called for "[f]resh efforts" at incomes policy arrangements (August 6, 1974, 17, 18). In 1975, Burns argued, "Sooner or later, in my judgment, we will move once again toward an incomes policy in this country. . . . I think the world will continue to look in this direction for part of an answer to its problems" (July 29, 1975, testimony, in Joint Economic Committee 1975, 145). In the same year Burns offered a specific proposal: "I think we ought to hold up for public airing those instances where we have some reason to believe that there is an abuse of economic power, whether on the part of our corporations or our trade unions" (October 2, 1975, testimony, in Budget Committee, House of Representatives 1975, 179).

Burns reaffirmed these positions in 1976 and 1977. In 1976, he observed,

"In the kind of world that we live in—with trade unions playing a large role in the determination of wages, so that competition in the labor market is very limited, and with not a few of our business firms having market power, as I think we all know—if we try to rely solely on monetary and fiscal policies to achieve general price stability, I believe we are likely to fail. . . . I am convinced that we will return to an incomes policy sooner or later" (March 22, 1976, testimony, in Budget Committee, US Senate 1976, 85). In 1977 Burns stated, "I feel, Senator, that some sort of incomes policy will have to be developed in our country" (November 9, 1977, testimony, in Banking, Housing and Urban Affairs Committee, US Senate 1977, 29).

Compared with an earlier period in US history when aggregate demand management was a sufficient tool against inflation, Burns said, structural change had produced a "catch"; there were now "tremendous nonmonetary pressures . . . tending to drive costs and prices higher" (August 13, 1977, speech, in Burns 1978, 417). A favorite formulation of Burns was that monetary policy in the new circumstances should do what it can against inflation, but that monetary policy was not enough. For example, Burns said in 1975: "The Federal Reserve is firmly committed to *do what it can* to restore general price stability in this country" (May 1, 1975, testimony, in Banking, Housing and Urban Affairs Committee, US Senate 1975, 173, emphasis added). He stressed in 1976: "Monetary policy alone, however, cannot solve our nation's stubborn problem of inflation" (November 18, 1976, speech, in Burns 1978, 250). Even at his final Federal Open Market Committee (FOMC) meeting (in February 1978), which he presided over on an interim basis, Burns described himself and his colleagues as "do[ing] what we can to reduce the rate of inflation" (FOMC Minutes, February 28, 1978, 31). G. William Miller adopted similar formulations during his tenure as Federal Reserve chairman (see, e.g., Nelson 2005).

Monetary policy within this framework was seen as able to provide a floor but not a ceiling for the inflation rate. As Burns put it, "if a 5 per cent rate of price advance were to be accepted complacently by Government, inflationary expectations would intensify, and the actual rate of price increases would then almost certainly move toward higher levels" (February 3, 1977, 123).

Like their UK counterparts, US policymakers erroneously saw the predominant situation of the 1970s as one of coexisting cost-push inflation and negative output gaps. Therefore, the perceived function of monetary policy became one of avoiding a compounding of the cost-push inflation that would occur if a positive output gap (and accompanying demand-pull inflation) were permitted. Thus Burns described his money growth target choices in 1975 and 1976 as designed to "facilitate substantial recovery in economic activity without aggravating the problem of inflation" (July 27, 1976, 671). Similarly, the following year Burns said that the "basic objective of monetary policy in the recent past has been to promote conditions conducive to substantial expansion in economic activity, while guarding against the release of new inflationary forces" (March 2, 1977, 229). "New" here refers to demand-pull forces on top of the existing cost-push forces. Or as Treasury Secretary Michael Blumenthal characterized the policy assignment in the United States in 1978, "Bill Miller has to keep the money supply from going through the roof."[16]

Burns summed up his necessary-but-not-sufficient vision of monetary policy in 1976: "Monetary policy—no matter how well designed and implemented—cannot do the job alone. Adherence to a moderate course of monetary policy can, however, make a significant contribution to the fight against inflation" (July 27, 1976, 671).

The series of papers of which this chapter is part provides a detailed chronology of the nonmonetary actions against inflation taken in both the United Kingdom and the United States during the 1970s. In particular, Nelson (2005) discusses not only the US wage-price controls of 1971 to 1974, but later US measures, including the Ford administration's "Whip Inflation Now" program of 1974, the Carter measures against specific prices in 1977, and the Carter administration's incomes policy initiatives in 1978 to 1979. It is true that the use of incomes policies in the United States was not restricted to the 1970s, as wage-price guideposts were pursued by the Kennedy and Johnson administrations in the 1960s. But the underlying theoretical rationale for the 1960s US measures was distinct from the pure cost-push view of inflation that prevailed among US policymakers in the 1970s. We discuss US policies against inflation during the 1960s in appendix A.

5. The growth rate of the output gap matters for inflation:

Burns took as a lesson from his studies of the business cycle that the first difference of the output gap mattered for inflation. Burns (1951, 198) observed, "inflation does not wait for full employment," and this belief carried over into his observations on 1970s developments. For example, in 1976, Burns argued, "Some step-up in the rate of inflation was perhaps unavoidable in view of the vigor of economic recovery" (February 19, 1976, 233). Later in the year he warned that underlying inflation "could well increase as our economy returns to higher level of resource utilization" (November 18, 1976, speech, in Burns 1978, 244–45). Likewise, in 1977 Burns stated: "As we should know by now, pressures on resources and prices can arise even at a time of substantial unemployment" (February 23, 1977, 226). He dismissed a negative output gap level as a restraint on inflation and emphasized instead the speed-limit channel: "Substantial amounts of idle capacity and manpower provide little assurance that price pressures will not mount as the economic growth rate speeds up. Indeed, the historical record of business cycles in our country clearly demonstrates . . . that the prices of final goods and services gather substantial upward momentum well before full utilization of resources is achieved" (March 22, 1977, 361).

16. Quoted in *New York Times,* July 4, 1978.

In Burns's view, the first-difference term mattered for inflation in a symmetric manner: not only, as noted above, did he believe that very rapid expansion promoted inflation, but additionally, slow growth in output (in relation to potential growth) restrained inflation (e.g., February 3, 1976, 5). This first-difference term could, however, be overwhelmed by the other factors mattering for inflation, so cost-push forces could raise inflation even during periods of a widening output gap (see his July 30, 1974, remarks on 1970 to 1971 developments, in Burns 1978, 170). Likewise, weakening cost-push forces could mean that inflation fell during a strong recovery, as in 1975 to 1976.

The speed-limit element in Burns's view of inflation helps reconcile his endorsement of cost-push interpretations with other, seemingly more standard, statements by Burns that are emphasized in other studies. Romer and Romer (2004, 141) interpret Burns's warnings of inflationary pressure in 1977 as reflecting "changes in [his] beliefs in the mid-1970s" toward believing that inflation responded to the level of slack as well as an assessment on Burns's part that output was exceeding potential, though they admit that they cannot reconcile the easy monetary policy of 1976 to 1977 with this change of beliefs. No inference of change in Burns's views is necessary, however; policy statements by Burns throughout 1974 to 1978 are consistent with the cost-push plus speed-limit views that we believe he held consistently over the 1970 to 1978 period.

Moreover, further examination suggests that Burns did not believe that the output gap was positive in 1977; the 1977 quotation Romer and Romer offer from Burns refers to "the pace of economic activity," that is, a speed-limit not a gap-level channel from demand to inflation. In the previous quotations Burns explicitly referred to a level of economic slack existing in 1977; that is, to a negative output gap. Indeed, Burns's statement that "there is now considerable slack in the economy" (February 23, 1977, 226) and his observation of "[s]ubstantial amounts of idle capacity and manpower" (March 22, 1977, 361) specifically refute Romer and Romer's contention that Burns believed that the gap had turned positive by 1977. In addition, Burns's views on potential output had not adjusted downward adequately in 1977, as he endorsed a potential output growth rate estimate of "3.5 percent or a shade below that" (May 2, 1977, testimony, in Banking, Housing and Urban Affairs Committee, US Senate 1977, 17).

Burns's speed-limit view can also reconcile his many statements about the limited power of monetary policy with his occasional observations that the Fed could, in fact, eliminate inflation. For example, Burns said in 1974, "we could stop this inflation in a very few months, and stop it dead in its tracks" (February 26, 1974, testimony, in Joint Economic Committee 1974, 747). In 1977 he stated, "For our part, we at the Federal Reserve know that inflation ultimately cannot proceed without monetary nourishment" (July 29, 1977, testimony, in Banking, Finance and Urban Affairs Committee, House of

Representatives 1977a, 69). Similarly, he also observed, "serious inflation could not long proceed without monetary nourishment" (in his August 13, 1977 speech, in Burns 1978, 417).

As discussed in the following, statements like these are often interpreted as implying that Burns really had a monetary view of inflation, according to which monetary accommodation is crucial in making cost-push shocks matter for inflation. This interpretation is untenable, as it contradicts Burns's many denials (including during 1974 to 1978) that a specific inflation rate was implied by a particular monetary policy choice. But we can reconcile Burns's statements in the preceding paragraph with these denials by using equation (1), which represents our characterization of official doctrine in the United Kingdom and the United States during the 1970s. With equation (1), it is possible, starting from conditions of a zero or negative output gap, for a monetary policy to offset cost-push forces by making the output gap more negative.

Such a monetary policy effect on inflation has different characteristics from those that arise in a standard framework for describing inflation determination. According to the latter, a given negative output gap exerts ongoing downward pressure on inflation, and no alternative policy can remove inflation. But equation (1), in which negative levels of the output gap do not matter for inflation, implies that a given degree of aggregate demand restraint would exert only a temporary effect on inflation; a widening output gap (i.e., continuous negative growth in the output gap) is required to maintain downward pressure on inflation. Moreover, since cost-push forces are an independent source of ongoing inflation under specification (1), that specification suggests that it is valuable to remove these forces directly through nonmonetary measures.

Thus, Burns argued, the Fed could stop inflation via a restriction channel, but "the only way we could do that is to bring the distress of mass unemployment on this nation" (February 26, 1974, testimony, in Joint Economic Committee 1974, 747). Similarly, Council of Economic Advisers (CEA) Chairman Charles Schultze stated in 1978: "We can't wring this inflation out of the economy through measures which promote unemployment and economic slack. Such policies have only a limited impact on the kind of inflation from which we now suffer."[17] Note the reference to a "limited impact"—that is, a temporary impact arising from the gap-growth channel.

6. Inflation cannot purchase permanent gains of output above potential: Chairman Burns repeatedly denied the existence of a trade-off between unemployment and inflation. For example, in 1975 he stated: "Whatever may have been true in the past, there is no longer a meaningful trade-off between unemployment and inflation" (September 19, 1975, speech, in Burns 1978,

---

17. Quoted in *Daily News* (New York), March 31, 1978.

221). He elaborated: "There was a time when there was a trade-off, and you could see it on a chart, between inflation rates and unemployment rates. Today, the nice relationship that previously existed no longer appears. In my judgment there is no trade-off any more" (September 25, 1975, testimony, in Budget Committee, US Senate 1975b, 164). Late in his tenure, Burns observed: "Economists and public officials used to argue about the trade-off between inflation and unemployment. Whether or not such a trade-off existed in the past, I doubt that it exists at the present time" (May 3, 1977, testimony, in Banking, Housing and Urban Affairs Committee, US Senate 1977, 15).

In contrast to the long-run trade-off view, according to which higher inflation can permanently buy an excess of output above potential, Burns saw low inflation as desirable and conducive to achievement of policymakers' real goals. For example, Burns testified in 1974: "There is no conflict between the objective of maintaining the integrity of the currency and the policy declared in the [Employment] Act of 'maximum employment, production, and purchasing power'" (February 26, 1974, testimony, in Joint Economic Committee 1974, 757.)[18] In a May 1975 appearance on *Meet the Press,* Burns repeated his view that full employment and price stability were compatible goals.[19] Two months later, Burns added that "among its several major objectives the Federal Reserve should seek over the long run to help this country return to a stable price level" (July 24, 1975, testimony, in Banking, Currency and Housing Committee, House of Representatives 1975, 219). In 1976 he stated that "elimination of our disease of inflation must therefore remain a major objective of public policy" (July 27, 1976, 671). He went on to be more specific: "Our objective ought to be a zero rate of inflation; no other objective, I think, will serve this country well" (July 27, 1976, testimony, in Banking, Currency and Housing Committee, House of Representatives 1976, 29).

Our recognition of Burns's rejection of a trade-off is incorporated in the specification of equation (1): while positive gaps have a positive relation with inflation conditional on expected inflation, the coefficient on the expected-inflation term is unity, so there is no relationship between the absolute levels of inflation and the output gap in the long run.

Incidentally, if there were evidence that the Federal Reserve during the 1970s internally used Phillips-style regressions that implied a trade-off, this would not be a reliable indication that the most authoritative officials believed in a trade-off. For his part, Burns said that he took computer models "with

18. Other 1970s policymakers expressed similar views. For example, George Shultz, while Office of Management and Budget (OMB) director in 1971, said that there was a "zone of full employment with relatively stable prices," which 1960s policymakers had missed by overstimulating the economy (*Omaha World-Herald,* February 14, 1971).

19. Burns's 1975 *Meet the Press* appearance is not included in the FRASER archive for copyright reasons, but it was reported in the May 26, 1975 edition of the *Washington Star.*

a grain of salt" (May 1, 1975, testimony, in Banking, Housing and Urban Affairs Committee, US Senate 1975, 194). He also noted:

> Economists these days have made life easy for themselves by using econometric models. I must say to you that, rightly or wrongly, I do not trust the results that are wrung out of these models. The models are based on average experience over a considerable period of time. I think we have been passing through a unique period and the characteristics of this period are not built into the econometric models that economists often rely upon. (October 2, 1975, testimony, in Budget Committee, House of Representatives 1975, 180)

Burns's belief that the US economy had undergone structural change that had given it a cost-plus style pricing system would only have reinforced his skepticism about the reliability of econometric estimates.

We have found that we can characterize Burns's views with a simple equation, but we do not suggest that this was estimated or reestimated econometrically. Indeed, equation (1) is not econometrically identified using aggregate data. Burns's intuition about inflation behavior was based not on macroeconometric estimates, but on the cost-push behavior (and implied source of the ξ_t shocks) that he thought he could observe directly at the firm and industry level.

8.4.1   Why Phillips Curve Trade-off Ideas Were Not Important

Baumol and Blinder (1982, 301), McCallum (1989, 1995), and Taylor (1992) all argue that US inflation outcomes in the 1970s reflect policymakers' belief in a permanent Phillips curve trade-off. More recently, that hypothesis has also been advanced by Sargent (1999). We have argued that belief in a Phillips curve trade-off was not an important factor driving US policymaking in the 1970s. It is true, as Taylor (1997) notes, that an empirical Phillips curve scatter diagram was discussed in the 1969 *Economic Policy Report of the President*.[20] But that report was issued by the outgoing administration. Statements by senior figures in the Nixon administration in 1969 suggest they had absorbed the natural rate hypothesis. For example, the Council of Economic Advisers stated that "there is no fixed relationship or 'trade-off' between unemployment and inflation" (in Joint Economic Committee 1969, 334). Furthermore, US monetary policy was tight during 1969 (Chairman Martin's final year as Federal Reserve chairman). If the 1969 policies had been continued, there would have been no Great Inflation of the 1970s. Instead, the policies of restraint ended, and were put into reverse, over 1970 to 1972, and the cost-push view of inflation came to predominate among US policymakers.

---

20. McCallum (1989, 181) also cites this scatter diagram as evidence that "inflation-unemployment trade-offs have been important in policy deliberations."

8.4.2   Comparison with Other Interpretations

We now compare our interpretation of US official doctrine with some others available in the literature. As noted earlier, an early study that attributed, as we do, cost-push views to Chairman Burns is Friedman (1972). We already have laid out some alternative interpretations of 1974 to 1977, as well as agreement on 1971 to 1973, with the studies of Romer and Romer (2002, 2004). We have also indicated problems with approaches (such as Sargent 1999) that attribute Phillips-curve trade-off views to policymakers.

Chari, Christiano, and Eichenbaum (henceforth, CCE, 1998, 467) claim that Chairman Burns "clearly understood" that inflation required monetary accommodation.[21] But they adduce no unambiguous evidence of this allegedly clear understanding on Burns's part. Indeed, both CCE and Christiano and Gust (2000) provide one quotation after another from Burns to the effect that excess demand no longer drives inflation and that higher growth rates of wages and other costs automatically push up inflation—which is to say, they provide Burns remarks that affirm the strict cost-push position on inflation. Chari, Christiano, and Eichenbaum do provide one seemingly orthodox statement by Burns regarding the monetary character of inflation; it is from a 1977 speech, near the end of Burns's tenure. In portions of the speech subsequent to the orthodox statement quoted by CCE, Burns repeated his claim that the character of inflation had changed to cost-push, and acknowledged only that lower money growth would "probably" reduce inflation.[22] Even late in his tenure, therefore, Burns would not grant that monetary restraint would reduce or eliminate inflation for certain, and he was emphatic that modern inflation conditions did not reflect a positive output gap. Even more crucially, via the speed-limit term in equation (1), we are able to reconcile Burns's 1977 statement with his other statements on inflation, without attributing a monetary view of inflation to Burns.

Hetzel (1998) is an important early study that stresses Burns's cost-push views on inflation. In one passage, however, Hetzel (1998, 35) seems to concur with the CCE position that Burns understood that sustained inflation required monetary accommodation. But he does not reconcile this claim with Burns's many statements to the contrary; and as we have stressed, the full record of Burns's views suggests a cost-push plus speed-limit view of inflation, not a modern or standard view of inflation.

The more general message that we believe should be borne in mind is that Burns largely accepted that monetary policy could determine aggregate demand but did not, we argue, accept that the same was true of the determination of inflation. His statements about accommodation should therefore be interpreted carefully: indeed, on one occasion, Burns observed, "I don't

21. A similar view was expressed by Lombra (1980).
22. See Burns's August 13, 1977 speech, reprinted in Burns (1978).

know what 'accommodate' means precisely" (March 13, 1975, testimony, in Budget Committee, US Senate 1975a, 835). If one believes that monetary policy can determine $\Delta m + \Delta v$ and so the *sum* $\pi + \Delta y$, but that monetary policy is powerless regarding π, then "accommodation" of a higher $\Delta m + \Delta v$ rate does not imply that the policymaker is *permitting* higher inflation. Rather, the exogenously-determined inflation rate would (according to this view) prevail *irrespective* of the $\Delta m + \Delta v$ value; in these circumstances, accommodating higher nominal income growth simply corresponds to giving room for output to grow. Or as Burns once framed the issue, "This is a rather high rate of [M1] expansion by historical standards, but it is not too high when idle resources are extensive and financing needs still reflect rising prices" (May 1, 1975, testimony, in Banking, Housing and Urban Affairs Committee, US Senate 1975, 172).[23]

8.5   An Estimated Structural Model for the United Kingdom

We have argued that the key to understanding UK inflation in the 1970s was the nonmonetary approach to inflation control, and that this flawed approach has even more to answer for because of its influence on US policymaking in the 1970s. In the remainder of this chapter, we provide a closer look at key policymaking episodes in the United Kingdom. We do this by examining output from the Smets and Wouters (2007) model estimated on UK data, and illustrating how UK data outcomes can be understood as resulting from the flawed policy framework of the 1970s.

The model is a dynamic general equilibrium system with sticky wages and prices.[24] The log-linearized version of the model is given in full in Smets and Wouters (2007), so we highlight only a few equations here. First, the monetary policy rule has the nominal interest rate (R_t) responding to quarterly inflation (π_t), the model-consistent output gap (gap$_t$), and the first difference of the gap:

---

23. Monetary targeting by the Federal Reserve therefore could be—and in the 1970s *was*—consistent with a rejection of the view that inflation was a monetary phenomenon. The study of Kozicki and Tinsley (2009) is marred by a failure to appreciate this point. Kozicki and Tinsley take adoption of monetary targeting by the Fed as tantamount to an acceptance of monetarism. They do not reconcile their account with the evidence (including those documented in papers that they cite) of US policymakers' adherence to nonmonetary views of inflation in 1970 to 1979 and, with it, a rejection of monetarist view of inflation. Kozicki and Tinsley's claim of a continuous powerful influence of monetarism on US policy decisions from 1970 onward is further contradicted by an authoritative account by a Federal Reserve governor (Andrew Brimmer) on the relation between Federal Reserve policymaking and monetarism. Brimmer (1972) notes, in line with our own interpretation of developments, that monetarism reached a high point of influence on FOMC deliberations in early 1970, and that its influence dwindled thereafter.

24. Previous work on estimation for the United Kingdom of dynamic general equilibrium models closely related to that of Smets and Wouters (2007) includes Harrison and Oomen (2008), Li and Saijo (2008), and DiCecio and Nelson (2007). The last of these studies provides a defense of the use of the closed-economy abstraction for the study of UK inflation.

(2) $$R_t = \rho_R R_{t-1} + (1 - \rho_R)[r_\pi \pi_t + r_y \text{gap}_t] + r_{\Delta y} \Delta \text{gap}_t + e_t^R.$$

It is important to note that our estimation sample for this rule, as for the rest of the model, is 1962:Q1 to 2005:Q4, notwithstanding our emphasis on the enormous difference between 1970s and post-1979 policies. Following Ramey (1993), we interpret results from a sample that includes regime breaks as depicting average behavior of the economy. For our data and sample, the relatively low inflation periods 1962 to 1969 and 1983 to 2005,[25] and the positive mean of the real interest rate associated with those years, will imply that the estimates of rule (2) will have fairly reasonable stabilizing characteristics (e.g., r_π above 1.0). It is consequently appropriate to think of the 1970s monetary policy actions as substantially consisting of *deviations* from this average rule, and to view these deviations as largely captured in the estimated monetary policy shock series. These deviations can be expected to be persistent, which makes it convenient for us to follow Smets and Wouters's assumption that e_t^R is a stationary AR(1) process.

Two other equations worth highlighting are the wage and price Phillips curves:

(3) $$\pi_t = \pi_1 \pi_{t-1} + \pi_2 E_t \pi_{t+1} - \pi_3 \mu_t^p + e_t^p$$

(4) $$w_t = w_1 w_{t-1} + (1 - w_1)(E_t w_{t+1} + E_t \pi_{t+1})$$
$$- w_2 \pi_t + w_3 \pi_{t-1} + w_4 (mrs_t - w_t) + e_t^w.$$

In equation (2), $0 < \pi_1 < 1$ is a function of the degree to which prices are indexed to lagged inflation; $\pi_2 > 0$; $\pi_3 > 0$; μ_t^p is the log of the inverse of real marginal cost; and e_t^p is a price-equation cost-push shock. In equation (3), w_t is the real wage, $0 < w_1 < 1$, w_2 and w_3 are functions of the degree of indexation of wages to lagged inflation, $w_4 > 0$, and mrs_t is the typical household's marginal rate of substitution in period t between consumption and contributing more labor input to production.[26] The shocks to the two Phillips curves are assumed to follow univariate autoregressive moving average (ARMA) processes:

(5) $$(1 - \rho_p L) e_t^p = (1 - \mu_p L) \eta_t^p$$

(6) $$(1 - \rho_w L) e_t^w = (1 - \mu_w L) \eta_t^w,$$

where η_t^p and η_t^w are white noise exogenous disturbances, and L is the lag operator.

It is worth dwelling on these equations, in order to consider the sense in

25. Of these subperiods, policymaking in 1962 to 1969 featured the same flawed doctrine that we attribute to 1970s UK policymakers. Inflation on average was nevertheless low compared to 1970 to 1979, in part because inflation rose over the 1960s from a zero initial level, and in part because the rise was slowed down by a monetary policy tightening in 1966 (when policymakers recognized an excess demand situation).

26. See Erceg, Henderson, and Levin (2000) for the justification for this type of wage Phillips curve.

which they contradict the cost-push view of inflation. The price Phillips curve in itself is not inconsistent with cost-push views, since it relates the dynamics of inflation to an average of marginal cost and to a cost-push shock specific to the price Phillips curve. But the cost-push view of inflation is largely contradicted when the wage and price Phillips curves are taken together. The wage equation makes wage inflation endogenous and, in particular, responsive in a symmetric manner to aggregate demand (via the presence of the $mrs_t - w_t$ term and the responsiveness of this term to aggregate demand).[27] Because of this endogeneity, inflation is a monetary phenomenon in the model, provided that $w_4 > 0$. Some elements of the cost-push view of inflation could nevertheless be salvaged if the cost-push shocks were very persistent. This would imply long systematic departures of inflation from target even if policymakers kept the output gap close to zero.[28] The price Phillips curve shock is particularly important in this regard; as Smets and Wouters (2007) note, the shock term in the wage Phillips curve can be interpreted either as a wage-push shock or a specific type of preference shock (a labor supply shock). Provided the shocks in the wage equation are interpreted as labor supply shocks, they can be thought of as affecting inflation via their effect on potential output; the price equation's shocks then provide the source of the truly "cost-push" shocks in the model (i.e., the e_t^p shocks in equation [3] are analogous to the ξ_t shocks in equation [1]).[29] Strong serial correlation in the price Phillips curve shock would support the idea that cost-push forces are important for medium-run inflation dynamics even without monetary accommodation. Absence of serial correlation in the cost-push shock would, by contrast, suggest that cost-push forces have only a short-run influence on inflation if not accommodated by the monetary authorities.

For our estimation, we use observations on the UK nominal Treasury bill rate, quarterly retail price inflation,[30] quarterly wage inflation, and per capita

27. Other equations of the model in turn make aggregate demand sensitive to monetary policy.

28. The lagged price-inflation term in the price Phillips curve does mean that a white noise cost-push shock that is not accommodated is still propagated somewhat into expectations of future inflation. But provided that the lagged-inflation coefficient is reasonably far below unity, this propagation is quite muted: for example, with $\pi_1 \leq 0.5$ and a 1 percent white-noise cost-push shock arising this period, the effect of the shock on one-year-ahead expected inflation is below 0.1 percent. Note also that the lagged inflation term makes inflation today sensitive to past monetary policy actions, not just to past nonmonetary forces.

29. Following Smets and Wouters (2007), the estimated policy rule (2) incorporates a response to the output gap, whose definition is based on the presumption that the wage Phillips curve shocks are markup shocks that do not affect potential output. If we accept the alternative interpretation of the wage Phillips curve shock as labor supply shocks, we must think of rule (2) as incorporating mismeasurement of the output gap. Specifically, policymakers must be assumed to be erroneously excluding the labor supply shock from their definition of potential output. In that case, policymakers are responding to an output gap estimate that contains a zero-mean error arising from their misspecification of potential output behavior.

30. In contrast to the series plotted in figure 8.1, the retail price inflation series used in estimation excludes mortgage costs. It also removes effects on the index of tax increases in 1979 and 1990. The adjustments are described in DiCecio and Nelson (2007).

values of log real GDP, log real consumption, log real investment, and log aggregate hours. The GDP, consumption, investment, and real wages are assumed to share a log-linear trend.[31]

Estimates of the model using Smets and Wouters's Bayesian procedure are given in tables 8.1 and 8.2. We focus the discussion on the estimates of the Phillips curves discussed earlier. First, we note that wages are estimated to depend on the discrepancy between the marginal rate of substitution and the real wage: the implied value of w_4 in equation (4) is 0.02, irrespective of whether the mode or mean value of the posterior distribution is used. Therefore, this condition for inflation to depend symmetrically on monetary policy actions is satisfied, rejecting one aspect of cost-push analysis. Second, we note from table 8.2 that the price cost-push shock term has only minor estimated persistence: although its autoregressive, AR(1), coefficient is over 0.90 (mode 0.97, mean 0.94), so too is the accompanying moving average, MA(1), coefficient (mode 0.93, mean 0.92), implying that a common factor virtually cancels from the dynamics of equation (5) and delivers a near-white noise cost-push shock process.[32] Third, the value of π_1 in equation (3) is moderate: using the mode values of these estimates, the implied value of π_1 is 0.21; using the mean values, it is 0.22. The dynamics of the price Phillips curve therefore do little to propagate a cost-push shock. Taken together, these results suggest that UK policymakers were wrong to attribute inflation movements to long-lasting special factors and to dismiss the scope for monetary policy to influence inflation.

Table 8.3 gives variance decompositions for the estimated model. For horizons of four quarters ahead or more, monetary policy shocks account for about 11 percent or more of variation in both inflation and output growth; indeed, for inflation they account for nearly 20 percent of the forecast error variance at a two- to three-year horizon. Several vector autoregression (VAR) studies for the United States find a lower fraction of output forecast error variance accounted for by monetary shocks at business cycle horizons than we obtain for the United Kingdom, while Cochrane (1998) argues that monetary policy shocks contribute trivially to the forecast error variance of US inflation. The comparatively larger fractions that we find in our estimated structural model may be due to our use of UK data instead of US data. But more likely, they are largely due to our deliberately imposing a constant-parameter policy rule over the whole sample. As noted earlier, this choice magnifies the variance of the deviations from the estimated full-sample rule. Effects of monetary policy are

---

31. Data sources for most of the series are given in DiCecio and Nelson (2007). The remaining data required for the VAR used here are: population (for which we use Darby and Lothian [1983] data to 1971, spliced into the UK Office for National Statistics [ONS] series mnemonic mgsl.q after 1971) and a nominal wage index (total compensation, ONS series mnemonic dtwm.q, divided by employment, obtained by *British Labour Statistics* data up to 1978, spliced into ONS series mnemonic bcaj.q).

32. There is substantial, but less complete, cancellation of the AR and MA terms underlying the wage shock process too.

Table 8.1   **Bayesian estimates of Smets-Wouters (2007) model on UK data, estimation period 1962:Q1–2005:Q4**

Parameter	Interpretation	Prior Mean (st. dev.)	Posterior Mode	Mean	5%, 95%
φ	Capital adjustment cost	4.00[a] (1.50)	7.60	7.18	5.55, 8.73
σ_c	Intertemporal substitution in consumption	1.50[a] (0.38)	1.13	1.43	1.02, 1.68
h	Habit formation	0.70[b] (0.10)	0.82	0.53	0.43, 0.81
ξ_w	Probability of wage adjustment	0.50[b] (0.10)	0.65	0.59	0.50, 0.72
σ_l	Labor supply elasticity	2.00[a] (0.75)	1.90	1.34	0.65, 2.33
ξ_p	Probability of price adjustment	0.50[b] (0.10)	0.58	0.63	0.51, 0.69
ι_w	Wage indexation	0.50[b] (0.15)	0.54	0.50	0.30, 0.71
ι_P	Price indexation	0.50[b] (0.15)	0.27	0.28	0.15, 0.37
ψ	Capital utilization	0.50[b] (0.15)	0.54	0.57	0.38, 0.76
Φ	Degree of fixed costs	1.25[a] (0.13)	1.79	1.79	1.64, 1.93
r_π	Policy response to inflation	1.50[a] (0.25)	1.20	1.74	1.34, 2.05
ρ_R	Interest-rate smoothing	0.75[b] (0.10)	0.85	0.90	0.86, 0.93
r_y	Policy response to output gap	0.13[a] (0.05)	0.03	0.10	0.04, 0.14
$r_{\Delta y}$	Policy response to gap change	0.13[a] (0.05)	0.10	0.18	0.10, 0.22
π	Steady-state inflation	0.63[c] (0.10)	0.59	0.59	0.46, 0.72
$100 \cdot ((1/\beta) - 1)$	Discounting	0.25[c] (0.10)	0.21	0.25	0.10, 0.41
l	Steady-state labor (in logs)	0.00[a] (2.00)	5.00	5.49	3.21, 8.17
γ	Balanced growth rate	0.40[a] (0.10)	0.52	0.45	0.38, 0.54
α	Capital share in income	0.30[a] (0.05)	0.18	0.17	0.10, 0.24

[a]Normal distribution.
[b]Beta distribution.
[c]Gamma distribution.

Table 8.2   **Bayesian estimates of Smets-Wouters (2007) model on UK data, estimation period 1962:Q1–2005:Q4, estimates for shock processes**

Parameter	Interpretation	Prior Mean (st. dev.)	Posterior Mode	Mean	5%, 95%
σ_a	Standard deviation of technology shock	0.10[a] (2.00)	0.61	0.63	0.57, 0.70
σ_b	Standard deviation of risk premium shock	0.10[a] (2.00)	0.51	0.29	0.20, 0.50
σ_g	Standard deviation of spending shock	0.10[a] (2.00)	0.81	0.81	0.74, 0.89
σ_I	Standard deviation of investment tech. shock	0.10[a] (2.00)	1.47	1.47	1.30, 1.65
σ_R	Standard deviation of monetary policy shock	0.10[a] (2.00)	0.28	0.31	0.27, 0.34
σ_p	Standard deviation of price eqn. shock	0.10[a] (2.00)	0.39	0.43	0.34, 0.45
σ_w	Standard deviation of wage eqn. shock	0.10[a] (2.00)	0.51	0.54	0.45, 0.60
ρ_a	AR(1) for technology shock	0.50[b] (0.20)	0.99	0.99	0.98, 0.99
ρ_b	AR(1) for risk premium shock	0.50[b] (0.20)	0.13	0.60	0.19, 0.77
ρ_g	AR(1) for spending shock	0.50[b] (0.20)	0.97	0.97	0.95, 0.99
ρ_I	AR(1) for investment tech. shock	0.50[b] (0.20)	0.09	0.14	0.03, 0.21
ρ_r	AR(1) for monetary policy shock	0.50[b] (0.20)	0.36	0.32	0.23, 0.45
ρ_p	AR(1) for price equation shock	0.50[b] (0.20)	0.97	0.94	0.89, 0.99
ρ_w	AR(1) for wage equation shock	0.50[b] (0.20)	0.99	0.99	0.98, 0.99
μ_p	MA(1) for price equation shock	0.50[b] (0.20)	0.93	0.92	0.82, 0.96
μ_w	MA(1) for wage equation shock	0.50[b] (0.20)	0.88	0.87	0.81, 0.94
ρ_{ga}	Correlation, spending and technology shocks	0.50[c] (0.25)	0.50	0.49	0.34, 0.65

[a]Inverse gamma distribution.
[b]Beta distribution.
[c]Normal distribution.

therefore likely to be manifested to a greater degree as contributions of monetary policy shocks to the variance of the model variables—rather than indirectly, as the effects of the monetary policy rule on the transmission of the nonpolicy shocks.

The wage Phillips curve and price Phillips curve shocks account for a

Table 8.3   Forecast error variance decompositions at horizon k

	ε_a	ε_b	ε_g	ε_l	ε_R	ε_p	ε_w	ε_a	ε_b	ε_g	ε_l	ε_R	ε_p	ε_w
				$k=1$							$k=12$			
Δ_y	6.7	33.1	30.4	20.9	7.6	1.1	0.3	7.3	30.1	26.2	18.5	11.6	1.6	4.8
Δ_c	1.2	87.8	0.1	0.1	10.4	0.3	0.2	3.9	72.4	0.5	0.2	14.4	0.9	7.8
Δ_i	0.5	6.4	0.1	86.6	5.6	0.7	0.1	1.9	6.1	0.4	78.9	8.7	1.6	2.4
l	20.6	27.7	27.0	18.3	6.0	0.2	0.1	7.8	11.7	17.5	6.2	22.0	5.5	29.3
π	2.2	1.1	0.8	0.1	8.2	62.8	24.7	2.7	1.6	2.1	0.2	19.2	17.8	56.4
Δw	1.2	4.1	0.1	0.4	2.6	25.5	66.1	3.2	4.1	0.3	0.7	6.2	23.4	62.2
R	2.2	17.5	1.0	0.8	62.8	8.7	6.9	5.0	7.8	4.9	1.1	19.4	4.3	57.5
				$k=4$							$k=30$			
Δ_y	7.4	31.3	27.9	19.4	10.9	1.6	1.6	7.3	29.8	26.0	18.3	12.0	1.6	5.0
Δ_c	3.2	78.3	0.3	0.2	14.2	0.9	2.8	3.9	71.7	0.5	0.2	14.8	0.9	8.0
Δ_i	1.6	6.2	0.3	81.8	8.0	1.6	0.5	1.9	6.1	0.5	78.2	9.1	1.7	2.5
l	14.8	22.8	24.5	12.5	21.2	2.1	2.1	4.6	5.6	10.1	3.2	10.7	4.2	61.6
π	3.2	1.9	1.7	0.2	17.6	27.7	47.8	2.8	1.4	2.2	0.4	16.6	15.4	61.3
Δw	2.5	3.9	0.2	0.7	5.7	24.5	62.5	3.1	4.0	0.3	0.7	6.7	23.2	61.8
R	4.9	13.4	3.2	1.5	40.9	7.8	28.3	4.8	5.1	4.9	1.2	13.1	3.0	67.9
				$k=8$							$k=100$			
Δ_y	7.4	30.7	26.7	18.8	10.8	1.6	4.0	7.4	29.7	25.9	18.3	12.0	1.7	5.2
Δ_c	3.9	74.3	0.4	0.2	13.7	0.9	6.5	4.0	71.3	0.5	0.2	14.7	0.9	8.3
Δ_i	1.9	6.2	0.4	79.9	8.0	1.6	1.9	2.0	6.0	0.5	78.0	9.1	1.7	2.7
l	10.4	15.9	21.1	8.5	26.4	4.5	13.2	6.2	3.5	7.1	2.1	6.7	2.8	71.6
π	2.8	1.7	1.9	0.2	19.7	19.8	53.8	4.2	1.1	2.0	0.3	12.8	12.2	67.4
Δw	3.1	4.0	0.3	0.7	5.7	23.9	62.3	3.2	4.0	0.3	0.7	6.7	23.3	61.7
R	5.4	9.9	4.6	1.3	24.2	5.4	49.1	7.5	3.0	3.7	0.9	7.6	2.4	74.9

Notes: Numbers reported are estimated percent contribution of the innovation to the variance of the row variable. The innovations (column headers) are to technology (ε_a), the risk premium (ε_b), spending (ε_g), investment technology (ε_l), the monetary policy rule (ε_R), the price Phillips curve (ε_p), and the wage Phillips curve (ε_w). The endogenous variables (row headers) are output growth (Δ_y), consumption growth (Δ_c), investment growth (Δi), log hours (l), price inflation (π), wage inflation (Δw), and the short-term interest rate (R).

large share of the variation in the nominal variables, while the wage Phillips curve shock accounts for a large fraction of the variation of hours, reinforcing our inclination to interpret it as a labor supply shock. Interest-rate decisions are driven by the wage Phillips curve innovation, because that innovation is part of a persistent shock process; by contrast, the price Phillips curve innovation accounts for a far smaller amount of interest-rate variation.

8.5.1   Great Inflation Episodes

In figure 8.2, panel A, we plot the short-term nominal interest rate and four-quarter inflation in the United Kingdom for 1969:Q4 to 1979:Q2. In panel B we plot the arithmetic first differences of these two series, a representation that helps to isolate the responsiveness (in sign and magnitude) of

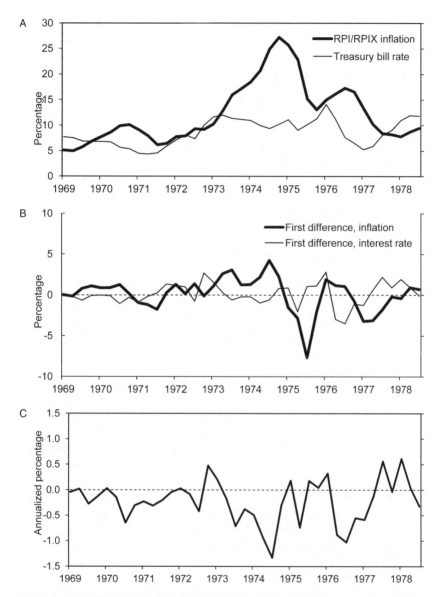

Fig. 8.2 **United Kingdom, 1969Q4–1979Q2:** *A,* **Nominal interest and four-quarter inflation rates;** *B,* **Nominal interest and inflation rates, first differences;** *C,* **Estimated monetary policy shocks**

monetary policy to movements in inflation.[33] In panel C we plot the behavior of the model's estimated UK monetary policy shocks over the 1970s.[34] As foreshadowed before, several of the observations on the monetary policy shock are notably negative in the 1970s, reflecting expansionary departures of monetary policy from the more orthodox rule estimated over 1962 to 2005. Four episodes stand out:

- There is a steeply negative value for the monetary policy shock in 1971:Q2. In April 1971, the government cut interest rates by 1 percent despite the fact that inflation was rising. The government was relying on its direct influence on specific prices (for example, on utilities prices) to control inflation. It even saw expansionary monetary policy as reducing inflationary pressure, on the grounds that output growth moderated unit labor cost growth (the denominator in the unit labor cost expression—nominal wages—being perceived as out of reach of monetary policy actions).
- There are some substantial, negative monetary policy shocks from 1974:Q2 to 1976:Q1. Even one former insider on UK policymaking seemed to be at a loss to explain monetary policy over this period: Cairncross (1992, 215–16) observes, "For some reason monetary policy had remained remarkably relaxed in Labour's first two years [i.e., to March 1976], with bank rate (or MLR [Minimum Lending Rate]) falling from 13 percent to 93/4 percent in April 1975, rising to 12 percent in October 1975 and then falling again to 9 percent in March 1976." Even more confounding is that the maximum level of the nominal interest rate over this period was well below the inflation rate, and several of the rate cuts were against the background of rising inflation. Faulty measures of the output gap do not seem to account for the extent of the ease of UK monetary policy over this period.[35] The reason for the relaxed stance of monetary policy seems to be the UK authorities' heavy reliance on wages policies (the series of "Social Contract" agreements between the government and unions) and their parallel belief that monetary policy tightening would not bring inflation down.
- In 1977, a sequence of negative monetary policy shocks appears, corresponding to a period in which nominal interest rates were brought down into single digits despite double-digit inflation. This period was again

33. That is, panel B of figure 8.2 plots $400*(R_t - R_{t-1})$, where R_t is the nominal interest rate in quarterly fractional units; and $\pi_t^A - \pi_{t1}^A$, where $\pi_t^A = 100*([P_t - P_{t-4}]/P_{t-4})$, P_t being the unlogged price level.

34. The shocks are constructed from the data and the median parameter estimates via the Kalman smoother. The Kalman smoother seems a more natural method for generating shocks than the Kalman filter in cases such as ours in which the assumption underlying model estimation is that the structural parameters and the policy rule responses are time-invariant (see Hamilton 1994, 394).

35. See Nelson and Nikolov (2004).

one characterized by reliance on the Social Contract as the inflation-fighting tool.

• Another notable negative monetary policy shock occurs in 1979:Q2. In April 1979, the UK government cut interest rates by 1 percent despite the fact that inflation was rising. This decision followed the government's signing of a new agreement with the unions, again intended to fight inflation by direct restraint of wages.

These results from the estimated model illustrate our contention that, while inflation in the United Kingdom in the 1970s was not in fact a cost-push process, the policy choices that led to the Great Inflation are traceable to the authorities' adherence to cost-push views.

8.5.2 Other Explanations for the UK Policy Episodes

Let us consider some more benign interpretations of the monetary policy easings that took place in the United Kingdom during the 1970s. One such interpretation is based on the fact that the UK stock market underwent an extraordinary decline during the 1970s. The *Financial Times* stock market index in 1974 was as low in nominal terms as it had been in the late 1950s (see, e.g., Bordo and Wheelock 2004). Could this stockmarket behavior justify the pattern of UK monetary policy decisions in the mid-1970s, explaining why nominal interest rates were so low compared with inflation rates? To us this proposed justification is weak. It may partially explain why policymakers behaved the way they did, but it does not establish that these actions were based on sound economics. We first note that if a period is associated with stock market weakness, that is *not* generally a sufficient reason in the monetary policy rules literature for rejecting comparison of actual policy decisions with simple rules based on macroeconomic aggregates. For example, the US stock market was weak in the 1970s, yet it is standard to compare actual policy against rules that respond only to inflation and an index of real aggregate activity such as the output gap, detrended output, or output gap growth (see, e.g., Orphanides 2003). Policymakers concerned with macroeconomic stabilization should not, according to this argument, care about stock market weakness per se. And monetary policy rules that respond to stock prices seem unlikely to contribute to macroeconomic stabilization better than rules that concentrate purely on responding to inflation and aggregate economic activity. Because the relationship between stock prices and macroeconomic aggregates tends to be very loose in practice, interest rate responses to stock prices are likely to detract from macroeconomic stabilization.

It also deserves emphasis that the weakness of the stock market was largely a symptom of the faulty UK policy framework in place in the 1970s—that is, of highly inflationary policy accompanied by nonmonetary interventions. These nonmonetary interventions were distortions that worsened for private corporations the costs of high inflation rates. Direct controls on prices, profits, and dividends, alongside an unindexed taxation system, magnified the collapse of the stock market (as well as other UK markets for corporate capital, such as the debenture market, which contracted dramatically in the mid-1970s). Among their other effects, the nonmonetary measures against inflation meant that prices were not allowed to have their optimal relation to costs, intensifying the squeeze on corporate liquidity in the mid-1970s. The UK monetary policy easings in 1974 to 1976 may have been partly undertaken to lessen this squeeze. For example, policymakers may have been more inclined to boost aggregate demand on the grounds that this would hold down nominal unit costs and also support profit margins. But that rationale for monetary policy easing reflects the flawed UK doctrinal framework, with its neglect of the links between aggregate demand and inflation. The decision to continue expansionary policy actually perpetuated the inflation problem. And there existed a variety of policy tools besides monetary instruments that can address a corporate liquidity squeeze.

Another rationalization for the policy easings of the 1970s might be found in the fact that the price index used to compute the "headline" inflation series in the United Kingdom, the Retail Price Index, gives a heavy weight to mortgage costs. This factor is not relevant to the consideration of the 1971 monetary policy easing, because the inclusion of mortgages in the RPI began only in the mid-1970s (Lawson 1992, 849). But, for the other easing periods examined earlier, it could conceivably be argued that an easing was justified by the connection between mortgages and price inflation. Might policymakers have thought that cutting policy rates would reduce mortgage rates, thereby helping to reduce RPI inflation pressure, and perhaps producing a favorable wage-price spiral via links between the RPI and wages? Again, such rationales might help explain UK policy decisions in a positive-economics sense, but do not seem to us to provide a good economic justification for those decisions. Any thinking by policymakers along "mortgage rate/price/wage spiral" lines is valid only in the faulty nonmonetary framework of inflation analysis. Judged from a more orthodox position on inflation determination, the "spiral" view is invalid except as a description of the very short run. Interest-rate cuts aimed at provoking mortgage rate cuts might deliver short-term inflation benefits, but do so at the cost of long-term inflation control. Over the long run, RPI behavior is similar to that of indices of UK prices that exclude mortgage costs, such as the RPIX series and the modern CPI. Fundamentally, this is because, when it comes to longer-term inflation determination, the path of aggregate demand tends to swamp other factors. Interest rate cuts ultimately raise RPI inflation via the stimulus to demand, so the cuts do not have a sound foundation as an inflation-control measure.

We therefore find no legitimate basis for the monetary policy followed in the United Kingdom during the 1970s in either stock market or mortgage rate behavior.

8.6 Conclusion

Economic policy in the United Kingdom during the 1970s was guided by a doctrinal framework that suggested that inflation arose from nonmonetary factors and could—and only could—be brought down by nonmonetary measures. This contrasts with the modern policymaking framework in many countries, which is guided by the notion that monetary restraint—and only monetary restraint—is the way to control inflation. We have argued that policymakers' adherence to the older doctrinal framework is useful for understanding why they made the choices that led to UK inflation outcomes in the 1970s. Seemingly nonstandard interest rate decisions during the 1970s can be understood as a consequence of policymakers using this framework, even though the decisions are unjustifiable from the point of view of more enlightened economic theory. Moreover, the US Great Inflation of the 1970s can be understood as arising from US policymakers' embrace of the UK nonmonetary framework. After pursuing an orthodox policy against inflation during 1969—which would have avoided the 1970s Great Inflation if it had been continued—US policy circles in the early 1970s inherited the faulty doctrine already in place in the United Kingdom. The similarities of the US and UK Great Inflation experiences can therefore be seen as arising not from common shocks, but from common elements in policymaking doctrine.

Appendix A

US Policy against Inflation during the 1960s

Wage-price guideposts—that is, federal government announcements giving recommendations for the maximum increases to take place in private sector wages and prices, sometimes laid out on an industry-by-industry basis—were used as an anti-inflation measure by the Kennedy and Johnson Administrations during the 1960s. In this appendix, we show that the thinking underlying these measures was not the same as that underlying the 1971 to 1974 US wage and price controls and other 1970s nonmonetary measures against inflation. We thereby reaffirm our position that 1970s US policy on inflation arose from the adoption by 1970s US policymakers of UK cost-push views, rather than from a continuation of the doctrines adhered to by 1960s US policymakers.[36]

We summarize the issues involved ahead of our detailed discussion. The major, and most authoritative, 1960s proponents of guidelines explicitly rejected the nonmonetary (a.k.a. pure cost-push) view of inflation. As we

---

36. As a related matter, we aim to show that our reference to the Great Inflation of the 1970s as a distinct entity is not a denial that the United States had an inflation problem during the 1960s; therefore, it is not subject to the criticism of Levin and Taylor (2008).

detail in the following, the 1961 to 1968 policymaking view was not as orthodox or modern as that prevailing in 1969 to 1970, but it *did* share with the 1969 to 1970 and modern positions the view that inflation was sensitive to both positive and negative output gaps. It follows that policymakers accepted that aggregate demand measures by themselves *could* produce price stability: that is, they conceded that monetary policy measures that resolutely restricted the level of aggregate demand would, if applied, be sufficient to remove all inflationary pressure. Policymakers opposed such an application, however, and instead favored a mix of aggregate demand and guideline policies. Guidelines had value, according to this view, as a complement to aggregate demand measures, and specifically could improve the inflation rate achievable under full employment; but if price stability was desired and guidelines were unavailable, it *was* accepted that aggregate demand measures were capable of securing price stability.

The 1970s US doctrine departed from both the 1960s US official position and modern views by embracing the "British" position that inflation was insensitive to negative output gaps. Monetary policy measures by themselves *could not* remove all inflationary pressure according to the 1970s view; which is to say, it was believed that even with demand restricted to a low level, prolonged inflation could occur. Pure cost-push inflation consequently could occur according to the 1970s doctrinal framework, so inflation was viewed as a nonmonetary phenomenon.

Samuelson and Solow

Prior to considering policymakers' views, we first consider the rationale for the US guideposts of the 1960s offered by Paul Samuelson and Robert Solow. Though neither was officially affiliated with the Johnson Administration, they were affiliated with the 1960 to 1961 Kennedy transition and 1961 to 1963 Kennedy Administration, and were the most prominent scholarly defenders of the guidepost policies.

As is well known, Samuelson and Solow (1960) are associated with a simple Phillips curve of the type:

$$\pi_t = a_0 + a_1 E(u_t - u_t^*),$$

or the same specification with an expectational term:

$$\pi_t = a_0 + a_1 E(u_t - u_t^*) + a_2 E_t \pi_{t+1},$$

with $a_1 < 0$, u_t^* being the natural unemployment rate. We include a rational expectation of inflation in specifying the abovementioned dynamic Phillips curve. It is true that an element of 1960s and 1970s controversies on inflation determination was how expectations were formed—for example, whether the expected-inflation variable should consist of lagged inflation with unit coefficient, lagged inflation with nonunit coefficient, or a rational expectation of current or future inflation. But this controversy is not germane to the issue of a trade-off between inflation and unemployment, which can emerge even with a rational expectation of inflation provided that the expectation has a coefficient a_2 differing from unity (specifically, $0 < a_2 < 1$).

The dynamic equation has a long-run form:

$$E[\pi] = b_0 + b_1 E[(u - u^*)]$$

with

$$b_0 = \frac{a_0}{(1 - a_2)}, b_1 = \frac{a_1}{(1 - a_2)}$$

Some observers have interpreted the position that policymakers tried to exploit a perceived inflation/unemployment trade-off as implying policymaker belief in this long-run condition coupled with a target for unemployment below the full-employment or natural rate; that is, an objective for unemployment of $E[(u - u^*)] < 0$. But this does not appear to be what 1960s advocates of a long-run Phillips curve relation had in mind in speaking of a trade-off; rather, the employment target was characterized as a full-employment concept, with the associated unemployment rate being a variable pinned down by real factors; see, for example, Samuelson (1970b, 42). Furthermore, at the policy level, Federal Reserve Chairman Martin articulated in 1967 the desirability of avoiding "a situation of overfull employment and overutilization of resources" (February 9, 1967, testimony, in Joint Economic Committee 1967, 416).

If the policymaker goal for real variables amounted to a zero output (and unemployment) gap, how does the Samuelson-Solow relation imply a long-run policymaking dilemma? Let us add a shock term to the dynamic Phillips curve,

$$\pi_t = a_0 + a_1 E(u_t - u_t^*) + a_2 E_t \pi_{t+1} + \xi_t.$$

Samuelson and Solow (1960) stressed the importance of variations in ξ_t and, as did later authors, they labeled it a "cost-push" factor. Provided it has a zero mean, however, this shock term does not generate a long-run trade-off between inflation and real variables. The shock term produces a trade-off in variances, not in means, and continues to do so if a long-run vertical Phillips curve replaces the one studied by Samuelson and Solow (1960). (See Taylor 1979, 1986.)

If, on the other hand, the cost-push shock term does have a nonzero mean, then we can decompose the long-run intercept of the Phillips curve as $b_0 = \pi^* + E[\xi]$, where π^* is the inflation rate corresponding to price stability and $E[\xi]$ is the mean of the ξ_t series. Then

$$E[\pi] = \pi^* + E[\xi] + b_1 E[(u - u^*)].$$

It is the long-run nonvertical, nonzero-mean shock term that delivers the trade-off or policy dilemma that Samuelson and Solow (1960) emphasized. Samuelson and Solow argued that inflationary momentum arising from cost-push sources meant that $E[\xi]$ could not be counted on to be zero.

Samuelson (1969) stated: "In 1960, when I prepared for President[-Elect] Kennedy a report on the State of the American Economy, I had to express pessimism concerning the ability of any mixed economy to achieve *price stability along with full employment and free markets*" (79, emphasis in original).

Similarly, Samuelson (1961) commented, "there is reason to fear that the cost-push spiral of creeping inflation may come back into being in 1962 while unemployment is still at the socially undesirable level of more than 5 percent" (8, 14). In 1970, he asked, "What can be done about cost-push inflation, this scourge that makes it impossible for us to have both full employment and price stability?" (Samuelson, 1970a, 57).

The guidepost policy came into force in the United States in 1962. Subsequently, Samuelson (1968, 60) argued that while a (permanently nonvertical) Phillips curve relation continued to be a structural feature underlying US data, guideposts could produce deviations from the historical curve by decreasing the mean of cost-push shocks:

> All these studies pick up what we all thought was there, namely, a strong cost-push element in the 1955–57 data. . . . There is a plus residual continuing for many quarters in that earlier period and there is a negative residual in the 1960s.

Reflecting this view, Solow (1968, 13) added an intercept-dummy variable when including post-1962 observations in his estimated Phillips curve equation, so as to capture the favorable effects on mean inflation claimed for the guidepost policies.

Samuelson and Solow repeatedly reaffirmed in the 1960s that they did not envision inflation as a pure cost-push phenomenon á la the United Kingdom (and later also, Burns's) conception. It was a time-varying intercept—equivalently, a Phillips curve shock term of nonzero mean—that was the source of a trade-off or policy dilemma, if aggregate demand policies alone were used to control inflation. The presence of this term was not seen as precluding a symmetric Phillips curve relation, whereby inflation depended continuously on unemployment or output gaps.

This position—that the tendency for the intercept of the Phillips curve to take undesirably high values makes it appropriate to take guidepost measures against wages and prices—must be distinguished fundamentally from the pure cost-push position, which is that no Phillips relation holds below full employment, leaving incomes policy the only feasible instrument against inflation. Solow made it explicit that his support for guidelines did not rest on a pure cost-push view of inflation:

> I want to make this very clear. I am not resting my case on a theory of cost-push inflation . . . [but instead] only on *the degree of tightness in the economy at which the price level begins to rise unacceptably rapidly.* (Solow 1966, 64, emphasis in original)

Thus Solow wanted to reduce the mean value of cost-push forces so that the permanently nonvertical Phillips curve, though implying an inverse relation between inflation and gaps, did not imply a trade-off between these series. Solow's was not a modern view of inflation, due to his acceptance of a permanent inflation/unemployment trade-off and his fear of a nonzero mean cost-push shock; but equally, it was not a 1970s-type view of inflation, because Solow accepted that inflation did respond continuously to monetary policy via an output gap channel.

Policy-Level Doctrine

Federal Reserve. It is unclear whether Federal Reserve Chairman Martin believed in a long-run trade-off between inflation and unemployment. But he recognized the need to avoid overfull employment, as noted earlier. Thus, even if he had a nonvertical Phillips curve in mind, his aims did not include exploiting it to purchase output levels in excess of potential output.

As far as cost-push views are concerned, Chairman Martin in the mid-1960s was not a believer in pure cost-push theories of inflation, but he did see cost-push elements as a component of inflation (see his February 9, 1967 testimony in Joint Economic Committee 1967, 421). Aggregate demand measures were not "necessarily the right tool" in the face of cost-push inflation, but were essential in the absence of other tools being applied (422). Restraint of aggregate demand could limit the extent to which inflation responded to cost-push forces (425).

Administration personnel. In 1966, Treasury Secretary Fowler conceded that pursuit of price stability via aggregate demand measures alone was feasible:

> The administration included price stability as a goal to be sought along with . . . full employment and a healthy rate of growth. It believes that there is a fundamental compatibility of these three objectives and that in seeking one of them it is unwise to sacrifice the others. If one objective, such as price stability or full employment, is sought with the utmost vigor without concern for the others, that is not wise national policy. (February 3, 1966, testimony, in Joint Economic Committee 1966, 180)

As the above quotation indicates, and in contrast to the case in the 1970s, the use of incomes policy as an anti-inflation instrument was seen by 1960s policymakers as desirable so as to avoid the need for trading off goals; it did not constitute a denial that, in principle, aggregate demand measures alone could deliver price stability. In keeping with this perception, CEA Chairman Gardner Ackley saw guideposts as moving pricing decisions in a direction that removed the need to trade off unemployment and inflation:

> We begin with the fundamental premise that this Nation must be able to enjoy the benefits of both high employment and price stability. We conclude that the wage-price guideposts offer the best opportunities for

encouraging behavior that will reconcile these two key objectives. (February 19, 1965, testimony in Joint Economic Committee 1965, 6)

This statement, like those of Martin, Samuelson, and Solow, reflects a view of inflation crucially different from pure cost-push view common to the United Kingdom in the 1960s and 1970s and to the United States in the 1970s. Despite his appeal to the presence of cost-push elements in the pricing process, Ackley's statements imply that the effect of cost-push elements on inflation *can* be counteracted by a maintained negative output gap. Cost-push elements existed according to 1960s US policy doctrine, and were a source of a trade-off (or, as Ackley put it, "of an inflationary bias of the economy at full employment"),[37] but 1960s US doctrine did not deny that, in principle, a desired inflation rate could be secured solely by the fixing of aggregate demand at a certain level.

US Policy from 1969 to 1970

As discussed in the main text, 1969 saw two important changes in official US doctrine. First, there was an explicit embrace of no-long-run trade-off view, as documented in the text from CEA statements.[38] Secondly, the administration (which initially included Arthur Burns as a White House advisor, ahead of his move to the Federal Reserve in 1970) took a truly monetary view of inflation by arguing that incomes policy was not necessary to eliminate inflation or to remove a long-run trade-off. The previous administration's position that there was an inherent tendency for cost-push forces to have a zero average effect on inflation, even in the absence of monetary accommodation, was not continued.

This new doctrine had a very short-lived initial influence on policy due to changes in views by Chairman Burns during 1970 and by the Nixon Administration thereafter, but it was distinct, as we have stressed, from both pre-1969 and 1971 to 1979 policymaker views.

Appendix B
Bibliographical Information

Material from Federal Reserve Publications

November 11, 1971: "Summary of Remarks by Arthur F. Burns, Board of Governors of the Federal Reserve System, at the New York Stock

---

37. Ackley (1966, 78). See Ackley (1978, 444) for a related discussion, which likewise concludes that a cost-push disturbance in the traditional Phillips curve is the source of the policy dilemma.

38. Romer (2007, 10–11) similarly notes that late 1960s US policymakers rejected any long-run trade-off.

Exchange." http://fraser.stlouisfed.org/historicaldocs/statements/download
/28999/Burns_19711111.pdf

August 6, 1974: Burns's statement before the Joint Economic Committee.
http://fraser.stlouisfed.org/historicaldocs/statements/download/28175
/Burns_19740806.pdf

August 21, 1974: Burns's statement before the Senate Budget Committee.
http://fraser.stlouisfed.org/historicaldocs/statements/download/28176
/Burns_19740821.pdf

September 20, 1974: Burns's remarks at the Financial Conference on Inflation. http://fraser.stlouisfed.org/historicaldocs/statements/download
/29556/Burns_19740920.pdf

February 3, 1976: Burns's statement to the Banking, Currency, and Housing Committee. http://fraser.stlouisfed.org/historicaldocs/statements
/download/29131/Burns_19760203.pdf

February 19, 1976: Burns's statement before the Joint Economic Committee,
Federal Reserve Bulletin, February 1976, pp. 231–36.

July 27, 1976: Burns's statement before the Banking, Currency and Housing
Committee, House of Representatives, *Federal Reserve Bulletin,* August
1976, pp. 668–74.

February 3, 1977: Burns's statement before the Banking, Finance and Urban
Affairs Committee, House of Representatives, *Federal Reserve Bulletin,*
February 1977, pp. 119–24.

February 23, 1977: Burns's statement before the Joint Economic Committee,
Federal Reserve Bulletin, March 1977, pp. 222–27.

March 2, 1977: Burns's statement before the Budget Committee, House of
Representatives, *Federal Reserve Bulletin,* March 1977, pp. 227–33.

March 22, 1977: Burns's statement before the Budget Committee, US Senate, *Federal Reserve Bulletin,* April 1977, pp. 358–62.

May 3, 1977: Burns's statement before the Banking, Housing and Urban
Affairs Committee, US Senate, *Federal Reserve Bulletin,* May 1977, pp.
463–68.

February 28, 1978: "Transcript, Federal Open Market Committee Meeting,
February 28, 1978." www.federalreserve.gov

Newspaper Articles Cited

"Britain's Economy Stalled," *Kansas City Star,* August 26, 1970, 2B.

Clifford German, "British Inflation Worst of the OECD Nations," *Daily
Telegraph* (London), November 11, 1970, 17.

Associated Press, "Signs Pointing Up for US Economy, Budget Chief Says,"
Omaha World-Herald, February 14, 1971, 25A.

Associated Press, "Burns, Ullman Differ on Upturn," *Washington Star,*
May 26, 1975, A5.

"Schultze: Inflation Pressures Are Greater Than Expected," *Daily News*
(New York), March 31, 1978, 32.

Clyde H. Farnsworth, "High Interest Rates: A Federal Reserve Inoculation to Cure the Inflation Disease?," *New York Times,* July 4, 1978, 32.

References

Ackley, Gardner. 1966. "The Contribution of Guidelines." In *Guidelines: Informal Controls and the Market Place,* edited by G. P. Shultz and R. Z. Aliber, 67–78. Chicago: University of Chicago Press.

———. 1978. *Macroeconomics: Theory and Policy.* New York: Macmillan.

Agriculture and Forestry Committee, US Senate. 1975. *Russian Grain Sales: Hearings.* Washington, DC: US Government Printing Office.

Banking, Currency and Housing Committee, House of Representatives. 1975. *Federal Reserve Consultations with Congress on the Conduct of Monetary Policy Pursuant to House Concurrent Resolution 133: Hearings, July 22, 23, and 24, 1975.* Washington, DC: US Government Printing Office.

———. 1976. *Federal Reserve Consultations with Congress on the Conduct of Monetary Policy Pursuant to House Concurrent Resolution 133: Hearings July 27 and 28, 1976.* Washington, DC: US Government Printing Office.

Banking, Finance and Urban Affairs Committee, House of Representatives. 1977a. *Conduct of Monetary Policy: Hearings.* Washington, DC: US Government Printing Office.

———. 1977b. *Federal Reserve Reform Act of 1977: Hearings.* Washington, DC: US Government Printing Office.

Banking, Housing and Urban Affairs Committee, US Senate. 1975. *Second Meeting on the Conduct of Monetary Policy: Hearings.* Washington, DC: US Government Printing Office.

———. 1977. *Fifth Meeting on the Conduct of Monetary Policy: Hearings.* Washington, DC: US Government Printing Office.

Baumol, William J., and Alan S. Blinder. 1982. *Economics: Principles and Policy,* 2nd ed. New York: Harcourt Brace Jovanovich.

Benati, Luca. 2004. "Evolving Post-World War II UK Economic Performance." *Journal of Money, Credit, and Banking* 36 (4): 691–717.

Bernanke, Ben S., Thomas Laubach, Frederic S. Mishkin, and Adam S. Posen. 1999. *Inflation Targeting: Lessons from the International Experience.* Princeton, NJ: Princeton University Press.

Beyer, Andreas, Vitor Gaspar, Christina Gerberding, and Otmar Issing. 2009. "Opting Out of the Great Inflation: German Monetary Policy after the Breakdown of Bretton Woods." European Central Bank (ECB) Working Paper no. 1020.

Blinder, Alan S. 1979. "What's 'New' and What's 'Keynesian' in the 'New Cambridge' Keynesianism?" *Carnegie-Rochester Conference Series on Public Policy* 9 (1): 67–85.

Board of Governors of the Federal Reserve System. 1970. "Inflation in Western Europe and Japan." *Federal Reserve Bulletin* October:743–55.

Bordo, Michael, D., and Barry Eichengreen. 2008. "Bretton Woods and the Great Inflation." NBER Working Paper no. 14532. Cambridge, MA: National Bureau of Economic Research.

Bordo, Michael D., and David C. Wheelock. 2004. "Monetary Policy and Asset Prices: A Look Back at Past US Stock Market Booms." *Federal Reserve Bank of St. Louis Review* 86 (6): 19–44.

Brimmer, Andrew F. 1972. "The Political Economy of Money: Evolution and Impact of Monetarism in the Federal Reserve System." *American Economic Review* 62 (1/2): 344–52.

Budget Committee, House of Representatives. 1975. *Second Budget Resolution, Fiscal Year 1976: Hearings.* Washington, DC: US Government Printing Office.

Budget Committee, US Senate. 1975a. *The 1976 First Concurrent Resolution on the Budget: Hearings, Volume II.* Washington, DC: US Government Printing Office.

———. 1975b. *Second Concurrent Resolution on the Budget: Hearings, Volume I.* Washington, DC: US Government Printing Office.

———. 1976. *First Concurrent Resolution on the Budget—Fiscal Year 1977: Hearings, Volume V.* Washington, DC: US Government Printing Office.

Burns, Arthur F. 1951. "Mitchell on What Happens during Business Cycles." In *What Happens During Business Cycles: A Progress Report,* edited by W. C. Mitchell, vii–xi. New York: National Bureau of Economic Research.

———. 1978. *Reflections of an Economic Policy Maker—Speeches and Congressional Statements: 1969–1978.* Washington, DC: American Enterprise Institute.

Cairncross, Alec. 1992. *The British Economy since 1945: Economic Policy and Performance, 1945–1990.* Oxford: Basil Blackwell.

Cecchetti, Stephen G., Peter Hooper, Bruce C. Kasman, Kermit L. Schoenholtz, and Mark W. Watson. 2007. "Understanding the Evolving Inflation Process." Report for the 2007 Meeting of US Monetary Policy Forum, March.

Chari, V. V., Lawrence J. Christiano, and Martin Eichenbaum. 1998. "Expectation Traps and Discretion." *Journal of Economic Theory* 81 (2): 462–92.

Christiano, Lawrence J., and Christopher Gust. 2000. "The Expectations Trap Hypothesis." *Federal Reserve Bank of Chicago Economic Perspectives* 24 (2): 21–39.

Cochrane, John. 1998. "A Frictionless View of US Inflation." *NBER Macroeconomics Annual 1998,* edited by Ben S. Bernanke and Julio J. Rotemberg, 323–84. Cambridge, MA: MIT Press.

Committee on the Budget, US Senate. 1974. *The Federal Budget and Inflation: Hearings.* Washington, DC: Government Printing Office.

Darby, Michael R., and James R. Lothian. 1983. *The International Transmission of Inflation.* Chicago: University of Chicago Press.

DeLong, J. Bradford. 1997. "America's Peacetime Inflation: The 1970s." In *Reducing Inflation: Motivation and Strategy,* edited by C. D. Romer and D. H. Romer, 247–76. Chicago: University of Chicago Press.

DiCecio, Riccardo, and Edward Nelson. 2007. "An Estimated DSGE Model for the United Kingdom." *Federal Reserve Bank of St. Louis Review* 89 (4): 215–31.

Erceg, Christopher J., Dale W. Henderson, and Andrew T. Levin. 2000. "Optimal Monetary Policy with Staggered Wage and Price Contracts." *Journal of Monetary Economics* 46 (2): 281–313.

Friedman, Milton. 1972. "Have Monetary Policies Failed?" *American Economic Review (Papers and Proceedings)* 62 (2): 11–18.

———. 1979a. "Correspondence: A Debate on Britain's Economic Policy." *Director* December:34–36.

———. 1979b. "Hooray for Margaret Thatcher." *Newsweek,* July 9.

Friedman, Milton, and Anna J. Schwartz. 1963. *A Monetary History of the United States, 1867–1960.* Princeton, NJ: Princeton University Press.

———. 1982. *Monetary Trends in the United States and the United Kingdom: Their Relation to Income, Prices, and Interest Rates, 1867–1975.* Chicago: University of Chicago Press.

Gorodnichenko, Yuriy, and Matthew D. Shapiro. 2007. "Monetary Policy When Potential Output Is Uncertain: Understanding the Growth Gamble of the 1990s." *Journal of Monetary Economics* 54 (4): 1132–62.

Hamilton, James D. 1994. *Time Series Analysis.* Princeton, NJ: Princeton University Press.

Harrison, Richard, and Ozlem Oomen. 2008. "Evaluating and Estimating a DSGE Model for the United Kingdom." Manuscript, Bank of England.

Hetzel, Robert L. 1998. "Arthur Burns and Inflation." *Federal Reserve Bank of Richmond Economic Quarterly* 84 (1): 21–44.

H. M. Treasury, United Kingdom. 1967–1970. Contributions to *Economic Trends,* various issues. London: Her Majesty's Stationary Office (HMSO).

H. M. Treasury, United Kingdom. 1970–1982. *Economic Progress Report,* various issues. London: HMSO.

Humphrey, Thomas M. 1976. "Some Current Controversies in the Theory of Inflation." *Federal Reserve Bank of Richmond Economic Review* 3 (4): 8–19.

Joint Economic Committee. 1965. *January 1965 Economic Report of the President: Hearings, Part 1.* Washington, DC: US Government Printing Office.

———. 1966. *January 1965 Economic Report of the President: Hearings, Part 2.* Washington, DC: US Government Printing Office.

———. 1967. *The 1967 Economic Report of the President: Hearings, Part 2.* Washington, DC: US Government Printing Office.

———. 1969. *The 1969 Economic Report of the President: Hearings, Part 2.* Washington, DC: US Government Printing Office.

———. 1974. *The 1974 Economic Report of the President: Hearings.* Washington, DC: US Government Printing Office.

———. 1975. *Midyear Review of the Economic Situation and Outlook: Hearings.* Washington, DC: US Government Printing Office.

Kozicki, Sharon, and P. A. Tinsley. 2009. "Perhaps the 1970s FOMC Did What It Said It Did." *Journal of Monetary Economics* 56 (6): 842–55.

Laidler, David. 1979. "Book Review: *The Political Economy of Inflation.*" *Journal of Political Economy* 87 (4): 896–901.

Lawson, Nigel. 1992. *The View from No. 11.* London: Bantam.

Levin, Andrew T., and John B. Taylor. 2008. "Falling Behind the Curve: A Positive Analysis of Stop-Start Monetary Policy and the Great Inflation." Paper presented at the NBER Conference on the Great Inflation. Woodstock, Vermont, September 25–27.

Li, Huiyu, and Hikaru Saijo. 2008. "Why Did Aggregate Volatilities Decline in the US, UK and Japan?" Manuscript, University of Tokyo.

Lombra, Raymond E. 1980. "Reflections on Burns' Reflections." *Journal of Money, Credit, and Banking* 12 (1): 94–105.

McCallum, Bennett T. 1989. *Monetary Economics: Theory and Policy.* New York: Macmillan.

———. 1995. "Two Fallacies Concerning Central-Bank Independence." *American Economic Review (Papers and Proceedings)* 85 (2): 207–11.

Meltzer, Allan H. 2003. *A History of the Federal Reserve, Volume 1.* Chicago: University of Chicago Press.

Nelson, Edward. 2005. "The Great Inflation of the Seventies: What Really Happened?" *Advances in Macroeconomics* 3, Article 3.

———. 2009. "An Overhaul of Doctrine: The Underpinning of UK Inflation Targeting." *Economic Journal* 119 (538): F333–68.

Nelson, Edward, and Kalin Nikolov. 2004. "Monetary Policy and Stagflation in the UK" *Journal of Money, Credit, and Banking* 36 (3): 293–318.

Newbery, D. M. G., and A. B. Atkinson. 1972. "Investment, Savings and Employment in the Long-Run." *International Economic Review* 13 (3): 460–75.

Orphanides, Athanasios. 2003. "The Quest for Prosperity without Inflation." *Journal of Monetary Economics* 50 (3): 633–63.

Parkin, Michael. 1976. "Wage and Price Controls: The Lessons from Britain." In *The Illusion of Wage and Price Control: Essays on Inflation, Its Cause and Its Cures,* edited by M. Walker, 103–31. Vancouver: Fraser Institute.

Ramey, Valerie. 1993. "How Important Is the Credit Channel in the Transmission of Monetary Policy?" *Carnegie-Rochester Conference Series on Public Policy* 39 (1): 1–45.

Robbins, Lionel. 1973. "A Crisis of Intellectual Error." *Financial Times,* December 14.

Romer, Christina D. 2005. "Commentary: Origins of the Great Inflation." *Federal Reserve Bank of St. Louis Review* 87 (2): 177–85.

———. 2007. "Macroeconomic Policy in the 1960s: The Causes and Consequences of a Mistaken Revolution." Lecture, Economic History Association Annual Meeting, September.

Romer, Christina D., and David H. Romer. 2002. "The Evolution of Economic Understanding and Postwar Stabilization Policy." In *Rethinking Stabilization Policy,* 11–78. Kansas City: Federal Reserve Bank of Kansas City.

———. 2004. "Choosing the Federal Reserve Chair: Lessons from History." *Journal of Economic Perspectives* 18 (1): 129–62.

Samuelson, Paul A. 1961. "The American Economy on the Move." *Financial Times,* August 3.

———. 1968. "Theoretical Problems." In *On Incomes Policy: Papers and Proceedings from a Conference in Honour of Erik Lundberg,* edited by Erik Lundberg, 58–62. Stockholm: Industrial Council for Social and Economic Studies.

———. 1969. "Lessons of the 1960s." *Newsweek,* July 14.

———. 1970a. "Price Controls." *Newsweek,* December 28.

———. 1970b. "Reflections on Recent Federal Reserve Policy." *Journal of Money, Credit, and Banking* 2 (1): 33–44.

Samuelson, Paul A., and Robert M. Solow. 1960. "Analytical Aspects of Anti-Inflation Policy." *American Economic Review (Papers and Proceedings)* 50 (2): 177–94.

Sargent, Thomas J. 1999. *The Conquest of American Inflation.* Princeton, NJ: Princeton University Press.

Smets, Frank, and Rafael Wouters. 2007. "Shocks and Frictions in US Business Cycles: A Bayesian DSGE Approach." *American Economic Review* 97 (3): 586–606.

Solow, Robert M. 1966. "Comments." In *Guidelines: Informal Controls and the Market Place,* edited by G. P. Shultz and R. Z. Aliber, 62–66. Chicago: University of Chicago Press.

———. 1968. "Recent Controversy on the Theory of Inflation: An Eclectic View." In *Inflation: Its Causes, Consequences and Control: A Symposium,* edited by S. W. Rousseas, 1–17. New York: New York University.

Taylor, John B. 1979. "Estimation and Control of a Macroeconomic Model with Rational Expectations." *Econometrica* 47:1267–86.

———. 1986. "Reply." In *The American Business Cycle: Continuity and Change,* edited by R. J. Gordon, 672–77. Chicago: University of Chicago Press.

———. 1992. "The Great Inflation, the Great Disinflation, and Policies for Future Price Stability." In *Inflation, Disinflation and Monetary Policy,* edited by A. Blundell-Wignall, 9–31. Sydney: Ambassador Press.

———. 1997. "America's Peacetime Inflation: The 1970s: Comment." In *Reducing Inflation: Motivation and Strategy,* edited by C. D. Romer and D. H. Romer, 276–80. Chicago: University of Chicago Press.

Comment   Matthew D. Shapiro

Riccardo DiCecio and Edward Nelson have produced a chapter that evaluates monetary policy during the great inflation from several angles. First, it takes a comparative perspective on monetary policy. In particular, it argues that British attitudes about monetary policy affected the US Federal Reserve during the 1970s. Second, it argues that policymakers emphasized nonmonetary factors in both the determination of inflation and in policy reactions to inflation during this period. The central claim of the chapter is that British thinking about monetary policy in the early days of the great inflation emphasized nonmonetary factors, and that US policymakers were affected by this thinking. Hence, the two lines of analysis in the chapter combine to shed light on economic policy in the 1970s. Indeed, the culmination of nonmonetary policies toward inflation in this period in the United States was the Nixon wage-price controls. Though implementing price controls was a presidential policy, they were supported by the Fed under Arthur Burns. While the chapter does not focus on these price controls, it illustrates the background of policymaking and thinking about the economy that led to them.

The chapter has two distinct parts. The first is a detailed narration of the policy perspective of UK and US central bankers. This narration is supported by extensive quotations from their policy statements. The second is estimation and simulation of a medium-scale New Keynesian macroeconometric model. Though the authors attempt to link these two parts of the chapter, the connection between the narration is weak. Hence, the chapter presents two separate, albeit complementary, approaches to understanding policymaking.

The first part of the chapter provides some valuable and compelling evidence on Arthur Burns's perspective on the function of the economy and how it related to policy choices. Here are what I take to be the central elements of the authors' characterization of Burns's perspective. First, the cost-push channel for inflation was important. Second, though monetary policy was viewed as an important regulator of aggregate demand, it was viewed

Matthew D. Shapiro is the Lawrence R. Klein Collegiate Professor of Economics at the University of Michigan and a research associate of the National Bureau of Economic Research.

For acknowledgments, sources of research support, and disclosure of the author's material financial relationships, if any, please see http://www.nber.org/chapters/c9173.ack.

as being insufficient by itself to control inflation. Third, Burns had a notion that the economy had a speed limit that, if exceeded, would (nonlinearly) trigger inflation.

Why is this characterization so important? From the perspective of modern policy analysis, the cost-push/demand-pull dichotomy is at best a curiosum. But when combined with the notion that monetary policy alone could not control inflation it provides a powerful intellectual foundation for price controls. Though the authors do not emphasize this point, their narrative of the Arthur Burns's policy perspective brings into sharp resolution his support of President Nixon's wage and price freeze and controls. The price controls are an important episode.

- The Nixon wage-price freeze is the only instance of price controls in the United States outside of wartime.
- They were about fighting inflation per se, instead of a policy to deal with wartime rationing and shortages.

The controls cast a shadow over the entire 1970s.

- The Council on Wage and Price Stability (COWPS) continued to exist throughout the decade.
- Nonmonetary approaches to inflation continued in the Ford Administration; for example, with President Ford's "Whip Inflation Now" initiative and the WIN button.
- Though most prices were decontrolled within a year or two of the Nixon freeze, oil prices remained controlled throughout the 1970s. These controls led to shortages and queuing during the second Organization of the Petroleum Exporting Countries (OPEC) price shock.

This episode of wage-price controls gets limited attention in the discussions of this period in general and this volume in particular. The authors' discussion of Burns's policy perspective leads me to an aside on the relationship between Burns and President Nixon. In particular, to what extent did Nixon pressure Burns to keep interest rates low in order to abet his reelection, and to what extent did Burns yield to this pressure? Abrams (2006) surveys evidence from the Nixon White House tapes as well as from memoirs of participants in the Nixon administration. This evidence makes clear that Nixon placed considerable pressure on Burns to keep monetary policy loose during the run-up to the 1972 election. He finds no direct evidence, however, that Burns acquiesced to this pressure.

I can add some evidence to this narrative. Arthur Burns's papers are housed at the Gerald R. Ford Library on the campus of the University of Michigan. I have looked through Burns's papers for evidence of political pressure on monetary policy. As on the tapes, there is evidence that the White House pressured the Fed to keep interest rates low. There is no evidence of acquiescence by Burns. Indeed, there are some annoyed notes written in the margins of the letters from the White House. The replies were, however, quite temperate.

I enjoyed reading the authors' narrative concerning nonmonetary issues in inflation and learned from it. I would, however, like to challenge the authors' central point that US policymakers acquired these ideas from Britain and that the ideas came to the fore in the late 1960s. In particular, nonmonetary control of inflation was very much a feature of US economic policy in the early 1960s.

- President Kennedy famously "jawboned" US Steel in 1962 to rescind a price increase that was feared to be inflationary.
- The Kennedy administration had wage and price "guideposts" that were meant to keep inflation in check.

Similarly, Britain pursued an "incomes policy" during the early 1960s. Hence, the nonmonetary approach to inflation control has earlier antecedents than is clear from the authors' narrative, and these antecedents are well-rooted in American soil. Hence, the authors' notion that the British way of thinking spread to the United States ignores these early, significant attempts at nonmonetary control on this side of the Atlantic. Their neglect of these earlier episodes also means the chapter is silent on how the Fed interpreted them. I would be very curious to know what William McChesney Martin thought of jawboning.

Now let me turn to the econometric section of the chapter. The authors posit an alternative Phillips curve for the United Kingdom in equation (1). It has some distinctive elements: the output gap enters only if positive, though the change in the gap is always in the equation. The authors do not estimate this equation. Indeed, it would not make sense to attempt to estimate it on actual data because the authors posit that this equation characterizes the Treasury's thinking rather than fits the actual data. One could imagine estimating the equation based on Treasury projections, or calibrating it. The authors instead estimate a version of the Smet-Wouters model for the United Kingdom. This model has a conventional New Keynesian Phillips curve, so equation (1) does not figure in the empirical work of the chapter.

The purpose of the estimates of the Smet-Wouters model in the chapter is to identify policy shocks for the United Kingdom. These shocks are then used to evaluate the monetary policy during the period that is the focus of the narrative. These estimated shocks are useful for policy evaluation. Yet, since they have a close resemblance to the real interest rate, perhaps focusing on the raw data is easier. Panel A of figure 8.2 shows that there were two prolonged episodes in the 1970s where the nominal interest rate was below the inflation rate. These episodes correspond to the two periods of persistent, expansionary policy shocks (low interest rates in equation [2]). Hence, the econometric model diagnoses the loose monetary policy that is readily apparent in the data. The authors only circumstantially relate the policy shocks to the nonmonetary inflation policy that is the focus of the first part of the chapter. Nonmonetary considerations have no role in the model. Therefore, it is correct to look for them in the residuals. The chapter would benefit, however, from a tighter link between the narrative in the first part of the chapter and the estimates in the second.

Let me close with a criticism of the chapter that applies broadly to a number of the papers in this conference. The story line of the conference is as follows: *Mistakes were made in the conduct of monetary policy from the mid-1960s through the 1970s. Policymakers now know better how to conduct policy.* This chapter, as several others in the conference, makes this point by showing that a modern model fit to the period of the Great Inflation diagnoses policy errors. The chapter connects these residuals to its narrative of nonmonetary factors only by their temporal coincidence. Since the nonmonetary features of policy, so well-documented in the chapter, are not explicitly modeled, the case is circumstantial. More importantly, the authors do not show that policymakers using the model would have done substantially better than the contemporary ones in dealing with the actual shocks the economy faced during the period of the Great Inflation. This chapter does, thankfully, not adopt the tone of self-congratulation of many of the contributions to this volume. Instead, it leaves implicit the "we know better" message that other papers make explicit.

This tone of self-congratulation at the conference was particularly grating given the timing of the conference in September 2008, when the financial system was crumbling. Perhaps monetary policy had nothing to do with the conditions that led to the crisis. I tend to think otherwise. Indeed, I suspect that the chapters in this volume will be fodder for an NBER conference some years from now about the complacency of monetary policy during the great moderation. Sustaining low inflation is, of course, an important goal. Central banks that achieve low inflation deserve commendation. Yet, I expect the message of that future conference will be that judging monetary policy solely by its achievement of low and stable inflation was a serious mistake.

Reference

Abrams, Burton A. 2006. "How Richard Nixon Pressured Arthur Burns: Evidence from the Nixon Tapes." *Journal of Economic Perspectives* 20 (4): 177–88.

Discussion

John Crow emphasized that the United Kingdom is rather exogenous and insular with respect to this issue. Where did the presented views of policy come from, particularly in regards to the Radcliffe Report? The Radcliffe

Report provided a muddy view of monetary policy, but to what extent did it influence policy? Remember that John Maynard Keynes was involved and Phillips was a huge influence. Why did these views persist for so long?

Gregory Hess provided his own story of attending Cambridge and meeting Frank Hahn, who believed that the United Kingdom was full of the best economists of the time, yet the worst economic performance. He attributed it to the Keynesian mentality that pervaded throughout the United Kingdom. There was a dearth of macroeconomics from the United States being sent to the United Kingdom.

Allan Meltzer stressed the upper tail theory of inflation as what is at play here. Inflation is caused by whatever price was rising at that particular point. However, what prevented hyperinflation? Favorable shocks? To comment on Shapiro's discussion, the Kennedy Administration had James Tobin, Paul Samuelson, and Robert Solow, all who wrote a report that said inflation begins before the economy gets to full employment, and therefore price/wage guidelines are needed. It was the Samuelson/Solow Phillips curve that brought this about in the United States. Meltzer continued on with some footnotes, adding that Chairman Arthur Burns criticized the policy of the Council of Economic Advisers in the 1960s, and for unknown reasons he changed his mind when he became chairman of the Federal Reserve. President Richard Nixon was often angry with Chairman Burns, and always believed that no one could lose an election due to inflation, but they could due to high unemployment. Price/wage controls were enacted simply to win the election of 1972. Chairman Burns was stroked by President Nixon many times; Nixon called him the greatest economist that ever lived in an effort to curb the recession that was predicted. Ironically, the entire Board of Governors at the time consisted of appointees of presidents Kennedy and Johnson, and Chairman Burns somehow convinced them to produce rapid money growth, and they made Congress believe it was the right thing to do. Unemployment was the first priority, and always remained the first priority until chairmen Paul Volcker and Alan Greenspan came into office.

Jeremy Rudd provided observations about Chairman Burns. He always seemed to argue that inflation came from fiscal policy, but he did not have a clear distinction of the difference between wage-push shocks and inflation expectations fitting into the picture, which is actually in line with the academic literature at the time. Even Robert Solow in the 1960s fluctuated between talking about wage-push and price expectations. Even as late at 1978, Chairman Burns said that wage-push pressures did not start because of workers' wages, but rather because of policies that brought about excess aggregate demand, like the Vietnam War and the Great Society programs. He clearly argued that monetary policy could affect aggregate demand, raise the unemployment rate, and reduce inflation, but that the cost of reducing inflation was too high. Rudd thought that this all stemmed from Chairman

Burns's misperceptions about the natural rate and slack in the economy. Since the economists who were estimating these animals back then were using techniques still used today, is it worrisome that we may not have learned a lot?

Alan Blinder wanted there to be more discussed of the "stag" part of "stagflation." In many European countries, there was a wage explosion with radical politics. Even from a modern perspective, there are supply shocks, and authorities have to balance this nasty trade-off. That was a big part of both the UK and US stories.

Benjamin Friedman began the discussion about rumors published in *Fortune* magazine some years ago about an FOMC meeting in which Chairman Burns was arguing for a rate cut, yet the rest of the FOMC would not go along. He was rumored to have left the room, called President Nixon, returned to the FOMC, said he had been on the phone with the president, and thus the rest of the FOMC went along with the rate cut. Meltzer was adamant that this rumor was not true, given his own experience interviewing people from the time. For example, George Shultz was around at the time and sat in on meetings when President Nixon was stroking Chairman Burns, but the published rumor is just not true. Meltzer continued by saying that it would have been a stupid thing for Chairman Burns to do, since most of the FOMC were Democrats. It also violates everything the FOMC knows about itself.

William Poole interpreted Chairman Burns's views as if the political process would not stand for unemployment, and that the UK situation might have a lot to do with the UK private sector sharing the same views. Why wasn't there a real explosion in credit markets with people fleeing from fixed-income assets? Interest rates went up, but there was no monetary crisis that one would expect from a standard rational expectations model.

Barry Eichengreen objected to some sources and conclusions from the chapter. He referred to the detailed documentary record on Treasury monetary policy thinking, which is in the public Treasury record files. While it is not a set of minutes, it provides a detailed set of memoranda. There is a thirty-year rule on releasing the documents, but many books have been published as more documents become available. Many of the contemporaries of the time thought there was no stable link between monetary policy and inflation outcomes, and Eichengreen agreed with Nelson's point about the lens through which dominant opinion viewed monetary policy being conducive to the development of inflation. All of the minds of the time were cost-push types. With regards to the conclusion of the chapter, Eichengreen found it wholly implausible to conclude that the balance of payments problems did not influence UK monetary policy. There are three examples. First, the stop-go policies, where you go as fast as you can to achieve a 1 percent unemployment rate, but then stop once you get into a balance of payments problem. Second, the 1964 and 1967 balance of payments crises. Third,

1976, where there was a tightening of policy, a balance of payments crisis, and upheaval in the exchange rate.

Christopher Sims was annoyed that the discussion still revolved around fighting the battles of the 1960s and 1970s by redefining the various ortho-doxies of the time. Sims thought that monetarism to Nelson was monetar-ism without money, and the emphasis on the ability of monetary policy to ultimately control inflation. James Tobin was fiercely antimonetarist, but not because he did not think that monetary policy could ultimately control infla-tion. He had a sophisticated set of equilibrium views close to what we have in modern times and thought it was ridiculous to tightly control the money stock. There was an L-shaped view of inflation at the time. At low capacity, there is no inflationary pressure. As you kick up capacity, so too do you kick up inflation. The Phillips curve in that context and sort of thinking was a move toward recognizing that as you approach capacity, you would begin to get inflationary pressure and it became a policy in which expectations began to matter. It was actually the route by which Keynesians began to appreciate the possibility that monetary policy was really important. Sims felt it was crucial to recognize that everyone back in those times was confused, and that confusion has been resolved slowly over time.

Martin Feldstein was a graduate student at Oxford in the late 1960s, and he remembered it as a time in which the notion of monetary policy as we think of it today as a mechanism for eliminating aggregate demand and infla-tion was not taught at the time. The lack of that permeated into the thinking of the Treasury. Recall that soon after, Alan Walters was expressing his views on how policy needed to change, and he later became Margaret Thatcher's advise on the subject. How did he happen upon the subject, given that he was, in all practice, an econometrician?

Andrew Levin recommended reading a biography of William Martin. President Lyndon Johnson exerted a large amount of political pressure on Chairman Martin. Then President Nixon exerted his political influence on Chairman Burns, and President Jimmy Carter even threatened to fire Burns. A positive change in the modern era is the extent to which politicians do not openly criticize the Federal Reserve. Referring to a comment made by Christina Romer, Chairman Burns was raising the real Federal Funds rate to around 5 percent during 1974 to 1975, even during a recession. While Nelson might want to say everything in the United States was repeating itself in the United Kingdom, the British were cutting rates at the time that Chairman Burns was raising them.

Nelson clarified that the 1960s guidepost included Samuelson and Solow thinking that the Phillips curve was symmetric. That is an important distinc-tion, and the United States changed its thinking and began to look at expec-tations more than the cost-push element. While this chapter did not deal much with the nonmonetary action, Nelson referred to his plethora of pre-vious work on UK monetary policy at the time. In reference to Eichengreen,

Nelson reiterated that he has an insurmountable lead in the amount of sources, and much of the materials that have been disclosed do not impress him. Were there any new revelations? The 1976 crisis caused them to raise interest rates, but they were fearful of cost-push stress again. In reference to Crow's remarks, Nelson recalled Anna Schwartz's description of the Radcliffe Report as the "coup de grâce" in terms of bringing together a lot of the hard-line views of the time. Keynes was not alive in the 1970s, but his associates were. Prewar UK economists had a large influence on the United States, and the reciprocation came later on. Meltzer asked about the lack of a hyperinflation, and Nelson felt there were limits to the extent the United Kingdom wanted to ease because they did not want a positive output gap. Therefore, there was an upper limit. Nelson refused to comment on the arguments made about Chairman Burns. Lastly, Nelson wanted to clarify Sims's belief that he was revising monetarism. In fact, Nelson is simply saying that there are monetarist principles and the United Kingdom did not believe they could be effective in using monetary policy to combat issues.

IV

International Perspectives

Bretton Woods and the Great Inflation

Michael D. Bordo and Barry Eichengreen

9.1   Introduction

There is no shortage of explanations for the acceleration of inflation in the late 1960s in the United States. A first interpretation is that policymakers mistakenly adopted a nonmonetary view of inflation as driven by idiosyncratic ("cost-push") factors and disregarded monetary policy as a tool for containing price-level increases.[1] A second cites price-level disturbances in combination with a monetary policy rule that caused policymakers to accommodate the resulting inflationary pressures.[2] And a third interpretation is that policymakers mistakenly concluded that they could attain a permanently higher level of output by accepting a higher rate of inflation.[3]

There is insight to be gained from each of these views. We neither dispute

Michael D. Bordo is professor of economics at Rutgers University and a research associate of the National Bureau of Economic Research. Barry Eichengreen is the George C. Pardee and Helen N. Pardee Professor of Economics and Political Science at the University of California, Berkeley, and a research associate of the National Bureau of Economic Research.

This chapter was prepared for the NBER conference on the Great Inflation, Woodstock, Vermont, September 25–27, 2008. We are grateful to Owen Humpage and Michael Shenk at the Cleveland Fed for facilitating our reading and analysis of the FOMC minutes. We also thank Hyun Hak Kim for able research assistance. For helpful comments, we thank Allan Meltzer and the referees from the University of Chicago Press and the NBER. For acknowledgments, sources of research support, and disclosure of the authors' material financial relationships, if any, please see http://www.nber.org/chapters/c9174.ack.

1. See Nelson (2005). In effect they saw inflation as unresponsive to aggregate demand and therefore to monetary policy actions.

2. See Clarida, Galí, and Gertler (2000).

3. As emphasized by Sargent (1999) and Romer and Romer (2002a). Some compounded this error by overestimating the output gap. This is the argument of Orphanides (2003, 2004), to which we return later. Others assumed the existence of an exploitable output-inflation relationship but perceived a steepening of the trade-off, encouraging them to accept higher inflation in order to maintain unemployment at low levels. See Taylor (1997) and Primiceri (2005).

their validity nor run a horse race between them.[4] But we argue that a full understanding of how and why policymakers allowed inflation to accelerate in the second half of the 1960s requires one also to understand why the same factors did not operate previously—what it was, in other words, that restrained inflationary tendencies in earlier years.

Here our emphasis differs from that in the previous literature. We argue that Federal Reserve policy prior to the Great Inflation—for present purposes the period 1959 to 1965—resembled that of a central bank following the gold standard rules of the game.[5] The stability of the dollar exchange rate (under Bretton Woods, the dollar price of gold) was a priority for policy. Balance-of-payments developments that could undermine the stability of the exchange rate drew a sharp reaction. An inflationary increase in aggregate demand that threatened to suck in imports and crowd out exports elicited an increase in rates. Accelerating inflation that augered a deterioration in international competitiveness similarly caused the Fed to tighten. The value attached by the Fed to the stability of the exchange rate was public knowledge. Thus, when demand increased and the balance of payments weakened, awareness that the Fed would tighten limited the inflationary consequences. The Fed's commitment to following the Bretton Woods rules of the game anchored expectations. It limited inflationary inertia and prevented inflation from taking off in response to shocks.

The attentive reader will note that we have shifted from referring to the gold standard rules to the Bretton Woods rules. This is intended to flag that we are referring not to the simple textbook characterization of the rules of the game under the gold standard (according to which a central bank mechanically responds to reserve increases and losses and disregards other possible influences on policy), but to a more nuanced version in which the central bank is also influenced by other factors. We are not arguing that balance-of-payments considerations were the only thing shaping policy.[6] We are not even arguing that they were always, or even usually, the most important factors in the decisions of the Federal Open Market Committee (FOMC), although as we show later they dominated on a number of occasions. But we are arguing that close attention to balance-of-payments concerns is necessary in order to understand why Fed policy was even less inflationary in the first half of the 1960s than one would expect on the basis of the Taylor rule.[7]

What then changed was not just the model of the economy and the priorities of policymakers, these being the emphases of much of the previous

4. Indeed, it can be argued that the three categories of explanation described in this paragraph are not entirely distinct. But that is a topic for another paper.

5. Prior to 1959 the same policy priorities prevailed, but this being the period of the dollar shortage the balance-of-payments constraint was rarely binding. For more on this see section 9.3.

6. In practice, precisely the same can be said of the nineteenth century and interwar gold standard years. See Eichengreen, Watson, and Grossman (1985).

7. A fact that we document in section 9.5.

literature, but also perceptions of the assignment of tasks. In the earlier period, defending the dollar had been perceived as a shared responsibility of the Treasury and the Fed, with the latter assuming a significant share of the burden. In the second half of the 1960s, in contrast, the Treasury and, more broadly, the Administrative Branch assumed more responsibility for defense of the dollar. The Fed perceived itself as freer to pursue other goals.

This perceptual shift was further encouraged by policies that can be thought of as quasi-capital controls, like the Interest Equalization Tax imposed in 1963 in order to limit foreign financial investment by American residents. Such policies loosened the link between inflation and the exchange rate. They relaxed the constraints shaping monetary policy and anchoring expectations in prior years. They allowed the Fed to rationalize more expansionary policies. If the central bank now adopted more expansionary policies, it did not have to worry to the same extent that this would cause the balance of payments to deteriorate. And if the balance of payments did in fact deteriorate, it was now the Treasury rather than the Fed that was primarily responsible for dealing with the consequences.[8]

On occasions when balance of payments pressure rose to alarming levels, the Fed responded as before. But it did so less regularly. Together with the knowledge that the central bank now felt freer to pursue other goals, this meant that the exchange rate commitment anchored expectations less effectively. Moreover, the view that a different government agency, the Treasury, was now primarily responsible for the stability of the dollar and the balance of payments, a responsibility that it also had the capacity to discharge, encouraged the belief within the Fed that inflation could be allowed to accelerate without violating one of its key objectives, which was to maintain the stability of the dollar. It fostered the belief that the central bank could pursue high employment more aggressively while exercising less vigilance over inflation than before.

How, then, does our account differ from the previous literature? We do not depart from other recent work describing a growing inclination, not just in the Fed but also in the Executive Branch, to enlist monetary policy in the pursuit of full employment and growth at the cost of price stability. We do not dispute accounts emphasizing how the Fed disregarded the inflationary consequences of its policies in order to pursue other goals. But we offer a different explanation for why the monetary policymakers felt free to do so. This explanation also points to a different periodization than most of the earlier literature. We see the Great Inflation as taking off in 1965, since this was when the reassignment of responsibility for exchange rate stability became clear. Scholars emphasizing other factors point in contrast to the late 1960s or the early 1970s. While it may have taken until then for the full extent of inflationary pressures to become evident, the precipitating shift, we

---

8. Which it could do by increasing taxes on foreign investments, reducing military spending abroad, and adopting other fiscal expedients.

argue, occurred around 1965. It critically involved the perception that primary responsibility for the dollar exchange rate had shifted to the Treasury.[9]

Section 9.2 presents an overview of Fed policy and its motivations in the 1960s based on the Board of Governor's *Annual Reports*. Section 9.3 then uses narrative evidence from the minutes of the Federal Open Market Committee to develop our view that balance-of-payments considerations exercised a restraining influence on inflation before 1965. Section 9.4 shows that this situation changed subsequently. Section 9.5 then supplements the narrative record with statistical evidence pointing in the same direction. Section 9.6, finally, concludes.

9.2   An Overview of FOMC Decision Making

If the dollar and the balance of payments were of concern to the Fed and influenced the conduct of policy prior to 1965, then this should be evident in the words and deeds of the Federal Open Market Committee. We take two approaches to determining whether this was the case. In this section we construct a summary of FOMC policy actions from the Board of Governors' *Annual Report*. Following that, in the next two sections we flesh out that summary with a narrative account featuring quotes from FOMC minutes.

For every FOMC meeting from 1959 to 1971 we describe the policy decision taken, the reason given for it (whether domestic or international or both), the number of dissents, the direction of the dissents, and whether the concept of "even keel" was invoked. ("Even keel" was the name given to the post-Accord policy of the Fed, which sought to facilitate Treasury funding operations by stabilizing the Treasury bill market while also pursuing other objectives; see Markese 1973.)

The upper panel of figure 9.1 shows policy actions: decisions to tighten are the positive bars, while decisions to ease are the negative bars. For decisions to keep policy unchanged, no bar is shown. In addition, we indicate whether the actions were taken primarily for domestic reasons (white bars), primarily for international reasons (black bars), or for a combination of both reasons (cross-hatched bars).[10] We also show in the upper panel of figure 9.1 the key policy instruments that the FOMC referred to at the time: the federal funds rate, the ninety-day Treasury bill rate, and the discount rate.

The lower panel shows the dissents. The bars above the line indicate that

9. Statistical evidence (following) suggests that the inflation process ratcheted up in several steps in the course of the 1960s and early 1970s; our interpretation points to changes in the perception and priority attached to balance-of-payments concerns as explaining the first ratchet around 1965.

10. Appendix B presents the data underlying figure 9.1. In addition to the information in the figure, it shows the number of attendees present and absent at each meeting and the vote taken. Information from the Federal Reserve Board's *Annual Reports* was gathered and summarized with the help of Michael Shenk of the Federal Reserve Bank of Cleveland.

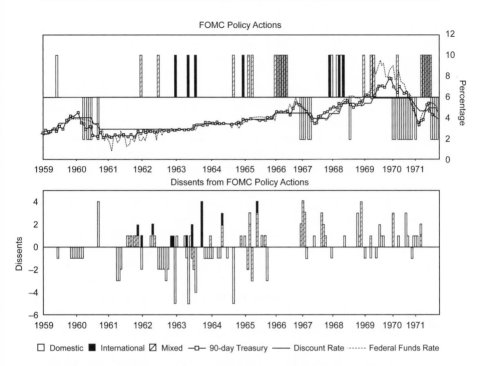

Fig. 9.1   FOMC policy actions and dissents from FOMC policy actions

the dissenter wanted a tighter policy than enacted, while the bars below the line indicate that the dissenter wanted policy to be looser than what was enacted. The length of the bars indicates the number of dissents. Their colors indicate the division between domestic, international, and mixed, as in the upper panel.

The number of meetings with black bars indicating policy actions motivated primarily by international considerations is not large (7 out of a total of 210), all of which indicated increased restraint. These cases are concentrated before late 1965, although they also appear occasionally thereafter at times that are associated with a dramatic deterioration in the balance of payments, such as the aftermath of sterling's devaluation in late 1967 and the collapse of the London Gold Pool in 1968 (more on that later). The number of meetings where there are cross-hatched bars indicating that a combination of domestic and international factors motivated the policy is considerable: there are twenty-three of these. These meetings, which also indicated increased restraint, occurred both before 1965 and during crisis periods in 1967, 1968, and 1971.

We do not read this evidence as indicating that balance of payments considerations dictated monetary policy decisions in the first half of the 1960s any more than they strictly dictated central bank decision making under the prewar and interwar gold standards. Rather, we see concern over the balance of payments as tipping the balance—but often importantly so, at least in the period before 1965.

9.3   Narrative Evidence, 1959 to 1965

Having shown what the FOMC did and provided a summary characterization of why, we now recount what it said about its decisions in more detail. In this section we focus on the period when balance-of-payments considerations repeatedly influenced the committee's policy decisions. Section 9.4 contrasts the subsequent period.[11]

Economic policy under the Eisenhower administration emphasized budget balance, price stability, and the Bretton Woods peg to gold at $35 an ounce. Federal Reserve Chairman William McChesney Martin was a firm believer in adherence to the gold peg. He was supported by a number of FOMC members, especially Alfred Hayes, president of the Federal Reserve Bank of New York, who throughout the Bretton Woods period advocated policy tightening to protect the monetary gold stock and offset incipient balance of payments deficits.

The year 1959 was the first time when significant concern was voiced about the stability of the dollar. The 1959 to 1960 recession, engineered by tight monetary policy, led to both deflation and a gold inflow in the classical manner.[12] The FOMC minutes document that the Fed's decision to maintain a tight policy was importantly influenced by balance-of-payments considerations. For example, at the FOMC on January 6, 1959, when the vote was to maintain policy, President Hayes said that "it was possible that when questions had been raised about the stability of the dollar, an action taken on the disciplinary side of System monetary policy would bring credit rather than discredit on System intentions. If nothing else it was quite likely that our upward movement of Treasury Bill yields in the United Sates to equality with or above, the yield on Treasury bills in the United Kingdom would tend to stem the outflow of gold from the United States. Moreover it might draw gold back to this country because of more attractive investment opportunities offered in the US Government securities market" (19).[13]

---

11. We also searched for other bits of narrative evidence, for example, in the memoirs of Treasury and Federal Reserve officials. One who speaks to the issues at hand is Charles Coombs, who was responsible for international operations at the New York Fed. He alludes indirectly to the kind of shift of perceived responsibility from the Fed to the Treasury that we emphasize here, although he places it somewhat later, at the time when Nixon administration took office and Fowler and Deming took over at the Treasury ("The role of the Federal Reserve in foreign financial policy was severely curtailed after the accession of the Nixon administration in January 1969"). See Coombs (1976, xii, 190–91).

12. For more detail see Meltzer (2010, chapter 2).

13. Page numbers indicated in parentheses in this section refer to the page in the minutes of the FOMC meeting cited on which the quoted material appears.

On October 4, 1960, when the action taken was to maintain the current stance of decreased restraint, Mr. Treiber, vice president of the Federal Reserve Bank of New York emphasized how it was "important that the United States act promptly and wisely to rectify the balance of payments deficit. Failure to do so will more and more circumscribe the ability of the Federal Reserve to pursue a flexible monetary policy" (16). The 1960 presidential campaign was in full swing, and investors had begun to worry that the Democratic candidate, John F. Kennedy, who was pledged to getting the economy going again, might not prioritize defense of the dollar. The priorities of the FOMC, however, were clear. President Leach of the Federal Reserve Bank of Richmond warned that "[m]ore ease . . . would not be of material assistance to the economy, but would affect the balance of payments adversely and could make the task of monetary policy more difficult in the future" (30). Also at the October 25, 1960, meeting, when the policy directive was to maintain decreased restraint, the accompanying statement explicitly acknowledged the balance-of-payments problem. The Federal Reserve Bank of New York was "directed to [conduct open market operations] in light of current and prospective economic conditions . . . with a view . . . (b) to encouraging monetary expansion for the purpose of fostering sustainable growth in economic activity and employment, while taking into consideration current international developments" (59).

Hayes elaborated:

> We have recognized right along, ever since our balance of payments became seriously adverse in 1958, that although domestic considerations must be our main concern, we could not ignore the international implications of our actions. It so happened that during this time our policies were well suited to both domestic and international conditions . . . but this has no longer been true during much of 1960, and last month's gold episode [when the London price of gold spiked to $40.00 per ounce on the fears that a Kennedy administration would be inflationary] should serve as dramatic evidence that we are dealing with a complex and sensitive problem with respect to the international financial position. Undoubtedly one of the causes of the gold speculation has been fear that this country might want to unduly loosen monetary and fiscal policies in an effort to combat recessionary tendencies. (16)
>
> It seems to me that the balance of payments deficit, with all of the complications which may accompany it in the way of gold sales and loss of confidence in the dollar confronts all Americans with an extremely serious if not almost intractable problem. . . . All of this argues strongly for our avoiding further overt measures of monetary ease, such as a discount rate cut, unless they are clearly called for by the state of the domestic economy . . . and I do not think they are at present. (170)

Canby Balderston of the Board of Governors agreed, stating that he "would favor a change in the directive such as Mr. Hayes had suggested [while inserting 'while taking into consideration current international developments']. The gold outflow was part of the total problem; to ignore it would be unwise and might reflect on the System in the future" (43).

On November 22, 1960, when the decision was to keep policy unchanged, even greater attention was paid to the balance of payments. Chairman Martin stated that "he continued to believe that the balance of payments problem was the most important problem for the country to deal with at this time. This was because he believed it to be the most significant shadow in the domestic business picture, and the only way he could point this up was to say that the credit of the US was now in danger" (41). Then on January 10, 1961, when the policy action continued to be to maintain the prevailing policy, A. L. Mills of the Board of Governors stated that

> In his view, it would be much more in order to permit the reserve position of the bank to tighten to a degree that would find the short-term interest rate moving up from its artificially low level which would be conducive to checking the outflow of funds and possibly recovering it . . . the economic affairs of the country had reached a point where it became necessary to use monetary policy as a surgical scalpel to correct dramatically a very difficult international financial situation. . . . It was a serious responsibility of the Federal Reserve Banks and of the members of Board of Governors to take into account first the international situation and to consider what detailed steps should be taken that would be most conducive to a more harmonious international financial position. (29)

There is extensive narrative evidence, then, that the balance of payments figured in the considerations of members of the FOMC, leading to a policy of a more restrained monetary policy than might have prevailed otherwise.

Although he was elected in the fall of 1960 with a mandate to restore full employment, President John F. Kennedy also believed in the importance of maintaining the gold parity. Pressure on gold reserves and a growing balance of payments deficit, reflecting US private and public foreign investment in excess of the current account surplus, emerged as important problems in these years. The US Treasury under Secretary Douglas Dillon and Under Secretary Robert Roosa supplemented the efforts of the Fed to stem the dollar outflow, intervening in the foreign exchange market, developing a network of swap agreements with other countries starting in March 1961 (in order to create credit lines big enough to finance short-term balance-of-payments pressures on the scale that might be suffered by the United States), issuing foreign-currency-denominated US Treasury securities (Roosa bonds), creating the International Monetary Fund's (IMF's) General Agreements to Borrow, and establishing the Gold Pool (an arrangement with seven European countries to jointly share the burden of selling gold on the London market as necessary to stabilize its price at $35 an ounce). While the Fed continued to pay considerable attention to the balance of payments when determining the stance of policy, the actions of the Treasury in complementing its efforts helped to set the stage for the subsequent period when the Fed felt free to delegate responsibility for the dollar and the balance of payments.

The FOMC meetings between 1961 and 1964 featured vigorous debate between those individuals (usually including Chairman Martin) advocating tight policy to defend the dollar and the proponents of looser conditions designed to stimulate growth and reduce unemployment. On multiple occasions, the two groups deadlocked, resulting in no change in policy. Policy almost certainly would have been loosened in a number of these instances absent the importance attached by the first faction to balance-of-payments considerations. In addition, on several occasions the FOMC voted to raise rates in part to protect the balance of payments: specific instances included December 18, 1962, May 7, 1963, and July 30, 1963. The second and third of these increases were part of Operation Twist, conducted in cooperation with the Treasury, under which the Fed raised short-term interest rates to stem capital outflows while the Treasury lowered long-term rates to stimulate domestic investment. Again, we would argue that these increases would have been unlikely had balance-of-payments considerations not tipped the balance.

At its meeting on August 1, 1961, the FOMC had voted to maintain its policy stance. The statement explaining this decision explicitly referred to the balance of payments and to the need "to encourage expansion of bank credit and the money supply so as to contribute to strengthening the focus of recovery, while giving consideration to international factors" (57). Several committee members argued vigorously for tightening policy in response to the deteriorating international position. According to Treiber, "[o]bservers abroad are likely to interpret excessive ease here, particularly as symbolized by a low T-bill rate, as indication of an unwillingness or inability on the part of the US to take the steps necessary to assure the soundness of the dollar" (23). Mr. Deming, president of the Federal Reserve Bank of Minneapolis, suggested further that "[a]s to the directive, in the light of recent developments in Europe [Germany had revalued in March, drawing attention to the comparative strength of its balance of payments] he would suggest the possibility of inserting the word 'increased' before 'considerations' in the phrase of clause (b) [of the directive] now reading 'while giving consideration to international factors'" (31). Rouse, manager of the System Open Market Account, warned that "[t]he questions that had been asked of him [by the BIS governors] about Government expenditures, the Federal budget, and related matters were indication of a background of concern about possible developments in this country over a period of time. They indicated a feeling that the US ultimately would have to resolve the same questions that the British were trying to resolve at the present time" (55).

In the meeting on October 3, 1961, the committee again voted to keep policy unchanged, and its statement again spoke of the need to attend to the balance of payments. Some members made the case for tightening in response to deteriorating balance-of-payments conditions. Charles Shepardson of the Board of Governors expressed his view that "it would be fortunate if there was some rise in the bill rate in the light of the international situation" (12). As Mills put it, "the disparity between short-term interest rates in this country and Great Britain argues for higher rates in this country as a hindrance against renewed gold losses and . . . to counter inflationary influences" (13). These last words are a reminder that concern over the balance of payments was not always the only or the most important factor, but this narrative evidence should make clear that it figured importantly in the minds of some members.

At its October 24, 1961 meeting, although the FOMC again voted to maintain the current policy, a growing number of committee members invoked deteriorating balance-of-payments conditions as reason for tightening. As President Irons of the Federal Reserve Bank of Dallas put it,

> In terms of the domestic situation . . . it would seem reasonable to continue about the same degree of ease that had existed during the past three weeks. However the international situation presented a problem calling for a somewhat different conclusion. The forthcoming Treasury refunding . . . suggests maintaining the status quo. Balancing these out, the Committee might do well to give more attention to firming short-term rates in order to provide relief on the international side without creating instability or undue restriction in the domestic market. (21)

Mr. Clay of the Federal Reserve Bank of Kansas City expressly referred to the impact of Fed policy on capital flows when he observed that "the Manager of the System Open Account would need to conduct open market operations with a view to keep the treasury bill rate from going too low relative to rates abroad" (29). Mr. Heflin of the Federal Reserve Bank of Richmond cautioned that "the delicate and uneasy position of the dollar suggested that it would be unwise to move toward additional ease" (31). Mills warned that "a start [must be] made toward implementing a moderately restraining monetary and credit policy. . . . The skeptical attitude to Federal Reserve system policies that has been taken by domestic and foreign monetary experts, and which is a factor in the weakness of the dollar on the international exchanges and in renewed gold losses, is perhaps the strongest reason that urges a revision of policy thinking" (33). Balderston asked rhetorically "whether the transfer abroad of gold and dollars plus the widened interest differential between New York and London, was serious enough to give concern. To this question his answer was in the affirmative" (49). Hayes, acting as chairman in Martin's absence, warned that "on balance the System would lose more by standing aside than by doing what it could to indicate that it saw danger on the international exchanges . . . he then said he thought that at least a goodly number of those around the table had expressed some concern about the international problem and had recognized that there was perhaps something the System could do to help, in a minor way, to show that it was aware of the problem, without doing damage to the domestic economy" (51).

At the meeting on November 14, the vote was again for no change, but now there were dissents in favor of tightening on balance-of-payments grounds. In the opinion of Treiber, "[t]he most disturbing factor now before us is our poor balance of payments. . . . The rise in short-term rates since last month . . . should be helpful from the international viewpoint. . . . As for the directive, it seems to me that in light of international factors and the basic strength of the domestic economy, the committee could properly change the directive so as to put less emphasis on encouraging credit expansion and greater emphasis on international factors" (24). Clearly, balance-of-payments concerns had tipped the opinion of at least one FOMC member in favor of tightening, although they had not yet convinced the majority.

Then on December 19, 1961, the FOMC voted eight to four in favor of increased restraint for both domestic and international reasons. Hayes was not satisfied; he pushed for even greater attention to the balance of payments. He recommended changing the directive to read, "giving special attention to international factors" instead of "giving consideration to international factors" (13).[14] Then at the next meeting on January 23, the FOMC voted to maintain the degree of tightening from the previous meeting, again mentioning the balance of payments. Once more Hayes pushed for tightening to help the international situation by raising the discount rate. As he put it,

This country is just too easy a place in which to borrow and not a sufficiently attractive place in which to invest. As the domestic economy continues to improve, we can very well afford to take steps to modify this set of conditions and try to induce some return flow of capital. . . . In terms of open market policy this means that we should edge towards less ease. . . . In our Bank . . . [we] have done a good deal of soul-searching lately on the subject of a possible discount rate increase. The balance of payments problem is serious enough to raise the question whether we could not act on the rate in advance of a market rate rise, in order to emphasize the increase as a signal of our determination to do our part in meeting the critical international problem. (11)

A series of meetings then passed without additional reference to the balance of payments. But at the December 18, 1962 meeting, the FOMC voted to increase restraint primarily for international reasons, over five dissents. Hayes was representative of those supporting the decision. In his judgment "the balance of payments situation was the biggest single shadow over the domestic business picture. He did not believe that a slightly less easy monetary policy [to alleviate the balance of payments deficit] would in any sense

14. His change was not adopted.

collapse the domestic economy. In fact such a change in emphasis might lead to a strengthening of confidence." (61)

There followed a series of meetings where the December 1962 policy was maintained, although both Hayes and Martin pushed for more attention to external balance. As Hayes put the case on February 12, "the magnitude of the balance of payments problem is much too great to be solved by monetary policy alone. Nevertheless, monetary policy can and should play an important part, and I would hope that it could do so simultaneously with a . . . well publicized program on the part of the Administration to achieve equilibrium in our international payments, including a substantial net reduction in military and aid disbursements abroad and a firm policy towards greater discipline in the area of production costs" (20). Chairman Martin reinforced the point, observing that "if the System had been derelict in 1962 it was probably in paying a minimum of attention to the balance of payments problem. There was little question in his mind but that a crisis was approaching" (48). At the next meeting, on March 5, the vote was again to maintain, and both Hayes and Martin again stressed the balance of payments. Hayes put it this way:

> The outflow of gold was resumed last week and the prospect is for substantial gold sales during the coming month . . . we are clearly getting closer to the danger point as the gold stock diminishes while the balance of payments deficit continues unabashed. . . . Admittedly a move toward lesser ease would involve some risk with respect to the domestic economy . . . they are minor risks compared with the growing danger to the dollar's international standing. . . . There might . . . be an opportunity later in the month for an increase in the discount rate if the System was willing to give a clear signal of its concern for our international position. (47)

And "[w]ith respect to the balance of payments . . . [Chairman Martin] continued to feel that conditions were gradually moving toward a crisis of some sort . . . too much attention has been paid to stimulating the domestic economy through monetary policy and not enough for dealing with the balance of payments . . . the balance of payments problem had become the real shadow over the domestic business scene" (82). On June 18, 1963, for a third time the vote was to maintain, although Hayes and others pushed for an increase in the discount rate to address the international situation. "[T]he time for decision is at hand," as Hayes put it. "[T]he continued gravity of the international position leaves us little choice, especially in the light of the Treasury's calendar. . . . An increase of one half percent in the discount rate in the near future could be expected to serve two very important purposes; 1. to signal to the foreign monetary authorities and to the world in general that the System is ready to use traditional tools of monetary policy to defend the international position of the dollar, and 2. to achieve a level of short-term market rates that should cause a substantial repatriation of short funds" (22). Braddock Hickman, an alternate member of the FOMC, was even more to the point. "The raising of interest rates," he stated, "might deter some investments but at the same time it would represent a forward step in dealing with the balance of payments problem" (54).

By the time of the July 9, 1963 meeting, sentiment for tightening on balance-of-payments grounds had become more widespread. Hayes said:

> [T]he dollar has clearly reached a vulnerable stage. The forthcoming gold losses caused by French purchases will tend to unsettle the exchange markets and there are increasingly ominous signs of apprehension and impatience among central banks in Europe . . . [it] behooves us to demonstrate that progress is being made on the balance of payments front before the apprehension reaches crisis proportions. For years there has been a heavy short-term drain . . . and it seems wholly reasonable to believe that an appreciable firming of short-term rates in this country would check the flow and might then bring a reversal. In addition it could have very important psychological effects by signaling . . . the determination of the System to have a strong dollar . . . the System would be prepared to take positive actions as soon as possible in the form of a one half per cent increase in the discount rate . . . [the New York Fed] directors have felt for some time that we should be giving greater emphasis to our international responsibilities . . . it would be important for the System to act in advance of rather than after, any administration announcement of a systemic attack on the balance of payments problem. (29–31).

Hickman again echoed the point: "In so far as policy over the next three months was concerned . . . a shift was not only appropriate but long overdue. The domestic economy continued to move ahead and the balance of payments to deteriorate. [I] would recommend moving immediately toward a higher term structure of interest rates" (40). Chairman Martin stated his willingness to "support an increase in the discount rate . . . [as] part of a concerted attack on the balance of payments problem" (70). Again, we are not arguing that balance-of-payments considerations were the exclusive or even the primary explanation for the 50 basis point increase in the discount rate decided on July 17. But they clearly played an important role in tipping the balance of opinion in favor.

There was little further discussion of the balance of payments for the remainder of 1963 or early 1964.[15] The Kennedy and Johnson administrations took a number of dramatic nonmonetary measures to address the external problem.[16] There was the Interest Equalization Tax adopted in July 1963. The Defense Department instituted a Buy America program to encourage sourcing in the United States. Both Kennedy and Johnson pressed European governments to shoulder more of the cost of stationing US troops

---

15. Although "contributing to improving the balance of payments" was always in the directive.
16. See appendix A for more information on these.

abroad and to purchase military hardware in the United States to offset US military expenditures there. Limits on the foreign goods that American tourists could import duty free were tightened, and a growing share of US foreign aid was tied to purchases of American exports. Still, these steps were less than perfectly successful at solving the balance-of-payments problem, which by mid-1964 had resurfaced. When on June 17, 1964, the FOMC voted to leave policy unchanged, Hayes once again pushed for tightening to strengthen the balance of payments.

> [Our] bargaining position in international financial matters has been dramatically weakened as our cumulative deficit has grown. We cannot afford to let the situation continue for long without taking decisive steps to check it. . . . the balance of payments outlook would justify our taking a clear step toward less credit ease at this time. [I admit] the difficulty of obtaining much public support for such a move in the virtual absence of immediate inflation development here in this country and against the favorable first quarter balance of payments. Also the imminence of treasury financing is an important inhibiting factor. Thus I am led to the reluctant conclusion that we should stay our hand, in so far as an immediate policy move is concerned. (24)

Again in the autumn of 1965 Hayes and others expressed concern about inflation and the deteriorating balance of payments and pressed for a 50 basis point increase in the discount rate. At the meeting on October 12, 1965, he noted that

> [C]oncern over prices and costs seems to be particularly warranted by the unsatisfactory state of the balance of payments and the prospect that we may have trouble keeping the US trade surplus up to its present level in view of the likelihood that imports will be strongly stimulated by the business expansion . . . the effort to reach ultimate [balance-of-payments] equilibrium without the need of artificial barriers will . . . call for a strong concerted effort including an appropriate contribution by monetary policy . . . , Looking ahead . . . [I] have a real basis for concern about potential inflation pressure, against a background of cumulative large increases in bank credit and a serious international payments problem that leaves us little margin for assuming inflation risk . . . [I see] an increase in the discount rate as the most appropriate method of signaling a move toward greater firmness in monetary policy and validating the firming that has already occurred in market rates . . . I think a one half per cent increase [in the discount rate] is fully justified if we look only at international factors. (24–26)

Balderston supported Hayes's position. "[A]n increase in the discount rate . . . internationally . . . should [lead to] a new measure of confidence in the dollar, and perhaps seek interest rate incentives to investment in the US" (67). This time Chairman Martin was more cautious. "With a divided Committee and in the face of strong Administrative opposition he didn't believe it would be appropriate for him to lend his support to those who favored a change in policy now . . . he hoped the debate about the role of monetary policy in dealing with the balance of payments could be shifted away from the question whether the deficit can be entirely overcome by interest rate action alone . . . he did not believe that was possible" (69–71).

Hayes reiterated the point on November 23. "In my judgment this combination of circumstances [inflationary pressure and adverse balance of payments] points to a clear policy conclusion. The time has come for an overt move to signal a firm monetary policy, and an increase in the discount rate by one half per cent is the appropriate means of affecting such a change . . . he is prepared to recommend that the New York directors vote a one half percent discount rate increase within the next week or so" (35–36). His argument drew support from new quarters. According to President Ellis of the Federal Reserve Bank of Boston, "it was evident that further measures would be required to restrain capital outflow. One such measure, a move towards lesser ease would not only buttress the special credit restraint measures being employed but would serve as a widely understood monetary signal that would strengthen the willingness to hold dollars abroad" (35). Dewey Daane of the Board of Governors added that "[l]ast but not least on [his] list of economic reasons for a System policy change was the deterioration in the US balance of payments" (69).

At the December 6 meeting Hayes observed that although the rise in the discount rate and the revision of Regulation Q ceilings would "prove valuable both in extending the duration of the present business upswing and in bolstering the international position of the dollar . . . [there is] need for Open Market policy to back up official rate action. . . . Any threat to reasonable price stability also has serious implications for our balance of payments deficit" (25). The Board of Governors agreed, and voted for a 50 basis point hike in the discount rate. This was the decision that led the president to verbally attack Martin during the chairman's visit shortly thereafter to the LBJ ranch, an experience that Meltzer and others argue significantly weakened Martin's anti-inflationary resolve.[17]

9.4   Narrative Evidence, 1966 to 1971

In the spring of 1966 the Fed tightened policy because of concern about inflationary pressures. This led to a credit crunch later in the year. In the face of pressure from the housing industry and Congress the Fed shifted its policy in favor of ease early in 1967 (Meltzer 2010, chapter 4). This loosening of monetary policy was reflected in the continued deterioration of the balance of payments. It appears that the Fed simply did not feel the same responsibility as before for addressing those balance-of-payments problems.

---

17. See Meltzer (2010).

Day-to-day responsibility for such matters now fell to the Treasury. Only when a major threat to the stability of the dollar developed did the Fed feel compelled to address it. We now discuss these threats in turn, if only to underscore their exceptional nature.

The first such episode followed the devaluation of the pound sterling in the autumn of 1967. Earlier in the year the Fed had postponed raising the funds rate in order not to precipitate a run on the pound. It also was constrained from raising rates in the face of rising inflation because of the prevalent view at the Fed and in the administration that what was needed to curb inflation was a tax increase. According to the Keynesian doctrine that then prevailed, tight fiscal policy should be matched with loose monetary policy. Chairman Martin repeatedly pressed the administration to raise taxes, an event that came to pass in June 1968 with a 10 percent tax surcharge.[18] Once sterling had been devalued—indeed, the first day after sterling was devalued—pressure shifted to the dollar (the investors' belief apparently being that if the second most important reserve currency could be devalued, it was at least conceivable that the same fate might befall the first). Moreover, when it became apparent that Congress would not pass the 10 percent surcharge that President Johnson had proposed, the Fed had another reason to raise rates.[19]

In addition to raising the discount rate by 50 basis points on November 20, 1967, the FOMC voted to raise rates further in the next meeting on November 27, 1967, and again on December 12. Not just this timing but also the minutes confirm that concerns for the stability of the dollar were of highest priority for these decisions. According to Mr. Treiber, not tightening would lead to "[i]nflation [that] would weaken the position of the dollar internationally at the very time our worldwide efforts require that confidence be sustained and strengthened" (40). Irons emphasized that "the deterioration in the balance of payments situation was a significant factor . . . [he therefore] proposed some reduction in the prevailing degree of ease" (48). According to Charles Coombs, Special Manager of the System Open Market Account, "In the event of [sterling's] devaluation, he would favor having the System devote all of its attention to protecting the dollar" (39). Andrew Brimmer of the Board of Governors "urged the need for contingency planning against a possible devaluation not only to the international finance area but also in connection with the use of domestic policy instruments" (39). Sherman Maisel of the Board of Governors concluded "that an increase in the Federal Reserve discount rate should be considered in connection with contingency planning against the probability of devaluation of sterling" (49).

At the meeting on November 27, 1967, Maisel again voiced concern that "the US might find itself in the same position as the British had recently"

---

18. Hetzel (2008, 73–74).
19. Hetzel (2008).

(43). A variety of expedients to defend the dollar while avoiding the need to tighten monetary policy were considered. Mr. McLaury, assistant vice president in charge of the foreign exchange desk at the Federal Reserve Bank of New York recommended that "the Fed use forward operations as a means of reducing the inflow of dollars into foreign central banks . . . he [viewed] the proposed provision of forward cover [as] an alternative to a tighter domestic monetary policy as a means of limiting dollar accrual by foreign central banks" (43–45). Ellis recommended augmenting the swap line. Still, he acknowledged that "[o]ne important ingredient of a program to defend the dollar in the short-run might very well be convincing evidence that the Committee intended to contribute to that defense in the long-run through its domestic monetary policy . . . the Committee should make it clear that it intended to validate the discount rate action through open market operations" (72).

There was then little discussion of the balance of payments in the minutes until the London Gold Pool collapsed in March 1968, rekindling fears for the stability of the dollar. The existence of the Gold Pool (see appendix A) had created at least the hope that other countries would support the dollar by sharing with the United States the burden of selling gold to the London market; its collapse therefore augured further gold losses. The FOMC voted to increase restraint at each of four consecutive meetings, and the collapse of the Gold Pool, with its uncertain implications for the dollar, was the dominant consideration in at least two of them, on March 14 and April 19. In all, the Fed raised the discount rate on March 22, April 19, and December 12. While the last increase, by 25 basis points, was motivated by the desire to counter inflation, a larger increase of 50 basis points was rejected on this occasion because of fears of how the dollar would be affected if the British were in the face of a large capital outflow to the United States to abandon their peg and float.

The minutes make clear what was motivating the FOMC. On March 5, Mr. Brill of the Board of Governors staff observed that "[o]n balance, the package of a half-point increase in the discount rate and a quarter point increase in Reg Q ceilings [offers] the best hope for achieving fairly prompt financial restraint on expenditures and attracting favorable attention from foreign investors, without engendering a panic reaction among financial institutions and financial markets" (61). Hayes warned that "[a] moderate tightening effort should be favorably received abroad as a means of defending the dollar. . . . Thus the present is an appropriate time for a policy move" (69). Mr. Coldwell, president of the Federal Reserve Bank of Dallas, "thought [that] the country was moving toward a serious and perhaps critical juncture of destabilizing forces . . . wage price pressures were increasing . . . the balance of payments deficit showed no improvement and runs on the gold market were occurring with increasing frequency. The overall situation demanded restraint in monetary policy" (79).

At the FOMC meeting on March 14, the decision to suspend the operation of the London Gold Pool was announced to the committee. Mr. Coombs warned that "the international financial system was moving towards a crisis more dangerous than any since 1931 . . . [it was] important to protect the exchange parity network . . . based on the official price of $35.00 per ounce for gold . . . or by making sure that the System swap lines were fully adequate to absorb the massive flows of hot money across the exchanges" (4). The directive that day included the following: "In light of recent international financial developments, the System open market operations . . . should be conducted with a view to maintain firm but orderly conditions in the money market, taking into account the effects of the Federal Reserve discount rate" (5). The discount rate was then raised on March 22.

At the meeting on April 2, 1968, Coombs warned that "the breakdown of the gold pool was . . . a major defeat for the central banks and governments involved . . . the system was now considerably more vulnerable than before" (5). According to Robert Solomon (associate economist at the Board of Governors)

> The gold pool supplied gold to private speculators in order to forestall a run on the dollar by official holders. . . . But the gold pool policy . . . designed to maintain credibility in the official price of gold . . . itself lost credibility . . . [a] much less happy scenario assumes that inflation continues in the US and [the trade balance worsens]. . . . In this unhappy scenario, the world begins to believe that the US balance of payments deficit cannot be reduced without drastic measures involving . . . [a] change in the relationship between the dollar and gold. . . . To prevent monetary chaos and to assure [a] more favorable evolution, the US must improve its trade balance . . . both domestic and international considerations call for restrictive monetary policy. (15–16)

Daniel Brill, an economist at the Board of Governors, voiced similar fears: "Our international payments position is more precarious, and inaction is proceeding more rapidly than we had estimated even just a month ago. . . . It seems to me . . . that we would be warranted in changing our sights on what is required of monetary policy. . . . there seems to be a sufficiently strong argument for turning the monetary screws a bit more this time" (42). Hayes, predictably, agreed:

> Although we have lived through a major financial crisis since our last regular meeting . . . the basic facts that should determine monetary policy have changed relatively little in that period. The crisis did . . . point up in a most dramatic fashion the perilous position of the dollar reflecting the current problems of inflation, lack of fiscal responsibility, and payment imbalances . . . my preference with respect to open market policy would be to move very gradually toward even further restraint. . . . The proposed policy will lead to a modest firming of the market interest rate and to expectations of another discount rate rise . . .

we should be contemplating the possibility of another one half point increase in the discount rate sometime before the end of April, when even keel restraint will commence so as to make crystal clear the System's determination to do what it reasonably can to uphold the dollar's international standing. (47–49)

According to Mr. Bopp, an alternate member of the FOMC, "further tightening would confirm that the committee meant business, and that was necessary for both international and domestic reasons" (57). Mr. Daane agreed that "greater monetary restraint in the US was necessary to support the decision at the recent meetings in Washington [where the two-tier gold policy under which the Gold Pool members would support the price of gold for official transactions and let the free gold market determine the price for other transactions, was agreed upon] and Stockholm [where provisional agreement was reached to issue Special Drawing Rights] . . . he would be quite amenable to another increase in the discount rate" (69–70). The discount rate was raised by 50 basis points on April 19.

This was not enough, however, to dispatch the problem. At the meeting on May 28, 1968, Brill stated that "[t]he most urgent need would be associated with our international financial problem . . . the main hope for keeping . . . in place . . . existing international financial arrangements lies in the promise that measures of restraint here will convince other countries that we are serious about our intention to curb inflation" (48). At the meeting on December 17, 1968, Mr. Hersey, an associate economist at the Board of Governors, urged the committee "to give full consideration to the long-run problem of checking inflation and halting the deterioration of the international trading position. . . . The principal contribution that monetary policy can make to the defense of our external financial position is through stability of the price level . . . monetary policy aimed at slowing inflation will bring higher interest rates . . . it is the slowing of inflation that is most needed for dealing with the balance of payments problem, not higher interest rates per se" (43). The discount rate was raised on December 18, 1968, preventing any further deterioration in the external situation through the end of 1968.

The Nixon administration that took office in January 1969 inherited inflation from the previous administration. Initially it wanted a tightening of monetary policy (based on monetary aggregates) but with increasing concern over rising unemployment, it followed Arthur Burns's advice and sought to deal with the problem using wage-price controls.[20] There was also discussion of floating the dollar. Balance-of-payments problems were seen as the responsibility of the Treasury and administration—to the extent that anyone took responsibility—and not of the Fed. In particular, Arthur Burns, who took over as chairman of the Federal Reserve in February 1970, viewed such international considerations as the Treasury's problem more

---

20. Hetzel (2008, chapter 8).

than his own. Over most of 1969 to 1970, there was little discussion in the FOMC of balance-of-payments problems. That the merchandise trade balance strengthened as a result of the 1969 to 1970 recession provided blessed relief.

In 1971, however, the exchange-rate problem then resurfaced a final time. As the trade balance began deteriorating again, capital outflows from the United States accelerated. West Germany, inundated with capital inflows, allowed the deutschmark to float upward against the dollar starting in May. Burns, under pressure from Nixon for expansionary monetary policy, lobbied the administration to impose price controls to defend the dollar and relieve the pressure for the Fed to tighten on balance-of-payments grounds. Some of his colleagues, in contrast, argued for tightening in response to the high danger of a payments crisis. In the April 6, 1971 FOMC meeting, the vote was for tightening. A minority led by Hayes wanted more tightening than the committee was willing to vote for to defend the dollar—Hayes emphasized that "the international financial situation should be given a high priority in the FOMC's policy deliberations" (35)—but the majority was preoccupied by the precarious state of the economy. Chairman Burns saw grounds for optimism on the external front, though he remained cautious.

> In the international area, he found it most encouraging that short-term interest rates in the US and abroad were finally beginning to converge. . . . He observed that the dollar had come under speculative pressure that had begun to reach dangerous proportions last week . . . the recovery was quite fragile, and economic conditions in general were at a delicate stage. He had a vivid recollection of 1931, when the Federal Reserve had raised its discount rate and acted to stiffen short-term rates because of a balance of payments problem, and an incipient recovery had been cut off. . . . He concurred in the suggestion that short-term rates should now be permitted to move up a little further." (56)

Hayes, predictably, responded that "on the international side we seem to be moving into the kind of major crisis that has long loomed as a probability in the light of our huge payments deficit, especially on the official settlements basis; and the sharp contrast between interest rates here and abroad. Under these circumstances I think we should promote a firming of short-term interest rates to the extent this can be accepted without causing major repercussions in the bond market" (57). He concluded that he found it "necessary to dissent from the proposed directive, which he thought gave inadequate recognition to the need for moving toward somewhat higher short-term interest rates in light of the international financial situation" (83).

At the May 11 meeting, the FOMC voted for increased restraint because of concern over the international situation, although it rejected the 50 basis point rise in the discount rate requested by the New York Fed, citing concerns over the weakness of growth. The chairman summarized as follows:

Toward the end of last month one Reserve Bank [New York] had proposed a discount rate increase of one-half point. The Board had voted to disapprove the increase for the following reasons. 1. . . . it was concerned about the effects on debt markets, which were in a highly sensitive condition. 2. . . . with the economic recovery still fragile, a discount rate increase could damage confidence. 3. The Board feared a rise in the discount rate might have a significant impact on long-term interest rates. (52)

Hayes, predictably, disagreed.

Last Thursday our directors voted unanimously to raise the discount rate by one half per cent to 5 1/4%. They recognized that under ordinary circumstances such a move would not be desirable, coming just after a Treasury refunding operation. They also recognized that the usual sequence in working toward a firmer monetary policy would be to start with open market operations and to use the discount rate as a confirming action. Finally they were aware that a 1/2% discount rate increase could have substantial unsettling effects on the delicately poised bond market. Nevertheless, the directors felt that in this major international crisis there was nothing the System could do that could be more useful and more timely than to give an overt signal of our concern and our willingness to move quickly toward narrowing the interest rate spread which was a major cause of the difficulty. . . . They felt that prompt action on the discount rate serves as an important signal both to authorities in Germany and other countries that were in the process of making crucial decisions (Germany as well as Austria, Belgium, the Netherlands, and Switzerland were considering floating. Germany allowed the deutschemark to float on May 1 1971 followed by the others), and to the unsettled foreign exchange market that the US intended to defend the value of the dollar while recognizing the risks involved in a general increase in domestic interest rates, they felt that these risks were outweighed by international considerations, more particularly against the background of rapid growth in money and credit aggregates . . . I regret that the Board was not willing to approve the increase last week. But it is still not too late to move, and a discount rate increase might well play an important role in the eventual resolution of the exchange market problem. (56)

His arguments registered. In June, the system raised the discount rate by 25 basis points to defend the dollar. It followed with another 50 basis point rise in the funds rate in July.

In the last meeting before the August 15 collapse of the dollar peg, on July 27, 1971, Hayes and the other members, while voting for increased restraint and acknowledging the seriousness of the situation, were reluctant to apply additional monetary restraint owing to concern for the domestic economy. Instead they pinned their hopes on incomes policy and other measures including the tariff surcharge (imposed on August 15) to strengthen the balance of payments—again indicating that defending the dollar was primarily the responsibility of the administration and the Congress. It was clear, as Hayes put it, that "the US balance of trade and the overall balance of payments were in an especially critical state" (32). "The firming of short-term interest rates that has already occurred has . . . helped in a major way, along with some interest declines abroad, in checking the interest induced short-run capital flow that paved the way for the May currency crisis." But further support for the dollar, as he saw it, should be the priority of the administration, not the Fed.

> While further firming of the money market might bring some additional benefit in this area, I think that for domestic reasons we have done about all we can afford to do at the moment in the monetary field for the balance of payments and by way of a control to combating inflation psychology. We cannot overlook the fact that the economic recovery is still rather fragile and that unemployment seems likely to drop only slowly over the coming year . . . my willingness to hold still on monetary policy in no sense implies the absence of great concern over the prospects for containing inflation and a drastically unsatisfactory balance of payments position. These conditions underlie the urgent need for an effective incomes policy. I also believe the time is ripe for a hard look at a new "package" approach to ways of reducing our international payments deficit. (55–56)

With monetary policy sidelined, the pressure on the dollar could not be contained. On August 15, facing the prospect of massive Western European conversion of outstanding dollar balances into gold, President Nixon closed the gold window, effectively ending the Bretton Woods system.

Thus, we also see in this second period sporadic mention in the minutes of the stability of the dollar and balance-of-payments concerns. However, these issues arose at longer intervals. Not only were they more widely separated in time, but one can see an even more explicit balancing in the statements of FOMC members of the need to defend the dollar against the need to support economic activity. This reflected the growing importance attached to stimulating output and employment, not just within the Fed, but in the Treasury and the Administrative Branch more generally. But it also reflected the perception that primary responsibility for dealing with the dollar crisis had been assumed by the Treasury, which would deploy an ever-widening array of nonmonetary instruments in the effort to resolve it.

9.5   Quantitative Evidence

Quantitative evidence can lend support to our view by showing that the Fed's commitment to defense of the dollar helped to anchor inflation through 1965. We show that monetary policy was even tighter in this period than concern with inflation and the domestic economy alone would predict, suggesting a role for factors like the weakness of the balance of payments. We show that inflation was less persistent and that expectations were better anchored than subsequently. The evidence points to a break in 1965 at the time when balance-of-payments considerations stopped figuring as prominently in the calculus of the FOMC.

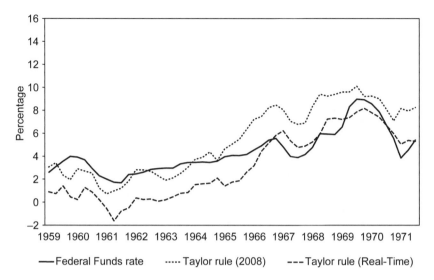

—— Federal Funds rate   ····· Taylor rule (2008)   --- Taylor rule (Real-Time)

Fig. 9.2   The classic Taylor rule

In figure 9.2 we show the Fed's monetary policy rule as calibrated by Taylor (1999).[21] We combined his parameters with data on inflation and on the output gap measured using measured real GDP less the most recent Bureau of Economic Analysis (BEA) estimates of potential real GDP. In addition, we calculate a Taylor rule using Orphanides's (2003) real time data on the output gap (using data from the original BEA sources, not data as subsequently revised, which is arguably appropriate as indicating what policymakers focused on at the time).

As can be seen, before 1965 policy was even tighter than would be expected on the basis of inflation and the output gap alone. The difference is minor when we calculate the output gap mechanically but quite dramatic when using Orphanides's method. Thereafter, policy is generally looser than expected, dramatically so when we use a simple measure of the output gap but more modestly when using Orphanides's approach.

Figure 9.3 shows three measures of inflation and inflation persistence: the percentage change in the CPI, in the GDP deflator, and in money wages.

21. We also estimated our own version of the Taylor rule using the forward-looking approach of Romer and Romer (2002b), focusing on the period 1959:Q1 to 1971:Q3. Romer and Romer evaluated Federal Reserve policy in the 1950s. They estimated the forward-looking Taylor rule in the manner of Clarida, Galí, and Gertler (2000), according to which the Federal Reserve chooses the federal funds rate in response to inflation and the deviation of output from trend. This method is forward-looking in that the Federal Reserve is assumed to respond to expectations of the variables. The equation is estimated using instrumental variables, where the instruments are contemporaneous and two lags of inflation, and output deviations. We used two measures of the output gap: one based on BEA potential output, the other based on a Hodrick-Prescott trend of real GDP. The coefficient on inflation was statistically significant and close to one and satisfies the Taylor principle, while the coefficient on the output gap is quite small.

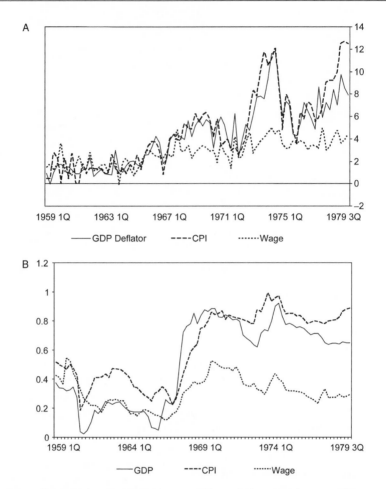

Fig. 9.3   CPI inflation and inflation persistence—G10, quarterly data 1959 I to 1979 III: *A,* **US Inflation Rates;** *B,* **US serial correlation of inflation;** *C,* **US median unbiased estimator for each series**

Sources: GDP deflator: Bureau of Economic Analysis, Department of Commerce. CPI: Bureau of Labor Statistics, Department of Labor. Wage = Nonfarm compensation per hour: Bureau of Labor Statistics, Department of Labor.

Notes: For panel C, model $P_t = \bar{\mu} + \alpha P_{t-1} + U_t$ for $t = 1, \ldots, T$ where $\bar{\mu} = \mu(1 - \alpha)$ and $\alpha \in (-1,1]$ where P_t is the inflation rate of each series from Andrews (1993). Also for panel C, part 1, GDP deflator; part 2, CPI; part 3, wage.

We plot the raw data in panel A and the serial correlation of inflation based on an AR(1) regression using a ten-year rolling window in panel B. To correct for the bias that arises when persistence is estimated using ordinary least square (OLS) (Andrews 1993), we show the median unbiased estimator for each series in panel C. As can be seen from the rolling regression and median unbiased estimates, inflation persistence increased dramatically after 1965.

C

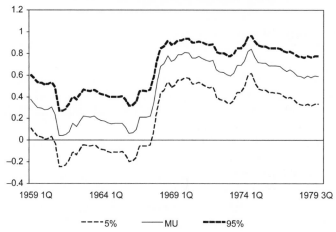

Median Unbiased estimator for GDP deflator inflation

- - - - 5%   ——— MU   ▬▬▬ 95%

Median Unbiased estimator for CPI inflation

- - - 0.05%   ——— MU   — • 0.95%

Median Unbiased estimator for Money Wage inflation

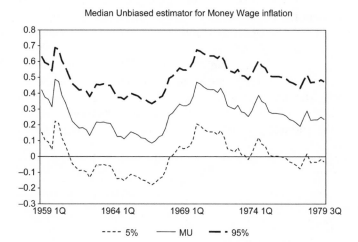

- - - - 5%   ——— MU   — • 95%

Fig. 9.3   (cont.)

We also use statistical methods to estimate underlying inflation persistence and ask whether there is evidence of a shift around 1965. Like Cecchetti et al. (2007), we use Stock and Watson's (2002, 2006) smoothed estimator to construct estimates of the trend (permanent) and transitory components of inflation using nonlinear methods analogous to the Kalman filter. In the top panel of figure 9.4 we separate inflation into a permanent or trend component and a transitory component. In the middle panel we show the first-order autocorrelation of the change in US inflation. This statistic summarizes the relative importance in the inflation process of the variances of the permanent and transitory components. The dotted line shows the break point at which the inflation process becomes persistent. Finally the bottom panel, for comparison, shows two measures of external balance: the official settlements balance-of-payments deficit (surplus) and the current account deficit (surplus).

As can be seen from the upper panel of parts A and B in figure 9.4, trend inflation follows actual inflation with a lag. Actual and trend inflation both rise in the mid-1960s, around the time of the shift in the locus of primary responsibility for managing the balance of payments. The calculated break in the inflation persistence process, in contrast, occurs in 1968, while the middle panel shows a steady pickup in the importance of the permanent component of inflation through the 1960s. The results for wages in part C of figure 9.4 are different from those on inflation. They show a much slower build-up of inflationary momentum, with the break in trend only coming in 1973.

Finally, there is evidence that these changes did not escape the attention of investors. In figure 9.5 we show the Livingston Survey of inflation expectations.[22] While the series is volatile, there is a clear break in 1965, as one would expect on the basis of our analysis.[23]

Even this limited empirical analysis confirms the complexity of the inflation process in the 1960s and early 1970s. Over time inflation accelerated, became more persistent, and exhibited greater volatility. There appear to have been a number of different break points depending on the aspect of the process under consideration: at or around 1965, at the end of the 1960s, and in the early 1970s. The break around 1965 is plausibly associated at least in part with the declining weight placed by the Fed in its policy decisions on the weakness of the balance of payments and the fragility of the dollar. The fact that monetary policy was even tighter in preceding years than one

22. Data are from the website of the Federal Reserve Bank of Philadelphia.
23. In addition, there is the evidence of Chen and Giovannini (1992), who used a target zone framework to estimate the probability, implicit in forward exchange rates and interest differentials, that the dollar would be devalued against the deutschmark during the Bretton Woods period. They find essentially no perceived probability of dollar devaluation before 1965 but a growing probability in the second half of the Bretton Woods period. The problem with this test is that the deutschmark price of gold could also change if the German currency was revalued against the dollar, as it in fact was on a couple of occasions under Bretton Woods.

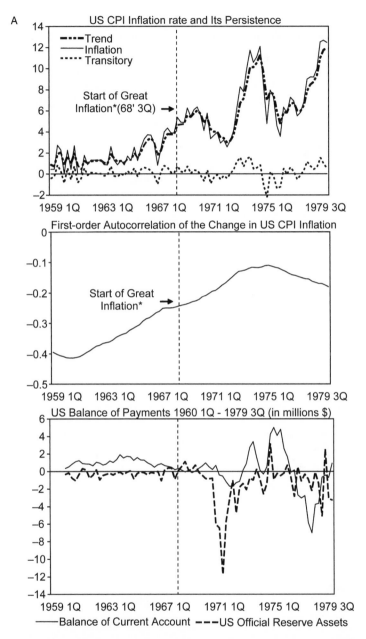

Fig. 9.4 Inflation persistence and the balance of payments 1959 I to 1979 III: *A*, CPI inflation; *B*, GDP inflation; *C*, wage inflation

* Break generated from the trend of inflation greater than 4 percent.

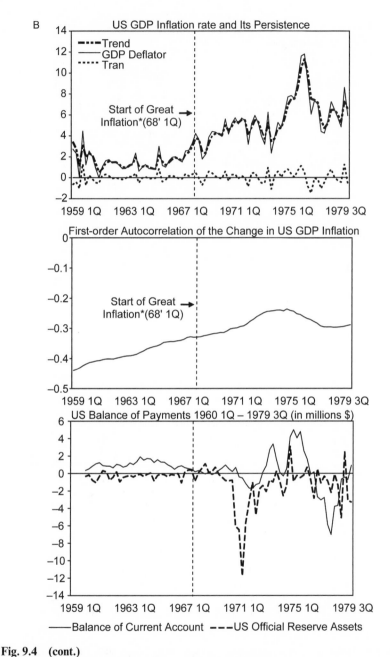

Fig. 9.4 (cont.)
* Break generated from the trend of inflation greater than 4 percent.

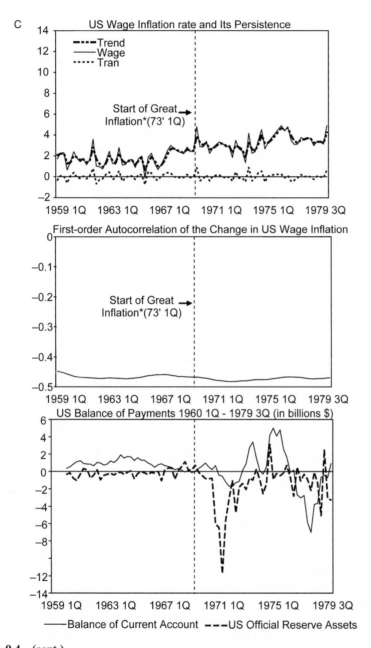

Fig. 9.4 (cont.)

* Break generated from the trend of inflation greater than 4 percent.

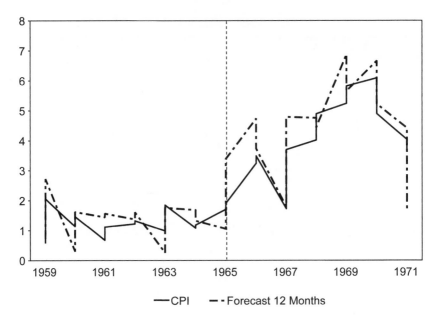

Fig. 9.5   The Livingston Survey twelve-month forecast of inflation, 1959 to 1971

would expect on the basis of inflation and the output gap alone confirms that the Fed had been factoring in other considerations to its policy decisions, plausibly the balance-of-payments considerations described earlier.

9.6   Conclusion

Explanations for the acceleration of inflation in the late 1960s and early 1970s emphasize a growing tendency to characterize the inflation problem as unrelated to Federal Reserve policy (Romer and Romer 2002a; Nelson 2005); as resulting from an excessively stimulative or overly accommodating monetary policy that failed to take inflation control as its central focus (DeLong 1997; Clarida, Galí, and Gertler 2000); and as reflecting a mistaken belief in an exploitable Phillips curve trade-off (Taylor 1992; Sargent 1999). There is insight in all of these interpretations. No account of the Great Inflation would be complete without them.

But neither would it be complete without recognition of the changing role of the external constraint in FOMC members' calculations. It is not as if it took until the end of the 1960s for the idea of an exploitable Phillips curve trade-off to come to Washington. Romer and Romer (2002b) show that this idea was already being advanced by the Council of Economic Advisors in the early 1960s. It can be argued that much of the decade had to pass before the ideas pushed by the council were internalized by the Fed. Or perhaps not until President Johnson gave William McChesney Martin his famous verbal lashing did the chairman disregard inflation as monetary policy's central focus and accept an unrealistically low estimate of the natural rate. To repeat, we agree that there is something to these points.

However, in addition, the record suggests that adoption of these ideas was delayed and willingness to act on them was constrained by the responsibility that FOMC members felt for defending the dollar and strengthening the balance of payments. This was a shared responsibility of Treasury and the Fed, but one that the Fed took seriously in the first half of the 1960s. And so long as it did so, the temptation to inflate was restrained.

What changed in the course of the first half of the decade was application by the Treasury, with the consent of Congress, of a series of fiscal measures like the Interest Equalization Tax, intended to strengthen the balance of payments. This affected the Fed's thinking through two channels. First, the Treasury's activism encouraged the belief that another agency had assumed primary responsibility for managing the balance-of-payments problem—that the Fed was now entitled to delegate the task. Second, measures like the Interest Equalization Tax that placed sand in the wheels of international financial markets encouraged the Fed to believe that it could loosen monetary policy and allow inflation to rise without posing as immediate of a threat to the dollar as before.

This is not the only set of considerations that distinguished monetary policy in the first and second half of the 1960s. But it is an important part of the story. The even more dramatic acceleration of inflation in the 1970s, when the exchange rate constraint was removed entirely, only reinforces the point.

Appendix A
Nonmonetary Measures to Strengthen the Balance of Payments

This appendix describes some of the nonmonetary measures pursued by the Treasury and the Administrative Branch in the 1960s with the goal of managing the balance of payments and strengthening the dollar.[24]

A first significant initiative was the Gold Pool, initially proposed by the Treasury to foreign governments and accepted by the latter in October 1961. Central banks managed the pool on a day-to-day basis, operating as a gold sales consortium in the effort to stabilize the dollar price of gold and limit US gold losses. The United States contributed 50 percent of the resources of the pool, while four large European countries—the United Kingdom,

---

24. The account here draws on Meltzer (1991) and Eichengreen (2000).

France, Germany, and Italy—contributed about 10 percent each. Three smaller European countries—Belgium, the Netherlands, and Switzerland—kicked in about 3 percent each. The idea was that when there was demand on the London gold market for gold at more than $35 an ounce, creating an incentive for foreign official purchasers to convert their dollars into gold in the United States, the price would be pushed back down by the consortium of central banks, sharing the burden in this fashion, and not simply by the Federal Reserve acting as agent of the Treasury.

The Gold Pool never worked perfectly. There was a tendency for foreign central banks to replenish their gold reserves by converting dollars into gold after selling gold into the market. The arrangement broke down entirely after 1968. But so long as it operated, it encouraged the belief that US gold losses would be limited.

A second notable initiative was the Interest Equalization Tax (IET) of 1963. The IET was designed to strengthen the dollar and balance of payments by discouraging long-term lending to foreign countries. A tax equal to a 1 percent rate of interest was imposed in 1963 on foreign bonds sold in the United States. To the extent that it was effective, this loosened the link between domestic and foreign interest rates and therefore the impact on the balance of payments of expansionary monetary policy. However, bank loans could be substituted for bonds—in response to which the tax was extended in 1965 to bank loans to foreigners with a maturity of more than one year. Short-term credits could be extended and rolled over as a substitute for long-term commitments. Some authors (e.g., Meltzer 1991) conclude that the IET, even as augmented, had relatively little effect, although others (e.g., Obstfeld 1993) point to them as explaining the magnitude of US-foreign interest differentials. But what matters from the present point of view is what policymakers likely believed regarding its effectiveness, and presumably such measures would have not been imposed had there been no confidence in their effectiveness.

A third initiative was to tie US foreign aid. New aid commitments in the early 1960s were limited to countries that agreed to spend the dollars they thereby received in the United States. The US commitments to the Inter-American Development Bank's Fund for Special Operations were similarly made subject to restrictions that made it difficult to use them except for purchasing US merchandise. Measures such as these are estimated to have doubled the share of US aid spent on American goods over the first half of the 1960s.

The Kennedy and Johnson Administrations adopted a series of initiatives designed to limit US defense spending abroad. In 1962 the Defense Department instituted a Buy American program in which preference was given to American suppliers even when their goods were as much as 50 percent more expensive than substitutes that might be procured abroad. Simultaneously with the announcement of the Interest Equalization Tax, it was announced that defense spending abroad would be reduced by $1 billion. Foreign governments were pressured to buy US military hardware as their quid pro quo for the stationing of American troops abroad.

Then there were various and sundry export-promotion initiatives. In 1963, for example, the White House held a conference on export expansion, at which the president and cabinet officials spent more than three hours exhorting business to sell more products abroad. Instances of such exhortation became commonplace in subsequent years.

Finally, in 1965 the Johnson administration negotiated a series of voluntary agreements with US corporations designed to limit their foreign purchases and investment commitments. Each company was asked to submit a corporate balance of payments account and to indicate what steps it was taking to improve its balance by 15 to 20 percent. Companies were then asked to commit to further improving in their corporate balances of payments in 1966. From 1968 the program was made mandatory and administered by the Office of Foreign Direct Investment. This initiative was also applied to US banks. Individual banks were asked to ensure that their foreign lending as of end of 1965 did not exceed end of 1964 levels by more than 5 percent. A similar ceiling was set for end-1966 lending, this time at 109 percent of end-1964 levels. From 1966, nonbank financial institutions were also requested to limit the rate of growth of their foreign investments.

Appendix B

Table 9B.1 FOMC policy actions

Date	Meeting	Attendance Governors	Attendance President	Absent	Vote	Even keel	Policy decision at meeting	Reason for directive Domestic	Reason for directive International	Total Dissents	Direction of dissent Maintain	Ease	Tighten	Nonmon.
1/6/1959	1	5	5	King (G), Shepardson (G)	10–0	Yes	Maintain	1	0	0	—	—	—	—
1/27/1959	2	6	5	King (G)	11–0	Yes	Maintain	1	0	0	—	—	—	—
2/10/1959	3	5	5	King (G), Mills (G)	10–0	Yes	Maintain	1	0	0	—	—	—	—
3/3/1959	4	6	5	King (G)	11–0	—	Maintain	1	0	0	—	—	—	—
3/24/1959	5	5	5	King (G), Martin (G)	10–0	Yes	Maintain	1	0	0	—	—	—	—
4/14/1959	6	6	5	Martin (G)	10–0	Yes	Maintain	1	0	0	—	—	—	—
5/5/1959	7	6	5	Martin (G)	11–0	Yes	Maintain	1	0	0	—	—	—	—
5/28/1959	8	7	5	—	11–1	—	Increase restraint	1	0	1	1	—	—	—
6/16/1959	9	4	5	Martin (G), Mills (G), Balderson (G)	9–0	—	Maintain	1	0	0	—	—	—	—
7/7/1959	10	6	5	Robertson (G)	11–0	Yes	Maintain	1	0	0	—	—	—	—
7/28/1959	11	5	5	King (G), Szymczak (G)	10–0	Yes	Maintain	1	0	0	—	—	—	—
8/18/1959	12	5	5	Robertson (G), Shepardson (G)	10–0	—	Maintain	1	1	0	—	—	—	—
9/1/1959	13	7	5	—	12–0	—	Maintain	1	0	0	—	—	—	—
9/22/1959	14	7	5	—	12–0	—	Maintain	1	0	0	—	—	—	—
10/13/1959	15	7	4	Johns (STL)	11–0	—	Maintain	1	0	0	—	—	—	—
11/4/1959	16	6	5	Martin (G)	10–1	—	Maintain	1	0	1	—	1	—	—
11/24/1959	17	6	5	Balderston (G)	10–1	Yes	Maintain	1	0	1	—	1	—	—
12/15/1959	18	7	5	—	11–1	—	Maintain	1	0	1	—	1	—	—
1/12/1960	1	7	5	—	11–1	Yes	Maintain	1	0	1	—	1	—	—
1/26/1960	2	7	5	—	11–1	—	Maintain	1	0	1	—	1	—	—
2/9/1960	3	7	5	—	11–1	—	Maintain	1	0	1	—	1	—	—
3/1/1960	4	7	5	—	12–0	—	Decrease restraint	1	0	0	—	—	—	—
3/22/1960	5	6	5	King (G)	11–0	Yes	Maintain	1	0	0	—	—	—	—
4/12/1960	6	6	5	King	11–0	—	Decrease restraint	1	0	0	—	—	—	—
5/3/1960	7	6	5	Mills	11–0	—	Decrease restraint	1	0	0	—	—	—	—
5/24/1960	8	6	5	Szymczak (G)	11–0	—	Decrease restraint	1	0	0	—	—	—	—
6/14/1960	9	6	5	Shepardson (G)	11–0	—	Decrease restraint	1	0	0	—	—	—	—
7/6/1960	10	7	5	—	12–0	—	Maintain	1	0	0	—	—	—	—
7/26/1960	11	5	5	King (G), Szymczak (G)	10–0	Yes	Maintain	1	0	0	—	—	—	—
8/16/1960	12	6	5	Martin (G)	7–4	—	Decrease restraint	1	0	4	4	—	—	—
9/13/1960	13	7	5	—	12–0	Yes	Maintain	1	0	0	—	—	—	—
10/4/1960	14	7	5	—	12–0	Yes	Maintain	1	0	0	—	—	—	—

(continued)

Date				Names	Score		Action							
10/25/1960	15	6	5	Szymczak (G)	11–0	Yes	Maintain	1	1	1	—	—	—	—
11/22/1960	16	7	5	—	12–0	—	Maintain	1	1	1	—	—	—	—
12/13/1960	17	7	5	—	12–0	—	Maintain	1	1	1	—	—	—	—
1/10/1961	1	7	5		12–0	—	Maintain	1	1	1	—	—	—	—
1/24/1961	2	7	5		12–0	—	Maintain	1	1	1	—	—	—	—
2/7/1961	3	7	5		12–0	—	Maintain	1	1	1	—	—	—	—
3/7/1961	4	7	5		12–0	—	Maintain	1	1	1	—	—	—	—
3/28/1961	5	7	5	Martin (G), Mitchel (G)	10–0	—	Maintain	1	1	3	—	3	3	—
4/18/1961	6	5	5	Martin (G), Mitchel (G)	10–0	—	Maintain	1	1	3	—	3	3	—
5/19/1961	7	5	5	Mitchel (G)	11–0	Yes	Maintain	1	1	2	—	2	2	—
6/6/1961	8	6	5	Mitchel (G), King (G)	10–0	—	Maintain	1	1	1	—	—	—	—
6/21/1961	9	5	5	Mitchel (G)	11–0	—	Maintain	1	1	1	—	1	1	1
7/11/1961	10	6	5	Mitchel (G)	10–0	—	Maintain	1	1	1	—	1	1	1
8/1/1961	11	5	5	Mitchel (G), Robertson (G)	10–0	—	Maintain	1	1	1	—	1	1	1
8/22/1961	12	5	5	Mitchel (G), Shepardson (G)	11–0	—	Maintain	1	1	1	—	—	—	—
9/12/1961	13	6	5	Mills (G)	11–0	Yes	Maintain	1	1	1	—	1	1	1
10/3/1961	14	6	5	Martin (G)	11–0	Yes	Maintain	1	1	1	—	1	1	1
10/24/1961	15	6	5	Martin (G)	11–0	—	Maintain	1	1	2	—	2	2	2
11/14/1961	16	5	5	Balderston (G), Shepardson (G)	10–0	—	Maintain	1	1	2	—	—	—	1
12/5/1961	17	5	5	—	12–0	—	Maintain	1	1	2	—	—	—	—
12/19/1961	18	7	5	—	8–4	—	Increase restraint	1	1	4	2	2	1	1
1/9/1962	1	7	5	—	12–0	Yes	Maintain	1	1	1	—	—	—	—
1/23/1962	2	7	5	—	12–0	Yes	Maintain	1	1	1	—	—	—	—
2/13/1962	3	7	5	—	12–0	Yes	Maintain	1	1	1	—	—	—	—
3/6/1962	4	5	5	King (G), Mills (G)	10–0	—	Maintain	1	1	1	—	—	—	—
3/27/1962	5	6	5	King (G)	10–1	Yes	Maintain	1	1	1	—	1	1	1
4/17/1962	6	7	5	—	11–1	—	Maintain	1	1	2	—	2	2	2
5/8/1962	7	7	5	—	11–1	Yes	Maintain	1	1	1	—	1	1	1
5/29/1962	8	7	5	—	12–0	—	Maintain	1	1	1	—	—	—	—
6/19/1962	9	6	5	Mitchell (G)	9–2	—	Increase restraint	1	1	2	2	2	2	—
7/10/1962	10	7	5	—	10–2	—	Maintain	1	1	2	—	2	2	—
7/31/1962	11	7	5	—	9–2	—	Maintain	1	1	2	—	2	2	—
8/21/1962	12	6	5	Robertson (G)	9–2	—	Maintain	1	1	2	—	2	2	—
9/11/1962	13	7	5	—	9–3	—	Maintain	1	1	3	—	3	3	—
10/2/1962	14	5	5	King (G), Robertson (G)	8–2	—	Maintain	1	1	2	—	2	2	—
10/23/1962	15	6	5	Robertson (G)	11–0	Yes	Maintain	1	1	1	—	—	1	—
11/13/1962	16	6	5	Shepardson (G)	10–1	—	Maintain	1	1	1	—	1	1	—
12/4/1962	17	7	5	—	11–1	—	Maintain	1	1	1	—	1	1	—
12/18/1962	18	7	5	—	7–5	—	Increase restraint	0	1	5	5	5	—	—
1/8/1963	1	6	5	Mitchell (G)	10–1	Yes	Maintain	1	1	1	—	1	1	—

Table 9B.1 (continued)

Date	Meeting	Governors	President	Absent	Vote	Even keel	Policy decision at meeting	Domestic	International	Total Dissents	Maintain	Ease	Tighten	Nonmon.
		Attendance						Reason for directive			Direction of dissent			
1/29/1963	2	6	5	King (G)	11–0	Yes	Maintain	1	1	—	—	—	—	—
2/12/1963	3	5	5	King (G), Mills (G)	10–0	Yes	Maintain	1	1	—	—	—	—	—
3/5/1963	4	6	5	King (G)	11–0	Yes	Maintain	1	1	—	—	—	—	—
3/26/1963	5	7	5	—	11–1	Yes	Maintain	1	1	1	—	—	1	—
4/16/1963	6	7	5	—	10–2	Yes	Maintain	1	1	2	—	1	1	—
5/7/1963	7	6	5	Mills (G)	6–5	—	Increase restraint	0	1	5	5	—	—	—
5/28/1963	8	6	5	Robertson (G)	10–1	—	Maintain	1	1	1	—	1	—	—
6/18/1963	9	5	5	King (G), Robertson (G)	7–3	—	Maintain	1	1	3	—	1	2	—
7/9/1963	10	7	5	—	10–2	—	Maintain	1	1	2	—	2	—	—
7/30/1963	11	6	4	King (G), Clay (KC)	6–4	—	Increase restraint	0	1	4	4	—	—	—
8/20/1963	12	6	5	King (G)	11–0	Yes	Maintain	1	1	—	—	—	—	—
9/10/1963	13	6	5	Mills (G)	11–0	Yes	Maintain	1	1	—	—	—	—	—
10/1/1963	14	6	5	King (G)	7–4	—	Maintain	1	1	4	—	—	4	—
10/22/1963	15	6	5	King (G)	11–0	Yes	Maintain	1	1	—	—	—	—	—
11/12/1963	16	6	5	King (G)	10–1	—	Maintain	1	1	1	—	1	—	—
11/26/1963	17	6	5	King (G)	10–1	—	Maintain	1	1	1	—	1	—	—
12/3/1963	18	6	5	King (G)	10–1	—	Maintain	1	1	1	—	1	—	—
12/17/1963	19	6	5	Balderston (G)	9–2	—	Maintain	1	1	2	—	1	1	1
1/7/1964	1	6	5	—	11–1	Yes	Maintain	1	1	1	—	1	—	—
1/28/1964	2	6	5	Daane (G)	10–0	Yes	Maintain	1	1	—	—	—	—	—
2/11/1964	3	7	5	—	11–0	—	Maintain	1	1	—	—	—	—	—
3/3/1964	4	7	5	—	11–1	—	Maintain	1	1	1	—	1	—	—
3/24/1964	5	7	5	—	11–1	Yes	Maintain	1	1	1	—	1	—	—
4/14/1964	6	6	5	Robertson (G)	8–3	Yes	Maintain	1	1	3	—	1	2	—
5/5/1964	7	7	5	—	12–0	Yes	Maintain	1	1	—	—	—	—	—
5/26/1964	8	6	5	Martin (G)	11–0	Yes	Maintain	1	1	—	—	—	—	—
6/17/1964	9	5	5	Balderston (G), Daane (G)	9–1	Yes	Maintain	1	1	1	—	1	—	—
7/7/1964	10	6	5	Mitchell (G)	11–0	Yes	Maintain	1	1	—	—	—	—	—
7/28/1964	11	7	5	—	12–0	Yes	Maintain	1	1	—	—	—	—	—
8/18/1964	12	6	5	Shepardson (G)	6–5	—	Increase restraint	1	1	5	5	—	—	—
9/8/1964	13	5	5	Martin (G), Daane (G)	10–0	—	Maintain	1	1	—	—	—	—	—
9/29/1964	14	7	5	—	12–0	—	Maintain	1	1	—	—	—	—	—
10/20/1964	15	7	5	—	12–0	Yes	Maintain	1	1	—	—	—	—	—
11/10/1964	16	7	5	—	11–1	Yes	Maintain	1	1	1	—	—	1	—
12/1/1964	17	5	5	Daane (G), Mills (G)	10–0	—	Increase restraint	0	1	—	—	—	—	—

Date	No.			Dissenter(s)		Vote	Yes	Action					
12/15/1964	18	6	5	Daane (G)	—	10–1	—	Maintain	1	1	—	—	1
1/12/1965	1	6	5	Mills (G)	—	11–0	Yes	Maintain	1	1	—	—	—
2/2/1965	2	7	5	—	—	10–2	—	Increase restraint	1	1	2	2	2
3/2/1965	3	6	5	Mills (G)	—	8–3	—	Maintain	1	1	3	3	3
3/23/1965	4	6	5	Mills (G)	—	8–3	Yes	Increase restraint	1	1	3	3	3
4/13/1965	5	6	5	Mitchell (G)	—	11–0	Yes	Maintain	1	1	—	—	—
5/11/1965	6	7	5	—	—	11–0	—	Maintain	1	1	—	—	—
5/25/1965	7	6	5	Balderston (G)	—	8–4	—	Maintain	1	1	4	4	4
6/15/1965	8	6	5	—	—	11–0	—	Maintain	1	1	—	—	—
7/13/1965	9	6	5	Daane (G)	—	11–1	—	Maintain	1	1	1	1	1
8/10/1965	10	6	5	—	—	11–1	—	Maintain	1	1	1	1	1
8/31/1965	11	7	5	—	—	11–1	—	Maintain	1	1	1	1	1
9/28/1965	12	7	5	—	—	9–3	Yes	Maintain	1	1	3	3	3
10/12/1965	13	7	5	—	—	12–0	Yes	Maintain	1	1	—	—	—
11/2/1965	14	7	5	—	—	12–0	Yes	Maintain	1	1	—	—	—
11/23/1965	15	7	5	—	—	12–0	—	Maintain	1	1	—	—	—
12/14/1965	16	6	5	Daane (G)	—	11–0	Yes	Increase restraint	1	1	—	—	—
1/11/1966	1	7	5	—	—	12–0	Yes	Maintain	1	1	—	—	—
2/8/1966	2	6	5	Balderston (G)	—	12–0	—	Increase restraint	1	1	—	—	—
3/1/1966	3	6	5	—	—	11–0	—	Increase restraint	1	1	—	—	—
3/22/1966	4	7	5	Robertson (G)	—	12–0	Yes	Increase restraint	1	1	—	—	—
4/12/1966	5	6	5	—	—	11–0	Yes	Increase restraint	1	1	—	—	—
5/10/1966	6	7	5	Daane (G)	—	12–0	—	Increase restraint	1	1	—	—	—
6/7/1966	7	6	5	Robertson (G), Shepardson (G)	—	11–0	Yes	Maintain	1	1	—	—	—
6/28/1966	8	5	5	Martin (G), Daane (G)	—	10–0	—	Maintain	1	1	—	—	—
7/26/1966	9	5	5	Martin (G)	—	10–0	Yes	Maintain	1	1	—	—	—
8/23/1966	10	6	5	—	—	11–0	—	Maintain	1	1	—	—	—
9/13/1966	11	7	5	—	—	12–0	—	Maintain	1	1	—	—	—
10/4/1966	12	7	5	—	—	12–0	Yes	Maintain	1	1	—	—	—
11/1/1966	13	7	5	—	—	12–0	Yes	Maintain	1	1	—	—	—
11/22/1966	14	7	5	—	—	10–2	—	Decrease restraint	1	0	2	2	2
12/13/1966	15	7	5	—	—	8–4	—	Decrease restraint	1	0	4	4	4
1/10/1967	1	7	5	—	—	9–3	Yes	Decrease restraint	1	0	3	3	3
2/7/1967	2	7	5	—	—	11–1	—	Maintain	1	1	1	1	1
3/7/1967	3	7	5	—	—	12–0	—	Decrease restraint	1	0	—	—	—
4/4/1967	4	7	5	—	—	12–0	—	Decrease restraint	1	0	—	—	—
5/2/1967	5	7	5	—	—	12–0	Yes	Maintain	1	1	—	—	—
5/23/1967	6	7	5	—	—	11–1	—	Maintain	1	1	1	1	1
6/20/1967	7	6	5	Daane (G)	—	11–0	Yes	Maintain	1	1	—	—	—
7/18/1967	8	5	5	Martin (G), Daane (G)	—	10–0	Yes	Maintain	1	1	—	—	—

(continued)

Table 9B.1 (continued)

Date	Meeting	Attendance — Governors	President	Absent	Vote	Even keel	Policy decision at meeting	Reason for directive — Domestic	International	Total Dissents	Dissent — Maintain	Ease	Tighten	Nonmon.
8/15/1967	9	6	5	Martin (G)	11–0	Yes	Maintain	1		—	—	—	—	—
9/12/1967	10	7	5	—	9–3	—	Maintain	1	1	3	—	—	3	—
10/3/1967	11	6	5	Martin (G)	9–2	Yes	Maintain	1	1	2	—	—	2	—
10/24/1967	12	6	5	Daane (G)	10–1	Yes	Maintain	1	1	1	—	—	1	—
11/14/1967	13	7	5	—	12–0	—	Maintain	1	1	—	—	—	—	—
11/27/1967	14	6	4	Hayes (NY), Daane (G)	10–0	—	Increase restraint	0	1	—	—	—	—	—
12/12/1967	15	6	5	Daane (G)	10–1	—	Increase restraint	1	1	1	1	—	—	—
1/9/1968	1	7	5	—	12–0	—	Maintain	1	1	—	—	—	—	—
2/6/1968	2	7	5	—	12–0	—	Maintain	1	1	—	—	—	—	—
3/5/1968	3	6	5	Daane (G)	11–0	—	Increase restraint	1	1	—	—	—	—	—
3/14/1968	4	7	5	—	12–0	—	Increase restraint	0	1	—	—	—	—	—
4/2/1968	5	7	5	—	12–0	—	Increase restraint	1	1	—	—	—	—	—
4/19/1968	6	6	5	Sherrill (G)	11–0	Yes	Increase restraint	0	1	—	—	—	—	—
4/30/1968	7	6	5	Mitchell (G)	10–1	—	Maintain	1	1	1	—	—	1	—
5/28/1968	8	7	5	—	12–0	—	Maintain	1	1	—	—	—	—	—
6/18/1968	9	7	5	—	12–0	—	Maintain	1	1	—	—	—	—	—
7/16/1968	10	7	5	—	12–0	Yes	Increase restraint	1	0	—	—	—	—	—
8/13/1968	11	7	5	—	12–0	—	Maintain	1	1	—	—	—	—	—
8/19/1968	12	5	5	Martin (G), Mitchell (G)	10–0	—	Maintain	1	0	—	—	—	—	—
9/10/1968	13	7	5	—	12–0	—	Maintain	1	1	—	—	—	—	—
10/8/1968	14	7	5	—	9–3	Yes	Maintain	1	1	3	—	—	3	—
10/29/1968	15	7	5	—	11–1	Yes	Maintain	1	1	1	—	—	1	—
11/26/1968	16	7	5	—	8–4	—	Maintain	1	1	4	—	—	4	—
12/17/1968	17	6	5	Martin (G)	11–0	Yes	Increase restraint	1	1	—	—	—	—	—
1/14/1969	1	7	5	—	11–1	Yes	Maintain	1	1	1	—	1	—	—
2/4/1969	2	7	5	—	12–0	Yes	Maintain	1	1	—	—	—	—	—
3/4/1969	3	7	5	—	12–0	—	Maintain	1	1	—	—	—	—	—
4/1/1969	4	7	5	—	10–2	—	Increase restraint	1	1	2	1	—	1	—
4/29/1969	5	6	5	Sherrill (G)	11–0	Yes	Increase restraint	1	1	—	—	—	—	—
5/27/1969	6	7	5	—	12–0	—	Maintain	1	1	—	—	—	—	—
6/24/1969	7	7	5	—	11–1	—	Maintain	1	1	1	—	1	—	—
7/15/1969	8	6	5	Mitchell (G)	11–0	Yes	Maintain	1	1	—	—	—	—	—
8/12/1969	9	7	5	—	10–2	—	Maintain	1	1	2	—	—	2	—
9/9/1969	10	5	5	Daane (G), Robertson (G)	8–2	Yes	Maintain	1	1	2	—	—	—	2
10/7/1969	11	7	5	—	11–1	—	Maintain	1	1	1	—	—	—	1

Date				Member		Vote	Yes	Action							
10/28/1969	12	7	5		—	12-0	—	Maintain	1	1	—	—	—	—	—
11/25/1969	13	6	5	Maisel (G)	—	11-0	—	Maintain	1	1	—	—	—	—	—
12/16/1969	14	6	5	Daane (G)	—	11-0	—	Maintain	1	1	—	—	—	—	—
1/15/1970	1	7	5		—	12-0	Yes	Maintain	1	0	3	3	—	3	—
2/10/1970	2	7	5		—	9-3	Yes	Decrease restraint	1	0	—	—	—	—	—
3/10/1970	3	7	5		—	12-0	—	Decrease restraint	1	1	—	—	—	—	—
4/7/1970	4	7	5		—	12-0	Yes	Increase restraint	1	0	1	1	—	1	—
5/5/1970	5	7	5		—	11-1	Yes	Decrease restraint	1	0	—	—	—	—	—
5/26/1970	6	7	5		—	12-0	—	Decrease restraint	1	0	—	—	—	—	—
6/23/1970	7	6	5		—	12-0	—	Decrease restraint	1	0	3	—	—	—	2
7/21/1970	8	7	5	Mitchell (G)	—	11-0	Yes	Decrease restraint	1	0	1	1	—	—	—
8/18/1970	9	6	5		—	9-3	—	Decrease restraint	1	0	1	1	—	—	—
9/15/1970	10	6	5	Mitchell (G)	—	10-1	Yes	Decrease restraint	1	0	1	1	1	—	1
10/20/1970	11	6	5	Daane (G)	—	10-1	Yes	Decrease restraint	1	0	1	1	—	—	—
11/17/1970	12	7	5		—	11-1	—	Decrease restraint	1	0	1	1	1	1	—
12/15/1970	13	7	5		—	11-1	—	Maintain	1	1	1	—	—	—	—
1/12/1971	1	6	5		—	10-1	Yes	Decrease restraint	1	0	1	1	1	1	1
2/9/1971	2	6	5	Robertson (G)	—	10-1	—	Maintain	1	1	1	—	—	—	—
3/9/1971	3	7	5		—	12-0	—	Maintain	1	1	—	—	—	—	—
4/6/1971	4	6	5	Mitchell (G)	—	9-2	Yes	Increase restraint	1	1	2	2	—	2	—
5/11/1971	5	7	5		—	12-0	Yes	Increase restraint	1	1	—	—	—	—	—
6/8/1971	6	7	5		—	12-0	—	Increase restraint	1	1	—	—	—	—	—
6/29/1971	7	7	5		—	12-0	Yes	Increase restraint	1	1	—	—	—	—	—
7/27/1971	8	7	5		—	12-0	—	Increase restraint	1	1	—	—	—	—	—
8/24/1971	9	7	5		—	12-0	—	Increase restraint	1	1	—	—	—	—	—
9/21/1971	10	7	5		—	12-0	—	Decrease restraint	1	0	—	—	—	—	—
10/19/1971	11	6	5	Daane (G)	—	11-0	Yes	Decrease restraint	1	0	—	—	—	—	—
11/16/1971	12	6	5		—	11-0	Yes	Decrease restraint	1	0	—	—	—	—	—
12/14/1971	13	6	5		—	11-0	—	Decrease restraint	1	0	—	—	—	—	—

References

Andrews, Donald W. K. 1993. "Exactly Median-Unbiased Estimation of First Order Autoregressive/Unit Root Models." *Econometrica* 61:139–65.

Cecchetti, Steven, Peter Hooper, Bruce Kasman, Kermit Schoenholtz, and Mark Watson. 2007. "Understanding the Evolving Inflation Process." Initiative on Global Markets, Graduate School of Business, University of Chicago, July.

Chen, Zhaohui, and Alberto Giovannini. 1992. "Estimating Expected Exchange Rates under Target Zones." NBER Working Paper no. 3955. Cambridge, MA: National Bureau of Economic Research.

Clarida, Richard, Jordi Galí, and Mark Gertler. 2000. "Monetary Policy Rules and Macroeconomic Stability: Evidence and Some Theory." *Quarterly Journal of Economics* 115:147–80.

Coombs, Charles. 1976. *The Arena of International Finance.* New York: Wiley.

Eichengreen, Barry. 2000. "From Benign Neglect to Malignant Preoccupation: US Balance-of-Payments Policy in the 1960s." In *Economic Events, Ideas and Policies: The 1960s and After,* edited by George Perry and James Tobin, 185–242. Washington, DC: Brookings Institution.

Eichengreen, Barry, Mark Watson, and Richard Grossman. 1985. "Bank Rate Policy under the Interwar Gold Standard." *Economic Journal* 95:725–45.

Hetzel, Robert. 2008. *The Monetary Policy of the Federal Reserve: A History.* New York: Cambridge University Press.

Markese, John D. 1973. "The Even Keel Policy of the Federal Reserve System—Origin, Definition, Implementation and Import." *Journal of Finance* 28:766.

Meltzer, Allan. 1991. "US Policy in the Bretton Woods Era." *Economic Review of the Federal Reserve Bank of St. Louis* 73:54–83.

———. 2010. *A History of the Federal Reserve System, Volume 2.* Chicago: University of Chicago Press.

Nelson, Edward. 2005. "The Great Inflation of the 1970s: What Really Happened?" *Berkeley Electronic Journal of Macroeconomics* 5:1–50.

Obstfeld, Maurice. 1993. "The Adjustment Mechanism." In *A Retrospective on the Bretton Woods System: Lessons for Monetary Reform,* edited by Michael Bordo and Barry Eichengreen, 201–68. Chicago: University of Chicago Press.

Orphanides, Athanasios. 2003. "The Quest for Prosperity without Inflation." *Journal of Monetary Economics* 50:633–63.

———. 2004. "Monetary Policy Rules, Macroeconomic Stability and Inflation: A View from the Trenches." *Journal of Money, Credit, and Banking* 36:151–75.

Primiceri, Giorgio. 2005. "Why Inflation Rose and Fell: Policy Makers' Beliefs and Postwar Stabilization Policy." NBER Working Paper no. 11147. Cambridge, MA: National Bureau of Economic Research.

Romer, Christina, and David Romer. 2002a. "The Evolution of Economic Understanding and Postwar Stabilization Policy." In *Rethinking Stabilization Policy,* 11–78. Kansas City: Federal Reserve Bank of Kansas City.

———. 2002b. "A Rehabilitation of Monetary Policy in the 1950s." *American Economic Review* 92:121–27.

Sargent, Thomas. 1999. *The Conquest of American Inflation.* Princeton, NJ: Princeton University Press.

Stock, James, and Mark Watson. 2002. "Has the Business Cycle Changed and Why?" *NBER Macroeconomics Annual 2002,* edited by Mark Gertler and Kenneth Rogoff, 159–218. Cambridge, MA: MIT Press.

———. 2006. "Why Has Inflation Become Harder to Forecast?" *Journal of Money, Credit, and Banking* 40:3–33.

Taylor, John. 1992. "The Great Inflation, the Great Disinflation, and Policies for Future Price Stability." In *Inflation, Disinflation and Monetary Policy,* edited by Adrian Blundell-Wignall, 9–34. Sydney: Ambassador Press.

———. 1997. "America's Peacetime Inflation, The 1970s: Comment." In *Reducing Inflation,* edited by Christina Romer and David Romer, 276–80. Chicago: University of Chicago Press.

———. 1999. "A Historical Analysis of Monetary Policy Rules." In *Monetary Policy Rules,* edited by John B. Taylor, 319–44. Chicago: University of Chicago Press.

Comment   Allan H. Meltzer

Professors Bordo and Eichengreen offer a welcome addition to the large literature on the Great Inflation. They do not dispute the findings in many earlier studies. They add to our understanding by considering some international and balance of payments responses. Many of my comments supplement their story, but I do not accept their conclusion that the Martin Federal Reserve raised interest rates for balance-of-payments reasons or that the public expected them to act that way.

One main theme is correct. The Kennedy and Johnson administrations put very different weight on the balance-of-payments deficit. President Kennedy had great concern about the gold outflow. He feared it, he said, as second only to an atomic attack. At one point, he threatened to pull US troops out of Europe, if the French and Germans continued to demand gold. DeGaulle did not believe him. President Kennedy's attention soon shifted to the Cuban missile crisis, so he did not pursue his threat. I cite this episode to reinforce Bordo and Eichengreen's evidence that international economic issues were a major concern in the early 1960s.

Concern is one thing. Policy and actions are different matters. I served briefly in the Kennedy Treasury Department in 1961 to 1962 and recall the discussions. The Treasury's first problem was to gain control of the policy response. Secretary Douglas Dillon was a Republican with close ties to Wall Street. His under secretary was Robert Roosa, who came to the Treasury from the New York Federal Reserve Bank. That background is important because New York was the strong supporter of a fixed exchange rate. Most of them wanted a dollar-based system tied to gold.

The Treasury's main rival for influence found a home in the Council of Economic Advisers, where James Tobin was a member and Robert Solow was on the staff. Paul Samuelson was not part of the administration but

Allan H. Meltzer is the the Allan H. Meltzer University Professor of Political Economy at Carnegie Mellon University.

My discussion is based on volume 2 of my 2010 book, *A History of the Federal Reserve, 1951–86.* For acknowledgments, sources of research support, and disclosure of the author's material financial relationships, if any, please see http://www.nber.org/chapters/c9175.ack.

served as an influential voice at the White House because of his relationship to the president.

The Treasury gained the upper hand after a compromise. Policy aimed at lowering long-term rates to expand output and raising short-term rates to slow the capital and gold outflow. This was an effort to "twist the yield curve" by lowering long-term and raising short-term rates. The policy called on the Treasury to finance the deficit by selling mainly Treasury bills, and it called on the Federal Reserve to buy long-term bonds.

In the 1950s and the 1960 election, the Democrats opposed the Federal Reserve's "bills only" policy. They claimed that the policy raised long-term interest rates and reduced economic growth. This was an error, part of a persistent failure to distinguish real and nominal interest rates. Chairman Martin at the Board agreed to cooperate with the new administration, but he would not resign, as some in the administration wished. He gave up "bills only" and agreed to buy long-term debt.

In my opinion at the time, there was not much chance that policy could twist the yield curve. The main proponent, Jim Tobin, believed the Federal Reserve failed to buy enough long-term debt, and he complained that the Treasury sold long-term debt. He kept track of weekly Federal Reserve purchases. When they slowed, he urged Walter Heller, chairman of the council, to ask the president to call a meeting of economic policymakers known as the Quadriad. He believed that Chairman Martin increased the rate of purchase before such meetings.

Once the economy recovered, policy changed. Tobin left the council and Roosa, at the Treasury, developed new techniques. He strengthened the London Gold Pool. Ten other countries agreed to buy and sell gold to sustain the $35 per ounce price. As part of the agreement, the United States agreed to purchase any gold that other countries bought, so the agreement gave only short-term support to the dollar. Roosa prevailed on the Federal Reserve to engage in "swap" agreements, under which the Federal Reserve purchased dollars by borrowing foreign currency. Also, because the Treasury lacked the resources to share equally in those transactions, the Federal Reserve loaned money to the Treasury. Such loans are illegal, so they were described as "warehousing." This, too, was a short-term palliative. Pushed by independent governors like James Robertson, Martin and others admitted as much. They did not offer a long-term program.

Roosa was creative and inventive, but he never considered parity changes as a solution. He believed the long-term solution was exchange rate stability. His policies responded to pressures and sought to rely on the US economy to produce a favorable long-term result.

In the 1920s the Federal Reserve, especially Benjamin Strong at the New York Bank, conducted international economic policy. Carter Glass blamed Strong for the Great Depression because he did not follow the real bills doctrine. Glass was influential. As a congressman in 1913, he had taken a leading role in the creation of the Federal Reserve. In 1933, as a senator he insisted on removing New York's role in international policy. The Treasury became the principal actor. Chairman Martin recognized that the Federal Reserve had a secondary role.

Inflation remained low in the early 1960s, lower than in major trading partners. There were a few months of falling prices in 1961. Relatively low inflation and a fixed exchange rate revalued the real exchange rate. By 1965, the balance-of-payments problem seemed on the way to solution.

Bordo and Eichengreen cite the minutes as evidence that the Federal Reserve took an active role in balance-of-payments problems. I agree that the minutes or transcripts contain the statements they cite. They do not note, however, that most of the statements were made by Alfred Hayes, president of the New York Bank. And they fail to note that Hayes's views were rarely the majority view. The Federal Reserve did not raise interest rates for balance-of-payments reasons, with few exceptions.

Chairman Martin did not have a balance of payments policy. He disliked economics. He was a market man with friends in the New York banks from his years as head of the stock exchange. His policy preference was to manage free reserves or "color, tone and feel." Connection to international or domestic economic outcomes was, at best, accidental. His aim was to regulate a short-term interest rate but never to acknowledge it out of concern for populists in Congress who usually wanted lower interest rates. As we know, free reserves and interest rates are not closely related. Martin banned forecasts until the mid-1960s. He did not ask the staff to analyze the relation between Federal Reserve actions and economic outcomes.

Why, then, did inflation remain low enough before 1965 to appreciate the real exchange rate? When I studied the period, I found Martin saying several times that the Federal Reserve was independent within government. Martin explained that he meant that the Federal Reserve could raise interest rates enough to stop a boom caused by strong private spending. But Congress passed the budget and the president signed it. The Federal Reserve, he believed, had to facilitate budgetary finance. That was his big mistake. In the 1950s and early 1960s, budget deficits remained low except during recessions. Monetary policy did not face the problem that came to the fore in the Johnson administration.

By 1965, Kennedy, Dillon, and Roosa were gone. President Johnson was a strong populist. He hated increases in interest rates. Many economists at the time favored coordination of fiscal and monetary policy. Council chair Gardner Ackley opposed Federal Reserve independence. Given Martin's beliefs about independence and President Johnson's concerns, the Federal Reserve helped to finance the enlarged budget deficit that financed the Vietnam War and the Great Society programs.

The Fed followed a policy called "even keel" of maintaining interest rates unchanged during Treasury funding. Reserve growth often rose at such times. The FOMC would not act to remove the excess. Average growth of monetary base and money (M_1) rose and inflation followed.

Coordination worked one way only. The Fed supported government borrowing. The administration would not agree to Martin's urging that it should ask for a tax increase. Many in Congress would not support a tax surcharge unless the president agreed to reduce spending, especially spending for the Great Society. Martin warned President Johnson about inflation several times. After one such warning in May 1965, Martin gave a commencement address at Columbia University warning about inflation and raising concerns about the return of the Great Depression. That got headlines, but it did not get a tax surcharge.

At its September 1965 meeting, many on the FOMC were ready to raise the funds rate. Martin opposed because the administration opposed and because most of the votes could come from the bank presidents, not the Board. The FOMC waited until December when on a four to three vote the Board raised the discount rate. Why did Martin change his mind? He explained at the time that for him the issue had become independence. Others voiced concern about inflation and the balance of payments.

Martin was called to Johnson's ranch and castigated, but he did not lower the discount rate. In the months between December 1965 and June 1966, total reserves rose at a 6.3 percent annual rate, four times the rate from the previous June to November. Sherman Maisel, a Board member at the time, recognized that policy had become more expansive. The reason, he said, was that the Federal Reserve used a money market strategy. Borrowing increased, so free reserves fell from $8 million in December to –$255 million the following March.

The money market strategy misled the FOMC on several occasions. It is not the whole story. In the late 1940s, Congress approved the Employment Act and the Bretton Woods Enabling Act. The only way to reconcile these guides was to maintain low inflation. Otherwise they were in conflict.

The vague language of the Employment Act called for maximum employment and purchasing power. In practice, that came to mean a 4 percent unemployment rate. The council and the Johnson administration believed that a bit of inflation was a small price to pay for a lower unemployment rate. They supported their predilection by appealing to a negatively sloped Phillips curve. President Nixon's council accepted that the long-run Phillips curve was vertical, but the president was not willing to accept higher unemployment to lower inflation.

The important policy change in 1964 or 1965 was an increased willingness by the administration and Congress to accept higher inflation to get lower unemployment. This combined with the Federal Reserve's commitment to policy coordination (and its frequent analytic errors) produced higher inflation.

In my reading of the minutes and the history, balance of payments was a secondary or tertiary consideration for most of the FOMC members. They regarded the balance as a Treasury responsibility. They saw their role as, at most, supportive of Treasury policy. Bordo and Eichengreen agree with that in part at least.

Academic economists shared, even sponsored, many of these views about inflation. Polling data suggests that until 1979, the public rarely gave much weight to inflation when asked about its concerns.

During the Kennedy and Johnson administrations, international payments called for two types of action. They put restrictions on mainly private spending whenever there was an apparent crisis. These included the Interest Equalization Tax, limits on foreign lending by banks and on foreign investment by corporations, requirements to ship in US flag carriers, and several other controls. The other policy action was a series of meetings to get agreement on Special Drawing Rights.

In 1969, Paul Volcker became Treasury under secretary for Monetary Affairs. In his first six weeks in office, he prepared a memo for the secretary and later the president. For the first time, his memo discussed exchange rate adjustment. Volcker proposed that this administration give two years to discussing exchange rate adjustment with other countries. After that time would run out, the gold stock would decline, and the United States would have to act unilaterally. His judgment was correct. A bit more than two years after he wrote, President Nixon closed the gold window.

The end of fixed exchange rates in 1973 did not eliminate either inflation or the balance-of-payments deficit. Until 1976, the government's estimate of the equilibrium unemployment rate remained at 4 percent. As Orphanides has ably shown, the Phillips curve continued to underestimate the inflation rate much of the time.

Inflation ended after the public told the pollsters that inflation was the most important problem they saw. Probably they mixed the increased relative price of oil with inflation.

President Carter appointed Paul Volcker. In his interview Volcker told the president he would work to reduce inflation. President Carter replied, "Good, that's what I want." Volcker changed the weights on inflation and unemployment in the Fed's objective function and restored independence. Concern for independence and credibility lasted until recently, and so did low inflation.

Discussion

Anna Schwartz had issues with two parts of the chapter. The chapter does not mention the Gold Standard Act of 1934. It appointed the secretary of the Treasury as the manager of the foreign exchange value of the dollar. The secretary needed the approval of the president for any actions he wanted to take, but once he had the approval no one inside or outside of the government could challenge him. So how could the Federal Reserve before 1965 believe that it was managing for the foreign exchange value of the dollar, and how it could it believe after 1965 that it could delegate that responsibility to the Treasury? Also, it seemed to Schwartz that even though the authors did not comment on whether the positions of the Federal Reserve were anomalous, should they have tried to verify that these positions were maintained? Look at the annual reports of the secretary of the Treasury. Was there any discussion in these reports about negotiations between the Federal Reserve and the Treasury about who should manage the foreign exchange value? If there was no such discussion, should the chapter have stated that one could not verify the Federal Reserve held those views?

Bennett McCallum felt the international aspects were important in thinking about crucial breaks in the historical record. You cannot have the Great Inflation if you are maintaining a metallic standard. The Bretton Woods system was designed to be a metallic standard. While other countries pegged their exchange rate to the dollar, the United States bought and sold gold at $35 an ounce only to other central banks. This was a huge restriction. There is reason to think why people at the time did not believe the United States was on a metallic standard, but the Bretton Woods system was set up to be one. When did the gold standard break down? Being on such a standard requires that you conduct monetary policy so as to keep the market price of the gold at $35 an ounce. But the United States was not really willing to discipline monetary policy so as to keep the price of gold at $35 an ounce, and this was revealed by the formation of the gold pool in 1961. By 1961, and probably even earlier, it was implicitly revealed that the United States was not going to stick to the Bretton Woods system unless monetary policy was conducted more strictly.

Marvin Goodfriend had issues with the authors' use of a Taylor rule in the 1960s. It gives the impression that policy was tighter than the Taylor rule would predict. It is crucial to realize that the country was on the gold standard, which created a constraint on US monetary policy. What was the inflation target used to get the results in the chapter? Was the gold standard a restriction if the inflation target in the Taylor Rule was zero? Goodfriend referred back to statements made by Paul Samuelson, Robert Solow, and James Tobin blasting the Federal Reserve and saying that staying on the gold standard was inconsistent with sustainable domestic stabilization policy. To Goodfriend, this undermined in an intellectual way the institutions that were established under the Gold Standard Act and Bretton Woods. The chapter should go back further and ask key questions. Is there really something inconsistent about the gold standard and doing the right thing domestically? Goodfriend continued with historical evidence. In 1951, the Congress was on the side of the Federal Reserve and good monetary policy. Senator Stephen Douglas was leading Congress to support independent monetary policy and inflation stabilization, which went against the administration at the time. Something drastic happened when the Federal Reserve went from pro-Congress and anti-president to anti-Congress and pro-president in 1965. What happened to undermine Congress's commitment to the Federal Reserve? It was a complete loss of belief in the institutional structure. Goodfriend also mentioned Chairman Martin's democratization of the Federal Reserve. While he felt it was a good thing, it may have undermined the Federal Reserve Bank of New York to make monetary policy and the commitment of the Federal Reserve to the gold standard and US institutions. Lastly, Goodfriend wanted to stress the ideas view of Christina Romer. Institutions are at play, and the United States had the right institutions. There needs to be commitment, but all the institutional agreements collapsed. Why?

Athanasios Orphanides felt that the fixed exchange rate regime somewhat helped the containment of inflation in the United States, and he focused on what happened in December of 1965. His interpretation of what really mattered was the encroachment of new ideas by academics in Washington, DC, to pressure monetary policy to work on better outcomes toward price stability. The pressure got so big that Chairman Martin in the fourth quarter of 1965 allowed the Federal Reserve staff for the first time to incorporate forecasts in the models of monetary policy decisions. The economy was approaching full employment, and he was stressing the need to tighten monetary policy and really wanted the support of the administration. But he gave a speech and said that he did not have the support of the secretary of the Treasury or the Council of Economic Advisors and regretted that. In December of 1965, the forecast for unemployment was 4.2 percent. Within a couple of months, the forecasts said it would drop below 4 percent. Orphanides referred to an earlier discussion about the famous split decision to raise the discount rate in December of 1965. Ten days after the meeting, there was a hearing where Congress dropped members of the Board of Governors, and made all members at the time explain why they made their decisions. What Orphanides found fascinating was that the explanations for support of the decision were all on domestic economic grounds, and the differences in outlooks for employment, growth, and the risks to inflation were driving the decisions. Even Chairman Martin stated that the critical forces at play that would determine price movements for the next several months were the expansion of total demand, potential output, expectations, and the success of the president's price-wage controls. Most projections of demand and supply available at the time when the Board of Governors made its decisions did not see the impending high inflation. What went wrong?

Eichengreen had several comments. As an economic historian, no one could argue that one should look at a longer period, but the authors were asked to consider the time right around the Great Inflation. Second, Bordo and Eichengreen did not see the balance of payments problem as the full explanation for the Great Inflation. It was a crucial element, but not the entire story. What about the timing of the shift around Bretton Woods? This chapter puts it on September 23, 1965, and there is a pronounced change in which the frequency of balance-of-payments considerations is involved. There was a tendency for the Treasury to unroll a caravan of policies designed to the deal with the balance-of-payments issue. In terms of the Taylor rule evidence reference by Goodfriend, Eichengreen stressed that if you just perform a mechanical Taylor rule analysis, policy looks unusually tight in the first half of the 1960s. One possible explanation is consideration of other issues, and another possible explanation is a lower inflation target. Are these two separate issues, or one in the same? The Federal Reserve internalized the balance-of-payments problem more before 1965 than after, but there was no evidence on them shifting their target level of inflation. Allan Meltzer often referenced that Alfred Hayes of the Federal Reserve Bank of New York was the dominant voice of the FOMC at the time, and did that add more punch? Goodfriend recognized Schwartz's comments, but quibbles with her questions of how the Federal Reserve believed it was responsible for managing the balance of payments given the Gold Standard Act. The authors are not arguing that the Federal Reserve was not solely responsible, but rather it was a shared responsibility with the Treasury, a sharing that began to shift over time as the Treasury assumed more of a role.

Panel Session II
Lessons from History

Lessons from History

Donald L. Kohn

My thinking about the Great Inflation period starts from the premise that high inflation could not have emerged without accommodative monetary policy, but policymakers did not seek the result that they obtained. At the time, many observers in addition to the Federal Reserve overestimated the response of inflation to rising interest rates and underestimated the persistence of inflation. These misperceptions are illustrated by the behavior of real interest rates. Medium- and long-term real interest rates were often zero or negative, calculated using backward-looking measures of inflation, indicating quite clearly that people in financial markets did not anticipate the inflation that occurred.

A lot of factors in addition to bad policy contributed to this episode of persistent high inflation: faulty ideas about the causes of inflation, underestimates of the costs of inflation and overestimates of the costs of disinflation, supply shocks, the unexpected slowdown in productivity growth, demographic shifts that raised the natural rate of unemployment, institutional factors such as labor contracts with escalator clauses, political pressures, and so on. My conclusion is that policymakers were dealt a bad hand, which they played poorly. My remarks on this panel will try to draw some lessons from this episode that can help us avoid a big mistake in the future, whether that mistake be sustained inflation or sustained deflation and recession.

Lesson 1: Central banks must remain focused on effective price stability over time as the most important long-run objective of policy, and long-run price stability is the responsibility of central banks. Central banks do not

Donald L. Kohn is a senior fellow at the Brookings Institution and a former member of the Board of Governors of the Federal Reserve System.

For acknowledgments, sources of research support, and disclosure of the author's material financial relationships, if any, please see http://www.nber.org/chapters/c11629.ack.

need convincing of this lesson, but they do operate in democracies. Political support for a price stability goal is essential. I was struck when looking at Ed Nelson's charts on the Great Inflation that both the US and UK inflation episodes came to an end in the late 1970s or early 1980s. Arguably, it took fifteen years for the political systems in both countries to become sufficiently unhappy with the results their economies were experiencing to be ready to back disinflationary policy. Even as late as 1977 and 1978, the Humphrey Hawkins Act was more focused on reducing unemployment than on achieving price stability.

The contrast between the economic performance of the 1970s and that of the 1980s and 1990s has greatly strengthened the support for central banks seeking price stability, and this support has been manifest over recent years in many countries in the adoption of inflation targeting. In my view, the overt political buy-in for a price stability mandate for the central bank is one of the most important benefits of inflation targeting. That support could be tested, however. I was struck by the last chapter of Alan Greenspan's recent book, in which he argues that the good inflation performance of the 1980s and 1990s was in part due to fortuitous circumstances that could reverse. He cites increases in globalization, deregulation, and greater productivity growth as contributing to lower inflation in the past few decades, and he questions whether they will continue to exert downward pressure on price increases.

The current turmoil in financial markets and the economy will pose interesting challenges to the focus on price stability as the main responsibility of central banks. Central banks need to deal with the present financial instability and its implications while keeping their long-run focus on price stability. The intellectual framework for inflation targeting is already being questioned in the aftermath of the turmoil. People are asking whether a macroeconomic policy focused closely on medium-term price stability was partly responsible for the bubble in financial markets, and whether central banks should take explicit account of the potential for financial instability as well as inflation in policy setting.

A corollary to the need for political support is the requirement that the political system be willing to grant a great degree of independence to central banks as they pursue their mandates. And independent central banks need to utilize the scope for action they get from this independence. As many have remarked, in the 1960s and 1970s, the Federal Reserve did not exercise its independence, perhaps because it sensed that it did not have political support for the actions that it would have needed to take. An aspect of the lack of true independence in the late 1960s was a great deal of coordination between monetary and fiscal policies. The fiscal and monetary authorities jointly considered the economic outlook and settled on a policy mix. For example, if fiscal policy was tightened through an increase in taxes, the central bank would agree to lower interest rates. Those sorts of agreements do not pay off over time. Circumstances change from the time of the agreement, or fiscal policy does not have the intended effect, and the central bank has committed to a policy path that turns out to be inappropriate. Importantly because of the experience in the Great Inflation, political support for independence is higher now, but we cannot take this support for granted.

Lesson 2: Inflation expectations are critical for controlling inflation. Increases in expected inflation make disinflation more costly. And changes in expectations feedback on the dynamic properties of economic activity and inflation in ways that are hard to predict, and make the appropriate policy setting that much more difficult to calibrate. The lesson of the importance of well-anchored inflation expectations has been taken on board by central banks as they have responded to supply shocks in recent years.

Lesson 3: Vigorous debate inside central banks, along with understanding and informed commentary by the public, provides safeguards against severe and persistent policy errors. Having alternative perspectives supported by good analysis and research heard and understood within the institution will help produce good policy. In theory, those discussions should be fostered by having a panel of experts making monetary policy. But the Federal Reserve under Chairman Burns did not seem to be a place that encouraged the development of differing viewpoints by staff members or policymakers. My experience on the Board's staff beginning in 1975 was one of vigorous discussions on the staff level, but limited opportunities for those discussions to bubble up to the policymakers. Publications by Board staff and by Reserve Bank staff were very tightly controlled to limit any hint of disagreement with the public stance of the institution. That sort of control feeds back negatively on incentives to do research.

Moreover, the difficult economic circumstances of the time might be expected to produce an unusual number of policymaker dissents. Yet, the number of dissents at meetings of the Federal Open Market Committee (FOMC) in the Burns era was a lot lower than under Chairman Volcker and for most of the Greenspan era. One can only infer that discussion of alternative perspectives was limited under Chairman Burns. Current practice does provide ample opportunities for putting forward differing perspectives at FOMC meetings, and these opportunities are routinely seized by meeting participants. And staff publications at the Board and Reserve Banks regularly express a variety of views about the appropriate practice of monetary policy.

Good external communication is critical for building support and for getting useful perspectives from outside the central bank. The public needs to understand why decisions were made. And it should have confidence that alternatives were considered and understand why they were not taken. To be sure, tension can exist between the diversity of views within the committee and the clarity of external communications. We have been through episodes in which the open expression of the diverse views of FOMC participants has confused the public about the considerations being weighed by policymakers at the center of the committee. But it is important to have those diverse views and public understanding of the complex calculus of policymaking if we are to avoid the persistent miscalculations of the 1970s.

Lesson 4: There are no shortcuts to price stability once inflation becomes embedded in practices and expectations. Attempts to reduce the pain of disinflation will not succeed for long, and those attempts distort market signals to private agents and central banks, further complicating policy decisions. Income policies of the 1970s and credit controls at the beginning of the 1980s made it hard to figure out the extent of underlying inflation pressures and how financial markets were reacting to policy initiatives. In addition, once the central bank had allowed inflation to rise, it could not expect instant credibility once it adopted a disinflationary policy. Moreover, gradualism in the face of an imbedded inflation problem will not succeed. Under such circumstances, slow policy adjustment will tend to allow inflation expectations to rise and pressures to build further. In such a situation, policy needs to make a major shift and find a mechanism for sticking to the vigorous pursuit of its price stability objective.

Final lesson: Humility! We need to be humble about what we know. As I noted at the outset, policymakers in the late 1960s and 1970s did not seek the results they got. In the Great Inflation, the Federal Reserve did a poor job predicting what would happen to inflation and what policy would be required to bring it under control. As I emphasized, expectations are critical to the inflation process, but we have little understanding of how expectations are formed, and we do not even measure them very well. Our ability to measure and analyze such key concepts in policymaking as the level and growth rate of potential GDP, the nonaccelerating inflation rate of unemployment (NAIRU), the nature and persistence of shocks, and economic dynamics as shocks work through the economy is quite limited. We must continuously remind ourselves of how little we know, we must be ready to acknowledge that developments are not working out as we expected, and, as a consequence, we must also be open to adjusting policies, to reconsidering our analyses, and to looking at different ways of accomplishing our objectives.

The Great Inflation
Lessons for Central Banks

Lucas Papademos

Introduction

The topical nature and policy relevance of this conference on the origins and consequences of the Great Inflation are underscored by the fact that over the past year real oil and food prices continued to rise significantly and persistently, despite the ongoing severe financial crisis that erupted more than twelve months ago. Before its recent decline, the real price of oil reached a historical peak in June 2008 that was higher than the previous all-time peak of April 1980. Moreover, an index of real world food prices has risen by more than 80 percent over the last three years, having increased by almost 50 percent over the twelve months to July 2008. The apparent parallels between the recent supply shocks and those of the 1970s point to the importance and pertinence of the topics discussed during this conference.

In my remarks, I will first assess alternative views concerning the determinants of the Great Inflation by comparing the inflation performance and the conduct of monetary policy in the United States and in a number of European countries. I will then summarize what I consider to be the key lessons for monetary policy that can be drawn from the experience of the Great Inflation in the 1970s and the subsequent period of disinflation in the 1980s, which led to the establishment of a high degree of price stability on both sides of the Atlantic. Finally, I will briefly explain that the lessons of the

Lucas Papademos is former governor of the Bank of Greece, former vice president of the European Central Bank, and former prime minister of Greece. He is currently visiting professor of public policy at the Kennedy School of Government, Harvard University, professor of economics at the University of Athens, and senior fellow at the Center for Financial Studies of Goethe University Frankfurt.

For acknowledgments, sources of research support, and disclosure of the author's material financial relationships, if any, please see http://www.nber.org/chapters/c12706.ack.

Great Inflation are embedded in the institutional framework and the monetary policy strategy of the European Central Bank (ECB) and have guided the conduct of the ECB's monetary policy since the launch of the euro.

The Role of Supply Shocks and Monetary Policy in Fostering the Great Inflation

Although conventional explanations of the Great Inflation largely ascribe it to the impact of commodity price shocks, there are several reasons why this view has to be regarded with scepticism.

First, in the United States the Great Inflation started around 1965, well before the supply shocks of the 1970s, thus posing a fundamental obstacle to this line of argument.[1] In October 1973—the date of the first oil shock—US Consumer Price Index (CPI) inflation was already running at 8.1 percent, clearly suggesting that inflationary pressures had been strong well before the oil shocks hit.

Second, a convincing case can be—and has been—made that the Organization of the Petroleum Exporting Countries' (OPEC's) dramatic oil price hikes in 1973 and 1979 would only have been possible under the conditions of significant increase in global liquidity after the breakdown of the Bretton Woods system. This view—which had originally been advocated during the 1970s and the early 1980s by Milton Friedman, Phillip Cagan, and Ronald McKinnon[2]—has been revived in a more recent paper by Barsky and Kilian.[3] According to this position, a large part of the commodity price increases in the 1970s should not be regarded as exogenous, but rather as an endogenous market response to the abundant global liquidity created following the collapse of the Bretton Woods system.

Third, and importantly, a comparison between the experience of the United States, the United Kingdom, France, Italy, and Spain, which suffered double-digit inflation rates, and that of Germany and Switzerland, which implemented a tight monetary policy during the 1970s explicitly aimed at keeping inflation under control, raises serious doubts about the notion that the Great Inflation was caused by a series of major negative supply shocks. Given that all countries experienced the very same adverse shocks and that their economic structures were not markedly different, it logically follows that the view largely ascribing the Great Inflation to commodity price shocks cannot account for the marked differences in their inflation performance.

So, what explains those differences in inflation performance? The chapter that was presented in the conference by Beyer, Gaspar, Gerbeding, and Iss-

---

1. This point has been forcefully made by Clarida, Galí, and Gertler (2000).
2. See Friedman (1975), Cagan (1979), and McKinnon (1982).
3. See Barsky and Kilian (2001).

ing clearly suggests that the divergence between the inflation performance of the United States and that of Germany in the 1970s was due to the tighter monetary policy pursued by the Bundesbank, compared with that of the Federal Reserve.

The difference between the two countries as regards the stance of monetary policy was reflected in the behavior of their exchange rates, with the nominal effective exchange rate of the deutsche mark appreciating during the entire decade, while that of the US dollar depreciated significantly. With the prices of oil and other commodities expressed in dollars, the strong appreciation of the deutsche mark partially insulated the German economy from the inflationary impact of the commodity price shocks.

Combined with the more restrictive interest rate policy implemented by the Bundesbank, this allowed Germany to escape the Great Inflation relatively unscathed, with German CPI inflation peaking at 7.8 percent in the mid-1970s, compared with the inflation peak of 12.2 percent recorded in the United States.

These arguments and the associated evidence strongly suggest that the monetary policy stance adopted by individual countries played a fundamental role in determining whether the inflationary impulses originating from commodity markets translated into persistent inflationary pressures, or whether—as in the case of Germany—they led to a relatively transient inflation hump.

Lessons from the Great Inflation for Central Bank Policy

A major challenge faced by policymakers pertains to the size and stability of the parameters, and sometimes to the very nature, of key economic relationships. The tumultuous 1970s clearly revealed the nature of the long-term unemployment-inflation trade-off. Following the publication of A. W. Phillips' 1958 paper,[4] and especially after Paul Samuelson and Robert Solow introduced the Phillips curve into the macroeconomic debate in the United States,[5] the notion of an exploitable unemployment-inflation trade-off, offering policymakers a menu of policy options they could choose from, became dominant within academia. The Great Inflation episode was akin to a large-scale "experiment." It showed that higher inflation and accommodative macroeconomic policy were not systematically associated with lower unemployment—and indeed in the United States they were accompanied by higher unemployment—thus refuting the proposition of a negatively sloped long-term Phillips curve. Moreover, the subpar economic performance associated with the inflationary outburst of the 1970s led a number of authoritative voices—notably, Milton Friedman and Friedrich von

---

4. See Phillips (1958).
5. See Samuelson and Solow (1960).

Hayek—to conjecture that higher inflation may actually be detrimental to economic activity.[6] This view has now become conventional wisdom among central bankers and academics alike.

A second proposition that the Great Inflation burned into central bankers' consciousness is the role of inflation expectations as a determinant of inflation and, consequently, the need to keep inflation low and stable, in order to prevent an unanchoring of inflation expectations. To be sure, this notion was not unknown before the 1970s. In his statement before the Joint Economic Committee of the US Congress in February 1965, Federal Reserve Chairman William Martin emphasized that:

> Expectations play an important role in price behaviour and the expectation of continuing price stability is vital to its current realization . . . if we fail to maintain a situation which is conducive to price stability, we could find ourselves caught up very quickly in an inflationary spiral.

Subsequent developments showed the prescience of his words, as US inflation drifted upwards starting from mid-1965, and inflation expectations became progressively unanchored.

Another important lesson concerns the dangers intrinsic to activist, overly ambitious policies striving to keep output close to its potential level. As extensively discussed by Orphanides,[7] although such policies perform well under perfect knowledge of the value of the output gap at each point in time, given the uncertainty associated with the estimates of the output gap calculated in real time, they may well produce markedly suboptimal outcomes. According to his explanation of the US Great Inflation, a key problem was the failure to detect the productivity slowdown of the 1970s in real time, which led to a systematic overestimation of the extent of slack existing in the economy, thus resulting in a comparatively accommodative monetary policy stance.

Over the past fifteen years, the macroeconomic profession has largely converged on a model of inflation dynamics embodied in the so-called "New Keynesian Phillips curve."[8] A distinctive characteristic of this theoretical framework is the forward-looking nature of the inflation process. To be sure, this feature has been criticized because of the model's inability to reproduce the high inflation persistence found in post-World War II data.[9] Recent research, however, suggests that this persistence reflects the shifts in trend inflation experienced in the post-World War II period, which have been associated with the Great Inflation.[10] When either controlling such shifts in trend inflation, or focusing on stable monetary regimes that exhibit no

6. See von Hayek (1978) and Friedman (1977).
7. See Orphanides (2002, 2003).
8. See, for example, Woodford (2003).
9. See, for example, Fuhrer and Moore (1995).
10. See Cogley and Sbordone (2008).

inflation trends, the purely forward-looking version of the New Keynesian Phillips curve fits the data very well.[11]

The forward-looking nature of the inflation process implies that a crucial element of monetary policy is the management of inflation expectations. Consequently, policy credibility, effective communication, and enhanced transparency are of paramount importance. For this reason, a credible and well-understood monetary policy framework, including a clear mandate for preserving price stability and a quantitative objective that can provide a "focal point" for inflation expectations, is essential because it effectively contributes to the anchoring of inflation expectations to price stability. The significance of firmly anchoring expectations offers a perspective on the emphasis placed on monetary analysis in the ECB's monetary policy strategy, as it can provide an additional means for assessing inflation risks and steering inflation expectations over the medium and long run.

Finally, the years since the Great Inflation have also seen important developments concerning the way uncertainty about economic relationships affects the optimal policy response to shocks. The traditional result that under "model uncertainty" policy responses should be relatively more cautious than under certainty has been shown not to be of general validity.[12] In particular, it has been shown that if uncertainty pertains to the lagged effects of policy, and if there is a positive probability that the dynamics of the economy may become unpredictable, the central bank should respond to shocks firmly in order to better control inflation.[13] This result is fully in line with the conclusions drawn from the Great Inflation episode about the appropriate policy response to shocks.

To sum up, the key lessons for monetary policy from the Great Inflation in the 1970s and the subsequent period of disinflation in the 1980s are the following:

- *First,* monetary policy can *effectively* control inflation over the medium and longer run, although the volatility and dynamics of inflation in the short run can be significantly influenced—and even dominated—by shocks and nonmonetary factors.
- *Second,* there is no stable trade-off between inflation and output growth that can be exploited in an effective and systematic manner by monetary policy in the long run. Although no such long-term stable trade-off exists, high and volatile inflation will adversely affect the economy's real growth performance. The first and second lesson clearly imply that the preservation of price stability should be the primary objective of monetary policy.

11. See Benati (2008).
12. See Brainard (1967).
13. See Gaspar and Kashyap (2006) for a pertinent discussion.

- *Third,* the uncertainty characterizing the short-term relationship between inflation and the level and pace of economic activity, which stems from (a) developments in productivity growth and labor utilization that are difficult to predict and measure in real time, (b) unanticipated shifts in inflation expectations, and (c) the effects of shocks, implies that in general attempts to fine-tune economic activity by monetary policy are unlikely to succeed and might even be destabilizing.
- *Fourth,* the ultimate impact of (significant and persistent) supply shocks on inflation performance crucially depends on the extent to which they will be accommodated by monetary policy and they will induce indirect and second-round effects on wage and price-setting behavior. The likelihood of such effects materializing in turn depends on (a) inflation expectations and (b) institutional features of product and labor markets, such as the degree of competition in product markets and the existence of (de jure or de facto) wage-indexation schemes in the labor market.
- *Fifth,* inflation expectations play an extremely important role in determining inflation dynamics and the effectiveness of monetary policy. Inflation expectations are influenced by the objectives, the strategy, and the conduct of monetary policy. The anchoring of inflation expectations to the policy objective of the central bank greatly facilitates its ability to effectively respond to inflation shocks and mitigate their impact on the price level and aggregate output.

These lessons were not self-evident forty or even twenty years ago in many countries. The painful experience of the Great Inflation and the disinflation that followed in the United States and in Europe, as well as the available empirical evidence in many countries over a long period of time, have contributed to their widespread acceptance and their embodiment in the institutional and monetary policy frameworks of most central banks. This is definitely the case for the ECB.

The Lessons of History and the ECB's Monetary Policy

Thus, let me conclude by briefly explaining that the lessons of monetary history—both in the United States and in Europe—over the past fifty years are well-embedded in the institutional framework and the monetary policy strategy of the ECB and have guided the conduct of the European single monetary policy. The Treaty on the Functioning of the European Union and the ECB Statute unambiguously state that the primary objective of the single monetary policy is to maintain price stability. No multiple objectives involving potential policy trade-offs are specified. There is a clear hierarchy of policy goals. In accordance with the Treaty and the Statute, "without prejudice to the objective of price stability, the ECB shall support the general economic policies in the Union with a view to contributing to the achievement of the objectives of the Union." These include "balanced economic growth" and a "highly competitive social market economy, aiming at full employment." It is therefore envisaged that the ECB shall contribute to economic growth and job creation provided that the preservation of price stability is not jeopardized. The mandated hierarchy of policy goals, however, has significant implications for the conduct of monetary policy.

The strategy adopted by the ECB in order to achieve its primary objective includes a quantitative definition of price stability, which aims at guiding and anchoring inflation expectations and provides a yardstick for assessing the central bank's performance and explaining its policy actions. It also includes a comprehensive analytical framework for the assessment of risks to price stability.

There are two pertinent features of the strategy of the ECB that I would like to emphasize. First, it has a forward-looking orientation and aims at maintaining price stability over a medium- and longer-term horizon. This is important for several reasons. It takes into account the fact that monetary policy affects price developments with relatively long time lags and that it cannot counter directly and promptly the effects of various shocks—especially those affecting the economy's aggregate supply—but only indirectly through a transmission process that is complex, possibly time varying, and characterized by intrinsic uncertainty. Second, the analytical framework for the assessment of risks to price stability incorporates alternative and complementary approaches to the appraisal of inflation risks. In particular, the analysis of monetary and credit developments provides a means to "cross-check" the risk assessment based on economic analysis and it is especially relevant and useful for the evaluation of inflation risks over a longer-term horizon. Such risks include those stemming from the potential effects of monetary and credit conditions on inflation via their influence on asset prices and risk-taking behavior. Monetary analysis also provides additional information that is pertinent for the formation of inflation expectations over a longer-term horizon.

But the effective management of expectations requires more than an unambiguously specified monetary policy objective and a well-defined strategy. It also requires credible actions that are consistent with the attainment of the objective and the adopted strategy. In order to protect the central bank's commitment to its primary objective and strengthen policy effectiveness, the legal framework of the ECB emphasizes the importance and meaning of central bank independence in the performance of its tasks. Of course, the essential counterpart to independence is accountability to the public and to its elected representatives in the European Parliament. Accountability requires effective communication and enhanced transparency of policy actions. Hence, central bank independence, accountability, and transparency are also vital for establishing monetary policy credibility and for anchoring inflation expectations.

Finally, let me stress that the conduct of the ECB's monetary policy has reflected the lessons from the Great Inflation that I summarized earlier. Over the past ten years, the ECB and other central banks often had to address challenges broadly similar—though not identical—to those faced during that historic episode. In particular, during the first year of the financial crisis, the ECB faced the extraordinary twin challenge of preserving price stability, which was threatened by sizable and persistent supply shocks and, at the same time, addressing the substantial risks to financial stability that stemmed from unprecedented market turbulence and banking system stresses.

To meet this challenge, the policy actions of the ECB were based on a separation principle: the monetary policy stance was effectively separated from the management of liquidity. For more than a year after the outbreak of the global financial crisis, the ECB did not ease monetary policy, as determined by its key interest rates, mainly because it was concerned about the materialization of second-round effects of supply shocks on wage- and price-setting and the potential unanchoring of inflation expectations. On the contrary, in July 2008 it raised its policy rates by 25 basis points to counter increasing upside risks to price stability. At the same time, the ECB provided substantial amounts of liquidity to the banking system and engaged in active liquidity management to alleviate money market pressures and protect financial stability. In line with the separation principle, liquidity management involved adjusting the intertemporal distribution of bank reserves and extending the maturity profile of the liquidity provided through refinancing operations, but without increasing appreciably the total supply of central bank money.

The policy pursued by the ECB proved effective. Inflation expectations remained firmly anchored in line with price stability and second-round effects were avoided, while financial stability risks were contained. Of course, the impact of the financial market turbulence on the real economy could be expected to reduce inflationary pressures and diminish inflation risks over the medium term. But this would not have been sufficient for ensuring the preservation of price stability, given the intensity of the adverse supply shocks and their potential effect on inflation expectations. The ECB's credible commitment to price stability has helped prevent the materialization of the unfavorable combination of rising inflation and contracting economic activity that characterized the 1970s. Central banks have learned the policy lessons from the Great Inflation episode.

References

Barsky, R. B., and L. Kilian. 2001. "Do We Really Know That Oil Caused the Great Stagflation? A Monetary Alternative." In *NBER Macroeconomics Annual 2001*, edited by Ben S. Bernanke and Kenneth Rogoff, 137–83. Cambridge, MA: MIT Press.

Benati, L. 2008. "Investigating Inflation Persistence Across Monetary Regimes." *Quarterly Journal of Economics* 123 (3): 1005–60.

Brainard, W. 1967. "Uncertainty and the Effectiveness of Policy." *American Economic Review* 57 (2): 411–25.

Cagan, P. 1979. *Persistent Inflation: Historical and Policy Essays.* New York: Columbia University Press.

Clarida, R., J. Galí, and M. Gertler. 2000. "Monetary Policy Rules and Macroeconomic Stability: Evidence and Some Theory." *Quarterly Journal of Economics* 115 (1): 147–80.

Cogley, T. W., and A. Sbordone. 2008. "Trend Inflation, Indexation, and Inflation Persistence in the New Keynesian Phillips Curve." *American Economic Review* 98 (5): 2101–26.

Friedman, M. 1975. "Perspectives on Inflation." *Newsweek,* June 24.

———. 1977. "Nobel Lecture: Inflation and Unemployment." *Journal of Political Economy* 85 (3): 451–72.

Fuhrer, J., and G. Moore. 1995. "Inflation Persistence." *Quarterly Journal of Economics* 109:127–59.

Gaspar, V., and A. Kashyap. 2006. "Stability First: Reflections Inspired by Otmar Issing's Success as the ECB's Chief Economist." NBER Working Paper no. 12277. Cambridge, MA: National Bureau of Economic Research.

Martin, William McChesney, Jr. 1965. "Statement of William McChesney Martin, Jr., Chairman, Board of Governors of the Federal Reserve System before the Joint Economic Committee, February 26, 1965." Statements and Speeches of William McChesney Martin, Jr. Accessed from FRASER (Federal Reserve Archive), http://fraser.stlouisfed.org/publication/?pid=448.

McKinnon, R. I. 1982. "Currency Substitution and Instability in the World Dollar Standard." *American Economic Review* 72 (3): 320–33.

Orphanides, A. 2002. "Monetary Policy Rules and the Great Inflation." *American Economic Review, Papers and Proceedings* 92 (2): 115–20.

———. 2003. "The Quest for Prosperity without Inflation." *Journal of Monetary Economics* 50:633–63.

Phillips, A. W. 1958. "The Relation Between Unemployment and the Rate of Change of Money Wage Rates in the United Kingdom, 1861–1957." *Economica* 25:283–99.

Samuelson, P., and R. Solow. 1960. "Analytical Aspects of Anti-Inflation Policies." *American Economic Review* 50:177–84.

von Hayek, F. 1978. "Inflation's Path to Unemployment." In *New Studies in Philosophy, Politics, Economics, and the History of Ideas,* edited by F. von Hayek, 192–96. Chicago: University of Chicago Press.

Woodford, M. 2003. *Interest and Prices.* Princeton, NJ: Princeton University Press.

Understanding Inflation
Lessons of the Past for the Future

Harold James

The study of inflation is always also a study of the ways in which inflation was understood. In the most dramatic cases of inflation that were not simply an immediate product of expensive military conflict producing an impetus for governments to devalue the currency, the inflationary process was propelled by intellectual arguments about why inflation (although it might produce some bad social consequences) was generally beneficial.

This was the case in the world's most famous hyper-inflation experience (though not quite the world's most extreme, which was post–World War II Hungary): Germany of the Weimar Republic. Representatives of the government explained that the inflation arose out of the circumstances of financing reparations payments and a trade deficit (rather than from the monetization of government debt) (Holtfrerich 1986). There were also many people who saw inflation as an interplay of organized interests, in which labor and employer organizations bid each other up (Feldman 1993). Inflation was thus simply a way of buying social peace in a politically precarious environment.

Not surprisingly, this interpretation became popular again during the postwar Great Inflation, in the 1970s. Again, a social science interpretation presented the inflation in Latin America (where it was generally higher), but also in the industrial countries, as a product of interest bargaining and of industrial corporatism, rather than as simply a monetary phenomenon. Again, it represented the power of organized interest groups, especially labor

Harold James is the Claude and Lore Kelly Professor in European Studies, professor of history and international affairs, and director of the program in Contemporary European Politics and Society at Princeton University.

For acknowledgments, sources of research support, and disclosure of the author's material financial relationships, if any, please see http://www.nber.org/chapters/c11174.ack.

unions, and the accommodation of those interest groups in the political process (Hirsch and Goldthorpe 1978).

A narrowly economic interpretation of the causes of inflation has substantial attractions relative to the broader social science view, with its quasi-apologetic depiction of inflation. Presenting the inflation as a monetary phenomenon was the clearest intellectual path to ending the inflation, both in the 1920s and in the 1970s. The view that the German Great Inflation originated in central bank policy was at first associated with the Allies, and was bitterly resisted by most German decision makers. Indeed, the central bank president depicted his monetary accommodation as a patriotic duty, and boasted about the number of printing works and plate presses that his institution had set in motion to tackle a monetary shortage. In the 1970s, also, the monetary interpretation depended on the notion that the measurement of money stocks was both possible and significant.

In this regard, it is not clear that we have learned the lessons of the inflationary episodes, or whether those lessons and policy responses have been overlaid by other, more pressing problems. In 2008 we are in the remarkable position of fearing inflation and deflation simultaneously.

Forecasts of the future are currently very confusing. Many people, including central bank policymakers, fear the continuing deflation that emanates from the collapse of financial institutions and from the unwinding of debt exposure by banks scrambling to improve their capital rations. Other people, including some central bankers, are worried about the inflationary effect of worldwide stimulus packages and government deficits on a scale unprecedented in peacetime. Money is pouring into index-linked funds.

Perhaps there will be some new term coined to describe the confusing mixture of apparently opposite expectations of inflation and deflation: conflation.

Our confusion is not altogether new, and it is not simply a product of the financial crisis. We now recognize the 2000s as an era of loose money, thanks to a combination of central bank policy and the global flows of funds from emerging markets like China and from oil producers. But there were also deflation scares, especially in 2002, when there was both a major academic and a policy discussion. The academic debate at that time justified a new inclination on the part of central banks to push down interest rates.

Most surprisingly, the inability to differentiate between inflation and deflation also existed in the 1920s and 1930s (which still figures prominently as a laboratory of bizarre monetary experiments).

Most modern economic historians like to characterize the 1920s as a time when the gold standard orthodoxy imposed deflation on the whole world (Eichengreen 1992). But at the time, it was much more common to diagnose a credit inflation as banks cranked up their lending.

Even John Maynard Keynes, who emerged as the major critic of deflation during the Depression years of the early 1930s, began to see the 1920s as inflationary, not deflationary. In a self-critical account, he later wrote:

"Looking back in the light of fuller statistical information that was then available, I believe that while there was probably no material inflation up to the end of 1927, a genuine profit inflation developed some time between that date and the summer of 1929" (Keynes 1930, 2:190).

In the early 1930s, when no one would now claim that there was anything other than dire deflation, many of the critics of government spending programs warned about the threat of inflation. Ramsay MacDonald convinced an overwhelming majority of British voters that he should lead the country by waving the devalued paper currency of the German hyper-inflation during election rallies.

The uncertainty about inflation or deflation would be only a footnote to the history of economic thinking were it not that as a result of the experiences of the past forty years, inflation has become the key to the way we think about monetary policy.

After the collapse of the fixed exchange rate regime in the early 1970s, the previous anchors of monetary policy disappeared. By the middle of the 1970s, some central banks began to argue formally for a replacement of fixed exchange rates as an anchor for stability by a targeting system for the growth of money. But then they found it hard to define what measure of money they wanted to target.

The disillusion with monetary policy produced a new interest in targeting inflation rather than monetary growth. In some cases, inflation targeting grew out of an intellectual conviction that it represented a superior way of dealing with the problem of inflationary expectations. New Zealand in 1990 and Canada in 1991 adopted this approach (Bernanke 1999).

First in academic life and then in policymaking, Ben Bernanke has been an academic pioneer of the concept. He started off by recognizing the novelty of the approach, stating in 2003 that many Americans considered inflation targeting "foreign, impenetrable, and possibly slightly subversive."

Some of the most spectacular conversions to inflation targeting occurred in the aftermath of currency crises, as previously fixed exchange rates disintegrated and policymakers looked for an alternative tool to achieve stability. That was the British experience, and the Bank of England can rightly regard itself as a pioneer of inflation targeting. The adoption in October 1992, as the logical response after sterling was forced out of the European Monetary System (EMS). Sweden, which experienced a similar currency crisis, also chose the same response in January 1993.

But just as monetarism in its classic form of the 1970s was frustrated and ultimately defeated by the inability to say precisely what money was and consequently how it might be measured, we are helpless in the face of all kinds of different measures of inflation. Should we include fluctuating seasonal food prices, or energy prices that move in unpredictable ways, or mortgage payments?

One of the most intense theoretical disputes over recent years was the extent to which central banks should attempt to correct or limit asset prices bubbles when there was no corresponding rise in the general level of inflation. Asset price rises lead to a general increase in purchasing power, because many asset-holders will use them as securities against which to borrow. Many Europeans tried to argue in recent years for the inclusion of some element to take asset price developments into account, while this approach was largely resisted by American policymakers and academics.

The problem is that asset prices and consumer price inflation may move in quite different directions, as they did in the 2000s, and that following both would produce inconsistent policy recommendations. Devising a formula to derive a rule on monetary policy would involve a nearly impossible exercise in weighting both factors. Central banks ran the risk as a result of no longer appearing to follow a clearly formulated policy guideline, and they might well lose credibility. But it was the search for a reliable rule, not susceptible to political interference, that had produced the desire for the inflation target in the first place.

The inflation targeting approach to monetary policymaking is in consequence facing its own moment of truth: the acknowledgment that there is an element of discretion in the application of rules, and that central banking is an art as well as a science.

References

Bernanke, Ben S. 1999. *Inflation Targeting: Lessons from the International Experience.* Princeton, NJ: Princeton University Press.

———. 2003. "Remarks at the Annual Washington Policy Conference of the National Association of Business Economists, Washington, D.C., March 25, 2003." http://www.federalreserve.gov/boarddocs/speeches/2003/20030325/default/htm.

Eichengreen, Barry. 1992. *Golden Fetters: The Gold Standard and the Great Depression, 1919–1939.* New York: Oxford University Press.

Feldman, Gerald D. 1993. *The Great Disorder: Politics, Economics, and Society in the German Inflation, 1914–1924.* New York: Oxford University Press.

Hirsch, Fred, and John H. Goldthorpe. 1978. *The Political Economy of Inflation.* Cambridge, MA: Harvard University Press.

Holtfrerich, Carl-Ludwig. 1986. *The German Inflation, 1914–1923: Causes and Effects in International Perspective.* Berlin, New York: De Gruyter.

Keynes, John Maynard. 1930. *Treatise on Money.* London: Macmillan.

Panel Session II Discussion

Allan Meltzer opened up the discussion: You should keep it simple, don't always state what you know, and tell them when you are going to deviate. The only thing missing from the papers presented at the conference, and it came up in the first panel discussion, was the fact that politics, certainly in the United States, play an enormous role. Chairmen Martin and Burns were not free agents. Chairman Volcker was more of a free agent, but he is an exception. Even Chairman Greenspan was sort of an exception. But, most Federal Reserve chairmen get called to Congress and are told over and over again what to do as an agent of the Congress.

Anna Schwartz felt that one lesson of the Great Inflation from a social welfare viewpoint is that the Federal Reserve assigned entirely too much weight to job loss that disinflation would impose and not enough weight on the losses that inflation imposed on households and firms, as well as on lenders who accepted loans when the price level was lower than when the loans were repaid. The irony is, of course, that finding reasons for not responding earlier to the evidence of inflation means that when the central bank finally took action to curb the inflation, the loss ratio was much greater for a disinflation than it would have been if it had been taken at a more timely point.

Contributors

Andreas Beyer
European Central Bank
Kaiserstraße 29
D-60311 Frankfurt am Main
Germany

Alan S. Blinder
Department of Economics
Princeton University
Princeton, NJ 08544-1021

Michael D. Bordo
Department of Economics
Rutgers University
New Jersey Hall
75 Hamilton Street
New Brunswick, NJ 08901

Don Brash
#311, 184 Symonds Street
Auckland 1010
New Zealand

John Crow
Public Accountants Council
1200 Bay Street, Suite 901
Toronto, Ontario M5R 2A5
Canada

Riccardo DiCecio
Federal Reserve Bank of St. Louis
Research Division
P.O. Box 442
St. Louis, MO 63166-0442

Barry Eichengreen
Department of Economics
University of California, Berkeley
549 Evans Hall 3880
Berkeley, CA 94720-3880

Benjamin M. Friedman
Department of Economics
Littauer Center 127
Harvard University
Cambridge, MA 02138

Vitor Gaspar
Banco de Portugal
Av. Almirante Reis, 71-8
1150-012 Lisbon
Portugal

Christina Gerberding
Deutsche Bundesbank
Monetary Policy Division
D-60431 Frankfurt am Main
Germany

Marvin Goodfriend
Tepper School of Business
Carnegie Mellon University
5000 Forbes Avenue
Pittsburgh, PA 15213-3890

Seppo Honkapohja
Bank of Finland
P.O. Box 160
FI 00101 Helsinki
Finland

Otmar Issing
Centre for Financial Studies
Goethe University Frankfurt
Mertonstrasse 17-25
D-60325 Frankfurt am Main
Germany

Takatoshi Ito
Graduate School of Economics
University of Tokyo
7-3-1 Hongo, Bunkyo-ku
Tokyo 113-0033
Japan

Harold James
History Department and Woodrow
  Wilson School
Princeton University
Princeton, NJ 08544

Robert G. King
Department of Economics
Boston University
270 Bay State Road
Boston, MA 02215

Donald L. Kohn
The Brookings Institution
1775 Massachusetts Avenue NW
Washington, DC 20036

Andrew Levin
Federal Reserve Board
Mail Stop 77
20th and C Street, NW
Washington, DC 20551

Bennett T. McCallum
Tepper School of Business, Posner 256
Carnegie Mellon University
Pittsburgh, PA 15213

Allan H. Meltzer
Tepper School of Business
Carnegie Mellon University
Pittsburgh, PA 15213

Frederic S. Mishkin
3022 Broadway, Uris Hall 817
Graduate School of Business
Columbia University
New York, NY 10027

Edward Nelson
Federal Reserve Board
Mail Stop 76, Monetary Affairs
20th and C Streets, NW
Washington, DC 20551

Athanasios Orphanides
MIT Sloan School of Management
100 Main Street, E62-481
Cambridge, MA 02142

Lucas Papademos
Kennedy School of Government
Harvard University
79 John F. Kennedy Street
Cambridge, MA 02138

William Poole
Federal Reserve Bank of St. Louis
P.O. Box 442
St. Louis, MO 63166-0442

Robert H. Rasche
Federal Reserve Bank of St. Louis
P.O. Box 442
St. Louis, MO 63166-0442

Christina D. Romer
Department of Economics
University of California, Berkeley
Berkeley, CA 94720-3880

Jeremy B. Rudd
Board of Governors of the Federal
  Reserve System
20th and C Streets NW
Washington, DC 20551

Matthew D. Shapiro
Department of Economics
University of Michigan
611 Tappan Street
Ann Arbor, MI 48109-1220

Lars E. O. Svensson
Sveriges Riksbank
SE-103 37 Stockholm
Sweden

John B. Taylor
Herbert Hoover Memorial Building
Stanford University
Stanford, CA 94305-6010

David C. Wheelock
Federal Reserve Bank of St. Louis
P.O. Box 442
St. Louis, MO 63166-0442

John C. Williams
Federal Reserve Bank of San Francisco
101 Market Street
San Francisco, CA 94105

Author Index

Subject Index